James K

James Knox was educated at Eton and Trinity College, Cambridge, where he read History of Art. After working as a feature writer on the *Antique Collector* magazine, he gained an MBA at INSEAD. Ten years were spent as Publisher of *The Spectator* before setting up his own consultancy to advise on commissioning works of art for public and private spaces. Other writings include a biographical essay on Sir Philip Sassoon, a history of the Trinity Foot Beagles and a column on the modern dandy for *Country Life*. He lives with his wife and twin son and daughter in London and Ayrshire.

Robert Byron

JAMES KNOX

JOHN MURRAY

First published in Great Britain in 2003 by John Murray (Publishers)
A division of Hodder Headline

Paperback edition 2004

1 3 5 7 9 10 8 6 4 2

A CIP catalogue record for this title
is available from the British Library

ISBN 0-7195-61744

Typeset in Sabon by Palimpsest Book Production Ltd,
Polmont, Stirlingshire
Printed and bound by Clays Ltd, St Ives plc

Hodder Headline policy is to use papers that are natural, renewable and recyclable products and made from wood grown in sustainable forests. The logging and manufacturing processes are expected to conform to the environmental regulations of the country of origin.

John Murray (Publishers)
338 Euston Road
London NW1 3BH

For Caroline,
most beguiling of editors

Contents

Illustrations ix
Preface xi
Map xvii

1. No Relation 1
2. Little Innocent 9
3. Lords and Rebels 19
4. Angry Young Man 32
5. Aesthetes and Dandies 39
6. Vivat Regina! 54
7. Grand Tour 80
8. Grub Street 91
9. The Joyous Life 100
10. An English Year 118
11. Seat of Angels 128
12. Dons and Counts 151
13. Byzantine Enthusiasms 166
14. Air Mail to India 187
15. Into Tibet 199
16. Analysis of Empire 215
17. The Higher Philosophy 228
18. Marx and Monuments 241

19. Cupid's Dart 252
20. The Charcoal Burners 270
21. Persia and Beyond 282
22. Towards the Oxus 302
23. A Pen in Each Hand 327
24. The Grim Orient 341
25. Travellers' Tales 356
26. Beset with Woes 364
27. Georgian Crusader 376
28. Warmongering 390
29. Crisis Pending 405
30. Called to Arms 421

Notes and References 437
Index 479

Illustrations

1. Eric Byron, Robert's father
2. Margaret 'Daisy' Byron, with Robert as a baby
3. Edmund Byron, Robert's grandfather
4. Robert's friends at Eton, 1921
5. Brian Howard's leaving photograph, 1922
6. Victorian party at the Hypocrites Club, 8 March 1924
7. Oliver Baldwin
8. Illustration by Mark Ogilvie-Grant recalling the Victorian Revival at Oxford
9. Henry Yorke
10. Gavin Henderson
11. The Hon. Hugh Lygon
12. Alfred Duggan, *c.* 1922
13. Coulsden Court, Surrey, the Byrons' country house
14. View of Savernake Lodge, Wiltshire
15. Leonard Bower, Alastair Graham and Robert in Athens, May 1926
16. Robert's drawing of the monastery of Chilandari, Mount Athos, 1927
17. David Talbot Rice and Mark Ogilvie-Grant with the guest-master at the monastery of Docheiariou
18. Simopetra, 1927

19–22. A *Sketch* article on Bryan and Diana Guinness's 1860 party

23. View of Mount Chomolhari, Tibet, October 1929
24. Michael Rosse with Mary Tehring and her father, Rajah Tehring
25. South Front of the Viceroy's House by Sir Edwin Lutyens, New Delhi
26. Birr Castle
27. The Hon. Desmond Parsons, younger brother of Michael Rosse

28. 'Sultaniya Mausoleum of Uljaitu, 1313 AD', Persia
29. Robert's caricature of his hostile exchange with Professor Ernst Herzfeld
30. Christopher Sykes, sketched by Robert in Persia, 1933
31. Sketch of the Musalla area
32. 'My lower middle-class Persian self'
33. The tomb tower of Gumbad-i-Kabus, 1006 AD
34. 'Me at one end of my big room writing'
35. James Lees-Milne, 1940
36. 'How We Celebrate the Coronation – a word to London's visitors'
37. Pair of Palladian houses saved by the Georgian Group
38. Robert Byron, 1930s

The author and publishers would like to thank the following for permission to reproduce illustrations: Plate 6, John Powell; 7, Christopher Walker; 8, Vogue; 9, The Cecil Beaton Archive courtesy of Sotheby's; 10, Lady Selina Hastings; 11, Estate of Lady Dorothy Heber-Percy; 26, courtesy of the Earl of Rosse; 35, Estate of James Lees-Milne; 37, The Georgian Group. All other illustrations are reproduced courtesy of the executors of the Estate of Robert Byron.

Preface

When rumour of Robert Byron's loss at sea in February 1941, two days before his thirty-sixth birthday, began to spread, it was greeted with incredulity. 'I can't believe that Robert isn't in the world any more,' one of his closest friends, Nancy Mitford, wrote, 'it doesn't seem reasonable.' Michael Rosse consoled Robert's mother with the thought that 'his will to live was so strong that I am convinced that he found some means of escape.' Robert's vitality was legendary, engaging him in an array of pursuits any one of which would have satisfied most individuals. He was at the forefront of the rediscovery of Byzantine civilization; he was an adventurous traveller with numerous books to his name; he was a crusader in the battle to save Georgian London; he stood out against Fascism and appeasement long before others saw the danger; and, on the outbreak of war, he threw himself into politics, arguing for the creation of a union of states to preserve world peace after Germany's defeat. Not surprisingly, when official confirmation of his death was finally received, another close friend, Ran Antrim, compared his loss to that of the 'intellectual giants, who were destroyed in the flower of their youth in the First World War'.

Brief obituary notices duly appeared, but his achievements had to wait until the end of the war before receiving fuller recognition. Christopher Sykes, his travelling companion for some of the journey described in *The Road to Oxiana*, wrote a long essay, part critical study, part memoir, which was published in *Four Studies in Loyalty* in 1946. Over the ensuing years this served as the main source of information concerning Robert's life and work, which, naturally, tended to focus upon his enduring achievements as a travel writer.

Robert's legacy as a traveller had already taken hold in his lifetime. His book *The Station* led one youthful admirer,

Patrick Leigh Fermor, to undertake a pilgrimage to Mount Athos. For good measure he set off equipped with a rucksack which Mark Ogilvie-Grant, a member of Robert's party in 1927, had taken to the Holy Mountain. Leigh Fermor, whose two volumes of travel-autobiography describe his walk across Europe, acknowledged that *The Station* 'altered my whole itinerary and, one thing leading to another, perhaps the course of a lifetime . . . Obviously I am under his spell; and mutatis mutandis, still am.'

Robert's own writings never quite disappeared from view. John Lehmann republished *The Station* in 1949 with an introduction by Christopher Sykes and, the following year, *The Road to Oxiana* with an introduction by David Talbot Rice. Over the next thirty years, his literary flame was tended by the cognoscenti, many of whom were inspired to make the journey, described in *The Road to Oxiana*, through Iran to Herat and on to Mazar-i-Sherif. His name was also kept alive through the appearance of memoirs of the 1920s and '30s written by his friends from Eton or Oxford. Harold Acton published *Memoirs of an Aesthete* in 1948, Evelyn Waugh produced *A Little Learning* in 1964 and Anthony Powell kept the ball rolling with two relevant volumes in the 1970s. Other books, such as *Brian Howard: Portrait of a Failure*, published in 1968, also indicated Robert's position as a central figure of that world, but inevitably these provided a sketch of his personality rather than a rounded portrait.

Robert's literary revival dates from 1980 when an American scholar and writer, Paul Fussell, published an encomium to him in a study of pre-war British literary travelling, entitled *Abroad*. His enthusiasm for all of Robert's writings encouraged readers to turn again to his earliest works. But the greatest praise is reserved for *The Road to Oxiana*, of which he writes: 'Its distinction tempts one to overpraise but perhaps it may not be going too far to say that what *Ulysses* is to the novel between the wars and what *The Waste Land* is to poetry, *The Road to Oxiana* is to the travel book.'

Fussell's eye-catching claim rests on the assumption that the book is a work of highly crafted fiction which Robert had spent years perfecting following the actual journey. This was based upon a misconception propounded by Christopher Sykes in *Four Studies in Loyalty*, and perpetuated ever since, that the book had cost Robert 'three years of hard work'. Sykes compounded the mistake by asserting that all non-English conversations in *The Road to Oxiana* were invented. This, too, was an exaggeration. Sykes himself, who spoke Persian, was invited by Robert to jot down in his diary any such conversations, which were relatively rare, immediately after their occurrence. As this biography will show, Robert spent a mere five months tidying up the travel diaries of his journey to Persia and Afghanistan for publication. During that time, he also skilfully inserted art historical material garnered since the journey. The result testifies to his natural ability as a travel writer and vindicates Paul Fussell's intuitive appreciation of his greatness.

Hot on the heels of Fussell came the travel writer, Bruce Chatwin. His introduction to a paperback edition of *The Road to Oxiana*, published in 1981, introduced the book to a wide readership at a time when travel writing was about to enjoy a massive revival. 'Anyone', he wrote, 'who reads around the travel books of the thirties must, in the end, conclude that Robert Byron's *The Road to Oxiana* is the masterpiece.' He went on to describe the book as 'a work of genius', acknowledging that 'Long ago I raised it to the status of "sacred text".' His copy, now 'spineless and floodstained', had accompanied him on his first journey to Oxiana in 1962. Chatwin, himself a traveller-aesthete, argued that Robert's descriptions of architecture were his greatest achievement. Byron, he wrote, scores over "experts" with his uncanny ability to gauge the morale of a civilization from its architecture, and to treat ancient buildings and modern people as two facets of a continuing story'.

The publication of *Letters Home* in 1991, edited by Robert's sister, Lucy Butler, an impeccable selection of letters to his mother, laced with fascinating introductions to each phase of his life, inspired many leading travel writers of the day to testify to his importance. Others, since, have continued to acknowledge their debt to him.

For some years, the question of a biography, based upon Robert's extensive archive in the possession of his family, had been under consideration. As Ran Antrim declared: 'There was no department of life that Robert rejected.' It was time to tell the full story. By studying the wealth of primary material at my disposal, aspects of his life, long shrouded from view, can at last reveal his complex personality and myriad achievements.

Without the support and encouragement of Lucy Butler and her husband, the late Rohan Butler, this task would not have been possible. By allowing me unrestricted access to her brother's papers and by granting me permission to quote from his published and unpublished material, Lucy Butler has displayed immense generosity. My debt to her is incalculable.

Many who shared with me their recollections, as well as giving me advice and information, are, unfortunately, no longer alive, but I would like to thank them nevertheless, along with those still happily with us. I was fortunate at the start of my researches to be able to interview some of the great survivors from Eton and Oxford of the 1920s, notably Sir Harold Acton, Anthony Powell, Lord Moyne and Tamara Talbot Rice. A slightly younger set also put up with my incessant queries, namely the Hon. Diana, Lady Mosley, James Lees-Milne, Lady Dorothy Heber-Percy, the Hon. Joan Leigh Fermor, Patrick Leigh Fermor, Alan Pryce-Jones, Billa, Lady Harrod, Harman Grizewood, Lady Cecilia McKenna, Etienne Amyot and Derek Hill. Others who had memories of Robert from his prep school days onwards were Mark Baker, Christopher Ryde, Cornish Torbock, Roger Mortimer, Lady Alexandra Dacre, the Hon. Daphne Fielding and Tony Bushell. Three Bright Young Things, Zita James, Teresa Cuthbertson (the Jungman sisters) and Loelia, Lady Lindsay, were also most informative. I owe a debt to Sir Steven Runciman, Sir John Pope-Hennessy, Thanos Veloudias, Robert Liddell, Professor Anthony Bryer, Bishop Kallistos of Diokleia, Graham Speake and Xavier Bray for assistance on Byzantine and related matters.

On questions of architecture Sir John Summerson, J. M. Richards, Gavin Stamp, Alan Powers and Robert Bargery of the Georgian Group proved unfailingly helpful.

Certain relations of figures from the period deserve especial thanks, above all for allowing me access to family papers. They are the Duchess of Devonshire, the Earl of Rosse, Francis Dineley, Sebastian Yorke, Sir Reresby Sitwell Bt., Francis Sitwell, John Powell, Nicky Talbot Rice, Elizabeth Talbot Rice, Anne Renshaw, Thomas Messel, Lady Morrison, Nicholas Monck, Lord Faringdon, Piers Dixon, Griselda Grimond, Mrs J. B. Ryan, Kate Russell, Gillian Sutro, the Hon. Hector McDonnell, Francis Wyndham, Charlotte Mosley and the Hon. Mrs Mulji.

I would also like to thank Jane, Lady Abdy, Sir Hugh Casson, the Earl and Countess of Cardigan, the Countess of Rosse, Edward Chaney, Anthony Hobson, Hugh Honour, John Fleming, Oliver Impey, Lady Chancellor, Michael Bloch, Lady Anne Hill, Christopher Walker, Duncan Fallowell, William Reese, Michael Meredith, Alan Bell, Marie-Jacqueline Lancaster, Michael Mallon, Princess Lobanov-Rostovsky, David Birt, Thomas Woodcock the Norroy and Ulster King of Arms, Michael and Anna Farr, Matthew Olex, Geoffrey Roome, Joss Graham, Christopher Marsden-Smedley, Philip Marsden, Richard Bassett, Ralph Pinder-Wilson, Noel Siver, Lindy Grant, Patrick French, Mark Roberts, Patricia, Countess Jellicoe, Taki Theodoracopulos, Philip Hooke, Jonathan Hunt, Sarah Bradford, Esther Whitby, Richard Ingrams, Rosalind Cameron, Joseph Friedman, Francis Hughes, John Daniel, Guy Penman, Simon Bailey, Betty Hussey, Jane Russell and Douglas Matthews who compiled the index.

Particular thanks are due to Bill Whelan for undertaking work on my behalf in America and to Posy Palmer for invaluable archival assistance in the UK.

At the conception of this book, Andrew Wheatcroft and Ariane Bankes, my commissioning editor, were essential. James Hughes, Grant McIntyre, Hazel Wood and Caroline Westmore kept me on track. John Murray gave me sage advice. Above all, Howard Davies, a rare editor of the old school, deserves heartfelt thanks.

I would like to record my personal gratitude to the following: my late mother, Patricia Knox, who inspired my love of architecture; my late father-in-law, Charles Owen, a fine writer, who offered practical support as well as wisdom when it was most needed; my mother-in-law, Felicity Owen, who likewise never lost faith; Charles Cator, a true friend, who gave me the chance to extend my knowledge of the period; Justin Coldwell, inimitable friend and travelling companion, who accompanied me to Mount Athos and did his best to keep his temper; and my twin son and daughter, Bryce and Constance Knox, for their growing curiosity in the book, not to mention the teasing; lastly Lady Selina Hastings, whose wit, sympathy and experience provided inspiration at many moments along the way.

Quotations from published and unpublished material by Robert Byron are by permission of the Executors of the Robert Byron Estate. Quotations from letters of Desmond Parsons in the Rosse Papers are reproduced by courtesy of the Earl of Rosse. Acknowledgement is also made to the Estate of Nancy Mitford for permission to quote from her letters. Every effort has been made to contact other copyright holders, but if any have been inadvertently overlooked the author would be pleased to hear from them.

All geographical names are given as used and spelt by Robert Byron.

James Knox

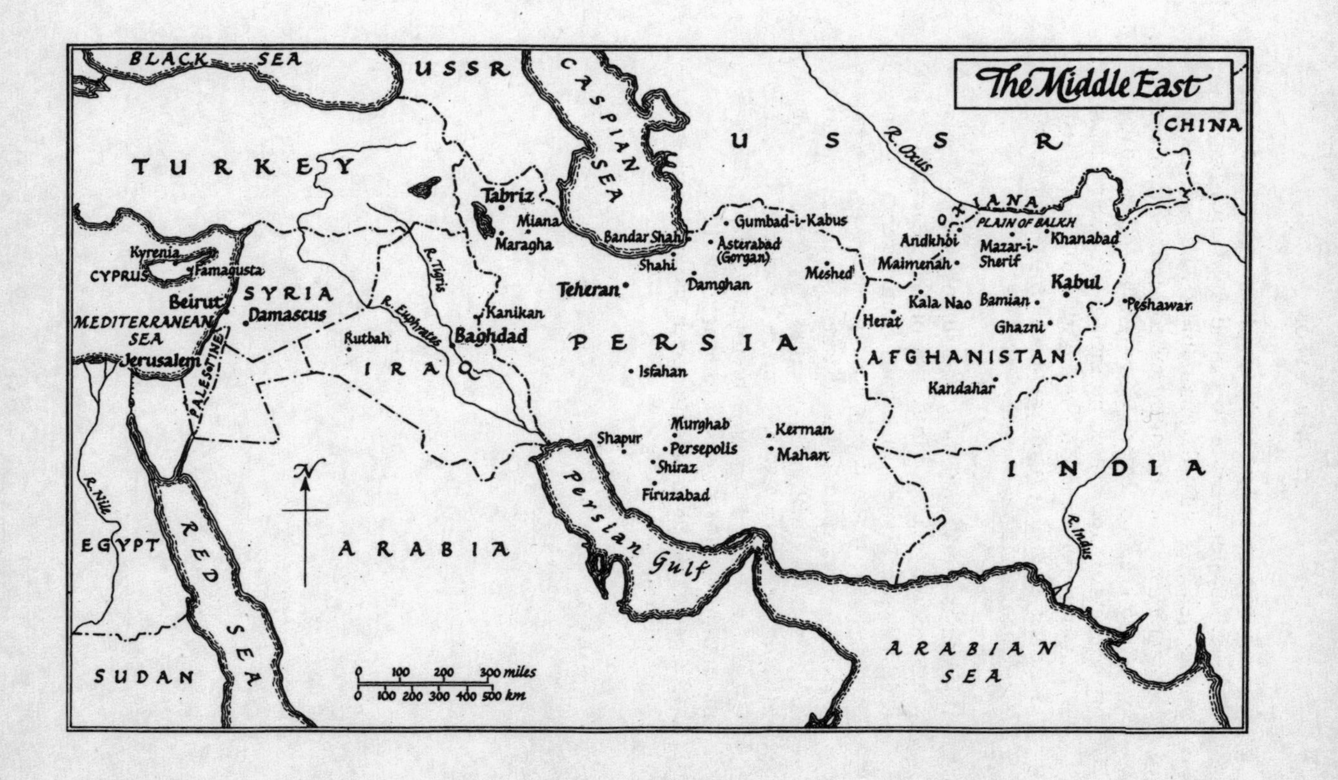

The Middle East
BLACK SEA
USSR
CASPIAN SEA
U S S R
R. Oxus
CHINA
TURKEY
Tabriz
Miana
Maragha
Bandar Shah
Gumbad-i-Kabus
Asterabad (Gorgan)
Shahi
Damghan
Meshed
IANA
PLAIN OF BALKH
Andkhoi
Maimenah
Mazar-i-Sherif
Khanabad
Kabul
Peshawar
Kyrenia
Famagusta
CYPRUS
SYRIA
Beirut
Damascus
MEDITERRANEAN SEA
Jerusalem
PALESTINE
Rutbah
R. Euphrates
R. Tigris
Kanikan
Baghdad
IRAQ
Teheran
PERSIA
Isfahan
Herat
Kala Nao
Bamian
Ghazni
AFGHANISTAN
Kandahar
Murghab
Persepolis
Shiraz
Firuzabad
Shapur
Kerman
Mahan
INDIA
R. Indus
R. Nile
EGYPT
RED SEA
ARABIA
Persian Gulf
ARABIAN SEA
SUDAN
N
0 100 200 300 miles
0 100 200 300 400 500 km

1
No Relation

'Oh, my dear, dear Lord Byron, How I did laugh over your letter . . . I read it on the terrace . . . and I near died of merriment.' In such Augustan tones did Cecil Clonmore address his close friend Robert Byron at Eton in 1921. Associating Robert Byron with his world-famous namesake proved irresistible to his Eton contemporaries. Robert Byron himself occasionally indulged the habit. Writing home from Ravenna, on his first trip abroad in 1923, he told his mother: 'Lord Byron liked it better than any town in Italy, and I was to have enjoyed the privilege of staying in my own hotel on my own piazza, but unfortunately it was shut up.'

In a number of respects, there are striking parallels between the two Byrons. Both were travellers and wrote about their travels, both fell under the spell of Greece, and both died close to their thirty-sixth birthdays engaged in the fight against tyranny.

The first member of Robert Byron's family to emerge with datable accuracy was Edmund Byron, born in 1634 of humble background and with the name Baron. By his death in 1702, he owned land in Lancashire and had changed his name to Byron. His second son, Edmund, an alumnus of Corpus Christi, Oxford, was a prebendary of Wells and vicar of Bishop's Lydeard in Somerset. The memorial in the Church of St John at Glastonbury marking his death in 1710 records that 'he was a royalist and a saintly man.' Of his five children, the youngest, also called Edmund, lived in London, serving as a Justice of the Peace in the County of Middlesex and in Westminster. Edmund married Elizabeth Green, according to family tradition, after falling in love 'by gazing at her of a Sunday across St Anne's, Soho'.

Their son Thomas, born in 1738, hastened the family's ascent in the world. Educated at Eton, he became a colonel in the army and made an excellent marriage to Lucy Anne Whettam, the daughter of Lieutenant-General Thomas Whettam, a cousin of General Wolfe. The Whettams had estates in Nottinghamshire and Surrey which, in 1781, Lucy Anne inherited from her brother. Such wealth enabled Colonel Byron to buy the estate of Coulsden in Surrey. There had never been a country seat built on the estate, so the Byrons acquired an attractive property close by, called Hooley House.

A further sign of social advancement was the granting of a coat of arms to Thomas Byron. No connection with the senior branch of the Byron family was established, but the design was based on their crest and shield with slight variations to differentiate the families.

The nineteenth century saw a consolidation of the Byrons' position. Colonel Byron's heir, his nephew Thomas, married a rich banker's daughter, Louisa Brassey, and became MP for Hertford. In 1841 the MP's son, also called Thomas, married his first cousin, Julia Jeffreys. Four years later, he inherited Coulsden and decided to settle there. Hooley House had been sold, so a suitable home had to be built to accommodate the new squire and his young family.

In consequence, a farmhouse was levelled on the northern part of the estate to make way in 1850 for Coulsden Court, a stark, gabled structure built of the local red brick. Evidently, the Byrons had little interest in outward display. The roof line is shorn of eaves; the long narrow windows are simple rectangles of plate glass, their lintels and sills mere strips of cream-painted stone. Only the porch, designed along Tudor lines with a coat of arms inset, provides any decorative flourish. The interior boasts an inner hall of immense height with a cantilevered wooden staircase and galleried landing which is decorated with Tudor motifs. In the Byrons' day, an immense drawing room and dining room dominated the ground floor with the result that the library and study were cramped, dark and unnaturally tall. Robert Byron described the mansion as 'one of the ugliest houses imaginable – yet not too ugly by reason of its simplicity'.

Such was the new seat of the Byrons, set high upon the Surrey Downs, a mere twelve miles from the centre of London. The surrounding estate comprised about two thousand acres as well as numerous cottages and other properties. Into this inheritance, at the age of nineteen, stepped Thomas's son Edmund, who, in 1865, settled into the life of a country gentleman, enlivening local society with balls and race meetings at Coulsden. Two years later, he replicated his parents' example by marrying his first cousin, Emily Jeffreys. The couple went on to have six children, three boys and three girls. The third son, Eric, born in 1875, was to become the father of Robert Byron.

Early in their marriage the Byrons had made an expedition to shoot game in South Africa, but this was not Edmund's first sporting adventure overseas. While still an undergraduate he had gone hunting buffalo in America, inspired to do so by a book called *The Boy Hunters*. Two magnificent stuffed heads, a buffalo and an elk's, had been brought home as trophies and duly mounted on the walls of Coulsden. Heads from the South African expedition joined them.

Although an excellent shot, Edmund's first love was hunting. He had ridden since boyhood with the Old Surrey Foxhounds and went on to become master of the pack for twenty-five seasons. His prowess in the field was acknowledged in an inscription on a silver hunting horn presented to him by the local farmers, which ran: 'a rum 'un to follow, and a bad 'un to beat' – a judgement supported by Edmund's hard-bitten features which were characterized by a powerful forehead, shrewd eyes and long thin mouth above a determined chin.

A strong vein of ruthlessness coursed through Edmund's veins. Taken to court in the 1870s for enclosing common land, he subsequently sold all his surviving commons, including the magnificent Farthing Down, for £7,000 to the City of London. But if he took with one hand, he also gave with another. Almshouses, a nurses' home and gifts to the church all formed part of his munificence as a landlord. He also sat as a Justice of the Peace for forty-four years as well as undertaking other civic responsibilities.

Most of the original contents of Coulsden Court had been removed at the time of Thomas Byron's death; the interior was thus largely of Edmund and Emily's devising. Handsome pieces of antique marquetry were supplemented with purchases from the workshops of modern cabinetmakers and upholsterers. Cases of stuffed birds adorned the drawing room complementing the menagerie of heads in the inner and outer halls. Overall, an air of discreet luxury pervaded the house, sustained by the efforts of a butler, a 'boots' and the usual bevy of kitchen staff and housemaids.

Despite having six children, neither Edmund nor Emily Byron showed much interest in them. Emily was astonished when Eric's godmother, on visiting the three-week-old baby for the first time, expressed a desire to kiss him. 'Ah give him to me,' exclaimed his mother to the nurse, 'I have not kissed him yet.' A few years later, Eric and his younger sister, Alice, contracted scarlet fever. The girl died, leaving little hope for Eric. Their parents, who had departed hastily for London, ordered the sexton to dig a grave for Alice and, while he was about it, one for Eric as well. Eric survived, but his travails were not over. An attack of pneumonia threatened his life as a schoolboy at Marlborough. Once again, his parents kept their distance at the critical time.

The effects of Eric's ill-health stayed with him into adulthood. Although tall, he was afflicted with a permanent stoop. And his oval face had a melancholy air, accentuated by the fall of a neatly trimmed moustache, making him look older than his years.

Of the two other Byron boys Thomas, the heir, a product of Eton and Christ Church, Oxford, had annoyed his father by going down from university in debt. Shortly afterwards, he left for Canada where, under conditions of great hardship, he tried to establish himself as a farmer. Cecil, as a younger son, had been sent to Marlborough. Later, he worked briefly in an office before deciding to start a new life with his brother in Canada.

On leaving school in 1893, Eric applied to join the Indian Army but was turned down on medical grounds. He subsequently enrolled at the School of Practical Engineering at Crystal Palace in south London, conveniently close to Coulsden. He proved an excellent student, passing out with top marks. His success led to an apprenticeship with a firm of civil engineers in Chesterfield. There, at the turn of the century, he met his future wife, Margaret Robinson.

The Robinsons had a streak of Highland blood in their veins. An ancestor, a Robertson of Struan, had fought for Bonnie

Prince Charlie at Culloden. After the defeat, he fled to France and spent the rest of his life in exile. A generation or so later, his descendants, having anglicized their name, returned to Britain, becoming land agents to the Miss Wyatt-Edgells of West Grinstead Park, themselves Jacobite sympathizers.

Their descendant, William Robinson, married into the well-off Chater family, who had made a fortune importing luxury goods from France. His father-in-law, an astute financier, had bought a large house in Holland Park and had also made generous provision for all his children.

The Robinsons had nine children, of whom Margaret, born in 1875, was the second oldest. After being educated at home by a governess, she went on to study at South Kensington School of Art. Thenceforth, Margaret, or Daisy as she was known, developed into an accomplished amateur taking further lessons from the artist Joseph Syddall after the family's move to Chesterfield.

Margaret Robinson was in her mid-twenties when she met Eric Byron. She was an attractive woman with a delicate, oval face and hooded eyes agleam with vitality and intelligence. Initially, Margaret rejected her 'tender' suitor's hand in marriage, but in so doing, she also revealed the strength of their attraction: 'I did not learn to love you through admiration . . .' she explained, 'I loved you because you wanted me & cared for me so & helped me & thought for me & brought out the good in me & because I saw & felt all the good in you & because I felt for you in your troubles & because I knew you were true & because I wanted to love you.'

Gradually, Eric wore down Margaret's resistance until she finally capitulated. 'I am not what I used to be . . .' she acknowledged some two years later, 'I should not care to have to live with myself . . . Oh darling I do so long for a little peace somewhere alone with you with only our two selves to think of and to worry about.' The couple were married in September 1903 at the fashionable church of St James's, Piccadilly. A honeymoon was spent at Church Stretton in Shropshire before they travelled on north to Bolton in Lancashire where Eric was to take up a new post overseeing a railway widening scheme.

Eric was now twenty-seven. For the past two years he had been working for a contractor called Strachan largely as the resident engineer on the construction of the Welshpool and Llanfair light railway. Just before his marriage, Eric had attempted to buy himself a partnership in the firm, but his father had blocked the idea, summarily transferring Eric's small sum of capital into the name of his trustees to prevent any possible transaction taking place. Eric's salary at the time of his marriage was £180. This was topped up by an allowance from his father and other income to give the Byrons just over £400 a year.

Keen to save money, the Byrons embarked on married life in modest rented accommodation in Bolton. Their stay, however, was of short duration. Eight months later, Eric was moved south to take on a railway construction job in London, where the couple rented a small, semi-detached house at 23 Swinderby Road in the growing suburb of Wembley.

This dull specimen of cheap suburban housing was the birthplace of one of England's most passionate lovers of architecture. Here, at 6 p.m. on Sunday 26 February 1905, Robert Byron was born. Congratulations from members of the family soon arrived by letter and telegram. His grandfather, Edmund Byron, dispatched a couple of rabbits shot at Coulsden explaining that 'they may be useful with your extra visitors.'

There was general satisfaction that the baby was a boy. Robert was not the first grandson to be born to that generation of the Byron family. Eric's sister Lucy, married to a lawyer Theodore Hall Hall, had also had a son. But Robert was the first in the male line. On 12 April 1905, he was christened Robert Henry Byron at St Stephen's Church, Ealing, the parish of his Robinson grandparents. The godparents were Eric's eldest brother, Thomas, still a frontiersman in Canada, a Byron cousin and the Byron family trustee. The Robinsons were represented by Margaret's sister, Gertrude.

With his very fair hair, blue eyes, pink cheeks and white skin, Robert was a nice looking baby. His uncle Wilfred, the youngest Robinson boy, described him at three weeks old as being like a 'model of Queen Victoria'. The similarity never left him.

Soon after Robert's first birthday, the family were once more on the move. His father's latest assignment took them to Cardiff where they lodged for a time in rooms. However, these proved so unsatisfactory that Robert and his nurse were sent to stay with Margaret's parents in Ealing.

The Robinsons' red-brick villa, called Netherleigh, which still stands within its leafy garden in Castlebar Hill, was a haven of moneyed comfort. Robert was to spend the next nine months there, the first of many extended visits that occurred during his early childhood. Numerous Robinson children had still not fled the nest, including Margaret's sister, Edith, known as Aunt Deedie. She immediately took the toddler under her wing, doing her best over the next few years to protect him from the harsh treatment of his first nurse, called Moon, whom she described as being 'smart, good looking, very trained, yet . . . without the least understanding of a child, and indeed was too hard on the little Bobby without excuse'. When Aunt Deedie remonstrated with her, Moon replied: 'Ah, you don't know him.'

She spoke with feeling. Despite his tender age, Robert was already proving to be a determined little enemy. He took delight in hurling the contents of the hated Moon's 'special cupboard' on to the floor. Once he was even discovered sticking needles and pins into her nightdress. Aunt Deedie had her own theory about the lifelong damage caused by this warfare. Many years later, she pronounced: 'There is no doubt that his experiences with his overstrict nurse had damaged his natural self-control. It was regrettable inclining him to be aggressive.' Many another childhood tantrum was cited in evidence. Robert himself had no recollection of Moon other than recording that 'I remember remembering that I hated her.'

Otherwise the gentle regime of Netherleigh proved much to his taste. He thrived on the enormous teas where plain nursery fare had been banished on doctor's orders in favour of cream-filled meringues and macaroons. Teatime also proved an aesthetic delight to the ever observant child. He treasured his own miniature Crown Derby cup and saucer reserved for his warm sugared milk. And his grandmother's magnificent tapestry tea cosy of gorgeous coloured wools and fantastic High Victorian design once provoked the precocious response: 'Isn't that beautifully worked.'

Netherleigh provided a series of cosseted interludes from the Byrons' peripatetic way of life. After nine months in Cardiff, Eric moved to Anglesey to assist in the construction of a railway across the island. The Byrons took a house in the village of Llanfair, where Robert joined his parents. They remained there for almost two years until October 1908, when Eric decided to set up his own engineering business in London.

The search for a suitable home began anew. This time, the Byrons plumped for the pleasant locality of Blackheath in south London, but, even so, their restless existence continued. They moved six times over the next four years, finally coming to rest in a Victorian house in Belmont Grove, Lewisham. During the course of this period, Robert's sisters were born. Anne arrived in August 1909, followed by Lucy in November 1912. The family was now complete.

2

Little Innocent

Robert's earliest memory of Blackheath was finding shepherd's purse growing on the side of a large pit. For a four year old, his knowledge of flowers and plants was already considerable. While living on Anglesey, he had, according to his mother's proud boast, learnt to name thirty-two species. Whatever the number, Robert's curiosity was genuine. 'Flowers made deep impressions on my early mind', he was to recall in an unpublished memoir, 'and still do more than anything else to revive associations.'

Margaret Byron had never doubted her son's intelligence. The tutoring of her precocious child had begun during their hours spent alone together living on Anglesey. She had taught him to read from the works of Beatrix Potter, and in turn read to him from Shakespeare and other classics so that he was soon able to recite long passages by heart. His education continued in Blackheath under two successive governesses until, at the age of six and a half, he was sent as a day boy to Lindisfarne School in neighbouring Belmont Park Road.

Owned and run by a Mr Arthur Kilby, this small preparatory school numbered about fifty-five boys, and had high academic standards, half the boys each year winning scholarships to many of the best public schools. As a day boy Robert was spared the brutal shock, common to most of his contemporaries, of having to leave home aged seven or eight to start at a traditional boarding school. This change eventually occurred in September 1916, when he was eleven, and was caused by the upheavals of war.

The outbreak of war in 1914 only gradually impinged upon the Byron family. The summer of 1915 saw Zeppelins over Blackheath and bombs dropped on Woolwich. Rumours of invasion, victory and peace swept the country, leading Margaret Byron to record in her diary: 'Heard an invisible host at the Marne caused the Germans to retreat.' At this time, her brother Norman, a civil engineer like her husband, was running a munitions factory in Russia. A visit from Burgess, their younger brother, resulted in the first family casualty of the war. He was drowned that August while swimming in the River Volga. The news hit Margaret hard, especially as it came just weeks after the death of her father. Her misery was compounded in December when her third brother, Wilfred, left for the front. Concluding her diary for 1915, Margaret wrote: 'so ends the saddest year of my life.'

Soon afterwards Eric Byron was also given the chance to play his part in the war effort. Too old and too unfit to enlist, he got a job working with the army on Salisbury Plain. This led, in October 1916, to a posting on behalf of the Ministry of Munitions to Sheffield.

The Byrons decided to set up home in nearby Chesterfield, familiar territory from their courtship days, where they rented a large detached house in an insalubrious part of the town. 'Very sorry indeed to come to the neighbourhood,' lamented Margaret in her diary.

The move coincided with Robert's first term as a boarder at Mr Kilby's new educational establishment in the country. Kilby had long wanted to leave the environs of London and the threat of bombs had spurred him on. His quest for suitable premises ended with the purchase of Abberley Hall, a palatial mansion situated in the heart of the Worcestershire countryside.

Abberley Hall was a monument to Victorian taste. A succession of nineteenth-century owners had refaced, remodelled, enlarged and embellished the original Georgian house, cloaking its brick core in an imperious Italianate façade. The extensive grounds boasted similar improvements which had been undertaken when the house passed into the hands of the cotton magnate, John Joseph Jones of Oldham. He had laid out rockeries, water gardens and grottoes, but his most grandiloquent gesture, dominating the countryside for miles around, had been the construction on a neighbouring eminence of a massive, pinnacled clock tower.

At Abberley Hall the rigorous academic schedule was maintained. Boys spent long days at their desks following a curriculum dominated by mathematics and classics with a leavening of drawing, poetry, scripture, geography and French. The intellectual regime suited Robert. In the autumn of 1917, aged twelve, he passed the Cambridge Junior examination, earning praise in the school magazine for being 'easily the youngest boy in England to pass the Cambridge Junior'.

For a nature-loving boy, the remote Worcestershire countryside was paradise. Hours were spent rambling through the surrounding woods and fields and up on to the neighbouring Woodbury Hill on the lookout for flora and fauna. His model was the eighteenth-century naturalist, Gilbert White of Selborne, and, like him, he set about recording the earliest flowerings of the year. First came catkins and primroses followed by an ever-lengthening list encompassing bird's-eye speedwell, dog violet, coltsfoot, white violets, spurge laurel and celandine. He also spotted a caterpillar in a cartridge case, a chaffinch's nest, and 'a horrible hibernating toad changing its skin', at the sight of which, he admitted, 'I was nearly sick.'

Borrowing another idea from Gilbert White, he compiled a 'naturalist's calendar', putting into chronological order the discoveries made during the first few months of the year. The information was readily at hand because since January 1918 Robert had been keeping a diary covering his life both in and out of the classroom. The habit had sparked a minor craze for Pepys. Some entries break into seventeenth-century spelling: 'it began to snow . . .' he reported, 'most colde beyonde everything.' His classics master, Mr Jarratt, one of the most acute masters in the school, 'is much intrigued by Samuel Pepys Junior', Robert noted.

Drawing was another favourite occupation. Lessons from Miss Harrison, an excellent teacher, frequently merited an entry in the diary. Under her instruction, he studied perspective, drew portraits and painted local views. At the back of his mind was also the example of his mother, herself a well-trained artist. After working up a painting of a courtyard, he wrote: 'I'm sure mother will like me doing that.'

His fluency as a draughtsman led him to fill sketchbooks with illustrations of scenes and anecdotes from his daily life. This practice replaced his diary which had lapsed after three months. Subjects included 'Blackberrying in Derbyshire', 'A Moor-hen's nest', 'Dawn on the way to Worcester' and 'Cuthbert, a pantomime horse'. Many pages were devoted to caricatures and cartoons. His technique was honed from copying illustrations in *Punch*, but the dry schoolboy humour was all his own. One cartoon entitled 'At the theatre' shows a man craning his neck behind rows of women with enormous hats. Another joked at the regular diet of scripture and sermons at school. It depicts a grotesque monk with a vast girth, and bears the caption: 'Thou art Peter and on this rock will I build my church!!!' Beneath, Robert appends: 'I am inclined to think it would soon wobble off.'

The war was a frequent topic in both diary and sketchbooks. Reminders at the school were everywhere. A handful of shell-shocked young men were given jobs as teachers, whilst German prisoners of war, distinguished by patches sewn on to their jackets, were commandeered to roll a cricket pitch. The fate of old boys, dead or wounded, was reported in each new issue of the school magazine. One of their number, Lieutenant Walter Stone, was awarded a posthumous VC and the school honoured his bravery with a whole holiday. Robert's family had their share of loss. In March 1918, Wilfred Robinson, still in his early twenties, was killed during the German offensive in France.

The privations of war did not suit Robert. A keen trencherman, he complained constantly about the lack of food. Breakfast, he moaned, consisted only of porridge, a baked apple and bread. Lunch was soup. There was no mid-morning snack or biscuits in the afternoon, and tuck was banned. 'I live in hunger now,' he wailed. 'One's life is spent in waiting for the next meal.' Even so, the school did not do too badly. The home farm provided milk and bacon just as the kitchen garden produced vegetables, and Robert duly put on weight.

The autumn of 1918 saw the Spanish flu epidemic sweep the school. No one died, but Robert, like many others, was laid low. However the end of the war was in sight. Robert noted each fresh victory in his sketchbook until, on 11 November, he was able to scrawl PEACE across the page.

The carillon in the Abberley clock tower rang out for the first time since the outbreak of war.

As usual, that first post-war Christmas was spent at Coulsden where the festivities were celebrated according to time-honoured routine. One of the most thrilling moments for the children was decorating the pictures and stuffed trophies with copious quantities of holly and yew. But even this had its rules. Year in year out, the greenery had to be arranged in exactly the same way. The final excitement of the day took place after dinner when their grandfather provided modest stakes for a game of commerce.

The Byrons' visits, which occurred two or three times a year, provided the children with a joyous release from their parents' assortment of rented suburban homes. Grooms were at hand to take them riding and, in Robert's case, a game-keeper to teach him how to shoot. Even so, as Robert recalled, their days spent roaming the beautiful gardens and ancestral acres were clouded by the 'grim shadow' of their grand-father.

Edmund Byron was now seventy-five years old and had been a widower for the past ten years. However his domination of the house and estate remained complete. One of the worst ordeals for the children, particularly for Lucy, the youngest, was having to bid their grandfather goodnight before he went up to change for dinner. This necessitated crossing the gloomy inner hall where the stuffed heads loomed out of the dark shadows. On reaching his austere study another fright was in store. Hung above the fireplace was the snarling mask of a fox with its fierce teeth, for once, especially well lit.

Although a remote and terrifying figure, Edmund Byron had long demonstrated a keen interest in the future of his grandson. This sprang from his desire to uphold family tradition by sending him to Eton. The family's connection with the school stretched back to the 1750s but had become established in the nineteenth century when three eldest sons in succession had been educated there, the last being Robert's uncle, Thomas Byron.

The question of the next generation came to be addressed

in 1909. By that time, the prospect of Thomas siring a suitable candidate for Eton looked unlikely. He showed no inclination to get married and remained a struggling rancher in Canada. Of the existing grandchildren, Robert was not the eldest boy. That distinction went to his cousin Owen, the son of Eric's sister Lucy and the solicitor Theodore Hall Hall. However Robert was the eldest in the male line, which, in his grandfather's eyes, justified his going to Eton. As a mark of his resolve, Edmund volunteered to pay the school fees and in so doing took charge of all the preliminaries.

Even though Robert was only four years old, there was little time to lose. Most boys destined for Eton were put down on a housemaster's list at birth in the hope of guaranteeing their admission to the school at the age of twelve or thirteen. Thus when Edmund paid a round of calls on potential housemasters in November 1909, he discovered that their lists were already full. Fortunately, one of them put in a good word for him with a colleague, Mr Todd. He still had vacancies for the proposed year of Robert's arrival and agreed to offer him a place in his house. An exchange of letters, following Robert's twelfth birthday, finally confirmed his place in Todd's house for the autumn term of 1918.

With everything signed and sealed, Mr Todd felt able to suggest a change to the arrangements. An unexpected vacancy had arisen for January 1918 and he wrote to Edmund asking if his grandson would like to fill it. Edmund's first reaction was to inquire about the fees. These had last been discussed in 1909 when the cost of board and tuition had been given as £150. Back came the unwelcome news that the figure had doubled.

Although Edmund could easily afford such a sum, he rejected Todd's offer out of hand. His next move showed him to be crafty as well as mean. He wrote to the school bursar about the cost to a parent of supporting a King's Scholar at Eton: these were the winners of Foundation Scholarships, who are housed in Henry VI's original college building and have their tuition paid for. The bursar reckoned that the cost for such a boy was a mere £60 a year. This proved too good to resist. The decision was taken at the end of 1917 that Robert should try for a scholarship.

Preparations were put in hand at once. A tutor was hired for the forthcoming Christmas and Easter holidays to coach him in classics, whilst during term time Robert began doing Eton practice papers. Already a well-trained examinee, he boasted to his mother of coming out 'second or top in everything'. Even Mr Todd was squared. He confirmed that if Robert failed the scholarship, a place would still be available for him the following autumn.

The exam took place at Eton in June 1918. It was held over three days and Robert and his mother stayed at the Bridge House Hotel in Windsor for the occasion.

Poor Margaret suffered agonies on her son's behalf. As the tension mounted over the days of the examination so did her fury at his grandfather's wilfulness. 'Poor old Bob was dreadfully depressed all yesterday –' she complained to Eric. 'I went to bed miserable – he'll just be heartbroken if he doesn't get it – I shall write to your father if he doesn't and jolly well have it out, I shall be so furious, dangling the thing in front of a boy and then not letting him have it – it's cruel.'

Adding to her woes was the arrival of her brother-in-law, Theodore Hall Hall. His son Owen had recently left the school, but Theodore, who himself was an Old Etonian and an Eton bore, welcomed any opportunity to return. The prospect of the arrival of her sister-in-law Lucy later that day led Margaret to express the hope that they would not meet. At the back of her mind was the fear of how Robert's possible failure might be viewed by the rest of the Byron family. Owing to Edmund's mishandling of the situation, Robert's name was down for no other school. In low moments, Margaret discounted Todd's existing offer and predicted a bleak future for her son: 'we shan't get him anywhere now except Cheltenham or Bradfield –' she pointed out to Eric, '& then your family will sneer.'

But all was not lost. On the final day, the list of boys to have got through to the viva voce was posted on the door of the examination hall. Robert's name was on it. 'I felt', he wrote, 'as if a lead weight was lifted from my heart.'

The oral examination was conducted by three masters including the Head Master, Dr Alington. Their topic was

English literature and in particular the Romantic poets. Fortunately, Robert had recently studied this period at Abberley. So when Alington asked him to quote a line from Shelley, he blurted out the words from 'Ode to a Skylark': 'Bird thou never wert.' Showing no respect for established reputations, Robert had originally memorized the phrase purely 'for its idiocy'. But the impact on Alington was immediate. He burst out laughing and replied: 'Wusent it really?'

News of the examination results greeted Robert as he stepped off the train on returning to Abberley. There to meet him was Mr Jarratt, exclaiming: 'Well done old chap! Well done!!' Robert had gained the thirteenth place out of eighteen. The decision apparently swung on the excellence of his mathematics which compensated for the poor quality of his Latin and Greek. The headmaster, Mr Kilby, though he taught Robert mathematics, had done little to promote his chances of winning a scholarship. He had written to Alington in the course of the exam stating that, although his pupil had all-round ability, as a 'classical specialist we have never encouraged him'. Robert however was overjoyed: 'Dr Alington didn't know whether he ought to have elected me as my CLASSICS were so desperately low. But as I was such a MATHEMATICAL GENIUS he thought he felt quite justified in doing so. Mr K's feelings on the subject were unimaginably furious.'

Even though he had won his scholarship, escape from Mr Kilby was not immediate. There was a shortage of places in College, as the residence of the King's Scholars is known, and Robert's entry did not look likely until May 1919. In the meantime, he would either have to stay at Abberley or enter Mr Todd's house on a temporary basis.

A decision was urgently required, but Eric Byron dithered. Finally he received the opinion of another housemaster, delivered via Theodore Hall Hall, assuring him of the 'strong possibility' of an eventual place in College: 'It will make no difference that he will be 14 before next Easter.' Thus it was decided to keep Robert at Abberley until the summer term of the following year.

It proved a disastrous miscalculation. At the turn of the year, the Byrons received the news from the Master in College that the ending of the war had greatly diminished the number of boys leaving school early. Hence, there were even fewer places available for the new batch of scholarship boys, making it most uncertain that Robert would be admitted the following May. Furthermore, he made plain that after that date, Robert would be too old to qualify for a place in College.

This bombshell effectively left Robert with no place at any school. Mr Kilby suggested trying for scholarships at the dreaded schools of Cheltenham or Bradfield, whilst Theodore Hall Hall, sensitive to passing on misleading advice about the age limit, offered every assistance. He trawled the *Public School Yearbook* for alternatives and even suggesting Oundle 'for science and business training'.

Hitherto, Margaret Byron had let her husband try and salvage the situation. But now she took the matter into her own hands. On 21 January she went to Eton where she sat outside the Provost's office until he agreed to see her. She also gained admittance to the Head Master and interviewed Mr Todd, who, she discovered, had a temporary vacancy in his house for the forthcoming half, as terms are known at Eton. This, she was strongly advised to take. The Provost even went further. He promised to do his utmost to find Robert a permanent place in the school. Margaret could not conceal a note of triumph from the telegram sent to Eric that evening. She ended: 'Good thing I came very strong case they say.'

Before taking up the place, one important matter had to be settled. With the scholarship no longer valid, Edmund Byron was asked to confirm that he would abide by his original offer to pay for his grandson's education. His agreement was given. Robert was now able to enter Eton as an Oppidan Scholar, one who receives no financial support, for the January half 1919.

Margaret Byron had snatched victory from the jaws of defeat. She had demonstrated in dynamic fashion the protectiveness she felt towards her beloved son. From the start, she had been intimately involved in his education, teaching him to read and write and encouraging him in his artistic hobbies. She knew better than anyone the key to Robert's creativity and the ease with which it could become obscured by his grumbling, awkward manner. Brought up on the idea of going to Eton, then forced to take the scholarship exam, Robert would have felt bitterly betrayed at not being given his promised reward. In seeing this, Margaret had proved herself a loving, sympathetic and ambitious mother. Her instincts were right. Getting him in to Eton was to prove one of the greatest prizes ever bestowed upon him.

3
Lords and Rebels

The last-minute offer of a place in Mr Todd's house saw Robert suddenly plucked from the familiar surroundings of Abberley and removed to Eton on a raw winter's day at the end of January 1919, one week after the half had begun.

His experience the following morning at Early School, the lesson held at 7.30 a.m., brought home to him the strangeness of his new world. Entering the room a few minutes late, he was met by the curious stares of his fellow pupils as the master in charge bore down upon him. This was A. B. Ramsay, the Lower Master (head of the lower school), and teacher of classics to the top form of Robert's year, known as the Select Division, into which, as an Oppidan Scholar, he had been placed. Ramsay, rubbing his mittened hands before him, asked Robert in his high sing-song voice: 'Dicis-ne Latine, puer?' Robert looked baffled at this pleasantry, forcing Ramsay to repeat in English: 'Do you speak Latin, boy?'

Having to converse in Latin before breakfast was not his only problem. He also had difficulty in finding his way about and complained to his mother in his first letter home of feeling 'so lonely – sometimes so watched'. His one consolation was the luxury afforded by all the boys' houses at Eton of having a room to himself. One of his first acts was to brighten it up with a hyacinth.

At the start of the following half, Robert was faced with yet more uncertainty. There was now no longer room for him at Mr Todd's but neither was there any other obvious place for him to board. Fortunately, the housemaster, F. E. Robeson, suddenly found himself with a temporary vacancy owing to a boy succumbing to appendicitis. Robert was transferred to his house but again on the understanding that it was for one half only. Gradually, however, the time limit was extended until in February 1920 permission was finally granted for him to remain at Robeson's permanently.

The coming of summer brought happier days. During the previous holidays Robert had had swimming lessons at the Corporation baths in Sheffield which helped him to qualify as a wet bob, enabling him to become a rower rather than a cricketer. Henceforth, enjoyable hours could be spent sculling by himself on the river far from the prying herd.

The end of the war also saw the revival of the Fourth of June, the famous Eton festival, in abeyance since 1914, commemorating George III's birthday. For weeks beforehand, a sense of expectation reigned. This was heightened by the arrival, like exotic birds of passage long awaited, of tiers of straw hats in the hosiers' windows, beflowered and beribboned, glittering with the names of the school's eights.

On the day, Robert dragged his mother round the various sporting activities on the programme, determined to miss nothing. The celebrations reached their climax after dark with a magnificent firework display and parade of boats. So great was the excitement that the crowd, Robert and his mother among them, overran the Head Master's private enclosure to get a better view of the river. The oarsmen, standing upright in their narrow craft, glided past, appearing against the showers of golden light as 'astonishing silhouettes' in their archaic uniforms and foppish headgear. As a final device, the words FLOREAT ETONA were emblazoned across the night sky.

The other fashionable event of the Eton summer was the cricket match against Harrow at Lords. This too had been suspended for the duration and its return, honoured by the presence of the King, evoked the glamour of pre-war days. Robert was caught up in the mood, not only – as he later recalled – because of the splendour of the festal celebrations, but also because of the atmosphere of 'historic excitement' that surrounded them. 'In sum', he explained, 'several thousands of people . . . were all using the school that summer as a focus for their various emotions.' It was, he continued, 'a spontaneous affirmation of the victory and the peace through homage to an old institution. Now, thank God, everything would go on as before; and what else mattered?'

Eton, like countless other schools, had suffered huge losses during the war. Eleven hundred old Etonians had died, the equivalent of the school's population in any one year, and fourteen hundred had been wounded. The fallen were remembered one evening in July at a sombre ceremony to mark the signing of the Treaty of Versailles. Masters and boys assembled in the ancient School Yard, each boy carrying a torch which smoked, stank and hissed in the drizzle. A hymn was sung composed by the Head Master in commemoration of the dead.

On a page of his sketchbook, Robert had noted down the time and date of the signing of the peace. But even as a young schoolboy he questioned its effectiveness. In an aside, he added: 'The only disadvantage being that the fulfilment of the terms and wars in other parts of the world will probably go on for another century.'

As a grown man, Robert speculated that the events of that summer, witnessed at such an impressionable age, had left him with an enduring legacy. 'The experience', he suggested, 'enrolled me as a child of the age then beginning, and may well have initiated certain habits of thought and conduct . . . whose imprint I shall bear as long as I live.'

In the meantime, he was having to come to terms with a more humdrum beginning as an unexpected arrival in Mr Robeson's house. Known as Penn House, it was a building dismissed by Robert as 'a gaunt pile of yellow brick closely resembling Wormwood Scrubs Prison'. No sanitary inspector, Robert claimed, would have deemed his particular 'cell' fit for human habitation. Such a verdict could easily have been passed on the whole house. Apart from a pervasive air of dirt, the plumbing also left much to be desired. Each room was provided with the usual washstand cum *table de nuit*, but otherwise there was only one bath and two outside lavatories to serve about fifty inmates.

Presiding over this Dickensian institution was the bachelor housemaster, F. E. Robeson, a dull man, not particularly clever, whose one claim to fame was having rowed for Oxford. Such an unprepossessing figure could not hope to establish a reputation with either conventional parents of Etonian pedigree or those ambitious for their sons. Far from it, as one old boy,

Roger Mortimer, later a distinguished racing correspondent, explained: 'Parents either did not know him or were put off by him. They would have thought he was dim.'

As a result, his collection of boys was, according to Mortimer and others, 'a very mixed bag'. Robert's future circle included the sons of a cultivated city magnate, a stockbroker, a northern industrialist, a tough Irish foxhunter, an impoverished younger son, an Irish aristocrat and an Australian. Others came from disrupted families. One boy had divorced parents whilst another, recently orphaned, was looked after by an American grandmother. Out of this group two of the more acceptable boys, at least on paper, Cornish Torbock, the industrialist's son but with ancient county roots on his mother's side, and William, Lord Clonmore, heir to the Earl of Wicklow, had both ended up at Robeson's owing to the sudden collapse of better laid plans.

During his first two years at Eton, Robert buckled down to the dictates of the academic regime. It was hard grind, as he made plain in a letter to his mother giving the timetable of a previous day's work. Classes, or divisions as they are known, had begun at 7.30 a.m. and ended at 5.45 p.m. When not in the division room, Robert was either writing up notes or revising for the next test. Two periods were set aside for physical exercise, which, on the day in question, took the form of recruit drill. The evening brought no respite. Over tea, Robert worked intermittently on a Greek construe in preparation for the 'pupil room' that followed with his classical tutor, H. E. E. Howson, the master responsible for his overall academic performance. The day ended with a long stint of maths prep, only interrupted by supper and prayers, until lights were put out at 9.50 p.m.

Classics and mathematics dominated the curriculum, but history, French, science and divinity were also taught. Robert's performance was somewhat erratic, especially in classics, although he did occasionally shine. His greatest triumph, which occurred in the Michaelmas half 1919, was winning the Lower Boy Rosebery history prize. He also achieved a measure of sporting success. Slightly built, but with a wiry frame, he turned out to be a good runner, winning a clutch of trophies.

Robert's entry into the conventional life of the house was reflected in his unadventurous choice of friends. Initially, he was happy to mess, or have tea every day, with a boy called Baker, described by Cornish Torbock as 'a perfectly decent ordinary type'; whilst another companion was Reginald Clay, a likeable athlete. Neither, in the long run, turned out to have anything in common with him.

In general, an unflinching reserve distanced Robert from the mass of his schoolfellows. The two masters who knew him best, Robeson and Howson, both attributed this to shyness. 'He appears uninterested in a large company,' Howson commented in one report, 'but the narrower the circle the more natural he becomes & therefore the less indifferent.' Robert, in later years, preferred to describe his condition as one of mental paralysis. 'I had accepted', he recalled, 'the conventions of whatever majority happened to be about me as immutable: if they were pleasant conventions I did not notice them; if unpleasant they had to be quietly endured.'

But behind the mask of acquiescence a fiercely independent mind was stirring. The effects were first felt in the division and pupil room where Robert was apt to kick against the time-honoured tasks doled out to him. If corrected in construe, he would, on occasion, blame the Greek or Latin author for being unreasonable rather than accept that he himself had made a mistake. Equally, he was capable of displaying such aversion to a piece of work that his behaviour became downright rude. Howson bore the brunt of this refractoriness, although he also ventured that 'others would agree with me in finding him tiresome to deal with when the mood is on him'. When his performance deteriorated in the Michaelmas half of 1920, Robeson too commented on his air of apathy, lack of interest '& apparent impermeability'. He urged him 'to look in everything & everybody . . . for what there is to admire than for what there is to criticize'.

Such sermonizing fell on deaf ears. Robert was now nearly sixteen years old and on the point of starting to shave. The onward march of puberty had already wrought other changes. His features, although still lacking the definition of maturity, had begun to take on their adult mould. He had developed a heavy jowl, high sloped forehead, prominent nose, full lower lip and hooded, protruding eyes. In some lights, his was already a knowing face, quizzical, slightly menacing and plain.

One other obvious change affected Robert's looks. An eye problem, which flared up just before Christmas 1920, forced him to start wearing a pair of 'prismal glasses' for reading. These were not sufficient in themselves to effect a cure. In addition, restrictions were placed on the amount of prep he was allowed to do as well as on the number of pupil rooms attended each week. Accordingly, his teachers had no option but to take a more lenient attitude towards his performance.

To enforce idleness upon an already difficult adolescent was asking for trouble. All that remained was for a rebel leader to step forward and claim him. Ready and waiting was William, Lord Clonmore, the eighteen-year-old heir to the Earl of Wicklow, who, by extending the hand of friendship, instantly changed Robert's view of the world.

William Clonmore, or Cecil as he was known to Robert, who used his second name, had been born into the highest ranks of the Irish ascendancy. His father, the seventh Earl, who had a posting at the War Office and sat as a representative peer in the Lords, sailed through life with an aristocratic detachment that rose above the social and political conventions of the day. His mother was dead, but her place had been filled, as far as that was possible, by his maternal grandmother, the Dowager Duchess of Abercorn.

An only child, Cecil had been brought up at the family seat of Shelton Abbey, outside Arklow in County Wicklow, a stately pile replete with buttresses, pinnacles, cloisters and crockets. Its appearance dated from the Regency period when an earlier, classical, building had been enlarged and gothicized in a late flowering of the Strawberry Hill style. The setting was no less fantastic. There were dense woods, rolling parkland, a subtropical garden and an avenue some two miles long bordered by high walls of rhododendrons. Robert evoked the scene when he wrote after a visit in the spring of 1927 that 'the house, of fabricated stone, sparkled like a porcupine of Gothic quills within its wooded cup.'

From this idyll, Cecil had been transplanted at the age of

eight to the fashionable English prep school of Wixenford. His circle there included a handful of artistic boys, such as Harold Acton and David Talbot Rice, but unlike them he was not destined for Eton. Instead, he was packed off to Osborne, the cadet college for the Royal Navy. If this were not bad enough, the move coincided with his mother's death. A miserable year ensued until his plight was finally recognized and the decision taken to send him to Eton where a place was found for him in Robeson's house.

By the time Cecil befriended Robert, early in the Lent half of 1921, he had become a schoolboy rebel par excellence. His chosen enemies were legion, numbering, as they did, virtually everyone of any consequence in the school from the Head Master downwards. To Robert, his junior by two years, idle yet restive, such individualism was intoxicating.

When analysing, many years later, Cecil's 'fearful skill' at dealing with his enemies, Robert pointed to the influence of his father and grandmother. The combination of their two worlds – the 'eccentric aloofness of Ireland' as personified by Lord Wicklow and the grand, gossipy milieu of the Dowager Duchess – was, he claimed, the source of the habitual expression of 'sardonic disdain' with which Cecil outfaced those presumptuous enough to sit in judgement over him. He surveyed the world through half-closed, almost veiled eyes, utterly impassive, his simian looks only flickering to life with a well-judged sneer or scowl. Such hostility left its mark upon Robert's contemporary, Cornish Torbock. He found Cecil unappealing and dismissed him as 'very Irish and slightly mad'.

By challenging the accepted precepts of the school, Cecil awoke in Robert 'the pleasure', as he put it, 'of questioning what I had thought unquestionable, of exchanging convention for my inner light and claiming the reward'. Robert was never to forget the sheer joy of revolt. 'We railed against the school,' he recalled, 'pitying the masters as being outside the pale of normal intelligence and looking forward to the time, now abundantly realized, when the captains and athletes . . . should have sunk into the limbo we so confidently reserved for them.' A favourite maxim, spoken, as stipulated by Robert, 'in that emphatic voice', captured their mocking tone.

'Education', they chanted one to another, 'is the backbone of the Nation.'

The determination of Cecil and Robert to combat all restrictions to their freedom knew no bounds. In league with a fellow inmate of Penn House, a self-possessed Australian called Simon Stoughton, they took to slipping out after dark to meet up with a pair of girls from Windsor. The only one with any serious intent was Stoughton, who had his eye on the more forward of the two girls. To further his suit, he persuaded Robert to chaperone them to the cinema in Slough. Disguise was essential. Stoughton stuck on a false moustache and changed into mufti whilst Robert, playing his part to the hilt, dressed up in widow's weeds hired from Madame Josephine, a milliner 'of pretension and refinement' in Slough High Street. Unfortunately, the intended effect of 'quiet resignation' was ruined by the addition of some brilliant orange curls to the sides of the hat. The colour had been the only tint available at short notice. Inevitably, his appearance attracted the glances of passers-by and Robert arrived at the cinema in a state of fright. Afterwards, he made it back to the shop undetected where a photograph was taken as a record of his daring.

On another occasion Cecil placed a notice in the window of Spottiswoode's, the booksellers, more usually reserved for announcements of sporting fixtures, informing the public that two rattlesnakes had gone missing and that their return was urgently requested to ensure public safety. Robert embellished the joke with the help of one of Cecil's staunchest friends, David Talbot Rice. Together, they appropriated a tame grass snake belonging to another boy and presented it to the terrified assistants behind the counter.

Sometimes, there was a more destructive edge to Cecil's antics which Robert refused to emulate. Returning together from a day out in London, where Robert had been visiting the eye specialist, Cecil, in Robert's words, 'was feeling so enlivened' that he broke a window on the train. Robert was promptly offered five pounds to pull the alarm cord, but he declined to do so out of fear of his father's anger.

The unruliness of Robeson's house was notorious. The senior boys, lodged on the topmost floor, took to drink, lobbing, or so it was alleged, their empty whisky bottles into the small patch of garden below. Gambling was also rife. The ring was organized by Reggie Lygon, the impecunious nephew of Lord Beauchamp, and Stanley Beale, 'a bully of a fellow', who rowed for the school. Beale was cited by the novelist, Anthony Powell, an almost exact contemporary of Robert's, as being the type of hard-bitten personality who earned Robeson's its reputation as 'an old, tough house'. In later life, Beale remained loyal to these values by becoming an all-in wrestler. According to Robert, both Lygon and Beale lost considerable sums each day on horses. Even so, he still subscribed to their sweepstake for the Derby and occasionally placed bets with them on other races. Under Robeson's loose regime, Lygon was made head of the house during Robert's last year, his gambling having proved no barrier to advancement.

Although in another house, Anthony Powell, an acutely observant boy, became a connoisseur of the rum cast of characters in Mr Robeson's establishment. His favourite was John Spencer, the model for the schoolboy Peter Templer in *A Question of Upbringing*, the first volume of Powell's novel sequence *A Dance to the Music of Time* covering the protagonist's years at Eton and Oxford.

Spencer, son of a smart London stockbroker, was a close friend of Robert's and the two ended up messing together. The contrast to Robert's earliest teatime companions could hardly have been greater. Spencer was a dandy, a rule-breaker and, though not averse to sleeping with other boys, a womanizer, famous with the junior ranks of Robeson's for having an affair with a shop assistant from Windsor. His looks were accurately caught by Powell in his portrait of Templer, in which he detailed the fixed expression of his eyes and his 'large pointed ears . . . like those attributed to satyrs'. Spencer's schooldays came to an abrupt end when he was sacked for getting blind drunk on a corps camp. Faced with a totally unrepentant son, his parents resorted to the traditional method of dealing with black sheep. They dispatched him on a one-way ticket to Australia.

A witness to the drunken spectacle had been Cornish Torbock. He was an exact contemporary of Robert's and was placed in many of the same divisions as they worked their way up the school. Apart from this daily propinquity, a shared interest in art and antiques brought them together. His friendship with Robert survived frequent rows about art because, as Torbock recalled, 'I liked his enthusiasms, his virility.'

Another boy in Robeson's committed to the cause of art was Oliver Messel, who already by the age of seven had decided to become an artist. Messel came from a highly cultivated milieu. His father, Leonard, descended from a long line of German Jewish bankers, had been a member of Max Beerbohm's coterie of dandies and aesthetes at Oxford in the 1890s. His wife Maud was the daughter of the famed Victorian illustrator, Linley Sambourne, and herself a talented draughtsman. Thus Oliver, along with his elder brother Linley and sister Anne, was brought up surrounded by beautiful furniture and objects in a society peopled by artists, collectors and scholars. When Oliver announced his decision to become an artist, he met no opposition from either parent.

Being one year older than Robert, Oliver only got to know him properly through Cecil Clonmore. The trio had much in common, not least their insouciant disdain for authority. One of Messel's most flamboyant gestures was witnessed by John Spencer, who lost no time in relaying the episode to the ever-curious Anthony Powell. 'He was standing', Powell recalled, repeating Spencer's account, 'in a group in the passage when a well-dressed woman walked past. They all took their hats off in the usual way as she moved up the passage and slipped into one of the rooms. Later he went into Oliver Messel's room and there he was taking tea by himself, dressed as a lady.'

Oliver's cousin, Rudolph Messel, was another subversive element in the house. His particular passion was for Wagner and he would sit closeted for hours in his room 'hypnotized by the emotion of the music'. Again, it was Cecil who encouraged Robert's friendship with Rudolph, who, following the death of his parents, was brought up by his American grandmother. Robert was invited to lunch with her and relished the opulent Messel taste. 'Lovely things in their house –' he reported to his mother, 'china, tapestry etc.'

Like his cousin, Rudolph showed considerable daring. He once took 'a local tart' up to London, leaving Cornish Torbock to field his grandmother who arrived unexpectedly to visit him. In reality, Rudolph would have had no designs upon his female companion. His tastes lay elsewhere, as his contemporary, Harold Acton, revealed: 'to some people he was very beautiful. Lots of people fell in love with him, but he was very precocious and over-sexed and had a tremendous number of affairs even at Eton.'

Such behaviour raised few eyebrows in Robeson's, where according to Roger Mortimer, a junior boy at the time, homosexual affairs were the norm: 'it was absolutely thick with it,' he recalled, 'although not taken very seriously.' Robert, according to both Torbock and Mortimer, was clearly 'homo', to use the argot of the day, whilst Cecil, in Mortimer's tactful phrase, 'was never heard . . . connected with women'.

In private, Cecil had few inhibitions. His letters to Robert, written after he had left Eton, ask fondly after particular favourites. One boy was referred to as 'the duck', another by the old slang word for prostitute or paramour. 'How is the dear Doxy?' he inquired. 'Give her my love, indeed my very best love.' But any suggestion of an affair between Robert and Cecil was strongly contested by Torbock, who, although utterly chaste, was kept abreast of the latest scandal by Rudolph. In Torbock's opinion, informed by his connoisseur's love of beauty: 'They were both too ugly.'

Cecil himself indicated the platonic nature of their intimacy when, having left Eton, he turned down Robert's suggestion of an illicit tea in Windsor: 'No, I don't think I will go to Fuller's with you . . .' he replied. 'Because if you should be caught . . . I will certainly be accused of immorality by Robeson (he always gets hold of the wrong end of the stick) and will be asked never to come down to Eton as an O.E. again.'

The summer half of 1921 saw their misbehaviour become even more overt. Most evenings they would head for a public house on the outskirts of Slough, called the Jolly Cricketers, where they would enjoy a glass of beer, out of doors, in full view of the wet bobs wending their way to and from the river. They took up smoking, although not furtively like other boys but, as Robert recollected, 'openly, like men of the world, as we went about our pleasures, to and from the bathing place, or up and down the streets of Slough'.

Tempting diversions were suggested, more often than not,

by the kindly, if irresponsible figure of Mrs Fagin, the matron, or dame as the role is referred to at Eton, of Robeson's house. In the summer half of 1921, Mrs Fagin laid on a picnic at the local beauty spot of Burnham Beeches for Robert, Cecil, the two Messels, John Spencer and a boy from another house called Hugh Lygon, a younger son of Lord Beauchamp. Apart from providing a vast hamper of food, she also produced cigarettes and numerous bottles of champagne and cider. They gambolled round the leafy glades until dusk playing hide and seek, fox and geese, French and English 'and every other imaginable game'.

For Robert, the enjoyment was tempered by the realization that Cecil, Rudolph and Oliver were on the point of leaving school. 'The rest of the house . . .' he wailed in a letter home, 'really are the incarnation of boredom – I shall be so lonely next half.'

Fortunately the summer holidays stretched ahead. A visit to Cecil in Ireland had been arranged and the two boys remained in touch thereafter. Cecil was due to go up to Oxford in October, but, until then, neither boy was quite ready to end the campaign against their more conventional peers. They decided, therefore, as the holidays drew to a close, to spring one final practical joke.

The scenario involved the invention of a character called Anne Doyce, a maidservant with a taste for music. Letters, heavy with innuendo, soliciting work were to be sent on her behalf to famously dull boys in the school. Although composed by Cecil and Robert, these purported to come from her current employer, one Olive Messel, resident at Nymans, the Messels' country house in Sussex.

Their first victim, a boy from Robeson's called William Walrond, was away from home at the time, so his mother opened the letter. She wired back to Olive Messel that she did not need a servant and 'certainly not one who played music'.

Walrond's mother, who was called Mrs Adams, having remarried since her first husband's death in the war, was then bombarded with telegrams and postcards, bearing slightly dubious messages. A woman of considerable self-importance, she had no hesitation in taking the collection to Dr Alington, the Head Master. Furthermore, she called in the Sussex police to investigate the identity of Olive Messel. A mystified Oliver was forced to proclaim his innocence and in so doing unmasked Cecil's role in the affair.

Initially Cecil was jubilant. 'My dear!' he exclaimed to Robert. 'Think of the police after Olive! My dear!' His euphoria evaporated when faced with the arrival of 'a real snorter' of a letter addressed to Lord Wicklow from Dr Alington demanding an apology from Cecil in order to prevent Mrs Adams from taking further proceedings. Lord Wicklow, however, was soon won round and dismissed Mrs Adams as 'a very stupid and genteel woman'. Cecil's equilibrium restored, he too adopted a loftier stance. 'I must say', he declared to Robert, 'she is behaving in (if you will excuse me using the word) a very unsporting manner.'

For all its absurdity, the Anne Doyce escapade carried considerable weight with Robert. He carefully preserved the correspondence and even considered turning the plot into a work of fiction. Here was proof of their valiant fight against the overwhelming forces of convention. The debt he owed to Cecil for leading him against such enemies as Mrs Adams and her ilk was never forgotten. 'His young example', Robert stated many years later, 'unwrapped the chrysalis in which I had bided till then. From it, at the age of sixteen, emerged the adult, a vain creature preoccupied with his own discoveries, but still adult in its refusal to accept face values until they had been confirmed by its own halting yet venturesome judgement.'

To his teachers and family, however, the benefits of this transformation were not so apparent, as their reactions to his current behaviour were to make abundantly clear.

4

Angry Young Man

Although Robert managed to turn in a reasonable academic performance during the summer half of 1921, his general attitude drew nothing but criticism. Howson was sufficiently alarmed to discuss the matter with him and warned that his overriding 'fatalism and indifference' could lead to wasting his talents in later life. Robeson confined himself to specific misdeeds. Topping the list was an 'outrage' perpetrated by Robert during trials, as exams were known at Eton, when he had illustrated an answer on the circulation of the blood with a drawing of a lady constricted by corsets. He urged Robert's parents to bring all their influence to bear upon reforming the outlook of their recalcitrant son.

In fact, a row was about to erupt on the home front, which would soon require them to do so. Its roots lay in the upheavals within the family caused by the death, in April 1921, of Robert's grandfather, Edmund.

The ailing autocrat had continued to dominate life at Coulsden until the end. Dinner remained the same long-drawn-out affair, even though, as Robert reported in September 1920, his grandfather was bent double throughout, fell asleep 'every other moment', and spilt his port. On Robert's next visit, his grandfather's condition visibly worsened. Indeed, by the end of the weekend, the Welsh housekeeper was 'filled with presentiment'. Her foreboding was justified in more ways than one. For when Edmund died, two months later, it signalled nothing less than the dissolution of the Coulsden estate.

This was caused, at least in the first instance, by the failure of Edmund and his eldest son, Thomas, to get on. A solitary individual, Thomas had remained unmarried and living in Canada for most of his adult life. He had returned home once, in 1901, but after that had shown no inclination to do so again, not even when his father had offered to pay the fare. Such behaviour had, in his father's eyes, ruled him out as a suitable heir to Coulsden even though the estate had been passed down through the senior male line since the death of Colonel Thomas Byron in the eighteenth century.

Cecil, the second son, was also out of the running, having predeceased his father by ten years. To complicate matters, he too had settled in Canada where he had married a Canadian and sired a son, christened Arthur, born a few months after Robert. By the rights of primogeniture, he should have been the next in line to succeed, but the estate was not entailed and this would have cut out Eric, who, alone of the three sons, had remained in England and kept in close touch with their father.

With no clear choice of male heir, Edmund's two daughters also merited consideration. Eva had lived at home, unmarried, until her mid-thirties when she had become engaged to Charles Hilton, a penniless sponge, dismissed by the Byrons as a lounge lizard. Edmund, by now in terminal decline, described the match as 'madness', but he also accepted that his daughter would require some form of financial support.

Meanwhile, Lucy, married to the eminently respectable solicitor, Theodore Hall Hall, had ideas of her own concerning the future of Coulsden, as she revealed after a visit to her father in January 1920. 'His brain last night was quite clouded,' she reported back to her brother, Eric. 'He is worrying dreadfully about money and his things and what to do with them all – and asked me if I would live in the house – I said no as we none of us had money for that even if we wanted to do so. I do hope he has left it all to be sold and divided among us three. I mean the land and everything and not attempted to make an "elder son".'

A mere two weeks later, her wishes were largely fulfilled. Edmund signed the final version of his will in which he stipulated that the entire estate be sold and the proceeds be divided amongst various heirs, but principally Lucy, Eva, Eric and the Canadian grandchild, Arthur.

When Robert learnt the terms of his late grandfather's will, he was outraged. It had been his belief, whether correct or not, that his father, being the only son to have remained in England, had always been considered the rightful heir to Coulsden. But now it emerged that not only was his father to be effectively disinherited, but also, in consequence, the Byron family were to be driven from their ancestral lands, 'uprooting the traditions of centuries'. And the villain of the piece? That was obvious. His unscrupulous aunt Lucy had quite simply prevailed over her father to alter his will when in his dotage.

She, still blithely unaware of her nephew's burning resentment, unwittingly lit the touchpaper by issuing one of her regular proposals to come down to Eton and take him out to tea. A volley of sarcasm was her reward. 'I feel', Robert replied loftily, 'it would be asking too much of your kindness that you should be seen associating in public with anyone belonging to my paltry family or bearing the despised name of Byron.' He then tore up his aunt's invitation and sent the fragments to his mother with a fair copy of his reply, adding proudly, 'In the real answer I got it all on one page as being more effective and curt.'

Unfortunately, the expected parental approval did not materialize. His father deemed his attitude ungentlemanly and insisted that he apologize. Robert's first attempt still bristled with defiance. 'I live in one long frenzy . . .' he wrote. 'I think of our eating lobster cutlets together at Tull's . . . and then suddenly I think of all the slights and cruelties heaped on my father & therefore on myself & I chew bits off my pen with rage.' Not surprisingly, he was forced to rewrite the letter in more abject terms, which, on receipt, merely earned him a pompous rebuke. 'These things', his aunt retorted, 'are not done!'

Although the case against Aunt Lucy was by no means clear cut, her 'brief but vulgar' reply, to use Robert's estimation, gave him added cause not to forgive her. In truth, unbeknown to Robert, his father had never expected to inherit Coulsden. On the other hand, nor had he wanted the estate broken up and he was furious with the Hall Halls for pressing the sale.

The lack of communication between father and son had been apparent when Robert submitted his first letter of apology for approval. 'Till now', he admitted, 'I have always used Mother as a sort of intermediary between you & myself & I haven't the very least idea of your views on the subject.' By contrast, letters had flown between mother and son with expressions of sympathy on both sides. Both viewed with dismay the inevitable transformation of Coulsden Court at the hands of a new owner. Robert expressed the hope that he and his mother might return just one last time to savour the singular atmosphere of the house: 'only you . . .' he wrote, 'can appreciate the place as I do.'

Certainly, the appeal of Coulsden was by no means obvious to the ordinary eye. However Robert was already capable of seeing beyond the boundaries of good taste. For him, the house was redeemed by its very oddity and unfashionableness, as he revealed in his list of cherished details. 'Why', he asked,

> can't the Duke of Wellington & the peacock embroidered biscuit tin in the double bedroom remain? . . . Why should . . . some swine alter the appalling hideousness of the housekeeper's room – some cultured monster execrate the ceiling papers . . . Think . . . of some potbellied magnate blustering past the Litany desk in the Chancel & gazing vaguely at those peculiar little windows just opposite.

Robert fired these questions at his mother, safe in the knowledge that she would commiserate. As his muse, she had inspired, even in this brief wail of complaint, a vivid evocation of Coulsden's genius loci.

Margaret Byron was to act as her son's artistic confidante for the rest of his life. But this was not her only contribution towards his development as an artist. For although Robert might bear the most romantic name in English literature, all his intelligence, taste and talent were inherited from his mother's side of the family. Physically speaking, he was also a 'Robinson' and as he grew older came to look increasingly like his maternal grandfather. His loyalty was pledged accordingly. The threnody to Coulsden, composed for his mother's benefit, inevitably degenerated into a rant against his Byron aunts and uncles, provoking him to exclaim: 'How lucky Father married you!'

In retrospect, Robert came to accept that the Byrons had also had an important influence upon his life. He suggested in an unpublished memoir that the many happy hours spent riding or shooting over his grandfather's estate had imbued him 'to the core with a love of England, her soil, her traditions, her countryside, her country houses'. In social terms, he defined his make-up 'as a particle of squireachy', equipped with an inherent desire, typical of that class, to play a part in the country's affairs.

Having said that, Robert still maintained that he had been debarred 'from the land and its pursuits, from the occupations I should have chosen'. But this sense of exile had already become a constructive force in his life. Rather than brood over what might have been, Robert welcomed the insecurity as a spur to his burgeoning ambition. 'I feel', he wrote, 'with a . . . deeprooted never absent assurance, that I shall triumph in the end, perhaps attaining greater things, than if wealth had been mine from the beginning.'

There were also other, more tangible, consolations for the loss of Coulsden. The contents were to be divided amongst the principal heirs and Robert swiftly put in a claim for some 'small thing' such as his grandfather's snuffbox or one of the hunting horns. He also had his eye on various other oddments including collections of coins and beetles and 'a little bit of blue and white oriental china' in the library.

Robert's passion for collecting had begun at prep school in the conventional way with fossils and coins. During the holidays, he had also made trips with his parents to pawnshops in Sheffield in search of silver plate. But it was in the many antique and curio shops of Eton, Windsor and even Slough that his mania had taken hold. Naturally, Coulsden, stuffed with the bric-a-brac of a bygone age, appeared nothing less than an Aladdin's cave. Robert read up the auction reports in *The Times*, passing on relevant tips to his parents in readiness for the moment when the more valuable items of furniture and plate were offered for sale to members of the family.

The acquisition of some decent possessions came at a good

moment for the Byrons, who, since the end of the war, had been settling down to a new life in unusually civilized surroundings. Having been released from his job as inspector of munitions, Eric had decided not to return to his original profession of engineer, but, instead, to follow in his father's footsteps and become a gentleman of leisure. He could afford to do so thanks to a modest private income from investments gifted to him over the years. His father's offer to pay the Eton school fees also helped. As a result, the Byrons could now choose where they lived and began looking for properties near Savernake Forest in Wiltshire. This location was the suggestion of Eric who had fond memories of the surrounding countryside from his days as a schoolboy at Marlborough.

The Byrons' search led them to Knowle, situated on the eastern edge of the forest. Dating from the 1730s, it is the epitome of early Georgian taste, a 'small square house', to use Robert's words, built of 'weathered plum coloured brick' with a generous pediment, handsome sash windows and bracketed door. At the end of the war, Knowle was in a sorry state. On viewing the house, Robert and his mother found the dining-room ceiling collapsed on to a pile of potatoes. Fortunately, the other, finely panelled, rooms were more or less intact, as was the hall with its chequered flagstones and carved oak staircase.

The house was being offered to rent by the Ailesbury estate for a nominal sum, provided the new tenants restored the property. The Byrons needed little persuasion. In November 1919, Knowle became their new home. For Robert, the move to Wiltshire meant immersion in country pursuits. Bird nesting, butterfly hunting, pigeon shooting and riding on his father's newly acquired horse were just some of the activities that filled his holidays.

The spoils from Coulsden arrived in the autumn of 1922 while Robert was away at school. His frustration was palpable. Even in his modest room at Eton, he was constantly rearranging the furniture, rehanging his pictures and dreaming up new ways of displaying his objets d'art. He thought himself, therefore, something of an expert. Instructions poured from his pen. 'Do put the silver candlesticks and the tea caddy on the commode,' he bossed his mother. 'China would look horrid on it.' Had the Cromwellian table been sent and was there damage to the French bureau? 'I am so sorry to be so boring with all these questions,' he explained, 'but I am so interested and longing to get home to see.'

One final act in the drama of Coulsden remained. In October 1922, the estate was put up for auction in London. The property was divided into forty lots from the mansion with its pleasure grounds to the four farms and other substantial residential properties, to the fifty cottages, five small holdings, the village post office, the school, the almshouses and the windmill. Much of the land was advertised as being ripe for immediate development.

Robert could not resist attending the auction, noting the ostentatious arrival of Uncle Theodore: 'that damned old swine . . .' he reported, 'fussed his way through . . . to the front of course: you would have thought he could have left snobbery out of an auction sale.'

A large number of lots were unsold, including the house, which was finally bought by the town council for conversion into a golf club, which it remains. When the last plot of land was eventually sold, Eric recorded bleakly in his diary: 'we are now landless.'

5

Aesthetes and Dandies

Robert had returned to Eton for the Michaelmas half 1921 determined to take himself in hand and work. His immediate goal was to sit the School Certificate, a national examination that was the most important hurdle to getting into Oxford or Cambridge. The exam was also used by Eton to judge whether boys could specialize in a particular subject.

Robert's determination to take the exam was proved right. He sailed through the various papers that autumn, picking up a clutch of credits in the key subjects, so clearing the way for him to specialize. After a short deliberation, he chose history in preference to modern languages.

One of the reasons for Robert's change of attitude had been the departure at the end of the summer half of his most intimate friend, Cecil Clonmore. His loneliness was mitigated by almost daily letters from Cecil who was going up to Merton College, Oxford, that October.

Life, however, was about to look up thanks to the discovery of a new friend in another house, called Henry Yorke. Until now, their paths had merely crossed occasionally as a result of their being placed in a number of the same divisions. Then one day out beagling with the school pack, early in the Lent half 1922, they struck up conversation. The rapport was instantaneous. In fact Robert became so absorbed that he totally forgot to beagle. Writing home that evening with the latest news, he had already come to the conclusion that Henry was 'only second to Clonmore'.

Yorke was, indeed, a captivating mixture of grandeur, exoticism, brains and wit. His father, Vincent, was the eldest surviving son of a cadet branch of the Earls of Hardwicke. His mother, Maud, was the daughter of Lord and Lady Leconfield, and thus one of the vast tribe of Wyndhams who had for generations inhabited the upper reaches of Society,

Government and the Services. Maud had been brought up at Petworth and, according to Anthony Powell, a friend of Henry's since prep school, regarded in consequence 'all other residences as small'. The Yorke seat, acquired through marriage in the eighteenth century, was Forthampton Court, a rambling house with a medieval core situated on the bank of the River Severn in sight of Tewkesbury Abbey.

Maud Yorke was a brilliant conversationalist, equal to any company however intellectual. The Oxford don, Maurice Bowra, remembered her as 'extremely quick and clever and witty and scored off one with great brilliance'. Henry had inherited much of her verbal accomplishment which was at the root of his charm for Robert: 'he can talk like no other person I've ever met,' he wrote in the first flush of friendship. 'It is a talent I have never seen so exaggerated.'

The liking between the two boys was mutual. In fact, Robert's friendship worked wonders for Henry's morale, releasing him from a stretch of adolescent misery. Convinced that his handful of friends in the house had begun to drop him, Yorke experienced not just 'a fierce, desperate' loneliness but a dread of persecution, a fate he compared to being 'mobbed by rooks'. None of this inner turmoil was obvious from Henry's outward appearance. Physically, he was mature for his sixteen years with a dark complexion and solid heavy-jowled face. But it explained his unremitting talk, which Anthony Powell later identified as a sign of his being ill at ease.

Another manifestation was his self-confessed snobbery. This, too, appealed to Robert, who lapped up the stories about Henry's grand relations. His social confidence dented by the impending loss of Coulsden, Robert, like Henry, had a need to impress. His feelings were made apparent one day over lunch with Cecil and his grandmother, the Duchess of Abercorn: 'the conversation turned on the family inheritance', he told his mother, 'which I turned off on to the family tree.'

Nonetheless, the row with Aunt Lucy was to propel Robert inadvertently into London grand society. In previous years, he had spent the Lent long leave as her guest in South Kensington, an option no longer available to him. Instead, Henry stepped into the breach and invited Robert to stay with his parents in their 'very large house' in Mansfield Street, just off Portland Place.

The usual activities such as visits to the cinema and the zoo filled much of the weekend, but there was also a foray to the theatre to see *The Bat*, a popular mystery. All rank and fashion were there from the King and Queen downward. Robert's account reflected his wide-eyed excitement. 'Wonderful dresses and lots of men in swallow tails: stiff with Etonians . . .' he reported to his mother breathlessly, 'Lady Dalhousie . . . her neck and bosom literally blazing with diamonds.'

The contrast with his own, less sophisticated, home life was exposed on the Sunday evening when Henry's aunt and uncle came to play bridge. Robert had been brought up not to play cards on the Sabbath, but he had not the face to refuse. Sheepishly, he owned up to his mother offering a string of excuses. 'I really don't see what I could have done without being rude,' he pleaded. 'When one is in Rome . . .'

Equally, Robert was no toady. He knew exactly how to handle the formidable Mrs Yorke as she reminded him of his own mother: he merely contradicted her when necessary. Maude Yorke warmed to Robert still further when they discovered a shared interest in decoration. This led to a tour of the house, built as a speculation by Robert Adam in the 1770s. 'It was too lovely –' he enthused, 'all Adam from garret to ceiling with Angelica Kauffmann ceilings.' Their incessant talk on matters artistic even led to the suggestion of a visit to Petworth.

Robert's enthusiasm for art was not confined to the past. Painting and drawing had been a favourite occupation since prep school. His arrival at Eton had given fresh impetus to his pen, causing sketchbooks to be filled with illustrations, cartoons and caricatures inspired by school life. The margins of exercise books and essays were similarly crammed.

His keenness gained him admission, even as a Lower Boy, which was not usually permitted, to 'Drawing Extra Studies'. These were run by Sidney Evans, the chief drawing master, who came from a dynasty of artist-teachers stretching back to the reign of George III. Members of the family had also run one of the boys' boarding houses for many years, and Sidney Evans retained the use of two interconnecting top-lit rooms, adjoining the old Evans house in Keate's Lane, as his drawing school, more commonly known as the Studio. Its atmosphere was fondly recalled by Anthony Powell. 'These rooms', he wrote, 'were always in a state of comfortable disorder; piled up with pictures, plaster casts, oddments of silver, china or glass, suitable for still life compositions.'

Here, Robert studied perspective and set about drawing classical heads, work that attracted praise from Evans for being 'intelligent and well-constructed'. Robeson, a keen supporter of his artistic endeavours, provided further encouragement by allowing him the run of his rock garden as a place to paint. His mother, as a competent artist in her own right, also kept him up to the mark.

Despite Evans's refusal to let him take the Certificate exam in drawing because – so Robert alleged – He feared that a poor result would bring discredit upon his teaching, the following Lent half 1922 saw Robert apply, as usual, for 'drawing extras' only to discover that they were oversubscribed. He admitted to being 'dreadfully disappointed' and had to make do with joining an overflow group.

The growing popularity of Evans's evening classes was a tribute to his gifts as a teacher. Highly experienced and with a bluff, good-natured manner, he knew how to bring out the best in his aspiring art students. 'All of us . . .' wrote Harold Acton, one of his most enthusiastic supporters, 'owed a great deal to Mr Evans's tactful encouragement.'

Coming from a highly cultivated background, Acton was a natural member of Evans's bohemian atelier. Born and brought up in Florence, he was descended from a distinguished Anglo-Italian family which had originally achieved prominence in the service of the Bourbon kings of Naples. The artistic strain had emerged with Harold's father, Arthur Acton, a man of exquisite taste and great artistic flair who had married an American heiress, Hortense Mitchell, daughter of the founder of the Illinois Trust and Savings Bank. Their union signalled the purchase of the Villa La Pietra, a Renaissance country house wrapped in an imposing baroque exterior standing within a demesne of vines and olive trees just one mile from the ancient city boundary of Florence, which provided the perfect setting for Arthur Acton's growing collection of furniture, tapestries, objets d'art and paintings.

Such cultivated taste rubbed off upon the child Harold. Hours spent in the Uffizi and other galleries fired the six-year-old boy with a passion for Botticelli, whilst the art magazines, monographs and catalogues piled high in his father's studio opened his eyes to the schools of other countries as well as to the work of designers such as Beardsley and Bakst. On his first day at Wixenford, his English prep school, another new boy, David Talbot Rice, saw Harold stand on a chair and recite a poem. Explaining his action many years later, Acton said: 'Coming from Florence, I did feel perhaps it was a way of making friends.' His impish looks, characterized by dark appraising eyes, tilted nose and pursed lips, contributed to the air of self-possession.

At prep school Harold had succeeded in gathering around him a handful of like-minded friends such as the aforesaid David Talbot Rice, a sprig of the Gloucestershire squirearchy, who, even as a prep school boy, was fascinated by archaeology. Another find was Mark Ogilvie-Grant, a gifted young draughtsman of Highland descent with whom Harold planned to found a museum of treasures from their homelands. Cecil Clonmore also emerged as a kindred spirit, collaborating with Harold on a hand-produced magazine on art and fashion.

Passing into Eton in 1918, Harold fell in almost immediately with a boy from another house who was to become his greatest ally. The backgrounds of Harold and his new friend, Brian Howard, bore certain similarities. Brian's mother also happened to be a rich American whilst his American-born father, having been largely brought up in London and educated on the Continent, was a talented amateur painter and highly successful art dealer. Like the Actons, they too moved in bohemian circles. The novelist George Meredith was Brian's godfather, whilst George Moore, a regular teatime visitor to the Howard house in Warwick Square, was credited by Brian with imbuing him at the age of six with a fascination for words.

Brian arrived at Eton with a past, having been seduced by

a master at his prep school. He was, in Henry Yorke's view, 'quite the most handsome boy' he had ever seen. His long sensual face, expressive of part-Jewish ancestry, was dominated by huge brown eyes which had even impressed George Meredith with their 'singular beauty'. Acton described them as 'brazen with self-assurance' while Anthony Powell opined that they 'seemed by nature to have been heavily made-up'. His manner also set him apart. A contemporary described the moment he first encountered him at Eton: 'It was raining. And there Brian was, immaculately dressed, holding up his trousers between thumb and finger . . . and picking his way through the puddles.'

Although relations between Harold and Brian were marked by constant bickering and, at one stage, a year's silence, they had by their mid-teens become inseparable. Both found one another's company intoxicating, both wrote poetry by the ream and worshipped Art, and both found a natural haven in Evans's Studio. By the start of the Lent half 1922, they were to be found at 'drawing extras' actively promulgating revolutionary precepts from abroad.

In their view, the innovations set in train by the Post-Impressionists and other modern masters provided the measure against which all living art should be judged. If this position caused a stir, then so much the better. Once, Brian announced to the assistant art master in the Studio that he had discovered the colour of shadows cast by bushes on snow. 'Blue, isn't it?' replied the unsuspecting Mr Powell who happened to specialize in Alpine scenes. 'Oh, no,' Brian drawled, 'it's a strange raspberry pink.'

One habitué unimpressed by their critique was Robert, who believed that art should be based upon accurate depiction of the objective world and that any attempt to do otherwise resulted in 'distorted form and distorted formlessness'. Battle lines were swiftly drawn. One day he marched up to Harold brandishing a reproduction of a rather 'difficult' Picasso. 'Do you think that's Art?' he challenged, before tearing it to pieces. Such behaviour led Harold Acton to remember him at Eton as being 'very like a British flag waving type', supporting 'Victorian values' and 'whatever was retrograde'.

The impact of Robert's painstaking work, which was often illustrative, could not, however, be denied. 'My "Journey over the Styx" caused great wonder', he wrote home, '& I think grudged admiration among the ultra artistic of Evans' Studio at whom I shout the most obscene epithets whenever they come near me.' The news that followed merely confirmed his standing in the Studio. 'They are getting up a club to discuss higher things', he went on, '& I know my name is on the list of members – but I am being so rude that it will probably be off it soon.'

There was little chance of that. The Eton Society of Arts, founded by Brian Howard towards the end of February 1922, was to rely upon Robert's fiery oratory to set the proceedings alight.

Membership, rather in the manner of a football team, was restricted to eleven boys. The nucleus consisted of Brian, Harold and his younger brother, William, a talented artist in pencil and oils. Others selected included Henry Yorke, who served as secretary, Anthony Powell and Alan Clutton-Brock, the son of *The Times* art critic. Some were picked for reasons unconnected with art. The choice of Hugh Lygon, the good-looking younger son of Lord Beauchamp, led Anthony Powell to surmise that 'his inclusion was to be accounted for by a tendresse (probably unvoiced) felt for him by . . . Howard or Byron.'

The role of devil's advocate came naturally to Robert as two opponents in particular, Harold and Brian, repeatedly found to their cost. 'I very much offended all the boys of American or foreign origin present by quoting Chesterton: "Good taste, the last & vilest of all human superstitions,"' he reported gleefully to his mother after one debate. 'They had all been harping on good taste in colour. Americans try so hard to have good taste and always just miss – poor fools . . .'

Meanwhile, Henry Yorke looked on with unbridled admiration. For him, the appointment as secretary of the society had marked a watershed in his life: 'after this', he wrote in his memoirs, 'there was no turning back. I determined to be a writer.' The result was his first novel, *Blindness*, published four years later under the pseudonym Henry Green, which, in the opening section, draws heavily upon this period of his life at Eton and remarks on 'the unrivalled powers of invective' of Ben Gore, the character modelled on Robert. 'His face, his voice, everything combines to make him a most formidable opponent in wordy warfare.'

Another chance to score off the enemy was occasioned by the imminent publication of *The Eton Candle*, a slim volume conceived and edited by Brian Howard largely as a vehicle for his own and Harold's poetry and prose. Brian's most notable contribution, an introduction entitled 'The New Poetry' in praise of vers libre, was a dazzling survey of the latest trends in Britain and America, which upheld the significance of modernist verse as revealed through the most radical poets of the day from the American Imagists to the Wheels movement of the Sitwells to the 'genius', Ezra Pound.

Where possible, Brian solicited contributions in line with his own thinking. The Sitwell brothers and Aldous Huxley were to raise the banner of the avant-garde in the Old Etonian section of the magazine, whilst luminaries of the Society of Arts were to represent present-day Etonians. From this select group there emerged one particular jewel of vers libre that was all the more welcome because it came from such an unexpected pen: that of Robert Byron.

Described by the author himself as 'a sonnet in vers libre to Kneller's little finger', the piece seemed tailor-made for *The Eton Candle*. Brian was thrilled. 'Robert has developed into a poet, my dear,' he announced to Harold, 'an English Apollinaire. You'll be amazed.' Against all the odds, Robert had become 'one of us'. But on congratulating him, Brian's illusions were cruelly shattered. The poem, dismissed by the author as 'poor prose divided into lines & dots at random', was a parody.

Brian's first instinct was to reject it out of hand, but sensing Robert's obvious relief he decided to mete out some poetic justice of his own. The verse would stand as a serious contribution under Byron's name. This embarrassing prospect was only avoided thanks to another blistering row at the Society of Arts when Robert drove Brian into 'such a frenzy of rage' that he vetoed the poem once and for all.

The Eton Candle, a handsome production in stiff covers of shocking pink with 'superlatively wide margins to the page', was published in March 1922, to great acclaim. Reviews appeared in the national press and sales were such that it reprinted. Robert gave all credit to Brian for his achievement, acquiring copies of both first and second editions which he asked him to autograph. From that moment on, the two adversaries warmed to one another, marking the start of an enduring friendship.

The summer half of 1922 saw Robert's own artistic gifts receive due recognition when he won a school drawing prize for his study of a beech tree, which was hung in the exhibition organized by the Eton Society of Arts for the Fourth of June. Robert also submitted some lacquer boxes and a tray. His craze for lacquering had started earlier in the year and had led him to take lessons in the craft from an antique dealer in Windsor. He saw his new-found skill as a way of making money because, as he informed his mother, 'painted furniture & lacquer is the dernier cri'.

That autumn, the Society of Arts pulled off a minor triumph by persuading the distinguished critic, William Rothenstein, to come down to Eton and give a talk. His theories on art delighted Robert as they vindicated his own stand against the avant-garde, a movement dismissed by Rothenstein as little more than an interesting experiment that was already petering out. French artists were a case in point. They were now turning away from abstraction in favour of 'the old set piece subjects'. Robert praised Rothenstein's performance as 'extraordinarily clear clever and thank heaven unaesthetic'.

Robert's appropriation of the term aesthete to denigrate the followers of modern art disregarded the fact that he, like the other luminaries of the Society of Arts, was utterly in thrall to the 1890s. Indeed, his new-found hero William Rothenstein had been one of the great dandy aesthetes of the age. Harold knew many of the other survivors – 'Florence was full of them,' he recalled – whilst Brian's outrageous ways made him a natural enthusiast of the era. Shortly before founding the Society of Arts, Brian had even suggested another club, to be called 'The Cremorne', at which 'members . . . must believe in the interpretation and appreciation of life as evolved in 1890'.

Ironically, Robert would have felt at home in such company, as he too was sounding increasingly like an aesthete of the old school. A phrase from his speech in a debate on Post-Impressionism, held in the autumn of 1922, was worthy of the high priest of aestheticism himself, Walter Pater. 'The function of art', Robert had pronounced, 'is to be beautiful . . . art is decorative; post-impressionism is not.'

The worshipper of beauty adopted other rituals. Rising at dawn, he attended Holy Communion at the Anglo-Catholic chapel at Clewer, a convent on the outskirts of Windsor. The plain fare of Eton College chapel was compared unfavourably to the atmosphere of Clewer where 'the very ticking of a clock . . . added to the solemnity & emphasized the silence'. Although quick to deny any plans to convert, he dwelt upon the attractions of Catholicism: 'Religion is an emotion,' he stated, 'not a set of statutes subordinate to the interests of national morals.'

On a less elevated note, his burgeoning friendship with Brian Howard inspired pranks with a nineties' flavour. One day, they dragged 'a little toy motor on the end of an enormous bit of string' down the High Street – an act which Henry Yorke claimed, in *Blindness*, 'outraged the dignity of the whole school'. In another episode, Robert summoned up the spirit of Wilde's nemesis, the Marquis of Queensberry, by having sent round 'the most gargantuan cabbages' to Brian and Henry at their respective houses. The greengrocer joined in the joke by presenting Robert's compliments on mourning cards.

Like proper aesthetes, Robert and his friends were also dedicated to the art of dressing. In this regard, Eton, the alma mater of Beau Brummell, provided them with the perfect schooling. The uniform of tails and top hat was a lesson in elegance and restraint, whilst the finery worn at the Fourth of June and set-piece sporting events, themselves highlights of the social calendar, added dash and glamour to the wardrobe. For his first Eton and Harrow match at Lords, Robert had equipped himself with a 'Lords silk tie', a buttonhole, suede gloves, an Eton blue favour, white silk socks and a silver mounted stick with tassel.

As time wore on, his passion for hosiery was taken to extravagant lengths. Acquisitions included a 'most delicious handkerchief', made from 'a sort of shimmering opalescent fabric of the brighter colours & butterflies', whilst for an outing to the opera, one long leave, he bought 'a huge black silk tablecloth' to wrap around his neck. The effect was 'too wonderful' and, he predicted, would be 'quite miraculous' once the material had been 'tutored' to remain in place.

The high seriousness with which the Etonian dandy took the subject of clothes was personified by Robert's teatime companion, John Spencer, who was always ready to share his expertise in matters sartorial. Thus when Robert mooted the idea of having a suit of plus fours made, 'to be paid for next year', Spencer wrote off to a remote mill in Scotland for 'the most amazing pattern of tweeds'. The result was a triumph. 'My suit has come from Scotland,' Robert told his mother; 'you may be sorry to hear that it is an unqualified success in every respect . . . that the coat fits like a glove, that the stuff is like autumn leaves with the sky shewing through and that everyone assures me it is perfect.'

His mother did not entirely approve of such purchases. In fact, she had been so displeased by his new pair of trousers and waistcoat worn at a Fourth of June that she had felt compelled to upbraid him. His response revealed the cause of his singular attire: 'I suppose you will learn better some day . . .' he told her witheringly, 'I am not ordinary.'

In parading his originality, Robert naturally liked to add a touch of menace to his appearance. On one occasion he decided 'to dress offensively' for a school concert by donning a double-breasted white waistcoat. A similar punch was landed on Mr Robeson whom he succeeded in intimidating with a pair of 'aggressively suede suede gloves'. But the knockout blow, which sent those in command reeling, resulted from an anti-militarist protest, when Robert committed the unpardonable solecism of appearing in corps uniform with an umbrella.

Such gestures reinforced the warlike image of Robert sallying forth to do battle with the philistines. So firmly was it etched upon the mind of one observer, Cyril Connolly, a cautious boy too conventionally ambitious to join the Studio set, that, many years later, he remembered him as a master of 'aggressive aestheticism'.

By no means all in authority were ranked against him. Robert enjoyed the venerable patronage of H. E. Luxmoore, a retired master ever alert to boys of unusual promise. He was an upholder of the values of William Johnson, poet, reformer and incomparable teacher, who had championed the radical belief at Eton in the nineteenth century that education should develop a boy's refinement and intellect. Early on in Robert's career, Luxmoore had allowed him to sketch in the beautiful garden which he had created on one of the 'broad island patches' in the Thames.

The Provost, M. R. James, a former pupil of Luxmoore's, best known for his ghost stories, also encouraged high-minded activities, once treating Robert and Rudolph Messel to a tour of the Provost's Lodge. 'Perfectly beautiful –' Robert declared, 'those Romneys in the flesh are marvellous & the lovely old panelling & woodwork & stained glass etc.' Accompanying them was Luxmoore who had his own dry contribution to make. Stopping before a portrait of Charles James Fox, he observed to Robert in his vibrating, 'slightly nasal bass voice': 'Yyoung eenough in yyeerrs perhaps; old eenough in wickedness already.'

S. G. Lubbock, the master responsible for much of Robert's work in preparation for the Certificate, sprang from the same cultivated tradition. His brother, the writer Percy Lubbock, testified to the resilience of Johnson's example which, through subterfuge, had survived the High Victorian ethos of character building and team spirit: 'under some of the roofs of Eton,' he observed in his memoir *Shades of Eton*, 'privately, informally, there reigned a spirit that ignored the order of the day.' Alone of all his teachers, S. G. Lubbock received Robert's wholehearted approval, being ranked as 'the most cultivated man I have come across except the Provost'.

Lubbock believed in exercising the minds of his pupils. He delighted Robert with his approach to divinity. 'Lubbock', he wrote, some months before his Anglo-Catholic phase, 'has more rational ideas that are more akin to my own on the subject of religion than anyone I have met.' Orthodoxy held no sway over the heirs to Johnson. One of his greatest strengths as a teacher had been to kindle in boys the arts of criticism, argument and reasoning.

Another mark chalked up by Lubbock was his ability to sharpen Robert's aptitude for Greek. Until then, his performance had been distinctly patchy, provoking one exasperated master, J. C. Butterwick, to complain: 'I may be wrong in thinking him a philistine, but he has not encouraged me to feel that "the Glory that was Greece" shines very brightly for him.'

Butterwick's accusation of philistinism revealed the source of nineteenth-century aestheticism at Eton. 'Taste began', said Percy Lubbock, 'in a just appreciation of ancient letters.' In the approach pioneered by Johnson to the teaching of the classics, dry exercises in construing had become a branch of literary inquiry that summoned up an idealized world. This glimpse of Elysium coloured the imagination of all manner of boys. Robert's grandfather, Edmund, who had been at Eton during Johnson's reign, never lost his love of the classics, invariably retiring to his study after dinner at Coulsden to translate a passage from Horace.

His grandson's enthusiasm was much shorter lived. He dropped Greek and Latin with scant regret as soon as the demands of examiners permitted. A modicum of interest led him to attend a series of lectures during his last half on Greek art, but even these received the thumbs down. 'They are', he complained, 'very dull.' In turning his back on classical civilization Robert was defining the modernity of his aestheticism. The cultural vacuum would be filled within six months of his leaving Eton when he discovered Byzantine art.

In matters of taste, Eton did bestow upon Robert one supreme gift. This was a passion for architecture. His awareness was first stirred by the 'Tudor dungeon, lighted in daytime by a single arrow-slit and at night by a popping gas bracket' which served as a pupil room for his classical tutor. Gradually, the other ancient buildings of Henry VI's foundation, especially the chapel, began to work their magic upon him. In his words, they 'dignified my life'.

So, too, did Windsor Castle where he would spend many of his free afternoons. His favourite view, as seen from the games fields or the river, was the 'long romantic pile, sometimes white against the rain clouds, or a dim silhouette in the dusk, or more often just a melancholy grey', the sight of which was guaranteed to relieve the tedium of compulsory games.

His pleasure in these surroundings awakened in him 'the critical appreciation of architecture' which, he acknowledged many years later, 'has since become one of the pastimes of my life'. Growing up amongst fine buildings moulded his character more profoundly than the public school mantra of team spirit ever could. 'Their example', he wrote, 'forms the taste, bringing tradition, quality and proportion to influence the mind and conduct. It is an insidious influence, because it is unfelt and exacts no time – and is therefore perhaps the more effective.'

Academically, Robert's final year was spent preparing for the entrance examination in history to Merton College, Oxford. He had never wavered from his long-held desire to join Cecil Clonmore at Merton and had, accordingly, nagged his parents without mercy until they finally allowed him to take the exam in October 1922. He passed with ease, securing a place at Oxford for the following January.

His remaining weeks at Eton saw him achieve a measure of conventional success. 'I do nothing this half but talk to m'tutors', he informed his mother, 'who hate me more than ever but who are quite incredibly polite because I am the fashion.' He played for the house football team and was elected to the Library, the group of prefects who run Eton houses. He now had fags at his disposal, junior boys to tidy his room and run errands, a system described by Robert as 'refined cruelty'. His one stipulation was that they should never, on pain of beating, clean his corps kit. 'This', he observed, 'worried them.'

His last weekend passed in 'a frantic turmoil of leaving'. First there was Brian Howard's leaving tea at the tuck shop, Rowlands. On the menu were oysters, turkey, Christmas pudding, trifle, foie gras, caviar and, according to Robert, who acted as the 'semi-host', 'such drink as one could smuggle'. When conversation ran out, Robert broke the plates. That evening, he had dinner with Mr Robeson and on Sunday heard with due sentiment the Head Master's farewell address in chapel.

The next day he was back in the chapel, standing at the

foot of the altar with Brian Howard, his mother, the Head Master, the Provost and Mr Luxmoore, gathered to choose a new carpet for the altar steps from a selection chosen by Luxmoore, which was to be paid for by Mrs Howard. The occasion was nothing less than the apotheosis of the aesthetes, ancient and modern. Finally, Robert conducted an auction of his possessions, raising £5 'for nothing'. And so his days at Eton drew to a close. 'It is', he admitted, 'all very depressing.'

Robert would remember Eton with affection for the rest of his life. Most of his closest friends were made there; his taste was formed there; and 'it was there', he recalled, 'I discovered how to use my mind and thus won the title of man.' These words were written in 1938, just after the Germans had marched into Vienna, when Robert was filled with an intimation of his mortality. In view of this, he judged Eton to have bestowed upon him the advantages of adulthood at an unusually early age. This, he realized, had brought him 'two extra years [of] real education, a longer lease of my own faculties'. His estimation was to be justified by events.

6

Vivat Regina!

Christmas in Wiltshire was enlivened with hunting, local dances and a visit to Henry Yorke at Forthampton Court. Borrowing his father's car for these and other outings, Robert, a novice at the wheel, had a number of narrow scrapes, not least hitting a cow on the way to Oxford with his possessions.

The official start of term, two days later, on 18 January 1923, saw Robert arrive at Merton College in the company of Cecil Clonmore, who, along with another raffish alumnus of Robeson's house, Rudolph Messel, promptly took him under his wing. As a result, Robert found himself 'shoved straight into the middle of a ready-made "set"', consisting principally of unconventional Etonians such as David Talbot Rice, Harold Acton, John Heygate, Gavin Henderson and Alfred Duggan.

An unsteady round of dining out in friends' colleges, visits to the cinema and 'orgies' of drinking ensued. One such occasion was a dinner party given later that month by Alfred Duggan, the immensely rich stepson of Lord Curzon, Chancellor of the University, which was followed by a visit to 'a sort of Los Angelos dancehall in the Cowley Road'. Having consumed quantities of champagne, port, cocktails and liqueurs, Robert found himself dancing the Boston two-step with abandon.

The evening ended in his first encounter with a proctor, one of the guardians of the University's morals, who fined him for attending the dance. Undeterred, Robert was again in trouble the following night when, having stepped over a recumbent body in the High Street, he fell flat on his face at the proctor's feet. The officer raised his mortarboard and politely inquired: 'Still at Merton, Mr Byron?' On this occasion, he was gated for a month, in other words, confined to his college after 9 p.m. Robert had been at Oxford for just over a fortnight.

Enforced leisure in Merton did not lead to his making any significant new friendships in the college. If anything, his fellow Mertonians, originally described by Robert as 'very nice & trying to be pleasant', now viewed him with alarm. Sitting in their midst in the Junior Common Room, he wrote to Henry Yorke: 'They all think I am mad.'

During his first weeks at Oxford, Robert was also in correspondence with Hugh Lygon, another close friend from Eton, who was currently studying in Germany. The upshot was an invitation from Hugh's father, Lord Beauchamp, to join him, along with Hugh and his eldest son, Viscount Elmley, on a trip to Italy during the Easter vacation.

Initially, Margaret Byron resisted the idea, but Robert soon wore her down by citing the 'unrivalled opportunity' to enlarge his knowledge of paintings, architecture and history; 'one feels it one's duty somehow', he concluded, 'to take these chances.'

The party left London on 23 March, boarding the wagon-lit at Victoria station, bound for Venice, the first stop on an itinerary that took in many of the most historic towns of northern Italy before continuing south to Naples and the island of Capri.

Immediately, it became apparent that this was going to be no picnic. 'Lord Beauchamp', as Robert pointed out to his mother, 'is one of those indefatigable sightseers, who map out every moment of every day, weeks beforehand.' In Venice they toured with Ruskin in hand, and in Florence and Rome with the guidebooks of the popular Victorian travel writer, Augustus Hare. The choice of restaurant was planned with equal thoroughness. 'Lord Beauchamp has a mania for Italian dishes', Robert complained, '& we frequent the grubbiest little restaurants in search of what I strongly suspect to be horse.'

For his mother's benefit, Robert kept a diary, starting a practice that was to be repeated on most future travels. Although interspersed with facetious anecdote and the occasional richly worded description, much of the content dutifully records the round of art galleries and churches made each day.

The most significant entry describes his day's sightseeing in Ravenna, the ancient town a few miles inland from the Adriatic which boasts a remarkable group of buildings, dating from the fifth and sixth centuries AD, that testify to the greatness of what has become known as the Byzantine tradition in art and architecture. To Robert, the basilicas, mausolea and baptisteries were a revelation: 'they were using designs and forms of decoration', he recorded, 'that one had always looked on as essentially the creation of the Renaissance.'

But it was not just the architecture that bowled him over. The history of the buildings swept him back to Ravenna's remote imperial past, as capital first of the Western division of the Roman Empire, then of the Ostrogoth kings and finally as an important province of the Eastern Empire. For him 'the culminating glory' was the Church of Sant'Apollinare Nuovo, built, and adorned with superb mosaics, by Theodoric, King of the Ostrogoths. 'I sat amazed', he wrote, 'to think that this was the work almost intact of one of the great names of the ancient world . . . To an historian this building was overwhelming.' The intensity of the experience was heightened by the sound of the organ suddenly swelling through the church and by the bells in the campanile first chiming, then pealing in harmony. In his rapturous estimation, it produced 'the most beautiful effect I have ever heard'.

Analysing the uniqueness of Ravenna, he decided that 'it was the atmosphere of the place – the absence of any trace of cosmopolitanism . . . and the extraordinary historical interest that made it'. He continued in lyrical vein: 'away in the great campagna it lies . . . with its sweet smelling pine woods, its mosaics, its churches & its old white houses, the last strand of the Empire of the West.' Without exaggeration, he stated, 'This was one of the most interesting days in my life.' His highly charged response was akin to the romantic enthusiasm felt by nineteenth-century aesthetes such as William Johnson for the literary and archaeological remains of Greece and Rome. Robert's curiosity was fired. His quest for Byzantium had begun.

In fact, some initial preparation had already been undertaken at Oxford where, at the request of David Talbot Rice, he had read a paper to the Asiatic Society on the 'Eastern influence on Western art'. His background reading had included 'some interesting books' on the Byzantine influence on Italian primitives including Cimabue. This knowledge was put to good use in Florence and Assisi where he unfailingly praised the work of Cimabue whereas, elsewhere, more familiar artists of the Renaissance often came in for criticism.

In Florence, the party lunched with Harold Acton and his parents at La Pietra. The house was deemed by Robert to be the most lovely he had ever seen, 'filled with priceless pictures, stuffs, bits of carving, statues, marvellous plate'. Since Robert's arrival at Oxford, where Harold was already at Christ Church, the two antagonists from the Eton Society of Arts had begun to warm to one another. Their meeting in Florence served to strengthen the bond: 'dear Harold', Robert wrote affectionately after their time together, 'idiotic as usual.' Acting as their cicerone, Harold took them to favourite haunts such as Doney's, the famous tearoom, and the nightclub, Raiola's.

These diversions came as a welcome relief to the other ex-member of the Eton Society of Arts in the party, Hugh Lygon, who, all along, proved to be a recalcitrant sightseer. Having climbed to the top of Giotto's bell tower in Florence, he insisted on reading the *Sketch* whilst Robert and Elmley swooned at the view; in Assisi, having missed breakfast, he merely pined for lunch. Hugh's lack of interest provoked even his doting father to call him 'something of a little philistine'.

Nothing, however, could dim Robert's affection for his travelling companion. Tall, languid, charming and blond, 'a man', wrote Evelyn Waugh, 'of the greatest sweetness', Hugh could get away with anything, justifying Anthony Powell's surmise that Robert harboured a 'tendresse' towards him.

Having reached Florence by train, Lord Beauchamp hired an enormous motor for the drive to Rome. The glare from the whiteness of the roads provided Robert with an excuse to buy a pair of smart tortoiseshell spectacles fitted with extremely dark glass and with joints in three places. Frequent wiping was required due to the great clouds of dust thrown up by the car as they raced from one destination to the next.

'I am looking forward to Capri –' Robert wrote from Naples, 'such a rest.' He was not the only one. Even Lord

Beauchamp was showing signs of fatigue; normally a stickler for punctuality, he turned up seven minutes late for one of his long-planned rendezvous. After ten days or so on the island, the party returned to England having been away for a month.

Despite his mania for timetables, Lord Beauchamp, a man of exquisite and unusual taste, had been the ideal bear-leader on Robert's first trip abroad. Thanking Robert for being such an appreciative companion, not least as an example to Hugh, he set down his own zestful approach to travel: 'It is . . . so much more delightful . . . to take an interest in everything – religious functions and daily customs everything that is different from England. Too many people bury their noses in a detective novel as they go thro' beautiful scenery & prefer internationalism in cookery to the native delicacies.'

Socially, the trip had established Robert as a favoured friend of the aristocratic Lygons. During the summer vacation he stayed with them at Walmer Castle where Lord Beauchamp, a man loaded with honorary duties, resided briefly each year in his capacity as Warden of the Cinque Ports. There, for the first time, Robert met the Lygon daughters, Sibell, Lettice and Dorothy. They were all to become firm friends. Lettice, despite one blemish, even caught Robert's eye. He judged her 'the most beautiful human being I have ever seen – oversize feet, & yet the most lovely figure'. Robert, in turn, made a lasting impression on the eleven-year-old Dorothy, who never forgot his café au lait suit and pince-nez spectacles.

When, in 1931, Lord Beauchamp was hounded out of the country by his brother-in-law, the Duke of Westminster, for his homosexuality, Robert felt unspeakable anger. 'I shall always be greatly in his debt,' he acknowledged, 'as he first took me abroad & first taught me anything about art.'

The summer vacation of 1923 was largely spent with his parents and sisters in Wiltshire. His month's absence over Easter had prompted complaints from his mother about not spending enough time at home. Furthermore, the Byrons were also moving house that summer, leaving Knowle, where they had lived for the best part of four years, for Savernake Lodge, situated a few miles away in Savernake Forest.

Originally the preserve of kings, Savernake Forest has been established since at least the Norman Conquest. Nowadays it extends to 4,500 acres, but not all the area is woodland; there is also farmland as well as hamlets within its boundaries. In the 1920s, the appearance of the forested area largely reflected the ambitious planting programme of the eighteenth century, principally of beech, but also of oak. By then, these trees were at the peak of their grandeur, especially when lining the 'Eight Walks', a network of formal rides, attributed to Capability Brown, that terminate in eye-catchers or distant views.

The Byrons had coveted their new house for some time. Like Knowle, it was owned by the Marquess of Ailesbury, the hereditary warden of the Forest, and had, until then, been let to a Lady Brownlow. Fortunately, she had decided to give up the lease and had supported the Byrons' request to take it over.

Savernake Lodge, more familiarly known as the Ruins, had been fashioned from the surviving stable block and servants' quarters of an eighteenth-century house that had been burnt down in 1861. The principal range was, in the Byrons' day, a plain, whitish block, roofed in slate, that incorporated the original stable clock tower and an attractive Dutch gable end. Annexed to this at right angles was a single-storey wing that once adjoined the now vanished house.

The L-shaped plan dictated a rambling arrangement of ill-assorted rooms. There was a huge drawing room, a tiny dining room, a den and a schoolroom. Six bedrooms, all in a row, including one for the cook, were reached by an unpretentious staircase. The wing, which ended in the schoolroom, also had a small bedroom and a study. Robert appropriated these for himself even though it meant crossing the courtyard to reach a bathroom or lavatory.

Neither grand nor particularly convenient, the house also suffered from a lack of daylight, no electricity and, in winter, intense cold. None of these drawbacks, however, deterred the Byrons who had fallen in love with this singular dwelling principally because of its romantic situation deep in the forest.

In the 1920s, the sense of isolation was total. A track led to the nearest public road, half a mile away, which happened to be a magnificent 'carriage walk', surfaced with flint and sand, known as the Grand Avenue. In the opposite direction, the section of forest visible at the back of the house stretched for two miles towards the town of Marlborough. Even the continuous process of thinning and felling added to the sylvan charm, with work horses, sturdy Suffolk punches, being used to haul out the timber.

Robert had fallen in love with the forest from his earliest days at Knowle. 'I did so enjoy Long Leave –' he had written from Eton, 'it was lovely, especially the walks in the forest . . . what a wonderful place it is to live in.' Once established at the Ruins, he took every opportunity to roam. 'Isn't the forest gorgeous at night,' he enthused, 'when one is going through the bracken smelling bits of honeysuckle.'

Contentment at home contrasted with a lingering discontent towards Oxford. Unfavourable comparisons were drawn with Eton, where he returned four times during his first year as an undergraduate. Gradually, however, he began to feel more settled, not least as a result of the pleasure derived from decorating his rooms at Merton.

Having rejected one set and been ousted from another by 'an infernal fellow', Robert ended up, in the summer term of 1923, on Staircase III of Fellows Quadrangle with a low square room, 'all old panelling . . . with deep window seats' and 'a huge bedroom'. As undergraduates were free to redecorate at their own expense, he immediately began making improvements. The eighteenth-century panelling was painted an 'egg-blue-green' to match some new coral curtains, the door plates were lacquered and the chairs covered in 'rich damask edged with gold'. Sconces, acquired at Eton, adorned the walls.

He had also been scouring the curio and second-hand shops in run-down areas of the city for bargains. An early find was 'the most exquisite glass casket', dating from the 1870s, bought for thirty shillings. Defending the purchase to his mother, he reasoned: 'when you come to think of it glass mounted with metal is very rare.' Rudolph Messel was so entranced by this eye-catching Victorian receptacle that he offered to buy it should the crash come. Another addition was a silvered alms dish of Italian Renaissance design, bought in a 'disgusting shop . . . full of horsehair sofas' in the Iffley Road. Even Harold Acton was impressed. However, Spinks, the London dealers, begged to differ. To his disbelief, they pronounced it modern and quite worthless. Robert redeemed himself by acquiring for nine shillings a blackened canvas which an expert at the Ashmolean Museum identified as being by a minor Dutch master.

By the autumn term, the stage was set for a hectic round of entertaining. Cecil's grandmother, the Duchess of Abercorn, called; so, too, did Lady Beauchamp. He gave breakfast and lunch parties and, on one occasion, thirty people came to tea.

'My room really did look magnificent', he boasted afterwards, with the rich colour effects, the candle-lit sconces, the alms dish over the fireplace, and, sitting in 'triumph' on the mantelpiece, the glass casket which had been transformed with the help of a concealed light bulb into an objet de luxe of glowing crystal, 'like the latest invention of Asprey's'. But the most original touch concerned the eatables. On a patchwork cloth, spread over two tables, lay an abundance of tempting fruit both real and wax, the latter having been 'modelled with care and tenderness' in the Victorian age.

Robert was not the only one to grasp the ornamental possibilities of so unfashionable an epoch. On coming up to Oxford, Harold Acton had turned his back on the beautiful quadrangles of Christ Church and opted for a set in a forbidding Victorian range designed in the Venetian Gothic style, known as Meadow Buildings. To lift the spirits, he painted the sitting room lemon yellow and started to fill it with Victorian bric-a-brac.

His collecting activities received a powerful boost, in the summer of 1923, when he first visited the house of one of his literary heroes, Osbert Sitwell, for a party to celebrate Edith Sitwell's recitation of *Façade* at the Aeolian Hall. Harold marvelled at the interior of Carlyle Square which he described as 'a shrine of . . . sailing ships of spun glass, humming birds under globes, petit point screens, porcelain spaniels'. If only, he wished, Robert had been present: 'How that "vaseline" Bristol would have made his mouth water.'

Osbert Sitwell had been the first person of taste to rediscover the 'fancy work' of Queen Victoria's reign, but fashion had stubbornly refused to follow his lead so that by the time Harold and Robert arrived upon the scene the furnishings of Victoria's reign were still more likely to be found in the servants' hall than back in the drawing room.

Elsewhere, the mood was changing. This was not lost on the cosmopolitan Harold, who visited, in the autumn of 1923, the '1840' exhibition at the Cà Pesaro in Venice. Writing to his publisher, Thomas Balston, himself a pioneer student of the Victorian arts, Harold described it as 'most interesting and entertaining' and as coming 'at a most appropriate moment'.

Now in his second year, Harold had already made his mark at Oxford. Co-founder of a serious literary magazine, the *Oxford Broom*, he also enjoyed the réclame of authorship, having seen his first collection of verse appear that spring. But his growing fame did not rest on the printed word alone. With typical brio, he had taken to declaiming his poems lustily through a megaphone often to the departing backs of rowers as they headed for the river beneath his balcony in Meadow Buildings.

During the Michaelmas term of 1923, Robert and Harold were constantly in one another's company, lunching and dining together as well as making jaunts into the surrounding countryside. Out of their conversations emerged a plan to mount an exhibition in Oxford, along the lines of that in Venice, celebrating 1840s taste.

As a first move, they sought the imprimatur of a suitable authority. Robert wrote off to Philip Guedalla, a fashionable historian famed for his pre-war presidency of the Oxford Union, who the previous year had published a history of the Second Empire. 'What a charming idea –' came the reply, 'I am afraid that I am an unworthy introducer, as 1860 is really my period . . . I shall be up for the Union Centenary . . . and hope for a preliminary glance at your treasures . . . You must mention portraits & . . . busts of Louis Philippe and his Queen: there are some dreadful ones.'

Guedalla's mocking tone summed up the post-war attitude

to the Victorians. It reflected the profound influence of one man, Lytton Strachey, who, in *Eminent Victorians*, published to huge acclaim in 1918, had ridiculed the ambition, pretension, superstition and repression of his four, previously revered, subjects, Cardinal Manning, Florence Nightingale, Dr Arnold and General Gordon.

His biography of Queen Victoria, published in 1921, although softer in tone, was an even greater success. Robert, at Eton, could not put it down: 'it is the way the book conveys the atmosphere of things that is so good,' he enthused to his mother, who was herself no mean critic of the era. 'Albert's horrid perfection – the suburban middle classness of it all – also it brings to me more and more the idea of what Coulsden must have been like in Father's childhood.'

Robert's fascination with Coulsden informed his response to the Victorian age. Every detail of the house, down to the last biscuit tin, was freshly imprinted upon his visual memory giving him a precocious understanding of the look of the period. The recollection of his grandfather added bite to his critique. In an unpublished memoir, he condemned him for selfishly pursuing a public goal, to 'behave as an English gentleman should', at the expense of loving his children. To any admirer of Strachey's acid pen, such an attitude, essentially allowing duty to crush natural inclinations, was by then understood to have been the cardinal sin of the Victorians.

The 1840 exhibition, especially now that Guedalla had turned him down, gave Robert the chance to seek Lytton Strachey's backing for their 'at present rather unsupported enterprise'. After praising 'the marvellous appreciations . . . of Victoria and Victorians', he went on to invite him to contribute a foreword, 'even one short sentence', to the exhibition programme which was to be printed in gothic type. He ended on a suitably ironic note: 'I hope you will agree . . . that a large number of people will be surprised to see what masterpieces were produced by an age they derided.'

Strachey politely declined despite 'the attractions of gothic printing'. Keeping up the bantering tone, he felt sure that Robert would be able 'to find someone else even more in sympathy with the Victorian age and all it stands for than I'.

By the Hilary term of 1924, the serious work of gathering

exhibits had begun. These were to include pictures, ornaments, 'articles of vertue', statuettes and even dresses. Lord Effingham, a fat aesthete picked up by Robert and Harold in a pub outside Oxford, offered to lend suitable pieces. So, too, did John Fothergill, the 'fantastic innkeeper' of the Spreadeagle at Thame, who was already a collector of 'Victorian truck'.

Meanwhile, a room was engaged and the posters and programmes planned. Announcements were also placed in the *Cherwell* magazine, edited by the organizers' friend, John Sutro. Further publicity was provided by Harold in a leader calling for a return to the simplicity of the 1840s as a means of opposing 'so tedious a period of refinement as the nineties'. For him, the Victorian Revival was a means of reinventing the Oxford aesthete, turning him from a latter-day follower of Oscar Wilde with a 'preference of rouge to roses' into a virile defender of beauty and a propagandist of the arts. The moment had indeed arrived, as Mark Ogilvie-Grant pithily remarked, when 'the drooping lily yielded place to the wax banana'.

A wider audience also received the clarion call. Robert won his first commission as a journalist for an article in the *Tatler* entitled 'The Victorian Revival at Oxford' which was timed to coincide with the date of the opening of the exhibition at the beginning of March. Oxford, he announced, always ahead in the race to be up-to-date, was poised to launch a new fashion: 'Victoria shall reign once more.' Undergraduates were already revolutionizing their wardrobes. 'Young Oxford . . .' he reported, 'affects the stock and side-whisker', abandons the turn-up and chooses 'the almost peg-top trousers of the double-breasted suit' to show off their 'Dickens hips'.

As for decor, the current mode was scorned. 'Today', he complained, 'we see light in swinging soup-plates, duresco walls and amateur lacquer.' Small wonder, then, that Oxford was turning 'to waxen fruits . . . to woollen flowers . . . to patchwork curtains; to fantastic paperweights . . . displaying some scene from the Great Exhibition; to needlework fire screens and beadwork footstools'.

The arts of conversation, prose and poetry also stood on the cusp of change. But his most outrageous claim was reserved for the paintings of the period, which, he asserted, were 'the only really Christian art that the world has ever seen [with] none of the crude horrors of the Primitives or the worldly magnificence of the Renaissance, but simply little girls taming lions by faith or early martyrs floating heavenwards in side-whiskers.' Just in case his readers should miss the point, Robert underlined the tease behind the craze: 'Oxford . . . turns to the things themselves, worships them, laughs herself to tears and imitates them.'

But even before his article was published, he discovered that not all Oxford appreciated the joke. Plans for the exhibition were now sufficiently well advanced to seek the necessary consent from the proctors. Their reaction was one of 'instantaneous disapproval'. Deaf to Harold's pleas, they banned the exhibition on the spot, claiming that it was 'entirely unnecessary'.

Furious, Robert dashed off a 'wild' letter to the *Daily Mail*, co-signed by Harold, which accused the authorities of conspiring to quash 'any fresh mental stimulus' by banning a scheme that had aimed to revive a 'great phase of civilization'. Were they, he challenged, 'alarmed lest Oxford should gain the reputation of being the home of bookworms instead of sportsmen'?

The letter caused an uproar. Journalists descended upon Oxford to interview the wronged. A gratifyingly thick sheaf of cuttings was the result. 'Oxford students indignant' ran one headline, 'Dons maintain their verboten ban' ran another. A trenchant condemnation, quoted verbatim from *Isis*, appeared in the *Morning Post*, whilst the *Graphic* published a photograph of Robert surrounded by wax fruit and a tower of woollen flowers with the heading: 'Victim of Oxford's latest ban'. Support was received from Philip Guedalla who telegraphed Robert with the suggestion: 'Why not include Proctors in exhibition?'

Although Robert and Harold hoped that the exhibition might be held at a later date, Robert's next move was scarcely designed to allay the proctors' fears. With his friend, John 'Widow' Lloyd, a precious, learned and wicked Wykehamist, he gave a fancy-dress party with a Victorian theme at the Hypocrites Club, a gathering place that had become the focus of Robert's social life at Oxford.

Situated above a bicycle shop in an ancient half-timbered house in St Aldate's, the club had been founded some three years earlier by a group of undergraduates, including John Lloyd and the young Georgian poet, Richard Hughes, who shared a taste for strong beer, plain food and convivial fireside chat of an artistic or literary nature. The motto of the club, 'Water is best', taken from Pindar's Olympian ode, had inspired, in the manner of a somewhat donnish joke, its name, the Hypocrites.

During the course of 1923, the make-up of the club had begun to change. Many of the founding members went down to be replaced by a more frivolous intake, including Harold Acton, Alfred Duggan, Evelyn Waugh, who served briefly as secretary, and Robert Byron. The club servant, much given to dry repartee, commented upon the new style: 'They call themselves an artists' club – all they draw is corks.' Even so, its character still reflected the relatively elevated intentions of the founders. As Harold recalled: 'At all hours I could find somebody here to talk to, somebody with a congenial hobby or mania.'

Topics covered, according to a list drawn up by Robert, ranged from Serbo-Byzantine primitives to Czecho-Slovakian composers, Nietzsche, Russian literature, the Restoration poets and the Tennyson Revival. Conversation, though, tended to drift into carousal. Evelyn Waugh described the atmosphere at the Hypocrites in its heyday as one of 'uninhibited revelry', encapsulated by Elmley's injunction, when secretary, that 'Gentlemen may prance but not dance'. At one stage, the brown papered walls, which were decorated with a changing display of murals drawn by members in chalk, boasted some 'subtly pornographic frescoes' by Robert. These were remembered by Anthony Powell as being of men wrestling or some such theme, although he dismissed the widely held assumption that the Hypocrites 'was a kind of queer club' as being 'quite absurd'.

Winding narrow stairs, suffused with the smell of sizzling onions, led up to the club premises, which consisted of a kitchen and two large rooms with Tudor archways, stone chimney pieces and uneven floors. An upright piano in the main sitting room catered for a range of musical talents from classical to jazz. One of the most enthusiastic songsters was Robert, who had only recently developed the ability to play by ear. Night after night he would make 'the rafters ring' with renditions in ear-splitting alto of Victorian ballads, 'contorting his features into fearful grimaces' at the more touching refrains.

The Victorian party at the Hypocrites confirmed Robert's position as one of the dominant personalities of the club. As impresario of the event, he summoned his old schoolfriend, Oliver Messel, currently studying at the Slade, to help with the scenery and props. Incidents and themes from the Queen's reign were drawn on the walls including 'Dr Livingstone, I presume', 'Alfred, Lord Tennyson nursing his whisky bottle' and, in pride of place, framed by a pointed arch, 'Queen Victoria – We are not amus'd'. Still-lifes of lobsters, rabbits and poultry, arranged in the manner of Edwin Landseer, were suspended like chandeliers from the beamed ceiling, whilst on the musical side a barrel organ, zither and xylophone were imported to supplement the piano. The invitation card served as the curtain raiser. Here, Robert was at last able to use the gothic typeface by designing it to look like an ecclesiastical announcement.

On the night, there was nothing sacred about the proceedings even though a particularly wanton undergraduate, Arden Hilliard, turned up dressed as a nun. Only a handful of guests respected the early Victorian theme. Harold Acton decided to don military uniform as 'a disguise of both body and soul'. But Robert excelled himself as a gentleman of the period in morning trousers, cutaway coat with silk striped facings and cuffs, low top hat, lace ruff and gloves. He leant upon a long silver-topped cane.

This was not his only impersonation. He also performed a party piece which was destined to run for years to come. Placing a napkin upon his head to resemble a widow's cap, swelling out his cheeks and pulling down his eyes with his fingers, he metamorphosed into Queen Victoria at the time of her Jubilee. The likeness was quite startling, with his yellowish complexion, slightly popping eyes and short stature adding to its verisimilitude.

Exaggerated rumours of the goings-on that evening soon

reached the ears of the proctors, undermining still further the case for the 1840 exhibition. Eventually Harold was forced to admit that the project was 'done for'. Instead, a Queen Victoria ballet was mooted with Harold appearing as Lytton Strachey taking 'historical notes in appropriate postures, at one time beneath a Balmoral sofa', but the idea fizzled out.

Nothing, however, could dampen Oxford's passion for the ornaments of Victoria's reign. Robert launched upon a frenzy of collecting, filling his rooms with a variety of articles from wool pictures to 'red & bubbled salt cellars'. Most notable of all, he assembled a group of glass domes sheltering wax fruit or confections made from shells, which became the trademark of the Victorian Revival.

Even at Eton, Robert had shown an interest in domes, idly drawing one in the margin of his history notebook. Now, he hunted high and low for specimens, which could be picked up for a few shillings. An antique shop in Windsor produced a dome of calceolarias made from small inverted shells. Cheltenham yielded another. But the most splendiferous was procured in a 'darkened warehouse' in Portsmouth while on his way to the Naval Review. So extravagant was the canopy of glass fruit, waxed roses, velvet pansies and cloth lilies, so affecting was the spun-glass scene, beneath, of a shipwreck, that Robert devoted an entire article to it in the *Cherwell*.

Not all domes incurred his mirth. He described his find in Windsor as 'quite beautiful' and drew real joy from the decorative effect of domes en masse. 'You will come and see my room once more won't you?' he begged his mother before he moved into lodgings. 'It is so depressing having to leave it.'

Harold likewise continued to enrich his 'Victorian chamber'. He even purloined the French word *rigolo* to 'express the humour of domes'. His clothes also bespoke the cause; he was, wrote Robert, 'a remarkable sight with his grey bowler on top of black side whiskers & black stock'. A. L. Rowse, a shy scholar on the neighbouring staircase, described him as 'the apostle of pure 1840'. No philistine was safe from his and Robert's evangelizing. As Mark Ogilvie-Grant recalled: 'in our young days . . . the Dome was a symbol of militant aesthetics.'

Their mettle was put to the test shortly after the Hypocrites party when Robert and Harold were invited by Elmley to a 'wine', an evening of after-dinner drinking and entertainment at Magdalen. The presence of two such noted aesthetes soon aroused the hostility of the company who shouted for them to stand up on the pretext of drinking their health, but really to have a good look at them. The occasion ended in uproar. Elmley's party kicked at the hearties when they refused to play ring-a-roses and tore down the ivy from the walls. The aesthetes only escaped, according to Robert's gory account, by 'clubbing people in the face till they bled'.

In light of that evening, Robert came up with new labels to describe undergraduate society. As he explained to Henry Yorke,

> You may divide Oxford into two, without adopting the old classification of athlete and aesthete. On one side are the Magdalen type, either athletes, hunting-men, hardworkers – or members of the OUDS & other societies formed for the display of superficial intellect. These are all essentially gentlemanly & they try to reduce everything to public school terms – grading, hero worshipping and toadying. Of course they are everywhere, not only in Magdalen: but it is a convenient name.
>
> On the other side are the Hypocrites' type, also everywhere, but rare, embracing also athletes and aesthetes, hardworkers and hunting men, but with boundaries to their minds a little wider than the snobbery of the moment, a living society (in the scientific sense of the word) – in which it's not necessary to give expensive dinner parties three nights a week to get enough people to talk to. And quite honestly it is conversation & contact with other people that constitute as far as I can see Oxford's sole benefits.

No wonder when the Hypocrites was finally closed down by the authorities in May, Robert lamented: 'What a blank Oxford will be.'

For one so social, Robert's conversational style was not for the faint-hearted. 'Trash. Muck. Rubbish,' he would shout in the face of conventional wisdom. Evelyn Waugh captured his performance thus: 'He leered and scowled, screamed and snarled, fell into rages that were sometimes real and sometimes a charade – it was not easy to distinguish.' His humour relied upon exaggeration for effect. When Mark Ogilvie-Grant proudly showed him a letter from the notoriously tall contralto, Dame Clara Butt, which she had signed with her married name, C. Butt-Romford, he remarked: 'I suppose she uses a pen made out of a pine tree.'

Honing his verbal sallies on the crowd at the Hypocrites had, he told Henry Yorke, made 'an enormous difference' to his prose style. A series of articles on Oxford, never published, set out to expose the 'town of factories and slums'. Friends, on seeing the typescripts, chorused that this unexpected approach was 'the best satire they [had] ever read'.

Satire was all the rage at Oxford. The *Cherwell*, subtitled 'The Journal of Satire', urged its readers to 'Squeeze the lemon, Let the juice fly where it will!' The Victorian Revival did just that, leaving proctors and hearties alike smarting with pain. As a sustained exercise in satire it provided the perfect vehicle for Robert's naturally sarcastic tone of voice.

The passing of time obscured the sharpness of his performance. Chroniclers of the period, Harold amongst them, fell into the trap of portraying Robert as a genuine Victorian throwback, resplendent in tweed and deerstalker, rather than as an energetic and resourceful campaigner determined to extract every ounce of publicity, amusement and trouble from an original idea.

There was, however, one undergraduate who did take the Victorian Revival at face value. Ironically, he was Evelyn Waugh, better known then for his stylish illustrations in undergraduate magazines than for the prose that was to turn him into the greatest satirist of the age. A devoted disciple of the movement, even to the extent of acquiring a grey bowler hat, he made a pilgrimage in the spring of 1924 to the Albert Memorial. This monument to Victorian craftsmanship had inspired one of Strachey's greatest flights of deadpan humour and was currently universally decried. Waugh saw nothing funny about it and studied every detail with care. He cited his visit, many years later, to James Laver, the social historian, as evidence that his generation had revived the 'appreciation of mid-Victorian art'.

Waugh was true to his word. On leaving Oxford, his first published works were an essay on the Pre-Raphaelite Brotherhood followed by a biography of Rossetti. The torch, so frivolously lit by Robert and Harold, was already being borne aloft by more devout hands.

The Victorian Revival, even when burning most bright, during the Hilary and summer terms of 1924, was by no means Robert's only preoccupation. He was also laying plans for a trip to Russia in the forthcoming long vacation with Cecil Clonmore and David Talbot Rice. Inspiring Robert's sense of adventure was the example of a new acquaintance met through David Talbot Rice. This was Oliver Baldwin, son of Stanley Baldwin, the recently toppled Conservative Prime Minister.

Following their introduction, Robert invited Baldwin, who lived near Oxford, to lunch: 'he was so amusing –' Robert reported home afterwards, 'the most bitterly sarcastic man I have ever met.' Oliver Baldwin, who was then twenty-five, had good reason to take a hardened view of the world. After surviving two years in the trenches in France, in August 1920 he had accepted a post in the newly formed state of Armenia, as infantry instructor to the Armenian army.

One month after his arrival, Turkey had invaded. The Armenians, facing insuperable odds, invited the Bolsheviks to set up a provisional socialist government in the capital, Erivan. Identified as an enemy of the people, Baldwin was thrown into a filthy and overcrowded prison until eventually freed on parole. By then, the subjugation of the Armenians was well advanced. A rebellion overthrew the soviets but did not save the imprisoned community leaders who were machine-gunned and hacked to death before help could reach them. Baldwin photographed their corpses as evidence of Bolshevik methods. The Soviet advance forced him to flee on horseback through deep snow, harried by wolves and afflicted with frostbite, into Turkey. There, he was immediately arrested as a spy, interrogated and condemned to months of near starvation in an ice-cold cell. Finally, he was informed that his execution would take place in four days' time. Instead, hardly daring to believe it, he was escorted to Trebizond, put on a steamer for Constantinople and deported from the country.

Robert sat at Baldwin's feet, spellbound. He was shown the photographs of the Erivan massacre and they talked for hours about the next area of conflict. Tempting new horizons unfolded, he reported to his mother:

> If we can't manage Russia I shall certainly go to Bessarabia: that is northern Roumania once Russian – there the fighting will start – and if one knew the country or happened to be there it might be a tremendous chance to get on the staff of a paper. It is certain to come and I suppose we are certain to back the Turk – or throw away the policy of over a century.

His mother was appalled at such suggestions. She had already forbidden a plan to travel through Poland to Vilnius in Lithuania and thence into Russia. Her intransigence infuriated Robert, not least because he felt humiliated before his proposed travelling companions. Scornfully, he had riposted:

> You would prefer, I suppose that I went with the rest of Oxford to Vienna & with them spent day & night drinking something new in rather dangerously attractive cafés . . . What enterprise, what economy, what experience! What food for thought & future literature!

This was exactly what his mother did want. And on 11 August 1924 Robert found himself setting off with Cecil Clonmore by train for Paris, bound for Vienna. His dispatches rang with complaints. 'The food here is disgusting', he wrote from Vienna, '& one always seems to have it in the open air on the pavement.' Budapest proved little better. Here he waded up to his chest into the Danube. A postcard announced: 'I have just bathed . . . amidst the sewage of this sweet little place.' Scenting 'unpleasantness' in Triestino, the former Hapsburg province of Istria, they travelled west to Trieste. The only site of interest was a remote village in the mountains. Their journey ended in Venice, whence they returned home.

Throughout the three-week trip, Robert had been in no frame of mind to enjoy the experience. 'How horrible most of Europe is,' he told Henry Yorke. 'Paris, Vienna & Budapest literally leave me speechless with repulsion, loathing, even resentment.' His lack of enthusiasm recalled Evelyn Waugh's account of Robert's self-caricature at Oxford shouting 'Down with abroad' at the mention of travel.

Oliver Baldwin was to remain a friend of Robert's for the rest of his time at Oxford, but his influence waned. Longing to experience a similar adventure, Robert did not appreciate the trauma that Baldwin had suffered, which led to depression and recurring nightmares. Defeated as a Labour candidate in the October 1924 election, he turned to chicken farming. Robert was dismayed by his hero's fall: 'it makes me sick to see Oliver amongst the chickens – I wish he would do something.'

On returning to Oxford for the Michaelmas term 1924, even Robert admitted that it was 'very nice to be back'. His immediate circle were all present and correct. There was Hugh Lygon installed in vast panelled rooms in Pembroke, Mark Ogilvie-Grant sporting a new tweed from Strathpeffer, Rudolph Messel bearing a Victorian paperweight, Cecil Clonmore, now in his fourth year, feeling 'like an old man at a dance', Harold Acton, straight from Paris, with an enviable collection of Charvet ties and, finally, Alfred Duggan, drinking nothing stronger than lemonade. A welcome new arrival was Henry Yorke, a freshman at Magdalen, where he was already 'miserably unhappy'.

The term spiralled into a vortex of parties. Two of the leading lights were the brothers, Richard and David Plunket Greene, a wildly irresponsible pair who had never experienced any form of parental control. Their father, a well-known concert singer, had abandoned them for his mistress, whilst their mother, the daughter of Sir Hubert Parry, had always treated them as her equals, indulging their every whim. Both boys were extremely musical. David imported jazz to Oxford and played the latest Harlem blues with great feeling on the piano at the Hypocrites.

Richard, having decided to stay up for a fourth year, now occupied the former premises of the club, playing host nightly to crowds of drunken undergraduates. Robert turned up one evening after dinner, lost track of time, and found himself, after midnight, assisting some Balliol men to climb back into college. The police arrived and, because a car was involved, threatened prosecution. Robert chivalrously produced his licence, saving the owner, Matthew Ponsonby, son of a senior Labour politician, from public embarrassment.

Only the intervention of Robert's long-suffering tutor saved him from rustication. This was the seventh time that he had appeared before the proctors for unruly behaviour and they warned him that the next would mean expulsion. A hefty fine was imposed and he was gated until the end of term. Robert retaliated by issuing a soon coveted invitation announcing that he was 'At Home' from 'Eight o'clock to midnight for the remainder of the term'.

He had never been more in demand. One evening, fifty people crowded into his rooms, each bringing a bottle. The noise was unbelievable and the last guest left at 2 a.m. 'This term', he concluded, 'has been one continual round of expensive parties – quite quite extraordinary. I owe more meals than I can count, yet feverishly ask people to lunch every week.'

Oxford was not their only playground. Robert and his friends also discovered Reading, where they marvelled at the commercial hotels and the dowdy refinement of the palais de danse.

Startling new fashions illumined the scene. The roll-collar jumper was first spotted by Evelyn Waugh in November at a party given by Cecil Clonmore in Merton. Next to make an appearance was the Oxford bag, described by Robert as 'an immensely wide turned down trouser . . . concealing the heel and billowing over the instep'. News of the latest modes brought accusations of depravity from the national press. Robert was swift to profit from the controversy, receiving a guinea from the *Daily Express* to counter the accusations. Both garments, he argued in a letter, drew 'their inspiration from the navy, and there seems nothing particularly effeminate in that'.

Robert's denial, as he well knew, did not hold water. The true picture was painted by Cecil Clonmore in a letter to David Talbot Rice, who was spending the year abroad. 'Oxford', he reported, 'has developed enormously in your absence.' It was now a 'whirl of Uranian antics', in which 'the streets are thronged with scented sirs, attracting hourly new candidates to their order'.

Although an added flamboyance was in the air, Robert and his friends had been falling in and out of bed with one another since first scenting the hedonism of Oxford. In recollecting his 'bygone loves', Harold referred 'to blue eyes, green eyes, eyes like black diamonds, to gentle struggles and showers of burning kisses'. Brian made unexpected conquests in the grand Bullingdon set, whilst Cecil yearned, hopelessly, for the handsome Peter Rodd, a cosmopolitan figure and already a success with women.

Robert had no particular emotional attachment. He was too preoccupied with his own ambitions to have time for love. Harold touched on his behaviour many years later when gently reproving Evelyn Waugh for drawing attention in print to one of his own passions whilst failing to allude to 'Robert's, Patrick's, Brian's and Hugh's promiscuities'.

Robert, however, was acutely aware that such behaviour would invite obloquy and even prosecution outside the hothouse of Oxford. Relaying a juicy piece of gossip in a letter to Patrick Balfour about a 'group of homosexual stock-brokers', who had arrived to see Hugh Lygon, he cautioned, 'Don't leave this lying about.' On the night in question, Anthony Powell saw Robert with the older men and made the mistake of passing on the news. Robert was furious, forcing Powell to retract. 'He thought', explained Powell long after the event, 'there might be a real (police) row if the truth got round . . . It all seemed to me a great joke, but to someone like Robert who was congenitally homosexual, not at all.'

Women, even if desired, were simply not in evidence at Oxford. Sequestered in their own colleges, undergraduettes, as they were known, also had to contend with stringent chaperoning rules that insisted on a married woman accompanying them to social engagements. Other indignities were heaped upon them. They could not debate at the Union, nor become members of the Oxford University Dramatic Society, let alone the Hypocrites. The female dons, as much as the males, upheld the need for segregation. Women students had only recently been given the right to become members of the University and their college principals dreaded this status being removed as a result of scandal.

There was little chance of that. A cup of cocoa in a small, bleak room, miles from anywhere, could hardly compete with hot lobster and champagne, overlooking a quadrangle of golden stone. The injustice was summed up by Christine Longford (née Trew), one of the few undergraduettes to make her mark at this time, who, in her novel about twenties Oxford entitled *Making Conversation*, had her heroine lament: 'What a lovely time men have compared with women . . . Lovely sitting-rooms and bedrooms and lunch-parties. They can enjoy themselves without women, but women can't enjoy themselves without men.'

Misogyny was rife. Robert complained at the end of his first summer term: 'Eights week is begun: the place is inundated by vulgar women.' Exploiting this mood for literary effect, he wrote in one of his unpublished articles on Oxford that lectures were to be avoided because of the 'horrible proximity of women undergraduates'.

An exception was Tamara Abelson, a spirited White Russian who had succeeded in escaping not only the Bolsheviks but also the confines of St Hugh's College. Wilting under the draconian restrictions, she won the right to become a 'home student' and thus live in rooms in the centre of Oxford. Exotic and clever, she swiftly made close friends with David Talbot Rice and his circle. Robert even invited her to sit for her portrait.

By the spring of 1925, Robert was tiring of the succession of parties but found himself continually led astray by David Plunket Greene. As he explained to Henry Yorke:

> If it were not for my work I feel that next term I should have to launch myself into some titanic (yr word) scheme to counteract the monotonies of rank and fashion with which David will surround himself – He drags me among them & I can't keep away from him personally as I like him so much – it is

very trying . . . but I must work or pretend to . . . However directly I return everything will be drowned in my beer and other people's champagne.

His note of alarm signalled the looming prospect of finals. He had last sat a university exam in his second term, otherwise he had merely had to pass the annual history 'collections' set by Merton each autumn, which had required some last-minute swotting during the summer vacation. Now he decided to pursue a similar course by joining a reading party during the Easter vacation on Lundy Island led by David Talbot Rice.

Much of the teaching for the Modern History tripos involved ploughing through weighty, nineteenth-century texts on economic and constitutional issues. Robert found these profoundly dull and only did the minimum amount of work. He preferred the past to be evoked in terms of personalities and in everyday details such as 'the journeys and the food'. One of the few set books to engage his interest was the autobiography of Metternich. Reading it at a sitting, he relished 'such facts as that the Venus by Canova in his library had its pedestal encased in a circular settee'. As he told Henry Yorke: 'To me this is real history.'

He had long known that the examiners would think otherwise. 'Please do not think I shall get a first,' he had warned his mother at the start of his final year. 'I couldn't if I wanted to even. You forget that a third is honours & besides that there is a fourth class & a pass.'

Robert was too ambitious to care about academic laurels. He had come to Oxford determined to make his mark as a writer. His first attempt was a series of articles on university life for the *New York Tribune*. These were rejected, but other commissions were forthcoming. His eye for an opportune story from abroad resulted in publication by *The Times* of a piece on the crowds visiting the Hapsburg tombs in Vienna. He also tried his hand at fiction, sending off a novelette, inspired by the 'atmosphere' of Reading, to Thomas Balston, the director responsible for discovering new talent at Duckworth, and to the eminent literary agent, Raymond Savage. Both turned down the manuscript but went to considerable lengths to encourage him to continue writing.

In February 1925, Robert decided to try his hand at undergraduate journalism. He was well placed to do so, having just started to share lodgings at 40 Beaumont Street with John Sutro, a financial backer and principal editor of the *Cherwell* magazine. Now in his fourth year, Sutro was a recognized star in the Oxford firmament. He was an incomparable mimic, excellent company, an inspired host, literate and rich. Under his editorship, the *Cherwell*, a rival to the establishment organ, the *Isis*, had published the work of numerous friends including Harold Acton, Christine Trew, Patrick Balfour, Evelyn Waugh and Anthony Powell.

Although a late arrival to its pages, Robert soon made up for his absence. His first topical contribution was an attack on the Oxford University Dramatic Society (OUDS), which was currently basking in the praise heaped upon its recent staging of *Peer Gynt*. The claque had been efficiently organized in both university weeklies. Apart from reviews, there were leaders, articles, notes and letters on the production. The star, Gyles Isham, had been named 'Isis Idol' and his minions, idolets.

Robert set out to expose their feet of clay. The OUDS, he sneered, was a band of public school prefects, 'a press-puffed galaxy', capable only of memorizing 'the words that they are set' and mouthing them 'as directed'. His argument focused upon the OUDS' practice of hiring professional directors and designers for their productions. With devastating clarity, he drew a comparison to their Cambridge peers, who 'create their own dresses, their own scenery, their own music and – most important of all – their own interpretation of the play in question'.

He scored a most palpable hit. The pages of the *Cherwell* were filled for weeks to come with furious articles and letters from members of the OUDS. One denounced Robert for his 'distinctly inerudite, thoroughly cheap attack', another railed anonymously at the 'petty sneers, the pompous superiority of tone'. But the field was his. He was appointed editor of the *Cherwell* in June 1925 and won the chance to become one of the leading players in Oxford's world of letters.

Although two issues appeared under his name after the exams were over, his appointment was planned to run into the autumn. Having come up to Oxford in a bye-term, he had sat his degree in just eight terms, which gave him a statutory right to return for a ninth. This, if all went according to plan, would be free of academic requirements. His finals, as predicted, resulted in a third. The editor's chair thus awaited him.

7
Grand Tour

At half-past ten on the sultry evening of 1 August 1925, Robert was to be found with Gavin Henderson and Alfred Duggan puzzling over a map on the pavement of Upper Brook Street, Mayfair. Parked alongside was a sleek, open-topped touring Sunbeam, the back piled high with cabin trunks, dressing cases and a Gladstone bag. The party needed to find the North Sea, but the route out of London was by no means clear. A policeman on the beat came to the rescue by pointing them in the general direction of East Anglia. Their adventure to the Balkans had begun.

They were lucky to have got this far. At one moment during the previous month, for one reason or another, the whole plan had foundered. As a result, Robert had only had three days' notice of their departure, entailing frantic hours in Thomas Cook's and the Passport Office.

The idea had first been mooted, back in May, by Gavin Henderson. He had been one of Robert's earliest Oxford friends and they had remained close ever since. A tall, elegant figure with a fine profile and a sharp wit, Gavin sprang from a background of civilized plutocracy, being the immediate heir to his grandfather, Lord Faringdon, a brilliant financier, who had formed a magnificent collection of pictures at his Georgian seat, Buscot Park in Berkshire.

Gavin had established his own aesthetic credentials at Christ Church by painting the ceiling of his sitting room black and the walls black and gold. His fascination with architecture and decoration was matched by a love of travel. Time spent in Berlin witnessing the violent upheavals after the war and a more recent journey by car to Poland and the Russian frontier had greatly impressed Robert. The Sunbeam had been bought by Gavin especially for the motor tour to the Balkans.

Alfred Duggan was a paradoxical figure. His career at

Oxford had been spent drinking, gambling, riding to hounds and escaping to parties and nightclubs in London. At the same time, he professed Communism, which to Robert did not ring true. 'Alf', he stated, 'is more conservative than anyone I have ever known', appearing utterly English, and yet 'without a drop of English blood within'. His father was from a rich Irish-Argentine family whilst his mother was American. They had moved to London in the year of Alfred's birth, but Alfred's father, betraying his son's inherited weakness, died of drink during the war; two years afterwards, his mother married the Marquis of Curzon. Only his stepfather's position as Chancellor of the University prevented Alfred from being sent down in his second year for repeated misdemeanors. Instead, he was packed off on the Oxford scientific expedition to the Galapagos Islands. Following this corrective he briefly took to lemonade.

Hook-nosed, bull-necked and short, Alfred dressed with great correctness favouring stiff collars, pearl tiepin, bowler hat and gloves. His closest friends saw through this starched façade which concealed a shyness and remarkable intelligence. Robert spoke of his reputation at Oxford as 'a brilliant historian' and was to appreciate his company on the journey ahead. Alfred, he acknowledged, 'being so very well read, is most interesting to travel with'. By the time they met up on the pavement in Mayfair, Alfred's university days were over. He had been caught, yet again, spending the night out of college and sent down.

From the start, their positions in the car never altered. Gavin was behind the wheel, Robert, with the narrowest shoulders, in the middle and Alfred on the other side, 'always the English Duke, sitting bolt upright studying a map'.

Taking a boat from Grimsby, they landed the following day at Hamburg. Their itinerary took them through Berlin, Nuremberg and Munich to Salzburg. Entering Italy by the Brenner Pass, they drove down the well-trodden tourist route to Rome and thence on to Brindisi where they embarked for Greece. Eventually, they hoped to carry on to Constantinople and return via Romania and Yugoslavia.

The long drives on the roughly surfaced roads were chequered with mishaps. Gavin and Robert were forever mending punctures, tying up bits of the undercarriage or unloading luggage to get at the spare tank. Alfred made little pretence of trying to help. A far more serious setback was caused by incomplete paperwork. This provoked an Italian customs officer at the Brenner pass to bar them entry to the country. The frontier had been redrawn since the war and as the Austrian officials pointed out: 'Since they've come this side of the mountains they've been above themselves.' Only Gavin's persistence prevented them from being stranded on the wrong side of the Alps.

His skill as a driver was also put to the test. The huge body of the car meant that on twisting mountain roads the back wheels were often suspended in mid-air. Overtaking on the flat was another challenge. Close shaves with horse-drawn wagons, piled with hay, left much of the load on Alfred's affronted head.

At each halt on their journey, Gavin and Alfred insisted on making straight for the most luxurious hotel. Both were used to the best and could afford it. Robert, on the other hand, only had £60 to last him the whole trip and would have preferred to live more cheaply. An initial awkwardness was smoothed over by pooling their resources rather than dividing the bills equally. In any case, Gavin was appalled that Robert might return home once his funds had run out, explaining how 'he cannot be left alone with Alfred who is not very competent at mending punctures.'

They went in for a good deal of sightseeing. Robert marvelled at the survival of Rothenburg in Bavaria with its walls, towered gates and streets 'like mountain paths'; Gavin opened his eyes in Vicenza to the importance of Palladio as 'the founder of English domestic architecture', whilst one of the highlights for them all was the castle of the Estes at Ferrara. Its effect was described by Robert, as seen against 'a smooth deep blue sky' which 'threw the exquisite workmanship of the towering pink masses of brickwork into prominence. While the moat, deep, green & slimy, reflected clear cut & dark, the sinister shadows of the past.'

His impressions were recorded in a diary that he had been keeping since the outset of the journey. He became increasingly pleased with the result, expressing the hope to his mother from Rome that, 'if we get far enough East to make it interesting, I might send it to Raymond Savage . . . & ask if it wld be any use.' Nor was he neglecting his journalistic career. An article was dashed off for *The Times* on a performance of Rossini's opera *Moses*, which they had attended during a thunderstorm in the Colosseum at Verona.

But his pen alone was not enough to occupy him. He had also brought his pencil and paints. 'I spent yesterday morning', he wrote from Siena, 'drawing the cathedral, the town & the surrounding country from the top of the "Mangia" – a terrific tower . . . I shall paint it from memory – as it was too windy up there.'

A week was spent kicking their heels in Bologna awaiting a new carburettor. Much of the time was whiled away in cafés where they met a man called Rossi 'encased from head to toe in black – black shirt, black tie, black handkerchief, black suit & black buttoned boots. Everything he had on clung.' Once a follower of d'Annunzio, he was now head of the Fascisti in Ferrara. They heard how he 'had fought, dislodged & drowned in the moat the communists who had taken possession of the castle'. Rossi proved difficult to shake off. He eventually disappeared after a drunken dinner taking Gavin's snakewood cane with him. Robert's early encounter with a Fascist left him with a feeling – unreasonable, he admitted – of 'overpowering revulsion'.

Another manifestation of the havoc wrought by the war were the numbers of young Germans, known as *Wandervögel*, trudging along the Italian roads. Robert described them with dandiacal disdain as 'couples of bare kneed khaki clad figures, packs on backs, dirty, smelly with burnt faces [and] flaxen haired'. Occasionally, 'this sordid exterior' was redeemed 'by the joint possession of a guitar'. They fell in with a pair on board the boat to Greece. Both were graduates of Heidelberg University, but had been driven to a life of wanderlust by the economic chaos at home. Now 'absolutely without funds', they raised small sums by selling photographs of themselves in *Wandervogel* garb, posed before a studio backcloth of urns and foliage. 'These', Robert discovered, 'are an indispensable part of the equipment of the professional young German beggar.' Their intention was to travel round the world, which they calculated would take them until 1935. On hearing this, Robert asked percipiently: 'What then?'

Dwelling on their meeting a few months later, he suggested that the two Germans would serve 'to recall not only the miserable tragedy of a European war, but also the unsettled mentalities and bitter disappointments created by the Peace that followed'. At least Gavin did his best to salve the wound by offering them a lift to Athens.

Robert was thoroughly invigorated by seeing Germany for the first time and by his return visit to Italy. However, he could not help admitting: 'I am all impatience as the saying goes to get to Greece –'

The last leg of their Italian journey, the drive from Rome to Brindisi, via Naples, was accomplished in three days. As they raced to reach Brindisi by nightfall, the car threw up blinding clouds of white dust 'so thick', Robert complained, 'that it came up through the gear holes and hit us in the face'.

The next morning they found their steamer moored by the quay. It was not the large and inviting *Lloyd-Trestino*, bound for Piraeus, the port of Athens, but a small, dirty merchant ship preparing to chug its way to Patras, situated many miles from the capital, on the south-west corner of the Gulf of Corinth. This destination had been chosen by Gavin when applying for the necessary paperwork in London because its name sounded so much less commonplace.

Three days later, after stops at Santi Quaranta in Albania and Corfu, they eventually sighted the lights of Patras twinkling 'out of a rather muddy dawn'. The ship dropped anchor some distance from the quay necessitating the winching of the car on to a lighter. At one point Robert, who was at the end of a guy rope, just prevented the precious cargo crashing into the sea. Once on land, the choice of Patras certainly proved original for anyone on a motor tour. Inquiries as to the road to Athens disclosed that none existed. The car would have to be loaded on to a train to Corinth, entailing further delay.

With time to spare, they found a small strip of beach and went for a swim. Robert recorded the moment:

> It was delicious, this the first of our Greek bathes, defying the heat from the cool shadows beneath the surface, lying back & blinking at the sun – with the mountains just across the other side – and foothills half brown, dotted with olives and rocks and patches of cultivation rising up to huge hills behind us. Then I trod on a sea urchin.

Athens was finally reached the following evening. They made straight for the Hotel Grande Bretagne Lampsa, where rooms had been engaged for them by their one contact in the city, an old friend of Gavin's, called Leonard Bower. An ex-soldier who had served in Constantinople, Bower had returned to the Levant on leaving the army, as an Honorary Attaché at the British Legation in Athens. They ran across him later that night at a nearby restaurant, dining with a party of diplomats. As they bore him off to their own table, he joked that he had been 'dreading this moment for six weeks'.

Leonard and Robert took to one another instantly. A plump figure, invariably dressed in Guards blazer and flannels, he too was staying at the Grande Bretagne owing to a lack of water in his flat. Each morning, over the next fortnight, Robert would accompany him to the Legation to pick up any mail. Leonard's duties there were slight. Only twice during Robert's stay did he have to decode a telegram, leaving him plenty of time to act as his guide. Their day always ended in the old Turkish quarter, 'like an eastern bazaar, narrow & crowded with awnings & dark & poky shops'. This was the preserve of antique dealers and where Leonard earned his living. As an honorary attaché he was unpaid, so an income from supplying London dealers, not to mention the Chargé d'Affaires at the Legation, with antiquities, rugs and icons came in useful.

Robert also enjoyed the assistance of John Stuart Hay, a well-known character in Athens with a finger in every pie. He was currently involved with winding up the affairs of a bank partly owned by Gavin's grandfather. Keen to make their acquaintance, he had bustled round to the restaurant on their first night having heard on the grapevine that 'Kurios Boover [Mr Bower] . . . was dining at the Petit Palais with

Lordos Vironos.' Hay well knew that Robert was not Lord Byron. But to the Greeks, it was irrelevant. As Robert was to explain in his published account of the journey: 'To avoid repeated self-advertisement I may admit at the outset that all Greeks feel a . . . pride in meeting a person bearing my name.'

Robert had arrived in Athens with his schoolboy prejudices intact. 'Ancient Greece', he wrote home on the first morning, 'so far we have been spared.' But his curiosity swiftly got the better of him. 'Honouring the famous ruin', as he called the Parthenon, was undertaken the next day in the company of Leonard Bower.

As their horse-drawn cab neared the foot of the mountainous platform, he could scarcely believe his eyes, so different was the reality from the familiar photographic image. Climbing up the rough marble steps through the pillared archway of the Propylaea, he was confronted by a scene of 'infinite beauty':

> Strewn in all directions lay blocks of white marble gleaming in the brilliant sunlight, their broken sides displaying the oldest, and at the same time the most modern architectural conventions, varied with now and then a fragmentary bas-relief, the hindquarters of a horse, a human arm, or draped hip. And at the top, rising from its massive double base, there stood the Parthenon . . . [its] pillars . . . Doric, plain, massive and fluted . . . against the brazen turquoise of the sky behind.

In this set-piece description, composed for publication, Robert pitted his pen 'against the lens of the Victorian photographer'. Their dreary prints, hung in schools across the land, accentuating every scratch and chip, were, he argued, 'responsible for the loathing with which the very thought of a Greek ruin fills the mind of any educated person'.

His new-found enthusiasm did not extend to lesser monuments. Most antiquities, especially late Greek and Roman, continued to receive short shrift. Making their descent into the city, they passed the Forum of Hadrian, which, with its 'rows of thin, grey, broken pillars', was deemed 'squalid and uninteresting'.

Robert continued to pursue his interest in Byzantine architecture, visiting the two best examples, the monastery church at Daphni and the 'Little Cathedral' known as Gorgoepikoos. However, as the majority of churches in Athens had been either destroyed or reconstructed during the nineteenth century, he found nothing to compare to the glories of Ravenna.

Trawling round the antique dealers with Leonard proved more instructive. Numerous icons were produced, many of late date but, to Robert's eye, of superb decorative quality. Occasionally one of 'real spiritual beauty' emerged. He described a panel, wiped with a damp rag as it was brought out by the dealer, of a life-size Madonna, her face 'a polished oval of grey ebony . . . her long straight-boned nose, like the visor of a Norman warrior'. It had previously been used as a lid of a chest on the island of Chios and some missing pieces had yet to be retrieved.

Present-day Greece also fascinated him. One day, he was taken by Leonard to meet Dr Skevos Zervos, the exiled leader of the Association of the Dodecanese, the chain of islands from Samos to Rhodes which lie along the southern Aegean coast of Turkey. The recent fate of these islands dated from 1912 when the Italians wrested them from the Ottoman Empire. Sovereignty was granted three years later, at the secret Treaty of London, as a condition of Italy entering the war on the Allies' side. Greece claimed possession at the Peace Conference but tortuous negotiations, which sometimes appeared close to resolution, had ended in failure. This was principally due to Greece's disastrous offensive against Turkey, launched from Smyrna in October 1920, which ended two years later in defeat and humiliation. The ensuing Treaty of Lausanne confirmed Italy's retention of the Dodecanese. From the point of view of the Great Powers, as well as the Greek government, the matter was closed. Only Dr Zervos, who had led a delegation of islanders to the Peace Conference, continued to fight for the union of the Dodecanese with Greece.

Originally a physician from the sponge-fishing island of Calymnos, he now occupied a lofty apartment off Constitution Square. Paintings of the islands, many by his own hand, hung upon the walls whilst all manner of sponges were perched and piled on every ledge. 'My house is yours

– everything I have!' he cried effusively in 'harsh and stilted French' as Robert and Leonard sat down to coffee, liqueurs and preserved oranges. Two hours later they were still discussing the plight of the Dodecanese.

Offering to send round his book on the subject, he asked Robert to write down his name. The magic word had an explosive effect: 'he . . . took me by the hand', Robert told his mother, 'and we swayed up and down sweating and shouting about Liberty and the new Byron in French. It was very gratifying.'

The next day, Robert lived up to his name by writing an article which exposed the oppressive rule of the Italians in the Dodecanese. Amongst other injustices, he cited the banning of Orthodox processions, the prohibition of sponge fishing and the exile of those who refused to take Italian citizenship. He ended by warning that the construction of a huge naval and air base on Leros posed a threat to the neutrality of the region. The article was published three months later in the *New Statesman*.

His meeting with Dr Zervos was not Robert's only foray into 'political interviewing'. That same night, he dined with a young financier, Sotiri Cartaliss, to hear about the destruction of Smyrna by Turkish forces three years earlier, in their final offensive against the Greeks in Anatolia. The horror for Cartaliss was still fresh. 'We drove down to the quay . . .' he told Robert, 'full speed over bodies and through blood. We pretended we were French, otherwise we should have been murdered.'

Robert interviewed many other witnesses. 'No one foresaw the barbarities of a seventeenth-century sack,' Robert reported.

> The Turks entered in the morning. Everyone went about their ordinary pursuits. Then the streets became unsafe. They were asked for money & if they did not give it, were butchered then & there . . . as the flames spread the crowds on the quay were joined by others fleeing . . . the foremost were pushed into the sea.

Placing the disaster in context, he explained that in England 'we talk of "after the War"', but in Greece 'they say "since Smyrna."'

The Treaty of Lausanne had insisted on a vast exchange of populations to prevent any irredentist uprisings in the future. Over a million Greeks arrived from Turkey and a quarter of them were housed in 'an extraordinary mushroom town' on the edge of Piraeus. Robert described it as 'miles & miles of wooden bungalows . . . intensely clean'. The inhabitants still displayed their cultural roots, 'wearing astrakhan caps or fezes & huge baggy trousers'. He went principally to meet Gladys Stuart-Richardson, 'one of those fabulous women of immense vitality' who, despite having no money, had launched a business employing refugees to weave high-neck jerseys and native textiles.

Despite Robert's manifold activities, he always met up with Gavin and Alfred for a leisurely lunch at the Grande Bretagne before spending the afternoon at the small harbour of Phaleron. A wooden pier led to their bathing cabins whence they descended 'by ladder straight into the sea'. Robert, unlike his companions, had no time for basking 'face downward on a splintery board in quest of sunburn'. Instead, he 'used to swim out two or three hundred yards & gaze at the Acropolis & Lykabettus'. In the evening, they dined either at the restaurants in the gardens of the Zappeion or at tavernas by the sea. Sometimes they took a midnight swim before ending up at the Griffon nightclub where entrance was free and champagne was not compulsory.

An idyllic day was spent at Porto Raphti, a horseshoe bay protected at its mouth by a conical island. They hired a boat 'with a high pointed sail & curving prows', carried on board an enormous amphora of Cretan wine as well as 'sandwiches, figs, goat's cheese, grapes, eggs, local beer', and set sail. Their swim was pure rapture: 'it was as tho' a million sun warmed beryls & ice cold aquamarines were rushing silently over the skin.' Having clambered up the small island to inspect an ancient statue, they rowed back in the dark. Crowds of holidaymakers were drinking under the trees; the small church glowed with the amber light of candles; the sea lapped against the shore; the Greeks at the next table began to sing. Recalling the day some months later, in the depths of an English winter, Robert mused wistfully: 'The voices seemed to wail farewell, the sea to murmur softly, "Come again".'

The end of his holiday drew near. Gavin had persuaded Sotiri Cartaliss to drive back with him to England, freeing Robert to return by faster means. Even so, he was faced with almost five days on a small boat to Marseilles. At one point, Alfred agreed to come too, but changed his mind at the last minute 'and went to his bath instead'. Gavin saw him off from the quay. Leonard with a diplomatic pass was allowed on board. Robert felt miserable at saying goodbye to both of them. A desolation overwhelmed him. 'I could honestly have wept', he confessed, 'as slowly we steamed out of harbour & beyond the masts and funnels appeared the brown hills; the far distant white acropolis; Lykabettus; Hymettus and the mountains.'

8

Grub Street

At the beginning of October, Robert returned to Oxford to take up his statutory right to a ninth term at the University. His only occupation was editing the *Cherwell* for which he was paid £2 10s. a week by the principal backer, Mr Sissons. Although one or two topics of parochial interest were addressed, Robert's recent travels provided him with more original copy.

'La Gazette', a section usually devoted to light-hearted snippets of local gossip and opinion, hummed with news from the Levant. One morsel, dropped nonchalantly on to the page, told of a failed plot to kidnap the Greek dictator, General Theodore Pangalos. This scoop went unremarked by Fleet Street, provoking a triumphant paragraph the following week, headlined: 'The *Cherwell* steals a march on Reuters'.

The dangers of the Italian presence in the Dodecanese were twice raised in the column. Robert also took the matter up with Lord Beauchamp, a prominent Liberal in the House of Lords, as well as with his friend Roy Harrod, a young economics don at Christ Church. Thanks to Harrod's connections, an invitation to tea was forthcoming from Professor Gilbert Murray, founder and chairman of the Executive Council of the League of Nations. The prospect filled Robert with the hope that '"the cause" may not be allowed to drop'. His harping upon the subject, as he gleefully admitted, led people to tell him to his face that 'what with the Dodecanese and The Cherwell I have become the greatest bore in Oxford.'

The trumpeting of his journalistic credentials was all part of Robert's hunt for a job. His best contact proved to be Jack 'Che' Murdocke, originally one of the notorious party of 'homosexual stockbrokers' who had come down to Oxford to see Hugh Lygon. He turned out to be a well-paid stringer, largely working for American newspapers. 'I am going to cultivate him assiduously', Robert schemed, 'and cover him with Cherwells.' A few days later, Robert was on his way to London armed with an introduction to the foreign editor of the *Daily Mail*. One interview led to another until finally, in January 1926, he landed a job as a trainee reporter on the paper.

Meanwhile, his Oxford career had come to an unseemly end. His downfall was precipitated by an incident on Guy Fawkes night when he and Henry Yorke had booed the mob of undergraduates in the Cornmarket from the windows of the Liberal Club and called them 'girl men'. A fusillade of rockets was the response. Appearing before the proctors for the ninth time he was fined and gated. But Merton had had enough. The College insisted that he leave Oxford straight after the official term had ended. He never bothered to collect his degree.

By the middle of January 1926, Robert had moved to London, taking rooms on the first floor of a 'dear little brick Georgian house' at 7 Upper Montagu Street in Marylebone. The next day, he arrived 'like a shy maiden' at the *Daily Mail* to take up his position at the news desk.

His task, termed space work, was to pursue minor stories suitable for filling up a few column inches. Topics investigated over the next few weeks included a ventriloquist vicar living in a disused public house in Peckham, the poisonous plants at Kew, aerial map-making in Croydon, a blaze at Ludgate Circus and the social acceptability of fish knives.

Each item was submitted to one of the two news editors who, to Robert's surprise, would pause 'in the midst of some world crisis' to attend to it. One editor, named Dimbleby, made no attempt to conceal his impatience, earning him the dismissive sobriquet of Fatman. He ticked Robert off for failing to produce pertinent information and made him rewrite stories over and over again, often finishing off the job himself. Robert's inability to type did not help.

Unadorned facts, which were meat and drink to Fatman, had little appeal to Robert. This had become apparent on his first day when he was sent to report on the crowds attending the Sargent exhibition at the Royal Academy. Although failing to elicit precise figures from the obdurate clerks in the office, he enjoyed an amicable chat with Henry Lamb, the Secretary, and summed up the atmosphere of the exhibition as 'one of Edwardian reminiscence, rather than artistic comment'. Much to his annoyance, this prized aperçu was cut from his copy.

The infrequent little paragraphs in the *Daily Mail* bore no comparison to the generous spread allowed him each week as author of 'London Letter' in the *Cherwell*. With no censor to cut him down to size, Robert assumed the role of dashing young man about town, making good use of the many leads picked up on his rounds for the *Daily Mail*. He divulged the recipe of the Yolanda cocktail, presented to him by M. Aletto of the Ritz; prescribed the latest in men's fashion, 'a very broad lapel, rolling . . . from the top button of the coat'; and conveyed alarming news from the dance floor: 'the Charleston is beginning to hold its own at clubs', ran his report. 'Its extreme difficulty lies not only in the complications of the step, but the necessity of having practised it beforehand with one's partner. The dancing instructors on the Riviera were taken completely unawares by it.'

His own London life was more humdrum. Many evenings were spent alone at Canuto's, a cheap Italian restaurant round the corner from Upper Montagu Street, often followed by a visit to the cinema. His greatest social prop was Gavin who was working at the Mayfair decorators, Turner, Lord & Co. They dined together at least once a week and made occasional forays into society, once ending up at the Cavendish Hotel where the drunken chatelaine, Rosa Lewis, 'tried to send us on to Lady Cork's at Claridges'. At the other extreme of respectability, they also attended one of Mrs Baldwin's 'Thursdays' at 10 Downing Street, Stanley Baldwin having been returned to power in the October 1924 election.

Robert's period in London gave him the chance to cement his friendship with Leonard Bower, who had come over to have his tonsils removed. Developments in Athens gave Robert cause for satisfaction. His article on the Dodecanese, recently published in the *New Statesman*, had appeared anonymously in Greek on the front page of *Empros*, the Athenian daily newspaper. According to Leonard, the Greek and Italian governments, who were hoping to establish an entente, were greatly annoyed. The Italians had even resorted to sending John Stuart Hay on a tour of the islands. 'I am delighted –' Robert crowed, 'one really does feel on the way to fame when one's things are translated into other languages & other lettering – So few people in this world can say that they have been "translated into Greek"!!!'

The *Daily Mail* remained a poor substitute, intensifying Robert's disillusionment. 'Rewrote map story', ran one glum account of his day, '& wrote what might for any other paper have been a good article on "George Robins auctioneer".' This, like many others, failed to appear. His frustration finally erupted when trying to gain an interview with the Duchess of Portland on the subject of wild birds. 'Insulted by man at the end of the telephone,' he fumed. 'Tore to Grosvenor Square & made terrific row with housekeeper.' Ominously, word got back to Fatman, who quizzed him on the incident.

Highly strung by nature, Robert's frustration tautened every nerve in his body. Let down one weekend over a social engagement, he consoled himself with a visit to the cinema, only to be refused admittance even though others were let in behind him. The ensuing argument ended in him being taken to Vine Street police station where he was detained until 2 in the morning. Appearing before the magistrate the next day, he was forced to plead guilty to insulting behaviour and 'say nothing' to keep the incident out of the papers. His fine was 19s. 6d. He did not arrive at the office until after one o'clock.

That Friday, 26 February, Robert celebrated his twenty-first birthday. The chief news editor let him leave early, which enabled him to reach Savernake in time for tea. The next day, he got in from a poor day's hunting to find a letter from the *Daily Mail* dispensing with his services. Robert felt humiliated. He left for London for a birthday celebration with Gavin; another in the foursome was Betty Baldwin, the Prime Minister's daughter. They dined at the Berkeley and went on to the KitCat Club. 'Charming evening', he wrote afterwards, 'but for the worry of having joined the ranks of the unemployed.'

Although without income, Robert was not without an occupation. Ever since arriving in London, he had spent his spare hours revising his travel diary from the previous summer. By the middle of February about half the book, up to his arrival in Greece, had been completed. Apart from eliding the dated entries into a continuous narrative, regularizing the chronology and adding passages of art history, no significant alterations were made to the original account of the motor journey. The most radical revision occurred in the second part of the book covering his stay in Athens. This was rewritten thematically covering topics such as the topography and monuments of the city, Byronism and the British community and the social life of cafés and restaurants.

Originally, Robert had planned to send the manuscript to Raymond Savage, the literary agent. This was obviated by his being given 'an absurdly complimentary' introduction by Roy Harrod to the publisher, Frederic Warburg, at Routledge. Having read the first part of the manuscript, Warburg accepted the book for publication that autumn.

Given that Robert was only twenty when the bulk of the book was written, it is a highly accomplished performance, engaging, informative and technically assured. His description of the Parthenon already shows an ability to convey the greatness of architecture. He also established a method, developed to great effect in his later works, of suggesting the spontaneity of speech through quick-fire, and often unattributed, dialogue.

Although very much his own man, Robert was also influenced by a handful of writers while preparing his first travel book for publication. The most improbable was John Ruskin, the Victorian critic and art historian who, to all appearances in both the diary and the finished manuscript, was the butt of Robert's derision. His championship of the Gothic Revival came in for a typical swipe in Verona where Robert admired the 'graceful Gothic arcading, so beautiful in its legitimate setting . . . so repellent as popularized by Ruskin'.

His literary legacy was another matter. Some eighty years earlier, Ruskin had developed a radical new style, opulent and ecstatic, that strove to reveal the pictorial drama of nature. Inspired by the paintings of Turner as well as his own meticulous observations as a watercolourist, he drew upon the language of the palette and the rhythms of Romantic poetry to invent what has become known as the purple passage. His discovery rapidly became the convention for countless writers keen to emphasize the unique beauty of some foreign scene.

Robert was no exception. Being an artist himself, he was well aware of the indivisibility of colour from landscape. Diary entries reveal his painterly eye, as in his description of the country south of Naples:

> Huge sweeping contours in every imaginable shade of yellow and brown rose and fell, disclosing here and there solid blue mountains on the horizon . . . The earth where ploughed shewed an ink-red brown. Occasionally a herd of black and brown goats would dot across the white road herded by a dog.

This unassuming plein air sketch was transformed for publication into a portentous tableau in the High Victorian manner.

> The country was like a work of art balanced and long premeditated in the soul of a celestial colourist. One felt . . . that one had been vouchsafed an insight not accorded to other men – a vision of some pagan divinity, some all-pervasive spirit of harvest and maturity, of roseate golds and the red, brown, black riches of the earth of the south, the south of Hannibal and Magna Graecia, the cradle of European civilization.

Tint was piled upon tint. The mountains were not just blue but also glassy and purple. The earth, which was tilled rather than ploughed, 'showed black and thick with burnt sienna lights'.

His struggle to control the impact of colour in description was to become one of the defining strands in Robert's growing maturity as a travel writer. Meanwhile, in this overwrought passage, the shade of Ruskin had its revenge upon the impudent young leader of the Victorian Revival.

His indebtedness to another writer was more overt.

Scattered throughout the book are references to the Sitwells, which, he states, find their 'analogy perhaps in the homage paid by the past generation to Ruskin'. Although acknowledging them collectively, one member of the family in particular had impressed Robert. This was the youngest sibling, Sacheverell, who in 1924 had published his masterpiece, *Southern Baroque Art*. 'It is most entertaining in parts and really learned,' Robert had enthused to Henry Yorke shortly after its publication. 'I am dying to go to Mexico: the descriptions of the churches are too marvellous.'

Sitwell's book, which revolutionized attitudes towards the baroque, is no ordinary art history. Time travel, historical romance, theatrical programmes, traveller's tales and guidebook commentary are just some of the genres used to summon up both the fantastic monuments and the exotic cast of tyrants, conquistadores, castrati, painters and architects who tread Sitwell's stage. The section on Mexico comes closest to straightforward travel writing, offering practical information about railway stations as well as lodgings where the author had stayed. In fact, Sitwell had only visited the country in his imagination. His persona of contemporary traveller was fiction. Such an approach, which mirrors the illusionism of its subject, is a virtuoso display of neo-baroque literature.

One notable trick is found in Robert's finished version of his travel diary. Sitwell makes giant leaps from country to country in search of far-flung outposts of the baroque. One moment the reader is dwelling upon the geometry of Neapolitan staircases, the next he is transported to the Esterházy Palace in Hungary. Similar detours are made by Robert. Contemplation of Bernini's 'ugly row' of statuary on St Peter's prompts a sudden departure, both in time and geography, to view the restrained neo-classical cathedral at Esztergom in Hungary, a building inspected by him the previous year.

Another addition was the introduction of a political motive to the journey. Drawing on an idea developed in a *Cherwell* leader, he expressed the hope that his observations of different countries would assist in furthering 'the new sense of "European Consciousness" that is gradually coming into being'. Little is heard of this theme in the rest of the book, but it inspired its title: *Europe in the Looking Glass*.

However, Robert did not shy away from inserting contemporary political material into his otherwise light-hearted book. The sack of Smyrna and the repression of the Dodecanese were both examined in detail. A timely precedent for discussing the consequences of the post-war settlements had been provided by Oliver Baldwin's account of his adventures, *Six Prisons and Two Revolutions*, which Robert had bought in Paris on his way home from Greece. He read it on the train 'with interest', commenting that it provided, like the outrages permitted in the Levant, 'another testimony to the Betrayal Era in English statesmanship'.

A growing fascination with Greek affairs gave Robert an idea for his next book. He determined to write a history of Greece from the birth of Byzantine civilization to the sack of Smyrna. 'I shall go round and see Warburg in a day or two', he told his mother, '& ask him what he thinks of the history book idea – I have been so obsessed with it that I literally dream of near eastern politics.' Warburg was impressed. Robert's written proposal was accepted and an advance received of £69. With the revisions to his first book complete, the way was now clear for Robert to return to Greece to continue his research.

To help tide him over financially, he tapped another potential source of income by seeking an introduction to the editor of *Vogue* magazine, Miss Todd, a woman of serious literary tastes. His go-between was Matthew Ponsonby's sister, Elizabeth, who worked as a mannequin, or assistant, in Lady Angela Forbes' dress shop. To pay her back, he offered to meet her after her work for a drink.

'Where?'

'Oh, the Ritz for a cocktail,' Elizabeth replied firmly.

Robert's introduction, including tips, cost him nine shillings, which in his days of employment would have amounted to almost a quarter of his weekly income.

Fortunately, Miss Todd commissioned two articles on the monasteries of Mount Athos, which, he calculated, would pay for his expenses from Athens to the Holy Mountain and back. She could hardly have picked a less suitable subject for her readers. And later in the year, to the rage of her literary contributors, she was sacked for her lack of interest in fashion.

Robert left for Greece on 19 April 1926, journeying second-class to Brindisi, and thence by 'cattle barge' to Piraeus.

9

The Joyous Life

Robert arrived in Athens at the end of April 1926. It was Easter week and he found 'the whole place thick with sheep'. Every family, he discovered, had one 'which it makes a pet of, then kills'. He and Leonard followed suit. Theirs was 'sacrificed by the Ilissus in accordance with the Orthodox rite' before being cooked and eaten at a party given by Gladys Stuart-Richardson, who had a little house on the bank of the river.

Leonard Bower had offered to put Robert up in his tiny flat at 4 Odos Mantzarou. The accommodation consisted of two rooms and an outside WC which had neither door nor running water. Cooking was restricted to boiling eggs in a cauldron heated over a broken forge. An old woman lived in a hovel across the courtyard whilst a large family lived above.

Robert started looking for rooms of his own, but it proved impossible as Athens was still struggling to absorb the refugees from Turkey. Although thousands had been housed in the 'mushroom town' on the edge of Piraeus which Robert had visited the previous year, this still left parts of the city looking like a shanty town. Alastair Graham, another lodger in Leonard's crowded flat, described how 'all the Palaces, Post Offices, public buildings and gardens are nothing more than dormitories. The refugees have built themselves sheds out of matchboxes and cigarette tins, and woven themselves tents out of old clothes.' There was nothing for it but to muddle along with Leonard and Alastair. To create more room, Robert bought a deckchair and turned the courtyard, shaded by vines and a strong-smelling honeysuckle, into his study.

Alastair had been a friend of Robert's at Oxford. A member of the Hypocrites Club, he had attended the Victorian party in the guise of a decadent god, swathed in a toga with laurels in his hair. Since childhood he had been fascinated by ancient Greece having been brought up on the tales of his great-grandfather, the 14th Duke of Somerset, who had travelled throughout the Levant in the 1840s reputedly with a shotgun under one arm and a copy of Homer under the other.

The decision to stay with Leonard had been made on the spur of the moment. Travelling home from Constantinople, Alastair had stopped off in Athens only to fall in love with the place. This meant abandoning both ship and his forceful American mother. He did not hesitate. 'I have got no clothes and my passport has been stolen by the Bolsheviks,' he protested, 'so that I cannot ever leave.'

Bookish and pleasure loving, he relished the slow pace of Athenian life. Leonard's eccentric ménage run by Nikola, his servant, and various hangers-on fascinated him. 'They hate Athens', he told Claud Cockburn, 'and say how lovely is Constantinople; and then they begin to weep because never again will they be able to go back there. It is all so sad.'

At Oxford, Alastair had embarked upon a passionate affair with Evelyn Waugh. Now he found himself much in demand from the locals: 'most of them mad', he informed Claud Cockburn, 'and the rest are homosexual nymphomaniacs, but they all have a certain amount of charm.' Two nights before Robert's arrival they had entertained a party of students from the university. 'One of them lechered with Leonard a good deal and then we all got drunk and danced on the bed,' he divulged to David Talbot Rice. 'They call me the Emperor of Lesbos, which I was rather pleased with.'

The easygoing ways of Athenian youth also appealed to Robert. He was remembered by Thanos Veloudias, a figure well known to Leonard and his circle, as having lovers 'but not really intimate ones . . . The English are discreet. When in Greece they were perhaps rather feminine but never effeminate. Since classical times, all the ancient heroes had so-called lovers.' Renowned for his own priapic tastes, Veloudias, recollecting this period in later life, described the uninhibited atmosphere of Athens at this time as 'not belonging to the cabinet of the psychiatrist. No not that. Something current [transitory] and not special. But not exaggerated. You see. Pointing towards the philosophical not the degenerate. The Greeks do not have the fear of sin.' Amidst such freedom, Robert and Leonard, for a while, also became lovers.

Thanos Veloudias was one of the great sights of Athens. An anglophile, a dandy, a historian, a scholar of ancient Greek dance, he was also a war hero who, during the Asia Minor campaign, had landed his Bleriot aeroplane at the Turkish military academy at Bursa and hoisted the Greek flag. Born into a family of academics, he loved to swagger round Athens with his English friends, dressed in his air force uniform, 'fashioned with a touch of Savile Row', declaiming on monuments, famous and obscure. One, which he showed Robert, was the site of Plato's Academy, marked only by an ancient boundary stone. He also took Robert and Leonard to tavernas to observe 'the solo, more or less ecstatic dances of the very plain working class, called zaybetico'. A jotting in Robert's notebook referred to the 'queer hesitation about dancing'.

With Thanos in command, inhibition fled. He even persuaded Robert and Leonard to dress up in ancient costume, designed and woven by Gladys Stuart-Richardson, and parade through Athens to the Theatre of Dionysius at the foot of the Acropolis. Each fold of their tunics was meant to represent, according to Thanos, 'musical tones in harmony'. Thanos recalled the occasion:

> They wore the ancient, long down to their feet, Ionian chiton a bit like the charioteer of Delphi . . . and I was wearing my smart air ensign's uniform tailored elegantly . . . I believe there was with us Alastair Graham in mufti, we were followed by a gang of jubilating children and we were greeted cheerfully all along . . . by gaping Athenians! When we arrived in the Theater, Leonard Bower started reciting in metric intonation the first verse of Homer's Odyssey . . . obtaining the applause of other Dionysos' disciples in His Theater. These were fantastic times indeed.

The week after Easter, Robert set off with Alastair on an expedition to the ruined Byzantine city of Mistra in the heart of the Peloponnese. Ten hours on the train brought them to Tripolitza, where they got into a taxi to take them to Sparta. Time passed whilst more and more people occupied the car, some in the front, some in the hood, some on petrol cans on the running boards, clinging to the side with their fingers. Eventually the vehicle set off bearing twelve passengers.

Robert jotted down his first impressions of the countryside: 'goats bells – red hills – mulleins – hellebore – rock roses, dog roses – orchids – Judas tree, margarets – crooks – fustinellas . . .' At one point, they stopped to set down a soldier 'who walked away singing into the green plain although there was no path nor habitation in sight'. It was Arcadia.

The city of Mistra, four miles from modern Sparta where they stayed, had been the most important centre of late Byzantine civilization outside Constantinople. Its magnificent defensive position, a conical foothill of the Taygetos range, combined with the enlightened government of successive despots of the Morea, had encouraged some of the finest scholars and philosophers to settle there. The most famous was Gemistos Plethon, whose Neoplatonist teachings had a profound influence upon Renaissance thought. Capitulation to the Turks in 1460 was the start of an inexorable decline, culminating in a final, brutal sack during the War of Independence.

Robert spent two 'entrancing' days exploring the largely deserted city. He found it 'the weirdest place – perched on a precipitous hill – all the houses and a huge palace still three-quarters standing and nearly uninhabited. Wonderful frescoes open to the wind and rain – cisterns, fireplaces, ovens . . .' Spotting a fragment of carving, he crawled into a vault in the Despot's Palace only to unearth 'four whole skulls and three skeletons'.

With no time to keep a diary, he scrawled an impressionistic sketch of the view from the recently opened café:

> wonderful late Roman trough – nude figures carrying grape vines . . . water flowing down all time – Sunset . . . seared red hills behind – turned purple – vast view – shadows of Taygettus looming over the whole plain – darkness – Birds

> like bells – peasants crying 'Kal 'Espera' – lighted shrines and glow worms – friendly frogs in ditch 'Brekekekex Coax Coax'.

Another overloaded car took them to the port of Gytheuri, where by a stroke of luck they found a boat leaving for the great Byzantine fortress of Monemvasia. Nothing was allowed to stand in the way of research. Frustrated at finding the entrance to the fortifications locked, they hurled 'great boulders' at 'the original iron clamped door' before a man appeared to let them in. A steamer took them on to Piraeus.

No sooner was Robert back in Athens than he was off with Leonard and Alastair to Constantinople, as he preferred to call the great Turkish city of Istanbul. The ship stopped at Smyrna where an afternoon was spent inspecting the wrecked area of the city which had 'forced open safes still lying beneath heaps of debris'. Even in the short time available, Leonard managed to acquire a Greek head that had been looted from the burnt-out museum.

A trawl of the antique shops in Constantinople on their first evening was not so fruitful. Many were merely filled with the personal effects of Russian refugees: 'dressing cases, each bottle and brush of which are quite obscured beneath enormous coronated monograms laid on in three precious metals'.

Over the next few days, Robert undertook a detailed exploration of the city. This was essential to his understanding of Greek history: 'the whole book', Robert acknowledged, 'hinges on it'. He was left feeling 'quite exhausted with the interest of the place – nervy in fact with a kind of intellectual satiety'.

Founded by Constantine in 330 AD on the site of an existing port on the Bosphorus called Byzantium, the city, known as the 'New Rome', had become capital of the Roman Empire of the East on the death of Theodosius in 395 AD, which it remained, barring a brief period of Frankish rule, for over a thousand years.

Under Theodosius the city became a predominantly Christian capital. Thenceforth, the link between church and state, although often strained, was never broken. The union between the eastern and western churches was not so durable. The Orthodox church recognized, and still does, Rome's primacy in the five great sees of the Church, but years of doctrinal argument culminated, in the eleventh century, in the Great Schism, which severed communion between the two churches and confirmed the status of Constantinople as the supreme seat of Orthodoxy. Gradually, the Byzantine Empire, as it was known, fell prey to crusaders and Turks alike. Even so, it was not until 1453 that the city finally succumbed to the overwhelming forces of the Ottoman Turks led by Sultan Mehmet II.

At the time of Robert's visit, the greatest monument of the Byzantine Empire, the Church of the Divine Wisdom, known as Santa Sophia, rebuilt by Emperor Justinian in the sixth century and now a museum, was then still a mosque with layers of plaster and whitewash concealing most of the mosaics. Disappointment tinged his visits. He attended Friday prayers only to be overcome by the smell of feet 'in places . . . a reeking stench'. His overriding visual impression was summed up in the phrase: 'Light in S. Sophia like that of a great deserted station.'

Walking along the outer walls of the city, he reconstructed 'all the main events of the last siege in 1453'. They were fresh in his mind from reading Edwin Pears' compelling history, *The Destruction of the Greek Empire*, published in 1885, which recounts in moving detail the fall of Constantinople. Studying the fortifications, Robert stumbled across vivid reminders of the siege in the form of 'cannon balls sheltering wood lice in lettuce beds'.

His researches were not just historical. He also called on the Chief Dragoman to the Ecumenical Patriarch at the Phanar, the historic Greek compound in the city, to collect more evidence of recent persecution. Constantinides had been present in June 1923 when the Patriarchate had been overrun by a mob of 'renegade Maltese' calling themselves the 'Turkish National Church', demanding the Patriarch's resignation. Robert heard how only the arrival of an international police force, called by Constantinides, had saved the Patriarch's life. The Metropolitan of Smyrna had not been so lucky. He had had been 'thrown to mob, hair and beard torn out by roots, stripped naked & crucified'. This account contained an element of exaggeration. The Patriarch had, in fact, been lynched.

The interviewing of useful contacts continued back in Athens. 'Modern Greek history exists almost solely in people's minds', he had written at the outset, '& has to be extracted by conversation.' Diplomatic gossip, military intrigue and telling historical detail were all confided to his notebook. He was ruthless in his quest for information. Meeting 'a deliciously common' Englishman working for Shell, he latched on to him as being 'just the person I wanted as the Treaty of Lausanne hinged entirely on oil'. A grander catch was General Phrantzes, whose ancestor had married a cousin of the last Emperor. He hoped to photograph a ring in his possession engraved with Constantine's initials.

He read widely round the subject, having brought out a weight of books borrowed from the 'Late Roman Empire' section of the London Library. The shelves of the Legation and the British School in Athens were also available to him. His studies were made easier by finally getting a room of his own when he and Leonard moved into a larger apartment, lent by Shirley Atchley, the translator at the Legation.

Not all his time was devoted to the book. On arriving in Athens, he had rushed round to Dr Zervos with another article on the Dodecanese, dashed off earlier in the year for the American magazine, the *Nation*. 'Vous êtes bien nominé l'autre Byron,' cried Zervos, entranced. Inevitably, Robert was drawn into further intrigues. A conference in Rome was mooted. Zervos palpitated with excitement, leaving Robert to draw up the terms for negotiation. 'I revel in it all, though not taking it too seriously –' he told Roy Harrod, 'anyhow I loathe the Italians.' For his pains, he was presented by Zervos with 'a monument of shells and sponges'. This proved too unwieldy to pack so he tore off the best sponge and buried the rest.

Gradually Robert was working his way through the most famous examples of Byzantine art and architecture. Another monument ticked off the list was the church and monastery of St Luke at Stiris. The route was not straightforward. An overnight boat trip followed by a three-hour ride in a horse-drawn cab brought him to Delphi. Food poisoning prevented him from viewing the ruins; however, he was strong enough the next day to face the eight and a half hour ride by mule to the monastery. The eleventh-century mosaics, some of the finest in existence, were briefly admired before he collapsed, exhausted, on to a flea-ridden bed. To escape 'this hell of fleas', he left the next day at 4 a.m. to retrace his steps to Delphi.

That night, despite the acute discomfort, he still managed to compose a prose poem on the scenery viewed that day:

> As we approached the monastery . . . sheer below to one side stretched great sort of flying buttresses of bluey grey earth, about 200 feet down, where they were met by smaller and more luminous ones, a purply pink – and on them very bright pink clumps of oleanders. Beyond a vast panorama of infinitesimal cultivated patches, olive trees and huge mountains rising again. Around one, yellow clumps of broom and hundreds of strange thistles, whose leaves looked as if they had been dipped in Reckitts blue – while huge iridescent beetles buzzed from bloom to bloom – and swallowtails, marbled whites, white admirals and all the blues flying everywhere.

By the beginning of July, he felt confident that most of his material had been gathered. He did, however, feel that a second, more thorough, investigation of Smyrna was necessary. He and Leonard set off for ten days or so which also gave them time to visit the great ruined city of Ephesus. Having spent a morning wandering around, Robert understood 'more than anywhere . . . the transition from the classical to the Byzantine'. He came away with 'a little piece of porphyry column' as a souvenir.

The rest of the visit was spent adding to his already considerable dossier on the Turkish atrocities. Armed with a Kodak camera, bought in Athens for £2, he prowled among the ruins snapping incriminating evidence. Photographs included the remains of an incendiary bomb in the ruined Church of St John, a cow browsing at the altar and desecrated Greek graves. An attendant, seeing him photographing in the cemetery, rushed towards him 'gnashing his teeth and shouting Tchuk Tchuk'.

Robert could hardly wait for the films to be developed. But the results were disappointing. A novice behind the lens, he had not realized that the camera 'was not good enough to stand such strong light and shade'.

Leonard's interest in Smyrna was far less altruistic. He was on the hunt for yet more booty from the burnt-out museum. In this, he was successful, returning to Athens 'laden with illicit antiques'. Robert did not question Leonard's activities. His own passion for collecting made visits to dealers, however shady, irresistible. He had, himself, managed to acquire a fine eighteenth-century icon in Athens. However, he did draw the line at organized attempts by London dealers to strip Greece of her treasures. The rumour that a party were about to descend upon Mount Athos led him and Leonard to raise the alarm with the authorities. Later it transpired that their friend John Stuart Hay, financed by the 'British and South Kensington Museums and Spinks', was the dealer in question.

The irrepressible John Stuart Hay bore no grudge. In fact his mission to Mount Athos coincided with Robert's own long-planned trip there and they agreed to meet up on arrival. Robert was to arrive a week after Hay as he awaited his other travelling companion to the Holy Mountain, his Oxford friend Bryan Guinness.

Although contemporaries at Eton, the friendship between Robert and Bryan had only sprung to life at Oxford where Bryan had served as Robert's deputy on the *Cherwell*. A gentle, dreamy personality with finely chiselled looks, Bryan had blue blood and stout coursing through his veins. His mother, Lady Evelyn, daughter of the 14th Earl of Buchan, was beautiful, fey and indulgent. His father, Colonel Walter Guinness, was a brewer and politician, who was currently serving as Minister of Agriculture in the Conservative government.

For long periods of the year, the Guinnesses moved from their large Georgian house in Hampstead to two neo-French Victorian mansions, knocked into one, in Grosvenor Place,

Belgravia. These had been transformed by Lady Evelyn into an evocation of the Middle Ages with plain pine walls, green leaded windows and furniture hewn out of leather and oak. Robert, who got to know the house on sprees up from Oxford, acknowledged that though the description sounded horrible, the effect 'was quite quite lovely' especially as peat smouldering in the hearths filled the rooms 'with a real smell of the country'. When persuading Bryan to join him on Mount Athos, he held out the opportunity of being able 'to design a Byzantine lift for Grosvenor Place'.

Bryan arrived in Athens at the very end of July and they departed a few days later for Salonica. An afternoon was spent on a tour of the churches although the finest, St Demetrius, had been ruined in the great fire of 1917. A friend of Hay's, who took them out to dinner, was another focus of historical interest. He turned out to be a Sephardic Jew, a descendant of those who fled from Spain in the sixteenth century. A night out on the town did not deter Robert from exploring the castle first thing the next morning whilst Bryan slept in. That night they caught the boat that was to take them overnight to Daphni, the tiny port of Mount Athos.

Looking at a map of Greece, the province to the east of Salonica, known as Chalkidiki, is distinguished by three narrow peninsulas that extend into the Aegean. The most easterly is Mount Athos, some 56 kilometres long and no more than eight across, that rises over its 'wooded hog's back' to a peak of over 2,000 metres before dropping sheer into the sea.

Robert described his first glimpse, at dawn:

> Framed in the cold circle of the open port hole . . . appeared the dark outline of a long finger of land, twisted by imperceptibly darker shadows into deep ravines and curving bays. And at its end, cut in terraced silhouette against the frigid gleams of the lower sky, rose a vast black steeple from the livid grey sea. The Holy Mountain. And ourselves the pilgrims!

In ancient times, Mount Athos was sacred to Zeus. Paganism, so Athonite tradition relates, was abandoned when the Virgin Mary arrived on the peninsula and converted the inhabitants. Her reward from Christ was possession of the Holy Mountain, a gift which the monks celebrate in everyday speech by referring to their surroundings as 'The Garden of the Mother of God'. Connected to this belief is the exclusion of women and domestic animals of the female sex from the Holy Mountain. Stories abound of the Virgin's own turning away of women from her preserve, although the precedent stems from the Church's primordial insistence upon the celibacy of monks. One of the earliest Athonite charters states: 'You will not own any animal of the female sex, for the purpose of doing any work which you require, because you have absolutely renounced all female beings.'

Monkish habitation dates from at least the ninth century. The earliest surviving monastery is the Great Lavra, founded in 963 by St Athanasios under the patronage of his close friend, the future emperor, Nikephoros Phokas. Within forty years, the spiritual life of Mount Athos was established. Monasteries multiplied. Of the twenty surviving houses, over half were founded by the twelfth century.

The principle of self-government is just as ancient. Caryes, which remains the seat of the Holy Community, was established as a meeting place of elders in the ninth century. Successive imperial decrees confirmed the freedom of the Holy Community to manage its own affairs. This autonomy, although modified, was respected by the Ottomans until they, too, lost sovereignty over the peninsula to Greece in 1913 following the Balkan wars. Uncertainty over the future was finally settled after the First World War when, as a condition of the peace treaties, the 'Athos Charter' was drawn up to clarify the privileges of the Holy Mountain and confirm its continuing independence.

The outcome was well summed up by Robert: 'there exists on the map of Europe the extraordinary phenomenon of an autonomous theocratic republic, voluntarily admitting Greek sovereignty, but upheld by international treaty in all its ancient rights of independence.' Stepping ashore at Daphni on the morning of Saturday 7 August 1926, he entered 'a single stronghold of Byzantinism, bound in a way of life unchanged since . . . the foundation of the Lavra'.

After breakfasting off 'liqueurs like fire, watermelon and tea' they set off by mule for the three-hour ride over the ridge of the peninsula to the capital of Caryes. He found it a 'weird little town with beggars and half-witted monks lying about the tiny streets – one or two shops kept by monks, and not a woman or a child, not a hen, a cow, a dog nor female cat to be seen'. John Stuart Hay was there to meet them. Robert was pleased to discover that his attempts to buy treasures off the monks were not prospering.

Ushered to the Assembly House, they were introduced to Father Adrianos, that year's primate of Athos. He proved to be fat, benign and 'terribly obsequious to me, Byron'. Later that afternoon, they presented their letters of recommendation to the Holy Community. 'The . . . head of the community occupies his throne', Robert wrote, whilst 'around on white divans sit the black gowned, tall hatted figures of . . . the representatives of the twenty ruling monasteries, who, elected yearly, constitute the parliament.'

No lesser personages than the former Ecumenical Patriarch and the Greek Foreign Minister had written on Robert's behalf. In return, a circular letter was drawn up to present on arrival at monasteries. The document was signed by the four members of the *Epistasia*, who were responsible for executing the decisions of the Community; each then produced one quarter of the Community's composite seal, the pieces were fitted together, the letter stamped, and the impression powdered with gold. Thus armed, Robert and his companions were free to wander as pilgrims, being lodged, fed and transported at the monks' expense.

Over the next eleven days, they managed to visit fourteen monasteries as well as dependencies, called *sketes*, and hermitages. Inland, they took mules, riding 'up the cobbled paths from the shady valleys of oak and ilex to the bare ridges of scrub, broom and bracken'. But most monasteries are built near the sea and were best approached by boat. These short voyages provided pleasant interludes. The monks rowed or set sail, whilst the English trio basked in the stern or hung 'to a rope trailing behind in the water'.

They never missed an opportunity to go for a swim. Monks viewed this activity with alarm and warned them against

sharks. Robert sought confirmation from a friendly abbot.
'Sharks?' Robert asked.

'They abound,' came the reply. 'They once ate a deacon 250 years ago – baited by lambs, they caught the shark & found him inside.'

All monasteries share certain characteristics. Robert listed them as follows:

> Within . . . fortified walls, sometimes rising hundreds of feet from precipitous spurs of rock, sometimes set amidst terraced gardens or on the sea shore, and entered by one gate which is locked every evening at sunset, stand the church, chapels, refectories, guest-houses and numerous rows of balconied cells . . . At the back rises usually a square tower, with machicolated balconies, now used as a library.

Numerous courtyards, he went on, are squeezed between these myriad buildings, some minute, others as large as Oxford quadrangles. The grandest have 'a phiale, a kind of pillared circular temple sheltering a fountain'.

Arriving at a monastery for the night they would be escorted by the guest master to their rooms. These, Robert discovered, were invariably decorated 'like Victorian nurseries' with coloured patriotic prints, heavy tablecloths and one-legged tables. A touch of orientalism was added by the Turkish divans around the walls. The abbot or a senior monk would join them for dinner which generally consisted of bean soup, octopus and greasy vegetables. Individual decanters of wine were placed before them. Breakfast was coffee, ouzo, jam and Turkish delight. Although each day was measured by the round of prayer and worship, Robert's party rarely joined in. Bryan complained that at the Great Lavra, while inspecting the frescoes, 'a service began and trapped us for a weary hour'. Nor did they scruple from interrupting the monks' afternoon nap. 'Furious all asleep' was Robert's curt comment on their arrival at Iviron after a choppy voyage. Eventually someone was aroused to provide them with food.

The Great Lavra laid on the best reception, 'Robert's name', Bryan testified, 'working miracles'. In honour of a Byron in their midst, the monks threw open the Synodico, a guest house usually reserved for great officials of the Church, which was 'lavishly furnished with carpets, cruets, and clocks under domes'. At their departure, a Union Jack was hoisted from the balcony and a carillon of bells pealed out as Robert processed with the Abbot 'in veil and orders' across the courtyard. An address concluded the ceremony. 'Today', declared the Abbot, though 'you quit our monastery, you leave [an] indelible memorial upon its history. We who have had the good fortune to entertain you shall pray always that the Great Pilot of the Universe, God, may fortify your powers and prolong your years to the welfare of your nation.'

Simple wonders lent enchantment to their days. The guest master at Docheiariou, 'whose hair, in the labours of the kitchen, had fallen in black ringlets on his shoulders', summoned them to lunch. 'But first watch,' he said, before calling: 'Frankfort! Frankfort!' Whereupon a large black cat walked obediently up, put its head between its front legs, and turned somersaults for their entertainment.

One night was spent in a hut with a chapel halfway up the summit of Mount Athos. After a few hours' rest on icy boards in the company of bugs, fleas, rats and mice they rose at 3 a.m. to climb to the top. 'The cold', Robert admitted, 'was ghastly.' Having reached the summit, their guide broke a piece of furniture from the church and lit a fire. Two hours passed as they crouched disconsolately trying to keep warm. 'Slowly, imperceptibly, the day lightened,' Robert wrote.

> The clouds seemed in a turmoil, tearing and swirling on, disclosing and shutting the tantalizing vision of a sun beyond. In a final agony the great black bank was rent . . . there lay beneath us the whole sea, and the other two of the three fingers of land; the wooded Athos twisting like a furry serpent back to the mainland . . . The sun shone and the golden morning seemed to penetrate the brain and suffuse the whole body. Half a minute – then with a rush of cold wind the curtain fell.

Before leaving, Robert and Bryan, as a record of their visit, pencilled their names 'in an indiscoverable corner of the church'.

The expedition provided a brief respite from Robert's hectic study of Byzantine art. At every monastery the monks took pride in showing them their finest manuscripts, books, icons, relics and other treasures. Sometimes they were left 'surfeited and dazed' as their holy guides rambled on about each precious object. 'Here is a piece of the Virgin's girdle,' ran one commentary. 'She wove it herself I expect . . . The eikon on the left has a curious history. You see the dent in the Virgin's forehead – that was done 400 years ago with this knife, by a monk who was annoyed with her . . . she struck off his arms and made him stand in that corner for thirty years – no not that one – here is one of his arms . . .'

Robert's prime interest was the frescoes in the churches and refectories. To assist him, he had to hand a newly published book covering the subject, the second volume of the *Manuel d'art byzantin* by the French popular historian, Charles Diehl. His methodology had been modelled upon the theories of Gabriel Millet, a French scholar who, in 1916, in a massive survey of iconography, had neatly categorized the far-flung oeuvre of Byzantine painting from the thirteenth to the sixteenth centuries into two schools, the Macedonian and the Cretan. Their individual characteristics, as delineated by Diehl, were duly summarized by Robert who jotted down in his notebook: 'Macedonian: Verges on impressionism and realism – open to Italian and Oriental influences.' The qualities of the Cretan school were copied word for word as being 'plus éprise de sobriété, de clarté, de noblesse'.

Unfortunately, such generalizations proved little help when standing before the works in question. Occasionally, Robert spotted a distinguishing feature, such as the 'lovely Cretan reds & blues' at Dionysiou, but, more often than not, he remained unconvinced. A cycle at St Paul's monastery, which Diehl had confirmed in ringing tones to be Cretan, appeared, at least in the treatment of the faces, to be 'definitely more Macedonian'.

Another area of confusion lay in the influence of the Italians upon later Byzantine painters. Diehl was clear about the Macedonian school, but contradicted himself on the Cretan. This caused raised eyebrows from Robert, who noted the inconsistency with exclamation marks. The point was important to him because already he was out to prove that 'Greek' painters, at least of the Cretan school, owed nothing to their Italian counterparts. Fortunately, another authority, O. M. Dalton of the British Museum, agreed with him. Robert had dipped into Dalton's hefty *Byzantine Art and Archaeology* at around the time of his visit to Mistra. Twice he had transcribed a passage asserting that stylistic developments, evident in murals at Mistra, came from 'Ferment of ideas, not due to copying such as Giotto'.

It was not just the past glories of Mount Athos that preoccupied Robert. He was also fascinated by the present-day survival of the monastic republic. Anyone of interest was quizzed on the situation. In this, he was greatly helped by John Stuart Hay who acted as interpreter. Some monks also spoke English, others German or French, both of which Robert could understand. If all else failed, he fell back upon his limited Greek. As his researches gathered pace, he conceived the idea of writing a series of articles for *The Times*.

His best material was garnered on the last full day of their trip. Returning to Caryes, they again paid a call on the Holy Community. One member, who spoke German, proved a fount of information on economic matters such as the market for their timber and the export of charcoal and hazelnuts. Robert also touched on the Greek government's threat to remove monastic treasures to a Byzantine museum in Athens. 'Stupid policy,' he was told, 'as they will immediately be hidden or sold.' Currently monks were disinclined to sell their birthright. John Stuart Hay had thus done little business, although he had gained the promise of 'one superb MSS' which the American collector, Chester Beatty, later offered to buy for £500.

Their last night was spent at the port of Daphni where they were put up by Father Boniface, who had provided them with breakfast on their first morning. Hay remarked that there was no church in which to say office. 'It doesn't matter,' replied the father. 'God gets drunk with too many people shouting at him.'

Formerly Archimandrite of Jerusalem, Father Boniface viewed his fellow monks with a jaundiced eye. Robert inquired about the two systems of internal rule practised in the monasteries: the coenobitic, based upon communal living, where property and tasks are shared, and the idiorrhythmic, which allowed monks to enjoy their own wealth, pursue their own devotional pattern and eat separately in their apartments.

Father Boniface did not stint on the abuses of both systems. Monks following the idiorrhythmic rule, he said, 'keep boys in their cells & train them & they succeed them. Then the 15 or so clever men [become] a close self-elected society – & the other 150 never get a look in.' Stavronikita was held up as the worst example. Its closure had recently been announced due to poverty, although the older monks had plenty of money and kept fifteen kitchens in operation throughout the building. At Boniface's own monastery, young monks were reduced to thieving to ward off destitution. His view of coenobitic houses was scarcely more favourable. 'Usually choose most illiterate & stupid man for abbot & the 4 behind him run the place,' he claimed. 'Eat meat in their rooms & then in refectory pretend they can eat nothing as they are fasting so vigorously.'

The opinions of Boniface noted, Robert's work was done. A day was spent lazing around Daphni before catching the boat to Salonica. Looking down from the upper deck, Bryan, who was genuinely fond of women, smiled upon the one or two shawl-covered matrons and girls below 'in gratitude for their existence'. Robert waspishly accused him of leering.

A few days were spent in Athens where Robert immersed himself in more research. He interviewed an official at the Foreign Office about the newly ratified Athos Charter and read up on past treaties. Exhausted, he decided to spend a day in bed, only for Nikola, their servant, to breeze in with the shaving water, saying: 'Bonjour! Il y a une révolution.' Robert felt obliged to investigate. Armoured cars were on street corners; and the army, he reported, 'has shaved for the first time this year'. A bloodless coup had deposed the dictator General Pangalos after just over a year in power.

One last trip was in the offing. Bryan's father had been so keen for him to see Constantinople that he had forwarded money for both Bryan and Robert to go there. Apart from visiting the usual sites, they also had an audience with the Ecumenical Patriarch who talked of his hope of union between the churches.

Discussion of spiritual matters sparked fierce arguments between the two friends. Bryan was already a sceptic, whereas Robert, despite grumblings at dull preachers and evangelicals, remained a sincere Anglican. He also claimed that the Anglican church enjoyed doctrinal ties with the Orthodox. This was the view of the English chaplain in Constantinople, the Reverend Borough, whom Robert knew well. Indeed, according to Robert, he had 'devoted 16 years of his life to the reunion of the Greek and Anglican churches'. Throughout these debates, Robert took a strong anti-Catholic view, insisting that the church of Rome, unlike Anglicanism, was 'at heresy' with the Orthodox church. His anti-Catholic crusade was on the march.

They returned to England by train via Constanza, Vienna and Paris. By the time he arrived at Dover in the middle of September, Robert had been away for almost five months.

10

An English Year

Making straight for Savernake, he returned to the full glory of an English autumn, 'to a garden of Michaelmas daisies; with the bracken turning to gold, and thin blue columns of smoke filling the air with the scent of burning leaves'. His first few days were spent sleeping off the exertions of travel but soon the pleasures of country life took hold. He went cub hunting in the forest with Mr Scarlett's private pack, enjoying 'those unknown hours when the dew sparkles thick in the hazy light and the trees and plants are twice alive'.

At the beginning of October, he set off with Gavin in his speedy 3-litre Sunbeam for the north of Scotland. They had been invited to stay by Nina Seafield, the twenty-year-old cousin of Mark Ogilvie-Grant, who, when still a child, had inherited an ancient Scottish peerage with vast estates to match. Nina adored Mark's Oxford friends and threw open her baronial halls to some of the worst shots in Europe. When asked how he had passed the time amidst Nina's moors and rivers, Harold Acton replied, 'We just loitered.'

Crossing the border proved an aesthete's nightmare: 'Horror of 1st view of Scotland,' shuddered Robert. 'Tin thistle at Gretna Green – also munitions factory. Red hair clashing with pink granite.' Their destination was Cullen House, a haunted pile in Banffshire which was ice-cold as the result of a coal strike. Robert sat in his room composing his articles on Mount Athos for *The Times*. 'It is so blessed being allowed to . . .' he told Henry Yorke. 'But I wish I had some woollen socks.' In the evening they drank martinis from enormous wine glasses. Every fashion has its moment, even in North Britain, and this was the cocktail's hour.

In November, Robert moved to London, taking another, smaller, set of rooms at 7 Upper Montagu Street. His arrival in town coincided with the publication to excellent reviews of *Europe in the Looking Glass*. The *Sunday Times* predicted: 'We shall hear more of Mr Robert Byron for he has written a book which calls loudly for others from the same whimsical pen . . . Mr Byron moreover writes with a sparkle. He is unexpected and paradoxical, and cares not two hoots for other people's opinions.' C. E. M. Joad in the *Daily Herald*, although no friend of 'public school England', also praised the book for 'a capacity of good, sometimes even for fine writing [and] a gift of provocative and often original comment'. The one sour note among the national press was struck by the *Spectator* which weighed in against the 'silly foreigners attitude' detected in Robert's narrative. The attack delighted him: 'the review . . . is incredibly rude – delicious –' he crowed.

Patrick Balfour, an Oxford friend now working on the *Glasgow Herald*, managed to review it for his own paper. 'How delightful of you –' thanked Robert, 'I shd. have thought they would have prevented you suspicious of a "puff".' Robert had no such qualms himself and 'advertised it a lot quite shamelessly' at parties. Eventually he was taken in by his own propaganda. Two fashionable girls of his acquaintance, Bridget Parsons and Daphne Vivian, had, to his amazement, both read the book: 'it is too extraordinary –' he marvelled, 'I keep on meeting people who have.'

Things were not going so smoothly on the journalistic front. *The Times* had rejected his outline for a series of articles on Mount Athos. A second attempt to impress the deputy editor, putting 'him right on several points' over lunch with the Greek Foreign Minister, met with another rebuff. Robert was dismayed to be told that he should continue submitting articles no matter how often they were returned. There was nothing else for it but to buckle down to his history of Greece. He did not underestimate the difficulties of getting to grips with Byzantine civilization; the prospect, he admitted, was 'terrifying'.

Distractions, however, abounded. A swarm of friends descended upon him as soon as he had set foot in London, turning life into 'one long temptation'.

Just returned from a prolonged stay abroad was Alfred

Duggan. His first night back in town, celebrated with Robert in tow, began sedately enough by dining in state at Lady Curzon's house in Carlton House Terrace before going on to a play. The Café Royal was their next port of call, where, according to Robert, 'the whole building rose like one man & shouted Alfred!!!' A similar ovation was accorded him at 'a lurid attic in Ham Yard'. The evening ended at London's most notorious nightclub, the 43, 'with Mrs Meyrick, Miss Meyrick & the entire staff at his feet'. Their unnamed host ordered so many bottles of champagne that the table could hold no more.

By day, Alfred was his usual correct self. He arrived at Upper Montagu Street attired for lunch in bowler hat and stiff collar, sitting bolt upright in a chauffeur-driven 1910 Fiat 'with a coronet as big as a cabbage' on the door. But the rake's progress was unstoppable. Alfred confided to Robert that he was suffering from locomotor ataxia, the unco-ordinated movement and lurching gait indicative of the later stages of syphilis. Equally, he might just have been drunk. Whatever the cause, Alfred had been assured that 'he was not immediately doomed.' Even so, Robert found having to accompany him an increasing strain: 'We had another rather lugubrious evening', he complained to Henry Yorke, 'when he broke all the chairs in a box at "Blackbirds" simply by sitting on them.'

The Blackbirds, a black American cabaret troupe just arrived in London and playing to packed houses, was a brief craze amongst Robert and his circle. He met them at lunch with William Acton, at tea with David Plunket Greene, and was invited to their party in Regent's Park where everyone ate chop suey in the kitchen. To him, their act throbbed to the savage beat of the dark continent. The performers thought otherwise, telling him how they disliked other black performers such as the nightclub singer Hutch 'who are not American'. They reiterated that Africa was not their home, but Robert would have none of it. 'Africa is', he asserted, 'v. *artistic.*'

Another exotic to arrive in England that winter was Harold Acton. Since leaving Oxford, he had been pursuing his career as a writer, settling first in Venice before moving on to Paris. A further volume of poetry was ready for the press, but this had only been accepted by the publisher on condition that a novel was produced as well. Harold found fiction heavy going and for 'the sake of discipline' betook himself to London.

Robert offered him one of his rooms in Upper Montagu Street while he was looking for a flat, but on the strict understanding that he never took the first bath. A more peculiar rule, unstated until broken, was never to help Robert on with his overcoat. When an unsuspecting Harold once made this friendly gesture, he was turned on violently. 'Don't do that!' snarled Robert before wrenching off the coat and performing a war dance over it.

Despite the odd squall, the two friends found one another's company invigorating. 'It is such a comfort that Harold is here –' Robert wrote home, 'his energy & real critical faculty is so refreshing.' Harold was one of the few people whose opinion was valued by Robert. He admitted to Harold that in *Europe in the Looking Glass* various opinions were 'straight out of your mouth', in particular the description of Epstein's bronze surfaces as those 'rough-hewn corrugations which he mistakes for patine'. Thereby, an authentic fragment of Harold's mannered diction was preserved.

Somewhat nervously, Robert had submitted to him the manuscript of *Europe in the Looking Glass* for his comments, urging him to be candid. Harold did not flinch from fulfilling the brief. The 'more slovenly phrases' were pointed out, whilst the overall form of the book was compared to a series of articles. Few others could have got away with such criticism. But Robert remained respectful. 'Please do not think I admire it,' he replied, 'or that, were it not for the money, I shd. choose to be "a journalist & a diarist".'

The relationship was not all one-sided. While at Oxford Robert had dished out some astute advice of his own regarding Harold's poetry: 'I believe yr. vocabulary is too much for humorous trivialities to occupy it for ever – why don't you work yourself into a terrific passion over something . . . it wd. be an interesting experiment, if you unloosed a few more hidden fires.'

Herein lay the counterpoint that gave their friendship such animation. Taking sides inspired Robert as a writer. 'I must get on with the cause,' he had told his mother at the start of his researches into Greek history. For Harold, who loved 'experiments with words', construction was more important than content. All the same, he viewed with affectionate amusement Robert's determination to foist some new theory or argument upon him, prowling, as he did so, about the floor 'with carnivorous tread' or fuming at him 'like an angry uncle'.

The very qualities that had made Harold the intellectual leader of their precocious circle, his cosmopolitanism, his high culture and unfettered mind, led him to appreciate Robert's particular gifts. Unlike other friends, Harold never tired of his latest traveller's tales. Robert, he recalled,

> was happiest poring over a bundle of photographs, evoking the exact colour of his impressions, explaining a detail, trying to reconstruct what had escaped the camera, adding some peculiar personal anecdote to etch the scene more deeply – and he could not avoid fantasy, for it pursued him everywhere – and, when the photograph had failed . . . he would dive into a portfolio of sketches.

This desire to share his journey was in Harold's view a 'charming act of friendship'. It was also a rehearsal for his future writing, which relied upon the same props and enthusiasms to convey the vividness of a journey.

Ever present during the social whirl that had enveloped Robert that winter, Harold observed that 'as soon as the excitement of his travels had worn off, he relapsed into cocktail urbanity, but not for long.' When Robert grew bored with social life, he was like a time bomb waiting to explode. Harold witnessed his startling rudeness at a party when he was trapped into listening to an interminable anecdote told by Harry Melvill, a famous raconteur of the nineties. Robert grew increasingly impatient, glowering and shuffling on the edge of the circle of deferential listeners, until quivering with fury, he shouted: 'Can't you shut up, you hideous old relic of the Victorian age?' Melvill could merely gasp in reply: 'I feared that society was coming to an end. Now I know it.'

The cause of Robert's growing dissatisfaction was the grind of writing his book. By the end of January 1927, he had completed the first chapter, but forecast dolefully to Henry Yorke that it would not be finished until 1940. Furthermore, 'out of all this wealth of occupation' no money oozed. His only source of income, apart from the odd dividend, was from the sale of a 'wonder working' icon bought jointly with John Stuart Hay for £3 in Salonica. This was sold to the South Kensington Museum for a handsome profit, netting him £10.

Escape, however, was on the horizon. Robert had stayed with David Talbot Rice for a weekend's hunting in Gloucestershire just before Christmas, when they hatched a plan to visit Mount Athos and Mistra with the purpose of preparing an illustrated book on the frescoes. Early in January, Robert had paid a call on Thomas Balston, at Duckworth's to discuss the project. One of his first contacts in the publishing world, Robert had been introduced to Balston by Harold Acton while still at Oxford. Since then, a further link had been established through Anthony Powell, who had recently joined the firm as a general dogsbody on going down from Oxford.

The outcome was a commission from Balston to write a light-hearted book about their adventures on Mount Athos, similar in tone to *Europe in the Looking Glass*. The advance was £70. Shortly afterwards, Balston invited Robert to a dinner party, given largely for the Sitwells, all three of whom were now published by Duckworth. His flat was in Artillery Mansions off Victoria Street; a block built around a courtyard with high wrought-iron gates that were closed at night. On leaving the party, Robert chose to ignore a side door on to the street and instead rushed at the gates with 'blood-curdling war-whoops', reached the top at a great rate and 'achieved descent into Victoria Street without impalement'. An awed Anthony Powell, who witnessed the event, remarked drily: 'Even in the twenties this was not the usual tone of Artillery Mansions residents and guests.'

Although Robert had known Anthony Powell since the Eton Society of Arts, he had always found him 'very boring'. Now his view began to change. Dining with Powell one night, he observed his anguish, 'almost suicidal', as he told Powell's close friend, Henry Yorke, 'at the prospect of impending social cataclysms, which might compel him to spend the rest of his life among people who referred to their "maters" & "guvnors"'. Unbeknown to Robert, or any of Powell's high-brow friends, he was currently enduring a spell as a probationer with the Territorial Army which gave him a chilling glimpse into the 'golf-and-bridge world'. Powell's neurosis made him more interesting to Robert. 'I think he is becoming much nicer,' he pronounced.

That spring, Robert took a short holiday divided between grand houses in Ireland and Scotland. He stayed first with Cecil Clonmore at Shelton Abbey before moving on to Birr Castle in King's County, the principal seat of Michael Rosse, which he had inherited along with an earldom in 1918 on the death of his father from war wounds.

Robert first remembered Michael at Eton, his junior by eighteen months, as 'a grave little boy with the face of an angel'. Following his arrival at Oxford in October 1924, the handsome young peer effortlessly joined the fashionable throng and within a term or two his friendship with Robert had blossomed. Not everyone found Michael so approachable. Anthony Powell, who had rooms in the same house at Oxford, thought him pompous and a snob. His perceived hauteur did not trouble Robert. He was drawn to a steadiness in his character that provided the ballast to their friendship. 'I do so want to see you again,' he had written during a summer vacation, 'I always feel that you are a rock against the storm of everlasting sex that pervades everything.'

For his part, Michael was fascinated by Robert's originality and bantered with him on the subject of domes. He longed to show off Birr. 'I have got some furniture that you will love,' he suggested. 'It is a bedroom set & is pale green with great gilt bobbles coming out in all directions.' Architecturally, his house was equally fascinating, boasting a robust Restoration staircase, excellent Georgian decoration, and, its glory, an octagonal gothic saloon, comprising a glittering network of white and gilt columns, tracery and canopied vault.

Michael's family, the Parsons, had acquired the castle and demesne of Birr in the early seventeenth century but the vicissitudes of war soon made their mark upon the stronghold, which was gutted by fire in the rebellion of 1643 and besieged again in 1690. In the 1800s the Parsons of the day, acting as his own architect, dressed up the battered fortress in a smart gothic uniform: Robert was quick to spot the architectural affectation. Comparing fragments of the old walls, still bearing the scars of cannonballs, to the new, he observed in an account written after his visit: 'The nineteenth century . . . had witnessed a reversion to more chivalrous methods of defence. Each bedroom had been slitted anew with openings for the cross-bow; each archway punctured for the engulfing of unwanted guests in boiling oil.'

He was struck, too, by the strange magic of the setting created not just by the tumbling river, the myriad streams, the lake and the lush planting. 'The garden . . .' he elaborated, 'was peculiar in that not only was it extensively and emotionally romantic, but was impregnated in addition with the excited phantasy of the early Victorian engineer.'

He was referring principally to the 3rd Earl of Rosse, one of the greatest astronomers of his age, who had built in the garden the largest telescope in the world, appropriately housed in a battlemented observatory. But this was not all. Robert, who came to adore Birr, compiled some years later a list of other embellishments initiated by the earl and his talented family, including one of the earliest known suspension bridges, a 'pseudo-moat', a gatehouse with an imitation drawbridge, an aqueduct to feed the lake and artificial ramparts riddled with 'a series of tunnels & subterranean stairways' – these elaborate structures, set down in the very heart of 'careless Ireland', the expression of a 'meticulous and eccentric precision imprinted by the playful ingenuity of mathematicians'.

As predicted, during Robert's first visit the mad suite of bedroom furniture, modelled on a past countess's tiara, proved an irresistible delight. Using the mirror to reflect Michael's classic profile, he whiled away the time by taking photographs of his host surrounded by choice Victorian pieces raided from the attic. The idyll came to an abrupt end with a grim journey of sixty hours by steamer and train to the Highlands. The final part of his holiday was spent with Nina Seafield at Castle Grant in Strathspey where his visit coincided with the arrival of plovers' eggs on the menu.

His return to London brought on a severe bout of mental dyspepsia. A wail went up to Henry Yorke who was working in the family factory in Birmingham: 'really I am driven to suicidal despair by the blank waste of stupid people, nasty champagne, stale food, mocking green leaves', he howled. 'At least you are doing something – it is physical action that I crave for – my body is distorted into a permanent L from sitting at the table writing this laborious unwieldy book which no one will read and about which I can get no encouragement . . . I have lost even a liking for drink.'

On the spur of the moment Robert drove to Yorkshire to witness an eclipse of the sun. Back in London, parties became 'freakish'. Night after night Robert donned some new disguise as invitations commanded him to attend a Sailor's party, an Impersonation party, an Episcopal party or 'some new variation on a theme of the pirate king'.

Towards the end of July, he shook London from his feet and retired to Savernake to make the final preparations for his return to Athos. It was to be a party of four, Robert and David having each agreed to take along a friend. David's choice was a scholarly type called Gerald Reitlinger, whilst Robert had invited Gavin Henderson.

He did so in order to help his old friend out. Gavin had been in a terrible state over the last few months because his ambitious mother, turning a blind eye to his homosexuality, had been determined to marry him off to someone as rich as themselves. His engagement was duly announced in November 1926 to the daughter of Lord Kylsant, a shipping magnate who, better still, sprang from an ancient landed family. Hearing the news, Robert reported home: 'Gavin is engaged to a girl called Honor Philipps – he leaves for Australia tomorrow.' En route, Gavin sent Christmas greetings from Colombo addressed in typically uncompromising style to 'Robert my poppett'. His absence abroad lasted four months. Back home, tension mounted as marriage loomed. Robert was present one evening at the Night Light when Gavin went on the rampage with the farouche MP Bob Boothby and broke up the club.

The wedding was jinxed in more ways than one. First a batch of forged invitations were sent out to well-known

Right: Eric Byron, Robert's father, a civil engineer, whose work led to a peripatetic life during Robert's early childhood.

Below: Margaret 'Daisy' Byron, with Robert as a baby. A talented amateur artist, Margaret encouraged her son's artistic pursuits and became his muse.

Left: Edmund Byron, Robert's grandfather. A Victorian autocrat who pursued the life of a country gentleman on his estate at Coulsden, only twelve miles from the centre of London.

Below: Group of friends at Eton, 1921: Cecil Clonmore (top left); John Spencer (top right), Robert's tea-time companion; Stanley Beale (middle centre); David Talbot Rice (centre right), already fascinated by archaeology; Robert lying in front.

Right: Brian Howard's leaving photograph, 1922, inscribed to 'LORD B'. Howard was founder of the Eton Society of Arts and editor of *The Eton Candle.*

Below: Victorian party at the Hypocrites Club given by Robert and John 'Widow' Lloyd, 8 March 1924. *Back row:* Viscount Elmley (third left), his brother, the Hon. Hugh Lygon in cap with pipe; *third row:* Alastair Graham (left) wreathed in laurels, David Plunket Greene (third left), David Talbot Rice (second right), and John Lloyd (standing second right) with lorgnette. Robert standing far left.

Left: Oliver Baldwin, son of the Prime Minister, Stanley Baldwin, whose adventures in Armenia and Turkey inspired Robert's thirst for adventure.

Below: An illustration by Mark Ogilvie-Grant in *Vogue*, 23 January 1929, recalling the Victorian Revival at Oxford. The setting is Robert's rooms in Merton: Harold Acton with megaphone through which he recited his poems; Robert seated; Evelyn Waugh, behind, 'a little gnome in checks'.

Henry Yorke, who went on to write modernist novels under the pseudonym Henry Green. He forged a close friendship with Robert at Eton and modelled a character on him in his first novel, *Blindness*.

Gavin Henderson, grandson and heir to the plutocrat, Lord Faringdon. One of Robert's most enduring friendships and regular travelling companion.

The Hon. Hugh Lygon, whose father Lord Beauchamp took Robert abroad with his two eldest sons, for the first time, in 1923. The trip to Italy awakened Robert's passion for Byzantine art.

Alfred Duggan, *c.* 1922, in his usual formal attire with bowler hat. He accompanied Robert and Gavin Henderson on a motor tour to Greece in the summer of 1925.

Coulsden Court, Surrey, the country house built in 1850 by the Byrons. Sold along with the estate and numerous houses and cottages by Edmund Byron's heirs in 1922. This led to a furious row between Robert and his aunt, Lucy Hall Hall.

Back view of Savernake Lodge, Wiltshire, more familiarly known as 'The Ruins', being the remnant of a house burnt down in the nineteenth century. Situated in Savernake Forest, it was rented by the Byrons from 1923 to 1936.

Right: Leonard Bower, Alastair Graham and Robert in Athens, May 1926. All three were living in Bower's tiny flat. Robert was researching a history of Greece from the Byzantine Empire to the 1920s.

Below: 'Built in the Forest', the monastery of Chilandari, Mount Athos, 1927, drawing by Robert Byron, made on his second visit to Athos.

Left: David Talbot Rice, official photographer of the frescoes, and Mark Ogilvie-Grant, naturalist and draughtsman, with the guest-master at the monastery of Docheiariou, Mount Athos.

Below: Simopetra taken by Robert in 1927. Considered by him to be the most beautiful monastery on Mount Athos, it inspired one of the finest architectural descriptions in his travel book, *The Station*.

people and then the bachelor party, held at a hotel at Henley, ended in conflagration. Before going in to dinner, the guests, including Robert, ordered from the garage 20 gallons of petrol in buckets. Afterwards, they poured the petrol on the river and proceeded to 'set the Thames on fire'. Flames were soon licking up the Cromwellian garden wall of the hotel, scorching the lawn and burning the chestnut trees. Proceedings were subsequently issued against Gavin.

To annoy his mother, Gavin invited the Blackbirds to his wedding, which took place in June at St Margaret's, Westminster. The marriage lasted a matter of weeks. The unsuspecting Honor was devastated; Gavin took to drink. Robert's invitation to Mount Athos was therefore a most welcome diversion. 'Did you ever conceive such a party . . .' Robert chortled to Henry Yorke: 'Gavin hurrying to the only place on earth where women are not allowed – within two months of marriage.' But the strain had proved too much. At the last minute, he was forbidden to leave by his doctor. With David and Gerald making their ways separately, Robert set off alone for Athens.

11

Seat of Angels

Robert crossed the Channel on 12 August 1927 bound for Marseilles. His heart lifted at the sight of the 'massive rotund coaches' of Le Train Bleu in its siding at Calais with the brass ciphers of the wagon-lit glinting on a 'background of dead ink'. A further treat was in store. It turned out that Gavin had booked him a single sleeper and private cabin when cancelling their original berths. Curled up on the garter-blue velvet seat, he passed the afternoon in 'comatose content'. He had the added pleasure on reaching Paris of idly observing the 'intimacies of slum life' as they were shunted round the *ceinture* to the Gare du Lyon where the great 'serpentine hotel', now doubled in size, gathered up more passengers. Dinner 'was a poem of snowy drapery, crystal glass, burnished cutlery, petit marmite, melon, trout, chicken, buttered beans & brown bread ice'. The night passed untrammelled, save for 'the hissing which foreign brakes emit whenever in action'. Dawn broke over Avignon and by 8 o'clock he was seated in the barber's chair at the Hôtel Splendide in Marseilles.

The journey begun in such style ended with a suitable flourish. Three uneventful days at sea brought him to Piraeus, where he was surprised to be met by a naval officer in a launch, who had been sent by his friend General Phrantzes to whisk him through the formalities ahead of all the other passengers.

For the next ten days, he stayed with John Stuart Hay in his basement flat, cool, shuttered and hung with icons, at 24 Alopekis Street, known in translation as 'the street of the little female fox'. Returning to Athens was like coming home. On his first morning, he made a round of calls including one on General Phrantzes who, as master of the President's military household, was now installed in the old palace of King Constantine, 'a spacious marble cooled house with pleasant empire furniture & a wealth of original Victorian chintz'.

Designed by the German architect Ernst Ziller in 1878, the palace is a late example of the Nordic neo-classical style that had taken root in the southern climes of Athens during the reigns of the first two kings of Greece, the Wittelsbach Otho and his Danish successor, George. When Athens was declared the capital in 1834, German-trained architects had both laid out the new city and designed its most prominent public and private buildings. They did so 'in accordance with the glory and beauty of the ancient city of Athens', creating, in the process, as Thanos Veloudias fondly recalled, the atmosphere of 'a little capital of a German duchy'.

Robert had great affection for the 'squared modern town', singling out the building that housed the British Legation as one of the finest examples of 'the Greek Revival in the country of its origin'. Since demolished, this was the domestic masterpiece of Stamatis Cleanthes, who had been a pupil of Schinkel in Berlin. The early architects were by no means wedded to the classic style. Robert visited Tour la Reine, the country retreat of Queen Amalia, wife of King Otho, which, to his great enjoyment, was 'in the most exaggerated gothic'.

It was not just the architecture that contributed to the city's unpretentious charm. 'Before the sun is up', Robert observed, 'the vendors are about, uttering the "cries of Athens".' Their wares included figs, brooms, towels, old clothes, fresh eggs and ice. Every morning the ice-man delivered his block to their apartment with due ritual: 'As he put it in the chest, still, almost beneath his breath, he wailed the chant, Ice! I-ce! as though mesmerized with the beauty of his calling.'

Robert and John Stuart Hay decided to give a *masticha*, a form of cocktail party, to pay off their social debts. Robert's perception of Athens 'society' was wreathed in folk memories of the Wittelsbach kingdom when the leading families of newly independent Greece assembled in national dress at Queen Amalia's court. The modern fashionables, bidden to Hay's flat, were served both Greek and British delicacies including 'small meat rissoles', sandwiches, wines from Crete and Samos, ouzo, gin and vermouth. The Miss Phrantzes and the other Greek debutantes fell upon the gin 'regarding it as an innocuous dilutant when combined with vermouth'.

His brief Athens season drew swiftly to a close. The time had come to board the Prague Express for the overnight journey to Salonica where he had arranged to meet his fellow travellers to Mount Athos. He arrived there just as the London train was pulling out. Hurrying in a two-horse cab to the Mediterranean Palace Hotel, he found the rest of the party standing on the steps, 'bobbing on a surf of greeting'. They were David Talbot Rice, Gerald Reitlinger and Mark Ogilvie-Grant.

David Talbot Rice had been a significant presence in Robert's life since Eton. Robert remembered him there as 'a familiar pillar in the battle of a public school; possessing at sixteen the figure & resemblance of a healthy bull; smoking in the school bathing place, drinking amid the aspidistras of the neighbouring public house, bawling at small boys in boats through a megaphone'.

Born into a long line of squires, soldiers and parsons, he had been brought up in Gloucestershire, where the family owned an estate and fine Regency house at Oddington. To all appearances, David was a typical product of the landed gentry, never happier than when helping out on the farms or, during the hunting season, 'flying the sedate walls of the Heythrop country like a dignified heron'. But this was not the mainspring of his life. At the age of twelve, to the astonishment of his family, he had developed a fascination for ancient Egypt. In this, he received encouragement from a Gloucestershire neighbour, the connoisseur and collector George Spencer Churchill, who used to invite him over to his treasure-filled house, Northwick Park, for tête-à-têtes. Soon David was building up his own collection of 'ancient' Egyptian artifacts, which were proudly displayed in a corner cupboard in his room at Eton. At the same time, he also acquired the burning ambition to become an archaeologist.

This was easier said than done if one chose to pursue an academic career at Oxford where archaeology was not taught as a degree. Instead, David had to take a diploma, or postgraduate course, in anthropology, principally designed for colonial civil servants, and at the same time qualify for a BA degree in another subject, in his case French. Although discreetly studious, he also became one of the great social figures of the day, often to be found carousing at the Hypocrites or throwing himself into some production of the OUDS. Having achieved his diploma, David was awarded a senior scholarship by Christ Church, which enabled him, at last, to pursue his archaeological interests. He twice went on digs to the prehistoric site of Kish in Mesopotamia, returning to Oxford between field trips to take up residence in the old premises of the Hypocrites Club. His most recent assignment in the spring of 1927 had been working on the excavation of the Hippodrome in Constantinople under the distinguished Oxford archaeologist, Stanley Casson. A short break in England, when he had become engaged to the Russian undergraduette Tamara Abelson, was the prelude to his expedition to Mount Athos.

His invitee on the trip, Gerald Reitlinger, was a friend from Christ Church where they had shared similar academic interests. Just old enough to have served in the war, Reitlinger had gone on to study painting at the Slade before deciding that art history was more in his line. A highly determined character, he had insisted in the face of donnish opposition on abandoning his degree to write a thesis on an aspect of Carolingian art. After Oxford, he became increasingly drawn to the ancient civilizations of the Middle East and Asia and being of independent means launched himself upon the path of scholar traveller. Robert had gone to a party earlier that year in his large house in Queen's Gate, which, he noted, was 'filled with rare austerely disposed oriental potteries'.

Reitlinger was an awkward customer who looked like Mr Punch, with a long curved nose sweeping towards an aggressively upturned chin. 'Totally argumentative, always contradicting' was Anthony Powell's verdict, and, true to form, this was the attitude on display in Salonica where David was already having to check 'the eternal cynicisms of his nature à propos . . . Byzantinism'.

There was nothing cantankerous about the third member of the party, Mark Ogilvie-Grant, who had been invited by Robert at the last minute to take Gavin's place. He too had been 'another of school's few mercies', an habitué of the art school and a brilliant chorister, capable of reducing Eton masters to floods with his solos in chapel. Robert had introduced him to the Hypocrites on his arrival at Oxford where his warbling had contributed to the club's closure. Music was not his only talent. He was also a promising draughtsman as well as a keen naturalist and botanist. This interest had been kindled by his late father, a zoologist at the Natural History Museum who, on their frequent visits to the Highlands, had taught him 'to see a moth flattened fifty yards away against the bark of a fir tree or a crested tit creeping through the branches of a larch'. Slender, with a narrow face and fine features, Mark was as decorative as the rare butterflies that he loved to spot. Always immaculately turned out, he wore a plus-four suit in small checks for the rendezvous on the steps of the Mediterranean Palace Hotel.

After two days, visiting churches and combing the 'tattered booths of the refugee town up the hill in search of antiques', the party boarded the steamer for Daphni. On their arrival the next morning, a police officer met them in a boat demanding their passports. This unwelcome innovation reflected the formalizing of the responsibilities of the Greek authorities on the Holy Mountain, following the ratification of the Athos Charter the previous year.

Within hours Reitlinger was complaining about his confiscated passport and obliged them to call on the appropriate official later that day in the village capital of Caryes. All went smoothly until the official demanded details of their professions. Robert, always wary of admitting to the 'wielding of a pen', suddenly tired of the petty bureaucrat.

'We have no professions,' he replied, 'but write down what you like!'

'What?'

'Although we have no professions, you can, if you wish, invent some.'

'. . .?'

'Electricians, painters, taxi drivers, thieves, soldiers, sailors, aeroplane makers . . . archaeologists . . .'

'Are you all archaeologists?'

'All.'

'Archaeologist – Archaeologist – Archaeologist – Archaeologist.'

A piece of paper bearing his approval was produced, but not their passports.

Throughout the interview, Robert had acted as interpreter.

Over the past few months he had been taking Greek lessons from the London correspondent of the Athens newspaper *L'Estia*, Christodoulou Hourmouzios, who lived round the corner from him in London. To supplement his grasp of basic grammar, he also relied upon 'Divry's Anglo-Hellenic vest pocket lexicon', lettered at the side like an address book to facilitate the looking up of words. His efforts did not go unremarked. A member of the Community, who remembered him from the previous year, congratulated him on his new-found proficiency. As the only member of the party to speak Greek, he acted as principal spokesman throughout the trip and his vocabulary enlarged accordingly.

Another task performed by his Greek tutor had been to compose a flowery supplication to the Ecumenical Patriarch in Constantinople requesting a letter addressed to the Holy Community supporting Robert's application to photograph the frescoes. The Patriarch had complied, urging the Community to afford him every assistance. Duly impressed, the Primate at Caryes had a suitable recommendation drawn up to present to the individual monasteries.

Their business done, the party set off for the monastery of Iviron in an impressive cavalcade of seven mules. Most visitors to the Holy Mountain travelled with their worldly goods packed into a knapsack, but Robert had insisted on bringing his saffron leather suitcase with canvas covering, a coming of age present from his parents that contained numerous 'pigeon holes, slots & pockets'. It was, he admitted, the 'heaviest & most inconvenient piece of luggage of its size that ever existed'. Apart from this, he also had saddlebags, made specially by Fortnum & Mason for Gavin, packed with glass jars of chicken in aspic, as well as a hatbox, a box containing a syphon and sparklets, a kitbag and a dispatch case. Neither were his companions travelling light. Their baggage consisted of paints, easels, another vast suitcase, a large, heavy camera, two wooden boxes of photographic plates as well as numerous parcels, holdalls and kitbags. Everywhere they went the monks blanched at the sight of their luggage. To the guest master of St Paul's monastery, it was a revelation.

'So that is how they travel in England,' he remarked.

Retiring to bed on their first night at Iviron, their room was promptly invaded by insects drawn to the lamps. Copious quantities of Flit sprayed through a tube saw off the attack, allowing Robert to fall asleep to 'the wittering of frogs & the fluttering of singed & drunken moths'. They left almost immediately the next day for the Great Lavra, but not before a larger boat had been found. The first, the length of a small canoe, would have sunk beneath the weight of the cargo.

Their reception at the Great Lavra would test the feasibility of Robert and David's plan to produce a book on the frescoes of Athos and Mistra. Neither the Ecumenical Patriarch nor the Community could force the individual monasteries to agree to their photography. This had to be negotiated at each monastery in turn.

Assuming that all would go well, Robert and David had settled before leaving on a provisional title for the book, 'The Byzantine Renaissance', and had agreed their respective responsibilities. David was to take the photographs and Robert was to research and ultimately write the text. The deal also stipulated that David would provide illustrations for Robert's other book, already commissioned by Duckworth, giving a light-hearted account of their adventures on the Holy Mountain.

Having pocketed the advance of £70, Robert had put pen to paper at the very start of his journey. 'My book is up to date – most voluminous,' he had reported just before his boat docked at Piraeus. One of his tasks in Salonica had been to bring his diary up to date so as 'to start fresh' on his first day on Athos. Thereafter, he attempted to write up extended entries every few days or so.

But all these well-laid plans could still founder upon monkish intransigence. Robert's stomach lurched with misgiving as he handed over his letters to the appropriate monk at the Great Lavra. 'We were now on the threshold of three of the most important cycles of frescoes on the Mountain,' he declared. 'What if the doors should be closed against us?' Some buttering up was called for. David had come armed with a parcel of sacred books bought in an Anglo-Catholic emporium in Oxford. A volume on Anglican vestments was presented without more ado to Dr Spyridon, the most influential monk in the monastery. Robert went on to explain their mission, punctuating his remarks with frequent references to the pocket lexicon.

'We are writing a book,' he began.

'You are writing a book?'

'The English public do not know that Byzantine art exists.'

'Why?'

'We want to show them . . . we want England and the entire world to talk of the frescoes at the Lavra.'

Robert's mission to photograph the frescoes was not the first. A massive survey had been undertaken at the end of the war by the French scholar, Professor Millet, promulgator of the Cretan and Macedonian schools of painting, who had spent, in all, eighteen months on Mount Athos. The results, *Monuments de l'Athos*, had been published in March 1927, but without any explanatory text. Robert had the volume with him and offered to show it to Dr Spyridon. Even so, Millet's example did little to further Robert's cause.

'Do you remember Millet?' Robert asked Dr Spyridon.

'Yes, he was here for three months.'

'Did he send you the book?'

'No, he was not well brought up.'

And so his petitioning continued until Dr Spyridon agreed to put their proposal to the monastery's superiors. He did so, successfully, early the following morning. Now their labours could begin.

One last-minute hitch occurred. David was entering the church with his huge camera and tripod when 'a little fanatic in spectacles barred the way with both his body & a spate of horrified disapproval'. His fellow monks seized him by the shoulders and pushed him out of the door.

Over the next four days their routine 'assumed a complexion of monastic regularity'. This was measured to the beat of Byzantine time, which varies daily according to the rising of the sun. Generally, Athonite clocks are set around five hours ahead of 'Frankish time.' Robert would rise at 6.30 a.m., or mid-morning on the Holy Mountain, and shave at a sink on the balcony. Monks crossing the courtyard below would glance upwards 'at this curious occupation'. After breakfast of ouzo and coffee, David began his photography whilst Robert either assisted him or made detailed notes of the colour and form of the frescoes. Meanwhile, Mark and Gerald went off sketching. Lunch was served in the guest quarters at 11.30, much later than usual as a concession to their 'barbarous' western timetable. A siesta followed. Work recommenced after vespers around 4 p.m. and continued until dark.

The three novices of the party were swiftly inducted into the discomforts of Athonite life. On the first night their table was laid with 'filthy cloth, filthy napkins, spoon fork & knife slimed with grease, a soup of haricot beans, then unmentionable vegetables . . . resembling large cut nails & filled with pips tasting of stale pharmaceutical peppermint'. Although the food improved, David still occasionally ate anchovies 'tasting of sewage'. The sanitary arrangements never failed to shock Mark. 'Sometimes', he wrote home, 'they are triangles in the floor hanging over precipices so that the wind blows the paper up and it eddies round the room.' In consequence, he continued: 'Robert is sending the monks beaded bromo for Christmas.' Sleep offered little comfort. Retiring to bed at the Lavra, they found 'flocks of ravening red bugs' frolicking over the rock-hard mattresses. The ensuing massacre with blood squirting everywhere left the 'denizens of the monastic beds' lying 'flat & empty like gooseberry skins'.

Tempers soon began to fray. Reitlinger grumbled incessantly about the food despite Robert producing delicacies from his own stores to supplement their diet. He also complained about the quality of the soda water, made with considerable effort using the gas sparklets, although content to down most of the supply without a thought for the rest of the party. Robert felt increasingly hard done by: 'he is very rich & I am very poor', he seethed, '& he did not once say thank you for all the food he ate & flit he used.' He subsequently took to eating his supplies in private. Reitlinger's other sin was to show insufficient respect for Byzantine art. Robert grew furious at having to justify himself and resorted to insult. When David joined in the fray, Robert bit him in his 'bovine torso'.

After a week of living at such close quarters, Reitlinger

classified his companions into artistic types. David was a Cranach emperor, Mark a Glyn Philpot fisherboy and Robert the 'adjunct of a Magnasco tempest'. Robert completed the quartet. He likened Reitlinger to a witch, drawn by S. H. Sime, the Edwardian illustrator, complete 'with bobbed hair and that wholesale disregard for cleanliness on which a witch's prestige depends'.

They left the Lavra with genuine regret. Robert pressed a donation into the palm of the guest master, uttering the usual formality, 'A present for the church.' He was rewarded with a bottle of the best raki. They then set off for the settlement of Kerasia to make an ascent of the summit.

This time the view was unimpaired; Robert could survey the world as though 'atop a pole a mile & a quarter high'. He gazed upon 'the tiny contours of Lemnos', the coastline of Cavalla and the distant peak of Mount Olympus. He fantasized that on a clear day, 'as all the world round here knows', one would see Constantinople and 'the flat white dome of Santa Sophia'. He turned to go just as the sun was setting and suddenly saw 'high up towards the horizon, a long pointed black cone . . . [with] two sides . . . ruled up on the water. The shadow [of the Mountain]! Stretching . . . seventy miles to Lemnos.'

The use of mules to convey them from one monastery to the next was free. Only when the party strayed into areas not bound by the rules of monastic hospitality, such as Kerasia, the settlement beneath the summit, were mules hired at a commercial rate often only agreed after bad-tempered bargaining.

This was the case prior to their departure, the following day, to St Paul's monastery. But if the start was bad, the actual descent caused Robert 'thumbscrews of agitation'. The luggage and, above all, the precious photographic plates wobbled precariously on the backs of the mules as the animals leapt and slithered down the precipitous path with 'stones falling from each clutching hoof a million-million miles to the sea below'. Panic set in when the muleteers appeared to redouble their pace. He bawled at them to slow down, hurling himself down the track, retrieving dropped coats on the way. 'My temper was real,' he attested; 'my Greek . . . cannonaded out like a piston would from a cylinder. Did we pay for mules in order to walk? Was he a thief? Need he drop the coats? And he smiled through the auburn beard.' This was the last straw. Robert forced him to the edge of the high mountain path, making as though to clutch at his throat, his fingers 'itching for his beard'. The smile vanished, apologies poured forth. Meanwhile, a horrified Mark had attempted to restrain him, only to receive a similar torrent of abuse.

Later that evening, Mark again remonstrated with Robert over the incident. They were swimming at the time. 'You, you slavering little toady,' bellowed Robert, 'I could drown you!' Henceforth, Mark determined to learn some Greek in order to oil the wheels of communication.

After the swim, they had to race back to the monastery before the gates were closed at sunset. Their progress was suddenly impeded by a flood of water, released by an upper sluice to wash away the mule droppings that coated the path from the day's work. Robert was enthralled by this example of traditional husbandry. Here was 'confirmation of the amenities of life which the Byzantines understood, & which are now with the solitary exception of the Holy Mountain, lost to the Levant'. He went on to praise the abundance of produce and the management of water through a system of aqueducts, reservoirs, piping and fountains. Other vivid survivals were the everyday utensils, the pots, ewers, plates, cups of beaten pewter and three-legged candlesticks. Strangest of all was the wooden gong carried on the shoulder, called a *semandron*, that summoned the monks to prayer. Robert had observed the procedure at the Lavra where a veiled monk marched round the outside of the church beating the long piece of wood metallically 'with weird almost savage rhythms'. The effect was 'terrifying in its unfamiliarity, neither European nor Asiatic'.

Life on the Holy Mountain was a continuation of the medieval empire. If proof were needed, Robert drew comparison between the items still in daily use and those depicted in the frescoes and miniatures preserved in the monasteries, where they were reproduced with astonishing accuracy.

His interest at St Paul's monastery lay in a tiny barrel-vaulted chapel built into the outer wall that ran beneath the summit of the mountain. He had studied the frescoes, depicting the traditional scenes of Christ's life, on his previous visit and judged them to be the finest on the peninsula. His second visit reinforced this view. They were, he considered, 'the very flower of the Byzantine Renaissance'.

Rapture swiftly turned to fury when he assessed the condition of the frescoes. The paintings on the slope of the roof nearest the mountain were already gone, rotted by damp, whilst the rest had gaping cracks, threatening to fall at the next thunderclap. 'Can nothing be done to save these incomparable works of art?' he fumed, before launching into a tirade against the money being wasted on excavating classical remains.

> Americans are paying a million pounds to convert the most picturesque quarter of old Athens into a broken-pillared playground for cats in the hope of unearthing on what they term the site of the Agora, yet another shoal of those inert stone bodies that have already rendered every museum in Europe unenterable to any person of artistic sensibility.

By contrast, at St Paul's, 'for want of a few hundreds pounds', the great frescoes must perish. This was not the only scandal. The surviving frescoes at Mistra, he went on, 'lie unroofed, crashing to the ground with every wind, open to every gust of rain'. May not someone come forward, he asked, and 'expend even five minutes with a hammer & tarpaulin?'

News of Robert's gathering prejudice against classical art reached England. 'How I hate it!' he wrote to Henry Yorke. 'It has really grown into a mania with me – as I get more and more hopelessly immersed in Byzantium.'

They continued by boat along the line of monasteries that fringe the western shore of Mount Athos. Their work progressed well, but not all of the party were content. Reitlinger, who had always intended leaving ahead of the others, had become increasingly anxious over making his escape, especially as his passport was still held at Caryes. Mercifully, his departure came sooner than expected. A mix-up over connections meant that he had to leave Gregoriou at a moment's notice to catch a boat to Daphni. 'He tore from the room,' Robert commented sourly, 'with a strangled goodbye stuck in his throat, and beyond it, not a syllable of thanks to the party he had joined and to which he had contributed no single element of spiritual or material happiness.'

A day was spent visiting the monastery of Simopetra which had captivated Robert on his previous visit – 'the most beautiful', he had jotted down after a swim.

> Lying back in water below with light just catching the Western side – whole thing reared up against the sky – with great deep wooded rift below in shadow – & one cypress reaching up from below the foundations to help the converging lines – the three piles at all different angles – a perfect composition . . . the grandest building in the world.

Rebuilt after a fire in the 1890s, the monastery rises from its towering rock in three balconied blocks. Robert had originally described it as 'Lhassic', drawing a comparison to the Potala, the Dalai Lama's palace at Lhassa in Tibet, a building known to him from photographs taken on the Younghusband expedition which he had seen in 1926 at the Royal Geographical Society.

Returning to London after his first visit to Athos, he had continued to puzzle over the similarity and began to read up on the Nestorians in China. 'There is no doubt', he ventured, 'that while the Buddhist theocracy in Thibet was actually taking shape, Nestorian Christianity . . . had many flourishing communities adjacent.' But this, he argued, when once again confronted by Simopetra, was mere scholarly supposition compared to a 'more important common factor'. The real reason for the 'astonishing resemblance' was the link between landscape and architecture. Athos and Tibet shared panoramic grandeur, which moulded the temperaments of their monastic inhabitants causing them to invent parallel styles of architecture: 'all this combination of man-made & God-made individuality; the distinction – distinction rather than seclusion – from the remainder of the world; cannot but have accelerated the impulse towards indefinable unanalysable emotion.' When expressed in architecture, the result was a fusion of 'the utilitarian with the abstract'. This assertion propelled him into his next critical leap: the Potala and Simopetra were thus unconscious forerunners of 'the dynamic style of architecture generated in the modern age'.

By linking the art of remote civilizations with that of his own day, Robert was promoting the attractions of Byzantine art to the moderns. Classicism, by contrast, now confined to 'letters and stones', had nothing to offer the 'possessors of the twentieth century'. Dressing up his theory for publication, Robert turned on an imaginary pedagogue, proclaiming: 'We run now with the soul, with the spirit that has escaped you, cobwebbed old man, paid instrument of enormous stagnation.' His arguments with Reitlinger at the Lavra provoked a similar outburst. Reitlinger's analyses displayed 'that pitiful trust in rational thought that betrays his generation (late war)'.

Robert's intuition, specifically his eye for architecture, was set alight by Simopetra. Determined to make a drawing, he slithered down a mountain path to the foot of the monastery. The impact of the building thrilled him to the core. 'My pencil,' he wrote, 'prone to the romantic, fled over the page in ecstasy exaggerating the tone of the sky to the ferocity of a thunderstorm.' His word picture, touched up only slightly for publication, was no less arresting.

> Far above, a huge tilted box, creamy gold, and striped with the shadowed silver of oaken struts and planks, was rocketed into the blazing turquoise sky. It lived; like the flowers of the mystic, it sang; insensate; irresistible; inexplicable.

Rarely moved by the church services on the Holy Mountain, the vision of Simopetra was for him a religious experience. The building had challenged all his gifts. It had stirred his intellectual curiosity, inspired him as an artist, and brought forth his voice, sonorous, speculative and passionate, as an architectural critic. His other great love, landscape, was also lauded in his hymn of praise. The psychological link between man's creation and God's earth was, in Robert's mind, indissoluble. It was to be a guiding light on his travels and a key to his unlocking of the creative genius of civilizations.

Towards evening they took a boat to Daphni where various pieces of luggage were dropped off. The last of the chicken in aspic had been consumed, liberating the saddlebags for clothes. Used photographic plates were also deposited. The party was rowed on to the 'huge barracks' of the Russian monastery of St Panteleimon, known as the Russico, just as the twilight deepened.

For once Robert was relieved of the negotiations attendant on their arrival. David had been learning Russian from an old man in Constantinople in anticipation of his marriage to Tamara. 'Wheedling his three dozen words into choking permutations', he obtained separate apartments for each of them. The walls were hung with 'ghastly scenes of wolves rushing at sledge borne damsels' and everywhere were portraits of Russian royalties including Nicholas and Alexandra.

At the turn of the century, Russian monks had outnumbered Greeks on Athos, fuelling their attempts to have a greater say in the running of the Holy Mountain. Now such ambitions were mocked by the vast derelict buildings. 'There are no visitors, no pilgrims,' a monk had lamented the previous year. 'Our house property in Moscow is confiscated.' A sign of their pre-war importance had been a visit from Rasputin. 'A remarkable man to look at, I suppose,' Robert had asked in French. 'On the contrary,' came the reply, 'a man of very ordinary appearance.' The Russian plainchant never failed to move Robert. He had attended a service the previous year when four men sang, unaccompanied, 'in tones of unfathomable sadness, they seemed to echo in exile the memory of a life always sad, now extinguished'.

On his second visit, Robert was the surprised participant in a less formal ceremony when a chanting monk bore down upon him and David, while both were shaving, sprinkled them with holy water using a bunch of fresh basil and enveloped them in Christian embrace. Inquiries revealed that this blessing, common throughout the Holy Mountain, took place on the first day of every month. By Robert's calculation, it was already 14 September, but the Holy Mountain follows the Julian calendar rather than the Gregorian, putting them fourteen days behind the outside world.

Their tour of monasteries along the north-west coast continued. 'A more benign air', Robert noted, 'overspread the landscape.' Cliffs gave way to beaches and the spine of the ridge flattened as the distance from the summit increased. Arriving at Xenophontos, he was struck by the well-tended vegetable beds between the shingle and the monastery. Inside the walls, the atmosphere of 'an industrious farmyard' prevailed. Piles of figs and walnuts were drying in the sun, alongside were pewter trays covered with tomatoes beaten into a paste. Fleets of mules, each bearing a pair of tall conical vats heaped with grapes, clattered into the courtyard. Later, when Robert and Mark went for a swim, a herd of long-haired swine arrived on the beach tended by a black-robed herdsman.

This atmosphere of peace and plenty was reflected in their welcome from the Abbot. Nothing was too great a trouble. Ladders were fetched to assist David in his photography. They proved to be single-sided stepladders supported from the apex by a pole that are, like so much else, peculiar to Mount Athos. Balancing precariously upon a pair of these fragile tripods, David released the shutter for a long exposure, only to find that a service was beginning beneath him. 'Don't', said the officiating father, 'interrupt your work for us.'

David was blessed with even temper, humour, common sense and tact. In order to photograph the frescoes of Athos all these abilities were tested to their limits. A monk was always in attendance, either intrusively helpful or acting as a lynx-eyed defender 'of the Lord's house' and ready to close the church on any pretext. The confined spaces added to his difficulties. He was often to be found 'clinging apelike to the ridge of the eikonastasis' in search of a good shot. Frequent crashes accompanied these gymnastics as plates or colour filters hurtled to the floor. Changing the plates meant retiring to some cupboard or crouching beneath a table shrouded in blankets from which he would emerge bathed in sweat as though from a Turkish bath. Leaving the camera unattended was never advisable. Once he returned to find a monk peering through the lens during a twenty-minute exposure, imprinting his eye upon the plate. There was no rest for him in the evening as the photographs had to be developed after dinner.

The obtaining of permission remained Robert's responsibility. He handled the matter with diplomacy and met with complete success. Robert also selected the frescoes to be photographed, although David occasionally disagreed. A fierce altercation was taking place in one refectory when a monk, who knew ten words of American, chose that moment to ask David his name. 'Holdjertonguedamnyou,' came the frustrated reply. At which Robert and Mark fled for a swim.

He and Mark were forever swanning off on some enjoyable expedition. Mark revelled in the strange butterflies, leaf insects and dung flies that abounded; he also busied himself with portrait drawings of the monks. Robert also drew, but much time was devoted to practising his new-found enthusiasm for photography. Before leaving London, he had bought a far more intricate camera than the one used on his previous visit. He had learnt to use it in Athens where the manager of the Kodak shop gave him lessons in the art of speeds and colour filters. As a result, he was always on the lookout for suitable 'art-views'. In all he took over 300 photographs. The best reveal his eye for a striking composition as well as the feel for architectural form that was to distinguish his later photographic work.

Recrossing the narrow peninsula, they started on the last stretch of their circuit of the mountain. Their final destination was Vatopedi, the largest and richest of all the monasteries. The clustering group of 'domes, towers, roofs and turrets, climbing within their walls from the water's edge', appeared like 'one of those imaginary cities on an old map'. Within the gates, a 'flawless satiety of colour' greeted the eye: 'the snow white campanile', Robert wrote later, 'against the fevered rust-coloured church, smooth as silken velvet . . . everywhere the inevitable Greek blue . . . outlining white buildings to make them colder, strawberry ones to make them hotter.'

They had stepped into a world of 'pomp and leisure'. Strips of thick, garter-blue carpet, once a single roll laid out to welcome a visiting Tsar, covered the floor of the guest salon, whilst overhead a grandiose ormolu lamp, converted from paraffin, blazed with electricity. All evening, the buildings resounded to the clang and throb of the generator. The next day, the engineer got drunk and broke his leg, so the visitors lit the ormolu lamp instead. Modern technology was not unknown elsewhere on Athos: the Lavra had a telephone, although it was broken when Robert asked for a call to be made.

In keeping with the surroundings the assistant guest master, Father Aristarchus, made the perfect gentleman's gentleman, having worked on a yacht belonging to an English colonel resident in Constantinople. When David went off to Caryes to collect the mail, Aristarchus remonstrated with Robert: 'Well, sir, I'm sure I don't know what Mr Rice is going to do about his lunch.'

Several days were spent photographing the frescoes in the church, which Robert considered the finest on Athos. Overall, Robert summarized their effect as that of 'a dull mist – like old dull ink – but not black or so sharp as indigo – very beautiful – with the changing sunlight the details of the building and figures stand out.' As at other monasteries, time was also spent inspecting the exceptional icons, relics, mosaics and other treasures as well as the manuscripts in the library.

Their stay was only marred by the arrival of an unwelcome guest on their last day, a Roman Catholic priest who appeared 'sweat-stained and odoriferous, with a permanent stubble veiling the lower half of his face like a tousled cock sparrow'. His presence in the guest rooms signalled the hasty departure of Brother Adrian, the previous year's primate, who had been sitting for his portrait. Father Aristarchus was equally furious. That night a conversational pall hung over dinner. The priest, who was English, drank copiously. 'Nor', Robert hinted, 'were we long left in doubt as to his toleration of the grosser excesses. Though these, after the nature of Roman Catholics in the Levant, he was mainly concerned to fasten upon the monks who were his hosts.' Robert's party assumed an air of puritan disapproval.

One last task remained. The church and a neighbouring chapel, known as the Prodome, still had to be photographed in Caryes. As they entered the outskirts of the capital, after three weeks on Mount Athos, they all felt a sudden urge to be free. 'We were irked', Robert explained, 'with ceremonies and good behaviour, with the early shutting of the doors, the attendance of services, and the punctuality of meals. Physically and mentally, our resolution was waning.'

David's self-discipline made him determined to complete the photography. Meanwhile Robert and Mark rode off to the nearby monastery of Xeropotamou for the feast of the Exaltation of the Cross. The food was delicious; the drink flowed. Afterwards, Robert pushed his way into the church where 'an exquisite shadowless radiance' suffused the interior. 'All the innumerable chandeliers, candlesticks, candle-brackets, candle-crosses, that had previously seemed but a superfluous obstruction were now in play.' Beneath on a brocade stool was the casket containing the piece of the Cross. A bishop, magnificently robed and veiled, formed a circle with attendants and paced slowly round the relic. Robert was transfixed. 'Rhythm of chant and paces,' he divined, 'that intrinsic rhythm independent of "time", caught the beholders from their human frames.'

Within hours, harbingers of the frivolous world were upon him. Forewarned of arrivals from Athens, he spied at sun-up the steamer nearing Daphni. Tearing down to the shore, he stripped off and swam out to meet it. John Stuart Hay, Alastair Graham and Alfred Duggan, closely watched by a keeper called Hogg, made up the party. They were the first of many friends and acquaintances to follow in Robert's footsteps to the Holy Mountain. Taking mules to Caryes, Alfred, who was unfamiliar with wooden saddles, rode bolt upright, gripping with his knees in the English manner.

Meanwhile, David had broken his way into the chapel like a burglar. Two more days saw their work complete. They resolved to leave that very afternoon for Daphni to catch a boat the following morning, even though it was heading in the wrong direction, for Cavalla. Their last night on Athos witnessed another massacre of bedbugs. Eventually, Robert and Mark threw their mattresses out of the window. Mark's, which was stuffed with hay, was eaten by a donkey.

Steaming from Byzantium, they passed the tip of the

peninsula; the peak was shrouded in cloud, but the scattered buildings of the Great Lavra remained visible until the boat struck out into the open sea. Nearing the modern port of Cavalla, Robert was already filled with regret, writing:

> There is a lament in the wind's talk . . . Turn south, it says, astern . . . There, carried high on a bank of clouds, hovers a shape, a triangle in the sky. This is the Holy Mountain Athos, station of a faith where all the years have stopped.

Another three weeks were spent in Greece. The main reason for delay was the need to photograph the frescoes at Mistra. Having done so, David left for England, whilst Robert and Mark made a 'flying visit' to Crete. This was viewed as a reconnaissance by Robert in anticipation of further researches into the inspiration of the Cretan school. Joined by Alastair Graham, they dawdled in the capital Canea before mounting an expedition to the Samaria gorge. Finally, Robert set sail for England, arriving back at Savernake towards the end of October 1927, where he immediately began the task of completing his travel book for Duckworth on his adventures on Mount Athos.

When Robert had first raised the subject with Tom Balston, he had proposed a straightforward history of the monastic republic with discursions on Byzantine painting and the Orthodox church. Chapters of descriptive writing were to interweave the weightier topics. Balston had rejected this approach and insisted, instead, 'over and over again', that Robert should produce a light-hearted work 'exactly like *Europe in the Looking Glass*'.

Robert had begun keeping his travel diary on the boat out from Marseilles. He soon discovered that the previous year of solid writing had oiled his facility. 'After the infinite pains and thought that I have been contributing to the Byzantine book', he told his mother, 'it seems trivial – but comes easily and is exactly what Duckworth's asked for . . . it is almost good enough to go straight to press – only illegible.' The only brake to his progress were the other preoccupations that resulted from his visit to the monasteries. By the time he got to the Russico, he was already a week behind with the finished account, but was noting 'every detail . . . in a lesser diary'. At Zographou, where a day was spent free of photography, he made a start on covering a backlog of five visits to monasteries.

Falling behind with the entries worked to Robert's advantage. The similarity of monastic life on Athos as well as the repetitive nature of the task of photography meant that a day-by-day account was inappropriate. Looking back over a number of days allowed Robert to treat certain aspects of life thematically. He also, cleverly, accentuated the particular atmosphere of each individual monastery. 'It is as though,' he wrote in summary, 'in the days of horse transport, a round of great country houses were in progress, each conducted on the tradition of centuries.'

Eventually, he left Mount Athos with two thirds of the narrative written up as far as their departure from the Russico. The rest was completed back in Wiltshire. Relatively few changes were made to the text as it stood. It brims with dialogue, pen portraits, evocative architectural descriptions and choice anecdotes, many of which were included from the previous year's visit. The quality of his account proved his ability to write accomplished prose, almost literally, on the hoof.

The major additions to the book concerned the history of the Holy Mountain and detailed descriptions of its treasures. Although inserted back in Wiltshire, where Robert had access to his books and notes as well as to his rejected *Times* articles, he had indicated while composing the original diary where these should fall. The start of the chapter entitled 'Government in the Fourth Dimension', which contains the early history of Athos, had already been roughed out, beginning with the memorable sentence: 'The Earth is behind us. We are back in that old Byzantine world with the spirit uppermost.' Similarly, he had planned in advance that further history should be included in the Russico chapter. One other major addition was made. In a Sitwellian leap, he interrupted the account of the Holy Mountain to describe his travels to Mistra and Crete.

Many references from earlier travellers' accounts were also

threaded into the narrative. One of the most picturesque was the discovery that both Robert and the nineteenth-century book collector, Robert Curzon, had eaten a picnic under the same mulberry tree at the arsenal of the Lavra. His other sources were the seventeenth-century diary of John Covel, the dense Victorian travelogue, published in 1887, of Athelstan Riley and the latest book on Athos, published in 1924 by the Cambridge don, F. W. Hasluck. This contained useful historical information, but was not up to date, having been written in 1912 and published posthumously by his widow.

Past travellers were usually mentioned with little comment, but Robert could not resist taking swipes at the unfortunate Athelstan Riley, a noted Anglo-Catholic, who was still alive in 1927. His own schoolboy dalliance with Anglo-Catholicism long forgotten, Robert quoted derisively from Riley's account of singing the Magnificat on reaching the summit. The book, though, had its uses. One of Robert's more intriguing discursions, calculating the cubic inches to survive of the Holy Cross, was lifted unacknowledged from an appendix on the subject by Riley.

The completed manuscript, entitled *The Station*, was delivered to Duckworth's at the end of February 1928, only four months after Robert's return from Athos. It did not meet with Balston's wholehearted approval: he 'was very disappointed that there was so much heavy matter in the manuscript'. Robert fought back, arguing that the book was 'intended only for people totally ignorant of the subject'.

Another bone of contention was the opening chapter, which describes the twelve months in Britain prior to his departure. Duckworth's wanted to drop it, even though Robert's intention had been to contrast this world with the 'romance' of Athos. Robert complained to his mother that 'as they don't like the book or understand it, they are not qualified to speak. It shall come out only over my dead body.' But he continued in far less confident tones, asking for her support: 'do write and say you agree or do you think it irrelevant? I am not calling it a chapter but a prelude – so that the hurried reviewer may be able to turn straight to the journey out.' Although the judgement of Balston and his assistant, Anthony Powell, was correct, they backed down in the face of Robert's intransigence. All rows were forgotten when Robert set eyes on an advance copy of the book, which made him croon with pride. Suitably contrite, he inscribed Anthony Powell's copy, 'Tony, with bitter remorse for his sufferings, Robert.'

Years later, Anthony Powell reassessed the book. He admired many of 'the splendid images and literary parallels' but accused Robert, in his 'obsessive repugnance for cliché', of overwriting and obscure language. Aspects of *The Station* are obscure, not least the title, which remains unexplained until the last sentence, 'This is the Holy Mountain Athos, station of a faith where all the years have stopped.' But Robert, at the age of only twenty-two, was attempting to convey a world, then as now, remote from the modern mind. James Lees-Milne, a later friend of Robert's, himself an historian, aesthete and lover of Athos, also reconsidered the book. Although admitting to the 'rash judgements' and 'lapses of style', he was bowled over by 'the lightning strokes of a prodigious mind!' Steven Runciman, the great Byzantinist, was also an enthusiast. When asked for his opinion by Christopher Sykes, he affirmed that 'the atmosphere comes across superbly.' Their more tolerant estimates stand. Robert made Athos his own. His account of the Holy Mountain has never been bettered.

12
Dons and Counts

While at home finishing work on *The Station* Robert's only distraction had been a project mooted with Brian Howard to publish a collection of essays by their literary contemporaries on the theme of values in modern life.

Brian and Robert's friendship, forged at Eton, had gone through an unsettled patch at Oxford where Brian, much to Robert's dismay, had aspired to join the grand hunting set: 'really', he informed Henry Yorke, 'I think every trace of intellect is almost vanished already.' Since coming down, however, the two had found one another's company increasingly congenial. Typical was an evening spent in conversation over the fire at the Gargoyle Club on 'the romantic spirit that can co-ordinate everything'. Prior to Robert's return to Mount Athos, he told Henry Yorke: 'It is perhaps curious to you but I must say that throughout my sojourn in London I have found Brian (Howard) intellectually far the most sympathetic person. He does not sneer when one is serious.'

In November 1927, Brian was in Berlin undergoing psychoanalysis with the fashionable Dr Hans Prinzhorn, who aimed to uncover his patients' 'dominion of life'. His creed, as outlined by Brian, ran as follows: 'To do with the mind is nothing. To do with the soul, which is life, is everything.' This belief was close to Robert's heart as he busied himself inserting into the manuscript of *The Station* triumphalist remarks about the modern soul overcoming the aridity of classical culture. Their shared enthusiasm led to an idea for a published symposium on the subject.

Having declared himself transformed by Dr Prinzhorn's analysis, Brian had returned from Berlin eager to throw himself into the project. Putting ideas on paper immediately threw up almost irreconcilable differences between the collaborators.

Brian, heavily influenced by Nietzsche, was anti-God, but pro-gods, citing the Dionysian and Apollonian classifications of human behaviour. Robert, fresh from the Holy Mountain, countered: 'Christianity (not the Xtianity of today as we see it) has been essentially anti-logical and pro-intuitive . . . historically Christianity has contributed more to man's progress than any single thing – progress being the search for the abstract.' Brian's continual rebuttals flushed out Robert's declaration: 'I have a God and you have not.' Eventually, Robert established the common ground between them: 'the instinct for the vital'.

During the project's conception Robert blazed with activity, despite having to meet a tight deadline on *The Station*. He submitted two draft synopses, visited Arthur Waugh, father of Evelyn, at the publisher's Chapman & Hall, and planned the editorial schedule. Brian spent his time criticizing the methodology and, much to Robert's annoyance, gossiping about the idea to their friends. The final proposal was divided into three parts under the headings Material, Transcendental and Aesthetic, each to be expressed through the work of contemporary writers and artists. The book was given the working title of 'Values', which stood for 'the pursuit of the Real' or 'that Essence of true satisfaction' which is man's goal.

The promulgators of this lofty theme, apart from Robert and Brian, were to be a clique of ambitious writers late of Oxford University. The prospectus sent out to the chosen few made no bones about the professional advantages of the scheme. 'Its primary intent', Robert explained, 'is to convert literary aspiration into income. It is a form of literary advertising, and as such best undertaken on a co-operative basis.' Acceptances were received by return from, amongst others, Peter Quennell, Cyril Connolly, Harold Acton and Evelyn Waugh. Only Henry Green prevaricated, but, he, too, finally came on board. The publishers had taken a similarly hard-headed approach. Arthur Waugh expressed serious interest as 'he wished the firm to keep in touch with the younger generation'. Their high hopes were never realized. The idea failed to become reality and by April had been extinguished. Brian's lackadaisical attitude throughout justified Dr Prinzhorn's diagnosis of his patient that 'young Englishmen like [Howard] never finish anything but their visky-sodas!'

The spring of 1928 brought a domestic upheaval to the Byron family. Robert's parents decided to move to Vienna for the year partly to save money and partly to widen the horizons of their daughters, Anne and Lucy. Savernake was sub-let for the summer and the Byrons left for Austria towards the end of March. Robert accompanied his parents to London before he too set off for abroad a few days later, to Spain.

Robert's companions were Gavin Henderson, now separated from his wife and enjoying bachelorhood once more, and a friend of his called Tony Alexander. The party travelled in Gavin's green Bentley, which he drove at great speed in pouring rain from Le Havre to San Sebastian in two days. Gavin only slowed down from seventy to fifty miles an hour, to swig from a bottle of Vouvray which accompanied lunches taken on the move. Robert sprawled in the back reading a book on Greece which he had been asked to review.

The purpose of Robert's journey was to study the works of El Greco. This would complete his survey of Byzantine painting in preparation for writing the accompanying text to David's photographs of the frescoes on Athos and at Mistra. He had also arranged to cover the Easter Week celebrations in Seville for the *Daily News*.

The party made leisurely stops on the way to Madrid staying a night at Burgos and at the monastery of Silos. On his first evening in the capital Robert stayed up late with Gavin drinking in a louche quarter of the city. The next four days were spent in haphazard sightseeing, which included a visit to the Escorial to inspect the famous El Greco of St Maurice and the Theban Legion. He stood entranced before the picture: 'it so wholly envelops the consciousness of the beholder', he recorded afterwards, 'as to translate him, physically and mentally, out of his environment into itself.'

Robert regretted his failure to organize himself on this first part of the trip. Recalling Lord Beauchamp's meticulous planning in Italy, he opined in his diary: 'in an unknown country, this is the ideal way of travelling. Then the sights are lifted from the conscience and it is possible to return another year and enjoy the country in greater detail. For those whose clue to a people's character and history lies in its creative art, the role of the thorough tourist is at first indispensable.'

Taking his cue from Lord Beauchamp, Robert planned his visit to Toledo in greater detail. In the course of a day, with tourist map in hand, he worked his way through all the El Grecos on view to the visitor. By the late afternoon, with the satisfaction of a task completed, he set off into the countryside to find a suitable eminence from which to draw a view of the city. 'This', he wrote, 'was the climax of my visit to Spain. I had seen the paintings . . . And now I saw the most beautiful town that I had ever seen, where the author of those paintings lived.' As the sun set behind him, the grouping of the city, the countryside and the river produced a feeling of total aesthetic satisfaction, when 'the whole earth seemed perfect, when no caprice remained ungratified, a minute robbed of desire, yet not merely content, but busy with enjoyment.' Dusk fell. Gathering his pencils, he climbed back up to the town. 'Life was shorter,' he concluded, 'yet now the more worth living.'

His response to the El Grecos in the city was far less intense. His remarks, jotted down in his diary, echo points made by the German art critic Julius Meier-Graefe in his extended commentary on the work of El Greco in *The Spanish Journey*, a book published in English in 1926, which Robert took to Spain and referred to constantly.

Meier-Graefe had visited Spain in 1906 to study at first hand the works of Velasquez, then considered the presiding genius of modern art. Within a week of arrival, Meier-Graefe experienced a dramatic conversion from being a conventional admirer of Velasquez to becoming a passionate disciple of El Greco: a revelation described in *The Spanish Journey*, first published in German in 1907, which helped to launch the rediscovery of El Greco. He lauded Greco for his 'inconceivable genius' and referred to Velasquez as 'a small creature', who borrowed from Greco's art. Robert disparages Velasquez in similar vein when writing to Henry Yorke from Toledo: 'as for El Greco – the point about him was that he was such a great man – it is that which emerges forcibly upon one – Velasquez on the other hand was only a great painter.'

In Seville, Robert had only one day to gather copy on the Easter Week celebrations for the *Daily News*. With mounting panic he spent Good Friday in the rain in search of religious processions, which did not emerge from their parish churches until the end of the afternoon. He watched the climax of the spectacle in the cathedral at dusk, with the showers of gold candle-points surrounding the floats as they paraded down the vast nave. Unlike the tourist-ridden scenes in the streets, Robert felt this ceremony to be an authentic display of religious emotion. It also caused him to revise his low opinion of Spanish gothic architecture; he accounted the cathedral of Seville the finest gothic interior he had ever seen. The following day, his article, glittering with ecclesiastical detail, was dispatched.

On Easter day they attended a bullfight. Driving away afterwards, having relished the drama of the spectacle, they found themselves swept by a stream of traffic into a promenade of carriages and antiquated automobiles. Each vehicle was emblazoned with an enormous coronet and coat of arms and bore two footmen on the box. Such an archaic social display was another example of the remoteness of Spanish life which Robert also found in the performances of flamenco and, not least, in the late hours of meals.

The Hotel Reina Christina at Algeciras, their next destination, had the advantage of being owned by Gavin's grandfather, Lord Faringdon, who had built it as part of his development of the Spanish railways. Heavily Edwardian in atmosphere, with stifling central heating, the hotel attracted a clientele of retired English colonels and upper-class family parties. Coming down to a high tea of ham and eggs, Robert encountered the unlikely figures of Osbert and Sacheverell Sitwell who were staying in the hotel to work. The Sitwells approved of Robert and in the lounge he overheard them recommending his work to another literary guest, the president of Harper's, the American publishing company.

Robert had formed a lukewarm sympathy for Moorish architecture after a visit to the Alcazar in Seville. At Granada it turned to pure loathing. He stomped round the Alhambra dodging the crowds of German and American tourists. 'The Alhambra was too awful –' he wrote to his mother, 'far uglier than we had thought possible.'

They took the road to Murcia and were astonished to come upon a settlement of troglodytes outside the town of Gaudix. 'As we approached,' he wrote, 'we saw all the hummocks contained houses . . . with doors and windows in the earth, and tall white chimneys sprouting from the top and sides like ninepins. The doors were all open, revealing normal lamplit rooms, full of normal household furniture.' Robert's last image of Spain was of the coastal road along the lagoons of the Mar Menor outside Cartagena, 'fringed with palms and windmills whose canvas sails hung listless in the hot air'. His working holiday of three weeks was over. He entrained to Barcelona and thence to London.

Robert's first task on his return was to find himself somewhere to live. He soon settled on a bed-sitting room in a small Georgian house at 6 Adam Street, next door to the Wallace Collection, where his rent including breakfast was £2 15s. a week. Over the next few months he would occasionally escape from there to Savernake, where he had to stay with the Byrons' cook, Mrs Clements, now that the house had been let.

Unlike most of his friends, Robert had no allowance from his family and he set out to support himself by journalism. His fee from the *Daily News* and for some photographs published in the *Sphere* paid for the Spanish trip; and he sold articles on Mount Athos to *Country Life* and the *Architectural Review* and another, on Spain, to *Vogue*. He undertook book reviewing for Oliver Locker Lampson, editor of the *Empire Review*, and he cultivated Desmond MacCarthy, who was planning the launch of *Life and Letters*, a literary monthly.

Robert hoped that once *The Station* was out, a publisher would pay a sufficient advance for him to undertake another journey, possibly to Russia or America, 'but I shouldn't go [for] under £200 down & another £100 in prospect from articles etc,' he wrote to his mother, having already mapped out the economics of travel writing. There were also two books on the stocks requiring attention. One was his history of post-classical Greece, commissioned by Warburg two years previously, the other was *The Station*, proofs of which were awaiting correction on his return from Spain.

Long before the book was finished, Robert had begun his publicity offensive. A long briefing note was dispatched to Patrick Balfour, gossip columnist on the *Daily Sketch*, with the request: 'do use it if you can – you know I am avid for publicity, so if you can work in my name, do.' Patrick proved a staunch ally, making frequent reference to 'Mr Robert Byron, the clever young writer and authority on things Byzantine'. On the morning of 14 June 1928, the day of publication, a prospectus of the book dropped through the letter boxes of Robert's friends and relations. Other targets included Orthodox bishops, tutors at Eton and Oxford, and unsuspecting neighbours of the Byrons in Wiltshire. That evening, with Gavin in attendance armed with two cocktail shakers, Robert gave a party 'to entertain all possible reviewers' in the house of George Schurhof, another old Oxford friend, in Mayfair.

The Station was widely and sympathetically reviewed, with the subject of the Holy Mountain providing critics with excellent copy. Of the popular press, the *Daily Mail* pronounced *The Station* to be 'a wholly delightful book . . . brimful of ideas', whilst the *Sketch* predicted for the author 'a big literary future'. One common complaint, summed up by the *Manchester Guardian*, was of 'the self-conscious facetiousness which is the bane of so many writers of such books'. However criticism was usually softened by generous praise. Arnold Bennett, who had been handed a copy by Osbert Sitwell over dinner, had reservations, but his influential column in the *Evening Standard* began: '*The Station* reveals a travel writer of sly urbane wit and all inclusive observation, with a sense of style and refreshing vocabulary.' D. H. Lawrence gave the book a glowing review in *Vogue*, opening: 'Athos is an old place, and Mr Byron is a young man. The combination for once is *really* happy.'

His writing on architecture attracted the warmest notices. In a considered review, the *Spectator*, which was critical of the opening chapter and the author's style, singled out the comparison between Simopetra and the Potala. The *Nation* quoted at length from the same passage. On the evidence of *The Station*, various reviewers placed Robert in the tradition of Kinglake and Curzon.

Another contemporary on the cusp of fame was Evelyn Waugh. His recently published biography of Rossetti had been generally well received and he was currently putting the finishing touches to his first novel, *Decline and Fall*. The two old Oxford friends saw a great deal of one another that summer. Evelyn had moved into rooms round the corner from Robert in order to be closer to his fiancée Evelyn Gardner, who was living in Montagu Place. The couple spent much of their time with Robert 'as their own rooms are so disgusting'. The Waughs' wedding at the end of the month was attended by only four people. Harold Acton was best man and Robert gave away the bride. Sensing an underlying lack of enthusiasm, he complained to his mother beforehand: 'It really is too awful – I have to fetch Evelyn Gardner to the church & I know she won't come.' In the event, all went according to plan. He saw the couple again that autumn when He-Evelyn presented him with a copy of the manuscript of *Decline and Fall*, recently published to huge acclaim. As a further token of friendship, he went on to name Robert, in the *Sunday Dispatch*, as one of five young writers to embody the spirit of their generation.

Robert's excitement over the publication of *The Station* made him restless. He could no longer concentrate on the history book and longed for a break from mental effort. His parents, who after a difficult start had adapted to life in Vienna, planned to take an apartment in the picturesque mountain resort of St Wolfgang in Upper Austria for July and August. Robert decided to join them. In mid-July he left for Salzburg, arriving two days later at the village of St Wolfgang by paddle steamer from the local station on the other side of the lake. 'I was immediately in the bosom of my family . . .' he wrote, 'the last dust of London cast from my soles.'

It was high season in the Salzkammergut. Various English friends were staying in the village, and Michael Rosse and John Sutro also came out to join the Byron family party. Robert spent the next few days overcome with exhaustion. Gradually the holiday spirit took hold: 'crags & trees –' he jotted down in his diary, 'the architecture cabin like – huge roofs – the flowers . . . hare bells, gentian . . . edelweiss –

steamers, motor boats fast and slow, yachts, rowing boats . . . train to Ischl . . . the wild strawberry ices . . . charabanc home . . .'

One month later, Robert left for Vienna to join Algy and Freddie Sladen, an English couple who had arranged for him and John Sutro to accompany them on a round of visits to Czechoslovakian country houses. The Sladens were well-known figures in central Europe and brimmed with introductions to good families. In return they expected to have their expenses paid.

Robert was entering territory where the new boundaries of Austria, Hungary and Czechoslovakia converged. His first destination was Pressburg, renamed Bratislava, but known by Hungarians as Pozony. Robert left ahead of the Sladens, driven by their friend the Count Charles Esterházy. He met up with John Sutro at the Carlton Hotel in Pressburg and the Sladens arrived after dinner. At 10.30 p.m. the party set off for the country house of Böös, forty kilometres away, a seat of the Count Vichlitz-Amade. Getting hopelessly lost, they did not arrive until 6 a.m. The butler and a bevy of housemaids ushered them off to bed. Robert rose at lunchtime to meet his host for the first time.

The Count and Countess Vichlitz-Amade presided over a large house-party of friends and relations who had come from Germany, Switzerland and most parts of central Europe to celebrate the Count's birthday. The Vichlitz-Amade family had owned Böös for centuries, although they only spent three months of the year at the house. Originally a fortress, it had been remodelled in the eighteenth century around a courtyard as a two-storeyed house with cream walls and a high shingled roof. The main rooms were furnished with provincial Empire furniture and hung with family portraits. Suits of armour, antique weapons as well as antlers adorned the public corridor on the first floor.

The next five days were measured out with heavy meals. Lunch and dinner were of five or six courses, waited on by the butler and three footmen, bearing in gloved hands silver platters of food decorated with flowers. In the evening the staff wore black livery with red waistcoats, black satin breeches and buckled shoes. After dinner, the butler placed two tureens of *bole* in large bowls of ice on the sideboard. The cup was flavoured with wild strawberries and made from brandy, champagne, pineapple and other ingredients. The party drank until the early hours and danced to old tunes on the gramophone.

Robert's schoolboy German became increasingly fluent under the pressure of making polite conversation. Particular members of the house party came into focus: the Baroness Hochberg, a member of the minor German squirearchy; the Countess Froissart, owner of coffee plantations in Brazil, and married to a Swiss arms dealer; the Countess Welchersheim, widow of an Imperial ambassador, now retired to Graz. Since the break-up of the Empire many members of the house party had acquired new nationalities. The Vichlitz-Amades themselves had switched from Hungarian to Czech nationality to prevent the confiscation of Boos.

Conversation often turned to the horrors of the post-war years. Count Amade related how his house in Hungary was saved from the clutches of the Romanians. Countess Froissart described the famine in Vienna in 1919 when tramloads of coffins creaked down the Ring at night. But the predominant topic was the Jews. 'Everyone says everyone is a Jew – in fact the conversation is about nothing else – I hope John doesn't mind . . .' Robert wrote to his mother, 'I suppose it is synonymous with every kind of success.'

The awkward social standing of prosperous Jews was revealed one evening when the Count invited 'some useful people' who rented land off him to dine. They turned out to be a middle-aged Jewish couple, the wife smartly dressed in red, and their exquisite dandy of a son. The young man spoke fluent English with an American accent and immediately addressed Robert on the subject of grouse moors and bridge. Robert abhorred his 'sophistication and arrogance' which he considered 'would have been antipathetic even in England'. However, he enjoyed talking to his mother about the antique shops in Pressburg. Only one tureen of *bole* was produced that evening. After dinner the young man danced the tango to universal admiration. Robert turned his gaze upon the rapt spectators: 'On the sofa . . .' he wrote in his diary with remarkable percipience, 'sat Countess Welchersheim, Jimmy the son of the house, and the little dark-haired woman in red – the whole problem of Germany and all Mittel Europa seemed to be symbolized in that trio.'

A grand dinner was held to celebrate the Count's birthday and the table was decorated with a mass of flowers and candles. At the end of the meal the shutters were suddenly thrown back to reveal a gypsy orchestra on the terrace. White and red wine, champagne, an ancient Swedish punch, liqueurs and coffee were brought. The Count and Countess danced the Csardas and the party foxtrotted and waltzed over the stone flags of the terrace. After midnight they went upstairs. Four tureens of *bole* were produced, two having already been consumed. Robert performed his imitation of Queen Victoria, using a face towel as a widow's cap, John Sutro yelled out patriotic songs at the piano to great acclaim. At dawn they danced wildly to the beat of 'Granada' in the manner of the Russian ballet. The sun rose and the butler appeared, still dressed in livery, having fallen asleep on duty. Robert went to bed in broad daylight only to be woken at 8 a.m. by Sladen, to pack for their departure in two hours' time.

Over the next four days, the Sladens' Buick became a familiar sight parked outside the portals of castles and country houses, as the party progressed north in the direction of Prague. They lunched with Countess Esterházy at Galanta and stayed with Count Chominsky at Wessels, walking up with his guns the next day. Guests at the same house party invited them to stay in their villa outside Brno. Robert undertook some diligent sightseeing in the town and visited the exhibition ground to photograph the 'excessively modern' pavilions, pioneering works in the Bauhaus style. Two more houses were fitted in before the weekend; and they also deposited John Sutro, looking quite helpless, at a station to catch the train for Vienna.

The Sladens' tour ended with a weekend at Castolovice, in eastern Bohemia, the principal seat of Count Sternberg. Life at Castolovice was on a far grander scale even than at Böös. On his first evening Robert's suitcase, full of dirty clothes, was unpacked for him and he had two men to help him change into his crumpled evening clothes. Colonel Sladen was in an even more shameful situation as he found himself in possession of John Sutro's evening shoes instead of his own.

The house itself, part Renaissance and part Gothic Revival, was heavily luxurious. Modern parquet floors mirrored the gilded and panelled ceilings. Portraits of kings and emperors stared down from the walls. Outside, the garden was bedded out on an elaborate scale and the stables housed a stud of yellow horses. The weekend was spent loitering by the tennis court, swimming, riding and visiting local sights.

Robert parted company with the Sladens in Prague. His desire to 'see Prague in a day' led him to consider taking a coach tour but in the end he tramped round the sights with guidebook in hand. The city was hosting a congress of the World Alliance of Churches and the day was spent dodging Anglican clergy and their wives. Despite his disgust at the clerical hordes, the beauty of Prague, which he found so different from that of Vienna, reconciled him to the nationalism of the Czechs.

Robert spent the next six weeks in Vienna. Apart from working on his history book, he was also gathering material for a travel essay on the city which he hoped to publish alongside a polished-up version of his country-house tour. Robert's researches led him to cafés, nightclubs and Madame Sacher's new bar where he drank gin fizz and met useful acquaintances. He lodged with the Countess Auersperg, who like many of her class had fallen on hard times. The bath water was rationed and he was only allowed one light in his room. Soon after his arrival she was declared bankrupt. The grasping natives, from grandee landladies to cloakroom attendants, increasingly irritated Robert, and his sojourn in Vienna was peppered with rows, although the presence of his family near by offered frequent distraction.

His life however was considerably brightened by the arrival of Bryan Guinness who turned up on 9 September, 'frantic with love'. Earlier in the summer Bryan had fallen for the eighteen-year-old daughter of Lord and Lady Redesdale, Diana Mitford. In July he had proposed marriage, which she had accepted, but her parents had still to approve the match. Another to express concern was Bryan's closest friend, Michael Rosse. A letter received from him in Vienna sent

Bryan into an even greater fever. Robert, who was proving 'inexhaustibly sympathetic' to his emotional turmoil, reproved Michael, but in so doing revealed unusual foresight.

> As a matter of fact, I think Diana Mitford is particularly charming, very pretty, & amusing in a way which one seldom meets & which is not at all that of the ordinary debutante trying to be clever . . . the truth of it all is of course that Bryan is still monstrously young . . . What he little knows is that he has fallen in love with a girl who will soon be much older than he ever can be.

Robert and Bryan went out of Vienna one day to meet Diana's brother, Tom, who, after Eton, was learning German as a paying guest at Schloss Bernstein in the province of Burgenland. Already steeped in Germanic culture, Tom appeared wearing lederhosen and an art blue silk tie. The acquaintance was renewed some time later when Tom visited Robert in Vienna. Afterwards Robert noted: 'we have a very enjoyable evening and morning discussing the ethics of the sexual act and wondering how much each knows of the other's past.' Tom, like Robert, had had schoolboy flings, which he was quite open about with his sisters. He was to confide to a friend, Etienne Amyot, met later in Berlin, that he had also had a brief affair with Robert.

Physically, Robert could not compete with Tom's matinée looks. According to Christopher Sykes' later description, Robert was 'moderately fat, short, with very fair hair, a penetrating rolling eye, a face of distinction, somewhat like that shown in portraits of the Bourbon kings'. The essence of his attraction, as Etienne Amyot pointed out, lay 'in his conversation, his use of speech, his feeling when asked his opinion'. The intensity of his manner was conveyed by Roy Harrod. He remembered him as having 'a very special voice, low toned, a little nasal, and also, although quiet, very emphatic. His words seemed to be forced out with some effort from some deep recess of body or soul. He often spoke with lowered eyelids, but then relented and revealed his beautiful eyes.' Robert's powers of attraction, however, did not seem to include a capacity for romance. His affair with Leonard

Bower had fizzled out towards the end of his long sojourn in Athens, and that with Tom, who was anyway poised to fall for women, settled down into a long and close friendship.

Gavin Henderson, who was returning to England from Athens with a friend, David Fyfe, also made an appearance in Vienna. He looked like death from various fevers picked up on the way, but was still capable of joining Robert on a tour of the bars. Both Bryan and Gavin happened to leave Vienna on the same day, at the beginning of October, plunging Robert into gloom. He had already complained to Henry Yorke of the dullness of the Viennese; however, he added: 'There is a revolution on Sunday – we are fearfully excited, except my father who takes it all quite seriously.'

On Sunday 7 October 1928 two rival demonstrations were planned in the town of Wiener Neustadt by the Fascists and the Social Democrats, both quasi-military organizations. The government mobilized thousands of troops to prevent a clash between the two, turning the small industrial town into a military encampment. On the day before the demonstrations Robert and his mother visited the town to inspect the arrangements. They found the market square ringed by grim-faced soldiers with machine guns. Political tension remained high and the following Sunday Robert witnessed 'a tremendous procession in the Ring with banners blazoned "Heil Hitler"'.

Robert's political and social antennae monitored the dislocation felt by a country ruthlessly cut down to size in defeat, but left with the outsize trappings of an empire. He was shocked by what he saw as the craze for all things modern: 'the modern hotel – the modern train – dreadful idea of modern life – instead of a development of old life – no continuity – why is this?' It also blunted his aesthetic sensibility. The masterpieces of Fischer von Erlach were dismissed as shallow 'like the people'. The only baroque which found favour with Robert was the plasterwork and mirrors at the Tabarin nightclub; and when the band was occasionally persuaded to play a waltz and the Viennese upper classes took to the floor, the effect, in his view, was magnificent.

Robert's train steamed out of Vienna on 15 October, leaving a knot of outraged officials on the platform, who had been worsted in his final row in the city, over railway regulations.

Robert's loathing of officialdom was not confined to foreigners. At Wiesbaden he was turned out of his carriage to make way for the British military. He vented his anger on the 'barbarity' of the Allies' occupation of the Rhineland, which so pleased the conductor that he put Robert in first class for the rest of the journey. He arrived back in London in time to attend Gavin Henderson's farewell dinner. He was escaping England for a while, flying off the following day to India.

13

Byzantine Enthusiasms

As soon as Robert returned to England in October 1928, Routledge pressed him for the delivery of the manuscript of his history book. The project had taken two years to come to fruition. The first draft had been written in London between November 1926 and June 1927 based on the research carried out during his five-month sojourn in Greece. This work was interrupted by his second visit to Mount Athos and his subsequent completion of *The Station*.

Returning to the subject in February 1928, Robert was faced with having to curtail the scope of his project. Originally, he had planned to write a history of Greece in two parts, divided between the Byzantine Empire and the upheavals in the Eastern Mediterranean at the end of the Great War. However, so far, only the Byzantine section had been completed.

Faced with further delay, Frederic Warburg decided to publish this as a separate volume in its own right. Bowing to the inevitable, Robert set about revising his existing work, which was to be published as *The Byzantine Achievement*, finally delivering the manuscript towards the end of November 1928.

The first chapter opens with a fanfare introducing the reader to the concept of the modern historian, whom Robert describes as 'the high priest of the instant'. His own generation, he announces, is poised on the footboard of a new civilization as it hurtles towards a future that brings with it scientific discoveries such as television and space travel. The historian alone can assist in the peaceful assimilation of the 'advancing epoch', for only by studying 'the centennially and millennially repeated incidents and trends of history' can one make sense of the present and the future.

His rhetoric was inspired by the theories of the German

historian, Oswald Spengler, the first volume of whose book *The Decline of the West* had been published in English in 1926. The long introduction, summarizing Spengler's visionary theories of world history, had been read avidly by Robert that December just as he was embarking on the opening chapters of *The Byzantine Achievement.*

Spengler's potency, which had already brought him a huge following in Germany, lay in his skill at pitching his arguments at the post-war generation, claiming that only they had been born with the ability to understand his theories. Addressing them as the 'leading minds of the coming time', he defined their qualities in terms that perfectly mirrored Robert's intellectual standpoint.

> A thinker is a person whose part is to symbolize time according to his vision and understanding. He has no choice; he thinks as he has to think. Truth in the long run is the picture of the world which was born at his birth. It is that which he does not invent but rather discovers within himself. It is himself over again: his being expressed in words; the meaning of his personality formed into a doctrine which so far as concerns his life is unalterable, because truth and his life are identical.

Spengler believed there was a layer of meaning to historical events deeper than mere cause and effect. He traces it to the 'logic of time' or simply 'destiny' which forms predetermined patterns in history, repeated across centuries and through the rise and fall of civilizations. Identifying such structures was impossible to the purely rational mind, he explains, as it requires the gift of 'the deepest inward certainty', allied to the scientific use of historical analogy.

The ranking of intuition above reason was singled out by Robert as the mark of Spengler's modernity. His acknowledgement occurs in a draft passage of *The Byzantine Achievement* concerning the transcendental element in civilizations, which he terms 'the great soul' that exists in man beneath his everyday appearance, 'ever striving to attain, to reach, to soar above the mental gravities of earth'. It is this, Robert went on, 'expressed in such philosophies as that of

Spengler which is in revolt today against that perennial governess of Western progress, Classicism'.

The Decline of the West reflected in its title Spengler's belief that classical civilization could no longer claim pre-eminence over other world cultures. Instead of hailing the Greeks as sophisticated exemplars for the contemporary age, he painted them as primitive myth-makers, slow to develop an alphabet, whose reputation rested upon a misleading body of ancient writings, termed by him a 'pedagogue's anthology', that had fixed an 'imaginary picture of "Classical Antiquity"' in the Western mind. Warming to his theme, Spengler stated that in 'all history there is no analogous case of one Culture making a passionate cult of the memory of another . . . We Westerners have sacrificed on the Classical altar the purity and independence of our art . . . We have projected our own deepest spiritual needs and feelings on to the Classical picture' which, he continued, was in reality 'a phantom, an idol'. Such radical precepts were enthusiastically applauded by Robert, who marked these and other passages with fierce scrawls of his pen. Here, at last, was a powerful voice bestowing authority upon his own anti-classical prejudices.

In Part I of *The Byzantine Achievement*, he did not hold back from attacking the allies of classicism. Chief among his targets were the 'classico-rationalist' historian, William Lecky, the nineteenth-century anthropologist Fallmerayer, and above all Edward Gibbon, author of the *Decline and Fall of the Roman Empire*, who were indicted for their moralistic prejudice against the Byzantine Empire. Reaching for an appropriate analogy, he likened Gibbon's choice of source material to a chronicler of contemporary America relying solely on the veracity of the Hearst press.

Having exorcized these malignant ghosts, Robert embarks on his analysis of historical fact. His approach is not chronological. The succession of imperial dynasties, of wars and of religious upheavals is recounted in one chapter. Five further chapters cover in turn government, trade, religion, culture and society. This structure was suggested by one of his principal sources, *The Byzantine Empire* by Norman Baynes, published in 1925, which Robert had read and noted at the outset of his researches.

Baynes's bibliography also proved to be of great value. It launched Robert upon an impressive course of reading that extended from early travellers' accounts to the most up-to-date authority on the bezant. Robert never disguised his reliance upon others. An author's note emphasized that the work was 'in no sense one of research among original sources'. As he explained to John Mavrogordato, a friend met through the Anglo-Hellenic League: 'My object is not to advance scholarship, but general appreciation of things Byzantine.'

In treating Byzantine history thematically, Robert, like Baynes, underlined the stability of Byzantine society, centred on Constantinople, regardless of the growing number of disasters both inside and outside the city's walls, from its foundation in 330 AD to its sack by the Fourth Crusade in 1204. One element, he argued, even provided a 'continuous link between the ancient world and the modern'. This was Roman law, preserved under the Empire and reintroduced to the West after the dark ages.

A vivid illustration of Robert's belief in the undying legacy of Byzantine civilization was his portrayal of Constantinople, a city, he claimed, which still preserved the original plan in all 'essential points of importance' as laid down at the time of its dedication. The reader is introduced to its topography as if on a boat sailing up the Bosphorus.

> Seventeen miles long, in places no wider than 600 yards, this magic creek winds through a double range of hills . . . The hills are thick with dwarf oaks, junipers and bay-trees, crowned occasionally with gaunt pines, and mingled with bracken, giant heath and yellow flowering broom. The air grows soft with a distant smell of pinks. There are signs of habitation, boats and gardens, then the villas and palaces themselves.

Robert based his description, not on any historical account, but on his own observations jotted down on one of his visits to Constantinople in 1926. His use of the present tense, however, refers not to that occasion, but to the day when Constantine chose Byzantium as the seat of his empire.

Borrowing Sacheverell Sitwell's technique of time travel, Robert suggests by this means the immediacy of the past before going on to describe the city under the first emperors.

The Byzantine Achievement culminates in a sweeping narrative of the events that brought about the downfall of the empire. Much of Robert's inspiration was drawn from the writings of Edwin Pears, which had so gripped him on his first visit to Constantinople. Apart from the volume entitled *The Destruction of the Greek Empire*, he had also read *The Fall of Constantinople*, a stirring account of the other great disaster to befall the city, its sack in 1204 by the Fourth Crusade.

Robert uses telling detail to condemn the barbarism of the crusaders. He enumerates one outrage after another, ending with their acts of sacrilege: 'the loading of church plate on mules brought to the very altars; the violation of the imperial tombs; the caparisoning of horses in sacred vestments; the enthronement of a prostitute in the patriarchal chair of St Sophia'. Their crimes rankled with Robert as though they had been committed within living memory. His consequent hatred of Catholic Europe is felt throughout the book. Of the Church's position since the Reformation, he wrote:

> Catholicism must appear a bastard aberration from the main body of Christendom; a product of obsolete Mediterranean materialism which henceforth played no part with Christianity in man's discovery of Reality . . . which extinguished all intellectual and material progress wherever its influence was strongest; and finally, which outraged, separately and in the aggregate, every canon of behaviour which enables a human being to dwell in amity with his neighbour.

If this were not enough, he warns readers in the bibliography against the 'feminine spite' of Catholic and Anglo-Catholic writers on the subject.

By contrast, the story of the last day of the empire before Constantinople finally fell to the Ottomans is elegiac in tone. On Monday 28 May 1453, a vast religious procession makes its way to Santa Sophia:

For the last time the Byzantines assemble. They receive the divine mysteries. Emperor and Patriarch bid public farewell: the temporal state doomed to extinction and the Church that must live. Then all go to their posts. And stationing themselves between the first and second walls, lock the doors behind them, so that retreat is impossible.

Writing *The Byzantine Achievement* had given Robert the education that Oxford had failed to deliver. In one chapter alone, on Byzantine civilization, he touches upon the spread of Mithraism, the spiritual roots of Judaism, the impact of Alexander the Great's sculptors upon the Buddhist carvers of northern India and the early Iranian influence upon Armenian church architecture. The geographical scope of his subject is conveyed in his description of the commerce of Constantinople: 'from every degree of the compass came the caravans and fleets . . . from India came pepper and musk . . . from Persia, sugar . . . and before the eruption of the Mongol races beyond the Oxus, porcelain from China and glass from Mesopotamia.'

His growing curiosity in the East found confirmation in Spengler's acclamation of alien cultures. Robert scored his pen repeatedly in urgent agreement alongside the following passage in *Decline of the West.*

> I see in place of that empty figment of one linear history . . . the drama of a number of mighty cultures, each springing with primitive strength from the soil of a mother region . . . Each culture has its own new possibilities of self-expression . . . There is not one sculpture, one painting, one mathematics, one physics, but many, each in its deepest essence different from the others.

Spengler had written Robert's manifesto for him. The time was shortly to come when he would spread his wings to become, in Spengler's words, a 'pathfinder for tomorrow', and explore the great civilizations of other continents.

As *The Byzantine Achievement* went forward to the press, Robert viewed the prospect of publication with increasing nervousness: no one at Routledge had found time to read the manuscript. Fortunately, John Mavrogordato, an experienced publisher's reader and an expert on Byzantine literature, agreed to check the proofs for factual errors. Robert also showed them to Sacheverell Sitwell during a visit to Weston, the Sitwells' house in Northamptonshire. His response was 'very favourable', causing Robert to feel more at ease. However, Sitwell's private opinion was less generous. He told his wife Georgia only that 'it is quite good and better than the book on Athos.'

Routledge was equally forbearing in the matter of the book's production, allowing Robert to design 'a heavenly' title page and choose coarse buckram of 'very deep delphinium blue' for the binding, which was stamped in gilt with a heraldic device. Great care was also taken over the illustrations. The book's handsome appearance was in stark contrast to the only comparable title published in recent years, Norman Baynes's *Byzantine Empire*, which had been both unillustrated and produced in the dull 'pocket' format of the 'Home University Library'.

The Byzantine Achievement was published on April 1929 to a flood of reviews. The author's violent opinions and, in the words of the *Manchester Guardian*, 'the very superabundance of his enthusiasm' gave the reviewers plenty to get their teeth into. His early reputation enhanced as a 'brilliant young traveller', Robert's latest work was hailed by the *Daily Mail* as 'a brilliant book [which] places its writer in the front rank of historical writers'. One or two reviewers expressed reservations about the style, whilst the critic Edward Shanks, in the *Saturday Review*, condemned Robert's bias against the Roman Catholic Church: 'exhilarating as it may be, it is as dangerous a fault in an historian as Gibbon's refusal to take a Christian state seriously.' Nonetheless, most reviewers came down in favour of the book, many conceding, in the words of the *Daily News*, that 'its subject is one which most of us have unduly neglected.' In making the Byzantines 'thoroughly alive', as the *Sunday Times* acknowledged, Robert had opened the eyes of the general reader to the importance of the Byzantine world.

Not all the publicity that accrued to Robert at this period

was connected to such highbrow causes. 'I am supposed to be going to a fancy dress lunch at the Trocadero,' he had informed his mother at the end of January, 'a bogus wedding party in Trocadero clothes i.e. 1921.' The invitation had been issued by the irrepressible Elizabeth Ponsonby, who was taking the part of the bride. Other members of the cast included John Rayner as the groom, Oliver Messel as an usher and Babe Plunket Greene, who had been briefly married to David, as 'the undesirable relation'. Robert, resplendent in bowler hat, buttonhole and waxed moustache, was to be the best man.

The party sat at a special table at the centre of the restaurant, causing a great stir amongst the usual lunchers. Oliver Messel proposed the toast and John Rayner stammered a reply. A clergyman seated at a nearby table, unaware that it was a mock wedding, was encouraged to join the party. He gave the couple his unofficial blessing and he too made 'a merry speech'. They were then seen off under a shower of rose petals, hotly pursued by the press.

'Mock Marriage Luncheon – Our Bright Young People – Parson Hoaxed', sang one headline. 'Mock Wedding Antics – "Best Man" In Old Bowler And Frock Coat', trilled another. After a relatively quiet period, the Bright Young People were back in the news.

The term had first been applied in 1924 to a thoroughly respectable set, led by Zita and Teresa Jungman, Eleanor Smith and Loelia Ponsonby, a first cousin of Elizabeth, whose father was Treasurer to King George V. At Zita Jungman's instigation they had devised a series of treasure hunts across London, consisting of ingenious clues, which usually ended up at a grand private house. Everyone joined in the fun. Lord Beaverbrook even printed a special edition of the *Evening Standard* for the benefit of one treasure hunt.

The precise moment when Elizabeth Ponsonby grabbed the mantle from her younger cousin and friends is lost in the noise and chatter of the freak parties, stunts and scavenger hunts which, to journalists' delight, she so loved to organize. Robert was appalled to discover that after the mock wedding his press cuttings account was exhausted in one day. News of the event even reached his mother in Vienna:

> I had another more horrible paper sent me about that mock wedding – I do call it third rate & can't *think* how you can let yourself be dragged into that sort of thing with that girl in it too – you are doing yourself harm by that sort of publicity – disgusting . . . you have got some friends of the wrong sort dear boy & I wish you'd drop them.

Margaret Byron need not have worried. That March, Elizabeth announced her engagement to Mr Dennis Pelly. She had only known him for a fortnight which caused many to suspect that it was another joke. 'It will not be a mock wedding this time!' she announced to the press and in July they were married. The era of the Bright Young People was over. Shortly afterwards, Evelyn Waugh, his marriage by now in ruins, completed its picaresque obituary in a novel published the following year as *Vile Bodies*.

The opening months of 1929 saw a number of adjustments to Robert's circle of friends. Alfred Duggan briefly re-entered his life, having returned from a sojourn in Constantinople engaged to the Ambassador's secretary, Miss Sylvia Nairn. He invited Robert to be best man, but explained that his fiancée, the daughter of a retired headmaster, had insisted upon a long engagement to test his ability to moderate his drinking. Alfred expressed optimism on this count. 'At the moment', he told Robert, 'I am doing a regime of being teetatoller [*sic*] in pubs and hotels and drinking with my meals in private houses.' In January Miss Nairn broke off the engagement. Part of the reason was that Alfred had refused to submit to psychoanalysis to effect a cure. 'I don't believe in psychoanalysis', he complained to Robert, 'and I don't want to be cured.' He was dispatched on a cruise to Barbados with a keeper who had rowed for Oxford in 1906. As Alfred sailed away, he wrote to Robert triumphantly of having thrice won the ship's sweepstake which required standing 'a drink to everyone in the bar and then to have one stood back'. This, he reassured him, 'has kept me going'.

One couple to make it to the altar was Bryan Guinness and Diana Mitford. They were married at St Margaret's, Westminster, on 30 January 1929, the Redesdales having finally given their consent the previous autumn, on Bryan's return from Vienna. Robert acted as Chief Usher although he avoided ushering a single person. Patrick Balfour fed readers in the *Daily Sketch* with a tit-bit on the marriage: 'Mr Byron has designed an original wedding present . . . It is a book-plate, and bears the legend: "Stolen from Bryan and Diana Guinness."'

Their engagement had resulted in Robert renewing his acquaintance with Diana's eldest sister, Nancy. They had first met earlier in the summer of 1928 through Mark Ogilvie-Grant and Nina Seafield when an afternoon had been spent at Savernake 'talking & playing the gramophone'. Nancy was much taken with her new friend and they went on to meet occasionally at parties. A passionate reader, she also immersed herself in *The Station*: 'quite brilliant,' she told her father, 'I am simply loving it although it overthrows all my hitherto most cherished ideas. It's very amusing too.'

That autumn Nancy wrote to Robert inviting him to stay at Swinbrook, the Redesdales' house in Oxfordshire, with Bryan and Diana. Not wishing to appear forward, she had begun her letter: 'Dear Mr Byron . . .' The acceptance came back: 'Dear Nancy, I won't call you Miss Mitford & should our correspondence develop please don't address me as if I were the local auctioneer.' Nancy, who had spent much of the past four years since her coming out dance practising the art of mockery on conventional young men, had finally met her match. The weekend proved a wild success. Robert charmed the Mitford parents, Lord and Lady Redesdale, and threw himself into the activities of the house party. They rode, visited Warwick Castle and, at his suggestion, organized a human hunt across the countryside with Nancy and Diana donning their old Girl Guide uniforms for the chase.

'Isn't Robert simply killing,' Nancy wrote excitedly to Tom. 'I love it when he talks about poetry & books, he seems to hate everything, which ordinary people like! Somebody mentioned Keats & he gave an awful look & said "That man".' Both discovered that they shared the same love of exaggeration. 'Robert wants you and me to go for a riding tour with him in Spain next Easter . . .' Tom was informed.

'We thought we could buy gored horses out of the bull ring and sew them up with straw.'

After the weekend, Robert reported back to Michael Rosse that he was 'prejudiced still further in favour of the Mitford family – I haven't laughed so much in a long time.' The two sisters, as he gleefully admitted to Nancy in his bread and butter letter, had quite simply bewitched him: 'your parents', he wrote, 'must be accustomed by now to demure, retiring & saintly minded people being transformed by you & Diana into human fiends.' For Nancy, the weekend had been unalloyed joy. 'I've never', she crowed to Tom, 'enjoyed a party in this house so much before.'

Many years later, she admitted to her sister Jessica that 'I would have liked to marry Robert . . .' Disappointment still lingered in the explanation that followed: 'but he was a total pederast . . . This wretched pederasty falsifies all feelings & yet one is supposed to revere it.' During the first burst of their friendship, the warmth of her affection was reciprocated by Robert as far as his nature would permit. Indeed, so solicitous was he of Nancy that Henry Yorke taxed him with being secretly engaged. 'His way with her', he told Evelyn Waugh, 'is rather that of "a man with a maid".'

Instead they settled for a deep, uncomplicated friendship. Nancy testified to their closeness when she wrote some years after his death: 'I found it almost impossible to convey to people who didn't know him what absolute heaven he was. I've never known anyone so complex – even his physical appearance was entirely unlike his character.' Reflecting upon him to another friend, she wrote: 'I think of all the dead, except relations, I miss Robert the most . . . It's the jokes.'

If Nancy was becoming one of the most important friends in his life, another, Henry Yorke, was on the point of drifting away. An initial upset had occurred after a party in February 1928 when Henry had complained about the behaviour of certain guests, including three of Robert's closest friends, Brian Howard, Bryan Guinness and Patrick Balfour: 'you must promise me', Henry had insisted, 'never to let me in for anything like that party again. Arty high life is not my line.'

An acid reply was dispatched forthwith: 'just because you

can discover human nature only in celebrities or the lower classes,' Robert retaliated, 'it is no reason to pour your yellow bile over the more normal . . . whom I . . . find the more interesting.' Their friendship was strong enough to survive this fierce squall. After all, they had been intimates since Eton and each was a favourite of the other's family – so much so that, for Christmas 1928, Robert went to stay at Forthampton whilst Henry journeyed to Vienna to spend it with the Byrons.

But one problem continued to undermine their relations. Both disliked the other's books and could not refrain from saying so. Henry's experimental fiction in the manner of Joyce and Woolf could not have been more different from Robert's richly hued works that were, to use Henry's expression, 'loaded on fact'. Eventually, their practice of 'aesthetic sincerity' turned sour. Mild criticism by Robert of the proposed title of Henry's new novel led to a furious spat. Countering a rebuke from Henry, he pointed out: 'I didn't really see as you had told me so often how disgusting you thought "The Station," & how even more disgusting, shocking in fact, its contents – I didn't see why I might not say I preferred one of yr titles to the other. I didn't think that could offend.'

The arrival of a copy of *Living*, an evocation of factory life in Birmingham, published in the spring of 1929 under Henry's pseudonym, Henry Green, gave Robert the chance to make peace. 'I do congratulate you,' he wrote. 'It is so much firmer, and the form so much more pronounced and economical than Blindness. The actual details of your prose are not, as you know to my taste – any more than mine to yours. But I must admit that you have redeemed that style from the mere Joyce "slice of life", and put it to its proper use.' If this were not enough, he even gave the book a glowing review in *Life and Letters*.

Their critical exchange thus ended in a fine display of good manners. This behaviour was to characterize their friendship from now on as they never regained their old intimacy. Another reason was Henry's marriage that summer to Adele Biddulph, known as Dig, the beautiful daughter of grand county neighbours of the Yorkes. Although Robert was fond of Dig, he had admitted to Henry long before the engagement, apropos their argument over the merits of 'arty high life', that conventional grandees such as the Biddulphs were a closed book to him.

One friendship that was deepening throughout this period was with Michael Rosse. They met whenever both happened to be in London, often joined by Michael's beautiful sister, Bridget. An early summer holiday in 1929 was also spent at Birr.

Since Robert's return from Vienna in the autumn of 1928, he had been living at Savernake, making only periodic visits to London, where he stayed with friends. His reoccupation of the house had been made possible by the premature departure of the Byrons' tenant, Lady Briggs, who had been driven out by the mice and the general discomfort. Considerable efforts had been made to relet the property, but there had been no further takers.

Robert immediately made himself at home, filling the drawing room with 'enormous sprays of dead beech leaves' and bowls of flowers. 'I find the solitude most delightful,' he wrote to Henry Yorke. 'I devour it – the wind is whistling and banging – the fire flickering with pretended gaiety – I can't *tell* you how gloomy it is and how I enjoy it.' Mrs Clements cooked for him although he found her food increasingly inedible. So, too, did Mark Ogilvie-Grant when he came to stay for five days and was served the same joint of salt beef and rabbit pie at every meal. Mark's abiding memory was going for long walks in the forest where Robert would stride out in his plus fours of pink and blue tweed, waving a walking stick and yelling after the family's elk hound, Gerda. When she bounded up to him, he would bury his teeth in the dog's fur.

The winter proved to be the harshest in fifty years, turning residence at the Ruins into an endurance test. The drawing room with three outside walls, one of them damp, became colder than outdoors. The food froze in the larder as did the soda water in the syphon, the tea in the pot and the water in the bath; 'when it does thaw . . .' Robert reported to his mother, 'the house will fall down'. By March, an improvement in the weather allowed the start of hunting and Robert followed hounds for the occasional half day. But his reign as squire of Savernake was coming to an end. His parents' arrival from Vienna at the beginning of April prompted his return to London where, after a spell in rooms, he became a lodger in Patrick Balfour's house in Yeoman's Row, Knightsbridge.

Throughout the autumn and winter, money worries had never been far from Robert's mind. His impecunious parents were also concerned and urged him to find a proper job. Their suggestion brought forth a robust defence of his chosen career. 'I could get something at £150–£200 a year – but what would be the use?' he countered.

> I am earning as much as that by articles now. I cannot help feeling that if I were . . . apprenticed to a solicitor and paying them the privilege, there would be no complaints. Just because it is writing, therefore mere play, I ought to be doing something else. In my opinion I work far harder than the average clerk drowsing in an office. Having begun to make a success of writing it must be writing to go on with don't you agree?

Certainly his freelance work as a journalist was burgeoning. Commissions came in from the *Observer*, the *London Mercury* and the *Pall Mall Gazette*. *The Times* published an article on Byzantine art which they had been holding over for months. Teaming up with Mark Ogilvie-Grant as his illustrator, he was much in demand at *Vogue* as a writer of light social pieces. He served as their political pundit in the run-up to the General Election, claiming that the outcome largely depended upon the looks of individual candidates. Oliver Baldwin, fighting for Labour in a neighbouring constituency to his father's, was tipped for his 'classic profile and buttercup tresses', whilst Lord Elmley's blue eyes, he claimed, 'have won all Norfolk with their mute denial of Liberal decline'.

His most noteworthy piece of journalism, which stirred considerable controversy, was an article in the *Architectural Review* on the ugliness of Oxford. His targets ranged from the demolition of ancient houses in St Aldate's to the unrelieved horror of Victorian Gothic. A prime example was the University Museum, which he dismissed as a 'curry of variegated slate, home-grown marble, and amateur carving'. His photographs of industrial chimneys and the gas works were equally eloquent, as were his deadpan captions. One described a grim stretch of cheap suburban housing as 'The backwaters of an ancient university town'. Robert's sarcasm was accompanied by some excellent advice. He proposed a bypass for the town and the listing of all buildings worthy of preservation.

As another string to his bow, he was also gaining experience as a public speaker. His first attempt, a talk at the Anglo-Hellenic League on the Dodecanese, had ended unpromisingly. The chairman, Sir William Ramsay, the eminent Byzantinist, concluded the evening by announcing that the proceedings were to remain secret. Robert, who had been hoping to turn his speech into an article, tore it up in Ramsay's face and threw the fragments into the fireplace. His distinguished audience, which included Professor Toynbee and other scholars, were aghast: 'they all leant forward', Robert recounted, 'in protestation & said M'dear fellow.' But no lasting harm was done. He was invited back some months later to address them on the subject of El Greco. A far wider audience opened up to him after he passed a voice test for the BBC. This led to a travel talk on the wireless in October 1928 on Mount Athos.

Such activities had to be fitted in around the one book project that remained outstanding. This was the text, provisionally entitled 'The Byzantine Renaissance', which was to accompany David Talbot Rice's photographs taken of the frescoes on Athos and at Mistra. Most of the research had already been done, leaving Robert free to put pen to paper as soon as *The Byzantine Achievement* had been delivered. He made swift progress: 'it is all so much at my fingers ends . . .' he wrote to his mother, 'having thought about it for so long, that it comes fairly easily.'

Although no contract had been signed, Thomas Balston at Duckworth, having published *The Station*, commissioned a reader's report, based upon the first chapter, from John Mavrogordato. Alarmed at the serious nature of the book, Balston requested something more 'popular'. Robert expressed incredulity. 'I can't think', he seethed to David

Talbot Rice, 'why they don't get Godfrey Winn or Michael Arlen to write it. As if such a subject would ever be popular.' Their discussions ended in a furious row. Fortunately, Robert's other publisher, Frederic Warburg at Routledge, accepted the book in May 1929 without any serious qualifications. The completed manuscript was delivered by the summer, but owing to Robert's travels abroad, the book, entitled at Warburg's suggestion *The Birth of Western Painting*, was not to be published until October 1930.

No expense was spared on the production. The book was half bound in russet cloth of the finest quality with a spine, lettered in gold, of white kid. There were almost 100 photographic plates.

The book opens with a statement on the meaning of life. In man's heart, Robert declares, is a longing to commune with God or Reality. For most, this is only achieved when 'the flesh is dust'; however, some, like the mystics, may strive 'to reach communion with Reality in the present'. Their ability to do so is also shared by artists who, through the depiction of familiar form, are capable of interpreting the emotions inspired by their perception of Reality.

Robert's views were strongly influenced by the critic Clive Bell, who in his book *Art*, published in 1914, had unveiled the theory of significant form. Bell claimed that for an artist to produce a genuine work of art, he must 'in the moment of aesthetic vision' see 'objects, not as means shrouded in associations, but as pure forms'. Only under these circumstances can the resulting work transmit to the spectator, through a combination of line, colour and form, an intimation of the 'significance of Reality'. Hence, he wrote, 'we, in turn, become aware of . . . the God in everything . . . [of] that which lies behind the appearance of all things.' Few artists, however, were capable of working such miracles. In his view, the finest examples were restricted to schools of what he termed 'primitive art'. 'For as a rule', he wrote, 'you will find no accurate representation; you will find only significant form. Yet no other art moves us so profoundly.'

Bell viewed the history of world art as a series of streams descending from the same range of mountains. Turning specifically to the course of Christian art, he maintained that its 'supreme summit' was occupied by the 'most majestic monuments of Byzantine art' as created in Ravenna and Constantinople in the sixth century. Thereafter, it was downhill most of the way. Exceptions were made for later Byzantine art, principally of the Basilian dynasty (867–1057), and for geniuses such as Giotto, who however was accused of breaking up 'the great Byzantine tradition', leaving 'the body of art a victim to the onslaught of that strange new disease, the Classical renaissance'. A handful of later artists were deferred to, including El Greco, but otherwise Bell's interpretation was one of inexorable decline ending in the 'fetid swamps' of nineteenth-century academic art.

Fortunately, salvation was at hand. Its prophet was Cézanne, founder of 'the contemporary movement', whose achievement held out the prospect of a new peak in the history of art. As such, Bell accorded his hero the ultimate accolade: 'since the Byzantine primitives set their mosaics at Ravenna', he attested, 'no artist in Europe has created forms of greater significance unless it be Cézanne.' The impact of Bell's thesis was widely felt and was acknowledged by Norman Baynes, who wrote that Bell had turned the tide in favour of Byzantine art.

Many of the critical opinions voiced in *The Birth of Western Painting* were the product of Bell's contentious reconfiguration of art history. Robert, like Bell, dismissed most artistic endeavour between the sixteenth and nineteenth centuries as being merely an expression of artists' desire to reproduce the natural world. Similarly, he held up Giotto as a genius but went on to state that his, and Duccio's, tradition became 'no more than a prison – a prison whence it has taken West European art five centuries to escape'.

Robert's thesis, however, as set down in the Introduction and expanded in succeeding chapters, differed from Bell's in that, though accepting that the twentieth century was now free from the 'blind alley' of naturalistic representation, he argued that the central principle of modern art was the revolutionary use of colour. Tonal harmony had been abandoned in favour of pure colours 'placed side by side in opponent fields'. This technique, he argued, had been developed more than a thousand years earlier in the art of the Orthodox church. Its inception sprang from the resolution of the iconoclastic controversy in the ninth century when a fixed iconography was invested with the same sacramental character as the liturgy. Given these restrictions, a new use of colour emerged as the principal means of expressing form.

'Here arose a compromise of austere and unearthly magnificence,' Robert explained, 'whereby the artist, in place of reproducing a subject in the exact likeness of his world, was now to reproduce his own emotional reaction to the central and One Factor in his and everyone else's lives.'

Continuing his line of argument, Robert accepted that the rigid conventions of Byzantine art were modified over the succeeding centuries, but he maintained that the central tenet of colour relation had been passed down, relatively unscathed, to the artists of the Cretan school on Mount Athos, who had become the final keepers of the flame.

The crux of his proposition was at hand. There was one other artist from the same epoch, Robert stated, who had also practised the revolutionary technique of 'contrasting colour-fields'. Until now, he declared, modern writers have never discovered 'the greatest of all Byzantine memorials: the paintings of El Greco'. Robert set out to prove by 'scientific co-ordination' that El Greco's genius was moulded not by Venetian, Roman or Spanish influences, but, as his name would suggest, by the great tradition of Byzantine painting. His interpretation had thus turned full circle: 'these later Byzantine frescoes', he wrote, 'exhibit exactly that principle of conception of form in terms of colour which is the basis of all Greco's Spanish pictures and of painting in the twentieth century.'

El Greco, claims Robert in his final chapter, is the last and greatest exponent of the technique which had enabled Byzantine painters to interpret the spiritual reality of the universe. His art anticipates by three hundred years the attempts by modern artists to express, through colour, the emotion inspired by the 'reality' behind pure form. His personality, too, was as attractive as his gifts as an artist. In the words of Robert's portrait sketch: 'He was witty; he was extravagant in living and violent of opinion . . . he wrote about architecture; he had a zest for legal battle . . . He was a man in whose acquaintance we should have delighted.' In short, his personality inspired Robert's pen. So, too, did the need to establish his Byzantine roots.

The case opens in Crete with a convincing account of a 'progressive native culture' that nursed El Greco's artistic personality. His period in Venice and Rome admit to the influence of Titian and Tintoretto, but their legacy, Robert asserts, was restricted to 'a supreme technical dexterity'. He moves swiftly on to Toledo where El Greco is revealed relishing the company of poets and scholars, of Greeks in exile, and of musicians hired to play to him at meals. He was, concluded Robert, 'above all . . . a Toledano; he loved the town; glimpses of it fill the corners of his pictures'.

In his view, Toledo transformed El Greco's art. Robert spoke from his own experience as an artist traveller: 'to watch the sun rise and set on the hills surrounding Toledo', he wrote, 'is to see reflected the ripple of light and shadow on the Cretan white mountains.' This liberated the dormant seed of El Greco's Byzantinism. 'All of Greco's palette, for which his native land can show no precedent,' he proposed, 'derives from here: particularly the grey and violet, those positive, steely colours with which he carried the luminosity of his ancestors to such astounding conclusion.'

Further stylistic arguments are put forward to prove his kinship with fellow Greek painters. Robert draws parallels between their handling of dramatic highlights, their elongation of figures and their shared Orthodox iconography. Hard evidence is provided by an art historical scoop. He made the incontrovertible connection, unearthed thanks to dogged research, between El Greco's painting of St Catherine's monastery at Mount Sinai and Orthodox 'paper eikons' of the same subject. This, he claimed, provided compelling evidence 'of Greco's habit of borrowing from the iconographic formulae of his native land'. Following publication of the photographs in the *Burlington Magazine*, Frank Rutter, the *Sunday Times* critic, rewrote sections of his own book on El Greco and praised Robert for having 'revolutionized everything'.

Robert, indeed, had ambitions for *The Birth of Western Painting*. 'I am setting great store by it,' he wrote to his mother. 'It is my first really original bit of work in the intellectual sense and will I hope be a definite addition to the history of European art.' There were signs that he might have succeeded. The book was widely and well reviewed, but its discursive nature cost it a place in the canon of El Greco scholarship.

Robert's thesis takes him into remote areas of Byzantine history without regard to narrative thread. The reader is soon lost in learned dissertations on the origins of iconoclasm, the development of Orthodox liturgy, the flowering of Platonism in Constantinople and the growth of dramatic interludes in church services.

Undermining his presentation, which hinged upon the exact definition of colours, was his unavoidable reliance upon black and white photography. Robert met this problem head on. 'Photographs', he declared, writing off a large percentage of Routledge's production costs, 'can add no force to the argument of colour relation.' Instead, Robert had to produce word pictures based upon his own painterly eye, which lack the 'scientific' authority necessary to prove his case. This was a pity, given that Robert's instincts were right. Recent discoveries of icons painted by El Greco have shown his early debt to Byzantine art. These, too, link to the iconography of some of his later masterpieces, adding weight to similar claims made by Robert. Above all, Robert was justified in stressing the obvious fact that El Greco was Greek. This was easily forgotten in the ensuing decades when the identification of mannerism as an artistic movement emphasized the artist's debt to Italian masters. Robert's equally partisan approach serves as a useful corrective.

One consequence of the book was of far greater importance to the history of art than its contribution to El Greco scholarship. In the course of describing the frescoes of Mistra, Robert had launched a tirade against their ruinous condition. This was picked up by Achille Kyron, the reviewer in the Athenian newspaper *L'Hestia*, with dramatic results. His reference to Robert's 'justified indignation for the desolate state of the precious reliques in Mistra' led to a donor stepping forward with 300,000 drachmas for the restoration of the churches. Not only that, but the Minister of Education declared that the 'works will begin immediately'. Robert's pen had secured in the nick of time the future of these precious survivals of Byzantine art.

While Robert had been completing *The Birth of Western Painting*, his travel plans had taken an ambitious new twist. Gavin, now living in Calcutta, had written to suggest a joint expedition to the state of Sikkim in the Himalayas. The only problem was finding the means of getting there. A helping hand was offered by Daphne Weymouth, an old friend married to his Oxford contemporary Henry Weymouth, heir to the Marquess of Bath. She introduced him to Lord Beaverbrook, proprietor of the *Daily Express*, who was constantly in search of young writers and had already expressed an interest in Robert.

At their first meeting, Robert made no bones about his desire to be sent to India. His timing was impeccable as Beaverbrook was formulating his plans for a crusade in support of Empire Free Trade. After further discussions, Robert suggested that the *Daily Express* should publish a series of articles by him on the newest and most spectacular means of imperial communication, the Indian air mail.

Launched in the spring of 1929, the service, which employed a relay of land machines and flying boats, reached India in eight days, halving the time of the fastest overland route. The idea had instant appeal. Beaverbrook hurried to the telephone: 'Baxter,' he instructed his editor, 'I'm gonna take a chance on this young man.' It was agreed that the paper should pay for Robert's air ticket to Karachi, costing £126, in return for articles describing the flight. In the guise of one of Beaverbrook's Empire Crusaders, Robert had found a way of working his passage to India.

14

Air Mail to India

In the run-up to his departure for India Robert fell into a state of mounting hysteria. Half blinded by an attack of pink eye the week before, he was left with only three days to complete his arrangements, which had to be fitted in around Henry Yorke's wedding and a farewell lunch given by John Sutro at the Ritz. Nerves finally snapped in the equipment department of Fortnum & Mason, after the general manager had informed him that his tropical suit would not be ready in time. He swore to take his revenge on the shop by exposing them in his next travel book. His rage was later rekindled when he learned that another new suit, ordered from a tropical outfitters, had been sent to Savernake by mistake.

At 9 a.m. on Saturday 27 July 1929, dressed in a Moss Bros suit purchased hastily the day before, Robert reported to Airways House in the Haymarket. A bus took him and his mother, who had come to see him off, to Croydon aerodrome where Robert was escorted straight to the aeroplane, its engines turning in readiness for take-off.

Apart from looping the loop in a tiny plane at Oxford, Robert had never travelled by air before. His first impression of a proper passenger aircraft with its narrow cabin, constricting wicker seats and cretonne curtains made him long for the blue velvet of the Wagon-Lit. The noise of the engines was like 'some gigantic dentist's drill' and the bumps soon had the other passengers retching over their aluminium cuspidors. They landed at Le Bourget for lunch before flying on to Basle. The next leg of the journey was by night train, through the Alps, arriving at the harbour of Genoa on Sunday morning, in time for breakfast on the Imperial Airways barge.

The white metal flying boat, with its Union Jack fluttering from the cockpit, glittered in the harbour. Robert described the sensation of the take-off: 'The engines roar; the floats on the wings dip, first on one side, then on the other; at each wave a great bump lifts the machine. The speed increases; clouds of spray lash the portholes; till suddenly we have exchanged elements, and the sea is beneath.'

Once airborne, Robert found the craft greatly to his satisfaction. The noise was subdued, the leather seats were spacious and there were only four other passengers. The heat of Genoa was soon dispelled by the opening of a porthole. They flew at a maximum height of 4,000 feet, and landmarks, pointed out by the wireless operator, were clearly visible. The captain, who equipped the passengers with large-scale maps mounted on boards, consulted them on making excursions over sights of interest. During the next four days, en route to Alexandria, they broke their journey for the night at Naples, at Athens and at Tobruk; they also stopped for lunch on Corfu. Customs and passport checks were negligible. On their last full day on the flying boat, they landed at Suda Bay in Crete. A swim was followed by a six-course lunch on the yacht *Imperia*, owned by the airline. When Robert parted company from Captain Stocks and his craft at Alexandria, like a guest departing from a house party, he was asked to sign the visitors' book. Robert now regretfully transferred to another land machine for the final part of the journey.

Flying east, stopping for the night at Gaza, at Baghdad and at Jäsk, the conditions became increasingly uncomfortable. Delays occurred leading to false starts at dawn; the heat grew intense whatever the altitude; the machine lurched violently in air pockets. Over the Syrian desert, while landing to refuel, the captain sent out rockets to find the direction of the wind. To the passengers the noise sounded alarmingly like engine failure. Between Baghdad and Jäsk, a flight of 1,070 miles, they breakfasted at Basra and refuelled at Bushire and at Lingeh. 'Here', wrote Robert, 'the heat reached a climax, a dancing white intensity over the arid, pebbly dust, which hurt the eyes and took away the breath.' As they flew over the Gulf of Oman towards Jäsk, the sun was suddenly obscured and the atmosphere became sticky. It was the Indian monsoon which greeted them.

On Saturday 3 August, eight days after he had left Croydon,

Robert landed at Karachi. His flight was ten minutes early. Along the route he had dispatched three articles to the *Daily Express*, handing one to the captain of a returning flying boat in the harbour at Alexandria. He finished his fourth in the air on the approach to Karachi and the final article, summing up his experience, was completed the following week. Robert delivered a successful mix of vivid report, purple passage, historical fact, and gossip about the characters he encountered on the journey. They were published six weeks later with few changes. In line with Beaverbrook's crusade, the opening headline ran: 'Halfway Round the World in a Week. Welding the Empire into One'.

The *Daily Express* flagged the journey as 'one of the most remarkable experiences of modern times'. In Robert's view this was no exaggeration. The flight fulfilled his prophecy, made in *The Byzantine Achievement*, that his generation were 'gathered to the brow of infinity by the initial achievement of the scientific revolution'. His words were borne out when, flying over Missolonghi, he stood in the cockpit of the flying boat with his head and chest protruding above the wind-screen into the open air:

> here was I . . . moving with measure and circumstance through the blue vault . . . Standing with head bare, drunk with the wind that tossed my hair and ran over my skin beneath a fluttering shirt, I travelled as sovereign of the universe, a solar emperor, a royal, emphatic master of space and time.

Robert was met at Karachi airport by two employees of Burmah Shell, who drove him to the Sind Club, where they had made him a temporary member. His welcome had been arranged by David Fyfe, the company's representative in Calcutta, whom Robert had met in Vienna the year before with Gavin Henderson. Robert's joy at the comfort of his suite of rooms was tempered by his sartorial inadequacy. Dressed in his Moss Bros suit, now crumpled and stained, he was informed by his new friends: 'Tonight, of course, you'll only want a dinner jacket.' Ruefully he explained that the weight restrictions of air travel had not allowed him to pack evening clothes. As a consequence he was made to dine that evening alone in his room. The next morning, he promptly refurbished his wardrobe by ordering new suits from an Indian tailor, including a white drill evening suit with pearl buttons. He also acquired high winged collars and a pair of patent leather shoes to ease his passage to the dining tables of Anglo-India.

After resting up at the Sind Club for five days, Robert sailed for Bombay on a small passenger steamer, arriving two days later on Saturday 10 August. His first sight of the Victorian architecture of Bombay had him gasping with horror: 'no town can equal it. Absolutely awful. Indian, Swiss chalet, French chateau, Giotto's tower, Siena cathedral & St Peter's are to be found altogether in almost every building.'

Gavin Henderson, who had been living in India for the past ten months, was in Bombay to meet him. They stayed only one night in the city before setting off by train, the following evening, on a tour of southern India and of Ceylon. In attendance was Gavin's servant, Nadjibullah, a dapper figure in frock coat, white trousers and turban, who was never without his umbrella. He oversaw the luggage, which in a matter of days had swollen to numerous suitcases and rolls of bedding, an ice chest, a portable washbasin and a spare topee.

Their compartment on the train was a self-contained haven of Victorian comfort, furnished with a pair of '1840' couches upholstered in black leather, a dressing table and a bevelled mirror framed in mahogany. Two ceiling fans circulated the air. And there was a separate lavatory and a shower room. Owing to the prevalence of bandits along the line, there were no corridors to the carriages. The dining car was reached only when the train was at a station. Over dinner, eaten between stations, an attendant guarded their belongings and made up the beds. On returning, the windows and the door of the compartment were bolted and barred until morning.

At noon the next day they changed trains at Londa Junction for Goa, the ancient Portuguese colony on the west coast of India. The splendours to be found there had been touched upon by Sacheverell Sitwell in *Southern Baroque Art*, but in the absence of photographs even he had been forced to admit, 'it is almost impossible, without a personal visit, to describe the nature and appearance of the churches and palaces.'

Over the next three days Robert explored the architectural remains, relying for historical information on a nineteenth-century guidebook by José Nicolau da Fonseca recommended in Sitwell's bibliography. Wandering round the former capital of Old Goa, he found 'the whole atmosphere absolutely extraordinary . . . one is simply confronted by a group of vast churches in the jungle.' The Goanese priests added a further touch of exoticism. A group of 'weird canons' were 'kneeling & muttering' in the aisle of the cathedral: whilst in the church of Bom Jesus, a naked acolyte announced the start of the service before the tomb of St Francis Xavier by igniting violent explosions with a flaming torch, a process he repeated during the elevation of the host. The population, Robert gathered, was largely descended from Franciscan monks; 'prostitutes work still –' he added, 'inspected weekly.' There had also been a deliberate policy of intermarriage which Robert compared favourably to the 'awful English snobbery about Eurasians . . . Disgusting attitude.'

They left by train for Madras in the pouring rain. For the next thirty-six hours they steamed south-east across India, under a sunless sky, observing the landscape becoming more and more arid. At Guntakal they changed trains on to the Bombay Mail which was crowded with English: 'a mass of Sahibs', Robert recorded in his diary, 'difficulty in finding a place – new carriage put on – frightful sahib turns on the ticket collector & says he bloody well won't have any bloody else in his compartment . . . with all his kit. We observed . . . that if he has only bought one ticket he can't keep us out to which he replies "But I'm an officer".' Only the prompt action of the ticket collector who found them a vacant ladies' compartment avoided a furious row. They arrived at Madras on Friday morning in time for breakfast.

In preparation for the journey ahead, Robert took a rickshaw to Higgenbotham's bookshop, housed in a nineteenth-century version of the Doge's Palace, where he acquired Murray's *Handbook for India*; other necessities were purchased at Spencer & Co., a vast emporium built round a courtyard in the Indian gothic style. The rest of the day was spent with

Murray's guidebook in hand. He inspected the ranks of nabobs, governors and generals staring from the walls of Government House, but afterwards passed up the other sights of the city to drive some miles out to the sixteenth-century Portuguese church of St Thomas's Mount. His goal was a Nestorian cross, dating from 800 AD, which he had read about in his researches into the eastern spread of the Nestorian church following its doctrinal separation from the Orthodox in the fifth century. Robert's original interest had been fired by a desire to explain the architectural similarity between the Potala at Lhassa and Simopetra on Athos, but he had become increasingly fascinated by 'the romantic tale' of the Nestorian missionaries whose remarkable feats he had summarized in *The Byzantine Achievement*.

That evening they caught the boat train to Ceylon, arriving in Colombo on the morning of Sunday 18 August. To recover from four consecutive nights on trains, they stayed at the luxurious Galle Face Hotel, with its own swimming pool. Robert toured the city, admiring the handsome eighteenth-century Dutch church, with its furnishings and painted hatchments recalling an earlier colonial regime. By contrast he awoke the next morning overcome by the artistic blight with which the English had affected India: 'awful churches everywhere – thousands all over Colombo & the impermanence or rather youthfulness of it all – everywhere enormous buildings springing up.' Pursuing Spengler's comparison between ancient Rome and the present day, he continued: 'Nothing reinforces so much the analogy with Rome as the pseudo classical style of these pompous mummified legislative creations . . . What will archaeologists say 2000 years hence?'

Robert and Gavin had come to Ceylon to attend the celebration of the Perahera, a series of processions around the ancient capital of Kandy, of the island's greatest treasure, Buddha's tooth. On the train to Kandy, Robert wrote to his mother describing his fellow passengers: 'I am surrounded by Buddhist monks in the most gorgeous butter cup and marigold yellow draperies (against a cedar coloured skin with shaven heads).' Towards the end of his letter, his aesthete's eye was further distracted when the monks started unwrapping chocolates from 'magenta tin foil, wh. looks too lovely against their robes'.

Kandy was *en fête* with a merry-go-round and peep-shows and enormous crowds milling through the streets. When Robert emerged from his hotel after dinner, he found the elephants lined up in readiness, caparisoned in spangled trappings and hung with silver bells. The appearance of the headmen of Kandy, in sequinned velvet jackets with tortoiseshell headdresses, like tiaras, preceded by their servants, signalled the start of the procession which was lit by flaming braziers swinging on poles. There were dancers and tumblers and fantastic figures on stilts. The route was lined by men, half naked, strung with coils of beads and bangles, wearing full white skirts. Most beat with both hands on sausage-shaped drums, to a rhythm of mounting intensity, throwing themselves from one foot to the next, then shuffling to keep in line with the procession. Robert lost himself in the crowd with its odd scent of Eastern bodies, of strange food from the vendors' trays and of incense and flowers. An old woman made a man from the crowd hold a white ceremonial umbrella above Robert's head. Returning to his hotel he encountered fat English couples in evening dress dancing to the jazz tunes of a naval band, with a crowd gaping at them through the windows. He found the contrast quite gruesome.

The next day they left by car to follow a route outlined in Murray's *Handbook*, to the great archaeological sites of Ceylon. The road, overhung with exotic fronds, took them through dense forest laced with creepers and roots. Robert, however, was disappointed with the jungle: 'But in all this there is no colour,' he wrote in his diary: 'It is not like a photograph, nor yet a coloured one, but a very old Victorian watercolour done in sepia and an unattractive green. Only these are always faded, & here everything is rather sharp and nasty.' But his decorator's eye was struck by the vivid highlights of the wildlife: 'Beetles with magnificent design, fearfully modern, red & black in diamonds – lizards, green & yellow . . . & chameleons – bright yellow with red heads.'

In a little over two days Robert and Gavin took in the most important historical sites of Ceylon from the vast ruined city of Anuradhapura to the rock fortress of Sigirya, along with numerous remains of temples and palaces on the way. 'I loathe ruins,' Robert complained to his mother after the trip, although as a disciple of Oswald Spengler, he recognized that 'they do enable one to form ideas of comparative civilizations.'

By the time Robert arrived at the rest house at Sigirya, he had spent the previous twelve days in hectic travel, much of it cooped up in trains. He began to find the pace irksome and regretted that there was no time for leisurely exploration. Even a stroll down the front at Colombo was frowned upon, as 'not done' by Europeans. When it came to attempting some minor expedition, Robert complained of the 'tendency in this country to exaggerate difficulties. A ghastly climb everyone told us of Sigirya. In reality rather like the cliffs of Bournemouth. Irritating feeling of being hemmed in. The traveller who likes taking the intiative shd. not come to India.' The frescoes, as opposed to the ruins, of Sigirya, were a different proposition, for they had to be approached by a shaky ladder up a cliff face tufted with bees' nests like 'great ginger & white pouches'. Pleased with himself at having made it to the top, Robert studied the frescoes with all the self-assurance of an expert.

Before leaving Ceylon, Robert found one more opportunity to stretch his legs. In 'blasting sopping rain', he made the strenuous climb of Adam's Peak, to view the Buddha's footmark imprinted on the summit. Having set out after lunch he returned in the dark, his lovely topee reduced to a pudding.

On Sunday 25 August Robert and Gavin caught the evening mail train to India. Their first destination, reached at noon the following day, was the island of Ramesvarem, which overlooks the straits of Adam's Bridge. The temple at Ramesvarem provided Robert with a textbook example of Dravidian architecture, the style applicable to temple buildings from the seventh to the seventeenth centuries, named after the ancient race of southern India.

At the railway station they were seized on by a guide and bundled off to the temple in an ox cart. Robert methodically marched round the temple enclosure, finding little to add to the descriptions in his guidebooks, until, that is, he turned his attention to the entrance towers, common to all Dravidian temples, and known as *gopurams*.

The eastern gopuram at Ramesvarem, which is typical, rises in tiers from a rectangular base, and recedes in pyramidal fashion to a decorated top shaped like 'an inverted boat'. Robert stood at an angle to it and observed the effects of shadow on three of the stepped edges of the tower: 'the genius of it', he wrote, 'lies in the fact that though it rises in tiers, yet the perpendicular lines, and not the horizontal, are calculated to catch the eye – the horizontal are made to merge with the whole, while the perpendicular stand out – a marvellous welded effect is thus achieved.' Robert's analysis of the tower as a simplified three-dimensional shape, given meaning by the manipulation of vertical and horizontal lines, detached it, in critical terms, from its architectural setting. During the rest of his journey he set about collecting further examples of gopurams at other Dravidian temples, just as a lepidopterist with his net might chase a single variety of butterfly, and ignore others of equal beauty.

The following day he visited the temple of Madura which possesses nine gopurams. During the tour of the crowded precinct, under the escort of an exasperating guide of great age and volubility, Robert took the opportunity to dismiss the acknowledged wonder of Dravidian architecture, the Hall of a Thousand Pillars, as 'low & unimpressive'. Yet he marvelled at the ingenious architectural plan of the gopurams still evident beneath their elaborate decoration. Later he filled three pages with notes and drawings devoted to the subject, concluding:

> In the Dravidian temples there is something native and organic – at last something new, not a mere adaptation of classicism, nor the creation of two dimensional shapes as in Mohammedan. Worth coming to India to see them alone. Faults – especially inside – but the Gopura is eternally impressive.

Robert spent the afternoon at Madura taking photographs, having bought a new supply of film at a branch of Spencer & Co. He also posted off numerous prints to England in the hope of selling them to illustrated magazines. The weather conditions were taxing for photography as they resulted in either not enough light or too much brightness, whilst in the middle of the day everything was drained of colour. During the photography session at Madura, Gavin, who had been a model travelling companion until then, suddenly lost patience, and the pair had a violent quarrel. At 4.30 p.m. they caught the train for Quilon in the state of Travancore on the Malabar coast. They arrived after a twelve-hour journey to sink gratefully into the Victorian four-poster beds of the government rest house.

One of the first things Robert did next morning was to go for a swim, letting himself be knocked off his feet by the huge breakers. His only other chance for a dip in the sea had occurred at Ramesvarem. After emerging from the water he and Gavin were informed by a passing boatman that the discreet little shelter, where they had chosen to undress, was the mortuary for bodies about to be burnt by the shore, and that the sea bed, which they had just waded through, was ankle deep in human ashes.

The object of his journey to Travancore was to 'make a fantastic pilgrimage to the Monophysite Christians' whose church, like that of the Nestorians, had been declared heretical by a General Council in the fifth century. There are five Monophysite churches in existence, the Armenian, the Syrian, known as the Jacobite church, the Coptic, the Ethiopian and the Indian. The precise origins of the Monophysites' presence in Travancore are unclear, although Murray's *Handbook* claimed 'without question' that the Nestorians had colonized the Malabar coast for almost a thousand years before the arrival of the Monophysites.

Robert spent the next three days rattling round in buses on the hunt for leaders of the church. One was away; another, Mar Francis, head of the Jacobite Syrians, was ill; but at a lecture at the YMCA in the town of Nottagam Robert struck lucky. The chairman, Mr Cheryan, a former recruiting officer for the Salvation Army in Travancore, turned out to be an expert. On the last morning of his stay, Robert was treated to a summary of the 'complexities of the ecclesiastical situation'.

According to Mr Cheryan, the present state of affairs dated from around 1600 when the existing Nestorian population, under threat from the Portuguese Inquisition, sought a new bishop. 'Antioch answered & got them,' Robert noted. 'They then turned Jacobite & now maintain that they never were Nestorian.' The Jacobites currently numbered 200,000, but there were various other sects, such as the followers of Mar Thomas, as well as 10,000 Nestorians. All were at one another's throats. Robert was later shown some ancient copper plates which were the subject of a legal dispute in the High Court between the Travancore Jacobites and the Patriarch in Antioch.

His mind reeling from the in-fighting, they drove off to the Old Seminary, a charming eighteenth-century building, where the chief priest turned out to be 'sweet and toothless . . . heavenly beard like a tassel of spider's web'. An animated discussion on the Monophysite heresy ensued. Sticking up for the Nestorians, Robert maintained that 'Jacobites weren't really monophysites'. In the end, however, 'we all agree that it is quite unimportant.' Of equal interest on the trip were his journeys through the countryside. Everywhere were 'lovely stretches of water (rice) with palm trees & woods in distance, sometimes flat sometimes undulating'. Churches punctuated the scene with their distinctive raised chancel roofs and elaborate 'Goanese' porches.

Once again Robert turned to his pursuit of gopurams. At the temple of Raghunathaswami, close to Trichinopoly, he insisted on entering one and climbing to the top. At the same temple he also attempted a drawing. It required huge mental effort to make sense of the architectural form beneath the mass of ornament. 'Wd not have thought', he marvelled, 'any building constructed by human hands wd have been so hard to draw . . . a great deal to be analysed – extremely subtle.' His concentration was not helped by the attentions of a whispering crowd of onlookers and of the temple elephant, 'painted to look like a mantelpiece ornament', which came and stood right in front of him. However even Gavin was impressed by the result. The following day he inspected two more at the temple at Tanjore, but his attention was equally drawn to the relics of eighteenth-century English taste in the town. The Rajah's Palace was 'an astonishing Adams building . . . windows straight out of the Adelphi'. The library, with its good editions of Scott and Byron, might have been that of an English country house. Two memorials by the neo-classical sculptor, John Flaxman, were also noted in detail in the church.

A visit to another early European settlement, Tranquebar on the Coromandel coast, ended their tour of southern India. Originally controlled by the Danish East India Company, it had been acquired by the British in the nineteenth century. The government guest house turned out to be the seventeenth-century Danish fort, considered by Robert 'the most preposterous building', all spikes and turrets, like a stage set for *Hamlet*. More charming survivals of the Danish occupation included a church complete with original furnishings. Tranquebar, now a backwater, was a perfect example of an early 'European' town in India, a type which till then he had only glimpsed in the 'Fort' quarters of the larger cities.

Gavin's servant, Nadjibullah, who had constantly despaired at their luggage, the weather, the trains and, as a Moslem, the lack of suitably prepared food, was ecstatic when he heard the news of their return to Madras. They arrived on the morning of 5 September, after almost four weeks of travel, and caught the night train bound for Calcutta.

15
Into Tibet

In Calcutta, Gavin and Robert rented a flat, found for them by David Fyfe, at 4 Elysium Row, whilst they spent the following three weeks preparing for their journey to Tibet. They also awaited the arrival of Michael Rosse, whom Robert had persuaded to join the party. Gavin's original intention had been to make a less ambitious trip to the small Himalayan country of Sikkim, but Robert had quickly overruled him. Getting to Tibet had been one of his schoolboy dreams. Furthermore, his experience of Mount Athos had served to sharpen his admiration 'for the few sanctuaries on our planet which have remained impervious to the missionary force of western materialism'.

The historical seclusion of Tibet had led Robert and Michael to assume that gaining access to the country would require recommendations from the highest in the land. Petitions were duly addressed to the Secretary of State for India and the Viceroy himself. Robert also waylaid the most influential figure of all in the eyes of the Tibetans, Sir Charles Bell, and invited him to lunch at Savernake.

Bell's passion for Tibet had begun at the turn of the century when he was transferred, as a member of the Indian Civil Service, from the plains of India to the Eastern Himalayas. The passes to Tibet remained closed to Englishmen, as they had been, apart from a few minor incursions, since the 1780s, but, from a distance, Bell learnt Tibetan and studied local customs. He first crossed the border in 1904, in the wake of the Younghusband military expedition when a British force fought its way to Lhassa. The political outcome was the establishment of a British trade agent at Gyantse at the head of the Chumbi valley. Bell was brought in to administer the area, which, until 1907, was occupied by British troops. When the Chinese invaded Tibet in 1910, the Dalai Lama sought sanctuary with the British. Bell was waiting to receive him at Darjeeling; and over the two years of the Dalai Lama's exile, Bell became his trusted friend. Much of the transformation of Tibet's perception of Britain, from conquering power to potential ally, was due to the diplomacy of Sir Charles Bell.

In Bell's view, Robert would have little problem in entering the country. His diplomatic mission to Lhassa in 1920 had negotiated the opening of the country to foreign visitors as far as Gyantse. As soon as Robert arrived in India he had forwarded a recommendation from Sir Charles Bell to the Foreign Secretary at Simla. This was passed on to Colonel Weir, the Political Officer in Sikkim, who issued a standard pass for Robert and his party to cross the frontier.

Only the practical details remained to be completed. To save money, they had jodhpurs tailored from carpet material in the bazaar where they also bought native blankets, sweaters and mattresses. The rest of their supplies came from the Army & Navy Stores, which was housed in a replica of its London headquarters. Their purchases included fingerless gloves, waistcoats, as used by the Everest expeditions, balaclava helmets and other equipment, 'all in fact that the polar-tropical nature of our journey could demand'. The grocery department sold them a large quantity of tinned food, already packed in wooden boxes in readiness for the backs of mules. This had recently been returned by a traveller who had been refused entry at the Tibetan border. Robert typed out menus for each day of the week, cheering up the remorseless fare of pastes and potted meats with the occasional suggestion of 'Selle de yak à la maison'. Five pounds was deducted from the total bill when he promised to mention the Army & Navy Stores in his next travel book.

Gavin took the initiative when it came to learning Tibetan. He found a Sikkimese with no previous experience of teaching a foreign language to give them lessons. The task proved almost impossible and at their daily tutorials Robert and Gavin ended up by asking him instead to translate useful phrases. Their vocabulary included the words for oracle, trumpet, bell, thunderbolt and intoxicating drink. They learnt how to ask to buy a carved mask, to borrow someone's yellow hat and to say: 'May I become a monk in your beautiful monastery?' Their teacher turned out to be far more useful on matters of etiquette, and he took them to the Chinese quarter of Calcutta to buy material for the ceremonial scarves which, in Tibet, are presented to one's host on arrival.

Thanks to Michael Rosse's approach to the Viceroy, he and his party received an invitation from Sir Stanley Jackson, the Governor of Bengal, to stay at Government House, Darjeeling, prior to the start of their journey. Robert's first sight of the town, 7,000 feet up in the foothills of the Himalayas, brought to mind 'Southend and Bognor reassembled in the form of an Italian hill town'. He took to his bed in the Everest Hotel suffering from an incipient cold and depression. The next day he met Mr Naspati, the local contractor who provided bearers and mules for such expeditions. He introduced him to a cook, Ah-Chung, and an overseer, Ah-Den. Robert tested them by asking a carefully prepared question: 'Po kyeh schingi yudgam?', meaning 'Do you speak Tibetan?' Their astonishment at his fluency evaporated when they realized that he could not understand a word of their reply.

On Saturday morning Robert made his way on foot to Government House followed by four ragged bearers with his luggage. At the end of a narrow garden he found what looked like a Victorian boarding house with a red tin roof; a guest bungalow stood to one side. Within, Robert found a world of high Victorian comfort: blazing fires in all the rooms, chintzed sitting rooms, well-appointed writing tables with sealing wax and gilt-embossed invitations to order horses or rickshaws whenever required. ADCs hovered about offering drinks. Meals were conducted with great ceremony. Their Excellencies, preceded by ADCs, processed into dinner. A double line of magnificent chuprassies salaamed as they entered and a band struck up. The meal ended with a toast to 'The King Emperor'.

During the day they were free to do as they wished. Robert met Laden La, a Sikkimese in the Bengal Police, who was excellently qualified to talk about the recent history of Tibet. A member of the Younghusband expedition, he was appointed by Charles Bell to look after the Dalai Lama during his exile. Later he was called to Lhassa to organize the police force there. The Dalai Lama had vented his indignation on Laden La, following the second Everest expedition in 1924, when the published photographs and the film of the expedition were thought to treat the Tibetans with undue facetiousness. The official photographer, Captain J. B. L. Noel, stood accused, and in 1929 he was refused entry to Tibet. It became clear that it was his boxes of food which Robert's party had acquired from the Army & Navy Stores.

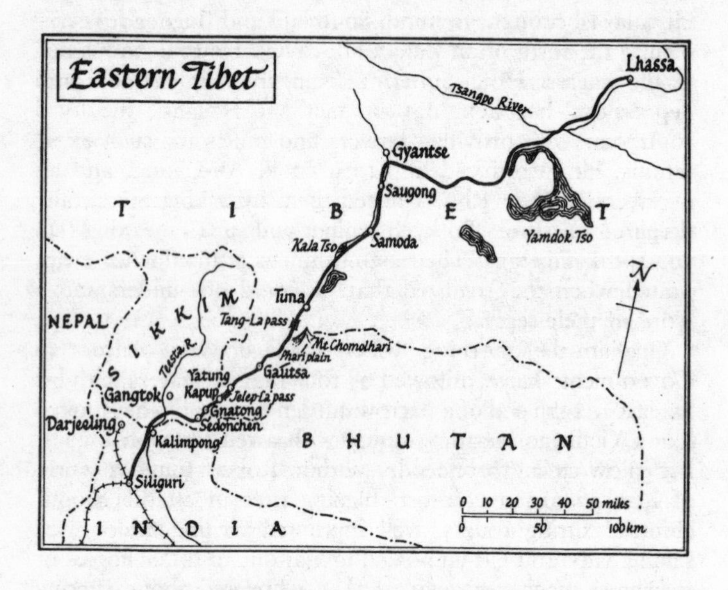

On Monday 30 September, in the pouring rain and with the town enveloped in cloud, they set off for Tibet. The journey began with a well-worn excursion by pony along the Teesta valley, descending through forest which exhibited three different zones of vegetation. Michael, who was a passionate horticulturalist, applied 'vast Latin names to every growth'. On crossing the Teesta suspension bridge they dismounted and were driven the rest of the way by car to Kalimpong. They retired to bed early, with Michael and Gavin complaining that they had already done quite enough riding.

Their hotel was run by another veteran of the Younghusband expedition, Mr Macdonald, to whom Robert had a letter of introduction from Sir Charles Bell. Partly of Lepcha extraction, a race akin to the Tibetans, Macdonald wrote and spoke Tibetan fluently. Appointed by Bell as British Trade Agent at Yatung in the Chumbi valley, he had assisted the Dalai Lama in his flight from the Chinese.

Macdonald offered to write letters of introduction to Tibetan officials at towns along their route, mentioning that Robert was a friend of Sir Charles Bell. He also coached them in Tibetan etiquette, taking Robert to buy more ceremonial scarves, which were to be delivered with each letter of introduction. For himself, Robert bought a traditional Tibetan cap, heavily embroidered, with ear flaps.

The next day they rode twelve miles through cultivated country, climbing from 4,000 feet to 7,000 feet, 'well into the clouds', to the bungalow at Pedong. Their caravan consisted of eleven mules, three ponies and about twelve men. Michael set off on the most expensive pony which immediately ran away with him, twice. Gavin mounted but was thrown off whilst lengthening the leathers. Robert eventually mastered the animal, finding him a splendid ride, very energetic, if a little venomous. After a picnic lunch, Robert dallied with his camera and was the last to arrive at the bungalow that afternoon, at a fierce gallop. Confusion reigned, as the men unsaddled the mules and unpacked, calling for their possessions. Ah-Chung, who had ministered to the first Everest expedition, served tea and received his orders for dinner. Apart from the boxes of tinned food, Ah-Chung had also brought several chickens in a wicker cage and some fresh eggs. They dined off tongue, French beans and cherries, waited upon by Ah-Den and a coolie.

The next morning they entered Sikkim, following the cobbled track which was the trade route between India and Tibet. Long mule trains carrying wool from Tibet passed them frequently, often forcing them to make way. Their destination each day was one of the series of government bungalows strategically placed along the route, which they had reserved before leaving. Ah-Chung, who set off in advance, was always there to greet them, with the fires lit and home-made scones for tea.

For two days they traversed steep valleys, descending into subtropical forest. The butterflies were miraculous, Robert recalled.

> There was one, very large & exaggeratedly tailed, of a deep emerald baize, with great squares of brilliant iridescent light blue on its lower wings. Another was of a demure soft brown, with a lower crescent border of pale blue. People always talk of the gorgeous butterflies. But one should describe them in a flash of speckled sky blue . . . a shower of hot golden yellow . . . rising from a clot of dung – all against the dark shadowy greens, of all forms and sinister shapes.

On reaching the bottom of a valley, they swam in a river to cool off, 'clinging to each stone in turn' against the incredible current 'until it became uprooted & one slithered down to another'.

Conditions changed dramatically on leaving the bungalow at Sedonchen. They climbed 5,000 feet in four miles, passing through the tree line to reach the bungalow at Gnatong for lunch, at 12,000 feet. In the afternoon the ascent continued through a bleak, almost Scottish landscape:

> On the hillsides, their tops towering into the clouds, lay great expanses of dark yellow grass . . . From this sprouted clumps of a star-leaved plant gone a gorgeous autumn red . . . And in addition, the hills were covered with enormous patches of dwarf rhododendrons, very small leaved, & growing about the height of gorse – so that looking at the scene as a whole, the hills stretched away dark yellow, red & this inimitable . . . rich blue-grey-green – a frightening melancholy colour – all darkening to purply blue in clefts & further valleys.

Robert developed a headache which, as they climbed, became so acute that he had to be led most of the five miles to the bungalow at Kapup.

When they awoke the next day, the pass ahead was covered with snow. The staff were reluctant to move on, and as it turned out that the bungalow had been reserved for two nights, they decided to rest up. Robert wrote letters and caught up with his diary.

Six days after leaving Darjeeling, they crossed into Tibet. The sun was shining when they left Kapup on Sunday 6 October, and Robert urged his pony on, ahead of the others, to the top of the Jelep La pass. The border was marked by two cairns, one with a branch protruding from it, hung with prayer flags. The mountain fell away at his feet to a sinister tarn that lay far below 'like a slab of ice'. His eye travelled across a valley, which unfolded in innumerable wooded declivities, to Mount Chomolhari. Even forty miles distant, its white peak rose above his own eye level of 14,000 feet, until minutes later it was obscured in cloud.

Slithering down through the snow to the tree line, they eventually reached Rinchingpong, a small town in the valley. There, turning a corner, Robert was confronted by a religious procession. Nothing had prepared him for the shock of his first contact with a society 'completely, terrifyingly strange'. The monks wore red habits, and hats of the same colour, either high pointed cones or caps. The women were dressed, like all the country people they passed, in 'thick mauve purple cloth' with high felt boots; they carried on their backs long boxes of sacred books. The most striking feature was their yellow complexions with brilliant apple red cheeks and lips, 'which had an effect of being painted'. The leading monk smiled politely, but gave orders to Robert's servants to take his party round another way.

They followed the course of the Chumbi river. On either side rose cultivated fields stretching from hill to hill. The villages of tall, broad-eaved houses, many carved and decorated, each had a *chorten*, or memorial pillar, surrounded by prayer masts. Near by stood the *mendong*, a rectangular structure enclosing prayer wheels. By mid-afternoon, they reached Yatung, the long-established post of a British trade agent, where they spent the night in the British Government rest house. It was furnished with comfortable armchairs; on the walls hung reproductions of paintings by Gainsborough and Romney, along with a portrait of the Prince of Wales, in the golfing fashion of 1924, holding a cairn terrier.

The road to Gyantse was much travelled by British officials and army officers; and the rest houses, where Robert's party stayed each night, had been originally established for their benefit. Not only was it the only trade route with India, but the road also marked the telegraph line to Lhassa. Primitive post and telegraph offices existed along the route where couriers to and from Gyantse collected the mail. Thus Robert dispatched letters home.

The next day they set off in a steady downpour following the River Chumbi across a marshy plain and through a gorge. 'We fell into a trance of gloom,' Robert recalled, 'as the wet percolated down our necks and up our sleeves.' By the time they arrived at Gautsa, a scattering of wooden huts, for the night, the rain had turned to snow. They awoke determined to continue, despite the pleas of the overseer, Ah-Den. Grimly Robert and Gavin donned their carpet jodhpurs and Michael his smart winter sports clothes. Most of the staff were ill-equipped for such conditions. A groom had neither shoes nor boots and had to be left behind.

Ah-Chung went ahead to pilot the cavalcade along the snow-covered path. Robert's pony soon lurched and slid its way into the lead and thenceforth displayed characteristic awkwardness whenever the path, which dropped sheer to the river, was blocked by falls of snow. Conditions improved somewhat. The sight of postal couriers coming from Phari lifted their spirits; it stopped snowing, and the track became easier to follow, although this did not prevent the mule bearing Gavin and Michael's luggage sinking up to its neck in a bog. The sun glimmered deceptively. After an hour or two Robert felt a strange burning on his nose. Ah-Den went snow blind.

In the early afternoon they reached the Phari plain, dominated from the far distance by the peak of Chomolhari, 24,000 feet high. Patches of snow gave way to bare earth and stones. A great herd of yak grazed. The tower of Phari Jong, the town's castle, came into sight but, with his pony now lame, it was another hour before Robert arrived at the British compound. Despite their exhaustion, they delivered letters from Mr Macdonald and Laden La with scarves to the two jongpens, the administrative officials, seated in the jong. The jongpens were absent, but their undistinguished representatives, 'squalid figures', paid a call.

The town is over 14,000 feet above sea level and Robert woke at dawn with a pounding headache. His face was also suppurating from the snow burns of the day before. Though it was barely light, the arrival of the two officials from the jong was suddenly announced. They had deemed the scarves of the night before valuable enough to merit, in return, the gift of a sheep's carcase and some eggs. Robert asked to see round the castle. Phari was a filthy town. Stacks of yak dung in kneaded pats, used as fuel, lay everywhere. The streets were strewn with bones and hides, and enormous ravens crouched on the housetops or flapped hungrily above their heads. The castle was less impressive than it looked from a distance.

The road sloped gradually up to the Tang-La pass, at 15,300 feet, the highest point of their journey. Always to their right reared the mountain of Chomolhari. Before them stretched the plain. Robert was now mounted on a pony the size of a large dog, with the shoulders of an eel. His saddle kept slipping and he found himself continually clinging to its neck. The party jolted along in an agony of tedium. They were equipped with neither whip nor switch to goad on their mounts, and there was not a stick to be had on the treeless plain. Their eyes focused desperately on the guiding line of telegraph poles, until at last the town of Tuna appeared in the distance.

Once again Robert woke, after a nightmare, with a headache. His face no longer dripped, instead it was covered in yellow scabs which clung to his stubble. Privately he contemplated turning back. During the night both Michael and Gavin's faces had started to ooze yellow pus. A breakfast of tinned sausages failed to lift their spirits, and Gavin high-handedly announced that he was returning to Phari. Robert immediately decided to carry on. The casting vote rested with Michael. When he announced himself so wretched that he was indifferent either way, Robert insisted on continuing.

At last they turned their backs on Mount Chomolhari, but there was no respite from the plains. The monotony was broken by a chance meeting with the British trade agent and two companions returning to Yatung. One of them, an army officer, had shot a gazelle and donated a haunch for their dinner that night at Kala. On this stretch of the journey, Robert was too exhausted to keep a diary, merely scribbling down his impressions. The landscape on the last day of their ordeal, between Kala and Samoda, was quickly sketched:

> plain six miles long . . . desolation – cracked formation as tho' a lake bottom . . . no trees – only shore plants that rattle like bones in the wind . . . get the colours & formation – microscopic clarity – & tone of sky gainst a pinky café au lait hill – as dark as a blot on blotting paper . . .

Their only recreation was tinkering with the effects of the snow burn on their faces. Each evening mirrors were produced, allowing them to gaze in rapt concentration upon their ravaged features. By now all three were covered with scabs and hard flakes of skin, which they delighted in disentangling from their respective beards and peeling from their faces. When it came to washing, they merely dabbed their eyelids with a half-frozen sponge. Since leaving Phari the bungalows no longer provided the suburban comforts of home, but conformed to simple Tibetan farmhouses. Yak pats were used to heat the primitive rooms, and at Samoda the confused odours of dung and lamp smoke compounded Robert's daily headache with nausea.

From Samoda the road descended into cultivated valleys, baking in the hot autumn sunlight, which were dotted with white fortified farmhouses. The harvest had recently been gathered. Peasants on threshing floors, up to their waists in golden chaff and straw, 'were jumping and beating to release the grain'. They chanted as they worked 'long drawn rhythmic utterances on one or two notes'. Others drove wooden ploughs behind pairs of yaks. On the second day they arrived at Saugong, to discover that Captain Blood, the officer in command of the Indian Army garrison at Gyantse, had sent fresh ponies for their ride into the town on the morrow.

Robert woke on Monday 14 October without a headache. He cantered the thirteen miles to Gyantse on Captain Blood's energetic mount, with a groom riding in attendance. As they neared the town, which was dominated by a great jong, pack animals and other riders hastened to make way for him. The headquarters of the British trade agency was in a small mud fort where Captain Blood gave them tea, before taking them to the government bungalow on the edge of the town. The rest house was large enough to provide each with the luxury of his own bedroom. After performing chilly ablutions in tubs before their fires and shaving off their beards, three sleek young men emerged from the chrysalis of filthy clothes, grime and facial hair, to dine with Captain Blood and his English staff that evening.

Blood, whose military duties were light, became their self-appointed escort in Gyantse. He also produced a young Tibetan, named Pemba, who worked at the trade agency, to act as their interpreter. The next day they climbed the steep path to the jong, passing on the way a convict in chains, who stuck out his tongue in supplication. The view from the top revealed the flat roofs of the houses immediately below, with their piles of drying yak dung. The courtyards were stacked with hay and everywhere the work of threshing continued. Larger houses stood on the outskirts, surrounded by groves of willows and poplars. Thence the intensely cultivated fields, broken by ditches into small squares, stretched away to the mountains. In another direction, the long street of the bazaar ran straight to the vast monastery complex, which spread over the opposite hill, surrounded by a castellated wall.

The Jongpen appeared, cutting a striking figure, with his hair pulled up into a small sausage on top of his head, knotted in red, and pinned with a brooch of turquoise and gold. This denoted the superior rank of his family. Immediately he invited them to his house for a bowl of *chang*, a pale green liquor distilled from barley. The room was furnished with divans and a variety of chests, some painted with floral designs, also a pile of hide trunks and a hatbox. From a crutch pillar hung two official hats. The walls were decorated with 'banners' representing Buddha and the Wheel of Life. Also on display were silver swords, a rifle and several umbrellas. A joss stick emitted a delicious smell.

On emerging, they spied a group of people on a neighbouring

roof, who turned out to be attending a wedding feast. Pemba reassured them that 'unscrupulous gate-crashing' would be acceptable. Just as Robert was about to enter the house, a cavalcade of mules and ponies 'gaily caparisoned' clattered up behind him. At the centre rode the Kenchung, the monk official, who was the Tibetan trade agent and the most important figure in Gyantse. Robert had letters of introduction to him from Macdonald and Laden La. The Kenchung invited them all to lunch in two days' time.

Their host at the wedding feast conducted them to the apartment of honour which Robert deemed the most astounding room that he 'had ever entered socially'. A vestibule hung with religious banners led, between crutch pillars draped in silk flounces, to an inner chamber, railed off, on a dais. The end wall was lined with religious statues in niches. Plaster reliefs of clouds decorated each niche. Painted on the clouds were minute deer '& other imperceptible fauna'. At the feet of a huge statue of Buddha were laid out the wedding presents consisting of tea, jars of butter, dried mutton and bales of cloth and silk. Servants appeared bearing gigantic silver beakers of *chang* which was decanted into bowls before being ladled into jade and porcelain cups.

Their social standing was confirmed the next day when the Kenchung granted them the signal honour of a visit, holding out with both hands, as he entered, a white silk scarf. In the afternoon two sons of Rajah Tehring, a local grandee, turned up; the eldest brother, Jigmed, to collect a wedding present delivered on behalf of Mr Macdonald's son-in-law. Another invitation to lunch was forthcoming.

Robert's long fascination with clothes and fabrics well qualified him to report on the fashions of Tibetan notables and their retainers. He marvelled at the Gyantse headdresses worn by the women servants at the wedding feast: arcs of stiffened red serge, soaring above their heads, studded with corals and speckled turquoises. But it was the robes of the Tibetan men, and in particular their hats, which he was unable to resist. The Kenchung made his appearance at the bungalow in a short jacket of buff velvet, embossed with a bamboo pattern and a skirt of flowered purple silk. The ensemble was magnificently set off by his hat of office, worn tilted over the brow. It was a cone of yellow silk, with a stiff brim, richly embroidered in light colours, surmounted by a large knob of coral.

Their invitation to lunch with the Kenchung at his residence in the monastery, at last gave Robert the chance to feast his eyes on a magnificent display of Tibetan architecture. He had long divined its significance from the evidence of photographs taken of Lhassa during the Younghusband expedition, one of which, of the Potala, he had illustrated in *The Station*, to support his claim that the buildings of Athos and Tibet were the forerunners of modern architecture. By 'modern', Robert meant buildings which expressed a dynamic sense of vertical movement.

The monastery complex at Gyantse was a small town in itself, made up of temples and dwellings. His first impression confirmed his view of Tibetan architecture. 'All these buildings', he wrote in his diary, 'are built with convergent perpendicular lines & lead the eye, mass upon mass, to the wall . . . & a small rich golden yellow house wh. tops the whole & provides a lovely harmony with the crushed strawberry wall & its cream crenellation & towers.'

He analysed the use of colour on the façade of the main temple to work out how this sense of movement and unity had been achieved: 'pink wash – white band – then a heavy cornice of deep plum coloured straw – wh. looks like velvet applied.' The roof line was topped with golden devices corresponding in height to the depth of the cornice. Robert summed up the virtues of convergence in architecture, as giving 'a sense of size & solidity wh. is often (tho' not always,) quite fictitious. And is extremely effective in groups of buildings, welding them to a single composition.'

The interiors of the temples, with their shrines, statues and rows of floor cushions, he declared to be of little merit. Robert found the smell from the butterlamps overpowering and the monks, who also stank of rancid butter, ragged and dirty in their red serge robes. Before lunch the Kenchung offered them Tibetan tea, which is made with flour, soda, salt and butter. Made squeamish by the smell of butter, Robert declined. Seated on divans before a low table, they grappled with their chopsticks, as dishes of sea slugs mixed with mutton, of liver, yak and noodles were placed before them. A saluki puppy gambolled at their feet eating the scraps 'that at times were necessarily spat on the floor'. They ate to the sound of mule bells from the courtyard below and to the thud and rumble of a drum, produced by a monk, close by, at prayer. A pair of doves fluttered in a cage by the window. The scene brought back memories of Athos.

The Tehring estate was six miles from Gyantse. The house was a grand example of typical Tibetan domestic architecture. Set in a grove of trees, the long, three-storeyed building was approached through a courtyard with open stabling on either side. Entering by a richly carved doorway, they climbed ladders to the first floor, where the family waited to meet them. Rajah Tehring had been heir to the Maharajah of Sikkim, but he had given up his claim to the throne, preferring to live in Tibet. His estate, along with another near Everest, had been given to him by the Tibetan government.

The family entertained them to a concert on Tibetan stringed instruments and servants performed a shuffling dance. They lunched and were shown round the house and grounds. Jigmed and his wife Mary had been educated in Darjeeling, and they spoke English. Robert promised to meet them in Calcutta, which they planned to pass through in a few months' time on a pilgrimage to the temple of Buddh Gaya.

On their sorties into the countryside Robert loved galloping about, like some medieval notable, mounted on one of Captain Blood's tough Lhassa ponies. His companions were not always so enthusiastic. On an expedition to the monastery of Dongtse, he had to spur on his pony to prevent Michael and Gavin from turning back when it started to rain. Not only was Robert determined to see the monastery, he also insisted on seeking out a country house near by which was illustrated by Sir Charles Bell in his book *Tibet Past and Present*. Gavin complained loudly at the detour. When they found the house, he compared it unfavourably to Blenheim. Robert, who by now brimmed with enthusiasm for the ancient culture of Tibet, found the house fascinating; and he clambered on to the roof, conveniently out of earshot of Gavin, to take photographs.

On the day of their departure, Sunday 20 October, Rajah

Tehring, wearing a beautiful hat, called with gifts. Their final engagement was lunch at the wedding celebrations, which were now into their eighth day. The cream of Gyantse society was present, led by the Kenchung and the Jongpen who were dressed in robes of the utmost magnificence. Rising from the sumptuous feast, with stomachs taut, Robert's party mounted their ponies, and rode off to Saugong.

After the festivities came the penitential journey back, across the Phari plain, to Yatung. This time they were equipped with green masks to protect their faces and with whips to urge on their mounts, but they were still overcome by depression; they were also hampered in places by heavy falls of snow. Robert enlivened the journey by taking a short ride on a yak; it butted his boots in displeasure whenever he attempted to steer. The memory of the courtly society of Gyantse remained untarnished by the discomfort of the return journey. From Tuna he wrote to his mother: 'One was in contact with a completely assured, sophisticated way of living absolutely unwesternized or unconscious of the west – probably the only place one could find such a thing – exquisite manners and everywhere a real love of beautiful things . . . I have never done anything so worthwhile.'

They entered Sikkim by a different pass, the Nathu La, as they wished to visit the capital, Gangtok. The final ascent was as challenging as any of their previous adventures. They were forced to drag their ponies by the reins through deep snow until losing all track of the path in the precipices below the summit. On the point of turning back they sighted a mule train above. A path between them was established, but a difficult climb remained. Robert had to negotiate it without the assistance of his groom, who was struggling far behind, burdened with an unwieldy Tibetan banjo which his master had bought on an impulse in Yatung. Once into Sikkim, however, the path became cobbled and graded and they reached the bungalow at Changu by lunchtime.

Gangtok was over a day's journey through the forested valleys. They cantered the last four miles into the town, where a chuprassy in Lepcha dress of red coat and skirt with a straw top hat adorned with a peacock's feather waited to guide them to the residency of the Political Officer, Colonel

Weir. Robert took an instant liking to Mrs Weir, a talented artist, who cosseted them after their journey. The following day they met the Maharajah and delivered a message of regards from his brother, Rajah Tehring. Two days later, on Saturday 2 November, they reached the bungalow at Rungpo where they dismounted and were driven to Siliguri railway station. Sitting in the station restaurant, incongruously dressed in their riding clothes, they drank quantities of claret, port and kümmel, until the arrival of their train, three hours later, for Calcutta.

The finale to Robert's Tibetan journey took place at the end of November with the arrival in Calcutta of Jigmed and Mary Tehring. Robert took them to dine at Firpo's, one of the city's smartest restaurants. They came in all their finery, Mary in purple and crimson silk, with a gold charm box studded with diamonds attached to her blouse, whilst Jigmed wore a robe of cinnamon brocade, tied at the waist with a scarlet sash. Robert was in a dinner jacket.

Robert joined them on a pilgrimage to the temple of Buddh Gaya, a night's journey south of Calcutta, where they spent two days in and around the temple. Robert remained fascinated by Tibet and in the evenings he grilled the Tehrings about every detail of their lives. He was horrified by some of Mary's views: 'I say that the monks don't want trains or motors. She says "Yes some people don't seem to want to be civilized." Civilized!' The country had seared his imagination; and like a nineteenth-century traveller in the grip of the Sublime, he experienced inner turmoil: 'Why has the whole trip left me in such a state of emotion?' he wrote on the last page of his diary: 'I think it is the romance of Tibet.'

16

Analysis of Empire

On returning to Calcutta from Tibet Robert succumbed to exhaustion, and he spent the first two weeks of November recuperating in the flat at Elysium Row. The Calcutta season was just beginning with a round of theatres and dinner parties. English society appalled Robert. As an antidote he attended a grand Indian wedding wearing the formal dress of Bengal. The arrival from Europe of the widowed Maharanee of Cooch Behar, one of the most fashionable figures in Europe and India, swept him into the orbit of princes. Her journey out, by the Air Mail, had made headline news when first one flying boat, then the relief machine, met with nasty accidents while taking off after refuelling. Her companion, the novelist, William Gerhardi, had decided to continue the journey by boat.

Sitting at Savernake, pining for her son, Margaret Byron had become thoroughly alarmed by the dangers of air travel, as the flying boat on which Robert had originally travelled out had since been lost at sea with no survivors. Now that Robert was planning his return journey, she wrote him an anguished letter:

> my darling boy I do beseech you not to fly any more on your way home. It would be the end of life for father and me if it happened to you; we couldn't bear it, you mustn't, you really mustn't darling, dear clever dear Bob, don't please fly – it seemed so safe but it is anything but safe – can't even survive a stone.

Robert acceded to her request not to travel by flying boat, but he reported that Cooch Behar, a vintage model of the jet set, had rather enjoyed her adventures and intended returning by air.

His own return to England was hampered by a lack of money. Only an invitation to deliver four broadcast talks on travel for the BBC decided him to reserve a passage on a ship to Venice, leaving India in mid-January. In the meantime he wrote articles for *Vogue* and the Indian press and made a start on his next travel book.

On the strength of his name, he auctioned the book between Tom Balston at Duckworth and Frederic Warburg at Routledge. An advance was eventually extracted from Warburg of £150 with a down payment of £100. Robert's resolve to hold out for the best terms was stiffened by financial adversity. At the beginning of December he owed over £300, including £50 to Gavin for his part-share of the Tibetan expedition; and he still had to raise money for the deposit on his fare home.

Just before Christmas, help came out of the blue from David Fyfe's company, Burmah Shell. The Calcutta office were urgently looking for someone to work for three months, writing articles for a publicity campaign. They offered Robert the job, agreeing to his terms of £100 a month. The company also threw in his first-class fare home. Robert was in no position to refuse, and he rearranged his plans to return to England in April 1930.

Robert spent Christmas, along with sixty other English people, as a guest of the Nawab of Rampur. His vast grey palace, a mixture of classical and Indian styles, set in a park laid out in municipal taste, was like a comfortable Edwardian hotel. On Christmas Eve they visited the Fort of Rampur which had been completely rebuilt in the modern Mughal style. 'The fort – horror of it – room after room of 1886 – makes one physically sick browns & yellow & bilious grey greens – what a pity that when Indian [princes] first went out to buy it was at the very worst period of European taste.' Amongst the collection of Victorian paintings, Robert spotted charming eighteenth-century Indian scenes. A fellow guest preferred the later works. 'What I admire', said a colonel, 'is that rhinoceros. Wherever you stand . . . it seems to be coming straight at you.'

On Christmas morning, as Robert was dressing, an ADC delivered a Christmas card from the Nawab and a present of an eighteenth-century bamboo stick with a silver knob.

The morning was passed attending church seventeen miles away. 'What induces me to go?' Robert questioned in his diary. 'Sentiment – respect for Christianity . . .' It had been nearly two years since Robert had stood up for the Church against Brian Howard's scepticism. Over that time his conventional Christian faith had evaporated, although his belief in 'God and Reality' had not.

A state banquet was held on Christmas evening followed by dancing. Robert's dance card remained blank but for scribbled notes of a conversation with the palace librarian whom he cornered after dinner. 'Delicious way of spending Xmas night –' he recorded later, 'to the sound of a jazz band over a bottle of champagne discussing Persian literature & the Mongol dynasties with a sage.' He left the next day for Delhi.

Three days earlier, Lord and Lady Irwin had officially taken up residence in the Viceroy's House, New Delhi, signalling the completion, but for a few flourishes, of the masterplan of the re-established capital of India, drawn up by Sir Edwin Lutyens and executed by Lutyens and Herbert Baker. Robert's visit was at the urgent request of the *Architectural Review* to gather material for articles on the new city.

Based on the evidence of other buildings thrown up by the British in India, Robert came to New Delhi with low expectations and his first reaction was one of astonished enthusiasm: 'I can't describe to you how beautiful it is –' he wrote to his mother:

> nothing but the Piazza of St Peter's can compare with it. The work of an Artist triumphing after 17 years' struggle over every stone, bush and drop of water with official India. The Viceroy's House is the first real vindication of modern architecture, it *succeeds*, where all the others have been only attempts. It is *really* modern, not quite cubist, or skyscrapery. My admiration for Lutyens is unbounded . . . People don't *realize* what has been done, how stupendous it is, and such a work of beauty, so unlike the English – one would never have thought of them – it will be a mystery to historians.

Writing to Henry Yorke, he described Lutyens as 'the genius of our age'.

Sir Edwin Lutyens was in New Delhi for the official opening of the Viceroy's House, and Robert lunched and dined with him almost every day. He found him 'a heavenly old man' full of mischievous gossip about grand Anglo-India. The only evidence of his wounds from the battles which were fought over the new city was the bitterness in his voice at the mention of Herbert Baker.

Their quarrel had originated in Baker's insistence that his Secretariat buildings should stand with Lutyens' Viceroy's House on Raisina Hill, the eminence which crowns the site of New Delhi. Originally they were sited at the foot of the hill with the Viceroy's House on its brow dominating the view along the two-mile processional avenue called the King's Way. Reluctantly Lutyens had agreed to the change which pushed back the Viceroy's House from its commanding position, although he still believed that the visual impact of his original plan would be protected. It was a fatal error which Baker did nothing to correct. When Lutyens realized his mistake and requested that the gradient of the King's Way be levelled between the Secretariats to clear a vista to the Viceroy's House, Baker fought off his demands. His victory left the Secretariats in possession of the heights. As a consequence, all but the dome of Lutyens' masterpiece was obscured from view for a considerable distance along the King's Way. Robert's dislike of Baker was immediate: 'It seems scarcely possible to explain Baker's action from any other motive than spite,' he concluded.

Although the *Architectural Review* had commissioned Robert to spend £20 on photographs, he felt confident enough to undertake the photography himself. His series of Tibetan architecture, particularly of the Gyantse monastery, had been a success, and he now owned a more reliable camera, which he had purchased in Calcutta as 'a £25 investment'. He was granted total access to the buildings of New Delhi, including the roof of the Viceroy's House, where he photographed Lutyens' magnificent dome, attended by a servitor in scarlet and gold. The Vicereine showed Robert round the interior when he went to lunch with the Irwins on their first Sunday in residence. 'It is almost completely unfurnished at the moment', he wrote to his mother, 'and magnificent in the extreme, a great deal of marble which I love and gorgeous inlaid floors of terrific coldness.'

Most of his five days in Delhi were spent examining the buildings of the new capital, but his visit also gave him his first chance to look at the architecture of Islamic India which Robert associated, irredeemably, with the Mughal style. His bias against the taste of the Mughal emperors, which had inspired masterpieces such as the Taj Mahal, sprang from his belief that its monuments, unlike his admired gopurams, appeared two-dimensional. He was not disappointed. Trotting round the sights, he dismissed the Humayun mausoleum, a prototype for the Taj Mahal, as 'frightful'. Summing up, he wrote loftily: 'There are moments of beauty but it is all so bad fundamentally.'

On 1 January 1930, Robert started work for Burmah Shell. He was responsible for planning and writing a series of 'bulletins' on the activities of the company and their benefits to the people of India, which were to appear as advertisements in the country's leading newspapers. Almost immediately he was sent on two tours across northern India to learn about the company, travelling as far as Sukkur on the Baluchistan border to view Burmah Shell's involvement in the construction of the world's biggest dam. Other destinations included a return visit to Delhi to study the excellent effects of 'Spray mex' on the roads. One spectacle was added to the itinerary for reasons not obviously connected with business. On the pretext of inspecting a display of kerosene lamps and cookers, Robert managed to witness the Kumbh Mela festival, which occurs once every twelve years, when millions of people celebrate at the confluence of the Ganges and the Jumna rivers. He returned to Calcutta in the middle of February to finish writing his thirty-five bulletins and to see them through the press. He also devised a national photographic competition on a similar theme to his articles.

The first column appeared on 15 March under the signature of 'An Overseas Visitor' who, roused by the complaints of politicians, had set out to examine whether big business and Burmah Shell in particular were motivated purely by greed or by a desire to serve the community. His efforts were attacked by the ultra-nationalist newspaper *Liberty* which described him as a 'propagandist lately imported into Calcutta with a fat emolument by Burmah Shell'. However he won plaudits within the company for the general success of the campaign.

Robert crowed as his overdraft shrank beneath the weight of his fat emolument. He found less satisfaction at the increase of his own girth, which had grown enormous after only a week of delicious free lunches in the managers' dining room. When he weighed in with only light luggage, to fly from Delhi to Karachi on his second fact-finding tour, the scales registered two kilos over the limit allowed for each traveller.

In December Robert and Michael Rosse had visited the Black Pagoda at Kanarak, the thirteenth-century Hindu temple three hundred miles south of Calcutta. Robert returned there at the beginning of March for a long weekend. In the Burmah Shell bulletins, ostensibly discussing lubricating oils, he had described the temple with its great carved wheels as the most beautiful building in all India.

Before he left, Robert felt duty bound to visit the Taj Mahal. The prospect filled him with dread. Lutyens told him that he liked the building, comparing it to a bubble. During his last week in India, en route to Bombay, Robert faced up to the chore. 'The Taj is beautiful, in spite of itself,' he told his mother. His considered opinion was given in an article for the *Architectural Review* when he compared it to the Black Pagoda. 'The beauty of the Taj Mahal is the beauty of an empty bubble, spat out by Shah Jehan and come to earth unburst.'

On 5 April Robert sailed from Bombay on the SS *Ranchi*. At Suez he disembarked to stay at the Residency in Cairo, where Mark Ogilvie-Grant now served as an honorary attaché to the Minister, Sir Percy Lorraine. Taking the opportunity to inspect another of the seven wonders of the world, he wrote to his mother: 'The pyramids and the sphinx lie in a suburb surrounded by advertisement hoardings. One would never have believed them to be so uninteresting. No doubt if one had come on them in the midst of the desert, all alone, they would have seemed very impressive. But the pyramids are no more interesting than Silbury.' Crossing to Athens he found all his old friends present, together with Sachie, Georgia and Osbert Sitwell. After a week in the city, and a round of dutiful calls, he caught the Orient Express, arriving back in England at the end of the month.

His first task was to prepare a lecture on the Christians of Travancore for the Anglo-Hellenic League which he delivered at the end of May. Diana and Bryan Guinness, Evelyn Waugh and William Acton were in the audience. 'I can't think why he does these things,' recorded Waugh in his diary. 'There was a scattered audience of about forty elderly people who none of them saw his jokes.' Waugh, however, savoured the humorous possibilities of the Nestorians and was to plot a prominent role for the Azanian branch of the church in his novel *Black Mischief*.

Robert spent the rest of the year at Savernake, making only periodic visits to London. He also flew to Holland for a few days with his sister Lucy. A feeling of depression which had settled on him when he returned to England lingered on through the year. At the end of August he broke his self-imposed exile with a visit to the Sitwells at Renishaw, travelling down by train with Evelyn Waugh, who complained: 'Robert . . . made me go third class. He says he only travels first class abroad because he thinks it is expected of Englishmen.'

Robert according to Waugh, shut himself in his room to work, but he was not as hidebound as his companion made out. 'We spent the morning', Robert wrote gleefully to a friend, 'preventing Evelyn Waugh from becoming a catholic. He has just had a letter from his priest telling him he has no faith.' But their mission failed. Evelyn was received into the Roman Catholic church one month later.

Another friend considering conversion was Cecil Clonmore. Torn between his dissolute life and a spiritual calling, he had worked since Oxford in an Anglo-Catholic mission in a poor area of north London, which eventually led to his ordination. Throughout, he had remained close to Robert and consulted him on his troubled conscience. 'C. is coming to stay to resolve his religious doubts,' Robert recorded. 'Fortunately there is an article in this morning's

Times on the intimidation of the lower classes in Liverpool by Roman Catholic priests. This is very opportune.' Again Robert's sermon fell on deaf ears. His anti-Catholicism was to undermine his friendship with both.

At Savernake Robert appropriated the self-contained bedroom and study, and even succeeded in having meals by himself. Here he began work on his survey of New Delhi for the *Architectural Review*, which was completed by October. Illustrated by his own photographs and by architects' drawings, it was published as an entire issue of the magazine in January 1931, one month before the official opening of the city and to coincide with the Round Table Conference on India.

The opening description is conveyed through the eyes of a traveller driving out from Delhi to view the imperial capital for the first time. He halts beneath Lutyens' monumental arch at the start of the King's Way, and sees in the far distance an accumulation of 'dome, tower, dome, tower, dome, red, pink, cream, and white, washed gold and flashing in the morning sun'. Succumbing to the imperative of Lutyens' masterplan, he is propelled down the processional route. He halts again to appraise the massive stone foundations of Raisina Hill and the Secretariats, but his eye is drawn onwards by the central dome of Lutyens' Viceroy's House, which beckons in the middle distance.

Robert tempers his initial intoxication at the sight of the dome with a sober analysis of the elevations of the Viceroy's House. He marvels at Lutyens' use of the Indian *chujja*, a thin blade of stone, which runs like a cornice round the building, both catching the sun and creating shadow, to bind the separate elements into a unified piece of architecture. He detects convergence in its perpendicular lines, which through their skilful juxtaposition to the horizontal elements in the design, result in a 'feeling of movement in mass'. This quality had already been identified in a handful of monasteries and temples, but never in contemporary architecture, save in 'raw and stark' industrial buildings. The unity of the Viceroy's House, combining severity, colour and ornament, proved that 'our age . . . has again discovered that joy in the sensuous beauty of the world perpetuated by the works of the Italian Renascence.'

The rhetoric which raised Lutyens to the level of a Renaissance architect emanated from the theories of Geoffrey Scott, himself a neo-Renaissance figure, who had lived in Florence before and after the war. Harold Acton had known Scott in Florence, and had encouraged Robert to read Scott's work of architectural theory, *The Architecture of Humanism*, first published in 1914, and reprinted after the war. The book defends and celebrates the Renaissance aesthetic in architecture, which, Scott argued, held sway for four centuries, from Brunelleschi to the coming of the Empire style. His definition of the tradition is simply stated. 'The architecture of the Renaissance', he writes, 'is pre-eminently an architecture of Taste.' By taste, Scott meant a preference for form in architecture which he defined as 'the values of Mass, Space, Line, and Coherence in the whole design'.

Never were these elements so extravagantly displayed as in baroque architecture, of which Scott wrote: 'the building must be realized as a *mass*, a thing welded together, not parcelled, distributed and joined . . . the parts should appear to flow together, merge into one another, spring from one another, and form, as it were a fused gigantic organism through which currents of continuous vigour might be conceived to run.' Robert enthused about Scott's 'remarkable' book and quarried his words for the construction of his own theory of convergence and movement in mass.

According to Scott, the long reign of Taste came to an end with the ascendancy of the Romantic movement and its offspring, the Gothic Revival. Architecture became a province of literature, as the evocation of a medieval past took precedence over the manipulation of plastic form. In his survey of New Delhi, Robert alighted upon the latest victory of the Romantic movement over Taste, in the work of Lutyens' co-architect, Herbert Baker. Praise for certain elements of Baker's design sank beneath the drift of his criticism. He reduced Baker to the level of a Victorian Goth, obsessed, in the manner befitting a creative pygmy, with the symbolism of detail.

Robert's disdain stemmed from his conviction that Baker was not only a Goth but a Vandal, who had deliberately undermined the status of Lutyens' masterpiece. In the *Architectural Review* he only hinted at Baker's culpability, but in *Country Life*, in an article on New Delhi published later in the year, Robert was openly to accuse him of opposing Lutyens' gradient and thus destroying the view of the Viceroy's House from the King's Way. Herbert Baker, though furious at the attack, was unable to muster any influential support and to defend his position in the press. Robert was thus left master of the field. Lutyens was thrilled by Robert's support, writing to him, after publication of the *Architectural Review*: 'Your article . . . cheers heartens and amuses me. I had no idea you were so brilliant an author & I offered that glass of milk punch to an angel unawares.'

In championing Lutyens' cause, Robert was upholding the principle of good in architecture. Ever since A. W. N. Pugin had laid down tenets to justify the Gothic Revival, morality had stained architecture, like veins in marble. His disciple, John Ruskin, had led a crusade against Renaissance architecture, claiming that the style was morally corrupt. Geoffrey Scott, by rehabilitating the baroque, showed that the principles of architecture were founded on the rules of design, not personal morality. He believed that the goal of great architecture was to convey, by adherence to the rules of Taste, a sense of permanence and strength. When man recognizes the quality in a building, he claimed, an echo sounds within his conscience, prompting him to bestow moral approval upon its architecture. 'We transcribe architecture into terms of ourselves,' Scott wrote. 'This is the humanism of architecture.'

Summing up Lutyens' achievement at New Delhi, Robert wrote that he had accomplished a fusion between East and West, 'and created a novel work of art'. The 'gorgeous façade, coloured and dramatic, of Asia' had been combined with 'the solid habit, cubic and intellectual, of European building'. His voice ringing with pride, he ended: 'but above all, in every rib and moulding, in every block of stone, he has revealed and given life to that perfect sanity and proportion which is the distilled essence of beauty, and which Europe calls the humanist ideal.' For this gift, he forecast, 'the English will be remembered.'

Closeted at Savernake until the end of 1930, Robert also completed the book which he had auctioned so successfully the previous year while living in Calcutta. The first draft, provisionally entitled 'The British Evening in the Morning-lands', was begun in November 1929, and opened with a description of his flight out to India and his journey to Tibet. 'I shall make it a short book . . .' he wrote to his mother, 'I feel that I have got beyond travel books at the moment – yet if one travels, what is one to do?' At the beginning of February 1930, soon after his contract with Frederic Warburg had been agreed, Robert elaborated on his plan for the book: 'The air and the Tibet pieces, which you will have seen,' he wrote to his mother, 'are to be the only bits in diary form – that is chronological – and even those will be much cut down. The rest will be definite essays on different subjects.' By June, he had persuaded Routledge to let him drop the idea of a travel book and to replace it with 'a political allegory'.

Essay on India, as it was finally titled, appeared shorn of all travel narrative. Rather than beguile his readers in the opening pages with tales of flying boats and Tibetan feasts, Robert chose instead to sound the tocsin on the future of world civilization. The conflict between the English and the Indians, in his view, mirrored the unequal struggle between the materialism of the West and the spirituality of the East. Unless these opposing cultures came to an accommodation with each other, as in the past, he argued, then civilization was doomed to the 'portentous barbarism' of the machine age, already rampant in Russia and America. In India, he concluded, a precarious balance existed between East and West, which if stabilized, offered the only hope of salvation.

Having set out the problem, Robert unveiled a double portrait of the Indians and the English. To his study of the Indian character, he applied his theory of *genius loci*, calculating the visual effect of landscape upon the activity of its inhabitants. In the fragmented landscape of India, drained of all colour and form by the noonday sun, Robert discovered 'the genius of disintegration', which had foiled all previous attempts by conquerors to impose political order on India. Against this backdrop, he depicted aspects of Indian society in a series of sketches, conveyed partly by generalized sweeps and partly by a detailed modelling from life. The atmosphere of remote villages, with kerosene lamps ablaze, was reworked from his propaganda for Shell. An incident at the religious festival of Kumbh Mela, when he was prevented from taking photographs, served as his illustration of the pent-up frenzy of the masses. His attendance at the Indian wedding was used to highlight the gulf between the intelligentsia and the English.

The portrayal of the English in India was complicated by the appearance of a self-portrait of the artist wearing a new topee. Robert described how, on his second day in Karachi, he ventured into the bazaar for the first time, where he immediately became the focus of attention:

> inside me, was something very, very strange. For here was I in a position which I had never conceived or wanted, a ruler among the ruled . . . It was written on every face, and if mine proclaimed a doubt, the topee hid it. I experienced a vague exaltation, an access of racial credit. Simultaneously a discomfort arose . . . and my companion noticed it, though without divining the reason. 'Look at them,' he said. 'It makes you realize what we are up against here in India.' It did. It made me realize that the thing we are up against existed in myself.

Robert accepted that, as an Englishman, he was incapable of suppressing the attitude of ruler, not least because it secured him comfort and efficiency on his travels. But he had to be forever on his guard against being lulled into believing that this position conferred upon him racial superiority. Racial snobbery was at its most pernicious in the stifling conventions of the British business community, which conspired to isolate the English from the Indians. Robert railed against Anglo-Indian society with the venom of one who has suffered at its hands, citing his fellow countrymen's obsession with evening dress and their rudeness on trains.

Focus of his blame were the Victorians, who, in investing their commerical imperialism with a sense of moral righteousness, had invented the British superiority complex. He called for a return to the equality between the races found in Georgian India, giving as an example of this happy state of affairs the monument designed by Flaxman at Tanjore which had been erected by the rajah to a European missionary.

His aim in *Essay on India* was to cure the English of their sense of racial superiority. Given that westernization was inevitable, Robert argued, the English must treat educated Indians as their equals. Only then would Western ideas be properly assimilated for the benefit of India.

Whatever Robert felt towards the social aspects of the English in India, he could not conceal his admiration for their administration of the country, which he described as 'the highest expression of a national genius'. As a result, soldiers, civil servants, and above all, the Viceroy, were spared his rod. He dismissed as absurd the prospect of the British leaving India. Rather, he foresaw the country eventually achieving Dominion status, a form of self-government within the Empire. He was encouraged in this belief by the first Round Table Conference on the Indian constitution, convened in October 1930, which had accepted the possibility of an All India Federation. In his eyes, the most serious threat to political coexistence lay not with Gandhi but with Winston Churchill who, in league with the *Daily Mail*, was braying for a return to old-fashioned imperialism. 'If Mr Churchill wishes to talk about India', he wrote, 'let him go there and discover what India is, instead of relying on the memories of a boastfully ignorant subaltern.'

Essay on India was published on 14 April 1931. One month earlier Lord Irwin and Gandhi had signed the Delhi Pact, vindicating, if only for a few months, Robert's hope for a future of harmony between the British and the Indians. Robert was disheartened by the lack of reviews, which in England were mostly either shared with other books or shorter notices. In the Indian newspapers he received wider and more sympathetic coverage. But sales were low. When Robert suggested to Warburg some months after publication that advertising might help, he received the frank reply: 'I'm afraid . . . it would be throwing good money after bad.'

17
The Higher Philosophy

In January 1931, Robert laid down his pen and escaped on a trip to central Europe. Although this gave him the chance of seeing his sister, Anne, who was living with a family outside Vienna, the real reason was to meet up with Desmond Parsons, the younger brother of Michael Rosse.

Desmond was one of the most magnetic men of his generation. Harold Acton described him as 'tall, fair and nordically handsome'. Robert conveyed the essence of his attraction when he composed a group portrait of the Parsons siblings: 'the beauty of the Parsonses as I knew them in early youth was real beauty . . .' he recalled in an unfinished piece written with a view to publication:

> it remains a favourite vision. There was no great regularity about it in the Greek sense. It was a matter of modelling, poise & movement, & in the last analysis of character, by which I do not mean innocence or virtue in the Christian sense, but candour & contempt for guile. This quality was physically evident in their eyes where humility of personal achievement & absolute pride of judgement were equally compounded. Strangers generally noticed the pride & missed the humility, so that first acquaintance with any of them was apt to be disconcerting.

Robert first set eyes upon Desmond at Birr in 1927. The memory never left him. Desmond was sitting on the library floor and having said 'How do you do?' returned with characteristic aloofness to what he was doing.

Over a year passed before Robert saw him again. He suggested coming down to Eton to take him out on the pretext that Desmond, now aged seventeen, was about to disappear into the army. He himself was soon to leave for Austria for several weeks. 'By the time I get back', he explained, 'you will have become a soldier and ceased to know me.' They met the following week when Robert motored down with Jack Murdocke, the wealthy Australian journalist who had originally helped him with his career. Robert let drop the news to Michael, telling him: 'I saw Desmond last night . . . [he] showed us the river, got very wet & was acutely bored. However we were in the most ostentatious Rolls Royce in five continents.'

Robert considered the decision to send Desmond to Sandhurst 'too extraordinary'. Certainly it would have been hard to find a less military type. As James Lees-Milne, his fellow aesthete in their notoriously athletic house at Eton, recalled, 'he was non-conforming, unreliable, unconventional, not particularly good (without being bad), and incorrect.' Their school days, Lees-Milne continued, were spent huddling 'in silent defence against the games-addicted hearties [who were] contemptuous of what we supposed was literature, art, and a dedication to the sublimer life'. It was only a matter of time before Desmond fell in with a thoroughly irresponsible set, led by the reckless charmer, Hamish Erskine. Thanks to him, his name cropped up in a Home Office report on the greatest Eton scandal of the day, when the actress Tallulah Bankhead was rumoured to have held an orgy with Hamish and his friends in a hotel at Bray. The incident, which was blown up out of all proportion, was more accurately described by the press as a jollification. However Desmond's sights were already fixed upon the frivolous world beyond school. Escaping up to London, he attended, along with Robert, the notorious 'swimming bath party' hosted by Brian Howard, Elizabeth Ponsonby and other bright young things.

The army, as Robert had predicted, proved a disastrous mistake. Desmond was finally permitted to resign his cadetship after a year, but the misery of the experience left him 'filled with feelings of resentment, and . . . disinclined to do anything to oblige'. Nineteen years old, rich and mutinous, he was in no mood to pursue a new career. Instead, his life assumed a leisurely pattern over the next few years, characterized by periods in France and Germany to improve his languages, travels on the Continent in pursuit of culture, spells of family life at Birr and bouts of party-going in London.

Wherever he went, his looks rarely failed to cause a stir. Describing a visit to Sarajevo during a tour of the Balkans, he confided to Robert: 'Life was made a little complicated by a most importunate guide who implored me to sleep with him from morning to night. In fact all the town seems to practise the "higher philosophy" as I was always finding my head being stroked by old merchants.'

Desmond was too self-aware not to realize that his life lacked purpose. To Roy Harrod, who persistently tried to improve him, he once temporized: 'I feel very deeply at times that I am capable of doing something – but WHAT!' If only, he pleaded, Harrod could 'exorcize the demon of uncertainty and pessimism from him'. Excuses came readily to hand. 'I am not interested in fame or money,' he admitted, 'and without either there is little incentive to demean oneself and publish some vulgarized account of one's travels.' Michael referred to his 'super-critical taste' which led to eternal grumbling. These exaggerated wails were often unintentionally funny. Lord Berners, who had Desmond to stay in Rome, was delighted one day when he arrived back with the complaint: 'I've had a *disastrous* morning in the Vatican.' Going in to lunch, Lord Berners inquired if he liked veal. 'Oh yes,' replied Desmond in gloomy tones, 'I'm a regular veal fiend.' Diana Guinness, who witnessed the exchange, said that 'the veal fiend' was 'not exactly consciously funny but never minded one laughing'.

His lethargy, or as he put it 'an inborn laziness', was indissolubly bound up with his health, which was almost always 'below par'. To Robert from Paris, he moaned: 'I have been feeling so ill lately, I just have not had the energy to write letters, especially as . . . having to write in my bedroom always makes me feel slightly sick.' London played havoc with his nerves. The Irish weather plunged him into gloom. At one point, 'these perpetual illnesses' forced him to retire to a sanatorium in Berlin. An abiding image for James Lees-Milne was of Desmond 'invariably lying voluptuously on a bed or couch with burning scent in the room'.

One detail was missing from this vignette. A stack of books always lay within reach. Desmond's passion for reading had been lit at Sandhurst, where, in order to survive, he had sought 'oblivion in books'. Literate in three languages, his enthusiasms revealed the range of his intellect. A weighty German tome on political economy, the complete works of de Nerval and the latest novel from Compton Mackenzie were devoured with equal hunger. His knowledge even kept Robert on his toes. Immersed in writing about India, he received advice from Desmond on the religious aspect. 'The idea of Buddhism as a great humanist influence is interesting,' Robert accepted. 'I had never thought of it in that light before – but of course it is obviously true.'

James Lees-Milne summed up the facets of Desmond's character as 'sulky, moody, beautiful, languid, wonderful but maddening'. To Robert, and many others of his circle, he was irresistible.

In the autumn of 1930, the relationship flared into life. Desmond had been out of the army since the spring but had spent much of the year in Ireland or abroad. He had seen little of Robert, although they had lunched at the Savoy in July. Finally, they managed to meet up over the course of a few days in London prior to Desmond's departure for Vienna. Afterwards, Robert returned to Savernake where he exulted in the turn of events.

He dashed off a letter to Desmond, having come in from walking in the forest 'buttoned up to the neck against the rain and dodging the red stags'. However, he confessed, nothing could seriously dampen his spirits:

> as I squelched along, my melancholy was coloured with a certain pleasure, as tho' I had spent the last week in another world, and having returned to earth, still kept the memory of it living inside me. I find it as unnatural to be sentimental on paper as in conversation. But I can't help telling you after having seen you again in London, I feel absolutely changed, physically and mentally, as though something I had been waiting for ever since July had at last happened. If only I could feel that you on your side had enjoyed your week in London the least bit more for seeing me, I should be the

happiest person in the world. This is not exaggerating. I write with the most painful restraint.

Letters from Desmond were greeted with joy. 'I had woken up depressed,' he wrote a few days later, 'but since the post have walked on air, reading them over and over again. You would probably think me absurd if I tried to describe the happiness it gives me to hear from you.' They agreed to meet in Vienna in January, which Robert anticipated with transparent excitement, going so far as to admit that at 'the prospect of seeing you again . . . I can't write a normal letter'.

Having settled their plans, the first week was spent in Vienna with Desmond's mother in tow. Numerous parties culminated in an invitation to a Rothschild ball. Robert grumbled of dancing a cotillon 'which was rather like trench warfare' and of there being no drink. A day or two was spent by Robert with his sister Anne, before he set off with Desmond on a tour of Prague, Dresden and Berlin. The ten days were an idyll marred only on the last by a tiff. Robert attempted afterwards to explain his 'own idiotic behaviour & wholly unnatural depression'. The cause was plain. He was returning to take up a job in London whilst Desmond was remaining in Austria for the foreseeable future. Separation was inevitable, although this did nothing to lessen the strength of Robert's feelings.

Robert returned home at the end of the month and three weeks later, on 22 February, after an absence of eighteen months, moved to London. He took a flat in 21 York Buildings, adjacent to the Adelphi, the terrace and streets designed by Robert Adam behind the Strand, overlooking the river. 'My flat is too heavenly –' he wrote to his mother, 'I adore it and pace the terrace every morning after breakfast.' His old flame, Leonard Bower, was living in the Adelphi, and together they gave a cocktail party there to celebrate Robert's twenty-sixth birthday.

On the strength of his work for the company in India, Robert had secured a six-month retainer from Shell, to come up with ideas for publicity. A visit to the oil refinery at

Shellhaven left him uninspired, and it was not until he suggested an exhibition of the posters and artwork commissioned by the company for their advertising campaigns, that he felt he had started to earn his fee. Since the early 1920s, Shell had been using artists to design advertisements, but the strategy only gathered pace after the appointment, in 1928, of Jack Beddington, previously a manager with Asiatic Petroleum in China. Beddington launched the 'See Britain First' campaign, employing artists such as E. McKnight Kauffer, Cedric Morris and Algernon Newton to depict famous beauty spots. He also commissioned humorous drawings from the likes of Rex Whistler for press advertisments.

Robert wrote an introduction to the catalogue and was responsible for the organization of the exhibition at the New Burlington Galleries. It was opened on 16 June by the architect, Clough Williams-Ellis, a well-known campaigner against vulgar advertising, who delivered a hymn of praise to Shell. The exhibition was also well received by *Country Life* and *The Times*. Robert's contract with Shell was renewed for a further six months.

Apart from working for Shell, Robert found himself in growing demand as a journalist. His most lucrative topic was New Delhi. In early February he had broadcast for the BBC on the subject, and had written an accompanying article in the *Listener*. His work for the *Architectural Review* also led to an invitation to lunch from Edward Hudson, the founder of *Country Life* who was a passionate advocate of Lutyens' work, not only on the page, but as a patron. Indeed, the offices of *Country Life* in Covent Garden were by Lutyens. Having attended the official opening of New Delhi in January 1931, he had arranged for a *Country Life* photographer, Arthur Gill, to record the new city. After some deliberation, Robert was commissioned to write the accompanying text in a series of five consecutive articles. It was here that Herbert Baker's mendacity received fuller treatment. A photograph, chosen by Robert, Lutyens and Hudson over dinner, also showed the effects of the gradient on the dome. Their efforts drew blood. When Baker tried to raise a posse of ex-Viceroys to ride to his defence, Lord Hardinge, speaking for his peers, replied: 'I think it would be derogatory to [our] position to be drawn into a controversy by a pip-squeak like Mr Byron.'

At the end of May, Robert took the Golden Arrow to Paris to review the exhibition of Byzantine art at the Musée des Arts Décoratifs for the *Burlington Magazine*. He stayed with Sir Robert and Diane Abdy at their eighteenth-century hunting box, the Pavillon de Noailles, at Saint-Germain-en-Laye. Abdy was a collector and dealer with a perfectionist's love for the finest examples of French furniture. The house was only partly ready for occupation, with most of the furniture and paintings stored in Abdy's shop, but it was still luxurious. Robert slept in hand-woven linen sheets and had a bathroom to himself. No one appeared before noon and the food was delicious. Even the Abdys' pekinese, Tulip, was lodged in a rosewood *niche de chien*, quilted with blue satin, which once sheltered the pet of Madame du Barry.

Robert's growing ability to make money attracted the attention of his impecunious father. Even before the depression, which was triggered in October 1929 by the Wall Street crash, the Byrons had been feeling the pinch. In July 1928 from Vienna, Robert's mother had complained: 'I don't believe we'll ever be able to live at the Ruins again comfortably, we just haven't the money.' Eric Byron's investment in a coal mine and his attempts at rearing poultry had done nothing to improve the situation. Robert returned to Savernake about once a month and would often invite friends over who lived within reach. The painter Henry Lamb and his wife, Pansy, a contemporary of Robert's, brought Lytton Strachey to tea. Lord Berners came from Faringdon with Sacheverell Sitwell. The use of the house by Robert led his father to request a contribution towards upkeep. Robert offered £10 a month, but rejected any further involvement, setting out his reasons in a letter to his father:

> With regard to the more remote future. Such earning capacity as I now enjoy is due to two things: my books and my travels. Each book and each long journey has increased it. According to the plan I have been following, if it is to be further increased, or even maintained, there will have to be more books and more long journeys . . . Also – I hope it will not

seem selfish if I say so – my impulse to write, the artistic impulse, transcends all other considerations. Without it, and unless it can be followed, I might as well not exist and should prefer not to.

Lack of money had acted as a useful goad in his literary progress. His most promising contemporary at Oxford, Harold Acton, experienced no such necessity, and, in Robert's view, his work had suffered as a result. In a letter from India to Evelyn Waugh, who also needed to earn a living from writing, he opined: 'Harold is the person I worry about. I have the most profound belief in his talents – and as far as my education goes, I think I owe more to him than to the whole of Oxford put together. Furthermore he is not a lazy person temperamentally . . . Let us be sententious, and say that too much money has its disadvantages.'

By his own efforts, Robert was well placed to ride out the depression, but he had little confidence in the ability of his family to do so. He told his mother to prepare for the complete breakdown of society: 'if it happens', he wrote, 'it is no good being hopeless – one must win.' He urged her to encourage Anne and Lucy to find jobs. Anne, now twenty-two, had long been a source of frustration to Robert. A beauty, as well as a talented artist and a brilliant horsewoman, she displayed little inclination to concentrate on anything that resembled work. Robert had done his best by asking her to design dust jackets for his books, including one for *Essay on India*. He had also put her in touch with his contacts in the publishing world. But she lacked her brother's determination to bring projects to fruition. Robert felt much more in tune with Lucy. She was pretty, clever and shared his sense of humour. In Vienna, although only sixteen, she had supplemented her pocket money by translating at two shillings an hour.

By the early summer, the pressure of life was taking its toll. Robert decided to consult a doctor on the state of his nerves. 'After an analysis, mental and physical, that lasted two hours', Robert wrote to his father, 'he told me that there was nothing wrong with me and that the pains in my head were only due to contraction of the scalp muscles resulting from a strained expression in my face.' He decided to visit

Greece in August, to be on his own, and, before leaving, to spend time resting at Savernake.

Socially, his final weeks in London were hectic. Robert had become a favourite of Lady Cunard, who encouraged his love of music by inviting him frequently to her box at Covent Garden. The Russian opera season had opened, and Robert attended her parties after the performances. His good behaviour was never guaranteed. One evening an altercation arose with Lord Lloyd, an arch imperialist, formerly Governor of Bombay and High Commissioner of Egypt. The opening shots were sketched out by Robert in a letter to Desmond. 'How long had I been in India?' inquired Lloyd. 'Eight months indeed! Then he would start writing a book on Byzantine art – rather a good answer I thought.' Robert refused to be browbeaten. He countered that if Lloyd had been in Irwin's place, at the time of the recent violence in India, then 'a good deal more bloodshed' would have resulted. As the row escalated, Lady Cunard became 'quite alarmed'. However, she well understood, as London's supreme intellectual hostess, the limitations of polite conversation. Robert explained: 'she now apparently expects me to insult her guests so it didn't really matter.'

During the frantic round of parties, a vapour of intrigue, fermented by Evelyn Waugh, clung stubbornly to Robert. Duckworth's had recently accepted for publication a collection of poems by Bryan Guinness. Waugh spread the rumour that Guinness had paid for their publication. When Robert teased Bryan about it, the rich young poet took great offence. To make matters worse, one of the poems, 'Tweed Sandwiches', which opens with the phrase 'Tough lids of bread on tongue-entangled hair / Fit close', had been written 'On a theme by Mr Robert Byron'. Peace was declared away from the hothouse of London when Robert retired to Wiltshire, prior to his departure for Greece.

Robert arrived home to find his father vacillating over the future of the house. One day it was announced that the family must leave, the next that they must sub-let the property and the girls be sent to a bed-sit in London. 'It is all so annoying and depressing . . .' Robert confided to Bryan, 'I am here for a week's rest . . . & feel ten years older as a result wh. is so helpful – the prospect of leaving here made tears come to my eyes whenever I looked out of the window.' The only comfort was the thought of his imminent departure for Greece; 'I hope to get there & to forget England exists for a month.'

One figure missing from his life at this time was Desmond. He had remained absent from London for most of the year, leading Robert to bemoan in July: 'I must see you soon . . .' An opportunity was supplied by Gavin who offered to drive him with Michael and Desmond to Munich for the opera festival. But by this time, his course was set for Greece.

The goal of Robert's trip was the monasteries of the Meteora in Thessaly. After spending a few days in Venice, growling at waiters and German holidaymakers, on 1 August he took a Lloyds steamer to the Albanian port of Santa Quaranti. His first destination was Janina, famous as the capital of the nineteenth-century Albanian tyrant, Ali Pasha. The unexpected appearance of Shirley Atchley, the translator from the British Legation in Athens, enlivened his visit. He insisted that Robert visit the monastery of Zitsa, twelve miles from the town and a two-hour journey by car. Lord Byron, who had spent the night there, described its situation as one of the finest in Greece. In honour of Robert's visit the village priest insisted on declaiming cantos from *Childe Harold* as well as his own lengthy ode in praise of Lord Byron.

Atchley was travelling with a friend, Kenneth Matthews, who later described Robert's behaviour: 'He spent most of the time in Janina cursing. He cursed almost everybody who did not speak English, sometimes violently, but more often in a pleasant conversational monotone, as though he were discoursing on the beauty of the countryside.'

The next stage of the journey, to be undertaken by car and mule from Janina to Kalabaka, began inauspiciously when his driver dropped him a good hour's walk from the meeting place with the mules and his guide. Later he demanded vengeance from the Governor General at Janina. In reply, the Nomarch wrote: 'I would be very happy had I been able to send you, as a present, the head of your chauffeur. But unfortunately we are very far from the time of my predecessor Ali Pasha.'

Robert was following the route to Meteora taken in the 1830s by Robert Curzon. At a khan in the valley of the Arachthos, he sheltered under the same walnut tree which shaded Curzon. At the town of Metsovo, the centre of the Vlachs, a Latin-speaking race of shepherds, he received a welcome equal to that granted to Curzon as a 'Milordos Inglesis'. The Nomarch at Janina had warned the elders of the arrival of a member of the Byron family and Robert had to push his way to the market square through a crowd of kilted Vlachs who had gathered to see him.

After a day's rest as a guest of the town's doctor, Robert rose at dawn to begin another journey by mule. He was determined to reach Kalabaka by nightfall. Undeterred by the threat of robbers, he refused to wait for a police escort and complained angrily at the slow pace set by his guide. In the heat of the afternoon, he became too exhausted to ride, preferring to drag his feet along the river bed, awash with rivulets, which formed the path. Then, to his astonishment, he saw a car. Forsaking his mule, he accepted a lift in the first motor vehicle ever to have attempted the drive up the river bed.

The ancient monasteries of the Meteora are built on pinnacles of rock which, in Robert's view, constituted 'one of the most extraordinary natural formations on the planet'. He visited first the monastery of Barlaam where Curzon had sent his two servants, his books and his sherry up the rock face in a net, preferring himself to ascend by rickety ladders. To his disappointment, Robert was forced to use a stairway, cut in 1925, which had rendered the nets mere objects of curiosity to tourists. He arrived at the oldest monastery, the Great Meteoron, at noon to find the iron-plated door shut. In response to his shouts, a head appeared far above from the old net house only to disappear, followed by silence. Exasperated, he climbed the hill opposite and yelled until he gained entry. The monks were hospitable: they offered him a bed to rest and showed him the treasury. But compared to Athos, Robert found the monasteries moribund, with the air of museums.

In the past, Robert's spirits lifted whenever he arrived in Greece. On this trip, the balm was slower to take effect.

Impatience and ill-humour marked every stage of the journey until the moment when he rode away from the monasteries. At that moment, he wrote,

> a radiant light gilded the black rocks above me while I turned in the saddle to see the tiny buildings on their summits silhouetted against the last rays of the sun. Suddenly my boy disappeared behind a hedge, to return with an armful of pink muscatel grapes, which he heaped upon my knees. My feet hung loose from the stirrups; a delicious relaxation, a perfect happiness, pervaded my being.

Back in England plenty of work awaited Robert as well as a few cheques. He also threw himself into an attempt at mounting an icon exhibition from Greek collections, including that of A. E. Benaki, at the Victoria and Albert Museum. Lack of funds halted negotiations at an early stage, leaving Robert free to make other plans. 'The time has come to move on,' he wrote to his mother in October. 'I shall be at home till March, when I hope to go off to Russia & Persia if it could be arranged financially & otherwise. I am at last on the track of a really fine and untouched aesthetic theme.' At the same time, he had gained an introduction to Sir Esmond Ovey, the British Ambassador in Moscow, who happened to be in London, in order to advance his cause.

Robert had conceived the idea of studying the Islamic monuments of Turkestan. Encouragement was received from Ovey, who told him to submit a proposal to the Soviet Embassy. Consequently, a week was spent at the School of Oriental Studies 'poring over atlases and Russian periodicals'. The result was a 'statement of the urgent need of a work in English dealing with the Timurid mosques'. Their aesthetic importance was explained: 'Various forces, historical and artistic, carried Islamic architecture to its climax in the districts of Merv, Bokhara and Samarcand. From the Turkestan style developed the early masterpieces of Moslem India.' Sorties across the River Oxus and into Persia, where Robert hoped to study 'the towers and minarets of Chorassan, were also suggested. Two assistants were to accompany him. The Earl of Rosse was to measure and to draw plans of the buildings and Alastair Graham was to act as photographer. The document along with curricula vitae and their photographs was duly delivered to the Embassy, but no permission was forthcoming. This decided Robert to take up Ovey's invitation to stay in Moscow after Christmas 'and see what can be done'.

Preparations were immediately put in hand. Robert took Russian lessons and trawled for introductions, including one from George Bernard Shaw. He also netted £150 worth of commissions from publications including the *Architectural Review*. Meanwhile, Michael Rosse expressed the wish to join him. Desmond's contribution, after a meeting with Robert in London, was the gift of a fine fur cap. On 30 December, after Christmas at Savernake, Robert left for Moscow.

18

Marx and Monuments

Robert travelled by train to Berlin, and thence to the Polish border, where he transferred to a Russian wagon-lit, dating from the turn of the century, with a ceiling as 'tall as a ballroom'. When he opened the window, the deeply banked snow alongside the tracks fell on to his bed.

The next day, 2 January, he arrived in Moscow to be driven in a Daimler with Union Jack flying to the British Embassy. which was situated on the opposite bank of the Moskva river to the Kremlin, in a mansion built by a nineteenth-century sugar millionaire. His bedroom, with a view of the Kremlin, led off an Empire dining room.

His host, Sir Esmond Ovey, who had taken up his post in Moscow in December 1929, was the first British Ambassador to Russia since the departure in 1919 of Sir George Buchanan from Petrograd. An Old Etonian with wide diplomatic experience, his appointment had met the Soviets' request for a gentleman instead of the trade union leader whom they had originally been offered.

The Oveys included Robert in their social circle, taking him to dine with the Norwegian minister, Miles Ubrye, and his family, who lived in an Empire house filled, Robert noted, with Russian Biedermeier furniture. Before the Revolution, it had belonged to a rich merchant family and the old mother still lived in the cellar. Robert struck up an instant friendship with the minister's daughter, Annelisa, who turned out to have a mania for all things Byzantine.

Benefiting from the free tickets offered to embassy staff to theatres and concert halls, Robert gave the performances mixed reviews. Commenting in his diary on a production of *Eugene Onegin* at the Stanislavsky Theatre, he wrote: 'a little rococo palace with a real proletarian mob . . . who stink & bite & push . . . hideousness of actors – but charming taste in decor. Soprano hideous – like a wild beast (her voice) . . . I hear the beasts stampeding as I put on my galoshes in director's office.'

The Ambassador was a passionate chess player and he challenged Robert to a game at every available opportunity. The boredom and strain of the Moscow posting were taking their toll on members of the staff. Robert heard how they had all turned up tight at Christmas dinner. One of them had had to leave in the middle, 'while the head of another fell into the soup'. W. G. Walton, the Third Secretary, had a Russian girlfriend, whom Robert met during an evening of drinking and dancing at the Metropole Hotel. Illness prevented him accepting another invitation to the Metropole. 'This perhaps lucky', Robert wrote, 'as Walton & his party were heard singing God Save the King at 7 a.m.' Neither Walton nor Alan Walker, the First Secretary, who was also present, appeared at their desks the next day.

Most visitors came to Russia on conducted tours, bought in advance and organized by the Intourist travel agency. They were obliged to keep to set routes and to take in visits to factories and other showpieces of the regime. As Robert was travelling independently, he had to negotiate his itinerary directly with the Soviet Foreign Office. Permission was also required to photograph certain buildings. Walker, the First Secretary, accompanied him to his first meeting with the official responsible, called Podolski, who wilted under Robert's string of demands.

His priority was to gather material for a Russian survey for the *Architectural Review*. Some days later, a guide, Miss Astrakhan, was provided to take him on a tour of modern buildings. These included a block of flats by the modernist architect, Grinberg, a member of the radical group ARU, which the tenants told him was inconvenient; the planetarium designed by Bartsch with a staircase in a glass tube and an 'amusing' curved porch; and the Izvestia building by G. Barkhin, constructed from 'dark forbidding concrete' which Robert deemed 'poor'.

Only Lenin's tomb, a simple form in richly coloured granite and labrador, met with his approval. He found it impressive and harmonious in relation to the Kremlin.

Robert interviewed the architect, Stchousev, who was old enough to have worked before the Revolution. 'Dear little man –' Robert wrote, 'obviously a real artist . . . said that "the Govt" were tired of all this dull grey concrete & wanted colours – good sign.'

His response to the architecture of Old Russia was far more enthusiastic. In his diary, Robert described his first view of Red Square as one of the greatest aesthetic experiences of his life. His sensibilities were aroused by a prelude of military choreography, which he witnessed as he was about to cross the bridge opposite the Kremlin. As he approached, there came towards him

> a company or two of the Red Army carrying skis – looking like goblins in their long dressing gowns & pointed hats – skis like old pikes – wheel round & cross the river singing – towers of Kremlin behind – fantastic . . . snow falling, lights coming out – the Russia that was & ever will be . . . this tremendous singing Russian chorus in parts – sing v. earnestly – & low sound of their tramp owing to snow.

About Red Square he wrote:

> I have experienced nothing more beautiful & romantic – Kremlin walls of Venetian brick with Venetian crenellation – lovely colour . . . all the towers different . . . one in big square v. fine [the belfry of Ivan the Great] – wonderful chimes – the whole square carpeted with white snow . . . the pineapple church [the Cathedral of St Basil] – what a mind that produced it – beauty of grouping – red with suspicion of green – snow on top halves of domes – in leaden sky.

A few days later, a concert performance of Beethoven's Pastoral Symphony at the Conservatoire moved him to compare the cultural achievements of the past with present Soviet ambitions: 'how small the wretched Gosplan [five-year plan] & all this communism seems by comparison . . .' he wrote, 'how unimportant – communists are right to hate beauty – it makes them small – & until that antithesis is removed, they will be in the wrong. The Kremlin makes them small & their modern building ridiculous.'

Permission was eventually granted to photograph the Kremlin as well as Lenin's tomb. Under the eye of Walton, the Third Secretary, and an official from the Soviet Foreign Office, he rushed around with his camera, attracting the furious stares of passing soldiers and riders. The man from the Foreign Office was convinced he was trying to photograph a gun emplacement, which unavoidably intruded into certain views. Walton made him hand over the film to be developed by the Russians to counter any suspicion of espionage. Robert called his behaviour 'idiotic'.

On 12 January, with Greenaway, the Second Secretary, Robert took the wagon-lit to Leningrad. He stayed with Reader Bullard, the Consul General, whom he had previously met in the Legation in Athens. The next two days were spent sightseeing. His eye was caught by the prospect of SS Peter and Paul across the frozen river 'with its incredible gold squewer [*sic*] of a spire'. He also loved the use of colour in the buildings, which drew his attention to the basins and vases in the Hermitage made from malachite, lapis, porphyry and other stones. These lavish objects disclosed 'the aesthetic instinct of the Northern barbarians'. A dutiful tour of the Hermitage produced an admission of indifference: 'I hate picture galleries', he confided to his diary, '& as soon as I have seen them all shall never bother again . . . 40 Rembrandts left – can't look at them – is there something wrong with my appreciation that I can pass by these masterpieces & yet go mad over a Scythian animal.'

With Bullard, Robert discussed the state of Russia based on the evidence of his past fortnight in the country. He had arrived sceptical of the Soviet experiment. On his first night at the Embassy, he had debated with Ovey the 'intellectual falsity' of the system. He had also garnered tales of repression. D. W. Keane, the consul, described the dominance of the GPU (the political security machine) and their use of a punishment cell called the cold chamber. Annelisa Ubrye told him of the arrest and exile of the distinguished Byzantinist, Professor Avisimov.

Robert repeated the gist of his conversation with Bullard in a letter to his mother the next day.

> Nothing could be more sinister than this regime based from top to bottom on a system of spying. No more shall I be deceived by English intellectuals who come on conducted tours – by our standards it is all evil, the sin against the Holy Ghost, the hatred of truth and denial of the spirit. If the five year plan works it will be industrial barbarism come true – apes in possession of machines, violently, madly nationalistic, hating and hated by the opposing human beings.

But, despite such loathing, Robert admitted to excitement at the novelty of Soviet Russia. 'They have cast off so much, all the futilities and extravagances that hamper us,' he continued; 'somehow . . . one breathes a fresher air, and however much their experiment may menace our civilization, one can't wish it different or fail to wish them a success up to a point.'

VOKS (the association of Russian intellectuals) provided Robert with a guide in Leningrad, called Mr Luknitsky, who also accompanied him on a trip to Novgorod. His father, a jeweller, had been shot during one of the first purges. Luknitsky, however, merely regretted the dullness of his father's life and relished the contrast between his bourgeois upbringing and the Revolution. 'He takes an interest in everything,' Robert wrote; 'the right attitude . . . that is the key to it all – that is what there is in the very air.' When Robert said goodbye to Luknitsky, he concluded that he would either be shot or go far.

Although only 130 miles south of Leningrad, the train journey to Novgorod took all night. Arriving in the early morning they were driven from the station in a sledge. The horse set off at a gallop leaping ditches and potholes, through the sleeping town to the kremlin. Entering by an arch in the crenellated walls, they drew up at the side of the cathedral before the former Palace of the Archbishops, now a rest home for scientists. Vestiges of its original use remained. Robert's room was furnished with a superb suite of late Empire furniture, of birch veneer upholstered with silk brocade.

The next two days were spent visiting the churches in and around Novgorod, identifying their Byzantine ancestry. At the church of Nereditsi, Robert examined the frescoes, spotting the influence of the Cappadocian and Macedonian schools. The church was twelve versts (about eight miles) from Novgorod and they made the journey by sledge. The young coachman, who belonged to neither of the Communist youth movements, drove like a free spirit. Suddenly he steered his sledge down a bank on to the frozen water of the River Volkhoff which still had a great stream flowing through the middle, and they tore along, in a snowstorm, passing sledges with hay coming from the other direction.

Another expedition, the following day, saw them conveyed at a fast trot down the broad streets of the town lined with wooden houses into the countryside, to the Church of the Dormition in the village of Volotovo. Inquiring after the key in a peasant's house, he found a woman making pies. He saw a carved and painted spindle in the room for twisting yarn and, in the corner, a group of icons with a lamp lit before them. As Robert entered the church, there was a thundering roar outside, as four grey aeroplanes with the red star beneath their wings flew low overhead. 'So unexpected,' he wrote, 'it really was the new Russia and the old. One becomes preternaturally susceptible to such impressions.'

Back in Leningrad for a day, Robert had dinner with Reader Bullard. The diplomat enjoyed his company. 'I like him,' he recorded in his diary, 'he is interesting and often amusing. And he laughs at my jokes as though they amused him – an endearing characteristic.' On his return to Moscow by the Red Arrow, the only Russian express, Robert moved into some vacant staff quarters at the Embassy. From now on, he usually ate in the staff mess, which released him from the Oveys' time-consuming routine.

Robert had come to Moscow with a sheaf of introductions. He had also brought out some parcels to deliver to a young Englishman called Marshall. Son of a bricklayer from the East End of London, Marshall had worked as a chauffeur in Britain. The turning point came when he saw a Russian film which offered him a vision of a new way of life. He became secretary of a workers' film society and eventually succeeded in getting to Russia. He now lived in a student village with other foreigners, dividing his time between studying Marxist philosophy and working in the Moscow film studios. In Marshall, a fervent believer in the Revolution, Robert found his ideal sparring partner.

The epic years were over, he told Robert, and the period of construction had begun which, artistically, was far more difficult to express. The two wrestled over the meaning of art. Beethoven's music, according to Marshall, was steeped in the class struggle. As Robert fought back, he demanded clarification. 'I discovered that all that is meant by the influence of class struggle . . . is that any . . . form of art is always the product of its age, social, political, environmental, etc, etc.'

The struggle between Etonian and East Ender moved on to the forced collectivization of the peasants. Now it was Robert's turn to go on the attack: 'when he said the country was ruled by its majority for the 1st time in history, I pointed out that this was not so. That it was a case of a million or two factory workers dragooning 100 million peasants to do what they don't want to do.' They clashed over the prophecies of Marx and Engels and over Marshall's own hope that in a few years' time he would be residing at Buckingham Palace. At their parting, Robert, replete with argument, felt nothing but goodwill towards his opponent.

A prominent blasphemer against the faith was A. T. Cholerton, correspondent for the *News Chronicle*, whom Robert first met after returning from Leningrad, in his tiny house, hung with Georgian primitives, close by the Church of the Late Redeemer. Married to a Russian whose family had owned an estate in the Urals, Cholerton provided a stream of evidence against the regime. He described the starving crowds shouting for bread who besieged his train on a trip to Samarcand, and the ruination of agriculture by the building of dams for industrial projects. He told of the night when he was raided by the GPU, and of his sister-in-law and her husband, who were sentenced to three years in labour camps on a trumped-up charge. He calculated that, in the autumn of 1930, the GPU were rounding up six thousand people a month. 'Pretty good', Robert wrote in his diary, 'for post-revolutionary construction period.'

On 26 January, Robert arrived in Yaroslavl, a provincial capital north-east of Moscow with fine seventeenth- and eighteenth-century architecture. He was accompanied by an Intourist guide, Mr Bender, a passionate Communist who spoke fluent American. They spent the day in a hectic round of sightseeing by sledge, driven by a magnificent figure in a skirted black coat tied with a red sash and trimmed with white astrakhan. Bender's authority gained them entry to every monument. Only once were they quizzed by a sentry: Robert asked Bender to explain on his behalf that he 'was a professional saboteur sent from England to blow him up'.

Cholerton had arranged for Robert to stay in the flat of a Swedish manager of an engineering works. Invited to dine by a Swedish engineer, he heard of the hopeless state of Russian industry and how the Russian managers and foremen were robbed of initiative by the constant fear of spying by the secret police. The engineer predicted that eventually Russia would have to hand over all management to foreigners or go bankrupt. Dinner turned into a titanic drinking session, lasting nine hours. The next morning Robert attempted to show intelligent interest going round the factory. The older workers touched their hats as he passed.

On his way back to Moscow, he stopped to visit the monastery of the Trinity and St Sergius at Zagorsk, the greatest walled group of monastic buildings in Russia. The vast complex was almost deserted: 'were told of course that monastery was shut on this particular day,' he complained, 'but it seemed open enough, formerly staff of experts – but now only one old man & dictator in office – both ignorami.' He succeeded in seeing the Metropolitan's apartments, which were still furnished as they had been when occupied by Peter the Great.

Robert spent his remaining days in Moscow in a scurry of sightseeing, photography and research. He also delivered a lecture to VOKS on Byzantine art. During a visit to the State Museum of Modern Western Art, which contained the collections of two merchant patrons, he came across *The Dance* by

Matisse, which he had attacked when debating Post-Impressionism at the Eton Society of Arts. The label alongside read: 'Period of distorted Imperialism – taste of rentier.' Similar explanations were given to the works of other modern French masters. 'The people who made these notices', Robert wrote, 'ought to be disembowelled.'

On 1 February, Michael Rosse arrived in Moscow. He had been keen to join Robert ever since the previous autumn, when the expedition to Turkestan had been mooted. His arrival had been delayed by the Soviets' initial refusal to grant him a visa. Meanwhile, Robert applied for an extension to his own visa in the hope of getting them both to Turkestan, but he was only granted a further fortnight in the country. A second appeal proved fruitless. His new guide, Mrs Halatoff, told him that the authorities felt Robert disliked Russia and the Russians. He strongly denied the charge, saying that he merely objected to being treated with suspicion.

On the evening of 8 February, Robert took the night train with Michael and Mr Bender to Kharkov, the then capital of the Ukraine. Arriving at noon the following day, they took one look at the acclaimed modern post office opposite the railway station, and decided to move on that evening to the Dnieper dam. Meanwhile, they were offered shelter in the hotel room of another traveller of title, the Duchess of Gramont, who was absent visiting the dam.

The Dnieper dam was one of the showpieces of Soviet Russia and a place of pilgrimage for tourists. A new town had been built near by. The hotel, where Robert's party rested, was already falling to bits. The dam itself was a scene of industrial bedlam, with a press of peasants and clerks, with trains 'suddenly coming this way & that', whistling and shrieking, and with cranes lowering cement bags to the sluice gates. They crossed a rickety footbridge to meet Tor Rubin, the manager of the office staff. Rubin, who had been warned that an important member of the English Parliament was in the party, was astonished by their total lack of interest in technical questions. At last, the Earl of Rosse, whose great-uncle Charles Parsons had invented the high-speed steam turbine, went off to inspect the turbine room. Robert crossed the frozen river to take photographs.

Over a lavish lunch with much to drink, Robert and Michael argued heatedly with Rubin. He believed passionately in the building of a socialist state and branded the culture of Western Europe as class dominated. At the end of the meal he turned to the subject of game. As the son of a landowner, he was a keen shot and had formerly hunted fox and hare with borzoi. They passed the evening at a concert given by a Ukrainian choir before returning in the middle of the night to Kharkov.

Leaving there for Kiev, they celebrated their first night in the ancient city with a magnificent dinner of smoked herring, clear soup, veal and cherries in liqueur. Afterwards they went to a performance of *Prince Igor* at the opera. The ballet scene, which was performed by almost naked dancers, the men wearing gold triangles on their chests and pouches under their arms 'to hide the hairs of manhood', ended in such disarray that it recalled one of Elizabeth Ponsonby's parties. The audience was quite different to that of Moscow: 'One felt as if one had got out of the shadow,' Robert wrote in his diary. 'A few real faces, people laughing and enjoying themselves.'

At the end of a day of intensive sightseeing, they attended evening service in the cathedral. Halfway through, the famous mosaic of the Virgin was floodlit. The sacristan took them behind the iconostasis which gave them a fine view of the Archbishop combing his hair before assuming a gold crown and emerging, magnificently coped in gold, to face the large congregation. As the service reached its climax to the chanting of the choir, Robert 'reflected on the history witnessed by the harebell blue Virgin with her shoes of royal scarlet, her pink girdle & ginger kerchief hanging from it – the queen of the world – Tartars, Poles, the hetman Mazeppa, the Tsars, the building of socialism – from 1035 – all but nine centuries'.

At a museum of religion the next day, Robert spotted a photograph of the Pope, labelled 'the agent of International capitalism'. He told Bender that this was the first time he had ever wanted to stand up for the Catholic church.

At 2 the following morning they left for the port of Odessa, where they were booked on a ship bound for Constantinople.

Owing to various mishaps, their train ran ten hours late and they had to wire Intourist to delay the boat. Mr Bender grew indignant with the conductor for letting Russia down. 'He felt it terribly that we shd. have so many accidents in a country that was building socialism.'

Once on board, customs officials rifled through their belongings, goggling at Robert's collection of books but failing to notice his exposed films, which he pretended were unused. Shortly after retiring to their cabins for the night, Robert woke up to find the boat moving through the ice floes in the path of an ice-breaker. He stood for an hour with his hand out of the porthole, watching the ice jostling along the side of the boat, until at last they reached open water.

19

Cupid's Dart

After spending over a week in Constantinople, Robert was back at Savernake by the beginning of March where he set to work on his report for the *Architectural Review*. It was published in May 1932 as the first part of a Russian survey. He writes as a self-confessed representative of European humanism, someone who believes that the fruits of civilization are produced by the creativity of individuals, as opposed to collective artistic effort. He describes the purloining by the Communist dictatorship of the trappings and symbols of religion and compares its techniques of oppression to the Inquisition. Russia, he predicts, is at the edge of a new Dark Age.

All the evidence gathered on his travels is marshalled to support this claim. The anti-God museums, the absurdities of Marxist aesthetics and, above all, the universal practice of espionage.

> Today Russia is ruled by men of meaner mould, men whose twisted outlook infects the whole Soviet Union with a spirit of malice and suspicion. The whole air is poisoned by this evil. Every man lives in fear of his neighbour. Even the schoolchildren are admonished, in the books from which they learn to read, to train themselves as spies in their own villages.

The victims of the terror, he continues, were not just the old intelligentsia who had been slow to ally themselves with the new regime, but also 'all the prophets of the modern age', such as inventors, editors, architects and film-makers. He turns with contempt on those English intellectuals who fail to offer them a word of support whilst hailing the achievements of Soviet Russia, and concludes:

> That this system, would immediately, on attaining power, annihilate these miserable hypocrites, these hypnotees of every windblown theory, these bastards by uplift out of comfortable income, is the one satisfaction I could derive from its introduction into England . . . What counts freedom of thought or scholarship or individual creation besides the regeneration of the Great Unwashed? Very little I daresay.

His exposure of the brutality of the Soviet regime anticipated by a year the famous articles by Malcolm Muggeridge in the *Morning Post*.

Apart from the photographs of buildings scattered throughout the text, until the final pages of the survey the subject of architecture is scarcely raised. Only then does Robert sweep through almost nine hundred years of architectural history, charting the succession of international styles which made obeisance to the Russian aesthetic. He looks to the landscape to explain the characteristics of Russian taste. The illimitable horizons as well as the neutral backdrop of snow, he argues, encouraged, in architecture, monumentality, bold outline, planes of colour and richness of texture and materials.

With the exception of Lenin's tomb, which had been designed by a pre-revolutionary architect, none of these qualities are apparent to Robert in the buildings of the Communist era. He refers to 'the banal mediocrity displayed in most of the accompanying illustrations of modern architecture'. And he dismisses the international entries for the Palace of the Soviets by leading modernist architects, such as Le Corbusier, Poelzig and Gropius, as 'one and all of that gasometer or packing-case type which may be suitable to factories and even to tenements, but must have inevitably disfigured the centre of Moscow'. He does not entirely abandon hope. The Russian architects Stchousev and Grinberg, he relates, had told him of a new policy 'which will eventually withhold its approval from the drab functionalism of the present era, and allow free play once more to the native genius of the country'.

Waiting in the wings to provide a stern corrective to Robert's optimistic forecast was the Russian-born architect

Berthold Lubetkin. As author of the second part of the Russian survey in the *Architectural Review*, he used it as a platform to explain the theories propagated by Russian architectural collectives and to display their achievements. He illustrates technical institutes, communes, workers' clubs and 'the first socialist town', all of which are designed in what Robert had termed 'the ferrocrete style'.

Arriving in Britain in 1931 the personification of the avant-garde – down to the wearing of the revolutionary zip fly, instead of buttons, on his trousers – Lubetkin cherished a romantic vision of Communism. He adverts in his contribution to the desire of Russian architects to invent new types of buildings to meet the needs of the proletariat. 'The problem', he concludes, 'surpasses individual capacity. What is wanted is the creation of a new style in accordance with the demands of the historical moment . . . Aestheticism, the admiration of abstractly beautiful things, is characteristic of the bourgeois aesthetic.' In contradiction to Robert, Lubetkin believed that architecture was determined by ideology, not by taste. Their exchange of fire in the columns of the *Architectural Review* presaged the war of styles to come between modernism and tradition.

In the more placid environment of *Country Life*, Robert was given the chance, over five articles, to tell of his adventures as a traveller in Russia. Well-crafted descriptions of art and architecture are strung between anecdotes of sleigh rides and shopping expeditions. His words reached as far as Tibet, whence Mrs Weir wrote to him from Lhassa: 'how vividly you tell it all to the nice fat comfortable readers of *Country Life*. I can picture them in their armchairs over the fire after the curtains have been drawn. "This Byron fellow has a pretty wit."'

Robert also turned to good account his sojourn in Constantinople, where the uncovering of the Byzantine mosaics in Santa Sophia had just commenced. Lady Cunard and the banker, Benjamin Guinness, had sponsored the undertaking by the American archaeologist, Professor Thomas Whittemore. Robert was shown round by Whittemore and in March he sought permission to write up his work for *The Times*. Whittemore impressed on Robert the delicacy of the situation. He did not wish to jeopardize his diplomatic triumph, which had resulted in the Turkish president Mustafa Kemal (later Atatürk) authorizing the unveiling of Christian mosaics in what was still one of the most famous mosques in Islam. In his article, Robert duly hailed the decision by the Turkish government as deserving the gratitude of the civilized world.

The rediscovery of Byzantine art was gathering pace. The exhibition at the Louvre, in the summer of 1931, was the first of Byzantine art ever held. In Athens, the Byzantine museum had opened as well as the private museum of A. E. Benaki containing a fine collection of icons and related works of art. Robert had visited both collections after his trip to Meteora, which had inspired his idea for an exhibition of icons at the Victoria and Albert Museum. Eventually a small exhibition was mounted by David Talbot Rice at the Courtauld Institute's temporary premises at the Adelphi. In the autumn of 1932, Talbot Rice also delivered a series of lectures on Byzantine art at the Courtauld using a number of Robert's photographs.

Robert's experience was being continually tapped by travellers, collectors and scholars, as they negotiated the inadequately mapped terrain of Byzantine art history. Hugh Casson, then an architectural student, asked for advice on visiting Byzantine monuments in Greece. Royall Tyler, one of the organizers of the Louvre exhibition, inquired about the availability of photographs of Kiev. Eric Maclagan, director of the Victoria and Albert Museum, consulted him on matters of dating. He was also called upon to review books relating to the subject. To the readers of the *New Statesman*, he gave a lofty welcome to *Byzantine Civilization*, the latest work from the pen of England's most promising Byzantinist, Steven Runciman. Robert's own efforts were acknowledged by the respected Byzantine Society, based in Athens, who conferred upon him honorary membership.

Robert affected disdain at the 'dubious popularity' surrounding Byzantine art. And he complained to Royall Tyler of his embarrassment when Viscount D'Abernon, who had lived many years in Constantinople, congratulated him with a wink 'on Byzantine art's progress'. Privately, his enthusiasm for the subject occasionally waned. In Russia, after preparing his lecture for VOKS, he recorded: 'Wrote my lecture till 2.00 a.m. V. curious sitting in a Swedish flat in Yaroslavl . . . writing about the same old boredom.'

In June 1932, Robert organized an exhibition of his drawings and photographs at Robert Abdy's new gallery in Carlos Place, Mayfair. In the introduction to the catalogue, Robert wrote modestly that the 'subject justifies his art and not vice versa', but the collection, covering his journeys to Mount Athos, India, Tibet and Russia, received high praise from serious critics. Robert drew with a modern boldness, reducing terrain and sky to patterns of simplified shapes, which, more often than not, provided a discreet backdrop to a complex architectural subject. Frank Rutter, the *Sunday Times* critic who had been influenced by Robert's views on El Greco, wrote that there was 'much to capture the delighted attention' of the student of architecture and that 'his records are of supreme interest.' The leading modern artist, Paul Nash, hailed him in the *Listener* as 'as an amateur of unusual distinction'.

His photographs attracted equal praise. His use of a reflex camera, which reflected the image in a mirror, allowed him, in his words, 'to compose to a nicety – an important consideration where buildings are the subject and the space around them limited'. The anonymous critic in *The Times* believed that 'his photographs . . . show a real gift of finding the most expressive lighting and composition.' Similar plaudits were received from many other publications. The warmth of the reception was summed up by the critic of the *Observer* who wrote: 'Mr Byron cannot be called anything but an artist.'

Unfortunately, such acclaim did not translate into sales. At the close of the exhibition, Robert Abdy hesitated to send Robert the accounts as he did not wish to depress him. Only three drawings were sold and no photographs. After framing costs had been deducted, Robert's profit amounted to £1 2s. One of the pictures, priced at four guineas, was bought by a friend, Penelope Chetwode, who negotiated paying in instalments over two years.

Penelope Chetwode, the twenty-two-year-old, culture-mad daughter of the Commander-in-Chief of the British Army in

India, had met Robert in Delhi when they had toured the new city together with Lutyens. When Penelope visited England, their friendship was renewed with an invitation to stay at Savernake. Out riding with Robert, she was surprised to find that his idea of hacking, a worthy form of exercise conducted no faster than the trot, was to career through the forest at a gallop. In 1931, Penelope consulted him on an article she had written on Indian temple architecture. At his recommendation she took it to the *Architectural Review*, where she was dealt with by the assistant editor, John Betjeman.

During the summer of 1932, while Penelope was in England, she and Robert corresponded at length over matters of archaeological and architectural interest to do with India. With her tipped nose, deep-set eyes and determined, sulky mouth, Penelope did not lack admirers and at the time of Robert's exhibition, three men were in pursuit, one of them being John Betjeman. Now she tossed out a line to a fourth, so crudely baited that the seriousness of her intent remains obscure. In a long letter to Robert, chiefly dealing with his exhibition, she wrote:

> Osbert Sitwell was talking to Mummy about the sub Ed of the A.R. [Betjeman] last week. He said: 'I don't know him very well, if only Penelope was going to marry Robert Byron I should be delighted.' A very nice suggestion but I dont know why he linked our names so closely together. I have only met you 3 times & thought you exceedingly delightful & attractive, but you have never on any of those occasions made any advances to me, so it is hard to say why O.S. imagined there was any likelihood of our being joined in Holy Matrimony (I am the last person for you to espouse because I should insist upon accompanying you on all your travels which you would not like at all).

She signed off with the words 'Kind Thoughts'.

The calm waters of their friendship remained undisturbed by Penelope's query. At the end of the year she was writing from Delhi with the appalling news of Lady Willingdon's alterations to the Viceroy's House. A loggia had been enclosed, the ballroom filled with lounge furniture and worst of all 'Sand & grass fill every alcove with stuffed tigers lurking in them.'

Penelope's naive approach occurred at a time when Robert was once again engrossed with Desmond. In April, he had taken the proofs of the Russian survey with him to Birr for a fortnight's working holiday. One member of the party who happened to glance through them was Desmond: 'it really seemed quite good', the fastidious young critic reported to Roy Harrod, 'though, as usual, I find the style rather difficult to read.' Desmond's presence transformed everything. Their days were spent riding and birds' nesting; they also went on an expedition with Michael and others to Killarney and Bantry on the south-west coast.

It had been over a year since Robert and Desmond had spent any length of time together. Robert lavished him with praise. 'I could not help noticing', he wrote afterwards, 'how you had changed since Vienna – like a flower in the sun – I hope this doesn't sound patronizing, but to see your interests and confidence expand makes me feel as if mine were expanding too.' Parting for him was agony, especially as Desmond was about to embark on a lengthy visit to Spain. One memory sustained him. 'Dear Desmond', he serenaded, 'I shall always think of you at Birr riding in a blue shirt.'

Within days such rosy sentiments had turned to wormwood and gall. David Fyfe, who had been another guest at Birr, bragged to Robert that Desmond had slept with him. Robert was overwhelmed with jealousy. Physically, he was attacked by facial neuralgia; mentally, he sank into 'a coma of depression'. His self-control broke after a week. The torture of loving Desmond poured out. 'Small coldnesses one can bear –' he told him witheringly, 'even those inevitable displays of downright aversion (tho' I don't think you realize how much they hurt & how deep they go) But it is rather bitter that others who have no deeper feelings and only want their five minutes of fun should be better rewarded.' With reasoned bitterness, he continued:

> Possibly it is my fault, I have always tried to avoid over emphasis on the purely sensual – perhaps too successfully – but though not the widest, sex is the *central* thing. The symbol one might say of all the other sides of a relationship & the completion of them . . . I think sometimes you don't quite realize what a degree of wretchedness you have the power to cause . . . occasionally you might shew a little more consideration or shall we say a little less reluctance – that is if you have any feelings.

The challenge hit home. Desmond telegrammed from Spain admitting his feelings and asked for reassurance. The response was calmer. Drawing upon his other great passion, architecture, Robert addressed the nature of their predicament. 'In every other way, Desmond, you were sweetness and kindness itself,' he began. 'I glow when I think of it. All your thoughts & interests & ideas seemed to form a harmony in which I could join. What does anything else matter? . . . Well, I quite agree in theory – what does a keystone matter to an arch? It is only the smallest stone and by itself nothing. But . . .'

Clear headed, yet unashamedly romantic, Robert parleyed with Desmond one last time.

> You say 'please reassure me' I haven't anything to reassure you of, except that you remain the pattern, the zenith, of all the world can give me. It is for you to reassure me that you can give me in return some of your affection – not all, though I should like it, but some. I mean something more than what is due to the 'good friend'.

Letters flew between them. Desmond's had a tonic effect, knocking Robert, as he put it, 'out of my tragic attitude'. The bookish swain suggested Goethe for consolation. 'Goethe', replied Robert levelly, 'is little comfort – I am not in love with being in love & never could be.' Gradually, peace was restored, but not without a final reiteration on Robert's part of the conditions: 'I on my side can't eliminate bed altogether – though I must admit I try and restrain myself. If this could be admitted between us once and for all, I do think things would be easier . . . Forgive all the bother I have caused you & try to think charitably of my brutish nature.'

Desmond now pressed Robert to join him on a trip to Morocco. He would pay for the fare and hotels whilst Robert, he suggested, could 'take over the unnecessary part of one's expenditure, sightseeing, cafés, bordeles and the thousand little things that crop [up]'. Robert had mixed feelings about the invitation, but, in any case, was forced to refuse: he was obliged in July to go into hospital to have his tonsils out. Meanwhile, Desmond continued his travels. Back in Ireland by the autumn, he tried to lure Robert over to Birr, but without success. His nervous system just was not up to it. With characteristic honesty, he replied:

> 'I am terrified of uprooting myself & being unable to settle down afterwards – it is partly the journey & change of environment that causes me these apprehensions – & partly the remembrance, which you also perhaps share, of how emotionally unsettled I became after my last visit, not to mention the strain of such self-control as I was able to exercise during it. This sounds possibly as if I don't want to see you which is grotesque . . . If I was rich and leisured, I should never willingly leave your side – so you may be thankful I'm not!

Their rift was finally healed in November when Desmond visited Robert at Savernake: 'how wonderful it was to see you again –' Robert exclaimed afterwards, 'I have been quite a different person since & you seem to have restored my spirits permanently – it was sweet of you to come.'

During these storms, Robert was helped by diversions from a few close friends. Mainstays were Bryan and Diana Guinness, who not only invited him to parties in London, but also saw him frequently in the country. In the autumn of 1930 they had acquired Biddesden, a distinguished baroque house near Andover. Robert's original high estimation of Diana had been fully vindicated. She was beautiful, clever, funny and had remarkable taste. His closeness provoked the envy of Evelyn Waugh, who later admitted to Diana, a month before he died: 'You ask why our friendship petered out. Pure jealousy . . . I felt lower in your affections than Harold Acton and Robert Byron and I couldn't compete or take a humbler place.' In the summer and autumn of 1932 Robert attended numerous parties thrown by the Guinnesses. The climax was a fancy dress ball at Biddesden where he went as Voltaire with a wig made from string.

Behind the mask of gaiety, the Guinnesses' marriage was in crisis. That spring, Diana had met Oswald Mosley, the maverick politician who was poised to found the British Union of Fascists. They launched upon a passionate affair, which grew in commitment as the year progressed. Robert, fresh from his trials with Desmond, provided Bryan with a sympathetic ear. 'Bryan invited himself to dine . . .' he informed Michael Rosse, 'what an unhappy life his is – it is all very well to be in love & suffer occasional tortures of jealousy . . . but to have one's whole existence made futile by it & to know it is dreadful . . . However I suppose nothing can be done. Diana is so unbridled.' In January 1933, Diana left Bryan, moving into a house in Eaton Square with their children.

By this time, Robert had also got to know Oswald Mosley's wife, Lady Cynthia, who in the spring of 1933 telephoned him one day with an invitation to the country. A few hours later, she was rushed into hospital with acute appendicitis which led to her death from peritonitis a week later. Robert was the first to break the news to Diana: 'she collapsed in my arms,' he told his mother, 'Diana is quite broken, & as for poor Mosley, he really adored Cimmie & is beside himself.' Robert remained a loyal friend to Diana, despite opposing political views. The following year, he reported to Desmond that she 'leads a cloistral existence & I am told has become very much disliked – tho' she seems to me more delightful than ever'.

Robert drew the greatest solace in the late summer of 1932 from the company of Nancy, who made frequent visits to Savernake from Biddesden. At the time, she was busy correcting the proofs of her second novel, *Christmas Pudding*, which, at Robert's suggestion, had been illustrated by Mark Ogilvie-Grant. As publication day approached, the tone of Nancy's letters to Robert sounded a note of girlish alarm. An invitation to a party to launch the book came with the warning: 'I have done a quite awful thing and you probably won't speak to me anymore when you know it.' Two days later, she urged him: 'Please you've got to come to my BOOK PARTY Quaglino's, 11.00 p.m. Thursday. Please there is a special reason (all connected with you not speaking to me any more) why I want you to come. And all your chums will be there so please be an angel.'

Nancy had dedicated *Christmas Pudding* to Robert. She inscribed his copy: 'Oh dear Robert please don't be cross about all this will you.' She need not have feared. The next day, Robert wrote:

> It was a heavenly party last night you looked so pleased and proud, wh[ich] is how I feel when a (decent) book of mine appears – I like to finger it & go over the best bits – I can't tell you how really delighted & touched I am by the dedication – it makes me feel as if I were being looked after by a sort of Not Forgotten Association – thank you so much – dear Nancy.

Far more alarming was Robert's suggestion that her next book be 'a wholly serious novel – that is to say one whose theme is serious, however much it may be filled in with jokes'. This was precisely what Robert himself was attempting to do, having begun writing, after his operation, a high-minded 'work of imagination'. By the beginning of December, he hit troubled water with his pompous craft, only managing to turn out 100 words a day. Sometime later he gave up the attempt and his abandoned novel sank without trace.

Meanwhile a cause far more suited to his talents began to occupy his time. In October, Christopher Hussey, architectural editor of *Country Life*, put to him an irresistible proposal. 'I know how much you admire the work of Sir Herbert Baker', he wrote, 'and particularly his splendid South Africa House, which is now practically complete, except for some very fine advertisement hoardings, which, if possible, improve the lower storey. If we took some photographs of this remarkable building, would you care to write an appreciation?'

The invitation was inspired by Robert's already published criticism of the plans for South Africa House, made the previous year in the *Weekend Review*. This was a civilized weekly launched by Gerald Barry, an editor with a rare passion for architecture who gave Robert frequent opportunity to voice his opinions. Baker's plans for the building to be erected in Trafalgar Square next door to St Martin-in-the-Fields had been savaged by Robert who accused the architect of ruining one of London's most important open spaces.

Christopher Hussey's enthusiasm for the fray was not shared by Edward Hudson. Between the typing of the letter and its dispatch, Hudson had expressed reservations. 'He is inclined to leave it', Hussey wrote in a postscript, 'in case he gets into trouble for always running J.H.B. down. But you may have suggestions.'

Unfortunately for Baker, his crime in Trafalgar Square was being uncovered just as another architectural outrage was being perpetrated, close by, at Carlton Gardens. In an unsigned leader in *Country Life*, dated 12 November, entitled 'The Unguarded City', Robert linked the two events. Using South Africa House as an example, he drew attention to the freedom of landlords and their clients to deface London. Unlike Paris or even New York, he pointed out, no government body existed here with the power to change or veto unsuitable plans. Then he turned on the Commissioners of Crown Lands, the body responsible to Parliament for the ancient estates originally held by the sovereign, which included Carlton Gardens and Trafalgar Square. In July, the Commissioners of Crown Lands had sold for offices the lease of number 4 Carlton Gardens, one of a group of houses at the western end of Carlton House Terrace. By the end of the month, the housebreakers had moved in and plans were submitted for an out-of-scale office block, part of a design for the rebuilding of the entire terrace. Robert accused the Commissioners of being 'less enlightened and less sensible of the public interest than the most rapacious private landlords'.

Carlton House Terrace had been conceived in 1827 by John Nash as a magnificent finale to the dramatic thoroughfare which he had laid between the poles of fashionable

London, from his crescents in Regent's Park, down Robert Adam's Portland Place, along the circuses and quadrant of Regent Street to Waterloo Place and St James's Park. Until 1920, his scheme had remained almost intact. But when the ninety-nine-year leases of Regent Street fell in, the Commissioners of Crown Lands pounced, destroying, in a frenzy of demolition, the exquisite riband of stucco, comprising work by Soane, Decimus Burton, C. R. Cockerell and others, besides Nash, which linked Carlton House Terrace to Portland Place. The dust had scarcely settled before the Commissioners turned to Carlton House Terrace for a second helping of London's finest Regency architecture.

As the rumour spread that the Terrace was to be demolished, Robert received calls to arms from Gerald Barry at the *Weekend Review*, and from de Cronin Hastings, editor of the *Architectural Review*: 'There are some glorious scandals which you must take a share in,' urged de Cronin Hastings. 'Carlton Gardens and Carlton House Terrace are going to be pulled down – did you know?. . . Surely this is your subject.'

On 10 December, Robert raised his standard in *Country Life*. He bore down upon Sir Reginald Blomfield, architect of the Carlton Gardens design, dismissing it as 'a medley of outmoded clichés, genteel and false in sentiment as a Cotswold tea shop'. Robert's sarcasm was born of frustration at the ease with which anonymous officials could sweep away one of London's grandest public monuments. The Commissioners of Crown Lands, he wrote, 'already branded by their destruction of Regent Street and disfigurement of Trafalgar Square, are still allowed to go their way of vengeance unhindered by concerted protest. Even the Zeppelins did less damage than these morbid officials.'

Three days after Robert's article in *Country Life*, *The Times* published a leader in similar vein. Christopher Hussey, who happened to meet a *Times* leader writer on the day of publication, wrote congratulating Robert: 'I cannot help thinking that the line you took was not without influence on *The Times*.' An alliance was now formed, one of the most unlikely in the history of English taste, between politicians and the press. An outraged group of MPs and peers extracted conflicting statements from ministers over the intentions of the Commissioners of Crown Lands. The almost daily coverage in *The Times* led to the exposure of the venality of Sir Reginald Blomfield. On 30 December, J. C. Squire, editor of the *London Mercury*, launched a defence committee, which Robert was invited to join. In February, Captain Cruikshank MP chose Carlton House Terrace as the subject for his Private Member's Bill. He called for reform of the administration of the Crown Lands and for public consultation on any future plans for the Terrace. The Government took the opportunity to beat a dignified retreat and agreed to the motion. The Terrace was saved. Nothing however could prevent Blomfield's office block being built on the site of number 4 Carlton Gardens, where it remains, a hard, white scar from the battle won.

Victory offered little respite. In June 1933, Robert drew attention in the *Architectural Review* to the latest disfigurement of London, an office block named Faraday House, which had arisen by Blackfriars Bridge obscuring the drum of St Paul's. This was the second act of vandalism to the City's skyline. Unilever House, he wrote, had already blotted the view from Hungerford Bridge of 'Wren's London still teeming on the north curve of the Thames, the vision of St Paul's dome, reigning over one of the grandest urban prospects in Europe'.

To save what remained of London's architectural distinction, Robert suggested that a planning body should be established with powers of veto. Streets and public monuments should be scheduled for varying degrees of protection, and areas of little merit should be marked out for redevelopment. He pointed out that the Royal Commission which advised on the preservation of buildings and archaeological sites could only propose monuments which dated from before 1714. 'Thus', he wrote,

> while the whole of England is now sprinkled with neolithic boulders, Roman valla, and Anglo-Saxon pig-sties which have been officially proclaimed as invaluable to our national heritage, the monuments of London, unless they happen to be Gothic or timbered, may vanish from the earth without

> so much as an official sigh. It is not merely Carlton House Terrace, but the whole of London surviving from before the year 1850, which cries, if not for rigid protection, at least for its case to be considered before the gangsters are upon it.

Robert did not wish to stifle good modern architecture in London. Each new building of any importance attracted his attention, including the Dorchester Hotel, Hays Wharf and County Hall. In the opening years of the 1930s, the future course of architecture was unclear. The building sites of London were under the command of vigorous Edwardians, such as Lutyens and Baker, and modern traditionalists who favoured unadorned façades of Portland stone and tiers of sash windows. To Robert, it represented a period of transition, with buildings of unprecedented height, sometimes constructed from novel materials, forcing their way on to the London streets. In the *Weekend Review*, he appealed for a display of good manners in the development of London. Architects, he wrote, should respect the ancient street pattern, harmonize their designs with neighbouring buildings and use Portland stone or London brick.

Modernism posed little threat to the architectural character of London. Apart from a handful of fashion-conscious interiors, the most striking example was the gorilla house by Lubetkin in Regent's Park Zoo. Robert kept an open mind on the merits of the style. In August 1932, he contributed to a survey in the *Architectural Review* on the newly completed Broadcasting House. Concentrating on the interiors, he praised the work of the radical designer, Raymond McGrath. 'In all cases', he wrote, 'the design is admirable, displaying, in conjunction with severe economy of form, the grace of true functionalism.' And he singled out the studios by the modernist, Wells Coates, as the 'finest achievement in the building'.

The *Architectural Review*, under the editorship of Hubert de Cronin Hastings, had been the first magazine in the industry to engage with modernism in architecture. Deploying glamorous layouts in place of banner headlines and expensive rag paper instead of newsprint, Hastings added his own gloss to each new landmark as it appeared in Europe or

America. He was the make-up artist who initiated English taste into concrete and steel.

The appointment of Hastings as editor in 1928, at the age of twenty-five, had been the not entirely disinterested choice of the proprietor of the magazine, his father. Despite his youth, he had a tyrannical streak which terrified members of the staff. He was also reclusive, fobbing off most visitors on to his assistant, John Betjeman. An exception was Robert.

Hastings had exerted a profound influence upon Robert's career. His boldness in commissioning an entire issue on New Delhi had established Robert's name as an architectural critic. His latitude over the Russian survey had extended Robert's range as a travel writer. Although underwriting the journey, Hastings had brushed aside Robert's concern over the brief. 'My correspondent,' Robert recalled, 'amidst whose constellation of natural virtues caution has never so much as twinkled, replied . . . that of course he left everything to me who was on the spot; but that what he really wanted was neither modern architecture nor old, but my "reactions to Bolshevism".'

In November 1932, Hastings was promoted to managing director. His replacement, Christian Barman, was, Hastings informed Robert, 'very much in sympathy with your effete un-functional and jazz-less credo'.

Robert's close association with the magazine continued under the new editor. An important link was John Betjeman who sub-edited his articles and undertook valuable research for him, particularly on planning laws. Urging him on from behind the scenes, Betjeman wrote: 'Look then at the terrific significance of what you have to write . . . This is all bloody important.' His assistance on the Russian survey, which involved retrieving information on Highgate cemetery, led to an acknowledgement to 'Bishop Betjeman, the father of necropolitan research'. Betjeman's correspondence was also laced with less serious asides. 'I do not feel at all well and I hope I shall soon die,' he interjected into a short note about an article, before ending with the bidding, 'Yours in the sure and certain hope of a speedy resurrection, John Betjeman.' His character acting was contagious. On his return from India, Robert complained to Bryan Guinness that in

Betjeman's company he found himself behaving like an old Indian colonel.

Socially as well as professionally, they paraded in the same ring, although Betjeman won no prizes for his appearance. Like Robert, he was an habitué of Biddesden, where he led hymn singing over the port after dinner. And he numbered two of Robert's oldest friends, Cecil Clonmore and Patrick Balfour, as his intimates. The chance of catching a glimpse of Lucy Byron was a further incentive to meet her brother. 'I saw Lucy Byron . . . yesterday,' he wrote to Lionel Perry, 'she always makes me want to cry she looks so nice.' He even went so far as to commission from Lucy a book review. This favour was but a posy compared to the bouquet laid at the feet of Penelope Chetwode. In October 1932 her article on Indian temples was published in the *Architectural Review*. Ten months later, after a marathon courtship, instigated by Robert's inadvertent match-making, John Betjeman and Penelope Chetwode were married.

Robert's final say on architecture for the year appeared in a slim volume, entitled *The Appreciation of Architecture*. His aim was to equip the public with the skills to differentiate between good and bad architecture. To do so, he first had to state his *raison d'être* as a critic. 'By good architecture is meant, not the style or styles in vogue at this or that particular moment', he writes, 'but good design, a constant factor transcending styles and susceptible to judgement by an absolute standard.' As someone driven by an unruly passion for architecture, he goes on to acknowledge the importance of critical instinct: 'Aesthetic judgement must always, in the last event, derive from sources outside the scope of reason and definition. Beauty may appeal to the one and be capable of the other. But primarily it must be felt.'

Robert devises two categories of design, the static and the mobile, one or other of which, he claims, is inherent in all great architecture. The static is generally found in classical buildings of the West, when the focus of a symmetrical building rests in a central point. The mobile is found in buildings of greater length or height, such as a gothic cathedral or Indian temple, where mobility of the structure or decoration unifies the building. Equipped with these classifications, the reader is dispatched on to the streets of London to identify for himself good and bad buildings.

Like all panaceas, the immediate effect of his rule of thumb was beneficial. Harold Nicolson wrote, in his influential column in the *New Statesman*: 'I have, I think, read most of what Mr Byron has written. I have always returned from his writings with a sense of increase. Yet in these thirty-one pages he has given me more excitement and more assuagement than I have experienced since *The Architecture of Humanism*.' The following week sales of the book doubled and by February 1933 they totalled five hundred. Over time, Robert found his black and white approach too simplistic to have any critical value. He referred to it as 'my little bastard book' and forbade Christopher Sykes from reading it, explaining 'rather shortly that he did not wish to be reminded of it'.

20
The Charcoal Burners

The first six months of 1933 saw the hatching of Robert's plans for his next journey. The idea had been laid during the preparations for his Russian trip when he had attempted to visit Turkestan. Though his application for a visa had been rejected in Moscow, Robert's ambition to visit Turkestan remained undimmed. During 1932, he kept in touch with Mark Dineley who had originally advised him on a route to Kashgar. Dineley lived near Shaftesbury. In May they met to discuss the matter. Afterwards, Dineley wrote: 'don't worry about Persia – it may come off it may not but just keep it in mind.'

Four years older than Robert, Mark Dineley was heir to a Quaker banking fortune and had travelled almost continuously since leaving Cambridge, reputedly as a gentleman spy on behalf of the Foreign Office. His journeys took him to the Baltic states and to Russia where he was caught up in the civil war. He spent a considerable time in Persia, ranging over the territory of the Turcoman nomads in the north of the country, where he was welcomed by tribal leaders 'as one gentleman of leisure receiving another'. From his maternal grandfather, a notable patron of Whistler, Dineley had inherited an acquisitive streak. In the district of Meshed in Persia, he had acquired 'some very jolly bronzes of the early Arab period', which were of sufficient quality to be accepted for the 1931 Persian Exhibition at the Royal Academy.

Another traveller whom Robert consulted before leaving for Russia was Bosworth Goldman, known as Boz, a neighbour living near Marlborough. In the summer of 1932 at the age of twenty-two, Goldman, a Russian speaker who knew Russia well, succeeded where Robert had failed, in visiting Turkestan. His route took him via Novosibirsk, the capital of Western Siberia. Wandering round the town, Goldman entered a building which turned out to be a hospital filled with wounded soldiers. 'I asked some of them where they had been', he related, 'and they replied that they had been fighting in the Southern Altai, in co-operation with some Chinese, against "anti-social elements" disturbing the advance of the class-warfare banner into Sinkiang.' Goldman had stumbled across evidence of Bolshevik penetration into Chinese Turkestan.

Boz had written to Robert from Tashkent requesting introductions to 'enlivening company' in Constantinople where he planned to stop off on his journey home. The next time Robert heard from him was at the beginning of November from the London Clinic where he was recovering from his ordeal. He asked Robert for assistance in writing 'a compendium of what I saw . . . and then a pamphlet or short book on the political interests'. Robert was intrigued by Boz's discovery of the wounded soldiers in Novosibirsk. The chance of investigating a Bolshevik presence in Sinkiang, with its attendant threat to the British in India, made him determined to visit the province.

From Boz's records and other sources, Robert wrote a memorandum on the Central Asian situation which he intended submitting to the Foreign Office in the hope of gaining their support for an expedition. He showed it to G. M. Young, the 'immensely learned' historian, who lived at Oare, close to Savernake. Young was the closest Robert had to a mentor. He gave him the run of his vast library and took over the task from John Mavrogordato of reading the proofs of *The Birth of Western Painting*. Young had also served in the civil service, so his opinion on Robert's memorandum was worthwhile. On reading it, Young counselled caution: 'you do not know what the F.O. are already doing: Dzungaria [a northern province of Chinese Turkestan] may be thick with Kim-like agents.' Robert received greater encouragement from Penelope Chetwode in India. In her role as Mata Hari, she showed his paper to her friend, Mr Williamson, the head of Intelligence: 'he seemed extremely interested,' she reported back, adding that Williamson was prepared to pay up to £400 for information of value.

Despite warnings of the difficulties faced by travellers who ventured into the region, Robert pressed on with his scheme. Michael Rosse was cajoled into putting his name forward as the third member of the party, alongside Boz and himself, and their application was submitted to the Foreign Office. Robert hoped to follow the route taken by the Frenchman, G. M. Haardt, in 1931, who crossed into Chinese Turkestan by the Gilgit pass in Kashmir. Haardt's expedition, which Robert wrote up for *Country Life* in March 1933, had travelled in a fleet of Citroën tractor cars across Iraq and Persia, entering Afghanistan at Herat. For political reasons, Haardt had to abandon his attempt to cross the Himalayas by car, but he continued to Kashgar in Turkestan by animal transport, eventually meeting up with the second part of the expedition which had travelled from Tientsin across the Gobi desert to meet him.

On 1 January 1933, Robert had introduced Boz to Mark Dineley over tea at Savernake to discuss the proposed trip to Turkestan. Dineley, however, did not agree to join the expedition until the spring, by which time Michael Rosse had withdrawn from the party. In April, he volunteered his Ford delivery van as one of the vehicles and it was suggested that Boz should acquire a truck. The practical difficulties of crossing the Gilgit pass were dismissed by Dineley: 'I think if we have sufficient funds', he wrote to Robert, 'it will always be possible to get one car into Kashgar by the simple process of pulling it to bits and loading it on yaks or horses.'

One of the problems faced by the relief party of the Haardt expedition had been the limited supply of petrol. For the return journey they had had to establish secret fuel dumps along the route. A novel element of the British plan was to travel in vehicles which were adapted to run on charcoal as well as petrol, thus avoiding fuel shortages in districts where petrol was unobtainable. The invention was well known, but not widely tested. In May, Mark Dineley sent his Ford van to have the charcoal burner put on.

Stressing the importance of Robert's role as the writer of the party, who might have to interview the Shah, Dineley chose for himself the role of driver-mechanic. 'I absolutely refuse to dress up and have meals with consuls anywhere,' he informed Robert. It turned out that Dineley had a dubious reputation in Persia, strengthening the rumour that he had once dispatched with his telescopic rifle someone who had taken a pot shot at him.

Meanwhile Boz could not resist boasting about their forthcoming adventure. To Dineley's disdain, he also hankered after a cine camera to film the journey. Unfortunately, the spirit of a diva lurked in Boz's swollen chest. After delivering a lecture to the Royal Central Asian Society on his Siberian journey, he took great offence at some imagined slight. Robert was dragged into the row and was obliged to pacify the baffled secretary, Miss Kennedy. None of these antics impressed Dineley. 'I do beg of you', he wrote to Robert, 'to cork up Boz's flights of fancy.'

Dineley's hard-headed approach began to give more realistic shape to the journey. He was sceptical of their chances of reaching Chinese Turkestan and argued that they should visit Kabul first before making a dash for the northern border. Robert, he suggested, should consider writing a book on Afghanistan. 'With regard to Persia and its monuments', he wrote, 'they are very well written up except the obscurer ones in Eastern Persia.' In his never-ending quest for booty, Dineley hoped to acquire twelfth-century bronze figurines from eastern Afghanistan. If successful, he explained: 'I could feel almost consoled for a failure to achieve the honour of sticking a Ford truck in the Gobi sand.'

Robert had long harboured a less materialistic goal. Researching the origins of Islamic architecture while in India, he had come across a photograph in a book by the German scholar, Professor Ernst Diez, of the eleventh-century tomb tower of Gumbad-i-Kabus in northern Persia. 'It was Diez's picture . . .' Robert wrote later, 'that decided me to come to Persia.' Situated in the heart of Turcoman country, it was a monument which Dineley had also photographed. In *The Appreciation of Architecture*, Robert illustrated the tower as an example of vertical mobility, describing it as Turcoman. To Robert's great interest, an article in *Country Life* in December 1932, on Persian brickwork, included photographs of other tomb towers. Edward Hudson put him in touch with the author, the Persian scholar, Arthur Upham Pope, who wrote back to Robert: 'it is a joy to me that somebody else feels this hysterical excitement in the brick-patterned minarets (I think we should call them Seljuk instead of Turcoman) and I have quite a number of photographs you have not seen. I can easily arrange an opportunity for you to see some of these towers.'

Arthur Upham Pope, scion of an old Massachusetts family, was a dynamic force in the world of Persian studies. Originally a professor of philosophy, he credited his interest in Persian art to the oriental rugs collected by a maiden aunt. By the 1920s Upham Pope, with his second wife, Phyllis Ackerman, had moved into the world of connoisseurship and dealing, advising American museums on their collections. After his first visit to Persia in 1925, he organized a congress and exhibition in Philadelphia. This was followed by his founding of the American Institute for Persian Art and Archaeology to 'encourage and extend an understanding and appreciation of Persian art'. His influence was recognized in his appointment as general director of the 1931 International Exhibition of Persian Art at the Royal Academy in London. The display of paintings, manuscripts, textiles, metalwork and ceramics was of unparalleled magnificence, the Shah having sanctioned loans from the Royal Library and from the treasuries of shrines. Many of the exhibits which had never before left Persia arrived packed in camel dung. Also shown were photographs of architecture taken by Upham Pope.

David Talbot Rice had been responsible for negotiating the loans of Persian treasures from the Turkish government. He was also asked to deliver weekly lectures in the Academy on the exhibits. Gerald Reitlinger lent the Talbot Rices his house in London for the duration of the exhibition. He too had a growing interest in Persian art and at the time was travelling in Persia visiting the principal monuments. The following year, Reitlinger's account of the journey, *A Tower of Skulls*, was published. When Dineley was considering the names of others who might join their expedition in May 1933, he suggested Reitlinger on the strength of his book. Reluctantly, Robert canvassed his old foe from Mount Athos who volunteered with alacrity, offering £200 towards costs.

Having received news earlier in the year of a Turki uprising in Chinese Turkestan, by June it had become clear that travel there would be closed to them. Robert decided to remain as the official writer on the curtailed expedition but on strict financial conditions. 'I shall, I think, definitely go to Persia and Afghanistan,' he wrote to his mother.

> The element of adventure is negligible, now that Sinkiang is impossible. I have stipulated for total expenses including 1. All preliminaries, equipment, visas, journey etc 2. Fare home under any circumstances 3. Enough to live on while working on material after returning home. And of course total keep etc during expedition. So I don't see how it can cost me a penny do you?

Boz was quick to enlighten him. Although he hoped to profit from the successful testing of the charcoal-burning plant, Boz resented the fact that he and Dineley were having to put up nearly all the money, over £700 each, to pay for the expedition. In the wrangling which followed, Robert agreed to pay back the cost of his passage from future literary earnings, but he deducted £100 from the debt to cover his advertising of the plant in books and articles.

Robert's demands sprang from the simple fact that he had no money. In the second half of 1932, apart from a small income from architectural journalism, he had made £35 from *The Appreciation of Architecture* and two guineas from a contribution to an anthology of childhood reminiscences. To improve the situation, in the spring of 1933, he worked up two proposals for books and appointed a literary agent, A. D. Peters, to negotiate with publishers on his behalf.

His most ambitious project was for a history of the 1914–18 war. Robert had never relinquished the idea of completing a companion volume to *The Byzantine Achievement* covering recent Greek history. In the autumn of 1932, he wrote to John Mavrogordato with regard to a copy of Compton Mackenzie's suppressed memoirs of wartime Greece: 'the fact is if ever I write my history of Greece 1912–23, it would be so extremely useful. And I fully intend to write this sometime.' Robert was undaunted by the leap from regional to world history. He planned a work of epic proportions in four volumes which linked the causes and course of the war to changes in society. Volume One was to open with a survey of the world at the dawn of the century. He undertook to commence this task in 1934 on his return from Persia.

In April, A. D. Peters offered the proposal to Macmillan, raising the prospect of an appropriately heroic advance of between £5,000 and £10,000. Their rejection came as a bitter disappointment to Robert. 'I was afraid that Macmillan's refusal of the history book would upset you,' wrote Peters. 'The scheme in toto is probably too much for any publisher to swallow, and I think you should bring your mind to fixing a minimum advance for the first volume.' Macmillan, however, swiftly agreed to Robert's other idea, which was for a travel book based on his journeys in Russia and Tibet.

Once previously, as a convenient way of making money, Robert had considered publishing two unrelated travel diaries, covering his journeys to Spain and Czechoslovakia. At the time, he had written to his mother: 'altogether I cd make the most amusing book & practically speaking in my spare time. It wd be child's play.' In March, exchanging his pen for scissors and paste he started putting together his writings on Russia. With only minor amendments, he took the Russian survey from the *Architectural Review* and joined it to the articles from *Country Life*. He also managed to stick in a stray piece from the *Weekend Review*. The only original material on offer was a chapter on 'Early Russian Painting'. Tibet was accounted for by the manuscript of 'The British Evening in the Morning-lands', the polished version of his travel diary, originally intended as the opening section of his book on India. On 18 May, Macmillan's bought the book, provisionally titled 'Wheels and No Wheels', for an advance of £100. Half this amount was to be paid to Frederic Warburg to release Robert from existing obligations.

By the end of June, the plans for the expedition were almost complete, with a date fixed in September for their arrival at Beirut. Robert wrote to the Persian minister in London asking him to smooth their way at the Iraq-Persian frontier. The aims of the journey were given as the testing of the 'Parker Producer Gas Plant', the invention 'which makes it possible to run motor cars and lorries on charcoal in districts where petrol and heavy oil are not available'. Its further purpose was stated as the gathering of material for a book 'which will describe the beauties of the country and . . . promote the cause of Anglo-Persian friendship'.

At this point Boz chose to transform the expedition into a serious business venture. Borrowing £5,000 on a life assurance policy he bought the Koela Producer Gas Plant Company, makers of the charcoal generating units, and appointed himself as chairman. Everything was now subordinated to the testing of these elaborate contraptions. The charcoal was converted into gas in a cylindrical furnace with a fuel hopper, fixed on the near running board. The fuel, enriched with water, was then fed from a small tank to a steel box on the other running board and thence to the engine. Boz, who had once briefly worked as an engineer for Rolls-Royce, had high hopes for the invention. If successful, he planned to manufacture the plants for use mainly in tropical countries. In Britain, he had visions of controlling charcoal dumps across the country. Dineley strongly advised him against the decision, fearing that Boz was buying 'a most expensive pup'. At the same time, he became increasingly wary of Boz's love of publicity, which, he explained to Robert, 'was a little bit too much Bertram Mills for me'. As a consequence, he withdrew from the expedition. For unconnected reasons, Gerald Reitlinger also dropped out.

Boz was unruffled by Dineley's desertion. Even Robert was swept along by his panache, writing to his mother in mid-July: 'Boz drove me (in a top hat) to the Ritz yesterday in the big lorry, wh. is just complete, with windows like a Tudor cottage! & a roof you can stand on. I am really beginning to look forward to it all.' Dineley's place was taken by a 'field naturalist', called John Henderson, who was keen to hunt rare species in Afghanistan. He was persuaded to invest in the Gas Plant Company and at the end of the month came up with £500 which finally signalled their departure. Provided that another driver could be recruited, Robert planned to travel out to Beirut independently, staying with the Abdys in Venice on the way. Eldon Rutter, an Arabist and author who had lived in Mecca as a Muslim, volunteered for the role.

Amidst all the coming and going one other traveller unobtrusively joined the party. A friend of Robert's, Christopher Sykes, who had lived in Persia and spoke Persian, now signed up as his companion on the journey. Late though the decision was, the idea had first been mooted in November 1931 when Robert was making his preparations for Russia: Sykes, on his first night back in England after a year in Persia, had encountered Robert with a group of friends at the Savoy Hotel. The following day, over a long lunch, Robert quizzed Sykes on the tomb tower of Gumbad-i-Kabus and, when they parted, suggested that they might visit Persia together one day.

The two had first met in William Acton's rooms in Christ Church on one of Robert's return visits to Oxford. 'I like Xtopher Sykes very much . . .' he wrote to Patrick Balfour in March 1927. 'I am meeting him at dinner in about a week – it is quite a light in the general gloom of existence.' To Robert, embarking on his study of modern Greek history, Christopher Sykes had an impressive provenance. He was the second son of Sir Mark Sykes, who had been one of the great authorities on the pre-war Ottoman Empire, and Robert had sought him out partly because he was keen to read his father's books on the subject. Mark Sykes, who had died in 1919, had also been co-author of the Sykes–Picot agreement assigning post-war spheres of interest over a dismantled Ottoman Empire, and had been an early exponent of Zionism.

Christopher had left Oxford after two years keen to sample the diplomatic world. He served as an honorary attaché at the British Embassy in Berlin, before deciding to learn Persian at the School of Oriental Studies in London. His slight stammer vanished when speaking Persian. In November 1930, he became an honorary attaché at the legation in Teheran, a post which he held for a year.

On his return to England, Sykes wrote a light-hearted travel book, based on two journeys he had made in Persia, entitled *Changed*. The book reached proof stage and was even advertised in the press for publication in the autumn of 1932. At the last minute, however, Sykes suppressed the book, realizing that certain remarks critical of the Shah and his government would, if published, prevent him ever being allowed to enter Persia again. After this act of literary immolation, the charcoal burners' expedition provided him with an excuse for returning. At the final gathering of the party, Sykes agreed to meet up with Robert in Cyprus before travelling on to Beirut.

In the weeks preceding departure, Robert's travel book was passing through the press. At Macmillan he dealt with the two junior family partners, Daniel and his younger brother, Harold. Ideas for the title were batted to and fro until they finally settled upon Robert's suggestion of *First Russia Then Tibet*. On 1 August, Harold Macmillan signed Robert up for another travel book for an advance of £100, provisionally entitled 'Travels in Persia'.

Arthur Upham Pope also supplied Robert with valuable assistance. At the time of the Persian exhibition, he had announced the preparation under his editorship of a three-volume *Survey of Persian Art* to be compiled by over forty scholars in ten countries. In August 1933, Upham Pope was living in Oxford working with the publishers of the *Survey*, the Oxford University Press. He armed Robert with letters of recommendation including one which certified that his party was 'engaged in serious research work in Persia for the SURVEY OF PERSIAN ART, and that they are making a special effort to secure some very much needed photographs, without which the book will be incomplete. They have been requested, if possible, to procure photographs of the various towers and minarets in North Persia.'

Against preparations for the expedition, one issue, central to Robert's life, had to be faced. His departure for Persia meant a prolonged separation from Desmond. So far, their reconciliation had held firm. Desmond had even offered to pay for Robert's fare to Birr in the spring and been accepted. As Robert admitted: 'that gave me I can't say how much pleasure, because it made me feel you really had wanted me to come over.' Part of the fortnight was spent on an expedition to Tory island off Donegal where they met the Queen of the island. An outpouring of feeling followed his return to England.

> I never felt so broken at leaving anywhere – or anyone – as when we parted on the quay at Dublin . . . I do wish sometime

> I could give more in return for all you give me – it is I who should give – yet I only seem to take of your sufficiency . . . Anyhow Desmond dear, thank you many times for being so sweet & kind in every way.

Robert's powerful ego was obliterated by his love for Desmond. Normally avid for publicity, he once reacted sharply to Desmond's news from abroad that a diplomat had referred to him as a celebrity: 'I'm afraid I'm not my idea of a celebrity', he replied, '& am thankful to hear that I am not yours either & trust I may never become so.' The thought of being in some way superior to Desmond was abhorrent to him. It was Desmond who was 'the great sufficiency', not he. James Lees-Milne divined the cause: 'Theirs was the love of opposites. Desmond was the stationary idol and seer, certainly the luminary to whom Robert the voyager was drawn . . . for perceptual sympathy and encouragement.'

The price of Desmond's self-possession was his coldness. Another show of indifference felled Robert in the run-up to his departure, reducing him privately to tears. 'You must understand –' he pointed out, 'however much it may bore you – when one person has for three years provided another with the most important of human relationships, the other is bound to feel seriously (to put it mildly) when that relationship is about to be interrupted.'

Robert's despair had been made worse because he foresaw a separation of several years. This was not entirely of his own doing. Desmond, too, had been making travel plans, having been seized by an ambition to go and live in China. Being Desmond, no decision had yet been made, but he had begun an intensive course of reading and with the aid of a grammar begun to study 'the roots of the Chinese language'. The personal consequences had been aired from the outset, forcing Robert to concede: 'I should never abandon my claims to you – but with regard to China . . . I'm afraid they can hardly be said to exist, as I see no prospect of being able to get there . . . all I can say is that once you have gone it would be the greatest possible inducement to me to find a means of joining you.'

The necessity of a meeting was, for him, paramount. He

was even prepared to defer his start for Persia to achieve it. But Desmond was at his most elusive. Robert finally lost patience. His outburst reflected the maturity of his love. 'I wish I weren't quite so serious about it,' he admitted.

> But after all our friendship has been more than mere bed, & I should like to think that by parting happily now we shall be able to continue it happily in the future. So don't be deliberately unsympathetic even if you can't share my feelings. Once in Pekin you can forget my existence. Try and bear with it while we are in Europe another three weeks . . . On the other hand, if you don't want to meet me, say so. This will be better than pretence. Then I will write goodbye & it may be irrevocable or may not.

As always, the force of Robert's personality, his honesty and his refusal to accept second best won Desmond round. They agreed to meet in Venice for a last farewell.

On 18 August, Robert left from Victoria station mightily relieved after days of frantic activity at suddenly having 'nothing to do and to think of nothing'. A week later, the charcoal-burning vans left London amid a fanfare of publicity with many curious sightseers stopping to watch the vans being loaded. *The Times* devoted a column to their departure and printed a picture. The *Daily Express* hinted at a secret mission, warning that a premature announcement of their destination 'MIGHT ENTAIL SERIOUS POLITICAL CONSEQUENCES'. Boz, as arranged, was heading for Marseilles and thence, by boat, for Beirut. His rendezvous with Robert was fixed for 6 September.

21

Persia and Beyond

Robert's host in Venice was William Odom, an American millionaire and art dealer, who had taken the Palazzo Barbaro on the Grand Canal. Diane Abdy had drawn up the guest list which included Sachie and Georgia Sitwell, the MP Chips Channon and his wife, and, of course, Desmond. 'Our host', Robert wrote to his mother, 'has succeeded in introducing one friend of his own . . . much to everyone's surprise and indignation.'

Over the next three days, Robert and Desmond said their 'long goodbye'. Robert described the life as that of 'a joy hog'. He bathed at the Lido, an experience which he dismissed as 'Water like hot saliva, cigar ends floating into one's mouth & shoals of jelly fish.' He toured churches and palazzos; he drank at Harry's Bar. On his last afternoon, a party, including the dancer Serge Lifar, drove out to the Villa Malcontenta near Mestre. As dusk fell, Robert stood on the lawn admiring the pure form of Palladio's masterpiece. Diane Abdy, who stood beside him, said: 'It is a mistake to leave civilization.' Robert spirits sank. Inside, the candles were lit, and Lifar danced.

At 5 the next morning, Robert was conveyed by gondola to the railway station, bound for Trieste and thence by ship for Cyprus. His parting from Desmond, later recalled triumphantly as 'that last morning in Venice!', had met every expectation. He wrote from the ship: 'You have sent me off happier than you have ever made me – despite the gloom of parting – because of a new permanence which I seemed to feel between us. I hope it wasn't only I that felt it. You were so kind & sweet (at times one might even say patient) Thank you a million times.'

Four days later, on 27 August, he arrived at Larnaca. Rupert Gunnis, who had served as secretary to Sir Ronald

Storrs when he was Governor of Cyprus, had placed his house in Nicosia, his staff and his car at Robert's disposal. Gunnis was away at the time, but he had warned Robert that he was likely to be viewed with suspicion by the British authorities. In 1931, after the burning of Government House by Greek nationalists, Robert had called for Britain to recognize the Cypriots' desire for union with Greece.

However, the purpose of Robert's visit was cultural rather than political and he spent the week gathering material for an article which he hoped to sell to *Country Life*. His timing was good. The British authorities had awoken to the problem of Cyprus's monuments and his survey was published to coincide with the setting up of a committee to study their preservation.

Passing through Nicosia, Robert received a telegram from Boz: 'Mishap necessitates delay one week so arriving Beyrouth fourteenth have informed Christopher stop car not plant at fault.' By the same post he received a letter from Ralph Stockley, ADC to the High Commissioner in Palestine, whom he had met on the voyage from Trieste. He was reminded of Stockley's descriptions of Jerusalem and decided to visit the city while waiting for Boz.

In light of the telegram, Robert assumed that his rendezvous with Christopher Sykes on 3 September at Larnaca was cancelled. Christopher, who had heard nothing from Boz, arrived as planned to find no sign of Robert. The two eventually met up and Christopher welcomed the idea of visiting Jerusalem. Recalling the scene later in *Four Studies in Loyalty*, he worked up for publication a bravura description of Robert's arrival, placing himself on deck rather than on the pier where they actually met.

> Twilight was falling rapidly and the boat due to sail in a few minutes, when to my relief I saw a round figure dressed in jodhpurs and a tweed jacket, and with a cigarette dangling from his lower lip, fairly charging along the jetty to a sound of clattering cameras, pencil-cases and folios which hung about him. A gigantic negro followed at a half run with his bags. I watched from the deck. Arrived at the boat he showed his ticket, returned it to his pocket, and then made a sort of dive

at the officials, as it were, swam through them on a breast-stroke, and mounted the gangway. 'Hallo, I'm late,' he said, and added as the official bellowings from below reached us: 'I had all my papers stamped this morning to save time. It never does to argue with customs people.' I went down the gangway, and not for the last time in my life with him, made peace with an angered crowd.

Their boat, like the vessel which Robert had taken from Trieste, was crammed with Jewish refugees fleeing the anti-Semitic persecution in Germany, which had escalated since Hitler's coming to power at the beginning of the year. That night, on the lower deck, their fellow passengers performed Hebrew dances to the accompaniment of their own chants. The next morning, as they disembarked at Jaffa in a lighter, there was a heavy swell and a Jewish woman was sick over Robert's hand. 'Her husband', he wrote, 'nursed their child while supporting, in his other arm, a tall plant of veronica in a pot. They were decent people. I was sorry for them.'

Arriving at the King David Hotel in Jerusalem in time for lunch, they took a nap, then walked to the old town. At the Church of the Holy Sepulchre, Robert was uncertain how to respond. 'To pretend to detachment is supercilious,' he wrote; 'to pretend to reverence, hypocritical.' His dilemma was solved by Father Gabriel, a monk from Mount Athos whom he discovered at the entrance to the church. Robert, having brushed up his Greek on Cyprus, hailed him. Gabriel led him inside, chatting all the time about his monastery, Docheiariou. Recording the visit in his diary, Robert wrote:

> I found myself in a small marble chamber carved in the Turkish baroque style. The way to the inner sanctuary was blocked by 3 kneeling Franciscans . . . Stepping through the Franciscans, Gabriel dived into a hole about 3 feet high, from wh. came a bright light. I followed. The inner chamber was about seven feet square. At a long slab of stone knelt a Frenchwoman in ecstasy. By her side stood another Greek monk.
>
> 'This gentleman has been to Mt Athos,' said Gabriel to his

crony, who shook hands with me across the body of the Frenchwoman. 'It was six years ago and he remembers Synesios's cat . . .'

Robert spent much of the week drawing and photographing the most famous sights of Jerusalem. With Christopher, he also visited the modern city of Tel Aviv, created since the war as a result of Jewish immigration. In honour of Mark Sykes's contribution to Zionism, they were given the red carpet treatment, with Joshua Gordon, the chief spokesman for the Jewish Agency, acting as their host. Robert put to him the Arab argument that the Jews were buying up all the land with international capital, thus pricing them out of the market. 'He was scornful,' Robert jotted down later. 'I said, wouldn't it be worthwhile, even at cost of inconvenience to themselves, for the Jews to do something to placate the Arabs, so as to avoid trouble in future. Gordon said no.'

A tour of the modernist architecture in Tel Aviv left Robert impressed: 'really v. good', he wrote, 'though all stucco, because there is no stone, but pleasant and amusing colours & not tiresome or affected. If this town were in Russia the whole world wd be raving about it, a planned city . . . it deserves a little raving really – inspiring pioneering atmosphere.' A few days later, on their way to Damascus, he was less taken with a Jewish farm settlement which the Agency had arranged for them to visit. They returned to Tiberias on the Sea of Galilee 'thankful to have escaped a communal meal among the hirsute & perspiring Abels who had offered to shew us round'. Nevertheless he had been impressed, and wrote: 'Palestine is so small; surely the Jewish experiment may be allowed to proceed.'

By 13 September, they were in Beirut to meet Boz and the lorries at dawn the following day off the ship from Marseilles. The ship docked a day late. When Robert went on board and inquired after Goldman and Henderson and 'deux camions', no one had heard of them. The only member of the expedition on board was Eldon Rutter, bringing with him a tale of disaster.

The lorries had reached Abbeville when the smaller one broke down. Another lorry was brought over from England

and three days were spent installing the charcoal plant. It was at this point that Boz had sent Robert the telegram warning of a week's delay. Setting off once more, it became apparent that even on the asphalt roads of northern France the charcoal plant was useless. Feeding the furnace proved more difficult than stoking the boiler of a railway engine. They could have driven on, using petrol, but Boz and Henderson were not prepared to jettison their investment. The party returned in secret to England, where, from the seclusion of a flat in Ealing, they were refitting the vehicles in order to depart anew in mid-October.

In the meantime, they were terrified that Robert would return to London and expose their failure. Originally, it had been agreed that he would pay his own fare to Beirut and thereafter rely upon the expedition's funds. Boz knew that Robert had little money left, and he dispatched Rutter to find out how much Robert would require to continue his journey to Persia, where he could await their eventual arrival. Robert felt sorry for Boz, but given his circumstances, he had no compunction in wiring him for £100 to be credited to him in Baghdad.

After spending a quiet day bathing to recover from the shock of the expedition's reversal, they decided, with Rutter in tow, to visit the famous Roman ruins of Baalbek on their way back to Damascus. The site, which was 'as closely guarded as a lion in a zoo', turned out to be a tourist trap. Robert successfully resisted the high cost of entry, only to be ensnared by a local guide.

'Alors qu'est-ce que vous êtes?'

'Je suis homme.'

'Quoi?'

'HOMME.'

'Je comprends. Touriste.'

Robert railed against his fate. Gone were the days when 'the traveller . . . was a person who travelled in search of knowledge & whom the *indigènes* . . . were proud to receive & entertain with their local monuments & peculiarities'. Now, he complained: 'You are a tourist as a skunk is a skunk, a parasitic & contemptible abortion of the human species whose sole function of nature is that of financial excretion.'

Despite his demotion to the tourist class, Robert upheld the standards of the Victorian traveller. He busied himself with his sketchbook and haunted the ruins with his cumbersome camera in its tin box with tripod and black cloth. Rhapsodizing like a true Victorian, he wrote:

> The 6 columns at dawn – indescribable beauty. Peach gold & sky exactly the same tone – equal interaction in colour of the stone & the air – even the empty bases looked superbly grand outlined by that radiant liquid blue with its violet depths – & then one looks up & up . . . to the huge broken capitals & the cornice. One understands now what one's Grandfather felt about 'ruins' & the grandeur of antiquity.

His words were composed the next day, set down in his diary without a single hesitation. Since Venice, he had kept a record of the journey, a compilation of conversations, gossip, art history, architectural and topographical descriptions, and chronological narrative. One understandable omission, save for a passing reference, was any mention of Desmond. Having signed a contract with Macmillan for 'Travels in Persia', Robert was writing with publication in mind. The first person to set eyes on the work in progress was his mother. 'I am afraid I can't write you good letters . . .' he wrote to her from Beirut, 'my diary takes all my effort.' In compensation, he sent her the first volume, a large brown notebook, which was completed in Damascus.

With Christopher laid low by fever, delaying their departure for Baghdad, Robert meanwhile dallied with one of his earliest loves. Each day he visited the Great Mosque to gaze upon the recently uncovered mosaics in the courtyard dating from the early eighth century. Here was proof that Western art was born in the East. To Robert, these early examples of landscape art foreshadowed the work of El Greco; he hailed them as 'the finest secular decoration . . . I have ever seen'. When it came to Arab culture, Robert was happy to be guided by Eldon Rutter whose book, *The Holy Cities of Arabia*, had been based upon his unrivalled experience of living in Mecca and elsewhere. But Robert felt no sympathy for the Phil-Arab group of English travellers and writers: '[it] makes me feel a little uncomfortable . . . A sort of pantheon – Doughty, Bell, Philby, Leachman etc etc & of course the inevitable Lawrence.' A parallel was drawn to the hero-worshipping of the philhellene world, which, somewhat to his embarrassment, he had benefited from, even though his success in Greece was all his own doing.

The convoy to Baghdad run by the Nairn Transport Company consisted of two coaches and a Buick with a two-wheeled trailer attached, which was hermetically sealed against the dust. Robert and Christopher, travelling second class, were in the trailer with six others. The journey lasted twenty-four hours with three stops for meals. 'I am still half dead from the crossing,' he wrote, swooning, to his mother the next day.

Awaiting him at Thomas Cook's was £80 from Boz. A fortune-teller in Damascus had predicted that he would receive the money and Robert only regretted not equipping himself with a charm to guarantee the full amount. Apart from sightseeing, they made final preparations for Persia. Although finding the city 'rather like the Edgware Road in a hot fog', Robert enjoyed his week. Christopher, on the other hand, hated Baghdad. His voice began to tremble with anticipation at the prospect of Persia.

On 28 September, they set off by car for Khanikin on the Persian border. On the same day, Rutter returned to await the arrival of Boz at Beirut. Whenever a ripple of foothills broke the monotony of the plain, Christopher, who had previously only flown the route, exclaimed: 'Behold the ramparts of Iran.' Crossing into Persia that afternoon, Robert felt, in contrast to the Arab world, as though he had returned to a European civilization. His only criticism was the squalor of the clothes and in particular 'the detestable Pahlevi cap insisted on by the Shah'. Christopher suggested that in future it would be prudent to refer to the Shah by a pseudonym. Dismissing names such as Smith or Jones, Robert settled on Marjoribanks, 'claiming that the traditional pronunciation of this surname as "Marchbanks" evoked the Emperor's ideals briefly and conclusively'. From now on Robert also used this name in his diary. A delay at customs meant that it was growing dark when they drove off. The dying sun and a fresh moon illumined the vast range of the Zagros mountains, the real ramparts of Iran.

For the next two days they bowled along the well-graded road to Teheran. On the final long stretch of their journey, Robert was granted his first insight into Persian civilization.

> At one point, as we were driving along the side of a mountain, I saw far away in the brown bare plain beneath a donkey bearing two huge jars of brilliant blue faience, wh. shone out like a symbol of all one has ever imagined of Persia. The peasants too . . . wore loose-fitting clothes of a strange fair blue . . . Just as the Russian colour is red – the word for 'red' & 'beautiful' are the same in Russian – so the Persian colour is blue. The word is 'ab' & it also means water. And this is the key to Persian taste; water & gardens, water and trees, water & shade & the sound of water, as an interlude from the scorching flats & cloudy dust storms.

'I have arrived in Persia', Robert wrote on reaching their hotel in Teheran, 'as a person might arrive in England who confused the identities of Edward I & Edward VII. It is humiliating.' At various sights along the route, his ignorance of Persian art had been exposed. Standing before the famous Sassanian bas-reliefs at Tak-i-Bostan, dating from the fourth century AD he was uncertain whether to ascribe them to Byzantine, Assyrian, Indian or Armenian artists. At Hamadan, he had visited the thirteenth-century Seljuk mausoleum but Christopher had rushed him, and he only had time to take three photographs; this was one building, he now realized, which Upham Pope had particularly wanted him to photograph. Robert determined not to stir from his room until he had studied his 'few books on Persia enough to tell me where & what things are'. Over two days, he drew up maps and schedules of possible journeys and two lists of monuments, 'one of Achaemenid & Sassanian carvings, the other of classic brick & tiled buildings'.

His sources included the book which had first drawn him

to Persia, Diez's *Churasanische Baudenkmaler* (Architectural Monuments of Chorassan), as well as Upham Pope's *Introduction to Persian Art* which gave a list of principal monuments. He was fortified with the work of two nineteenth-century travellers, *Persia and the Persian Question* by George Nathaniel Curzon and *Ten Thousand Miles in Persia* by his disciple, Percy Sykes (a consul in Persia, unrelated to Christopher).

Laying aside his books, Robert ventured out on a round of calls, including one to the Minister of the Interior, who furnished him with introductions to provincial governors. T. L. Jacks, head of the Anglo-Persian Oil Company, had him to lunch, and promised help with transport. Through Christopher's contacts, they were adopted by members of the British Legation, and spent much of their time at Gulhek, the summer retreat in the foothills of the Elburz.

Architecturally, Teheran had little to detain him. The city had been modernized over the previous two years and Robert found the streets 'wide, straight and ugly'. After ten days, he and Christopher set off in search of the towers, mausolea and mosques of Azerbaijan in north-west Persia. The first building on Robert's itinerary was the mausoleum of Uljaitu at Sultaniya, a gigantic structure which dominates the plain from ten miles distance. Completed in 1307, it is the surviving masterpiece of the Mongol dynasty: a massive octagon of 'brown satin brick' with the remains of a circlet of minarets on its parapet, capped by an egg-shaped dome. Robert photographed the building from the mud roofs of the surrounding village, composing each picture to emphasize the massive form.

Over a leisurely weekend in Tabriz, Robert ticked off the next two monuments on his list, before heading due south for Maragha, an unprepossessing town with modern streets cutting through the bazaar. Despite appearances, it possessed some tomb towers as well as the remains of the thirteenth-century Observatory, built by the Mongol emperor Hulagu. The Chief of Police provided horses and an escort for the ride into the surrounding hills to view the site of the Observatory. Naturally, he assumed that Robert and Christopher were spies. While photographing an ancient cave dug into the hillside beneath the Observatory, Robert overheard the police chief question 'why the British govt. wld want photos of such things'.

In need of exercise and fresh air, they decided to hire horses and ride due east to the town of Miana on the main road from Tabriz to Teheran. Upham Pope had told him that the route was unknown from an architectural point of view 'and that there might be monuments'. The party consisted of two muleteers and a member of the 'roads' police, called Abbas, who was to act as their guide on the three-day journey. The first night was spent at a road house a few miles out of Maragha. Abbas lit an opium pipe, administering Robert a puff, like a nurse. During the night, Christopher was savagely attacked by fleas. Robert was tickled but unscathed.

The road through the bare highland landscape was almost deserted and they averaged twenty miles a day on agonizing wooden saddles. Apart from an ancient brick bridge, Robert spied one building of consequence, a big tower on a distant hill, which he hoped was only a watchtower. Each night they stopped at the house of a village headman. Dinner was invariably chicken and potatoes with flaps of bread, mast and melon, served on a round tray on the floor and eaten in their fingers.

On the first morning, Abbas and the chief muleteer were silly with opium. They were slow to start and laughed openly when criticized. That night, Robert shooed them from the room, refusing to put up with the stink of their hubble-bubble. Christopher was furious. He understood Persian society with its easygoing, yet formal conventions and told Robert that his action was dangerously insulting. Drawing himself up like a sahib in India, Robert retorted: 'I have my customs also and one of them is not to be inconvenienced by the presence or pipe of the muleteers I am employing.'

By the end of the journey, Christopher's legs were covered with huge water blisters as a result of flea bites. They returned to Teheran as fast as possible by lorry and car and he spent the next two days in a nursing home. Robert settled in to a French pension, the Coq d'Or. A few days later, snow fell on the Elburz mountains 'so that the common streets of Teheran, at least such of them as point North,' observed Robert, 'have suddenly become enchanted by this Alpine . . . backcloth'.

A telegram from Rutter broke the news that Boz and the lorries were leaving Beirut. Robert resigned himself to waiting for their arrival, but became increasingly bad-tempered as the days passed. 'My visit to Persia', he wailed, 'is faced by a portcullis of frustration.' Almost all his photographs had failed. He also discovered that he had missed some of the key monuments in Azerbaijan. And now, just as his taste buds were beginning to respond to Persian architecture, his stay in the country was to be cut short by having to join Boz's expedition. 'I am anxious, now, to do a book on Persian brick bldgs – pre-Safavid. I know what I want to see: I need 5 or 6 months, a car, & the assistance of a Kufic epigraphist. For this', he claimed, 'I have exactly £10 & am being swept off to Afghanistan.' The threatened arrival in Teheran of his old friend, Patrick Balfour, only added to his siege mentality. His choleric air was accentuated by a newly grown moustache which, bleached by the sun, blazed against his burnt skin, 'the colour of lightning in a sunset'.

After two weeks with no word, a rumour reached Teheran that the lorries had completely broken down. Robert decided to leave for Meshed, the site of one of the holiest shrines in Persia. A visit had been first suggested by Upham Pope who wanted him to photograph two sacred tomb covers from the shrine. Accordingly, he had already written to the Governor for assistance. Robert persuaded Christopher to go half shares in a 1926 four-seater Morris which he bought for £30. 'As second hand cars are very expensive here & this seemed in good working order,' he reasoned, 'it seemed cheap – not more certainly than I shd. have to pay for the hire of a car to Meshed.' Three days were spent battling with Persian bureaucracy and seeing to the overhaul of the engine. The key negotiations were undertaken by Robert without Christopher to act as interpeter. 'I am at an advantage, being alone', he realized; 'for I cd. speak just enough Persian to say what I wanted, and cd. understand just so little as to make any refusal or excuse useless.' On the fourth day, Robert took his car on a successful test drive.

Originally he planned a leisurely journey to Meshed photographing buildings en route, but events forced him to plan only a quick trip. News came through of the assassination of King Nadir Shah of Afghanistan, which curtailed his ambition of continuing to the frontier. Furthermore, Patrick Balfour, who turned up one evening at the Coq d'Or, brought news of Boz. The expedition had spent five nights in the desert between Damascus and Baghdad, breaking two big ends on the way, but was now on the point of leaving Baghdad for Teheran. Balfour was a member of Colonel Edward Noel's party, which was driving out to the North-West Frontier in two Rolls-Royces. Although never the *raison d'être* of the expedition, one of the cars had been fitted with a charcoal-burning plant supplied by Boz's company. By Dover the furnace had burnt a hole in the running board and they had thrown it away. Noel was now in dispute with Boz over a refund.

On 11 November, Robert set out without Christopher for Meshed. Sixty miles from Teheran, the car broke its back axle and had to be pushed by a gang of labourers to the nearest village. Communicating with the aid of a dictionary, Robert made arrangements to garage the car while his driver returned to Teheran for help. Meanwhile he planned to continue the journey by lorry. 'It is rather depressing', he wrote, 'that all the effort of the last week shd have ended in fiasco – apart from the financial loss. I ought to feel that Persia is too much for me. I don't.'

For four days Robert travelled by bus and lorry through the region of Chorassan, only breaking the journey at Damghen to photograph the monuments. Otherwise, he persuaded drivers to stop for half an hour while he dashed out to a shrine or tower with his camera. As a guide, he had brought with him Diez's *Monuments of Chorassan*, 'a gigantic quarto whose weight probably broke the Morris's axle'. Most nights were spent at garages which were modelled on the traditional caravanserai: a quadrangle guarded by huge doors, with rooms for eating and sleeping.

Arriving in Meshed he observed the mass of pilgrims crowding the entrances to the shrine: the tomb of Ali Reza, eighth Imam of the Shiites, who died in the ninth century. Elsewhere in Persia, mosques were being opened to non-believers, but at Meshed the authorities remained powerless before the fanaticism of the pilgrims. Robert's only view of the buildings was of the domes and minarets which could be seen from the new road surrounding the walled complex.

There being no news of further trouble in Afghanistan, he was encouraged to move on. Over the past year, the town of Herat in Afghanistan had featured 'as the goal and gateway' of Robert's plans for travelling to the region. Now that he was so close, he could not resist booking a seat on a lorry to Herat leaving in three days' time. However, the Noel party had arrived, with Patrick Balfour, and once Noel had succeeded in acquiring visas for Afghanistan, Robert chose to drive with him to Herat rather than take the lorry. 'I don't relish the party', he confided to his diary, '& Patrick also is writing, & we mustn't overlap.'

At the end of a day of frantic preparation, Robert received a wire from Boz telling him that the expedition was heading for Meshed as soon as their guns had cleared customs. 'This was the crowning bewilderment,' Robert moaned. 'The only thing to do is to take no notice & hope to meet it in Mazar-i-Sherif.' To calm his nerves, he retired to bed with Boswell's *Life of Johnson*.

Boz meanwhile, stuck in Teheran, was seething. 'Robert', he wrote to his fiancée, Stella Buchanan, 'has failed entirely to organize the authorities on our behalf. He has been so preoccupied with his own affairs and social gaieties . . . Our guns were seized at the frontier so now we have to undertake what Robert should already have done.'

On the same day that Boz was venting his rage, Robert left Meshed in Colonel Noel's party. Having crossed the border without incident, he took the wheel of the open-topped Rolls-Royce for the drive to the walled city of Herat. Such style did not extend to their hotel, which proved to be unfinished. Robert's bedroom lacked window-panes and his door refused to shut. As the Park Hotel was situated in the metalworkers' bazaar, the noise was appalling.

The next day the Noel party left for Kabul. 'I must confess to low spirits at their departure,' Robert wrote. 'To find oneself alone in an Afghan town with no plan, or rather too many plans, is trying.' Should he go north to Mazar-i-Sherif or east to Kabul? Alternatively, he could wait for Boz '& go off into the blue with them'. However, half his films were in Meshed, and the rest of his luggage, including his typewriter and the second volume of his diary, was in Teheran.

The one consolation was the beauty of the Afghans. After a day going about town on visits to government officials, he wrote: 'Afghans as a race are tremendously good looking – terrific features, breeding – large of stature – many armed . . . Attractive after Persians to look at – & not coarse-grained like Arabs.' His dandy's eye admired their couture: 'magnificent clothes, great white cloaks of serge falling from square shoulders with false sleeves embroidered, or quilted coats, or even European coats, waisted, & always surmounted by a great mass of wound turban – all the country people seem to dress in white.' Even the metalworkers' bazaar had its attractions: 'A superb physical sight – 8 men hammering iron in rhythm with all their strength in loose trousers, gorgeous movements.' When polishing up his diary for publication, Robert added a postscript: 'Now and then a calico bee-hive with a window at the top flits across the scene. This is a woman.'

On his second day, Robert explored the area to the north of the town popularly known as the Musalla, where most of the surviving monuments are situated. The contrast with Persia fascinated him. Much of Persian art appeared anaemic and 'ninetyish' when set against the 'terrific scale' of Herat. The only building was a domed mausoleum, but scattered across the orchards and fields were seven free-standing minarets: 'when one thinks they were wholly covered in tiles,' Robert concluded, 'the approach to Herat is inconceivable – the splendour of it . . . they really are a wonder of the world.'

The minarets and mausoleum were all that remained of a complex of religious buildings constructed in the fifteenth century, when Herat was capital of the Timurid Empire. The founder of the dynasty, Timur, the Tamerlane of English literature, notorious for his atrocities as a conqueror, was also an artistic despot, who embellished his capital, Samarcand, with superb buildings. His son, Shah Rukh, with his principal wife, Gohar Shad, emulated the beauty of Samarcand at Herat. Gohar Shad employed the greatest architects of the day to build a madrassa (college), a mosque and her own mausoleum. The last Timurid emperor, Hussein Baikara, followed her example by commissioning an imposing madrassa in adjacence.

The fall of the Timurids brought obscurity to Herat which lasted until the end of the nineteenth century. By then, the town had acquired strategic importance as the key to Russia's threatened advance on India. In 1885, after a bout of Russian aggression, an attack seemed imminent. The Emir of Afghanistan, with British approval, ordered the demolition of all buildings to the north of the town which might provide cover for the enemy. Only Gohar Shad's mausoleum, and nine minarets, which had originally been attached to particular buildings, were spared. A few years before Robert's arrival, two of the minarets had collapsed in an earthquake.

So unknown was the architecture of Herat that the first significant account of its monuments had not been written until a British officer, Major C. E. Yate, serving on the Afghan Boundary Commission, had inspected them in the process of their demolition. He did his best to identify what remained, publishing the results in his book, *Northern Afghanistan*. The only recent survey had formed part of a picture book of life in Afghanistan by a German, Oskar von Niedermayer, published in Germany in 1924, with a preface by Ernst Diez. Robert came armed with both books which, although valuable, provided little background information to the monuments. Apart from jotting down a few scanty impressions, much of his time in the Musalla was spent with his camera 'trying to compose the minarets and mausoleum into pictures'.

For three days, Robert busied himself around the town with sightseeing, sketching and photography. He was driven out in a two-horse barouche to the shrine of Gazar Gah: 'peace, pine trees, water, & a charming decagonal, 2 storey garden house – an idyllic spot.' Other sights included the ancient Friday mosque and the citadel. An arresting view of the old town was gained from the massive tenth-century bridge to the south: 'v. magnificent –' he recorded, 'triple lines of mud walls . . . with moat – top wall has towers – others a lacework of loopholes – all v. battered & jagged. V.

romantic outline.' At all times, he was accompanied by an attendant from the Governor's office, who had been sent to keep an eye on him. Straying too close to 'a broken down artillery park' in search of a good photograph, Robert was subsequently prevented from re-entering the citadel. The order was rescinded by the commander-in-chief, but only after a furious row.

By the end of the week, Robert had resolved to take a lorry leaving that Saturday, 25 November, for Kandahar, whence he would make his way to Kabul. Heavy rain delayed the departure of the lorry, and he spent the next few days in a state of uncertainty, whiling away the time in his room, reading Boswell and polishing up his drawings. On Tuesday morning, it was confirmed that a lorry was leaving at one o'clock for Mazar-i-Sherif, north-east of Herat, on the Russian border. Without hesitation, Robert climbed on board.

A few miles out of Herat, the Bedford lorry, painted on the outside like a piece of embroidery, turned north off the main Kabul road. The passengers, who were mostly soldiers, cried out: 'To Turkestan.' At last Robert was nearing the original goal of his journey.

After spending the night at a shrine only thirty miles from Herat, the serious drive began. 'The road', Robert wrote, 'led up one of those interminable valleys that twist in & out of hills that meet, from opposite sides, like the teeth of a cog wheel – till at last it got a bit steeper and we began to ascend.' It snowed briefly, and Robert caught sight of the occasional Afghan hound well-rugged. Suddenly, as a result of snow, the earth road degenerated into a muddy track. For the next seven hours, Robert slithered on foot, whilst the soldiers helped to manoeuvre the vehicle with chains over the pass. Eventually they reached a sound stretch of road, but it was now dark, and the lights of the lorry had begun to fail.

The driver stopped for the night in a narrow defile. Robert, who had had no food all day, ate some bread and cheese. Parched with thirst, he was forced to drink 'white mud, melted snow, mixed with oil from a petrol tin'. Changing into pyjamas, and putting on a fur helmet as protection against the howling wind, he lay down on the road in his sleeping bag covered with his pushteen, a shaggy leathern coat, and blankets, and had a remarkably good night.

The small market town of Kala Nao was reached the following morning, where the Governor provided him with a room and servants. Robert was exhausted. In the afternoon he climbed to some caves outside the town, but was overcome with vertigo. During the night, it rained and blew a gale. At 2 a.m. both doors of his room flew open. Robert described the next event: 'At 5.00 a.m., descending to perform an act of nature on the dung heap, I slipped and cracked my head on the last step – wh. fortunately was only mud. The hurricane lamp went out. It was hideous.'

The weather trapped Robert in Kala Nao for three more days. On the second day, he did not even bother to get out of his pyjamas and merely added layers of clothes for warmth. He now realized that even if he reached Mazar-i-Sherif, it could take a month to travel from there to Kabul. Another anxiety beset him. 'I am strangely worried', he recorded, 'at the prospect of not being able to telegraph home for Xmas.'

A violent attack of diarrhoea followed by acute stomach pains made him determined to turn back. Early on the third day, he called on the Governor and managed to explain his predicament in his limited phrases of Persian. Both a permit for the return journey and horses were forthcoming for the next day. In his diary, Robert sought to justify his decision: 'It is a fearful disappointment – to be so near Turkestan at last & not to reach it – but it's useless to overstrain one's capacities.'

With three government horses and a guide, he reached the village at the foot of the pass in a day. The following morning, he made such excellent progress, cantering along in the sun, that it was decided to make for the shrine of Kharouk where he had spent the first night on his outward journey. As the day wore on, the seemingly endless gorge, in which 'each new spur refused to disclose the plain', began to take its toll. 'On & on & on . . .' he groaned, 'my inside, a sort of stitch, on the left, feeling like angina pectoris. One's thighs and behind eaten away by the saddle – & at every rise almost castrated.' At sunset, the 'dank yellow plain' stretched before them. Eventually, by the light of a lamp, the guide recognized a short cut to Kharouk. As they deviated on to smaller and smaller paths, Robert became querulous:

'Does this road go to Kharouk or not?' he demanded.

'I don't know. I don't know anything. You say Kharouk, Kharouk, Kharouk. I don't know where Kharouk is,' came back the reply, according to Robert's translation. Whereupon, the guide sat down on an aromatic tuft, placed his head in his hands, and groaned.

Enveloped in cloud, the unhappy party made camp. The guide hobbled the horses, threw the luggage on the ground and curtly refused food. In a gesture of goodwill, Robert covered him with a blanket, but all the same, he decided to sleep with his knife at the ready. He awoke a few hours later at midnight. A bright moon revealed that they were perched on the edge of a ravine. The guide took his bearings and, after an hour, they reached Kharouk. They had ridden fifty miles. Just before going to sleep Robert recorded: 'It has been the worst day I have ever done.'

When Robert rode up to the hotel in Herat he found that Boz and his companions were already in residence, having arrived from Meshed the previous evening. This came as no surprise, as news picked up at halts on the ride had led him to expect them. As he sat down to tea, they walked in: 'a disappointed pathetic little party, pleased with nothing & each dwelling, in my ear, on the shortcomings of the other two'.

After retiring to bed for two days with a bad cold, Robert at last made a trip on foreign soil in one of Boz's lorries. Neither vehicles any longer ran on charcoal, but he pronounced the short journey to the shrine of Gazar Gar as 'v. slow – but comfortable'. He now planned to accompany the expedition at least as far as Kandahar, although he grumbled at having to pay for his own expenses. He then discovered that Rutter was also writing a book and, even worse, that Boz had been aware of this from the start. Finding such concealment 'unforgivable', he decided to return to Persia.

Robert's journey back to Meshed was undertaken in increasing pain. A small pustule on his left thigh had led to the swelling of the knee joint so that he could hardly walk. Crossing the Persian border, the lorry stopped for the night at an inferior garage at Turbat-i-Sheik. Robert noticed soldiers eyeing his saddlebags from the threshold of their room. When he next turned, the soldiers and saddlebags were gone. 'I was not in a suave mood', he wrote, '& supposing that the doors, if shut, were probably locked, took off with [a] hop from my sound leg & hurled my whole weight upon them. They were not even fastened – with the result that I entered that room like a 10-inch shell.' Screaming maledictions in English, which he varied with his two phrases of Persian abuse, 'Son of a dog' and 'Son of a burnt father', he retrieved his bags.

At Meshed, Robert stayed as a guest of the acting consul. After the effort of the journey, he collapsed for ten days doing little more than read. His leg was cupped at the American hospital, with fascinating results: 'after a disgusting & incredible discharge', he wrote, 'a large hole has formed & it looks like a volcano though not yet quite extinct.' He spent Christmas at Meshed before returning to the Coq d'Or in Teheran just in time for the New Year's Eve Ball at the English Club.

In the pile of correspondence which awaited him was a reprimand from his mother, complaining of the upset caused by his disappearance into Afghanistan. Before venturing there, Robert had tried to warn her that communication might be difficult. From Meshed he had scrawled in a hurried note: 'it may be 2 or 3 weeks before you hear again – & I don't want to telegraph at all, as I have so little money . . . So don't worry at a protracted silence.'

He did not take kindly to his mother's anxiety, and wrote at once to answer her complaint. 'I suppose it was rather upsetting, the vagueness about my address,' he began.

> But you can imagine it was a good deal more upsetting for me, not knowing myself where I was going or what I was to do . . . you know perfectly well by this time (20 years since I first went to boarding school) that on the rare occasions when I don't write regularly, it is because I can't – either through exhaustion or lack of postal facilities. Travelling is difficult enough here without the added misery of feeling you are worrying because I haven't been able to get to a post office.

Having put his side of the story, he went on to reassure her:

> You know quite well that you are always with me – that everything I write or draw is done with the subconscious & often conscious purpose of its being for you . . . & one of the chief reasons that made me give up my journey to Turkestan was that if I went on I shdn't be able to reach you for Xmas . . . as I say you know perfectly *well* that mentally I am writing to you all the time. I wonder you don't get the messages by telepathy.

There was a good deal of truth in his assurances. After his death, Margaret Byron admitted to Michael Rosse that 'I was always surprised when he struck out or changed any words I didn't like – immediately – I was a very hard critic & he always read his things to me.' Margaret Byron had the strength of character to make Robert perform for her, having from an early age encouraged his acute powers of observation. In his stream of letters home, he set out to entertain her, filling them with amusing, slightly exaggerated anecdote and vivid pictorial detail. Similarly, he never failed to report on his latest sketches. Uncomfortable hours spent capturing some exotic view were made worthwhile by the prospect of her appreciation.

But the descriptions of his travels, deposited faithfully at her feet, were the price of Robert's independence. Sudden changes of plan, often involving extended delays to his return home, were decided without consultation with his mother. He would merely soften the blow with a few half-hearted regrets. Nothing ever deflected him from his course, as another victim, Boz Goldman, discovered to his cost.

Margaret Byron was not the sole person in his thoughts that Christmas. At the same time, he was writing to Desmond: 'I miss you so much & wish we could meet somewhere in Asia.' Unbeknown to Robert, Desmond had already set out for China. When the news finally caught up with him, Robert talked of joining him in the distant future, but in the meanwhile requested: 'remember sometimes that I still exist & still think of you, always every day.'

22

Towards the Oxus

For the first time since he had arrived in Persia, Robert no longer had to worry about Boz and the charcoal burners appearing over the horizon in hot pursuit. Also, after three months in the country, he had a much clearer idea of what he wanted to achieve. 'I now know, at last, exactly what I want to do here, which is such a relief –' he wrote to his mother in the New Year, 'what I want to see, & where to go to complete a book about the buildings that will have permanent value. How far I can fulfil my plans I don't know – so I can't give you any idea yet of when I shall be home – it may be in April or May, it may not be till July or August –'

Although not entirely destitute, much depended on Robert's ability to raise more funds. He turned to Macmillan's for help, submitting to them his latest idea for a book. 'My object now is this,' he wrote to Daniel Macmillan in mid-January:

> To make a complete survey of the chief monuments of Persia, and in the spring to return to Afghanistan, and make another complete survey of the chief monuments of that country. I plan the book in diary form, that is to say in sections under date entries. But in each case where a monument is described, or a series of monuments, this would occupy another section, suitably headed. Thus those who wish to read the book as a travel book can concentrate chiefly on the dated sections, while those who want to use it as a guide book can concentrate on the others.

He gave Meier-Graefe's *Spanish Journey* as an excellent example of a guide and travel book combined.

After assessing the potential sales of such a book, Robert turned to the question of money:

> I am in a very awkward position financially; and if it were not for the project which I have just outlined to you and on which I have set my heart, I would come straight home. In fact it was for the sake of that project that I left the expedition, which otherwise [he fibbed] would have financed me the rest of the way home. Would it be unreasonable to ask you if you could see your way to advancing me a little more money.

Harold Macmillan, who took over the negotiations, used the opportunity to secure a second book from Robert. He refused to increase the advance on 'Travels in Persia', but raised £100 on a general royalty account 'on the honourable understanding', he wrote to A. D. Peters, 'that any books he may write will be offered to us on similar terms to past books'. Macmillan suggested that the subject of the second book should be decided when Robert returned to London. The receipt of the money in the first week of February prompted the resolution from Robert: 'No more dawdling'.

Since the middle of January, Robert and Christopher had been trying to reach Isfahan. At first, their escape from Teheran was thwarted by heavy snow and ice on the roads. Then, on the morning of their second attempt, Robert woke in agony from a swelling on his back. Although the abscess on his leg had finally healed, others had continued to develop. Christopher left without him, and Robert spent the next few days being 'poulticed, lanced, squeezed, purged & cupped' at the English nursing home. Finally he was given permission to depart, but he took with him 'a little box of injections' to be administered over the next few weeks.

The Hoylands, a diplomat and his wife, who were on their way to Shiraz, south of Isfahan, offered Robert a lift. Before their departure on Thursday 8 February, it rained for twenty-four hours without stop, making driving conditions so bad 'it wld.', Robert reported, 'have been easier in a boat'. Rounding a corner, on the second day, they were faced by a rushing torrent with three lorries and a Ford embedded mid-stream.

The continual mishaps led him to question whether he was cursed like Jonah. The drive from Teheran to Isfahan was one of the easiest in Persia, which normally took a day. 'Is there such a place as Isfahan?' he asked while stranded in a nearby village. 'If there is, I doubt if I shall ever see it.' After thirty-six hours, the river briefly subsided and the cars made it across. Robert was left cheering on an island until a stocky peasant boy, half his height, carried him to the other side.

On his arrival in Isfahan, Robert made a cursory tour by cab of the principal sights.

> It was a delicious evening, clouds clearing from the sky & a faint caress of spring in the air. I realized suddenly what it was to have escaped from that vile stinking hideous intrigue-ridden pretentious vulgar parody of a capital, Teheran, that weighs on one's soul without one's knowing it – I felt uplifted, like a bird in song on a May morning – I hate living among a people who have no dignity . . .

After two days, mainly taken up with appointments, Robert left with the Hoylands for Shiraz where Christopher was waiting for him. He too was busy researching a book. His subject was Wassmuss, the German agent who, during the war, had stirred up tribal unrest against the British. Only after numerous skirmishes and a final battle at Firuzabad had he been defeated. By the time of Robert's arrival, Christopher had already gathered a great deal of information from the locals on the brilliant German spy. His book, when published in 1936, was to include photographs by Robert.

Shiraz captivated Robert: 'A delicious place – the black spires of cypresses against the eggshell coloured mountains . . . blue onion domes of a late period standing up, a cloudless sky, tangerines on the trees in the hotel garden, and a feeling of spring – almost of the Mediterranean.' An added sense of well-being was provided by the flagons of Shiraz wine: 'it is pleasant', he concluded, 'to be in a place where one can drink again & get tipsy before lunch.'

Within forty-eight hours, the charm of Shiraz had evaporated. On consulting the Chief of Police about an expedition to Firuzabad, they were informed that Christopher was forbidden to leave the town. The order had come from Teheran and prevented him even from going into the surrounding countryside to shoot. Robert was outraged, assuming the cause to be fear of Christopher criticizing the regime in print. 'As for their treatment of Xtopher,' he wrote, 'who is probably modern Persia's only living apologist, it passes belief.'

The Persians were justified on other grounds in being suspicious. Christopher had recently been offered the job as *The Times* correspondent in Persia, a useful cover for espionage. A second person was involved in the appointment, discovered in Robert's diary in a cryptic aside: 'Xtopher has become a fairy, seduced by an old man named Basket from Jerusalem at night in a garden. This perversion seems to hinge on his getting the Times correspondentship.' Years later, Christopher was to tell his sister, Freya, that he had been recruited as a spy.

Firuzabad, due south of Shiraz, was only accessible by horse or mule. It had, until recently, been out of bounds to travellers owing to the threat of brigands and to tribal unrest. But in the autumn of 1933 the archaeologist, Aurel Stein, had succeeded in visiting the town with an escort of soldiers to survey the remains of a Sassanian palace. It was also the site of the last stand against the British of the Kashgai tribe, followers of Wassmuss. Robert now planned to inspect the palace, and, on Christopher's behalf, the battleground.

The ride to Firuzabad of forty-five miles produced an impressive list of natural wonders: a sounder of wild boar, a dead wolf, bushes flowering in all shades of icing pink, grape hyacinths and a spectacular gorge, in which the river appeared to be flowing uphill. Halfway along, massive fragments of ancient masonry topped the cliff before a 'stupendous bldg', identified as a Sassanian fortress, came into view. They arrived in Firuzabad at 9 at night, after thirteen hours in the saddle, to find the streets deserted and only a few people left in the bazaar. The Governor was roused at home, 'a minute residence of one room & that small, with a room beneath it'.

'I ascended,' Robert wrote.

> In the middle of the floor on the carpets, burned a brilliant white light in a tall paraffin lamp. On either side of this stood two tall pewter bowls, one filled with bunches of gt. big sweet smelling jonquils, arranged in a pattern, the highest centre bunch being surmounted by a posy of violets – the other being filled with large pink fruit blossom. Gazing at them, cross-legged, sat the governor and his small son.

Robert made obeisance before the tableau. 'After cursory salutations', he continued, 'I lowered my creaking frame to the floor & buried my head in the jonquils.' To the Governor's invitation to share his room for the night, 'I asked nothing of him on earth, not a crumb,' he responded, 'except a room to myself. So the basement was got ready.'

After a day spent recovering from the ride, Robert headed back towards the gorge to explore the various Sassanian ruins which he had passed on the outward journey. The first was the palace of Ardeshir, dating from the third century AD, thought to have been built by Ardeshir I, founder of the dynasty. A part, consisting of three domed chambers, was well preserved.

Robert clambered about on the roof, took photographs and drew rough plans. Sensing that he had made an important discovery, he later minuted: 'I was very excited by this huge & practically unknown structure . . . Forerunner of all Moslem structure with domes here.'

A similar investigation was undertaken at the 'stupendous building' in the gorge, known as the Kala-i-Dukhtar. Both sites demanded intense concentration: 'Photography single-handed is v. hard work,' he wrote.

> Here in addition the bldgs were completely unfamiliar in plan. I was unlikely ever to see them again. As far as I knew there were no books of reference to help one afterwards. It *is* hard work – one has to apprehend the plan of the whole, make rough guesses at dimensions, mentally reconstruct what is missing, & all the time be at the camera with an eye on the light. And in addition, the bldg may suddenly present a kind of revelation, as these did to me – of the reality of the Sassanids – every faculty becomes alert when

> it is all against time & when to mistake the time means a night in the open.

With the serious work over for the day, Robert set off with a Kashgai tribesman to explore a mysterious 'hammam' or, rather, 'a domed cavern carpeted with squares of caked yet quaking mud'. They had only ventured in a short way when Robert turned and fled, pursued by bats. His bodyguards, meanwhile, were busy picking jonquils, having descried a patch on their way to the cave.

Descending to the river, Robert jumped in. 'My escort', he wrote, was 'seriously perturbed – they thought I shd die of cold.' A bonfire was lit. Pied kingfishers flew about. And Robert polished off a bottle of wine with lunch. Afterwards, he inspected a Sassanian rock carving: 'the whole thing made a rather terrifying expression', he noted, 'solitary in this gorge – they must have been terrifying, the Sassanids.'

The party galloped off at breakneck speed to escape the gorge before nightfall. In a village beyond, his servant had set up camp in a mud room. 'Ali Asgar . . .' Robert wrote, 'had arranged my comforts, wines, spirits, books etc – with tea ready on a tray – & to all of wh. were added the jonquils, whose smell, as I lay in bed, conflicted with those of flit and horsedung from below.' In sum, he felt:

> Yesterday was the perfect day, the day for wh. one leaves home . . . the day in fact wh. rewards all effort & consigns previous disappointments, hardships & irritation to oblivion . . . plans accomplished, mind excited, flowers – scenery, hammam the unexpected, *bathe*, *wine*, a difficult gallop . . . But the wine was the thing, the wine & the bathe – spirits wd not have done. Wine gives just that pearl of content.

Returning to Shiraz, he found that Christopher was now permitted to proceed to the port of Bushire, provided that he left the country forthwith. On 26 February, Robert's twenty-ninth birthday, they drove together to Kuzerum, which lies on the Bushire road. Both were researching their respective books. An ally of Wassmuss still lived in the town; and close by are the Sassanian monuments of Shapur. As Christopher was now determined to fight his expulsion, they parted in the hope of meeting up later in the spring to travel to Afghanistan. If not, they planned a reunion at the Ritz.

Robert's next destination was Persepolis, the capital of ancient Persia founded in the sixth century BC by Darius the Great. Although the ruins had been famous since the Middle Ages, only now, thanks to the excavations of the German archaeologist, Professor Ernst Herzfeld, were they being revealed in their true extent. Herzfeld, one of the outstanding scholars and archaeologists of the day, had been appointed by the Oriental Institute of the University of Chicago, in 1931, as field director of Persepolis to excavate and restore the ruins. Two further stairways, carved with reliefs, had been uncovered, as well as other important structures. The most sensational recent finds, made in September 1933 by Herzfeld's assistant, Fritz Krefter, were the gold and silver foundation plaques of the city.

A week or so after this event, Robert had met Krefter at the English Club in Teheran. Krefter's reluctance to show him photographs of the objects confirmed Robert's suspicions about Herzfeld's control over Persepolis.

> Archaeological jealousy gleamed from his eyes . . . Herzfeld, it must be remembered, has turned Persepolis into his private demesne, destroying the whole beauty of the place & refusing to allow anyone to photograph there; at least, so report says . . . It remains to be seen how Herzfeld, or this blond gnome, behaves on the spot.

On arriving in Shiraz, which is only forty miles south of Persepolis, he wrote a letter to Herzfeld, recording his purpose in his diary: 'I want to know if & what I can photograph before going to Persepolis. If nothing at all then I must refuse H's hospitality – as I shall not hesitate to publish what I think of him.' Nine days later, on his return from Firuzabad, Robert was still awaiting a reply. The only news came from Krefter, who happened to be in town. As reported by Robert, he told him: '[Herzfeld] had been heard to remark that if I wanted photos – he thought it wd. be better I shd. write to Chicago for them.' Krefter then pointed out that under the terms of the concession all photographic rights were held by Herzfeld. Robert decided from now on to refer to the Herzfeld regime as 'The Persepolis OGPU'. At this stage, Herzfeld had little reason to be concerned by Robert's request. They had lunched amicably together with Christopher in Teheran. And Robert had left his card at Persepolis as he passed through with the Hoylands on their way to Shiraz. When a letter from Herzfeld finally arrived, it began: 'Excuse my late answer, I simply forgot.'

Herzfeld confirmed that no photography, apart from the taking of souvenir snaps, was permitted on the site. In the past, he explained, whenever foreigners had taken photographs and sold them for publication, Persians had complained of discrimination. Hence, he had arranged for the Oriental Institute of Chicago to hold photographs which were available for reproduction. Krefter delivered the letter to Robert just as he was leaving for Persepolis. 'You'll find the Professor all alone,' Krefter said. 'He'll be glad of company.'

That night, in a tea house a few miles beyond Persepolis, Robert made his riposte: 'As far as I am concerned he can remain alone.' His accommodation was a stable piled with heaps of fresh dung. 'It is tantalizing', he wrote, 'to think of the comforts of Persepolis so near & open to me. But if one has a personal grudge against a man, disapproves of him on principle, one doesn't go & stay with him. It is all v. boring because if there is one man in Persia I really want to talk to, it is H. Also I don't expect anyone to take 10 days to answer an important letter.'

The following morning he rose early to inspect the rock tombs and reliefs at the royal necropolis of Naksh-i-Rustam. 'No OGPU,' he reported, 'tho' I was alarmed, when two men emerged by a goat hair rope from one of the tombs & ran towards me. But they saluted politely (ridiculously German) & helped.'

In the afternoon, he visited Persepolis with a letter from the Governor of Fars to Dr Mostafavi, the Persian representative at the site. Mostafavi confirmed that those remains which had been visible before the current excavations could be photographed. They went off to find Herzfeld 'whose ample, hermaphroditic bulk was encased in tight, carefully creased Oxford trousers & an untidy green jumper'. From a distance, Robert had mistaken him for a washerwoman.

They retired for tea to Krefter's house, a reconstruction of Xerxes' harem, incorporating original stone features. Herzfeld defended his attitude towards photography by claiming to be a victim of theft and harassment. A principal villain was Arthur Upham Pope, who, in Herzfeld's absence, had taken about 100 photographs and sold them in Teheran: 'not that it really mattered v. much,' he conceded, 'they were so bad.' The situation was the same all over Europe, Herzfeld told him. 'When I was a young man, doing excavations, we were never allowed to photograph anything. It is much better so.'

'But that is no reason why you shd. follow a bad example now,' Robert argued.

'I think it is perfectly rrright,' Herzfeld replied. With which, in Robert's words, he 'tossed his head like an insulted housemaid'.

Robert was outraged to hear a 'supposedly educated' man talk like this. 'His reasons I cld. appreciate – but here one had this little feminine spiteful creature bursting out into the German authoritarian attitude – good for young not to be able to take photos of things in fact – not the smallest consideration that Persepolis is a world property.'

Krefter having entered the lounge, Robert praised his ingenuity at unearthing the famous foundation plaques. This, he knew, would needle Herzfeld, who over lunch in Teheran had dismissed them saying: 'they were really of no importance, & gold was such a bore, it always caused such a fuss.'

In the hope of compromising his independence, Herzfeld pressed Robert to stay the night. When he refused for the second time, both Germans 'looked positively haggard'. To their chagrin, Robert was prepared to suffer for his art.

Early the following day, Robert called on Dr Mostafavi at the site, bringing a letter addressed to Herzfeld. It read:

Dear Dr Herzfeld, Since both the Governor of Fars & Dr

Mostafavi have stated categorically that you have no right to prevent my photographing the portions of arches and columns wh. have always been above ground, the only means of stopping my photographing them are either

1. To shew me the wording of your concession proving that you *have* the right, or

2. Force.

Please choose your means.

Yours truly Robert Byron.

Dr Mostafavi, acting as his second, delivered the note. In reply, an ashen-faced Herzfeld appeared and said: 'I have simply come to tell you this, that I have never known such an illoyal action.' And with that, crowed Robert: 'He turned on his heel and wiggled away.'

Robert's choleric nature had triumphed: a private grudge, fiercely nursed, had been turned into a fit quarrel for a duel on the great terrace at Persepolis. But there were no victors. As Robert himself admitted: 'On the whole, I have lost far more than I gained. H's conversation on ancient subjects wd. have been worth far more to me than a few paltry photos. of a much photographed subject. Besides I was longing to ask him about Firuzabad & Shapur etc.'

The following day, Robert was back in Isfahan, staying with Wishaw, the local manager of the Anglo-Persian Oil Company (APOC). Over the next ten days, he photographed the monuments of the city, rising at 6 a.m. to catch the dawn light on 'the northern faces of domes & eiwans [large, vaulted porches] where the tile work is best preserved'. In a city crowded with architectural marvels, he would work for ten hours on a stretch, sinking exhausted into bed each evening with a cup of Ovaltine.

The Friday Mosque at Isfahan dates from the eleventh century, when the city was capital of the Seljuk Empire. Successive dynasties rebuilt, enlarged and adorned the Seljuk building, whilst in the surrounding district are numerous minarets, mausolea and tombs of medieval origin. In 1598, the Safavid emperor, Shah Abbas I, made Isfahan his capital. Working on a huge scale, he created an imperial city to the south-west of the old, laying out a grand avenue, a park of palaces, and at its heart, a vast square, known as the Meidan-i-Shah. Splendid monuments punctuate the four arcades which frame this space: the Bazaar portal, the pavilion of Ali Qapu, the mosque of Shayk Lutfullah and the Shah Mosque. The two mosques, aglitter with painted tiles and tile mosaics, represent the apogee of Safavid art: 'Grandeur & space & proportion not grandeur in our manner but the grandeur of emptiness confined in a shape & relieved [by] ornaments of ethereal colour.'

Robert's receptiveness to the beauty of Isfahan had by no means been guaranteed. On returning from his tour in Azerbaijan, he had written to his mother: 'Persian *brick* buildings are what excite me – much more than the later tile work.' His enthusiasm for the citadel at Tabriz was typical: 'Brickwork of this v. lovely – a pale dusty pinkish russet brick . . . gt. richness of texture . . . facet at edge of this [central panel] had bricks roughed criss cross, wh. the Germans & Dutch think so modern.'

Medieval Persian brickwork, unlike tiled decoration, accorded with his passion for form in architecture. On taking a second look at the mausoleum of Uljaitu at Sultaniya, he noted: 'The use of glazed brick in the Mongol things is *exactly* the same as Babylonian – same feeling, not non-representational . . . The tile, the patterned tile flowing everywhere, is later & is *much* less architectural in fact non-architectural.'

The magnificent fragments of Timurid architecture at Herat opened his eyes to the power of decorated buildings. On returning from Herat to Meshed in December 1933, he scrutinized through field glasses, from a roof overlooking the precincts of the holy shrine, the most important group of tile- and mosaic-decorated buildings which he had so far encountered. 'The minarets have an affinity with Herat tho' they look a bit later,' he wrote. The courtyard he described belonged to the mosque of the Empress Gohar Shad which was commissioned in 1416. The dome of the mosque was easily identifiable and 'very beautiful, & the design tho' twisty, is conceived with the utmost simplicity & delicacy, one may say it has elegance, but it is elegance still with strength – not run riot and grown bul-bulish.'

By associating the bulbul or Persian nightingale with bulbous domes, Robert was casting aspersions on Safavid taste. 'The thing about Persia', he wrote to his mother from Meshed, 'is that it isn't all Bulbuls and lovers under trees and pretty stuffs and all that Omar Khayyam idea. That side exists – it dates from the 16th century . . . But it is all that came before that is so interesting and so much more worth-while.'

But even before these words were written, Robert had already denied his puritanical creed. Visiting the mausoleum of Khaja Rabi outside Meshed, he had been swept off his feet by the attractions of the Safavid exterior. He arrived in Isfahan with no inhibitions left to declare. In his notes on the monuments, he gave as much emphasis to the domed chamber of the Sheik Lutfullah Mosque, ablaze with tiles and mosaic, as he did to the sober purity of the brick Seljuk interiors of the Friday Mosque. A day of photography in the Sheik Lutfullah led to a flood of superlatives:

> The whole is without exception, save perhaps the Gumbad-i-Alivan at Hamadan, the richest decoration I know – terrific contrast of textures – the bold Arabic borders, the yet bolder arch panels with their squares and arabesques, the fine wain-scot & pendentives, the incredible richness of the window traceries (upper windows double, inner & outer, so you get a double richness[)], the bold yet decreasing ceiling, the minute detail of the mihrab, like a daisy field – the bold brilliant liquid sea-blue corkscrews of the arches – effect is unbelievable.

In the grandiose Masjid-i-Shah, the epitome of Safavid swagger, he discovered that tiled decoration was compatible with architectural form. 'The whole mosque,' he wrote, 'tho' poor in tiled detail (save dome) & not to compare with S. Lutfullah, is unique in its cubic sense – really has a 3-dimen-sional virtue . . . The main entrance v. beautiful – tall & slender, & the minarets carry on the proportions instead of being disastrous stumps.'

Robert's initial aversion towards tiled architecture provided

Sykes with a rich source of anecdote for his biographical essay in *Four Studies in Loyalty*, which he published only in 1946, twelve years after the journey. Robert is evoked snarling at the tiled buildings of Isfahan until, one day, he saw the light. According to Sykes: 'He did not recant . . . until I had taken him inside the mosque of Shayk Lutf'ullah . . . After that he had few hard words for the Omar Khayyam fiends, and there were no more eructations.'

Sykes's version of events is fictitious. During Robert's first visit to Isfahan, he was in Shiraz; and on the second, he was incarcerated in the British Residency in Bushire. As an inveterate raconteur and skilled caricaturist, it is possible that Sykes simply confused fable for fact. Whatever the case, his account of Robert's behaviour fitted the not unreasonable view 'that he was a man of extremes, that his talents were wrought to extreme heights of intensity'. It also served to bolster Sykes's authority as Robert's travelling companion, at a time when they had, in fact, been apart for almost eight weeks.

Whilst Christopher languished in Bushire, Robert set off on a ten-day journey to Yezd and Kerman, south-west of Isfahan. Travelling by car and post lorry, he saw almost every monument on the route, which range in date from the tenth-century Abbasid mosque in Nayin to the nineteenth-century Kajar additions to the mausoleum at Mahan. With his mind cleared of aesthetic prejudice, Robert now had a chance to achieve his ambition of surveying in Persia 'every building of real *aesthetic* importance'.

Returning to Isfahan, he found that Christopher had been set at provisional liberty in order to collect his things from Teheran. On Easter day, 1 April, they drove to Teheran where Lady Hoare, wife of the Minister, Sir Reginald Hoare, had them to stay at the Legation. A cousin of Christopher's, she had been campaigning on his behalf by refusing all official invitations. Her husband, meanwhile, with mounting impatience, had been lobbying members of the government. 'The Minister', wrote Robert, 'is working up for the hell's own row over Xtopher's treatment.' Even though another Englishman was expelled at this time,

Hoare finally secured Christopher's freedom. His persecution was attributed by the Minister for Foreign Affairs to the fact that 'he talked to peasants.' Robert traced this to a conversation with a gardener of the Shah, when Christopher had 'asked if the old boy was interested in flowers or words to that effect'. Unaware of Christopher's espionage, or unwilling to confirm it in his diary, Robert appeared satisfied with this explanation.

Soon after Robert's arrival in Teheran, news reached him that Herzfeld had agreed to allow photography at Persepolis. His capitulation was prompted by a complaint from the Governor of Fars over Robert's treatment. The immediate beneficiary was Arthur Upham Pope, who had recently arrived in Persia by private plane with one of his patrons, an American millionairess called Mrs Moore. When Robert met him in Teheran shortly after Pope had visited Persepolis, he reported: 'Herzfeld appears to have gone mad – after abusing Pope like a *maniac* for the last 2½ years, he fell on his neck & fawned on him the whole time they were at Persepolis, begged him to take any photos he wanted, etc.'

Awaiting Robert in Teheran had been a cheque from Pope for £30. 'I have just received some v. welcome & unexpected help from Upham Pope in the shape of money –' he informed Macmillan's, 'so must allow him the use of photos for the *Oxford Survey of Persian Art*. This being a 12 guinea book won't conflict with mine – and it is really owing to Pope's recommendation that the Persian authorities have been so helpful.' Pope was an inventive fund-raiser and had already, for a survey whose costs would run to thousands, secured £500 from the Persian government and, so Robert reported, 'was trying to raise another £500 out of Marjoribanks personally'. Christopher was appalled by the toadying that went on, but Robert knew well 'the advantage of financial solidity behind artistic enterprise'.

Making preparations for departure, Robert arranged for the dispatch through APOC of all his drawings, diaries, photographs and undeveloped films. The precious box was laced into a sack 'and addressed in indelible pencil on a wet surface to Eric Byron Savernake station G.W.R.' Finally, on 22 April, he left with Christopher in an open-topped

Chevrolet, bound for the monument which had first drawn him to Persia, the tomb tower of Gumbad-i-Kabus. Heading north-east across the Elburz mountains, they descended into luxuriant forest 'out of whose depths . . . came suddenly a piercing whistle, a puff of smoke & a goods train'. They had met up with the new railway line, which was still under construction, between the Caspian Sea and Teheran. After spending the night in Shahi, 'a curious "pioneer" town', they put the car on a train to Bandar Shah, a port on the Caspian, and thence drove to Asterabad (Gorgan), the regional capital, on the edge of the Turcoman steppe.

Robert described their journey of the following day:

> We set off after lunch, a little way down the Bandar Shah road, & then . . . suddenly we were out on the steppe – absolutely *dead* flat like a sea – a most beautiful sight – a rich grass green, as far as eye cd. see, this green made more yellow by the distant range of blue mountains, Elburz – running all along with steppe – snow capped here & there . . . everywhere groups of kibitkas [circular tents made of felt] like mushrooms – white topped, like highlights – but so small, & so far apart, that they gave size of steppe, like towns on a map – or from an aeroplane – then the droves of animals – mares & foals, cattle, camels – the latter more apart – & black & brown sheep – at different distances – occasionally a slight hump – 10 feet – looking like a mountain – the grass all wild oats & wild barley really – filled with flowers, tiny poppies, myriads of purple irises 9″ high – buttercups, & other familiar blossoms – larks overhead . . . one almost knocked my hat off as I sat on a knoll.

It was an ideal spring day with blue sky and cloud fleeces. Traffic on the smooth green tracks consisted of 'high wheeled carts some with hoods – one strange high-wheeled gig – parties on camels & horses – ladies all in red chintz, with flower patterns . . . One party of three men in turbans on horseback, one wearing a gorgeous sort of batik coat.' After driving about fifty miles, they caught sight of the tower: 'Suddenly a cream needle v. small stands up against the blue mountain[s] behind.'

Built in 1006 AD by a local prince as his mausoleum, the tower of Gumbad-i-Kabus is sited on an eminence to the north of a small market town. In *The Road to Oxiana*, Robert describes it thus:

> A tapering cylinder of café-au-lait brick springs from a round plinth to a pointed grey-green roof, which swallows it up like a candle-extinguisher . . . Up the cylinder, between plinth and roof, rush ten triangular buttresses, which cut across two narrow garters of cufic text, one at the top underneath the cornice, one at the bottom over the slender black entrance.

The tower fulfilled his every expectation. The Kufic panels, he noted, were 'as exquisite as in Diez'. The interior was sublime: 'Absolutely plain brick circular chamber going up to a point – *most* impressive – terrifying in fact – also terrific.' In conclusion, he wrote: 'The whole thing is *superb* in its boldness of design – unequalled among brick bldgs & somehow suits the edge of the steppe where it stands, a lighthouse over the terrestrial sea.'

After leaving Gumbad-i-Kabus, numerous setbacks occurred. At Bandar Shah, they were arrested for assaulting the stationmaster, who had let the train steam off without them. 'X[topher] dealt him a symbolical punch', Robert admitted, 'self clutched symbolically at his throat – upon wh. a squad of soldiers marched in with raised rifle butts, led by a v. small puffed out officer . . . Both of us were manhandled as tho' by mice.' Eventually, they were released after making a written apology and shaking hands with the stationmaster. Retracing their route across the Elburz, a lorry collided with the car, dislodging Robert's Revelation suitcase, a sturdy companion since India, and squashing it flat. As a result, £10 worth of unused films were destroyed. The next day, the back axle broke. Driving conditions worsened: 'the sky', Robert reported, 'was dropping water like a tank with the bottom fallen out.' Bumping at speed over a watercourse, they landed in a bog. At last, on the fourth day, in the wake of a rainbow arc, which moved 'like a harbinger' before them, they reached Meshed where they were put up by the consular staff.

On this visit, Robert hoped to gain entry to the sacred precincts of the shrine to inspect the mosque of Gohar Shad. The religious authorities turned down his request, but 'a v. natty young man', whom Robert met in one of their offices, offered to act as a guide. In order to keep the plan secret from the consulate, which would have forbidden it, they mounted the expedition from the Hotel de Paris. It was also agreed to make the attempt under cover of darkness. Robert dressed up as a lower middle-class Persian with a grey coat, a collarless shirt with a gold stud, tight black trousers four inches too short, a battered Pahlevi cap and a mackintosh. Christopher made less effort, but both blackened their fair complexions with burnt cork.

Their contact appeared after dinner with some friends. 'They watched me make up,' Robert wrote. 'But in haste, by the light of one candle, it was necessarily impressionist.' Ignoring the main entrance to the shrine, the trio entered a tunnel-like passage, which eventually led to the courtyard of Gohar Shad. They circled twice, then visited the two other courtyards. At Robert's insistence they returned to Gohar Shad's court before leaving by the main gate. Throughout, Christopher had had to cover his face with a handkerchief lest his beard betray them. He decided not to accompany them the following day when Robert planned to repeat the exercise in daylight.

In a private room, after lunch, Robert made up as usual. At the last minute, the guide dropped out, leaving Robert to venture into the shrine alone. 'I kept an exact pace, short, high steps from the knees,' he wrote, 'Persian looking & calculated to prevent my tripping over any uneven paving stone . . . Everything depended on keeping the pace exact – I was keyed to it & by it.'

He trotted down the passage, determinedly pushing past a group of mullahs, through a small bazaar and into the courtyard. Immediately, he felt insecure. His intention had been to make a slow circuit, but crowds of pilgrims were blocking both ends of the court. He grew conscious of the fairness of his moustache, which, he knew, showed through the burnt cork. Adjusting his pace, he moved slowly between the two crowds taking in what he could. Then, realizing that he was attracting attention, he retreated back down the passage. His rendezvous outside the main gate went according to plan: 'I passed Xtopher who had agreed to wait there & leered at me like a bearded wanton, while I looked disapprovingly in the opposite direction.' They drove straight to the photographers 'as it seemed a pity not to record so much art'.

If caught, Robert learnt afterwards, he could have been 'mauled about' and thrown into a gaol within the sacred precincts. Release would have been dependent on an appeal to the Governor. Reflecting on his escapade, he wrote: 'Even now I daresay nothing wld have happened if I had been discovered – the old prejudices are wavering.' That autumn, the shrine was opened to unbelievers. Upham Pope was even allowed to study a tomb cover of the sarcophagus of the Imam; he also took nearly fifty photographs of the court of Gohar Shad.

The mosque of Gohar Shad had been constructed between 1416 and 1418 by the architect Kavam-ad-Din, who was also to design the empress's complex at Herat. As the mosque has no exterior façade, all the decoration is concentrated on the courtyard. Robert recorded its impact upon him: 'A blaze of colour – bewildering – as though one saw the stars by day light.' In a separate note, he remarked: 'To know what mosaic is one must see this & Yezd. A sort of liquid quality about it, as opposed to the jigsaw puzzle [size]. Everything is interlaced in the most wonderful way. Arabesques in fact, look not like arabesques, anymore than a carpet looks like stitches.'

The next day, they left for Afghanistan. Robert warned his mother that his flow of letters might be disrupted:

> There is the possibility that the Afghan post won't work. So you must *not* fuss . . . You must remember that I don't travel merely out of idle curiosity or to have adventures (which I loathe). It is a sort of need – a sort of grindstone to temper one's character and get free of the cloying thoughts of Europe . . . I must develop my life in my own way as my instinct bids . . . If you worry, it is an obstacle – I feel caught in a net . . . When you read this, promise,

promise me to be unconcerned at a silence that may last till August and be astonished at any letters that arrive before.

Heavy rain again delayed their journey. At the Persian frontier, they were stranded for two days before being able to make the final stage to Herat. Awaking the following morning in his old bedroom in the Park Hotel, Robert was filled with optimism. On going to fetch his tea, he had seen the minarets shining in the dawn light. 'But how different is that light,' he wrote; '5 months ago it was a mournful pathetic gleam . . . that weighed on my spirits . . . Now every day the light will be stronger. We have the summer before us. We can walk to Mazar if we want.' Lying in bed, he looked down on the bustle of the streets: 'everyone', he noticed, 'is carrying roses or has roses in his mouth – perhaps roses have replaced rifles – a summer fashion . . . A man has just walked across the street with a *tray* of roses.'

On 15 May, after three days spent making preparations and studying the monuments, Robert embarked on another attempt to reach Mazar-i-Sherif in the Afghan region of Turkestan. Their problems began on the pass which had so tested his endurance the previous winter. On the descent, the low-slung car became 'stuck on a steep slope, shipwrecked as it were on a bed of enormous jagged rocks'. Putting up the hood and side flaps, they settled in for the night. While Robert slept, Christopher kept watch against brigands and wolves. In the morning, a gang of labourers came to the rescue, but, at the foot of the pass, the car again ran aground. The following day, twenty miles beyond the town of Kala Nao, the front axle struck a grass hummock; there was a slight jar and the engine stopped for good. A passing merchant lent them horses and they rode back together to the nearest caravanserai. The following morning, Christopher sold the car to the merchant for £50, and a team of oxen were dispatched to fetch the vehicle.

Resorting to horse power, they reached the town of Murghab two days later with a caravan of six baggage animals and an armed attendant. In all, they had spent six nights on the road. Normally, the journey by lorry from Herat to Murghab would have taken a day.

The town gave Robert his first glimpse of Central Asia. In a courtyard, he saw Turcoman women wearing tall head-dresses covered in floating veils: 'the gt. beauty', Robert pointed out, 'is in the various reds – the view of that court-yard . . . with all those nodding top hats was like a flower bed of geraniums roses & sweetwilliams.' They lodged for the night at the Governor's house which looked on to a garden running down to the river. Along the bank, a row of mulberry trees 'sheltered conversation parties, readers, solitary prayers, and people at their ablutions'.

The only available transport to Maimenah, ninety miles due east, was a ramshackle Ford owned by a Persian boy-chauffeur. The chance of reaching their destination appeared so remote that they made no preparations for the journey, apart from changing into their best suits. Against all odds, and with a great deal of clanking and fizzing, the vehicle slowly covered the distance. They spent the night at a cara-vanserai, in a carpeted room perfumed by roses drying in a niche. Before leaving, their host, a holy man, gave them bunches of dark red roses from his walled garden. Soon after, they crossed the regional frontier into Turkestan.

The weather had turned hotter, and since leaving Murghab the country had appeared 'rich beyond belief'. The hills on either side of a valley were rounded and glossy 'like a horse's flanks'. Poppies flourished on the tilled soil, so that 'one might see the top of a distant hill dappled with bright scarlet among the golden green.' Along the road, yellow-buff snakes basked in the sun and Azar jays flitted from 'earthen holes'. Tortoises crept across their path. The final approach to Maimenah ran through a fertile plain dotted with groves of poplars and mulberries.

Settling into his room in the caravanserai, Robert succumbed to a bout of retrospection. At last he had reached Turkestan, which had been his dream since the autumn of 1931, when he had first applied for visas to visit Russian Turkestan with Michael Rosse and Alastair Graham: 'all the novelty and pastoral romance implied in the name Turkestan have come true.' Food was produced: 'Milk in great quantities, plum jam, pilau with raisins, kabob on a skewer well-peppered & salted & new bread.' This was the standard fare. In the evenings, they added their own delicacies such as prunes in gin, chocolate, tomato ketchup and Ovaltine. They also had a supply of whisky. For breakfast, Robert cooked porridge. Usually, two armed men stood guard on the veranda whose other duties included lighting the fire and doing the washing up.

A walk through the bazaar revealed all the pageantry of the East. Here, Robert enthused,

> the hirsute, fiercely bearded Uzbegs, are all dressed in long robes of chintz or silk, brilliantly coloured, patterned with roses, stripes, or the jazz-lightning effects favoured by the old Bokhara fashions. Turbans vary between white, deep blue, pink, & black. Slippers are like boats & worked in gold thread. The tall black boots have high heels and embroidery on the top.

Even a troop of grim-faced soldiers sported roses in their rifles. In the evening, Robert and Christopher walked to a meadow just outside the town where men sat in tea houses listening to 'banjo' players and wrestling contests and partridge fights took place.

Their transport problems were solved by hiring a new Chevrolet lorry, owned by an Indian, to take them to Mazar-i-Sherif. 'Words can't describe the luxury of the lorry,' Robert wrote, 'in wh. we sprawl on narrow benches propped by pushteens – with all our necessities about us & the heavy luggage on the top. This is the way, the only way to travel here.' Apart from the owner-driver, they also acquired three servants.

They drove, due north, to Andkhoi, the centre of the lambskin trade. Robert had always been curious about the origin of 'Persian lamb'. Now he inspected skins drying in the bazaar and met a merchant, who, each year, sent a batch to London to be turned into fashionable collars and cuffs. The next day, spying a flock of sheep from the lorry, he walked across the sparse crackling pasture to interview the shepherd. Continuing his quest for local colour, he tried to photograph a Turcoman woman outside a kibitka, 'admirable portable houses' made from felt and rush matting. The young woman advanced upon him brandishing a large pole and screaming denunciations. Although this made a fine subject, Robert was too flustered to take a successful shot.

On the two-day journey from Maimenah to Mazar-i-Sherif, the landscape changed dramatically. The lush green hills turned to brown, then these too receded. A hot breeze blew up and a leaden light appeared in the sky. At length, they debouched on to the Oxus plain, which was the colour of steel. The atmosphere remained oppressive. Nearing Mazar-i-Sherif, Robert detected a slight shift in tone: 'the lead & steel gave place to a sort of aluminium colour, pallid & deathly . . . Occasionally one saw a field of barley – it was ripe . . . But it was not gold – there was no hint of brown, of Ceres, of plenty. It was like the hair of a fairhaired man turning prematurely white.' They had reached the plain of Balkh, named after the city which is reputedly the oldest in the world. The geometric forms of ancient remains arose on either side of the road. By degrees, the country became greener. Suddenly, dilapidated walls appeared on the horizon. Passing through, they found themselves in a vast metropolis of ruins. It was the city of the plain.

In the inhabited core of Balkh is a Timurid shrine. Near by, a group of officials were discussing plans for the rebuilding of the city. From them, Christopher learnt that Mazar-i-Sherif was only fifteen miles away. As a storm threatened, they dashed off in the lorry, reaching the town just as the deluge began. 'I must confess that, for me at least, our arrival here last night was a solemn occasion,' Robert pronounced. 'I left England last August with 2 intentions: one, to see the monuments of Persia; two, to reach this town. Neither of them v. formidable – but they have taken some effort to carry out.'

To their astonishment, they discovered a modern hotel. Each bedroom had sprung beds and its own tiled bathroom with soap, a bath mat, and a pail of water for washing. The dining room had Sheffield cutlery and finger bowls. The lavatory doors, however, only locked on the outside. Robert suggested pointing this out to the proprietor 'but Xtopher said he liked it & wldn't have them touched'. Elsewhere, the town had evidently been smartened up. There was a public garden with a band playing European ditties. The bazaars were new and the streets cobbled. The dresses were not so picturesque. 'One feels here the remoter parts of the country are behind us,' Robert wrote. 'Maimenah & Murghab are *untouched* – we shd. have stayed there longer.'

Immediately, they sought permission to visit the River Oxus, which lies only thirty miles north of the town. After being fobbed off at various ministries, they petitioned the Minister of the Interior with a letter composed in excessively flowery language. Word came back that they must abandon the idea. The matter could only be dealt with in Kabul. Another reason put forward by the Indian doctor who acted as their intermediary, was the risk of their kidnap by Bolshevik agents operating with lawless bands of Russian Turcomans along the south bank of the river.

Christopher scored a minor diplomatic triumph by gaining entry to the Russian consulate to request visas for Samarcand. Without delay, the acting consul, who was delighted to meet another European, telegrammed Moscow and Kabul. With the serious business over, he then invited them to a party that evening. As the decanter of vodka circulated, Robert was induced to drain his glass in the Russian manner. They conversed in Persian. 'But . . . as the drink infused,' Robert recalled, 'all speech became intelligible, so perfect was our understanding. We danced, wildly, and sang.' Sinking into a deep slumber he was carried into the garden. Christopher was left to endure the soulful conversation of drunken Russians. According to Robert: 'When I woke up, I put the souls to flight, & announced when X.[topher] said it was time to go . . . that . . . the party had only just begun. I even threatened him with a bottle.' Christopher gave a different version. Robert, he claimed, woke up and knocked out the consular doctor who was attempting to give him artificial respiration. 'The next morning', Robert admitted, 'was painful beyond the usual run of next mornings.'

Rather than wait for the decision over their visas, they left in another Indian-owned lorry for Khanabad. Two armed guards from the foreign ministry travelled with them. Their purpose soon became obvious when they tried to prevent Robert from taking photographs. An explosion of rage put a stop to their demands. 'I suppose it will be v. amusing afterwards to say one was regarded as a spy etc', fumed Robert, 'but how boring it becomes after 8 months of incessant suspicion.' At Khanabad, they received some straight talking for once. The Governor ruled out another request to visit the Oxus. He also dismissed their idea of travelling to Chitral in India, owing to snow in the pass. Robert had no alternative but to head south for Kabul.

Following, through plains and valleys, the course of the River Kunduz, their Indian driver doggedly overcame all obstacles. On the pass over the Hindu Kush, they looked down upon the 'great, rushing broad torrent with huge waves', which on the third day led them to the ancient Buddhist site of Bamian. Robert set the scene:

> Incredible beauty of the valley, with dark rhubarb red cliffs across river, electric green fields & trees below, snow capped indigo peaks, blue sky & white puffy clouds, & then gt furious clouds – at last the gt cliff on the right, pinky orange ochre, with the thousands of caves & the gt Buddhas.

On a closer viewing of the two giant Buddhas which stared out of niches in the cliff face, Robert was less enthusiastic: 'loathsome effort artistically – if I lived with the Buddhas I shd be ill.'

Two days later they were in Kabul. At the British Legation, Robert at last learnt the reason for being refused permission to travel to the Oxus. Under pressure from the Indian and Russian governments, the Afghans had banned the British and Russians from straying too close to each other's border. Inquiring at the Russian Embassy about their visas to Samarcand, they were told to return in a week. 'This is evidently hopeless,' wrote Robert, 'so, thank God, we can make preparations for India & home.'

Invited to stay at the Legation, Robert passed uneventful days, feeling too lazy even for the Kabul museum. He roused himself to visit the twelfth-century minarets at Ghazni: 'before the lesser tower of Ghazni,' he recorded triumphantly, 'I took my last scheduled architectural photograph – the end of 10 months' effort, wh. I rushed back to celebrate in whisky. This was far from discreet in hot thundery weather with sandstorms blowing up, & I regretted it for the rest of the day.'

At the end of the week the Russian visas had still not come through. The following day, they left at dawn for India and by 7.30 p.m. were drinking gin fizz in the marble lounge of Dean's Hotel at Peshawar.

On Sunday 8 July, three weeks after leaving Kabul, Robert arrived at Savernake. As he recorded it:

> The last journey from Paddington left me dazed, dazed at the thought of coming to a stop, at the impending collision between the momentum gathered from 11 months of new experience & the immobility of a cherished home . . . The collision happened . . . I stepped from the car. Our dogs ran up. And then my mother. To whom, now it is finished, I deliver the whole record – fondest of mothers, earliest of teachers, & most just of critics.

And with that, both diary and journey came to a full stop.

23
A Pen in Each Hand

For the next six months, Robert was based at Savernake. By the end of his travels, his overdraft stood at over £600 and he had been forced to sell £500 of equity, a third of his capital, to clear some of the debt. Fortunately, commissions were plentiful. Within days, Robert had picked up the threads of his literary career. His last book, *First Russia Then Tibet*, which had been published in his absence, in October 1933, had sold about 800 copies. A letter awaited him from Harold Macmillan: 'The sales of "First Russia, then Tibet" are not so satisfactory as they might have been and I think perhaps the price was rather against it. Nevertheless . . . I believe the book added very materially to your reputation, and this is a great thing as far as the future is concerned.'

The book had been widely and favourably reviewed. 'It is refreshing', wrote the reviewer in *The Times*, 'to read a book on Russia by a man not obsessed by the Five-Year Plan but concerned with the art and architecture of the country.' The weakness of the structure was obvious. Cecil Roberts in the *Sphere* commented: 'The book on Russia proves him the born traveller and the born reporter . . . It is a pity Mr Byron has joined two books into one.' As a stylist, Robert caught the eye of L. P. Hartley, 'The Literary Lounger' in the *Sketch*, who wrote: 'His prose is stately and rhetorical, and recruited from an exceptionally large vocabulary; it wears long words like jewels. I am all in favour of this.'

Robert sought advice from Harold Macmillan about his next step. Having received a second advance from Macmillan's earlier in the year, he was effectively under contract to produce two books for the firm. After their meeting, Macmillan wrote: 'I think you would be wise to write a general travel book on the lines we discussed, leaving the technical archaeological discoveries and descriptions to a scholarly book of a different type which you might embark upon later.'

Macmillan also expressed interest in a satirical novel which Robert and Christopher had been working on together during their travels. The idea had been Robert's, but of the early drafts Christopher's were the more successful. His confinement in Shiraz had offered an opportunity to make further progress. '[Christopher] has now developed a real style,' Robert wrote after departing for Firuzabad, 'wh. made me laugh to tears last night. So I hope this encouraged him. I am looking forward to putting pen to it myself again now.' In caravanseries across Afghanistan, they whiled away their evenings writing the novel; and on the ship home Robert perfected the plot. Macmillan promised a quick decision on sight of the finished manuscript, and talked of publishing before Christmas.

Meanwhile, Robert wrote three articles on his journey for *The Times*. In dealing with the attitude of Persia and Afghanistan towards the West, he called for an Anglo-Russian convention to relieve tension in the region. In Teheran, as a consequence, the Shah's blood pressure soared. According to Robert: 'The Persian Minister [in London] was in an awful state – his life is in danger, almost, because his filthy old Shah thinks that after 2 months he ought to have the English press under control.' Robert was obliged to write an explanatory letter to the newspaper to calm the situation.

Another form of report also claimed his attention. Its instigator had been Major Hamber, secretary to the Consul General in Meshed, who had suggested to Robert that he record details of his route through Afghanistan as a brief for Military Intelligence. The road linking Herat, Mazar-i-Sherif and Kabul had only been opened in 1933 and Robert and Christopher were the first Englishmen to have attempted it. Robert duly made notes of the distances between towns and villages, the condition of the roads and the geography of the surrounding countryside.

Back in London, he was supplied with large-scale Indian Survey maps of the region by the War Office. He marked in previously unidentified place names and bridges, as well as gradients and other relevant details. The accompanying report admitted the difficulties of his task. Of the stretch between Murghab and Maimenah, he wrote: 'Our only concern was to reach our destination before the Ford fell in half, and there was no opportunity of taking notes.' However, he discovered a number of discrepancies between the maps and the actual distances as measured by the milometers on Christopher's car and the two lorries; and he made plain the true state of most of the roads. 'The Afghan method of making an earth road', he explained, 'is simply to dig it over till it looks level. Rolling is done by the infrequent traffic, which often collapses into cavities that have formed unseen beneath the loose surface.'

His factual report came spiced with political observations. True to the tradition of the Great Game, Robert retailed every scrap of rumour and gossip concerning the Russian presence. Diligently, he recorded the drinking session at the consulate in Mazar-i-Sherif, concluding his account: 'At 2.30 a.m. the party ended, and M. Bouriachenko got out the "consulski Vauxhall" and drove us back to the hotel, which was only 400 yards away. This he did, lest the Afghans should have observed anything peculiar in our gait, which would have shocked them considerably and might have got us into trouble.'

The document, along with photographs of bridges, fords and typical views, was forwarded by the War Office to Colonel Bruce Scott, Deputy Director of Intelligence, the Government of India. Robert had added the following proviso: 'In the event of its being printed, I would ask that its circulation should be confined solely to Military Intelligence. Not that the contents are of any great significance. But it is of the utmost importance to the author that his authorship of such a document should not be known to any one, English or foreign, outside M. I.' Robert had already aroused suspicion with his drawing and photography. He knew that if his association with Military Intelligence, however slight, should leak out, his future as a traveller would be imperilled. When the report reached India, an intelligence officer acknowledged: 'I have been most interested in going through it', and Grindlay's Bank were instructed to pay £25 to cover Robert's expenses.

Country Life also moved quickly to harvest Robert's fresh

crop of experiences. By the end of August six articles had been agreed, which were published between October 1934 and April 1935, under the heading 'Between Tigris and Oxus'. Readers were regaled with the tale of German intrigue at Persepolis, of a mysterious bubbling 'hammam' outside Firuzabad and of Robert's entry in disguise to the sacred precincts at Meshed. Only one article, on medieval brick buildings, avoids the garnish of anecdote; its description of tomb towers, mosques and mausolea has the gleam of unearthed treasure. Of two early masterpieces, a tower at Maragha and a Seljuk mausoleum in Isfahan, he concludes: 'We have lighted on a golden age in architecture.'

The articles provided Robert with an ideal opportunity to display his photographs, which included landscapes, portraits and scenes of local colour. The strongest images are architectural. In his views of buildings, picturesque composition is rare. The tower of Gumbad-i-Kabus rears above its eminence; the mausoleum of Uljaitu dominates the flat-roofed village of Sultaniya, presenting an image, to use Robert's words, of 'fabulous enormity'.

Robert accepted that black and white photography could not do justice to the brilliance of tile- and mosaic-decorated architecture. To convey their effect, therefore, he had reverted on his travels to pencil and crayon. 'My art is very active,' he wrote from Meshed. 'Yet how long each picture takes . . . The great shrine here . . . I drew from a roof, keeping the police officer who accompanied me up there 3 hours, till he nearly went mad.'

Country Life took the unusual step of printing colour plates to reproduce four of his drawings. Executed with Robert's usual verve, they made striking illustrations of coloured architecture. Their publication, in the 1934 Christmas number, previewed an exhibition, which Robert had mounted on his own behalf at Walker's Galleries in New Bond Street. Friendly notices appeared in *The Times* and the *Morning Post* and the exhibition raised over £80 before commission.

Robert's homecoming had been warmly welcomed by Arthur Upham Pope, who was working at Oxford on the Persian Survey. 'I am all a twitter to see you at the earliest possible moment,' he enthused. 'It goes without saying that you are to do something for the SURVEY.' At their first meeting, he commissioned him to write an article on the architecture of Afghanistan, dispensing at a stroke with the services of André Godard, the distinguished Director of the Archaeological Service of Persia, who had, so far, failed to deliver on the subject.

In 1931, Pope had launched a photographic survey of Persian architecture. Since then, on a number of expeditions across the country, he had amassed almost 8,000 prints or negatives of monuments. Robert had taken around 1,000 photographs on his journey, which, Pope realized, could usefully supplement his own collection. 'If you could identify yourself with the work in Persia for the Institute,' he wheedled, 'we would forget that little sum I sent you last year, and we might be able to get a little more, say another £30 or £50, so you could say your photographing this year was part of the Institute's architectural survey of Persia.'

Pope proved most persuasive. In the next *Bulletin* of the Institute, it was announced that 'Mr Robert Byron . . . has joined the staff of the Institute's Architectural Survey Expedition in Persia.' There followed an account of the outstanding shots taken by Robert on his journey, illustrated by fine specimens mounted on the covers of the journal.

The *Bulletin of the American Institute for Persian Art and Archaeology* was another part of Pope's empire, which Robert had been urged to colonize. In the same issue, there appeared an article by him on the Sassanian palace, known as Kala-i-Dukhtar, outside Firuzabad. Before committing himself, Robert had been assured that 'an exhaustive discussion on the subject is not at all necessary.' Pope had gone on to suggest: 'There are two ways of dealing with discoveries; one can sit on them like crockery eggs, as Herzfeld does, without sharing them and only publishing them inch by inch . . . I think the other method is better, for the objects discovered to be published even with brief designations as to their character and location.'

In his dealings with Pope, Robert made a point of distancing himself from the attainments of scholarship. Mindful of this, the *Bulletin* printed the following disclaimer: 'Mr Byron has always kept in mind that the ultimate interest of architecture is aesthetic, and that by this criterion architecture must finally be judged, and that scholarship in architecture has its *raison d'être* in what it may reveal about buildings as works of art.'

Towards the end of the year, Pope arranged for his protégé to lecture in America. Miss Elkins, secretary of the American Institute, undertook to find Robert places on programmes, offering as credentials his articles in *Country Life*. Early in January 1935, Robert sailed for New York.

Until now, Robert had viewed America with hostility. On his early travels, he had sneered at American tourists and referred to their country as 'that great menace to civilization'. His attitude softened when the American publisher, Knopf, bought editions of *The Station* and *The Byzantine Achievement*. However, Robert's mood soured on seeing reviews of *The Station*. 'I had the American press cuttings the other day about the size of a thumbnail each . . . both stupid and illiterate,' he complained. His encounter in Teheran with an American wishing to travel to Afghanistan had only reinforced this prejudice. Robert described him as 'one of those weedy prognathous creatures . . . hunched in figure, of loping tread, a sort of anaemic anthropoid reversion, a familiar product in fact of transatlantic industrial barbarism'.

Accustomed to visualizing America as the birthplace of twentieth-century materialism, Robert was surprised to discover, on arriving in New York, a tribe of old-fashioned English people. 'Their standard of manners is what ours was before the war,' he reported back to his mother. 'They strike one as the real thing, rather boring perhaps, but essentially non-vulgar.' Social life, he remarked, was equally archaic: 'people have At Home afternoons. At a large lunch at the Lewisohns . . . half the men were in tail coats. One sees old ladies out in their broughams.' Robert started a collection of eighteenth-century words still in use.

Initially, he stayed with one of Upham Pope's richest supporters, Mrs Otto Kahn, the wife of a multi-millionaire financier, who was a great traveller and collector. After a few days, he left to settle in to the Shelton Hotel. His first engagement was as guest of honour at the American Institute's annual dinner, where he gave a talk entitled 'An Architectural Adventure in Persia and Afghanistan'. It emerged, however, that no lectures had been booked until the middle of February. To retrieve the situation, he set about pursuing contacts on newspapers and magazines. This included visiting the *National Geographic* in Washington.

In the end he delivered three lectures. The first took place in Philadelphia museum, before an audience of over a thousand. 'The lecture', he boasted, 'was really quite a success – a travel lecture, they saw my jokes and I had arranged my pictures so that they illustrated what I was saying automatically.' After another good reception in New York, Robert felt 'a new confidence'. He also met with success as a journalist, receiving commissions for travel articles from the *New York Times* and *Asia* magazine. By the time he left for England, at the beginning of March, he had just about covered his costs.

Awaiting him was news that Harold Macmillan had accepted the novel which Robert had jointly written with Christopher Sykes. After incorporating revisions, Robert had delivered the manuscript just before Christmas. Macmillan and his principal reader, J. C. Squire, now asked for a number of further changes. By mid-April, the book was finished and in July, *Innocence and Design* by the pseudonymous Richard Waughburton appeared on the bookstalls. Comic illustrations, drawn by Sykes, enlivened the text.

Set in a country called Media, ruled by a tyrant bearing the title the Sanskrit Potshaw, *Innocence and Design* is something of a *roman-à-clef*. The geographical location of Media corresponds to Persian Azerbaijan and her cities are named after ancient Persian sites, whilst the plot centres upon an attempt by the Russians to undermine British influence in the region. A cast of inept spies and secret policemen do their best to thwart one another, and confusion is added by the arrival of an innocent Scottish baronet, Sir Constantine Bruce, in search of examples of coloured architecture. Thanks to his unwitting assistance, the Russians receive their come-uppance, and the Potshaw is forced into making a diplomatic apology to the British.

Many of the characters are modelled on friends and

acquaintances of the authors. The aesthete-baronet was inspired by Sir Robert Abdy; Tolstoy, an incompetent Russian spy, was sketched from Hannibal, a well-known Russian who lived in the bazaar in Teheran. The one character requiring no key to his identity is the Potshaw who, with his determination to impose westernization upon his subjects, is clearly a portrayal of Reza Shah. 'Chief among the instruments of this degradation is the new sumptuary law', it is related, 'where-by . . . all Medes, at all times and under all circumstances, are forced to appear in peaked skiing-caps.' One of Robert's abiding impressions of Persia had been 'the detestable Pahlevi cap insisted on by the Shah'.

The authors' visit to Persia had coincided with a bout of political repression, particularly against the southern tribes. Returning to Teheran from his first trip to Afghanistan, Robert observed: 'Teheran is v. changed. Tremendous atmosphere of intrigue . . . All the Bakhtiaris in prison – Assad, Minister of War, sent back from Turcoman races in a lorry.' Many incidents in the book echo actual events. In the novel, the Median foreign minister, an hereditary khan from the south, is murdered in prison; the cause of his death is given as epilepsy. On Robert's return from Isfahan he had heard that Sardar Assad, the Minister of War, had died in the prison hospital, apparently from apoplexy. Robert remained unconvinced, noting that it was: 'The second murder of that sort since I have been here.'

A number of reviewers recognized the novel's charm. The *Spectator* described it as 'a solemn leg-pull which Mr Waughburton has succeeded in sustaining with great skill for the length of the novel . . . As farce it is of the best.' Like all *romans-à-clef*, it attracted the charge of exclusiveness. The *Evening Standard* wrote: 'No doubt there will be hearty chuckles in service clubs and other appropriate places. I found it rather hard going.' Others criticized the undoubted weakness of the book, the intricacy of the plot. The *Daily Mirror* complained that it was 'rather too complicated and overloaded', whilst *Punch*, in a generally favourable review, described the opening chapters as congested. Evelyn Waugh, modish satirist of exotic realms, found the book unreadable.

Outside a small circle of friends, the authorship of the

book remained a mystery. Nancy Mitford reported the following exchange: 'I sat next to Sir Ronald Storrs at lunch & he said, "I think your last book was far and away your best – how did you manage to get the atmosphere of Persia so vividly?" I said you mean my first book & the atmosphere of Perthshire. No no he cried your book about the Potshaw which I read with so much enjoyment & admiration.'

With *Innocence and Design*, Harold Macmillan had hoped to repeat the success of the comic novel, *England, Their England*. Indeed, its author, A. C. Macdonell, a close friend of J. C. Squire, had lavishly praised the book in the *Tatler*. However, initial sales of 600 copies were deemed to be very disappointing. Harold Macmillan wrote to Robert: 'I think a simpler story with an English setting would be very different. People have been a little puzzled by the complexity of the plot and by the oriental setting . . . After all, a satire is more amusing when it satirizes what one knows. This was, I think, the secret of Macdonell's success.'

In April 1935 another of Robert's literary tasks came to fruition with the publication of the *Shell Guide to Wiltshire*. The idea for a series of guides aimed at the motorist had been conceived by John Betjeman, who had persuaded Jack Beddington at Shell to sponsor the project. In 1934, the *Shell Guide to Cornwall*, written and designed by Betjeman, was published under the imprint of the Architectural Press. This slim volume, with its entertaining miscellany of information, arresting illustrations and eye-catching typography, had, as Betjeman wrote to Robert, taken 'the wind out of the sails of the other [guide] books by being unlike them'.

That autumn, three further guides were proposed, including one to Wiltshire. At first, Robert refused to write on the subject of his home county as he took a dim view of the idiosyncratic approach adopted by Betjeman, who had become general editor of the series. At Beddington's intervention, he changed his mind. 'The Wiltshire Guide book is all arranged . . .' he announced to his mother, 'it is to be a proper guide book after all.'

On submitting his synopsis, Robert's original fears were confirmed. His suggested coverage of the 'Antiquities' of the county, ranging in date from Pre-Christian to Georgian, did not meet with Betjeman's whole-hearted approval. 'I think there is a little too much medieval *antiquities*,' he advised. 'All guide books illustrate stinking little gothic churches. Views of Salisbury Cathedral are countless. We need hardly bother about it at all. We certainly do not want a photograph of Bradford-on-Avon Church.' Instead, he called for illustrations of Georgian terraces in Devizes, of ironwork from the Close at Salisbury and of 'any amount of country houses'.

In his annoyance, Robert quite forgot that during the battle for Carlton House Terrace, he had scorned the English preference for ancient monuments over Georgian and Regency architecture. He informed Betjeman that only buildings which were 'worthwhile' would be included; and he rode to the defence of the Saxon church at Bradford-on-Avon. Betjeman was forced to retreat. 'I really don't mind if you make the book into a monograph on Bradford on Avon church', he conceded, 'so long as you produce some good and unhackneyed illustrations.' He then made a further plea for Georgian buildings: 'This is the stuff that is newer than Stonehenge from a popular point of view and can be made just as interesting.'

Ignoring such advice, Robert took his readers on a tour of the pioneering monuments of Wiltshire. Stonehenge, he writes, 'marks the dawn of artifice and aesthetic instinct on English soil. We smell the beginnings of form and order, of the subordination of natural material to human taste.' He dwells upon the significance of the church at Bradford-on-Avon, choosing a worthy photograph as illustration. He dilates upon a pair of Norman carvings at Malmesbury Abbey and lauds Salisbury Cathedral as a supreme work of art. Georgian architecture is dismissed in a short paragraph, which opens: 'Wiltshire is comparatively poor in monuments of the eighteenth century.'

Other sections of the *Guide* covered topics such as local industries, agriculture and sport. Much of this information had been gathered by Robert's father and his sister, Anne, who had also compiled a gazetteer. Unbeknown to Robert, their version had been dropped by Betjeman in favour of one commissioned from Edith Olivier, a well-known literary figure, who lived at Wilton. On seeing the finished guide, Robert reacted with fury, accusing the Architectural Press of deceit.

Since his return from Persia, Robert had peppered his correspondence with acrimonious complaints against various companies and organizations. His bad temper coincided with an increasingly tense atmosphere at home. Both his parents were turning sixty; money was short; and they felt unable to carry on at Savernake. Robert loved the house, which had been his home since he was eighteen. When abroad, he suffered intense pangs of homesickness. In the depths of despair at Kala Nao, he had written: 'I am getting homesick – I mean for my own home, not England or London . . . its details haunt me – I smell the house & see every plant in the garden. I must get back before the Spring and have a few days hunting.' His days with the Tedworth Hunt and Mr Scarlett's forest pack had rooted him in the Wiltshire countryside. When, in anticipation of a move, Robert sold his beloved hunter, he wrote afterwards: 'It breaks my heart to think of Aubrey really gone – I didn't realize I should mind so much.'

There were problems however in disposing of Savernake. Under the terms of the lease, the Byrons had to stay in the house until another tenant was found. In the New Year, Margaret Byron heard from a friend of J. C. Squire, who was house-hunting in the neighbourhood 'and seemed to want everything we haven't got . . . central heating, electric light, 11 bedrooms etc.' The house, she bemoaned, 'is down with all the agents, but no one comes, & if they do, they won't take it.'

By the following summer, there was still no progress. Anne complained to Robert: 'they must be moved soon, I am really frightened about Punch [Eric Byron], he is so mad, he is determined he is going mad & is quite angry if one says he isn't, mother is frightened too . . . I feel nearly off my head with all the interminable arguments.' Anne, in turn, was proving a worry to her mother. Her beauty drew many admirers: 'young men are incessantly ringing her up,' Robert was informed, 'heaven only knows who they are, she never leaves the neighbourhood.' Lucy had already made her escape. In October 1934, she had married Rohan Butler, a sub-editor on *The Times*, and now lived in London.

Amidst this unsettled family atmosphere, Robert completed his essay on the architecture of Afghanistan, which had been commissioned by Pope the previous summer for the Persian Survey. Before doing so, Robert visited Professor Joseph Hackin in Paris. A member of the French Archaeological Mission, based at the Buddhist site of Bamian, he was one of the few scholars to have travelled widely throughout the country. Hackin provided Robert with up-to-date photographs of inscriptions at Ghazni and with photographs and descriptions of the monuments in the southern region of Seistan.

The finished work catalogues the Islamic monuments in Ghazni, Seistan, Herat and the region running north to the Oxus river, termed Cisoxiana. Each entry gives dates, dimensions, details of inscriptions and a description. However, Robert also had a wider goal. In the longest section, devoted to Herat and Cisoxiana, he sought to resurrect the reputation of the Timurids as rulers over the 'golden age of the Iranian Renascence'.

Centre stage is the Empress Gohar Shad. 'The fame of Shah Rukh as a patron of architecture', Robert states, 'is eclipsed by that of his wife . . . she is still remembered by the people of Herat as "the most incomparable woman in the world". It remains for us to crown [her name] with the laurels of a Medici.' He did so by reconstructing her great architectural complex at Herat. Working from a photograph in the India Office of a drawing made by a Major Durand just before the demolition, Robert maps the vanished portals, eiwans, domes and walls of her mosque and madrassa, to which he adds, like the final pieces of an elaborate model, his accounts of the surviving minarets and mausoleum.

His exploration into the lives and buildings of the Timurids resulted in a treatise exceeding 30,000 words. In July, when Pope finally received the manuscript, he realized at a glance that it was much too long. As he afterwards admitted: 'I had never dreamed of anything more than 4–5,000 words.' Robert had fallen victim to the chaotic conditions surrounding Pope's activities which allowed him little opportunity to keep track of commissioned articles. During the previous twelve months, apart from editing the *Survey*, Pope had visited America, undertaken a lecture tour of French universities and mounted an expedition to Persia.

With regard to Robert's Timurid essay, he devised a solution. Since the launch of the *Survey*, its scope had considerably widened. In June 1934, it had been announced that the first section, in four volumes, was 'rapidly approaching completion' and that a second was being planned, to appear in two or three years' time. This would deal with the influence of Persian art upon other cultures. Pope suggested that Robert's contribution should appear in the second section. He also offered to publish it in instalments in the *Bulletin*.

With mounting pique, Robert rebuffed Pope's offer. Claiming that he had spent six months on the task, although the actual time was nearer three, he replied: 'Naturally I don't expect to make money out of this kind of work . . . But what I do expect is that . . . [it] will be read by somebody.' He dismissed the option of publication in the *Bulletin* out of hand.

In making his response, Pope drew upon his ample reserves of sympathy, flattery and tenacity. 'I was dismayed, disturbed, and quite astonished to get yours . . .' he wrote by return, 'and I am glad you wrote so fully and strongly.' Launching into a defence of the structure of the *Survey*, he reasoned: 'If the architecture of Afghanistan is to receive 55 pages of text, what should the architecture of the central plateau receive, with its 500 or so monuments? . . . the Survey is primarily a survey.' As for the second section, its preparation was well advanced. 'If only you knew some of the sensational material that was going in . . .' he enthused, 'and some of the great names that are writing for it, you would feel it was no afterthought, but rather the culmination of the whole undertaking.' His salesmanship worked. Robert replied in such emollient terms that Pope was forced to command: 'Stay, oh, stay those contrite tears!'

Robert's outburst had coincided with the collapse of longheld plans to return to Persia. Fortunately, the prospect of another foreign journey remained in place. That summer,

Robert had been invited to deliver a paper at the Third International Congress and Exhibition of Persian Art and Archaeology to be held in Russia in September. David Talbot Rice, the Treasurer of the Congress, had granted him a free passage; and Robert had arranged with *The Times* to act as their correspondent. Christopher Sykes agreed to accompany him; and on 28 August, they left by boat from Hull, bound for Copenhagen.

24

The Grim Orient

The Third International Congress of Persian Art and Archaeology opened on 11 September in Leningrad in conjunction with a magnificent exhibition at the Hermitage. As *Times* correspondent, Robert filed reports on both events, not forgetting to mention his own contribution to the congress, which was a short lecture with slides on the monuments of Afghanistan. 'You don't seem to realize', he explained to his mother, 'that all the news in the Times has been sent by *me*!! So of course my name is mentioned!'

Many of Robert's acquaintances were presenting papers at the congress. Others joined as observers. Mrs Otto Kahn had flown in with thirty-five pieces of luggage and a ladies' maid. Kenneth Clark was also present, an old acquaintance from Oxford who was now director of the National Gallery and 'had his eye' on some of the Russian pictures for the Gallery. Joan Eyres-Monsell, a talented young photographer who was to become a great friend of Robert's, was also of the party. In the evenings, delegates were entertained on a pre-revolutionary scale, as Tamara Talbot Rice, who had fled Russia in 1918, recounted: 'They gave us a banquet every evening after the ballet or theatre performance about midnight with partridges and sour cream and the table was laid as in Czarist times with animals moulded out of ice.'

At the end of the week-long congress, Robert's plans remained uncertain. He had hoped to travel to Russian Turkestan, but permission was refused. However, by a stroke of luck, the Soviet Foreign Office renewed his pass as a *Times* correspondent for a further two months, granting him considerable freedom of movement. 'We are thinking of going off to Siberia', he wrote home, 'and just seeing where we may get to.' At the last moment, Christopher was denied an extension to his visa, leaving Robert, on the morning of 28 September, to venture forth on his own.

He flew by mail plane due east, from Moscow to Novosibirsk, staying three nights en route at Sverdlovsk, formerly Ekaterinburg. 'The flights were really wonderful –' he wrote home, 'one saw the great Russian rivers unfolding as though on a map.' Robert's interest in Sverdlovsk, where the Tsar and his family had been murdered, had been aroused by a propaganda broadcast heard on his first trip to Russia. The announcer had told how 'smiling children and workers might be seen going in and out of the house of Ipatiev – now a museum – where the family of Romanov met the fate it justly deserved,' to which, in his account in the *Architectural Review*, Robert had responded: 'I should like to go to Sverdlovsk and see the children smiling in the death-cellar of those other children.' On visiting the house, he found that the contents of the 'Museum of Revolution' were being packed up. As for the execution chamber, 'a grave old man with pointed white beard' told him that it contained party archives and could not be seen.

Novosibirsk owed its importance to the construction of the trans-Siberian railway. Originally a trading post, the site had been chosen for the bridging of the River Ob. Robert's visit coincided with another period of expansion: under consecutive five-year plans, the town was being transformed into a giant industrial centre. A few days after his arrival, a tour was arranged of the latest showpiece developments, including two office buildings designed for 'the railway administration'. One, in modernist style, he likened to 'a grey gasometer'. The other, in the words of his guide, 'was Renascence adapted to modern taste with [a] touch of baroque'. The guide, who proved to be a well-informed town planner, was, Robert noted, 'v. insistent on the constructivist style being the *old* style – 1930 – now the other is correct.'

Three years earlier, in Moscow, Robert had heard tell of the new architectural policy, instigated by Stalin, which, in the interim, had led to the polarization of Soviet taste. His information had come from, amongst others, the traditionalist Stchousev, designer of the Lenin mausoleum, and the modernist Grinberg, a member of the radical group,

ARU. They had assured him, with regard to the proposed Palace of the Soviets, 'that the authorities were now casting about for ideas of a different character, being convinced that the ferroconcrete style of the present was entirely unsuitable to the dignity of a great capital or to the Russian scene'.

The next building on Robert's itinerary, the theatre at Novosibirsk, had been designed originally by Grinberg as a series of functional geometric shapes faced with Ural stone. Robert learnt, however, that the whole project had been held up during the 'recent battle of the styles'. Now, Stchousev was overseeing its completion, equipping Grinberg's structure with a portico, pilasters and entablature. Robert commented: 'Dome constructed of cement, boarded over (so that it looks like a ball of wool) & on this iron pattern being applied – pretty – classical.'

The district behind the theatre exposed the reality of industrialized Russia. It was, Robert wrote, 'cleft by a gigantic ravine at bottom of wh. is malarial trickle . . . In this are crowded hundreds of little wooden houses. It is really a most ramshackle town, deep in dust . . . no flowers in windows, all out of repair, miserable.'

In Novosibirsk, Robert finally settled on China as his ultimate destination. The decision, he told his mother, was due to the uncertainty surrounding their life in Wiltshire which made work difficult. The real reason was to stay with Desmond who was still living in Peking. 'At last, after all this time', he wrote to Desmond from Novosibirsk,

> I have a hope of seeing you again . . . I have no idea what I shall do in Peking – I have to write a book on Persia, wh. is long overdue – I thought I might do that . . . I can hardly tell you how excited I am – that morning in Venice seems a very long time ago . . . I fear even my intention of spending some time in Peking may seem rather a bore to you . . . so please don't feel that a burden is descending upon you, if you want to be alone, you have only to say so, & I will try not to disturb the tenor of your life.

For the next forty-eight hours, he rumbled eastwards on

the trans-Siberian railway in the comfort of a turn of the century wagon-lit. He disembarked at Irkutsk, capital of Eastern Siberia. 'Compared with Novosibirsk,' Robert observed, 'Irkutsk is a pleasant conservative old town – very little construction, & population not increasing very fast . . . dignified main street and bldgs . . . obviously some tradition of culture here.' A rougher side was evident in the restaurants. Brawls interrupted one meal; and in the hotel, Robert sat at a table next to that of a man who 'was heaving, niagarily sick, & then went on eating without even getting up!!'

Irkutsk is situated forty miles above the southern tip of Lake Baikal, one of the largest lakes in the world. Accompanied by a government official and an interpreter, Robert boarded an English-built steamer which plied the length of the lake. 'This is a curious old hulk', he wrote, 'battered & bent – & towing two large black barges – taffrail generally gone, or with bits of wood & rope substituted – decks filthy with coal, coils of wire, broken machinery – In fact the Russian genius doesn't show to advantage in maritime affairs.' However, the food was edible; and he also had a cabin to himself with a porthole which opened.

They steamed up the western shore, passing 'barren hills, escarpments rising straight from water . . . either rock or dead brown grass'. The ship called at Olkhoi island inhabited by Buriats, the settled Mongol race. 'Drab-dressed' though they were, Robert conceded that 'fur always lends a certain picturesqueness.' Their destination was the fishing port of Nishi Angarsk at the northern end of the lake. From there the boat, loaded with barrels of omul fish, headed back south.

On the return voyage, after dinner one evening, the saloon filled up for a public meeting, at which Robert took the following minutes:

> a raucous voiced member of the crew with beard got up & said it was all too much on this ship, the crew were heroes, but the officers were perpetually drunk & stole part of the fish cargo. Officer . . . replied . . . rebutting accusation about fish & saying if the ship was too much that was the fault of the disgusting passengers who were always drunk, threw their

> cigarettes on the floor, & blocked up the toilette with tins so that it overflowed (this morning). Then the ship's bursar said the officers were delicious . . . while the crew were boors & she quite agreed it was the passengers who made the ship insupportable (she is a retired Jewish tart & not too retired either).

The meeting broke up when a member of OGPU began reading a leader from *Pravda* on the subject of transport.

Afterwards, the spokesman for the officers assured Robert that 'these confessional meetings were really a great help to the Captain, enabling him to find out the faults of the ship. His word is law – no one can disobey his orders.' The officer, Robert added, 'seemed to think it all v. natural and pleasant but was a bit worried about the fish accusation'.

Not everyone on board was so convinced of the benefits of the Revolution. A 'genial unshaven gentleman' had observed Robert playing vingt-et-un with his guide and his interpreter. Later, he asked him if he played preference, a genteel card game fashionable before the war. '"Last night you played 21 didn't you?" he continued. "Pshaw!" (gesture of disgust). "The Bestprezorny [drifters] play that – not cultivated people."' When Robert teased his companions about the remark, they both stood on their dignity. One stalked from the room, whilst the other 'retorted that Preference was a game of the aristocracy'. The same gentleman joined in the celebrations on the last night on board. '[He] had a most *beautiful* voice', Robert wrote '& sang by far the most beautiful Russian song I have ever heard – about Baikal, composed by one of the exiles in the middle of the last century, describing how he escaped.'

Catching boats and trains in Russia was an exhausting occupation. On taking the ferry to the scientific station on Lake Baikal, which involved much clambering to and fro, Robert remarked: 'Such effort is typical of the simplest proceedings in this country – & must be endured, proportionately, in everything down to the purchase of a pin.' The next few days in Irkutsk were a case in point. Hours were spent shopping for a pair of common quilted trousers and it took twenty minutes and three queues to acquire a collar stud. Nowhere was there 'a single morsel of paper of any sort on wh. one cd. write a letter'. This particular shortage, Robert declared, marked 'a return to barbarism'.

After the usual battle at the railway station, he boarded the trans-Siberian railway for Khabarovsk. His arrival, four days later, coincided with the celebrations of the anniversary of the Revolution. 'General impression of the town', he wrote, '& its crowd & the coloured modernist bldgs & the banners & radios playing from the lampposts was like a Brussels exhibition.'

In each town on his itinerary, Robert was chaperoned by local officials. His escorts showed him the latest triumphs of Soviet planning and took him, in his capacity as *Times* correspondent, to the offices of the local newspaper. Evenings were spent at the cinema or theatre. Not until the journey's end did Robert realize that he might have been under surveillance. A Danish expatriate disabused him. 'The Dane', Robert wrote, 'derides my contention that my interpreters on this journey were anything but GPU spies – & says that after 7 yrs in VV [Vladivostok] he hasn't one Russian friend whom he can greet in the street, for fear of embarrassing him.'

When Robert's articles appeared, some months later, in March 1936, they strove to give a balanced view of the 'New Russia'. His first impression, on arriving in Leningrad, coloured his muted reaction to the country. 'Russia is now becoming rather a bore, to my thinking,' he wrote home, 'the novelty of Bolshevism is wearing off . . . and its attendant inconveniences remain.' Compared to 1932, food was abundant and clothing had improved. Also, Stalin's purges had yet to gather force. 'For the moment', Robert reported, 'the indiscriminate prejudice against persons of education, which threatened to wreck the five year plan, is over.' He detected a new morality amongst Russians: an 'unselfishness, spontaneous and impersonal, the result of circumstance rather than a creed . . . It is this good . . . which has made the sacrifice of happiness to theory worthwhile.'

But the cost, as Robert reiterated, had been the enslavement of every man, woman and child. He told of the mass deportations to Siberia and of the fear which paralysed society; and he cited the distortions and inefficiencies in the economy. The truth about Soviet Russia, he wrote, could be found at Sverdlovsk:

> A low grey house overlooks the town . . . There, in a room at the east end, the Tsar and his family were killed; and there may the idle stranger, as the town goes about its business, devise a text for the understanding of modern Russia. The text is this: that Bolshevism was founded, has grown, and will endure on a basis of absolute inhumanity towards any individual who fails to surrender his body and soul to the Bolshevik state. To accept this condition as permanent is to avoid misunderstandings in the future.

Robert spent over a week in Khabarovsk fruitlessly trying to plan his route to China and obtain visas. 'Day exhausted in formalities', ran a typical entry in his diary. Finally, he gave up and took the train to Vladivostok, the terminus of the trans-Siberian railway, where a visa was forthcoming. From there he sailed to Seishin, a port on the north-east coast of Korea, travelling thence by train to Hsingking, capital of the Japanese puppet state of Manchukuo. On his brief passage through Korea, the men's hats made the greatest impression. A souvenir of Manchukuo was the sight of passengers at a station: 'grotesque magnates in furs, swords, revolvers, capes etc'. After a weekend with the British consul in Mukden, Robert caught a vintage train to Peking where he was met at the station by Desmond. It was over two years since they had seen each other in Venice, on the eve of Robert's departure for Persia. At last, Robert was poised to achieve the previously unthinkable prospect of sharing a house with Desmond.

Throughout the intervening period, Robert's letters had been filled with the longing to see Desmond again. 'You might have thought my feelings would have cooled over 14 months & half a hemisphere . . .' he had written on his return from Afghanistan, 'just the contrary.' He had, however, shown a realistic attitude towards both their sex lives. Writing to him from New York, he had been amazed by Harlem: 'the old Berlin isn't in it . . . I have been celibate since arrival, why, heaven knows, but I suppose it is the result of curiosity, which drowns the grosser impulses at first.' Desmond, on his part, told of his success, or lack of it, at sampling 'the pleasures of the east'.

Desmond's decision to uproot himself to China had revealed his strength of character. As he explained to Roy Harrod:

> To remain in Europe much longer is out of the question . . . my power of resistance would be sapped away, leaving behind the stereotype, boring dilettante, content to wander round . . . looking at old buildings, going to operas and concerts, reading the newest books . . . so there remains nothing for it but to find me some useful position in China.

He finally left at Christmas 1933, reaching Peking the following April after a leisurely progress through India and South-East Asia.

Although stepping into the unknown, he did have the comfort of an old friend from London to help him settle into his new life. Harold Acton, who was already well established in Peking, found him a house two minutes' walk from his own.

Harold had abandoned Europe over two years previously, his literary promise unfulfilled. Slim volumes of poetry and prose had met with indifference; a novel had been slated; and his latest book, *The Last Medici*, published by Orioli in Florence, had led to complaints from the Home Office at its more scandalous contents. Acton was viewed by conventional London society with similar disapproval. Robert observed his behaviour at a dinner given by Lady Cunard: 'Harold was magnificent. There were people there . . . who detest him. So he took the opportunity of shouting across the table to one: "You old d-d-duck!"'

A gift from an American uncle of five thousand dollars had enabled him to travel to China. His fascination with the country had been first nurtured by a Chinese cook, whom he had once employed in London. 'Unconsciously he had watered a seed long dormant within me: an innate love of China beyond rational analysis and an instinct that I had some vocation there,' he stated. 'Until I went to China my life could not be integrated and I knew it.' By the time of Desmond's arrival, Acton had become a successful lecturer and teacher of English at Peking National University. He was also busy with other projects, including the translation of contemporary Chinese poems.

Desmond, on the other hand, settled down to nothing in particular. He studied Chinese in a desultory manner and, most days, dropped in on Harold. Both were devotees of the classical theatre, losing their hearts to a pair of actors. 'But as usual they are quite uninterested & need continual urging to come & visit one,' Desmond lamented to Robert, 'so that such a friendship is most exhausting & unlikely to endure.'

Suddenly, his life assumed an unexpected dynamism. In May 1935, he set off on an expedition by cart and horse into the remote province of Kansu to photograph the Buddist murals in the Tun-Huang caves. Arrested on a trumped-up charge of stealing ancient Buddhist carvings, he was thrown into prison where an attack of dysentery made his plight more acute. Diplomatic pressure, combined with an outcry in the British press, secured his release two weeks later. Needless to say, Robert was enthralled by his adventures. 'As you foresee', he wrote to Michael, 'I am quite sick with jealousy.' Desmond's photographs of the murals were of sufficient quality to be accepted by the Courtauld Institute.

The experience did nothing to undermine Desmond's contentment: 'life here is so pleasant', he wrote to Roy Harrod, 'that I do not feel like returning.' He even began translating a German edition of Chinese fairy tales into English. Such notes of optimism left his grumbling unimpaired. Indeed, it had reached such a pitch that Harold christened him 'The Perpetual Wail'. By this time, Harold had reverted to the life of a littérateur, his lectureship having been terminated apparently as a result of the machinations of jealous colleagues.

Robert's arrival in Peking, in November 1935, coincided with visits from Desmond's mother and from Michael and his bride, Anne, who were on their honeymoon. Anne was the sister of Oliver Messel and had previously been married to a barrister, Ronald Armstrong-Jones. The Rosses' long courtship had been fraught with difficulties. During a particularly low moment, Robert, whose relationship with Desmond was never mentioned, offered Michael his affectionate support. 'I have suffered so much myself at times', he responded, 'that you must forgive this unasked sympathy.' Robert, who had known Anne since his schooldays, was thrilled to see them. 'Anne really charming again,' he reported home, 'though a little too gushing and slightly inclined to be gracious (not to me! God forbid).'

Throughout the round of sightseeing trips and entertainments, laid on largely by Harold for the Rosse family party, Desmond had been feeling unwell. On the eve of their departure, the diagnosis was delivered. 'A great blow has fallen on us all,' Robert wrote home. 'Desmond, after suffering for some time from swollen glands in the neck . . . is informed that he has a rare & serious disease known as Hodgkin's Disease.' Rushing to a medical dictionary, Desmond discovered that his illness was fatal. The doctors, however, prevaricated. Whatever the prognosis, he was ordered back to Europe for immediate treatment.

Robert was plunged into 'an abyss of gloom'. Acton described his condition to Roy Harrod: 'he is, of course, deeply dejected and unsettled: he cannot sit down to write and drinks like a fish and has financial worries to boot. He does not appear in the least way enthusiastic about Peking and mostly sits alone in his room.' Desmond decided to keep on the house and servants in the hope of returning after his treatment. It suited Robert to remain. But he told his sister, Lucy: 'The prospect is one of unmitigated gloom – icy winds make it impossible to go out – the monuments here bore me – my muse is dead – & altogether I wonder why I exist.'

The Rosse family departed on the Trans-Siberian Express, just before Christmas, leaving Robert in charge of a large residence, staffed by a head servant, who spoke English, a personal servant, a rickshaw boy and a cook. The house was arranged in groups of pavilions around courts; the pavilions were brick-built apart from the fronts, which consisted of wooden lattices covered with paper.

Having retreated to two pavilions on the main court, Robert wrote mournfully to Desmond:

The *Sketch* reports on the 1860 party given by Bryan and Diana Guinness at their house in Buckingham Street, Westminster, in the summer of 1929. Robert, close friend of the Mitfords, appears as a Victorian angel; Nancy Mitford as 'her ancestress, Lady Georgiana Mitford'; Tom Mitford as 'a well-bred lady of 1860'; Bryan and Diana (née Mitford) Guinness, the latter 'in her "Mariette" crinoline'.

Tibet, October 1929. A view of Mount Chomolhari by Robert Byron showing the unforgiving plain near the settlement of Tuna, where the party considered turning back.

Michael Rosse with Mary Tehring and her father, Rajah Tehring, once heir to the throne of Sikkim. Robert and his party visited the family who lived on an estate about six miles from Gyantse.

New Delhi. South Front of the Viceroy's House by Sir Edwin Lutyens, *Architectural Review*, January 1931. Photograph by Robert Byron. This building, he wrote, 'is the first real vindication of modern architecture'. His illustration reveals the effect of the Indian chujja (cornice), which binds the separate architectural elements into a unity.

Above: Birr Castle, previously in King's County, now County Offaly, Ireland. Acquired by the Parsons family in the seventeenth century; the present appearance dates from the 1800s.

Left: The Hon. Desmond Parsons, younger brother of Michael Rosse. Educated at Eton, followed by an unhappy stint at Sandhurst, he went on to lead a life of leisure, largely occupied by reading and travel.

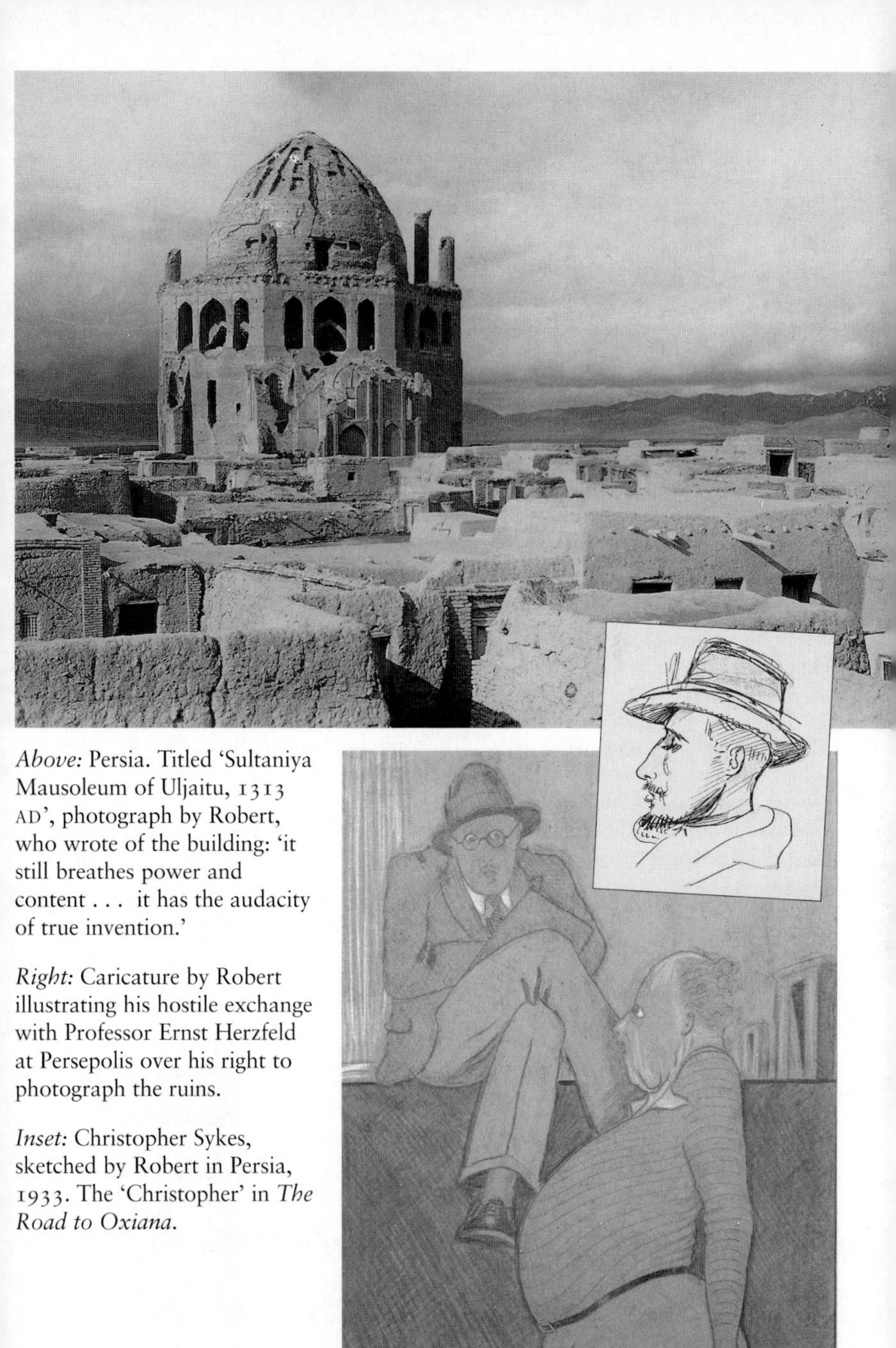

Above: Persia. Titled 'Sultaniya Mausoleum of Uljaitu, 1313 AD', photograph by Robert, who wrote of the building: 'it still breathes power and content . . . it has the audacity of true invention.'

Right: Caricature by Robert illustrating his hostile exchange with Professor Ernst Herzfeld at Persepolis over his right to photograph the ruins.

Inset: Christopher Sykes, sketched by Robert in Persia, 1933. The 'Christopher' in *The Road to Oxiana*.

Sketch by Robert of the area, popularly known as the Musalla, showing all that remained of a complex of religious buildings built by the Timurids at Herat in the fifteenth century.

'My lower middle-class Persian self', Robert's disguise which allowed him to enter, undetected, Gohar Shad's courtyard in the sacred precincts of the shrine at Meshed.

The tomb tower of Gumbad-i-Kabus, 1006 AD, the monument that had first drawn Robert to Persia, described by him as 'a tapering cylinder of café-au-lait brick'. The tower, he maintained, 'ranked with the great buildings of the world'.

Peking 1935–6. 'Me at one end of my big room writing.' Robert spent much of his time in Peking editing the five volumes of diaries on his travels in Persia and Afghanistan, which were published in 1937 as *The Road to Oxiana*.

James Lees-Milne, 1940, who worked for the National Trust. An early member of the Georgian Group, he was greatly influenced by Robert's approach to architecture.

The front cover of 'How We Celebrate the Coronation'. Robert's polemic against the architectural destruction of London, published in May 1937.

Above: Old Palace Yard, Westminster: the stone-faced pair of Palladian houses on the left were saved largely thanks to the efforts of Robert and the Georgian Group. The brick house to the right was demolished to make way for the statue of George V.

Left: Robert Byron in the 1930s.

> There is a wild howling wind lamenting through the empty house. It was a dreadful moment when I woke up next morning & found you gone . . . You looked so sad as the train went off . . . I do wish I wasn't so inhibited about the past . . . And being equally faltering in speech, I probably never *shall* be able to convey to you, except by a sort of dumb cow's gaze, what I want to convey. So we must leave it at that . . . Only let me just say if ever at any time you want me to do anything for you . . . from a pin to going round the world, I will do it as well as I can . . . Goodbye, my dear boy – relax, be lazy & enjoy yourself – I may yet be on the platform here to welcome you back.

With Desmond's departure Robert's most pressing task was to finish the articles on Russia for *The Times*. On Christmas Day, the struggle ended in defeat: 'I don't know what has come over me,' he confessed in a letter to his mother. 'I *cannot* write . . . I realize now that when I got here I was utterly exhausted – not physically at all, but mentally . . . and then on top of that, this terrible business with Desmond.' A few days later, a doctor found him shivering with a high temperature, and packed him off to the German hospital. The fever was followed by agonizing attacks of neuralgia. He was also in a highly emotional state. Opening a book at a picture of a Sussex village, Robert found himself crying.

A week in hospital brought about a gradual improvement. By the end of January, the articles were finished, and Robert talked confidently of 'emerging from a nightmare'. Then depression descended once more. The breakdown reached its crisis at a dinner with the Third Secretary at the Embassy. Some remark ignited Robert's pent-up rage and in the ensuing storm, he smashed all the china and glass. His host was forced to call out the guard, who succeeded in locking Robert up for the night. The next morning, Harold Action found him bruised but in excellent humour. The broken goods were replaced and peace restored with the Embassy. From now on, Robert rationed himself to medicinal stout, he rested after lunch and took regular walks; parties were to be avoided. Slowly, the regime began to work, although he did not recover completely until May. Meanwhile, the weather added to his gloom. After snow came roaring winds, which turned the sky yellow with dust. 'This winter', he stated, 'has been the worst time in my life.'

Harold Acton offered scant sympathy. On withdrawing from the social round, Robert had rightly predicted: 'Harold will be furious – he has a great sense of social duty.' Robert's views on Chinese architecture were another major irritant. Within days of arrival, he had pronounced: 'of architecture in the real sense of the word, there is nothing. That I can see straight off. They can build a wall, and make it very big – they have an exquisite capacity for space and layout . . . but cubically and intellectually it is all a vacuum.' Harold retaliated by branding him a crank.

As the weeks passed, Robert began to enjoy delusions of wealth. Much to his embarrassment, an elderly admirer, Mrs Stuart Wortley, to whom he had written about an introduction, sent him £50 with the command: 'Don't hesitate to use the money, I can so easily spare it.' And *The Times* paid him over £100 for his various reports. His expenses, by comparison, were only £20 a month. Robert started to buy old Chinese paintings, building up a collection of over forty works.

In February, Gerald Reitlinger took a house in Peking. He was once more on good terms with Robert, who had admired his book about Persia, *A Tower of Skulls*. But Harold's dislike of Reitlinger had remained intact since Oxford, where he had found him a bore. Thus Robert had to divide his hour prescribed for socializing between the two. For the rest of the day, he shut himself away to write his travel book on Persia.

After Robert's return from Persia and Afghanistan, he let a year elapse before he started editing the five volumes of travel diaries, which were to form the basis of his account of the journey. The first two volumes were polished off during the summer of 1935. Russia intervened, but once the decision had been made to head for Peking, Robert wired home for the diaries and the existing typescript to be sent out by sea to China. The precious bundle arrived by Christmas, but work did not recommence until February. To supplement his diaries, Robert also asked Harold Macmillan to dispatch a copy of his essay on the architecture of Afghanistan. By the end of May, the first draft was complete. All along, Robert had expressed satisfaction at its progress. Now he wrote to Harold Macmillan: 'The book is done – finished yesterday . . . It has come out quite different to what I expected – a real *book*, instead of a mere compilation of incidents – & I venture to think it is the best thing I have written.'

With the last notebook edited, Robert took ship for Japan. A brief stay in Tokyo effected a re-entry to the real world. Over lunch at the British Embassy, the Ambassador drew him out on the subject of the Russian Far East. Afterwards, Robert announced: 'All my interest in things, which died in the mortal atmosphere of Peking, has revived now.' He took a week's holiday in the Nikko National Park, a region of mountains and lakes to the north of Tokyo. Gerald Reitlinger joined him for a few days. His other companion was a Japanese student, whom Robert 'got hold of' in Tokyo to act as an interpreter. To get off the beaten track, Robert tried walking over a mountain pass, only to find that 'a friendly beer bottle was always glinting in the bamboo undergrowth to shew the path'. Reitlinger's abiding memory, relayed to Anthony Powell, was his discovery that Robert had had an affair with a Japanese 'train attendant' on the journey. On 19 June, he left the Orient for America.

The voyage to San Francisco lasted thirteen days. Having negotiated a large cabin to himself, Robert spent the time revising his manuscript in preparation for a final read-through on his eventual return to England.

No sooner was he on dry land than he took to the air, flying across America to stay with his sister, Lucy, in Washington, where her husband, Rohan Butler, was the acting *Times* correspondent. After a few days in the city, Robert treated himself to a tirade against the New World. 'The barbarity, hideousness, discomfort and uncouthness of it all strike me more forcibly after China,' he cried. 'One just has to close one's senses to the external world altogether.' The Washington police caused further outrage by preventing him from photographing the building of the Supreme Court. In protest, Robert abandoned plans for a survey of the new buildings and layout of the city. When officials begged him to reconsider, he responded: 'whereas one gets a certain amusement out of doing down a Bolshevik Commissar or the Shah of Persia, the American cop lacks glamour as an adversary and the struggle becomes nauseating.' Robert decided to sell his camera, declaring: 'it is the end of architectural photography as far as I am concerned.'

Apart from seeing Lucy, his main reason for lingering in the country was to pursue an idea for a book. At the Persian Congress in Russia, Robert had hatched a plan with Eric Schroeder, a fellow protégé of Upham Pope, to collaborate on a scholarly work on Persian architecture. This was the subject for which the second advance from Macmillan's had been earmarked, but by the start of the congress Robert had particular reason to feel sensitive about embarking alone upon such a task. A few days before, Macmillan had forwarded an unflattering opinion from a young scholar, Basil Gray, on his essay 'Islamic Monuments in Afghanistan'. Robert was stung by its comments, deriding them as 'the criticism of a museum official who resents the amateur's interference'. However, teaming up with a specialist such as Schroeder would make him less vulnerable to such attacks. In proposing the idea to Macmillan, he argued: 'It would be a good combination, because while I . . . can write on aesthetic values of architecture & can provide good illustrations, I lack technical knowledge, I cannot read Arabic inscriptions & I am no good at plans. These deficiencies he is admirably qualified to fill.'

Schroeder, a friend of David Talbot Rice at Oxford, had worked with him on the university excavations at Kish in Mesopotamia. A skilled draughtsman, he was later recruited by Upham Pope to undertake measured drawings for the Institute's architectural survey. Before starting work on their book proposal, Schroeder invited Robert for a few days' relaxation on Naushon Island, off Cape Cod, which belonged to his wife's family. Out riding on the second day, Robert misjudged an obstacle and was unseated by an oak tree. He came to 'lying in a paste of blood and leaves', totally disorientated. A doctor staying on the island ordered complete rest for a fortnight.

By August, the synopsis was beginning to take shape. Using much of Schroeder's unpublished material, they planned an epic work in two volumes, entitled 'Persian Classical Architecture'. Every significant monument in Persia, Afghanistan and Central Asia, dating from the seventh to the eighteenth centuries, was to be included. Over 200 catalogue entries were sketched out, and introductory essays planned. 'It will be impossible to write a book – such as this is becoming – on both sides of the Atlantic . . .' Robert explained, 'unless every section is carefully worked out & designed beforehand.' By the end of the month, the job was finished. On 2 September, Robert sailed for home. He had been away for just over a year.

25

Travellers' Tales

During Robert's absence, his parents had finally succeeded in disposing of the lease on Savernake. Currently, they were living in a small house in the village of Easton Royal before taking possession of the vicarage at Overton, on the edge of Savernake Forest, which Eric Byron had bought from the Church Commissioners. With little room to work, Robert soon moved to London, ending up with a furnished flat in Brick Court in the Temple.

In the meantime, he had delivered the manuscript of his travel book to Harold Macmillan. Few changes were required and it passed smoothly through the press to be published, on 6 April 1937, as *The Road to Oxiana*.

The bulk of the book, following his previous practice, is closely modelled upon Robert's travel diary. However, this time he maintained the dated entries in print. The result is uncompromising. This version conforms throughout to the immediacy of the original, minor excisions only serving to enhance it. The structure of five parts corresponds to the five notebooks kept on the journey and most of the dated entries are those of the diary. Where necessary, Robert rearranged the sequence of events within entries to improve their narrative flow; he also tightened the prose and cut material which was obviously redundant. The process encouraged him to write more simply. From Peking, at work on the last three notebooks, he informed Macmillan: 'I have developed a new style I believe, more concise, yet more conversational. This is not a conscious development. It has come of its own accord . . . I am sacrificing everything to maintain this style at one easy level.'

One subject thus 'sacrificed' was that of the Charcoal Burners. Despite a number of cryptic references, the only hint of their involvement in the trip occurs towards the end of the book, when he admits that 'another expedition was formed, but preferred, at the last moment, to undertake a research into the combustive properties of charcoal.' Thus are Boz and his fellow charcoal burners dismissed.

Another adjustment was to remedy Robert's initial ignorance of the history and architecture of the region. In the book, there is no reference to his two days spent swotting in the hotel room in Teheran. Instead, he arrives in the country with an impressive command of the subject, which is first deployed to greatest effect on his arrival in Herat. Turning to the Timurids' architectural legacy, Robert refers to the handful of published accounts by earlier visitors before unfolding the 'miserable story' of its large-scale destruction in the nineteenth century. Finally, he tours the surviving monuments of the Musalla, calling forth well-judged measures of scholarship and descriptive art to convey their artistic importance.

Understandably, no such mastery is exhibited in the original diary. Apart from expressing wonder at the minarets, Robert's observations on the Musalla are minimal. Most of his knowledge was acquired on return to London when researching his essay on the architecture of Afghanistan for Upham Pope. At work in Peking on the third notebook, which covers his first visit to Herat, Robert had written to Macmillan for a copy of the essay, explaining: 'where Afghanistan is concerned, I have collected so much really new architectural and historical information that it is a pity not to give it.'

Wearing the mantle of the scholar-traveller, Robert rearranged the original entries, interspersing discourses on ancient monuments with incidents from his actual stay. By reproducing the episodic form of the edited diary, his ambition for the Timurid essay was fulfilled: 'It would', he had written to Macmillan, 'give the book a core which it would otherwise lack if I can work in some of that information.'

With equal craft, Robert incorporated into the final part of the book his findings on the Empress Gohar Shad. Having returned to Herat, he walks out to the Musalla, diary at the ready, where the sight of some mullahs and their pupils, seated by the mausoleum, prompts another leap into the past.

This grouping, unremarked in the original diary, had been the subject of a photograph, which for added verisimilitude illustrates the finished version. Robert's eulogy to Gohar Shad contrives a fitting conclusion to the entries on Herat:

> It is cold. The sun has gone down. The mullahs have gone in, and their pupils with them. The lustre has gone from the blue towers and the green corn. Their shadows have gone. The magic scent has gone. The summer has gone, and the twilight brings back the spring, cold and uncertain. I must go. 'Goodbye Gohar Shad . . . Sleep on there under your dome, to the sound of boys' lessons. Goodbye, Herat.'

Despite the assurance of his performance, Robert remained uncertain of its success, confessing to his past mentor, John Mavrogordato: 'As for the relationship between "learning" and entertainment, I know it is the chink in my armour – not so much with regard to references [to previous travellers] but as it affects the composition. Did Gohar Shad bore you? I should like to know.'

Although no reply is known, Mavrogordato was uniquely qualified to give an opinion, having served for many years as literary adviser to Norman Douglas, the greatest living exponent of travel as a learned pursuit. A Scotsman, Douglas was born in 1868 in Austria, and after a brief career in the British Foreign Office, had retreated to a villa on the Bay of Naples, moving, a few years later, to Capri. At first, his literary output was confined to scholarly monographs on the island and its history; eventually, such labours were abandoned, but they were not allowed to waste: a travel book was written, entitled *Siren Land*, crammed with his researches, antiquarian, historical, pastoral, literary, epicurean, which was published in 1911 by Dent, on the recommendation of the firm's reader, Mavrogordato.

Siren Land was the precursor of Douglas's greatest travel book, *Old Calabria*, an account of his wanderings through the region's remote valleys and ancient towns and villages which gives full rein to his manifold enthusiasms. Douglas ranges between the past and the present, one moment detailing the sights along his route, the next embarking upon some elaborate digression, such as the history of a local saint. This approach had particular appeal to Robert, who was an avid reader of Norman Douglas, quoting from his novel *South Wind* at the opening of *First Russia Then Tibet*. As a result, parallels were drawn between the two writers: 'throughout the book I am constantly reminded of . . . Norman Douglas, who is probably the most civilized man now living,' wrote a columnist in the *Architects' Journal* of *First Russia Then Tibet*. 'Both Mr Byron and Mr Douglas refuse to be stampeded by spurious intellectualism into accepting half-baked or part-worn ideas about anything. The robustness of their sense is matched by the profundity of their scholarship and the range of their observation.'

Thanks to Mavrogordato, Douglas and Byron began to correspond. At his suggestion, Douglas wrote with a request for information about Goa, ending: 'I liked your *Russia and Tibet* immensely and wonder whether you would allow me to send you a copy of some book of mine? Have you read my *Paneros*?' In due course, his slim volume on aphrodisiacs was received. Meanwhile, Byron expressed admiration for *Old Calabria*, asking Douglas to inscribe his copy. In doing so, Robert acknowledged Douglas's influence. The autographed book would stand, he told him, as 'the imprint of one mind upon another'. Douglas willingly agreed. Byron remained in touch, and once tried to meet up with him in Italy, but their paths were never to cross.

Robert was the natural heir to Douglas. But by rigidly adhering to the entries of his original diary, he modernized the literary form of the cultivated travel book. His method displayed an indifference to the conventions of storytelling, which, although not without precedent, was, for its time, wholly original. All his contemporaries took the safer route of retailing their experiences as a continuous narrative – none more so than Robert's greatest literary rival, Peter Fleming, who only eight months previously had published his classic tale of adventure, *News from Tartary*.

Born into a rich family of Scottish bankers, Fleming was two years younger than Byron. At Eton, he had risen effortlessly to the top, the school crowning him with her highest honours. Gaining a scholarship to Christ Church, Oxford, then a First in English, Fleming left university ripe with promise. After a brief stint in the family bank, he exchanged commerce for the world of letters, landing a job as deputy literary editor of the *Spectator*.

Ill-suited to a sedentary occupation, one year on, he signed up for an expedition to Brazil to ascertain the fate of the explorer, Colonel Fawcett, who in 1925 had disappeared with his eldest son on an expedition into the Mato Grosso. Fleming's book about the journey, *Brazilian Adventure*, published in 1933, was reprinted eight times in four months. In spite of certain reservations, Evelyn Waugh hailed it as 'arresting and absorbing', stating: 'The first chapters, before the expedition gets into the real jungle, are delightful, in the modern manner of Mr Robert Byron.'

First Russia Then Tibet was published two months after Fleming's triumph. Commercially, as we have seen, it proved to be a disappointment. At a post-mortem, held during Byron's absence in Persia, Macmillan blamed the high price, caused by the cost of illustrations; in retrospect, he considered it a mistake to have combined travel with art history. As to Robert's current, Persian, journey, A. D. Peters reported that in consequence the Macmillans 'hope that it will produce a travel book suitable for general reading (they instanced as an example Peter Flemming's [*sic*] book on Brazil which has sold very well indeed).' On reaching the Legation at Kabul, Robert had a chance to sample Fleming's work. 'I have just read *Brazilian Adventure* – or part of it,' he wrote home. 'Very disappointing – in fact I have ceased to feel jealous.'

Meanwhile, Fleming's career continued its ascent. *The Times* appointed him Special Correspondent to report on the political and military upheavals in China. His experiences became the subject of his next book, *One's Company*, which was also very well received. In 1934, he set out once more for the East, travelling across Russia, via the Ukraine, Georgia and Turkestan. By gaining permission to travel through Turkestan, Fleming succeeded, where Byron had repeatedly failed, in visiting Samarcand. However, his brief report on the city, which Byron kept along with all his articles from

The Times, referred only superficially to the surviving masterpieces of Timurid architecture. As Fleming had earlier admitted: '[I am] wholly lacking in either an historical sense or the ability to appreciate architecture . . . The sight of any edifice, however imposing, however drenched . . . with historical associations, merely embarrasses me . . . I gape dutifully, but without pleasure, without profit.'

Naturally, Robert deprecated such philistinism. 'I have got back to my book at last [*The Road to Oxiana*] . . .' he informed his mother from Peking. 'I think it is mostly funny – there is very little else, in fact, except an occasional landscape – but I am noticing a few buildings, as I don't like the Peter Fleming kind of thing, which deliberately avoids anything of interest. At least, that is how it strikes me, though this may be sour grapes really.'

Fleming's journey across Russia was the prelude to a far more ambitious enterprise. Byron had got wind of the scheme, months beforehand, while still in Persia, when he heard from another traveller that 'Boz is replanning an assault on the Sinkiang, in company with Peter Fleming.' In the event, Fleming joined up with a Swiss woman, Ella Maillart, and by luck and endurance they succeeded in penetrating Sinkiang, which had been closed to foreigners since the outbreak of civil war two years earlier, and, thence, in crossing the province to India.

In *News from Tartary*, Fleming handled the experience with characteristic reticence, relying upon understatement, plain English and the perspective of hindsight to deliver 'an honest account' of the journey. Critics acclaimed the result, anointing Fleming one of the great storytellers of the age; a position confirmed by sales of the book, which soon outstripped his previous records.

A voice of dissent was raised in the *Architects' Journal*, which opined: 'True, this last journey of his took him through places where building was often rudimentary; but I found myself longing for some of the descriptive felicities of Robert Byron whenever I visited a town in Mr Fleming's company.'

In *The Road to Oxiana*, Robert offers a series of remarkable descriptions of cities, buildings and monuments, which drew widespread praise from the critics. As the anonymous reviewer in *The Times Literary Supplement* commented: 'His prose is economical and edged. That sense of design to which his photographs bear testimony is partnered by a delicate appreciation of colour; he can convey, with a kind of inspired fidelity, the distant prospect of an ancient city or the decorative detail of a shrine.' One of the few to carp was the novice travel writer, although experienced novelist, Graham Greene, who found the descriptions too 'drily instructive'.

Robert's eye for landscape won him plaudits, which included a comparison to Virgil for his picture of a Persian garden in early spring. Evelyn Waugh rated his use of dialogue to be 'of outstanding excellence' and also praised 'the savage and pungent narrative of the actual events of the journey'. Christopher Sykes was another defender of Byron's irate tone: 'As may be imagined most of this book was written in discomfort and a state of boiling fury,' he attested. 'There is much to be said for writing in these circumstances; they are the realities of the traveller's experience.' The *Manchester Guardian* declared: 'Mr Byron . . . has produced an almost ideal book of travel . . . much candid criticism of men and ideas, some admirable descriptions.'

Robert had been vindicated in preserving the tenor of the original diary, rightly confident that the humour, gusto and beauty of the prose would propel the reader, from one entry to the next, along the wandering road to Oxiana.

The review which went to the heart of Robert's approach as an artist was written by his mentor, G. M. Young, in the *Sunday Times*. 'The power of making every situation yield all it contains of comedy and beauty at once is the best gift of a mature culture to its elect children,' he wrote. And this, Robert had achieved in abundance. Alluding to Lord Byron, he placed Robert in the same tradition of the 'last and finest fruit of the insolent humanism of the eighteenth century'. By humanism, Young meant 'a determination of the mind to maintain its own poise, and to view the world in its own perspective: and I call it insolent for the readiness with which it turns to aggression if its poise is disturbed by sectarian clamour or its perspective blurred by fashionable sentiment'. When Robert read the review, he told Desmond that it made 'me feel as if I had at last come into my own'.

Sales of the book did not reflect its literary achievement. Eight hundred copies were sold in the first three months of publication, a figure which increased to fourteen hundred over the following year. However, the book's true worth was recognized at the 1937 National Book Fair when it was awarded a gold medal as the outstanding travel book of the year.

26

Beset with Woes

On returning to London in the autumn of 1936, Robert had begun work on a series of articles for *Country Life* describing his recent peregrination around the world. A commission from London Transport was also received to write a short guide to the capital and its environs, aimed at visitors from the Dominions. Robert dutifully followed the brief, giving prominence to monuments and institutions associated with the Dominions. He even curbed his loathing of South Africa House, noting merely that it was the headquarters of a Dominion High Commissioner. With his nose for publicity, he promoted the booklet on the BBC's recently launched television service.

Early in the New Year, the British Council invited Robert to undertake a lecture tour to the Low Countries, the Baltic states and Poland. His chosen topics were 'The English Home', a survey, illustrated with lantern slides, ranging from fifteenth-century manor houses to the work of Lutyens; and 'What is English Civilization?', an exposition centred upon the nation's deep-rooted respect for liberty.

From Holland, Robert travelled to Tallin, capital of Estonia, before working his way through Latvia and Lithuania to the Polish port of Gdynia on the frontier with the free city of Danzig. The audiences, usually members of Anglophile societies, were appreciative. Of his reception in Kovno, then the capital of Lithuania, he noted in his diary: 'the best audience I have had for my lecture on English Civ . . . They all seemed . . . deeply impressed by the fact that the English can afford to laugh at themselves – this is just the effect that I had intended.'

Sightseeing between lectures, Robert admired Tallin and Riga, but expressed greatest enthusiasm for Danzig: 'what a lovely town', he wrote, 'Dutch style bldgs, high & narrow, but somehow different & better – lovely colours, pistachio green, cream, pink etc – the stoops [raised platforms] in front of them announced by great balls & railings – Renascence reliefs on the balustrades . . . many bldgs covered with gilt.' He judged it one of the most beautiful towns he had ever visited.

While there, he also introduced himself to the local Nazi party. His entrée was provided by Unity Mitford, a younger sister of Nancy, who since 1933 had been an ardent supporter of Hitler. A letter of introduction from Unity put him in touch with various prominent Nazis, including a spokesman on foreign affairs who delivered a stream of 'loathsome womanish sarcasm . . . about the League of Nations, Versailles, Ll. George – much worse than downright open resentment'. Appalled by the invective, Robert concluded: 'The man was a revelation of unconstructive bitterness – & hatred of England – one of the most unpleasant conversations I have ever had. The Russians are angels by comparison.'

Even so, the Nazis had their comic side. 'I hardly know how to contain myself when they say Heil Hitler to one another down the telephone . . .' he reported home, 'and that salute, when a couple of friends happen to part in a crowded bus, also has an hysterical effect – but I suppose one will get used to it.'

Warsaw was next on the itinerary, where he was greeted with press interviews and a banquet in his honour. Thence, he travelled to Berlin for a few days' holiday before giving a final lecture in Brussels.

His return to England, at the end of March 1937, coincided with the Byrons' move into their new home at Overton, a rambling vicarage dating mainly from the eighteenth century which, as his mother remarked, was 'a proper house & not a cottage & will enable us to spread out everything we've got'. During the months that followed, Robert threw himself into the role of decorator. He planned the hanging of some of his old Chinese paintings, and busied himself with the selection of colours and finishes, even tracking down samples of Empire wallpaper made from the original blocks.

Unfortunately, his father hankered after something more Victorian. At the last minute, he proposed that the stuffed trophies of game, which had once adorned the walls of Coulsden, should now form part of the decor. Robert was dismayed at the news. 'I am haunted by the heads . . .' he remonstrated.

> If you put them into the middle of a house wh. is done with a certain amount of taste, the effect is to announce either that it is inhabited by bores . . . or by nouveaux riches . . . Personally I don't much care if this is the effect . . . But what I do care about is that . . . the general ensemble shd. be shattered by objects which, whatever their sentimental interest, even you cannot call beautiful . . . We can store the brutes in camphor – or lend them to Devizes Museum.

Robert's opinion of the new house had long been a cause of anxiety to his mother. Writing to him in America, she had confessed: 'I am getting very nervous about your liking the place – it will be so awful if you hate it.' Robert's ill temper during a weekend visit, following the move, did not bode well, and earned him a rebuke from his mother. In mitigation, he blamed the inadequacies of the new domestic arrangements, but went on to admit a deeper source of dissatisfaction: 'there is always, all the time, the forest in the back of my mind – a sort of endless regret . . .' he lamented, 'I shd. love Overton otherwise – but as it is, the only thing to do is to make it so nice in every possible way that the regret will disappear.'

To aggravate matters, Robert was also experiencing a crisis in his working life. After the year abroad, he had been faced with an overdraft of over £900. The bank had insisted upon its liquidation, forcing him to sell the last of his capital. In consequence, he felt 'doomed either to get a job, & give up writing altogether, or to retire to the country for ever, to write & live in poverty – without pocket money even'. Forthwith, Robert began putting out feelers to his friends in the oil industry, hoping to capitalize on his previous experience in India and with Shell in London. Meanwhile, his hopes as a writer rested upon his long-planned history of the Great War. He had been reading up on the subject since his stay in China, and, in addition, had questioned various diplomats and politicians in the Baltic states about their wartime experiences. Apprised of his ambition to write the book, Harold Macmillan invited Robert to stay at Birch Grove, his family's house in the country, to discuss the project.

The invitation was a sign of the friendship which had sprung up between author and publisher over the past four years. Early on, Macmillan had won Robert's respect by displaying a taste in book design to rival his own. 'I have just seen [*First Russia Then Tibet*]', Robert wrote from Teheran, '& hasten to congratulate you on a really superb production . . . I think the title page is particularly felicitous . . . Also I like the jacket so much. It is far nicer than my idea of red and green.' Between them, they devised an amusing binding for *Innocence and Design*. Byron suggested a cover, impressed with an appropriate motif, in 'that coarse, hard, shiny cloth wh. Victorian novels so often have'. Macmillan obliged with a specimen case, stamped with an 'oriental' design. When it came to a colour for the boards of *The Road to Oxiana*, he requested 'as bright a blue as possible', whilst expressing confidence that Macmillan would make the right choice.

In all matters, Robert was handled with the care befitting a young thoroughbred in the Macmillan stable. He was generously backed, and received nothing but counsel and encouragement after the disappointing results of his first two books with the firm. Macmillan watched over him during the gestation of *The Road to Oxiana*. His vigilance was rewarded with the delivery of a 'general travel book', as opposed to a work of a more scholarly nature. Such an outcome had long been prized by Macmillan, who had reminded Robert in China: 'travel books with anything of a personality behind them seem almost certain of success.'

The visit to Birch Grove, at the end of April 1937, marked a decisive change in Robert's life. Macmillan deliberated over the war book, but failed to hold out much hope of publication. In light of this, Robert's search for a job in the oil industry took on a sharper edge. The ground had already been prepared in talks held previously with Jack Beddington. Now, Robert brought the matter to a successful conclusion, receiving an offer of a position attached to the Anglo-Iranian Oil Company (AIOC). Before committing himself, yet another discussion with Macmillan took place; thereafter, he went ahead and accepted the job.

Thus, at the beginning of June, Robert reported for duty to Colonel Medlicott, head of publicity and press relations for the AIOC. Apart from his other responsibilities, Medlicott ran a committee set up by the international oil companies to promote their interests in Parliament and the press. Robert had been hired to further this endeavour, and labelled himself accordingly a 'crypto-public relations buffer'. To carry out the task, he was given his own private office in Bishopsgate, an entertainment allowance of £40 a month and a salary of £1,000 a year. Nor was he subject to the usual restrictions of office life. Before his arrival, a future colleague assured him: 'we are certainly not expecting you to keep office hours.'

Corporate intrigue came naturally to Robert. Within a few months of his arrival, he was plotting to write a book about the oil industry. Having drawn up a synopsis, his next move was to secure the support of Harold Macmillan, who went on to propose the idea, as if it were his own, in a letter circulated to Robert's superiors. Medlicott's committee reacted to the letter with alarm. The central thesis of the book, as outlined by Macmillan, trespassed upon dangerous ground: 'It seems to me', he had propounded, 'the oil industry is an extremely interesting example of a problem which will become more and more acute in the future. The relation of an international commercial organization to the national political organization within which it works . . .'

Not surprisingly, serious doubts were cast upon the project. 'I find now that what really frightened my various directors', Robert relayed back to Macmillan, 'was the idea of dealing with politics at all. No matter if it were a vindication of the industry – it wd. be bound to raise controversy etc etc.'

On a more routine level, Robert threw himself into the task of entertaining journalists and other influential figures on behalf of the oil industry. Favourite venues were the Savoy Grill, conveniently located for the headquarters of Shell-Mex and BP, and Boulestin. His guests included men of substance such as Ralph Deakin, foreign editor of *The Times*, and Sir

Richard Maconochie, director of talks at the BBC, whom Robert had first known as a diplomat in Kabul. But usually the selection was less worthy. Numbered at his table were the veteran gossips, Patrick Balfour and Tom Driberg; so too was Christopher Sykes, accredited for accounting puposes to the *Geographical Magazine*, and Brian Howard whose claim to a free meal rested upon the occasional review for the *New Statesman*.

The political world was largely represented by Harold Macmillan, their assignations providing useful opportunities to chew over plans. With regard to foreign affairs, Unity Mitford merited lunch, thanks to her unimpeachable connections in Germany, whilst for his technical expertise Boz Goldman at last had the pleasure of being paid for by Robert. He had bounded back into Robert's life, unscathed by the failure of his expedition, and remained chairman of the Koela Producer Gas Plant Company. Many guests qualified solely as friends, among them various Sitwells, as well as Adrian Stokes, William Acton and the Yorkes. Robert deployed his contacts with professional skill. Elected to the Garrick Club in 1937, he had a portion of his membership fee paid by his employers.

In counterpoint to the social round, Robert's private life grew increasingly dark. For almost a year, Desmond Parsons had been fighting Hodgkin's disease, seemingly with some success. On Robert's return from America, they had spent weekends together in Northamptonshire, where Desmond had rented a black and white timbered house from Sacheverell Sitwell. Despite his own sufferings, Desmond was solicitous of Robert's needs, offering to lend him money at the time of his financial collapse. By November, Desmond's condition had worsened. His looks were swollen and doctors recommended the removal of his tonsils. He wrote to Roy Harrod of attending a party 'to drown my sorrows in drink, until the cool air of dawn blows in to remind me of my fate'.

As the months passed, Desmond succumbed to repeated attacks of the disease. Robert was at hand to cheer him up with supper at the Savoy or to accompany him to consultations with his doctor. Finally, it was decided that he should enter a clinic in Zurich. The journey was made with his brother, Michael, in attendance. 'Ghastly insomnia has been my chief trouble since my arrival,' Desmond complained to Robert, 'though everything else is also worse. I hope for an improvement with the X-ray treatment, which begins today.' His anguish was heightened by the prospect of Michael having to leave his side: 'I shall feel quite lost without M. to fight my battles for me. Do write a chatty letter.' Robert not only kept up a flow of news, but also flew out to see him. His brief letter of farewell read: 'I couldn't say goodbye because I couldn't speak. But in case we don't meet again, you know I wish you happiness. God bless you. Robert.'

Soon afterwards, the illness took hold with added intensity. Michael had to rush to Zurich, scribbling Robert a note en route, warning him of Desmond's deterioration. Robert lent his support by writing another diverting letter for Desmond's amusement. A bulletin, a fortnight later, conceded all hope. Michael, who was accompanied by his sister, Bridget, told Robert: 'It has become simply a question of how long his strength can last out . . . I hate having to write so absolutely despairing a letter, but I know that you would only want to know the truth. Bridget read him your letter this morning, which he loved getting & he sent you all his love.'

Desmond died on 4 July 1937. He was twenty-six years old. Two days later, his body was brought home from Switzerland. That evening, Robert dined at the Savile Club with Jim Lees-Milne, one of Desmond's closest friends. Over coffee, Robert composed a short obituary notice for *The Times*, breaking down in tears at remembrance of the man he loved. At its heart, the epitaph runs: 'What people valued in him was his truth. He never let a lie pass; he never compromised with the pretentious or second best. It was this essential honesty, combined with a half-laughing, half-sulky grace, which so endeared him to so many friends.'

After attending the funeral at Birr, Robert received a few veiled words of commiseration from Michael, the closest he ever came to acknowledging his friend's love for his brother. 'I think you know better than most people how utterly void the gap that his death had made in my life must always remain . . .' he mourned. 'I will not write more, as I believe you understand my feelings about it all as perhaps I understand yours a little.'

In his misery Robert turned to Jim Lees-Milne for consolation. The two had a great deal in common. Jim had once been in love with Desmond and had known him since his schooldays. But there were also other ties to bind them. Jim, too, was passionate about architecture and, by 1937, was working for the National Trust, launching schemes for the preservation of country houses. Robert's influence was apparent in his aesthetic prejudices. Busily engaged on guidebooks to National Trust properties, he voiced his disdain to Robert of archaeological remains, pointing out that one guide was to 'the Roman Baths at Wall . . . of which nothing remains but a rim of discoloured grass which can only be detected from an aeroplane'.

However, beneath the surface, there had always been tensions between them. Robert had never been able to resist making teasing advances towards Jim, who had willowy good looks, but such signs of affection often turned, just as swiftly, to rage. The first occurrence was sparked by Jim's defence of his then employer, Lord Lloyd, whom Robert had attacked in print following the fierce exchange at Lady Cunard's. 'Don't harrow me with Lloyd's wounded feelings,' Robert snorted.

> Surely a man of that arrogance is fair game . . . To me, he & his type represent quite sincerely a sort of imperialist anti-Christ, of considerable menace to the world . . . And how could my attitude be personal? I have only met him once & thought him charming and witty till he suddenly turned offensive . . . I dislike being accused, even by so gentle an implication as yours, dear Jim, of unfairness.'

Jim, who was described by his old friend, Wilhelmine Harrod, as 'utterly gentle, friendly and affectionate', found Robert's bursts of aggression hard to take. Matters were not helped by his conversion to Catholicism, which gave Robert ample opportunity to bait him.

Desmond's death brought their simmering relationship to

the boil. Robert felt that it marked a turning point, uniting them through loss. His physical advances were made with more serious intent, but he received nothing but rejection. Jim, who was 'repeatedly falling in love with somebody or other', simply could not reciprocate his feelings. In consequence, Robert threatened to break off all contact. 'I am very sad about all this,' Jim responded. 'It seems to me an unnecessary interruption to a relationship whch I otherwise have valued enormously & wld have continued to do. I do not think you should blame me unduly. It is your decision and wt. else can I do?' Adding to their predicament was the prospect of having to spend a summer holiday together at the Rennells' villa in Italy. Once a few days had elapsed, Jim urged Robert not to back out: 'I wd so much like you to be there as you know.'

His plea was answered. Robert duly joined the house party in the villa belonging to Lord and Lady Rennell at Posilipo near Naples. His hostess was their daughter-in-law, Nancy Mitford, who had married Peter Rodd, an old friend of Robert's since Oxford, in December 1933. This had come as a great relief to Robert, who had thoroughly disapproved of her hopeless entanglement, lasting almost four years, with the homosexual Hamish Erskine. 'He is really the most utterly amoral creature on earth,' he had confided to Bryan Guinness. Her engagement to Peter was far more satisfactory, even though he had always found him rather a bore. 'I'm so glad everything is so perfect –' he wrote on hearing her news, '& I like to think I had a hand in it, as your happiness is one of my chief concerns . . .' The congratulations ended on a slightly anxious note. Referring to his involvement he added: 'I hope it won't prove to be the hand of a Jonah – or shd. one say the fin.' Robert had been on his Persian travels at the time of the wedding, so Lucy and Anne had represented him.

On holiday, Jim remembered, Robert was a picture of calm:

> he would set forth after breakfast for the shore in his butterfly-catcher's suit, a wide brimmed panama, a tight, striped, sailor's shirt, a pair of buff shorts, and sandals. From nine till long after midday he would swim fierce breast strokes, then

> overarm strokes, and finally float on his back spouting sea water like an indolent whale . . . In this attitude he would recline for three-quarters of an hour at a stretch while from a boat we plied him at intervals with chocolates, and cigarettes which he smoked through a holder.

For all the appearance of contentment, Robert, even in Italy, was actively engaged in a war of words with Arthur Upham Pope. The latest row was over a new contribution to the Persian Survey, which had been commissioned by Pope, at the beginning of the year, to replace the previously rejected essay on 'The Architecture of Afghanistan'. This, in the end, had worked to Robert's advantage, as he had been able to reuse the material on the Timurids in *The Road to Oxiana*. To avoid any misunderstanding with the present commission, the subject matter and length, about 7,000 words, had been agreed in advance. The subject agreed was a general introduction to the architecture of the Timurids.

Much of the essay is taken up with descriptions of the Timurid monuments in Russian Turkestan, Afghanistan and Persia. Robert relied for his analyses upon the detailed catalogue entries, already compiled by himself and Eric Schroeder for their projected book, 'Persian Classical Architecture'. Robert also pronounced judgement on the artistic significance of the Timurids. Their impact, he argues, was akin to that of the earlier Turkic invaders from the north-east, the Seljuks and the Mongols, who brought 'an influx of foreign muscularity' to the 'Persian habit of surface decoration'.

The work was delivered to Pope at the end of February 1937, having been completed in under six weeks. On receipt, Pope managed one or two phrases of admiration before delivering his first thrust: 'I think probably if you had had more time', he ventured, 'it might have been a little more dashing in style.' In separate memoranda, he went on to enumerate over forty suggested amendments. Soon, Robert had issued the first of repeated threats: 'I warn you quite frankly', he fumed, 'that if this chapter is altered in any way I don't like after I have passed the final proof, I shall put the matter in the hands of a solicitor.'

A meeting, which had to be postponed owing to Desmond's

death, solved little. Eventually, Robert took his case to Sir Humphrey Milford, head of the Oxford University Press, publishers of the *Survey*. A second salvo was fired from Italy, and, as a result, an editor from the Press was appointed to act as referee. Under his jurisdiction, Robert's contribution survived intact.

The most contentious issue had been his theory that 'structure came from the north-east and the established Iranian mode was simply that of surface decoration'. This assertion, Pope made plain to him, 'simply isn't true'. Fear of reviewers' attacks on 'this kind of wildness' led Upham Pope to add a series of signed footnotes to Robert's article, one of which baldly states: 'A more generally accepted view is that the structural impulse was indigenous to Iran and was maintained there with remarkable continuity through the various political changes.'

Robert retaliated by accusing Pope of indulging in 'schoolboy scoring of points', but he was helpless to prevent his damaging annotations. No sooner had the quarrelling subsided than it flared up again, over a trifling sum of money. With neither side giving way, the correspondence, blazing and spitting to the last, was forced to a close.

The imminent publication of the *Survey* in seven vast volumes postponed any intention of writing 'Persian Classical Architecture'. Macmillan agreed, and the project was allowed to lapse, leaving an unearned advance of £100 on Robert's royalty account.

During the twelve months following his lecture tour, Robert had never experienced such unhappiness. Much of this became focused on his parents' new house in Wiltshire. To compound the problem, he was the only sibling left in need of a family home, as in February 1937, Anne had married and moved to Yorkshire. In a letter to his mother, written in the spring of 1938, Robert summarized his feelings:

> In a way, I suppose, the house is a symbol of what is over or rather of the fact of its being over: travelling, hunting, Anne & Lucy, the forest, even writing, in fact my youth & independence . . . it was unfortunate that the change of house coincided with the change of so much else, because visibly

> the house bears the blame, & you know how sensitive I am to visible surroundings . . . it will always be an enemy & I fear therefore that I shall never be happy in it or cease to resent the fate that linked me to such a place.

Robert faced stalemate in his life. Fortunately, a cause was at hand which was to engage in worthwhile combat all his fury and invective.

27

Georgian Crusader

Amidst all the upheavals in Robert's life, his dedication to architecture remained constant. The thunder of demolition was rumbling with ever increasing frequency through the streets and squares of London. In 1936, the Adelphi, the magnificent terrace of houses designed by the Adam brothers, fronting the Thames, had been torn down to make way for offices. Waterloo Bridge, completed in 1817 to the design of John Rennie, had been reduced to little more than a mountain of debris overlooking the Embankment, whilst in the City, Wren's church of All Hallows in Lombard Street, largely intact and unrestored, was poised to meet its doom.

Robert could not stand idly by. Towards the end of March 1937, he joined forces with de Cronin Hastings and his editor at the *Architectural Review*, J. M. Richards, to denounce the perpetrators of these and other crimes against London. The polemic, entitled 'How We Celebrate the Coronation – A word to London's visitors', was published both in the *Architectural Review* and as a pamphlet, in May 1937, to coincide with the coronation of King George VI. In language aflame with anger, Robert sounds the alarm over London's ruination, warning that 'Slowly and furtively, but only too surely, England and the Empire are being defrauded of their ancient capital.'

His finest vitriol is reserved for the Church, and especially those 'befrocked and dog-collared vandals' responsible for the destruction of All Hallows, Lombard Street: 'this beautiful building . . .', he fulminates,

> is to be sacrificed as a financial hors d'oeuvre to the orgy of speculation in real estate which our pastors are preparing for the future . . . Even the Bolsheviks, when they sold up the Hermitage, had not the effrontery to sell anything Russian.

> But in England, property is sacred. Yes. In England, the Church is sacred too. Yes. And art? Art! Good God! We don't want any of that sort of stuff.

As final evidence of the degradation of architecture, Robert turns to the case of Bedford Square, one of the most perfect examples of Georgian town planning to have, thus far, survived. Under consideration, in 1937, was the demolition of the entire east side of the square at the behest of the British Museum. 'That an institution', he submits, 'devoted to the diffusion of knowledge can contemplate an act of this description is a phenomenon so far removed from the canons of civilized behaviour that it seems at times as if the English were really as mad, as gross and as intolerant of art and culture as their foreign detractors pretend.'

The Ancient Monuments Act of 1900 authorized the Office of Works to draw up lists of monuments whose preservation was considered to be of national importance. Once scheduled, a monument or site was afforded conditional protection should the need arise. However, all occupied dwelling houses and church property were excluded from the lists. Moreover, the Royal Commission on Ancient and Historical Monuments for England, charged with publishing inventories of monuments 'worthy of preservation', was forbidden to notice any structure erected after 1714. In practice, therefore, the law favoured almost exclusively the survival of ruins and archaeological sites. Architecture was offered no significant protection.

The Town and Country Planning Act of 1932 gave local authorities the power to protect buildings of architectural or historic interest, but it also stipulated that owners had to be compensated for any resulting loss of value to their property. In consequence, not a single building had been saved under this provision. Robert also attacked the latest Housing Act, which denied government grants, ordinarily available for rebuilding, if the façade of the previous structure was to be retained. 'This extraordinary clause', he writes, 'would seem to have been specially designed to defeat that excellent rule whereby Paris and Rome have preserved so many of their ancient beauties.'

Powerless under the law, Robert resorted to guerrilla tactics. In an epilogue to the pamphlet of 'How We Celebrate the Coronation', he listed, 'for the convenience of inquirers', the telephone numbers of the villains of the piece. His directory included the Ecclesiastical Commissioners, the Archbishop of Canterbury, the Bishop of London, whom he had described in his first draft as 'this mitred serpent', and the Trustees of the British Museum.

Fortunately, Robert was not alone in making an outcry. Some months earlier, in December 1936, Lord Derwent, a young peer of refined taste and artistic sensibility, and a pioneering advocate of Georgian and Regency architecture, had initiated a debate in the House of Lords in response, as he put it, to 'the tide of careless destruction that is daily menacing the architectural beauties of our country'. His motion proposed that a census be undertaken of all buildings constructed between 1700 and 1830, with the aim of protecting those of sufficient importance. The proposal had no chance of becoming law. However, outside Parliament, it provided the spur to action.

In preparing his speech to the House of Lords, Derwent had consulted other people who shared his concern, including the writer Douglas Goldring, a veteran campaigner against the capital's demolition squads. In 1936, Goldring began to focus his attention upon the perils facing Georgian buildings. 'At the present rate of progress', he predicted in the *Daily Telegraph*, 'relics of Georgian London will be almost as rare in ten years' time as relics of Tudor London are today.' That autumn, he was put in touch with Lord Derwent, then researching his speech for the Lords. Apart from briefing him on recent demolitions, Goldring also outlined an idea for a society dedicated to the saving of Georgian architecture. Drawn by a common cause, the two met again some weeks later, when both happened to be in Paris. 'As a result of that discussion', Goldring recorded, 'the society I had been brooding over and trying to bring into existence for so long was finally procreated.' The Georgian Group, as it became known, had been born.

Derwent sought the support of Lord Esher, chairman of the Society for the Protection of Ancient Buildings (SPAB), the organization founded by William Morris in 1877 to combat the disastrous 'restoration' of medieval cathedrals and churches by Victorian architects. Esher counselled against setting up as an independent unit, arguing that 'a distinct loss of power, of public weight is entailed when one powerful society is divided up into many less powerful ones.' Instead, he recommended the creation of 'an active Georgian Group' within the framework of the SPAB. Derwent swiftly accepted Esher's proposal; Goldring expressed himself 'wholeheartedly in favour', and agreed to act as unofficial secretary.

On 22 April 1937, the Georgian Group was formally instituted by the committee of the SPAB. Goldring was present, and it was decided to defer any public announcement until after the coronation in May. Meanwhile, likely candidates for the Group's committee were approached. At this point, Robert also became involved. Coincidentally, he and J. M. Richards had arranged to meet Lord Derwent to discuss ways of prosecuting the attack commenced in 'How We Celebrate the Coronation'. Robert was promptly invited to join the committee, 'for the purpose', suggested Goldring, 'of rousing public opinion (or canalizing public rage)'.

At the end of May, a letter to *The Times*, largely written by Goldring, but appearing under Lord Esher's name, announced the formation of the Georgian Group. Membership inquiries were directed to Goldring at his home address. The preliminaries were completed a few days later when, at the first committee meeting of the Group, Lord Derwent was elected as chairman, Robert Byron as deputy-chairman, Henry Everett, an appointee of the SPAB, as treasurer and Goldring as secretary.

From the start, however, the secretary of the SPAB, William Palmer, and his colleagues had eyed their offspring with suspicion. To keep the upper hand, the committee had drawn up stringent conditions of affiliation, including the right to vet all articles, letters to the press, even the contents of speeches, issued by the Georgian Group. The rule was put to the test over a publicity paragraph destined for the news agencies. Goldring obediently submitted his draft to Palmer, who took a week to reply, and then quibbled over the opening sentence.

The delay led to the item being released over the August Bank Holiday.

Robert and Goldring were united in their impatience with the SPAB. 'What is not to be borne is Palmer's censoring of every announcement we wish to put out,' Robert wrote to Lord Derwent. 'This must surely be put an end to, as otherwise our technique will be exactly the same as theirs, which is the last thing we want.' As the summer wore on, relations between the two organizations reached breaking point. Esher stressed to Palmer the importance of cooperating with 'so virile & modern a movement'. He commanded his secretary to maintain amicable relations, and decided to undertake the delicate task of censorship himself.

By the autumn of 1937, the Georgian Group was established in a small office in Cork Street, lent by the architect Basil Ionides. Membership stood at over a hundred, and a formidable committee had been assembled, bristling with architects, scholars and committed amateurs. A younger core included John Betjeman, Christopher Hussey, James Lees-Milne, Michael Rosse and John Summerson. Initially, meetings took place at the SPAB offices, a seventeenth-century house off the Strand. After a few months, the committee opted for a 1920s flat in Piccadilly, belonging to one of their number, Baroness D'Erlanger. Meetings were held weekly, and as Derwent was frequently away, Robert in all but name assumed the role of chairman.

Thanks to his encouragement, an ideal candidate stepped forward to apply for the post of assistant secretary. She was Wilhelmine 'Billa' Cresswell, a friend of some years, who had previously worked for a branch of the Council for the Preservation of Rural England. 'She would make a wonderful agitator,' he urged. Still in her twenties, Billa had long adorned the social world of the young Georgians. At her first ball as a debutante, she had caught the eye of Christopher Hussey, who, after a night on the dance floor, had presented her with a copy of his book on the Picturesque. A year or two later, John Betjeman had fallen recklessly in love with her. Briefly, they had become engaged. Her appointment as sole employee of the Georgian Group was carried unanimously. The typist was paid off, and the Group's affairs, which from the start had suffered administrative problems, at last appeared to be placed upon a professional footing.

Meanwhile, the committee was faced with a growing list of buildings from all over the country under threat of demolition. The most urgent case was Norfolk House in St James's Square which, in November 1937, was reported to have been sold for development on the instructions of Bernard, the 16th Duke of Norfolk.

Begun in 1748, for the 9th Duke, by the Palladian architect Matthew Brettingham, Norfolk House, with its reticent brick façade occupying a double frontage on the square, concealed one of the most glorious eighteenth-century interiors left in London. Much of the plasterwork and carved decoration had been designed by the Piedmontese architect, Giovanni Battista Borra, who had embellished the state apartments in the continental rococo style. Apart from minor nineteenth-century additions, the rooms and their furnishings had remained intact throughout the residence of six successive dukes.

The property also comprised a stable block on Charles II Street, and, more importantly, the relic of a previous ducal mansion, dating from the early 1700s, which stood across a courtyard at the back of Brettingham's building. Most of 'Old Norfolk House' had been demolished to make way for its successor, but part of a baroque saloon had survived with a painted ceiling attributed to Pellegrini or Sebastiano Ricci.

Unfortunately, sentiment played no part in the calculations of the 16th Duke of Norfolk, a twenty-nine-year-old ex-cavalry officer with a penchant for racing. Although laden with assets, including valuable property elsewhere in London as well as estates covering 49,000 acres, he was determined to be rid of Norfolk House down to the last exquisite door-handle.

On hearing the news, members of the Georgian Group, including Robert, toured the building. It was agreed to fight for the preservation of some of the interiors, particularly the Music Room, a dazzling ensemble of white and gilt boiseries with an especially fine ceiling. Time was against them. The sale of the contents and fittings by Christie's was planned for the new year. When Lord Derwent pressed for a meeting to discuss ways of saving the house, the Duke replied: 'There is really no more I can say,' adding mendaciously: 'It is very sad to think it has to go.' Eventually, Lord Gerald Wellesley, son of the 4th Duke of Wellington, an architect and leading member of the Georgian Group, secured an audience. Afterwards, he was able to announce to the committee that the Music Room had been saved, and would be given to the Victoria and Albert Museum. The Georgian Group claimed no credit for this achievement as they did not wish to detract from the Duke's gesture.

The sale of Norfolk House lasted three days. 'I see the Norfolk House prices were fruity –' Derwent commented to Robert, 'the wicked wax fat . . .' Throughout the campaign, Robert had been impatient to discover the identity of the new owner of the building. But for tactical reasons, he had been persuaded to hold back. Once the Music Room had been saved, his investigations began in earnest. The trail led to Rudolph Palumbo, 'a man', Robert noted, 'behind all these monster flats . . . in Maida Vale'. A year or two earlier, Palumbo had demolished one half of a semi-detached pair of Regency villas, and constructed a block of flats on the site. From then on, the Regency half had become known as 'The Mutilated House'.

Robert acquired sufficient evidence of Palumbo's involvement to justify telephoning his office for confirmation of the fact. After receiving a denial, he followed up the call with a letter, which ran: 'I was much interested to hear this morning that neither you nor Mr Pybus [a financier] were concerned in the purchase of Norfolk House . . . I should be very grateful for a contradiction in writing . . . over a question of such urgent national importance.' Palumbo avoided the question. Instead, he referred to two queries raised by Robert on the telephone: whether Pybus was the purchaser; and whether Palumbo was the agent in the deal. Neither was strictly true, leaving Palumbo free to reply: 'The answer to both these questions is in the negative.' In fact, Palumbo had long agreed to buy Norfolk House. In November, his plans for an office block on the site had been submitted to the London County Council. And two weeks prior to Robert's letter, these had been approved in principle. Palumbo's anonymity had been preserved because there was no compulsion to name the landowner on a planning application.

One last cry of protest was made on behalf of the house. In April 1938, Gwendoline, the Dowager Duchess of Norfolk, joined the Georgian Group, enclosing with her subscription the message: 'would it be possible for the society to save Norfolk House from being pulled down?' All along, the Dowager Duchess had opposed her son's decision. For her pains, she had seen the entire contents of her bedroom going under the hammer.

As for the Duke, the grandest philistine of the age, Robert had the last word. 'The Duke of Norfolk', he wrote in the *New Statesman*, 'still refuses to divulge the purchaser of Norfolk House . . . When noblesse ceases to oblige, it is not surprising that richesse should do likewise. The law not only condones the speculator; it protects him with anonymity.' With ruthless indifference, Palumbo sent in the housebreakers. The destruction of Norfolk House, one of the architectural masterpieces of London, was to make his fortune.

The battleground moved to Bloomsbury, where the north side of Brunswick Square had been torn down by London University to make way for a new Pharmaceutical School. At the suggestion of the Georgian Group, the BBC staged a debate on the wireless, entitled 'Farewell Brunswick Square', which considered the future of Georgian buildings in London. The Group was represented by Robert and John Summerson, whilst an MP and an estate agent made up the opposition.

Robert's speech conveyed both the greatness and vulnerability of London's Georgian architecture, as typified by the classic streets and squares of Bloomsbury. Such architecture, he argued,

> corresponds, almost to the point of dinginess, with our national character. Its reserve and dislike of outward show, its reliance on the virtue and dignity of proportions only, and its rare bursts of exquisite detail, all express as no other style has ever done that indifference to self-advertisement, that quiet

assumption of our own worth, and that sudden vein of lyric affection, which have given us our part in civilization.

Brunswick Square, of which not a brick remains, had been conceived in the 1790s as part of a grand development centred upon Thomas Coram's Foundling Hospital. To balance the composition, Mecklenburgh Square, with a similar three-sided plan, had been laid out on the opposite flank. This, too, was endangered. Behind the houses on the south side, a residential hall for Dominion students had recently been built by Sir Herbert Baker. The intention, given time and money, was to extend the premises on to the square, replacing the Georgian terrace with another range by Baker.

The scheme presented Robert with an irresistible target. 'The style of the new building in the adjoining streets is a gruesome foretaste of the intended deformation,' he warned readers of the *New Statesman*. 'It was designed by Sir Herbert Baker, and other than this, comment is hardly necessary, except to remark on his new whim of introducing flints into London architecture.' The article, written in the name of the Georgian Group, caused a stir in committee. Baker was a distinguished member of the SPAB, and William Palmer rushed to his defence, suggesting that, in future, 'personal attacks on architects should not be made in the Press.'

In the summer of 1938, the Group joined forces with local residents to rally support against the proposal. Together, they organized a 'Georgian Ball and Fair' in the gardens of the square. Queen Mary, who only a few months earlier had opened Baker's new hostel, agreed to act as patron. The rout took place, on a chilly night in July, against the backdrop of the graceful pillared façade of the east side, floodlit for the occasion. Oliver Messel decked out the gardens with lanterns, and decorated the marquee as a circus tent. Ancestral phaetons and barouches, drawn up among the trees, were provided for sitting out between dances. There was a beer garden and coffee stall, hoop-la and a coconut shy. Hermione Baddeley ran a darts competition, and members of a local boys' club performed a ballet. London's Intellect and Beauty mingled with Pearly Kings and Queens. Young men in sweaters joined the strings of Lambeth Walkers; old women from the neighbouring streets warmed themselves by the braziers, enjoying free beer. The evening, as the *Spectator* remarked, 'was the most enchanting occasion imaginable'.

The Georgian Group had good cause to celebrate. In June, they had played a vital role in the saving of a pair of Palladian houses in Old Palace Yard, one of the most historic and important spaces in London, which lies between the eastern precincts of Westminster Abbey and the Palace of Westminster. The stone-fronted houses, with a unified elevation, date from the 1740s, and have been attributed to John Vardy. At the time, these houses belonged to a charming enclave of Georgian architecture tucked beneath the gothic wonders of Church and State. Attached to the west side of Vardy's building, at a right angle, was another large house, taller and of brick, whilst to the south, facing Victoria Tower and its gardens, ran the pleasing row of Abingdon Street.

The entire group had been in peril since March 1936, when the Archbishop of Canterbury had suggested that all the houses in Old Palace Yard and Abingdon Street could be swept away for the purpose of creating a fit setting for a memorial to King George V. He pointed out that a new vista of Westminster Abbey, 'rising above its cloisters', would be revealed, and also of the Jewel Tower, a structure (heavily restored) dating from the fourteenth century, currently obscured. Two months later, the idea was officially adopted by the General Committee of the King George V Memorial Fund.

By the autumn of 1936, this ambitious plan had been curtailed. The Lord Mayor, who was in charge of the appeal, announced that only the three houses in Old Palace Yard would now be pulled down to make way for an area of lawn and pavement around the statue. Even so, a view of the 'ancient' Jewel Tower would still be disclosed. The gothic architect, Sir Giles Gilbert Scott, and the sculptor, Sir William Reid Dick, were invited to draw up proposals.

In 'How We Celebrate the Coronation', Robert censured the Memorial Committee for its decision to do away with the building by Vardy. To make matters worse, the reprieve of Abingdon Street was short-lived. In October 1937, a confidential planning application was submitted to the London

County Council for an office block on the site. The Georgian Group was tipped off by Basil Marsden-Smedley, a member of the Chelsea Society, who also sat on the LCC planning committee. Billa Cresswell made a seemingly innocent inquiry, and elicited from the council that the application had been approved in principle. Soon afterwards, the project was announced in the press. The new building was to be developed jointly by the Church Commissioners and the Association of Local Government Officers, the owner of a further two houses in the street.

As the block would abut Old Palace Yard, the architects of the development, Culpin & Sons, proposed that the side elevation, facing north, should incorporate the re-erected façade of Vardy's building, thus forming a backdrop to the George V Memorial. Ewart Culpin, the senior partner of the firm, was uniquely placed to exploit the possibilities of both sites. Not only was he a member of the LCC planning committee, but he also sat on the 'site and statue committee', the body responsible for overseeing the complete design of the memorial.

One formality required of the statue committee was the submission of its plans to the Royal Fine Art Commission. On seeing the drawings, the Commission promptly came up with an alternative scheme, less radical and more coherent, which recommended the preservation of the Vardy building, but the demolition of the adjoining house to the west. In effect, this would create a square of green lawn, offering an 'unexcelled' position for the King's statue. Unfortunately, the statue committee were determined to ignore such advice, and Sir Giles Gilbert Scott was asked to finalize his proposals.

The future of Old Palace Yard looked grim. Judgement day was set for 14 June 1938, when Lord Macmillan, chairman of the Memorial Fund, would receive the committee's detailed recommendation.

The Georgian Group had been monitoring events closely. MPs had been lobbied and letters written to the press. But as the deadline approached, their activities gathered pace. A council of war was set up, including Robert, Jim Lees-Milne, and a new adherent to the Group, an employee of the *Architectural Review*, Osbert Lancaster. It was decided to focus their efforts on a petition to be launched on the eve of the official announcement.

As a preliminary, Robert softened up the enemy with a long-planned tirade in the *New Statesman*. Foremost in the line of fire was Culpin, by now chairman of the LCC, whose plans for Abingdon Street, Robert observes, 'will have to pass the withering test of his own approval'. He notes in conclusion: 'The public at large, as usual, has not been consulted. Theirs is not to reason why, but to pay. Their money will bring them a memorial not so much to King George V as to avarice, apathy and irreverence, whose example in high places, during his reign and after, have consigned his capital to destruction.'

The article brought an outraged response from Culpin, who remonstrated:

> It is . . . with amazement that one reads the innuendo, the disgraceful innuendo . . . that because I happen to be chairman of the London County Council, as well as the architect of certain buildings, my plans have undue preference. This, sir, is a suggestion which I believe no one having any knowledge of the integrity of the administration at County Hall would have the impertinence to make.

Meanwhile, opposition was growing in Parliament. A meeting of the Amenities Group of MPs and peers, run by Georgian committee member, Alfred Bossom, came out strongly against the current plan. The Prime Minister, alarmed at the prospect of unseemly argument in the House, privately advised Lord Macmillan to consider the option put forward by the Royal Fine Art Commission.

By this time, the Georgian Group were in full cry. An illustrated circular was sent to members of both Houses of Parliament and all London councillors, urging them to come to Abingdon Street and sign the petition. Contrasting photographs, chosen by Osbert Lancaster, showed, on the one hand, the elegant façade by Vardy, and on the other, the squat Jewel Tower, hemmed in by later accretions, and to all appearances in use as a garage. The opening of the protest office on 13 June was heralded by sandwich-men parading round

Parliament Square and Old Palace Yard. Newspapers reported the event. Peers, MPs, writers and artists flocked to sign the petition. Nancy Mitford volunteered to chain herself to the railings.

The next day, as predicted, the statue and site committee recommended their own scheme for Old Palace Yard. Lord Macmillan, however, had taken fright. In an embarrassing volte-face, he rejected their proposal in favour of that drawn up by the Royal Fine Art Commission. In explaining his decision, he acknowledged that 'nothing could be more unfitting or ungracious than that the memorial to a revered Sovereign should become the subject of public controversy.'

Although the Vardy houses were saved, the fate of Abingdon Street remained in doubt. Later that summer, the LCC approved a new plan for an office block by Culpin, but it was never realized. Instead, Abingdon Street was demolished after the war to create College Green, which, to this day, offers an unrivalled view of the Jewel Tower.

Despite the Group's growing reputation, problems remained back in the office. 'You wouldn't like to run the Georgian Group I suppose for £2 a week – doing about £20 a week's work?' Robert asked John Mavrogordato in desperation. 'We are on the crest of a wave after our success in Abingdon Street, but held up for lack of a directing brain.' Billa Cresswell's efficient regime had been cut short by her engagement to Roy Harrod. After her departure, the roles of secretary, both honorary and clerical, were never satisfactorily resolved.

Robert's tenure as deputy chairman lasted two years. In May 1939, owing to pressure of work, he too resigned, but agreed to remain on the committee. His contribution to the Group was acknowledged by Professor Albert Richardson, who, in his vote of thanks, referred to 'the enormous amount of case-work and day-to-day details of administration that Mr Byron had personally supervised, quite over and above his formal duties as Deputy Chairman'.

Robert's architectural interests were not limited to preserving the past. He had begun to write regularly on architectural matters for the *New Statesman* and in his role as their correspondent had reviewed, in January 1938, the

MARS (Modern Architectural Research) exhibition at the New Burlington Galleries. The MARS Group, founded in 1931, which numbered Lubetkin as a member, promulgated the most advanced theories in architecture and town planning. Robert questioned their desire to relegate architecture to a branch of social service. 'These architects', he wrote, 'want to build what is good for people. Who are they to judge what is good for me and mine?'

Robert believed that the architect's duty lay elsewhere. Buildings had to be functional, but they also had to delight. The MARS Group, which exhibited as an anonymous collective, implicitly denied this belief by refusing to accept that their designs sprang from the creativity of individuals working within a particular style. Robert was having none of it. 'Of course the modern architect has a style . . . A more pronounced style . . . never decorated the earth.' Certain principles of modernist design were praised, but he warned that an over-emphasis on functionalism threatened to 'swamp the whole idiom'. This could only lead, when in the hands of an inexperienced architect, to the fallacy of 'mock-utilitarianism' which was often the reverse of functional. The modern movement, he concluded, was at a crossroads. Unless the practitioners developed a grammar of 'valid form' then they were destined for 'obscurity or the hate that now pursues their kind in Russia'. Robert underestimated the future might of modernism, which in 1938, had still had a limited impact upon the urban scene. But his analysis of its stylistic flaw has been vindicated.

28
Warmongering

Despite the demands of his full-time job and the Georgian Group, Robert's central preoccupation, as the 1930s wore on, was the deteriorating situation in Europe.

To him, the source of danger was obvious. His distrust of Fascism stretched back to his first visit to Greece in 1925, when he had learnt of the oppressive Italian regime on the Dodecanese. Back at Oxford, he had warned in the *Cherwell* of the territorial ambitions of Mussolini, urging the 'Powers of Europe' to stand up to him. He returned to the attack in his first travel book, *Europe in the Looking Glass*, pointing out that 'Italy is the victim not so much of a dictatorship, but of an ochlocracy, the rule of an armed mob, and an immature mob at that.' The rise of Hitler met with equal distaste. His reaction on seeing a propaganda film put on by the German Minister in Teheran, which showed 'Hitler, Goebbels & the rest of them roaring away', was to conclude: 'I cd only say I felt glad I was not a German.'

Even so, Robert still believed that another war in Europe was an impossibility. This conviction rested upon his faith in the League of Nations, the organization established in 1920 to preserve the new-found peace and settle international disputes. As an undergraduate, he had been filled with optimism at the League's potential, predicting in a leader in the *Cherwell* that its benign influence in post-war Europe could result in 'universal fellowship throughout the continent'.

A critical test of the League's authority occurred in October 1935 with Mussolini's invasion of Abyssinia. Within days, fifty member states had agreed to institute 'collective measures' against Italy. An arms embargo was immediately imposed, followed by an impressive array of financial and trade sanctions.

Robert, who was crossing Siberia at the time, only managed

to pick up snatches of the latest news. However, in retrospect, he viewed the autumn of 1935 as being a 'landmark of our age . . . when the nations joined forces under English leadership to try and defend the idea of international law'. He described the use of sanctions as that 'great movement', which had engendered, even in faraway Siberia, a 'feeling of hope in the world'. It proved a false dawn. By May 1936, the Italian army, supported by an air force equipped with mustard gas as well as bombs, had conquered Abyssinia. Two months later, all sanctions were lifted by the League.

Meanwhile, Hitler had taken his first step as an aggressor on the world stage. In March 1936, he had occupied the demilitarized zone of the Rhineland, thus violating the treaties of Versailles and Locarno. His boldness paid off. Neither the French nor the British had the stomach for military retaliation. Despite being a guarantor of the Locarno treaty, Britain strove to conciliate rather than condemn, muffling her diplomatic thunder in an extended round of talks.

Returning home in September 1936, after a year abroad, Robert was filled with shame at his country's failure to deter the dictators. He gave vent to his feelings in a letter to *The Times* which supported the line taken by another correspondent that Britain had to champion the cause of freedom in the world. In a similar message, dispatched to the *New Statesman*, Robert accused the Prime Minister, Stanley Baldwin, and Foreign Secretary, Anthony Eden, of inviting war through muddle. Reluctant to join up merely for their sakes, he suggested that all men of military age should 'levy a blackmail on the Government, by opposing recruiting and rearmament, until it declares itself for principles they can decently fight for'.

In advocating pacifism, if only to force the Government's hand, Robert found himself 'driven further to the left than Labour' on the political scale. Being a natural conservative, such a stance was quite alien to him. Once, he had even dallied with the idea of writing propaganda for Conservative Central Office. But his only active involvement had taken place during the Westminster by-election of March 1931, when he had rallied to the support of the Tory candidate, Duff Cooper.

Five years on, Robert's easy certainties were being buffeted by the growing turmoil in Europe. Almost immediately, his political conscience was again on the rack, torn between the ideological extremes of the warring sides in Spain. Having visited the country in 1928, he knew what was at risk.

Initially, Robert had felt a sneaking sympathy for the nationalist cause. But after the first few months of the war, his position veered to the left. His change of heart had been brought about by the realization that Germany was covertly supporting the nationalist forces. To Jim Lees-Milne, who was ardently pro-Franco, he explained: 'I can't help feeling that the interests of England are the most important thing, & the mere suggestion of a German fortress at Ceuta [the Spanish possession in Morocco] makes me hope the Reds will win – if that is the only way of stopping the Germans.'

The decision had not been reached lightly. In the same letter, Robert admitted to detesting both sides. In fact, only weeks before, he had penned a ferocious attack on Communism for the American *Mercury* magazine. Unlike most of his contemporaries, Robert had observed at first hand the workings of the Soviet tyranny. His article enumerates the loss of individual liberty, the fettering of intellect and creativity, the subjugation of the peasants and the near starvation of the urban proletariat. The imposition of Communism in Russia, he concluded, had caused 'a degree of misery and destruction without parallel in recorded history'.

His dilemma over Spain was rekindled by a circular sent to writers and poets in June 1937, soliciting statements for a pamphlet to be published by the *Left Review*. The signatories, who included W. H. Auden, Nancy Cunard, Brian Howard and Stephen Spender, made no secret of their loathing of Fascism. After an emotive preamble, they demanded: 'Are you for or against the legal Government and the People of Republican Spain? Are you for, or against, Franco and Fascism? For it is impossible any longer to take no side.'

Robert bridled at such a loaded question: 'You condemn the impartial view of politics,' he replied. 'Perhaps you will allow me an impartial view of myself. Had I been a Spaniard when the rebellion broke out, I cannot say for certain that I wouldn't have favoured it. Now that it means Fascism, I hope for its defeat.' But he could not leave the matter there. Irked by the imputation that Spaniards on the Fascist side lacked integrity, he continued: 'But my sympathies are with those Spaniards on both sides, whose honesty, which you despise, brings their loyalty and their reason into conflict.'

The vast majority of those questioned, well over one hundred, came down in support of the Republicans. Only five, including Evelyn Waugh, were against them. Robert was one of sixteen to fall into the category of 'Neutral'. Others of the group were T. S. Eliot, H. G. Wells, Vita Sackville-West and Norman Douglas. The latter declared: 'Nobody's going to compel me to take sides. To hell with sides. If Fascists annoy me, I hop it. If Communists annoy me, I hop it. Everything that ends in "ism" is just b***s, so far as I am concerned.' But escapism was not an option for Robert. With uncommon prescience, he realized that each transgression by the Nazis meant a further ineluctable slide towards war.

On 11 March 1938, German troops invaded Austria. There was no resistance. The following day, Hitler made short work of the country's sovereignty by reducing her status to an administrative province of Germany. The *Anschluss* provoked only qualified condemnation from the British Government. Nerves were soothed by the announcement of a defence review. But the awkward matter of policy was postponed.

Coincidentally, on the night of the Commons debate on Austria, Robert was also marshalling his thoughts on the subject. The next day, he sent the resulting article, which appeared a fortnight later, to Kingsley Martin, editor of the *New Statesman*, expressing the hope that '[it] might help as little things sometimes do in a telepathic way, to make the leaders realize how wrong they have led us, & reinforce their resolution (if it yet exists . . .) to get back on to the road at the 11th hour.'

Robert's opening words signalled his descent into the arena of politics. 'Every writer . . .' he explained, 'is a citizen as well as an artist, and there are times when his citizenship is more urgent than his art; times that is when public policy threatens to submerge the truth on which his art depends.' His platform was patriotism; not the conventional brand, symbolized by sword and crown, but a vision based upon the virtues of English civilization. Having previously lectured on the subject, he had a definition readily to hand: it was 'a condition of life' rooted in democracy, justice and liberty. 'Thus the achievement of English civilization', he suggested, 'is outwardly political. But its end is freedom, the freedom for every man to be true to the light within him.' This ideal, he continued, has influenced the fate of almost every nation. Consequently, if Britain and her Empire falls, so too will freedom and 'the rational faculty' throughout the world. 'The hour glass', he proclaimed, 'has begun to empty . . . with Austria gone, with the tide of tyranny and obscuranticism at our garden's edge, the danger is too close. A man at bay can no longer reason, no longer ask who led him to such a pass. He must fight. We must all fight.'

This was no idle boast. The previous autumn, Robert had already tried to join the Royal Naval Volunteer Supplementary Reserve, but had been turned down. Now he decided to pursue a civilian tack, and promptly offered his services to the War Office as a propagandist. The approach, made through his old friend Lord Elmley, Parliamentary Private Secretary to the Minister of War, led to a meeting at the beginning of May with Sir Stephen Tallents, controller of Public Relations at the BBC. Tallents had recently been appointed Director-General designate of an embryonic Ministry of Information and, as such, propaganda fell within his sphere.

Robert sent Tallents a proposal for instigating propaganda overseas, singling out Germany as the preferred target. Next, he invited him to lunch at the Garrick Club to meet another potential recruit, his brother-in-law, Rohan Butler, who, in March 1938, had been posted to Berlin as the second correspondent for *The Times*. Having effected the introduction, Robert asked Rohan as a personal favour to assess the opportunities for propaganda in Germany. He then used the resulting report to press Tallents for a decision. This did the trick. Two days later, he was given the go-ahead to start preparations for a propaganda offensive against Germany.

The assignment was resolutely low key. Butler remained his sole confederate, and no official resources were made available. Furthermore, Robert still had his job in the oil business to keep him busy. He therefore took advantage of the Whitsun bank holiday at the beginning of June to spend three days with Rohan in Berlin planning their next move.

Robert flew in under the cover of authorship. 'It is good news that you are coming and that you are getting to work on the history,' Rohan had written beforehand. 'There is plenty of material to be collected here, and I will try to decide how the short time can be used to best advantage.' That weekend, Robert and Rohan mapped out various lines of strategic inquiry. For his part, Robert determined to observe the full might of the Nazi propaganda machine at first hand. Accordingly, he asked Unity Mitford to try and get him invited to the Parteitag, the Nazi Party Congress, to be held at Nuremberg that September.

Unity, known as Bobo to her intimates, was ideally placed to pull strings on his behalf. Her fascination with Hitler dated from 1933 when, as an impressionable eighteen year old, she had been electrified by his performance at the first Parteitag. Since then a warm friendship had sprung up between them. After the *Anschluss*, she had rushed to Vienna to witness her hero's triumphal occupation of the city. Hitler had greeted her with the words: 'They said England would be there to stop me, but the only English person I saw was on my side.'

'Red Robert', as she called him, was not put off by her taste in friends and remained genuinely fond of her. A similar affection tied him to Diana, despite her marriage in October 1936 to Mosley – which Hitler and Goebbels celebrated with them. He also remained on close terms with Tom, an admirer of Hitler's statecraft, if not his anti-Semitism. Nancy, by contrast, was unequivocal in her scorn of Unity's Fascism. In letters, she would address her troublesome little sister as 'Darling Stone-Heart Bone-Head'.

No lesser personage than Ribbentrop, the German Foreign Minister, had been the recipient of Unity's request for an extra invitation to the Parteitag. Some weeks later, word came back that Robert would be added to the list of *Ehrengäste* or 'honoured guests', joining the Redesdales in Unity's family party. The purpose of Robert's mission was clear. 'I want to see the enemy for myself', he told Christopher Sykes, 'and do a little warmongering.'

His bulldog spirit was in stark contrast to the emollient attitude of the British Government. In effect, the *Anschluss* had made little impact on policy. Chamberlain remained convinced that peace in Europe could only be secured through appeasement. But with Austria in his grip, Hitler turned his attention to the Sudetenland, the border territory of Bohemia occupied by some three million Germans, which after the war had become part of the newly-formed state of Czechoslovakia. In May, a spate of anti-German incidents in the Sudetenland was followed by rumours of German troop movements along the border. The Czech government ordered partial mobilization. Jolted into action, Britain and France squared up to Germany, but the show of resolve swiftly evaporated.

Renewed pressure was put upon the Czech government to agree terms with the German Sudeten Party. Funded and advised by the Nazis, its leaders continually raised their demands, until the Czech cabinet could take no more. In mid-July, they voted to reject the reform programme. To repair the damage, a British mediator, Lord Runciman, was dispatched to Prague. Whilst his diplomacy got underway, Germany called up reservists of all ages. The massive exercise, passed off by Berlin as 'small manoeuvres', resulted in an estimated one million men under arms. Robert could draw only one conclusion. It was the 'prelude to invasion of Czechoslovakia'.

Finally, the Czech government announced its intention to concede 'self-administration' to the Sudetenland. In response, the leader of the German Sudeten Party, Konrad Henlein, crossed into Germany for discussions with Hitler. It was the eve of the Parteitag. The countdown to the Final Rally, when Hitler was expected to pronounce on the Sudetenland, had begun.

By now, Robert viewed the British Government's efforts with deepening scepticism. On the train to Munich, 'in the heart of the enemy country so to speak', Robert delivered his verdict on the present policy: 'worm Chamberlain's "appeasement" . . .' he declared, 'has not only failed and in the process accelerated the prospect of war; it has vanished altogether, leaving us rudderless as before, but now in much narrower waters.'

The Parteitag opened in Nuremberg on 6 September. Robert, along with Hitler's other 'honoured guests', was put up at the Grand Hotel, where he found his room equipped with a bootjack. The Redesdales had arrived the day before. Throughout, as Robert remarked afterwards, Lord Redesdale behaved as though at a house party 'to which five hundred thousand rather odd and unexpected guests had turned up'. On the first evening, he spotted him in the hotel lobby, 'among the surging mob of fascists, Phalangists in red berets, Germans in every kind of uniform all covered with orders and medals and badges, with his head bowed, walking slowly this way and that'. It turned out that he was searching for a needle which Lady Redesdale had dropped from her tatting.

Over the next week, Robert was assiduous in his attendance at the rallies, parades and formal sessions of the Congress. Allocated a prime seat, he had an unrivalled view of the choreography of each event. At one session of the Congress, Robert was embarrassed to find himself seated alongside Unity in the front row. The problem of hailing Hitler now arose. Foreigners were not expected to make the Nazi salute, but not having a hat to doff, Robert was in danger of drawing attention to himself. Thus he decided to fall in line, and stick out his arm. Suddenly, Hitler, walking at a great pace, swept around the corner: 'my fingers', Robert reported, 'were nearly bitten off by the Führer and I half withdrew my arm, thus assuming a position of grotesque flabbiness.' Throughout the performance, Robert kept catching the eye of either Goebbels, Himmler or the Führer. The last, he noticed, had 'eyes like peas, but a good-humoured face obviously very moved by music'. Himmler, on the other hand, was sketched as 'terrifying, he sucks his teeth and keeps them bared.'

Despite the artistry of each performance, Robert found them demoralizing. The opening ceremony conveyed 'a feeling of death – of the absence of the vital spark', leaving him with the impression 'of a people doomed on earth and in heaven'. Unexpectedly, he found solace in church. Early in the week, Robert had attended an organ recital at the Church of St Lorenz, the finest in the city; 'it came to me,' he confessed, 'perhaps for the first time, how very deeply our civilization is bound up with Christianity.' His aesthete's belief in the supremacy of beauty was toppled. Western civilization, he now saw, was infused with Christian principles of untold value. 'They are life,' he stated, 'the others death.'

The continuing uncertainty over the Sudetenland guaranteed a fevered atmosphere amongst the foreign observers at the Parteitag. Robert kept in close touch with the latest developments through his friends in the press, especially Virginia Cowles, an American journalist working for the *Sunday Times*, and Jimmy Holburn, chief *Times* correspondent and a colleague of Butler's.

The German Sudeten Party, it emerged, had turned down the proposals for self-administration. Henlein left for Nuremberg, where as Hitler's guest of honour he was also put up at the Grand Hotel. On the same day, Wednesday 7 September, *The Times*, as recorded in Robert's staccato diary entry, 'published leader saying Czechs better divest themselves of the Sudeten territory before it is too late'. Virginia Cowles testified to 'the buoying effect it had on German officialdom'. Dr Dietrich, the German press chief, explained to her that Hitler did not want war, adding slyly, 'He can get what he wants without.' When Robert paid a call on Jimmy Holburn that evening, the telephone never stopped ringing with news of Runciman's late-night negotiations in Prague. Robert stayed till the early hours. His depression, the next morning, was acute.

Gradually, the tension began to undermine Robert's composure. The inevitable eruption occurred during a seemingly friendly conversation with some German journalists and officials. One of the company was Dr Silex, a rabid Nazi and editor of the *Deutsche Allgemeine Zeitung*. Referring to the leader in *The Times*, Silex argued that Britain would soon come to her senses, and realize that the present quarrel was one for Germany and Czechoslovakia alone to settle. Virginia Cowles recorded Robert's reaction:

> I saw a red flush rising on Robert's neck and the next moment I heard him saying in a deadly voice: 'What happens on the

> continent is always England's concern. Every now and then we are unfortunate enough to be led by a Chamberlain – but that's only temporary. Don't be misguided. In the end we always rise up and oppose the tyrannies that threaten Europe. We have smashed them before, and I warn you we will smash them again.'

A terrible silence fell round the table. When Robert and Virginia made to leave, none of the party urged them to stay.

By the end of the week, Robert could hardly take much more. An interlude was spent with Virginia in the old town eating grilled sausages. 'A pleasant scene', Robert wrote, 'and to us it seemed one of the last of such evenings. We resolved, whatever else we accomplished, to see that the blood of this generation, should it be shed, should be on the heads of the Appeasers.'

The day of the Final Rally arrived. Robert woke with a sore throat and an attack of the jitters. After an aircraft display, they went to the Congress Hall for Hitler's speech. A great swastika, floodlit, known as 'the Blood Flag', formed the backdrop. The pillars were red and gold. Beneath the tribune stood a line of black-uniformed SS men. The speech, delivered in a whining, cajoling, bullying tone, was filled with threats and imprecations against Czechoslovakia. Hitler's voice rose to a scream with the declaration: 'If these tortured creatures cannot obtain rights and assistance by themselves, they can obtain both from us.' Robert was filled with foreboding. Of Hitler's performance, he wrote: 'As his fury mounted, and his hair grew untidy, the nightmare of the whole week came to its climax . . . one finally realized it was a nightmare from which one might never wake up.'

Back at the hotel, the dreadful truth appeared to be dawning upon Unity. All week she had been in the limelight. Senior Nazis had greeted her in the stadium and the Führer himself had cast her warm glances during conference speeches. Above all, he had invited her and the Redesdales to his suite for a private chat. As one of the few people with access to Hitler, she was also fiercely courted by foreign journalists. Nuremberg was her finest hour. One evening, her dinner plans with Robert and Virginia were upset by preparations for a storm troopers' parade. The streets had been closed to traffic, but, without more ado, she commandeered a 'delicious Stormie' to race them in an open-topped car through the waiting crowds to their restaurant. Of her success that week, Robert observed: 'It is amusing to see people taking her so seriously.' But after Hitler's speech, Robert noted sadly:

> Bobo's confidence all gone – for the first time, she admitted the possibility of war – and wondered what to do with herself – she can't come back to England, yet would be an enemy alien in Germany. She sent her love to her family, and seems to contemplate a time of unhappiness, though bravely keeping up her spirits by saying she would be in Prague for the Einmarsch [marching in].

At one o'clock the following morning, Robert left by car for Frankfurt. Thence, he flew to London, where he lost no time in briefing Sir Stephen Tallents on the lessons to be drawn from the Parteitag. The outcome was a memorandum, produced within a week of his return, on the dissemination of propaganda in the event of war. On the moral front, his argument ran, Germany should be projected as an international outcast. The swastika, he said, 'should be exposed . . . as the symbol of EVIL outside the Reich – a symbol which must be erased from the earth before men can find peace and security.' To press home the attack, he proposed that ordinary Germans should be reminded, via leaflet drops and broadcasts, of their sufferings after the last war. Vulnerability on this point had been evident at Nuremberg. Robert cited the 'frenzied assurances of Goering and others that the food supply was adequate to any emergency'. The screws could be tightened further by spelling out the consequences of defeat: namely, that after two world wars, the angry victors 'will inevitably make it their aim to exterminate the German nation by dividing it, placing large parts of it under the rule of other races'. As a final string to his bow, Robert included an analysis of German society which identified possible sources of opposition to the regime. This had been completed by Rohan Butler earlier in the summer and represented his contribution to the campaign.

On 23 September, within forty-eight hours of receiving the document, Tallents summoned Robert from the country to an urgent meeting with Sir Hughe Knatchbull-Hugessen at the Foreign Office. There and then he was asked to draft the text of a leaflet to be distributed in Germany immediately war broke out.

The danger was very real. Hitler's speech at the Final Rally had been the trigger for violent demonstrations in the Sudetenland. Martial law was imposed in certain districts and when the Czech government refused to back down, Henlein declared that further negotiations were impossible. Determined to find a peaceful solution, Neville Chamberlain flew to Munich on 15 September for talks with Hitler at Berchtesgaden. He emerged two and a half hours later having all but conceded the principle of self-determination for the Sudetenland.

On 22 September, Chamberlain travelled to Bad Godesberg for a second meeting with Hitler, believing peace to be within his grasp. He was swiftly disabused. Hitler now laid claim to the entire Czech frontier with 'military defensive works' intact; he also announced his intention of holding plebiscites in other areas. A deadline of 1 October was set for the handing over of territory. Naturally enough, the Czech government, which had already announced general mobilization, rejected Hitler's terms.

War now seemed inevitable. On the evening of Tuesday 27 September, Chamberlain broadcast to the nation. His speech was infected with the frustration of failure. 'How horrible, fantastic, incredible it is', he said, 'that we should be digging trenches and trying on gas masks here, because of a quarrel in a far away country between people of whom we know nothing.'

Robert's foresight had landed him in the thick of the last-minute preparations for war. On the previous Saturday, he had attended a second meeting at the Foreign Office when a representative from the Air Ministry put forward a more detailed scheme for the dropping of 10 million leaflets over Germany on the first night of war. Robert was to take responsibility for the text, layout and schedules. He relished the task. From Whitehall, he made straight for the Stationery

Office to discuss timing with the government printers. His next stop, with rough layout in hand, was Harrison's in St Martin's Lane, the typesetters responsible for much of the propaganda material during the last war. They agreed to produce a trial leaflet, using a German gothic typeface from their wartime stock. The initial proof, although modified, settled the question of design and format. Meanwhile, the text was also revised to good effect. All was accomplished in the nick of time. On the day of Chamberlain's broadcast, instructions were received to go ahead with the printing of the leaflet.

The operation now fell foul of departmental rivalry. At the last minute, Sir Alexander Cadogan, Permanent Under-Secretary at the Foreign Office, produced a new message for the German people. A rapid translation was made by Military Intelligence, who handed it over to Robert for delivery to the typesetters. Loyally, he returned at midnight on 27 September to correct the proof. But by this time, the Foreign Office was no longer in command. That day, the Ministry of Information had come into existence as an independent body, under the direction of Tallents, within the Board of Education. One of the first decisions of Lord Stanhope, the minister responsible, was to reject Cadogan's effort as being too weak. Robert was instructed to start afresh. His latest draft ended with the words: 'When the war is over; when we have mourned the children & counted the dead; when the victors have had vengeance & the cities of Europe lie in ruins; then, German people, we shall ask one another. Why did it happen?'

Germans were never given the chance to ponder this question. The Munich conference, dramatically convened by Hitler at twenty-four hours' notice, brought Robert's activities to a halt. The agreement signed in the early hours of 30 September appeared to overturn Hitler's previous demands. The deadline of 1 October was abandoned in favour of a gradual occupation over ten days. The total area was to be divided into five zones. Of these, the first four covered little more than half the territory claimed by Hitler at Godesberg. The extent of the fifth was to be established by an International Boundary Commission. Chamberlain exploited the goodwill engendered by the conference to promote a new

Anglo-German détente. Following a further meeting with Hitler, he read out to waiting journalists the text of their joint declaration, which affirmed 'the desire of our two peoples never to go to war with one another again'.

Chamberlain returned home in triumph. The roads from Heston aerodrome were thronged with cheering crowds. A similar sight greeted him at Buckingham Palace, where he made a balcony appearance to wild acclaim, urged forward by a grateful King. A *Times* reporter outside the Palace summed up the mood of the nation. He described the mass of people as having 'their hearts full of relief and a deep sense of thankfulness towards the man who had lifted a great weight of anxiety from their minds'.

There were a handful of spectres at the feast. The following evening, Robert attended a party given by Diana and Greville Worthington, friends met through the Sykes family. It was the day when Germany, under the terms of the agreement, was to march into the Sudetenland. Robert decided to stage his own demonstration, as a fellow guest recalled: 'Robert Byron took up a firm station immediately beyond Diana and Greville, and wiped the smile off every guest's face with the abrupt demand, "Are you proud to be English tonight?"'

The sham of Munich was self-evident to witnesses of the German advance. Virginia Cowles had flown to Prague in anticipation of war. After the agreement, she stayed on long enough to report Hitler's entry into Carlsbad. Arriving in the town, she caught sight of Rohan Butler standing behind a long line of SS men. He was covering the story for *The Times*, and had already been through the first three zones of occupation with the German army. The experience had been so depressing that he could scarcely summon a smile of greeting. His pessimism was justified. The International Boundary Commission, currently mapping out the fifth zone, was under German domination. Its ruling, enforced ten days after Munich, ensured that the total area surrendered was greater than that originally demanded at Godesberg.

Over the next few months, Robert continued to pursue his interest in propaganda. He produced a short note on the technical problems thrown up by the Munich exercise, and he kept in close touch with Tallents in the hope of securing a job in any future agency. Unfortunately, Tallents was himself losing influence, as the Ministry of Information returned to its shadowy existence and ministries reclaimed responsibility for their own propaganda. When responsibility for enemy propaganda passed back to the Foreign Office, its first victim was Tallents, who was summarily dismissed from his post of Director-General designate.

Not all doors were closed to Robert. An *éminence grise*, Sir Campbell Stuart, invited him to dinner. Stuart had been responsible for propaganda during the last war, and had been secretly recalled by the Prime Minister in March 1938 to help plan for any future emergency. One of Tallents' roles had been to act as his official persona. Although Stuart encouraged him to talk, Robert was uncertain how much to reveal of his propaganda activities. Instead, he discussed the issues of the day, particularly the editorial line of *The Times*. As a director of the paper and an old friend of the proprietor, his host had a close interest in the subject. 'I told him', Robert reported to his mother, 'that it was difficult to suppose the Times was not in German pay. I don't know if this was a success or not.' It proved an unproductive line in chat. A subsequent meeting went some way to retrieve the situation, but ultimately Stuart felt unable to make use of Robert's considerable talents as a propagandist.

Meanwhile, the prosaic world of Robert's business career lifted him from the fevered atmosphere of Europe. On 19 October, he sailed for New York on a fact-finding mission for the Petroleum Information Bureau.

29

Crisis Pending

Arriving on 25 October, Robert spent the first ten days in New York under the wing of a manager appointed to help him plan his itinerary. One of his current projects, a report on the expropriation of foreign-owned oil companies in Mexico, was examined by a head of publicity, who made various amendments to it. However, the representative of Shell in America, an Englishman named Wilkinson, was less helpful, taking the view that a 'junior associate' had no business to be concerned with such matters of policy as the crisis in Mexico. He also warned him against going to stay with Victor Mallet, Counsellor at the British Embassy in Washington, claiming it would arouse American suspicion. Robert told him curtly: 'I dislike being given a job & then prevented from doing it.' As regards Mallet, whom Robert had first met in Teheran, he informed him crushingly: 'it wd look very odd if I had to put off all the arrangements the Mallets have made. Victor M. is a very old friend of mine – [I] discussed the whole Mexican question at length with him last summer.'

Robert's address book had also provided him with an excellent billet in New York. Stepping off the ship, he had been whisked uptown in Mrs Otto Kahn's Rolls-Royce to her apartment in Sutton Place. Since first staying with her, at Upham Pope's behest, three years earlier, the two had become firm friends, and that summer had met frequently in London. As her guest, he was made to feel thoroughly at home, accompanying her most evenings to either the theatre or the ballet. After a weekend party on Long Island he was driven home at 3 in the morning by Mr and Mrs Irving Berlin.

Following a social weekend with the Mallets, Robert headed south for Houston on the first of a series of train journeys, which would take him across America and back.

At Houston, three days were spent inspecting oil fields, workers' housing, coastal drilling, and the massive Baytown refinery. 'This coastal country is very fascinating . . .' he wrote home, 'all the trees hung with gt. festoons of Spanish moss, lots of birds, rather seedy cowboys driving cattle among the oil fields . . . Huge copper coloured butterflies that settle on the innumerable motors as though they were flowers.'

On the train to the west coast, a journey stretching over three nights, Robert befriended an aspiring film star called Bill Null. Not surprisingly the young man was much exercised over the choice of a screen name. He thought 'Robert Byron' ideal and threatened to purloin it. News of this outrage reached Tom Driberg at the *Daily Express*, who reported in the William Hickey gossip column that the real Robert Byron was thinking of taking out insurance at Lloyd's against the theft of his name.

After a round of oil fields and installations in southern California Robert's impression was of 'a country where the victory of man over nature has been too violent – too sudden . . . I am uncomfortable. I like the balance to be equal: man triumphant in a motor car is not my ideal of man . . . I want the solitude of Asia or the civilized instincts of a Mediterranean crowd. But this, I fear, stamps me at 33 as the child of a past age.'

At a personal level, the oilmen were looking after him well, so much so that his attitude to Americans mellowed; he listed their strengths as 'reasonableness, helpfulness, good nature, personal independence'. However, after four consecutive nights on the train, gloom set in: 'I am bored at the idea of more oilfields,' he moaned, 'I don't know what more I can get out of them.' Fortunately, the tour was reaching its conclusion. A few more days of interviews and site visits brought the bulk of his researches to an end. The following week, after a month away, Robert returned to New York. A few days later, on 10 December, he left on the SS *Aquitaine*, bound for France.

His parents were waiting for him in Paris. The Byrons, in a bid to save money, were planning to let Overton and winter in Neuilly. After a brief reunion, Robert returned to London for a week at his desk before setting off to spend Christmas with Lucy and Rohan in Berlin. Part of his luggage consisted of 'a huge plush football with bells inside it', destined for Georgia, his five-month-old niece. Predictably, German customs officials suspected a bomb, delaying his arrival in Berlin until the early hours of Christmas morning.

The Butlers had moved into a spacious flat in a large house in a respectable quarter of the city overlooking the River Spree. The interior had been stylishly arranged by Lucy with a scattering of Biedermeier furniture hired from a repository. A blue and white porcelain stove in the drawing room added to the comfort and charm. Robert found that his sister had blossomed. 'She has suddenly grown up', he told his mother, '& is losing some of her diffidence . . . She is on top of things in Berlin. In America things were on top of her.' A frequent visitor to the same house was Dr Goebbels, the presiding genius of Hitler's propaganda ministry, whose mother happened to live on the ground floor. Once Lucy sent her German maid down to pass him on the steps. She returned with the news that 'Herr Doktor stinks of scent.'

On Christmas day Virginia Cowles, who was passing through Berlin on her way to Russia, joined the party. After dinner, they ended up at the Golden Horseshoe, a nightclub where the dance floor was ringed by a dirt track occupied by three circus horses which the clientele could ride for a mark. It was a far cry from the 1920s when, as Robert noted, the premises had been occupied by the Eldorado Club, the most famous haunt of homosexuals in Berlin.

Robert and Lucy found the temptation to ride the horses too much to resist. Both in evening dress, they cut a dashing pair. Lucy was wearing a long blue satin dress, which spread over her horse's tail like the caparison of a medieval knight. Their many seasons on the hunting field stood them in good stead. As the riding-master cracked his whip, they broke into a spectacular gallop. Lucy, in particular, caused a sensation, her dress billowing behind her in a blue cloud. A storm trooper at the next table shook his head: 'We will never understand the English,' he told Virginia, 'they always do the thing you least expect.'

The persecution of the Jews was being pursued with added

ferocity. On the night of 9 November, known ever since as Kristallnacht, Jewish property throughout Germany had been looted and destroyed. Many Jews were murdered, thousands were rounded up, and heavy fines were imposed to pay for the damage. At the same time, a decree forbade Jews from engaging in economic activity. An exhibition, entitled 'The Wandering Jew', opened in the Reichstag in Berlin. Many of Germany's greatest writers, scientists and intellectuals were pilloried, their images displayed against black draped walls. The list included Heine, Walter Rathenau, the post-war statesman, and Einstein. Also on display was a photograph showing Jewish 'enemies of the state' in Dachau concentration camp.

Robert visited the exhibition with Lucy just before leaving Berlin. The experience left him in no doubt as to the fight ahead. 'It confirmed more vividly than any previous experience', he wrote later that day, 'that there can be no compromise with these people, that there is not room in the world for them & oneself & that one or the other must go under.' He told Lucy that the 'technique of showmanship' reminded him of the anti-God museums in Russia. She asked him why the German version was worse. He explained: 'it seemed to me quite legitimate to argue over the Virgin Birth – but . . . an anti-Jew exhibition is an attack on humanity itself – by which I mean, on that . . . which enables [man] to conceive & apprehend God.' Despairingly, he added: 'Has any people ever sunk so low . . .?' Voicing his disgust at the exhibition to Christopher Sykes shortly after his return, he announced: 'I shall have warmonger put on my passport.' It was not long before Christopher himself was at the receiving end of Robert's belligerence. The trigger was his anti-Zionist stand on the Palestinian question, viewed by Robert as treachery to the anti-Nazi cause.

Back in London, Robert's professional duties took second place to his preoccupation with current affairs. His trip to America had been largely designed to furnish material for articles on the oil industry commissioned by *The Times*. But Robert put off the task, choosing instead to produce a long report on America's attitude towards the outside world in the light of Munich. Throughout his travels, he had grilled anyone from oil managers to film stars, journalists and diplomats for their views. His snapshot of American opinion revealed a growing belief that isolationism was no longer possible; that if Britain was involved in a war, America would inevitably follow. The report, which his old patron, Sir Stephen Tallents, had encouraged him to write, stressed the importance of bolstering the alliance between the two countries. In the near future, he predicted, 'the goodwill of the United States may prove a matter of life and death to the British Empire and the principles on which it rests.'

Any flaws in the historic relationship, his argument ran, could be smoothed over by subtle use of propaganda. A golden opportunity was the forthcoming visit to America by King George VI and Queen Elizabeth. His interviewees had universally welcomed the news 'as a gesture against the dictators'. However, he warned of America's obsession with the Windsors: 'Many people', he reported, 'treasure the gramophone record of the Duke's abdication speech as a romantic possession.' Robert harboured no such feelings. He had listened to the broadcast on the night of the abdication in 1936, and had pronounced it 'a miserable performance'.

The final section of his report offered advice on influencing the American press in advance of the royal visit. He recommended that any related literature 'or other propaganda' should explain the constitutional role of the King, making clear that his personal freedom, particularly 'doing as he likes with his private life', would always be curtailed. Ideally, the King and Queen should be portrayed as 'active hardworking partners in a joint defence of the rights of man'. This, he suggested, would redress any lingering grievance felt on behalf of the Windsors.

A copy of the report landed on the desk of Jock Balfour, Acting Counsellor in the Foreign Office with America as his special area of responsibility. Another was sent by Sir Stephen Tallents to Sir Alexander Hardinge, the King's Private Secretary. So effective was the distribution, G. M. Young assured Robert, that 'wherever the K**g turns, someone respectfully hands him a copy.' Comment surrounding the monarch's visit later that summer took a similar line to Robert's. 'It is everywhere accepted', reported *The Times*, 'that the visit is personal and symbolical, and the newspapers are at pains to explain the difference in the Constitutional position of the King and President.'

With the report out of the way, Robert was free to concentrate on his articles for *The Times*. Unfortunately, all inspiration now deserted him. After two arid months, Robert was forced to admit to Colonel Medlicott that 'I have got to the point where I cannot write a word.' Acting on doctor's orders, he took a fortnight's holiday in Ireland. The tonic worked: two articles were produced on his return, part descriptive, part technical, illustrating the impact of the oil industry on the American way of life.

The source of Robert's paralysis had been identified by a colleague in the Information Bureau, E. F. Richardson. 'I am quite sure', he consoled him, 'that the political situation is more than anything else responsible for your despondency.' Robert had good reason to despair. On the morning of 15 March, German troops had entered Prague unopposed. The disintegration of Czechoslovakia left her erstwhile President with no room to manoeuvre. Presented with an ultimatum by Hitler, he had signed a communiqué placing 'the destiny of the Czech people and country with confidence in the hands of the German Reich'.

Initially, Chamberlain avoided outright condemnation of Germany. 'I cannot believe', he said, 'that anything of the kind which has now taken place was contemplated by any of the signatories to the Munich Agreement at the time of its signature.' He reiterated his determination to seek peace through discussion rather than force. Two days later, however, his rhetoric had stiffened. At a speech in Birmingham, he warned the German Chancellor that 'any attempt to dominate the world by force would be resisted by this nation.'

Following the broadcast, Robert wrote to his mother:

> I could not help feeling that it was the most complete justification of my attitude during the last 3 years that could possibly have been uttered. Not that this is any satisfaction. I find that the average conservative has begun to realize that

> the blood of millions will probably be on his head in the next few months if not the next few days. Damn their stupid souls.

Shortly after the seizure of Prague a prominent appeaser, sitting opposite Robert at the Beefsteak Club, began praising the Prime Minister's achievements in extravagant terms. Robert, his impatience mounting, leant across the table and asked him a question. The speaker, appearing not to hear, or at least to misunderstand, continued with his panegyric. Robert's next interjection was loud and clear. Letting loose one of his favourite insults, he demanded: 'Are you in German pay?'

In fact, Chamberlain was on the point of abandoning appeasement. Beset with rumours of Hitler's next target, he announced in the Commons, on 31 March, that Britain would support Poland in the event of any threat to her independence. Scarcely was the ink dry on the agreement than another vulnerable nation fell to a Fascist dictator. On 7 April, Mussolini invaded Albania. Two further pledges, to Romania and Greece, were swiftly issued by Britain.

Even before the Polish Guarantee, Robert had written to the Minister of Labour offering to speak on behalf of the National Service Campaign, set up to support the introduction of conscription. A few weeks later, his search for a suitable job in the run-up to war began in earnest. His best hope lay with D. B. Woodburn, a contact in the Civil Service Commission, who was acquainted with his propaganda work at the time of Munich. Turning to him for advice, he dropped the fact of 'the rather special position I occupy in Greece owing to my name & books'. At first, Woodburn held out considerable grounds for hope, but, a few weeks later, these were dashed. The rejection letter, received at the end of May, came with the dismal sop: 'we have you on our list.'

Away from politics, another target for Robert's agitation at this time were the authorities of the British Museum. Early in 1939 rumours had begun to circulate with hints in the press that some damage had been done to the Elgin Marbles. On 14 May, Robert raised the alarm in a letter to the *Sunday Times* calling for a statement to be made in Parliament. It emerged that Lord Duveen, who had paid for a gallery to house the marbles, had requested that they be cleaned. Robert had recently inspected the marbles and claimed: 'It is not necessary to be an authority on Greek sculpture to see that the cleaning process . . . has not restored them to their original appearance . . . The lumps of stone remain, robbed of life, dead as casts.' Three days later the museum admitted that 'unauthorized methods' had been introduced for cleaning. However, the statement went on to reassure readers that 'To anyone but an expert their effect is imperceptible.' *The Times* expressed its satisfaction in a leader, but a report the next day in the *Daily Express* confirmed the worst fears. The cleaner in charge admitted to using a blunt copper tool to remove some of the dirt. 'Some of them were as black with dirt as that grate.'

Writing again in the *Sunday Times*, Robert argued that as the museum claimed they had not been injured by unauthorized methods, then 'the methods which have in fact succeeded in removing the entire patina of the marble and the last remaining traces of ancient colour must presumably be those which the museum authorities did authorize.' He claimed that the marbles had now 'lost their virtue', and he called for a more explicit account to be given. Robert took his cause to Parliament, drafting questions for MPs to put to various ministers. One was accepted, concerning whether payment of the work had been undertaken by the museum or the donor of the new gallery. The answer was the museum. On 28 May Sir Frederick Kenyon, a past director of the British Museum, accused Robert of gross exaggeration, and hinted that he could not tell the difference between a cast and an original.

Meanwhile, Robert continued to cause mayhem at fashionable gatherings across London. One of his most devastating attacks occurred at the end of a dinner when the men of the party were sitting over their port. Predictably, an argument was soon raging between Robert and two eminent guests over the Government's ability to handle the approaching crisis. On the sidelines sat Christopher Sykes, who was to recall the final exchange. Robert, grim with anger, rounded on one of his opponents with the words: 'What you mean is that in spite of Munich, in spite of everything that's happened since that surrender, in spite of all the passes being sold, you still believe in a British guarantee.'

'Yes I do,' came the reply.

Robert filled his glass with port before delivering the *coup de grâce*. 'I'd like very much', he went on in his deadly voice, 'to have you under a glass case with a pin stuck through you. I'd have a label tied round your neck. I'd show you to people with strong stomachs. A perfect specimen of the British ruling class today.'

No putative member of the 'British ruling class' was safe from Robert's broadsides. Hostilities had first been declared in the *New Statesman* in March 1938 as part of his call to arms following the *Anschluss*. The 'English governing class . . .' he argued, 'in so far as it now dictates our policy, has taken a wrong turning, has begun to prefer what it thinks its own interests to those of its country.' In short, the Conservative Party had been 'seduced by the cares of property' away from 'the simpler programme of freedom'. A celebrated variant of this theme, as reported in the *Evening Standard*, was his retort to Henry 'Chips' Channon, the American-born MP, who was a besotted adherent of the Prime Minister. Hearing him sing the praises of the Fascist dictators, Robert observed caustically: 'I see you put your adopted class before your adopted country.'

By the summer of 1939, Robert had become a liability in polite society, so much so that even Nancy Mitford, an implacable opponent of Fascism, banned him from her bridge parties. 'Pity you're so red', she lectured her bosom friend. 'I have had to supply Paul Hislop as a MALE BRIDGER on account of you being no longer suitable.'

Christopher Sykes captured the nightmare of Robert's life at this period. He spoke of him as a man 'persistently haunted by the monstrosities which his clear vision could not allow him to disregard for a single second'. His suffering was intense, as Sykes explained:

> There is a point where heightened intelligence incurs anguish, where the too-seeing eye and the too-sensitive ear inflict sometimes unendurable pain. Many great artists and men of abnormally capacious mind have paid this price for the

bounty of the gods, and I believe that Robert, endowed as few are, belonged in his later days to this enviable though unhappy company.

To make matters worse, home life in Wiltshire offered no solace. This was largely of his own making. By the summer of 1938, Robert's relentless complaints about Overton had successfully undermined his parents' confidence in their pleasant house, and between them, they had begun looking for an alternative.

The house-hunting even extended to other counties. In Northamptonshire, a derelict eighteenth-century folly known as the Menagerie caught Robert's eye. The building had first come to his attention via the Georgian Group, which had expressed concern over its future. Jim Lees-Milne was taken by Robert to inspect it. They were greeted on arrival by a cow looking out of a window. However, according to Jim, 'in the central chamber enough was left of an exquisite rococo ceiling and walls to intoxicate Robert's love of the audacious in architectural composition . . . It became for Robert his Eldorado, the golden citadel, the dream which would be realized only when the loathed dictators were vanquished, the war was over and sanity had returned to the world.'

In the meantime, the problem of 'Nightmare Hall', as Robert dubbed Overton, remained. Just to confuse matters, he suddenly changed his mind about the house, having made a flying visit when his parents were away in France. 'Inside . . .' he reported to his mother, 'the house looks extraordinarily nice . . . I saw it all with a new eye. I must say I don't like it any better – it cd. never be a home – but I can't help considering if it mightn't be wiser for you to stay on there a bit.' But by now it was too late. His father was convinced that the upkeep was beyond his meagre income. Robert offered to contribute to the running costs, but the sum required proved too steep.

Eric Byron's resources were no match for his son's high architectural standards. The problem came to a head when Robert alighted enthusiastically upon Marshwood House, an eighteenth-century building situated in the Wiltshire village of Dinton. The price was £1,500. Faced with finding such a sum, Eric had to come clean over his finances. '[I] am sorry the make of houses is so important to you,' he wrote plaintively to Robert. 'It is almost true to say that such a house would absorb all my remaining free capital . . . next year my financial position will inevitably be such that Ma & I must have a cottage. It's got to come. Short of someone's death, it must be.'

Providentially, Eric's finances were indeed saved by a death in the family. That autumn, his eldest brother, Thomas, died in Canada, leaving him a share of his estate. The need to sell Overton was removed.

Throughout this time of uncertainty, Margaret Byron had borne the brunt of her son's ill humour. To all appearances, his affection remained unquestioned. Every letter was warmed with the habitual terms of endearment. 'Darling Mib', he would begin, invariably ending: 'Good bye darling Best love Bob'. He also cherished her in other ways. After their unhappy sojourn in France, which had proved unsuccessful owing to the expense and his parents falling ill, Robert helped pay for his mother's ticket to Berlin, enabling her to visit Lucy. But in Wiltshire, it was another matter. There, his thin-skinned behaviour hurt her deeply.

Pained beyond endurance, Margaret Byron summed up their shared misery in a letter written after one such visit:

> I feel worried beyond words about you my darling – you don't seem yourself – are you never happy now darling? And I feel so dumb when you give me anything to read, you have so often snubbed me, I can't express what I feel . . . But you are not a bit *certain* you want to live at home any more are you – oh I wish so many things for you – I wish you had a real house of your own – I wish I knew what you really want – it seems to me a coil – we can't get what you'd like unless you contribute, & you don't want to contribute unless you really like it & have plenty of room.

In contrast to the country, Robert's accommodation in London provided him with a civilized retreat. Since March

1938, he had rented part of a small white-fronted Georgian house, set back from the street behind high railings, at 1 Swan Walk overlooking the Physick Gardens in Chelsea. His landlady, Mrs Clarke, a semi-invalid who spent long periods abroad, proved most obliging, even allowing members of the family to use spare bedrooms on her side of the house. An added attraction was the small garden planted with fruit trees including almond and pear. His life became even more agreeable with the arrival of Fay, a highly respectable manservant, proficient at cooking, valeting and coping with telephone calls. In February 1939, Robert signalled his satisfaction with these arrangements by renewing the lease for a further year.

Early on in the tenancy, Robert had lured Jim Lees-Milne to join him as a lodger. Until then, Jim had been renting a bed-sitting room in a house in Cheyne Walk filled with other indigent but respectable young people of both sexes. With a familiar snarl, Robert insisted upon a more sinister interpretation, inviting Jim to leave 'that refined brothel' in favour of his more commodious premises. The arrangement only lasted a few difficult weeks before Jim was told to 'get back' to his original lodgings.

One year on, the pleasures of peace were increasingly overcast by the growing certainty of war. Even so, the 1939 London season drew to a close with a burst of glamorous parties, principal among them the Georgian Ball and Fête Champêtre held on 13 July at Osterley Park, Lord Jersey's magnificent seat on the western outskirts of London. The house, celebrated for its state rooms and majestic 'double' portico by Robert Adam, forms the centrepiece of an eighteenth-century Arcadian landscape, dotted with ornamental buildings and laced by a string of serpentine lakes.

Jersey had decided to open the house to the public and allowed the Georgian Group to announce the news at its first annual general meeting. This scoop produced excellent coverage of the Group's activities in the press. Concurrently, inquiries had been put in train into the holding of another ball. The idea had been suggested by Robert as part of his ceaseless campaign to attract new members to the group. Originally, Mecklenburgh Square had been the preferred venue; however, after some delay the residents turned down the request. Cancellation of the ball seemed inevitable until Lord Jersey stepped into the breach offering Osterley for the occasion.

Once again Queen Mary graciously consented to be patron. Grandees, scholars, writers and artists were persuaded to join the committee; press releases were issued; posters and circulars were produced; a costumier was appointed to assist with fancy dress; motor coaches from central London were laid on; even a reduced price dinner for ball-goers was offered by the Hyde Park Hotel. Over 1,000 tickets were sold.

On the night, London Society danced to Jack Harris's Band in a huge marquee in the courtyard. It was decorated on a rustic theme with 'sheaves of ripening corn and surrealist equine bustos'. The designers were Oliver Messel and his old friend Felix Harbord, an artist-decorator inspired by all things Georgian. The sideshows run by John Sutro included wrestling, darts and a palm-reader known as the Alchemist. At midnight, a firework display cascaded over the principal lake to the accompaniment of Handel's *Water Music*. The musicians, moored on a raft, were dressed as eighteenth-century peasantry.

Although fancy dress was not compulsory, many guests obeyed the request of the organizers to 'wear eighteenth-century dress as a tribute to the Romantic Period in which the house was built'. Lord Jersey himself appeared in a costume copied from the portrait of his banking ancestor, Francis Child, considered at the time to have been Adam's patron at Osterley. Lady Jersey, the American beauty and former film star Virginia Cherrill, ablaze with diamonds, performed her role as chatelaine in a silver and sky-blue brocade dress designed by Oliver Messel. Many ladies dyed or powdered their hair and wore 'rats'. Anne Rosse, who never did things by halves, coloured not only her hair but also her eyelids and eyelashes blue. In keeping with the pastoral theme, Nancy Mitford had an air of the 'Petit Trianon' about her with a panniered dress of white satin with blue bows and a flowered headdress. Camilla Sykes, Christopher's beautiful wife, was resplendent in a 'Gainsborough' hat, whilst Cecil Beaton glittered in a toile de jouy frock coat and floral knee breeches. Robert did not stint over his appearance. His crowning glory was a wig, hired, along with assistance at putting it on, for a guinea from L. Gustave, 'Private, historical and theatrical wig maker'.

But the sensation of the evening proved to be the loss by Lady Jersey of a diamond and sapphire bracelet. Private detectives mingling with the crowd were immediately informed, and the following day a detective inspector from Scotland Yard descended upon the grounds with his squad to comb the debris. The popular press also flocked to the scene drawn by the irresistible combination of crime and high society. The most likely explanation was that a loose clasp had caused the bracelet to fall from the Countess's wrist as she brushed against her own or some other period costume, but the *Daily Express* added spice to the story by drawing parallels to the loss of fur capes reported recently from other grand parties. For an instant, the ball was headline news. Illumined, thus, in the flashlight of notoriety, the Georgian Group took a final swaggering bow before the curtain came crashing down upon its world.

At the beginning of July, the march towards war had suddenly gathered pace. The focus was Danzig where large numbers of German 'tourists' had begun to arrive from the Reich, as well as quantities of arms brought in under the noses of Polish customs officers. In the House of Commons, Chamberlain felt compelled to reaffirm Britain's pledge 'to give our assistance to Poland in the case of [a] clear threat to her independence'. Any attempt on Danzig, he made clear, would qualify for such action. In London, the expectation of war was heightened by the staging of a trial 'Black Out' in preparation for bombing raids.

Against this backdrop, Robert packed his bags and left on 18 August for a holiday in Northern Ireland. Although anticipating war, he was in escapist mood: 'please don't write unless it is v. necessary,' he instructed his father. 'I don't want to hear about the war or Berlin or anything of that sort.'

His travelling companion was a French bulldog puppy which had been reserved for him by Nancy Mitford from a litter born to her beloved bitch, Millie. The new arrival, originally called Agnes but swiftly renamed Sarah, came with the warmest recommendation from her proud breeder: 'Really Agnes is such a pet', clucked Nancy, 'I can hardly bear to let her go – couldn't to anyone but you . . . She is very anti-appeasement.' For the voyage to Ireland, Sarah travelled with her own trunk 'full of biscuits, cutlery, cushions, plates & rubber bones'.

Their destination was a cottage at Glenarm, the estate belonging to the Earl and Countess of Antrim. The Antrims had become firm friends with Robert over the past few years through Christopher Sykes, who was Angela Antrim's brother. This was Robert's second visit to them that year; he had already stayed with them for part of his rest-cure in the spring. Angela Antrim had trained as a sculptor, first in Brussels and later at the British School in Rome. Since then her career had met with growing success, including an exhibition at the Beaux Arts Gallery and numerous private commissions. Well travelled on the Continent, she had developed an unshakeable loathing of Fascism.

In Northern Ireland, most of Angela's creative energy was devoted to undoing the disastrous redecoration of Glenarm Castle by her mother-in-law after a fire had gutted the interior in 1928. Angela had turned to Robert for help and together, that spring, they had conceived a grandiose design enriched with giant caryatids, bas-reliefs and neo-baroque marbling. An inscription was also planned stating that the work was undertaken as a distraction from the horrors of Chamberlain's premiership.

That August, Glenarm brimmed with guests. Robert's arrival coincided with a large house party up at the castle including the Harrods, the Worthingtons and Cyril Connolly. After a few days, Connolly returned to England, whilst the others set off with the Antrims on a motor trip to the South leaving Robert in splendid isolation at his cottage in the deer park. But the outside world could not be kept at bay for long. The announcement of an impending German-Soviet pact signalled the final lurch towards war. Even before the documents were signed, Hitler had made plain to the British Ambassador that Germany would no longer 'allow her vital space and vital interests to be prejudiced by the British guarantee'.

With events moving towards a climax, both Houses of Parliament met on 24 August to pass the Emergency Powers Bill. 'The crisis has supervened rather sooner than I calculated . . .' Robert wrote to his mother. 'I still think it is possible that there will be a last minute wriggle on someone's part that will provide an escape.' This fragile hope offered scant comfort. 'It is very beautiful', he continued, 'as I sit here looking out across the valley, with a terraced lawn and roses in front and the sound of the river. But I must confess I feel depressed.'

His thoughts turned to Lucy who had remained resolutely in Berlin with her young daughter throughout August, not leaving until the 25th, after a friend, a baron from one of the Baltic states, urged her to get out. Rohan timed his departure even more finely. He escaped to Denmark only twenty-four hours before Hitler launched his 'blitzkrieg' against Poland. At news of the invasion, Robert delivered his verdict on the conduct of Britain's foreign policy over the past few years: 'Appeasement', he remarked, 'seems to have had its final success.'

Britain did not declare war until two days later. Listening to Chamberlain's broadcast on 3 September along with the rest of the party at Glenarm, Robert was in robust mood. 'Well, there's one thing to be thankful for . . .' he observed, 'the post-war decadence ought to be even better than the last one.'

30

Called to Arms

Immediately on his return to England at the outbreak of war, Robert sprang into action in search of a job. Strings were pulled, letters written, interviews arranged. A conversation at the Foreign Office was followed up with a personal memorandum citing his unique qualifications for undertaking propaganda work in Greece, not least his name, his books and his past championship of the Dodecanese. Predictably, these compelling arguments fell on deaf ears. The War Office proved more receptive to his advances. Presuming on 'a slight acquaintance' with Leslie Hore-Belisha, the Minister for War, Robert offered his services as someone trained 'to observe, analyse and state facts, and if necessary to draw deductions'. Here, his reports on the Afghan road system, German propaganda and American public opinion were brought into play. A week or so later, an interview was arranged with an officer in Military Intelligence. It took place in the overcrowded conditions of the War Office where, according to Robert, 'the squalor was Crimean' with old beds and mattresses filling the passages. His interviewer expressed tentative interest in Robert's capabilities, modifying his enthusiasm with the query: 'I don't know that we can very well have another Old Etonian in this room.' For whatever reason, no position at the War Office was immediately forthcoming.

As a stopgap, Robert decided to join the European News Department at the BBC. The work involved composing propaganda bulletins to be translated for broadcast overseas. After only a few weeks, the Corporation was pressing him to sign a contract, but Robert procrastinated. Apart from the War Office, he was also waiting to hear from the Ministry of Information, having put to them an idea for a series of lectures 'to inform the peoples of the Empire what they are fighting for'. Past endeavours, such as his tour for the British Council to the Baltic and elsewhere, lent authority to the proposal. But his trump card was linking the lectures to his authorship of an unpublished book on the very same question. 'I have thus given . . .' he asserted, 'intense thought to the analysis and simplification of the issues now at stake and could expound them in terms intelligible to everyone.' The men from the Ministry were impressed. Accordingly, a synopsis was dispatched for their perusal.

The book had originated twelve months earlier on Robert's long train journeys across America. Its writing had continued intermittently until the outbreak of war, by which time only about half the planned chapters had been completed. Nevertheless, Robert presented Harold Macmillan with an optimistic assessment of his progress to date: 'I have nearly finished that political essay . . .' he told him, '& it has now turned into a book. The bulk of it is applicable to the present time in that it shows people not only what they are fighting against but what they are fighting for. It is the latter that needs making clear.'

His answer was a vision of a new world order, governed not by political expediency but by a God-given principle capable of inducing a 'law above states'. The first espousal of this 'emanation of wisdom' had been the sanctions imposed by the League of Nations upon Italy. Although a failure, they provided concrete evidence of a 'principle of association' operating between states. This principle sprang, at one level, from man's age-old desire to pursue a communal life; and at another, from his spiritual aspiration to achieve a greater good. Lasting peace had never been delivered, because, as he argued: 'so long as a number of societies, each enjoying sovereign rights, are in active contact with one another, yet possess no law to regulate their contact, those societies are in a state of potential anarchy.' Now, however, there was a chance to break the destructive pattern of history. It lay in the creation of an international law, fair and enforceable, founded upon the 'principle of association'. His revolutionary plan, which at this stage of the book's composition still lacked definition, envisaged 'an improved League' with the character of a federation.

Robert's prose style matched the earnestness of his theme:

'[it] is very quiet & even . . .' he informed Macmillan, 'there is no abuse & hardly any sarcasm.' Unfortunately, his lapse into good manners did not make for light reading. On receiving the synopsis, his contact at the ministry, H. V. Hodson, was less than enthusiastic: 'the highly theoretical nature of the early part of the book', he opined, 'renders it doubtful whether a very large circulation could be secured.' All talk of a lecture tour was subsequently dropped. So too, for the time being, was any suggestion from the War Office of a job with Military Intelligence. Thus, at the end of October, Robert was left with no alternative but to commit himself to the BBC.

Some consolation was to be drawn from the fact that, by this time, he had found a political platform in tune with his views. It was the Federal Union, a far-sighted organization born out of the failure of the League of Nations, which was already promoting a new system of international government for implementation once the war was won. The idea had germinated, spontaneously, on both sides of the Atlantic. But the seminal figure in its development was an American journalist, Clarence Streit, who, in his book, *Union Now*, published in March 1939, suggested that a union of democracies should now be formed, comprising the United States, the British Commonwealth, France, the Netherlands, Switzerland and the Scandinavian countries. National sovereignty, he proposed, should be conceded in five fields where 'common government' would 'clearly serve man's freedom better than separate governments' – namely, citizenship, defence, trade, money and communication. Home affairs would remain the prerogative of each democracy 'according to its own customs . . . whether by republic or kingdom'. 'The Union's existing and potential power from the outset', he argued, 'would be so gigantic, its bulk so vast, its vital centres so scattered, that Germany, Italy and Japan even put together could no more dream of attacking it than Mexico dreams of attacking the American Union now.'

The book became an immediate best-seller. Groups were formed across America championing the cause, whilst in Britain the home-grown version, already known as the Federal Union, saw its membership soar. Founded shortly before Munich by a handful of concerned individuals, the movement had, from the start, advocated an almost identical solution to Streit's. Propaganda was disseminated from an office in Bloomsbury under the direction of Charles Kimber, a young man who had previously been attached to Colonel Medlicott's committee lobbying on behalf of the oil companies. As such, Kimber was an old ally of Robert's. He asked Robert for help in approaching Macmillan about publishing a book on the Federal Union.

Hard at work on his own political essay, Robert, in turn, tapped Kimber for information. He responded with nothing but praise for Robert's theories: 'the more people I talk to on this Federal Union stunt,' he wrote, 'the more apparent it becomes that you've got hold of the question that is at the back of all their minds.' So far, he admitted, one of the best-received ideas coincided with Robert's own: 'that there should be an international constitution . . . In fact your approach rather than that of our present memorandum.'

With both thinking along the same lines, it was only a matter of time before Robert threw in his lot with the Federal Union. The perfect opportunity occurred at the end of August when he was invited to take part in a wireless discussion on the subject along with Clarence Streit and Sir Alfred Zimmern. The programme, scheduled for 12 September, was to be broadcast in both Britain and America. On the day, Robert did not actually meet Streit, who expounded his views direct from New York. However they spoke as allies, whilst Zimmern, the Professor of International Relations at Oxford, opposed them. The advance notice in the *Radio Times* billed Robert as 'adviser on public relations to the Union'.

His original script, which had to be cut to fit the programme, boldly tackled the issue of national sovereignty. The Federal Parliament, he emphasized, unlike the League of Nations, would be empowered to enact laws binding on all states equally. Priority would be given to the formation of an armed force 'sufficient to keep order among the states . . . and to resist any attack . . . from outside'. The other immediate subject for federal legislation would be the unification of the financial system 'which', Robert stated, 'means some form of common currency or banking system'. The safety net underlying these revolutionary proposals would be the democratic nature of the Union. All members of the Federal Parliament, he emphasized, must be elected by popular vote. 'If they are nominated by governments,' he explained, 'as happened in the case of the League, they become simply the agents of their separate governments, in other words diplomats.' Universal suffrage, by contrast, would engender in every individual 'a direct and personal loyalty to the union as well as his own country'. The difficulties were enormous, he admitted: 'it isn't easy to get used to the idea of one's own country surrendering a part of its sovereignty to an international parliament composed largely of foreigners.' But what was the alternative? Apart from living in a state of perpetual war, there was none. 'The time is coming,' he concluded, 'slowly perhaps . . . when all the nations that want peace in the world will be prepared to contribute to the maintenance of peace. Our job now is to think out a scheme in advance which will enable them to do so.'

At a conference in Oxford, held shortly after the broadcast, Robert was elected to the governing council of the Federal Union. The position was by no means purely honorary. In fact, an urgent task, ideally suited to his skills, awaited him. It was to establish a club in London, which could provide a focus of metropolitan support in the otherwise regional organization.

Friends were immediately mobilized to get the idea off the ground. Astutely, he invited Sir Michael Assheton-Smith Bt., known as Michael Duff, to become membership secretary. Duff knew *le tout Londres* and the minutes of an early committee meeting acknowledged his usefulness. Two other stalwarts on the committee were Michael Rosse, who became chairman, and John Sutro. The latter, who had remained a constant friend of Robert's over the years, successfully negotiated a share in the magazine *World Review* to gain a voice for the Federal Union on the bookstalls.

On hearing of Robert's recruitment activities, Angela Antrim noted drily that he 'seems to have collected some particularly unimpressive supporters: playboys, nitwits and philanderers – but of course Gentlemen'. The Antrims' adherence to the Federal Union predated the war. Until then, Ran

Antrim had contented himself with leaping to its defence in the pages of the press, but now he pursued a more ambitious strategy. Through blatant string-pulling, he gained an interview with the Foreign Secretary to brief him about their goals. His success was evident in Lord Halifax's broadcast to the nation on 7 November when he looked ahead to the post-war world. 'There are some', he said, 'who believe that the new order can only come through surrender in some measure by the nations of their sovereign rights in order to clear the way for some more organic union.' His speech was music to Angela Antrim's ears: 'but for the mention of the word Federal Union . . .' she wrote in her diary, 'he openly espoused its cause.'

Five days earlier, the Federal Union Club had been inaugurated at a cocktail party in borrowed offices in Brook Street. Robert, as the newly elected president, marked the occasion with a speech. As far as the party went, he reported to his mother, the evening was 'a wild success' although it had struck some guests such as the Bishop of Lichfield, who had come up specially from the country, as 'a little frivolous'. The atmosphere was caught in a cartoon drawn by Angela Antrim. One caption floating above the crowd reads: 'Champagne cocktails for our party don't you think?'

By December 1939, the committee had found a home for its growing band of members. Premises were acquired off the Junior Constitutional Club at 101 Piccadilly, which also provided the use of a large room for meetings. Robert had already been hard at work soliciting guest speakers. He succeeded in getting the MP, Richard Law, an ex-foreign correspondent, and Count Huyn, formerly the Press Attaché at the Austrian Legation. Officers from the Federal Union organization also spoke. Robert chaired both meetings. At the second, in January 1940, he rightly boasted of the Club's rapid achievements, but reminded his audience that 'it is absolutely imperative [to] increase our membership as quickly as possible if we are to become a really stable body destined to influence public opinion in this country.'

Inevitably, the fierce tide of war swept away any such ambition. The Club's activities, along with Robert's own involvement, grew more sporadic in succeeding months, until eventually, with the onset of air raids, all further meetings had to be suspended. Meanwhile, the Federal Union fell into increasing financial difficulties. Even so, Robert never lost faith in the movement. As late as October 1940, he agreed to broadcast once more on its behalf. Ever alert to the lessons of war, he spoke of the offer made by Churchill to the French that June, on the eve of their capitulation, to unite with Britain in common citizenship. The proposal, drafted in part by Jean Monnet, future founder of the Common Market, had suggested a single government with associated parliaments. 'So you see,' Robert argued, 'when I talk about Federal Union, it is not just a vision or a panacea . . . The present British Government was actually prepared at one moment to put into practice something very like it, and may one day perhaps be prepared to do so again.'

Escape from the BBC, variously labelled 'the beastly place' or 'that odious institution', was never far from Robert's mind. A post in Budapest was mentioned, but failed to materialize. A meeting at the Admiralty led nowhere. Suddenly, his line of communication with the War Office sprang to life. The upshot was an invitation in April to undergo a four-month course with the Officer Cadet Training Unit (OCTU). Since there was no guarantee of a job at the end of it, Robert was forced to weigh up the value of his work for the BBC.

In the process, he encountered stiff opposition at the prospect of his departure, particularly from diplomats involved with his broadcasting activities. As a result, he decided to stay. The challenge was now clear. 'I do feel', he told Rohan Butler, 'that the only way to get our propaganda going properly is for persons of independent judgement to speak their minds about it, and that to some extent I am in a position to do.' His new-found enthusiasm inspired a memorandum, sent to his friend Kenneth Clark, now Controller of Home Publicity at the Ministry of Information, outlining a strategy for transforming the propaganda machine from its current 'haphazard series of unrelated and often discordant individual efforts' into 'the full status of a war instrument, saving lives and limiting ruin'.

The target of Robert's verbal missiles was south-eastern

Europe, principally Romania and Hungary, both, until the autumn of 1940, neutral countries. His words, translated into the appropriate language, aimed to instil fear and suspicion into the hearts of listeners regarding the intentions of the Axis powers. After the 'Second Vienna Award', imposed by Germany and Italy upon Romania, which ceded part of Transylvania to Hungary, he avoided direct criticism of Count Teleki, the Hungarian premier. Rather, he warned Hungary of the imminent danger of political instability stirred by her restive German minorities. Furthermore, he predicted 'a rude awakening for the Hungarians when they discover the price the Axis will exact in food and material'. He went on: 'Hungary will find before long . . . that the Führer and the Duce intend for her no future but that of another slave state.' As a parting shot, Robert hinted that German troops were massing on the eastern frontier in preparation for a Russian invasion.

'News talks' directed at Romania covered the revolt of the Iron Guard, the abdication of King Carol II and the arrest of British oil men. Press censorship was attacked in both countries, as were the 'Lie Factories of Berlin and Rome'. Listeners were frequently reminded that only the broadcasts from London gave an accurate view of the course of the war.

In tandem with his propaganda work, Robert drew up a proposal for the formation of a 'Civil Infiltration Corps' with the goal of establishing resistance movements in occupied countries. For him, this type of activity was a logical development from his current role. 'The present opportunity . . .' he wrote in a related, unpublished article, 'demands the transformation of the propagandist into a professional combatant.' With his usual panache, he sent the document to a number of influential people, including Clementine Churchill. Thence, it reached the desk of the Prime Minister's Parliamentary Private Secretary, Desmond Morton, who informed her: 'there is no new idea in Mr Byron's note. Nevertheless it is interesting to find an independent person who has reached such intelligent conclusions.' One of Robert's contacts to receive details of the plan was Peter Fleming, himself engaged on training the first British resistance group in anticipation of a German invasion. Fleming duly forwarded Robert's proposal to the War Office.

Outside working hours, Robert reviewed books for the *Sunday Times* and *Country Life*, and continued to write and broadcast on the oil industry. Financially, however, his situation was parlous. Accumulated bills and demands from the Inland Revenue dating back to 1938 swiftly ate into his salary, even though this was topped up by the Petroleum Information Bureau to its pre-war level. There were attempts at economy. Elected to Pratt's Club, he tried to postpone joining to avoid paying the subscription. But nothing could stop his cheques from bouncing. Finally Gavin Henderson, who had succeeded to the title of Lord Faringdon, and, later, Michael Rosse, came to the rescue by guaranteeing his overdraft.

For the first nine months of the war, Robert carried on living at Swan Walk. However, in the summer of 1940, he moved in as a paying guest to Nancy Mitford's house in Blomfield Road, Little Venice, a far more convenient location for the BBC. The arrangement was short-lived, but he soon found alternative accommodation around the corner with Patrick Kinross in Warwick Avenue. The onset of the Blitz forced Robert to spend nights at the BBC before returning 'with the all clear & the milk' to Warwick Avenue. By November, he had moved in to the Langham Hotel, across the road from Broadcasting House, where he stayed until the end of the year.

Wiltshire offered the occasional escape. Margaret Byron had avoided taking in evacuees by filling the house with family. This had mixed blessings for Robert, who, in anticipation of a few days off, wrote: 'I really do want to be quite sure of having a rest next week, so without wishing to be unkind, may I stipulate that the house shall be free of brothers-in-law.' At least, that autumn he was able to get in a few days cubbing in his beloved Savenake Forest.

Throughout the summer of 1940, Robert was in buoyant mood. Christopher Sykes took some credit for the improvement in his morale which dated from the decision to remain at the BBC. Boldly, he had informed him that, according to his sources, Robert's inability to land a first-rate job had stemmed from disapproval in high places at his violent pre-war outbursts. 'To my surprise', Sykes recalled, 'he received this news with relief: he knew now where he was, and the natural resilience of his spirits began immediately to assert itself once more.'

Robert relished the theatre of war. In July, he stayed with Michael Rosse, now an officer in the Irish Guards stationed at Dover Castle. Together they observed an air battle over the Channel. Writing to Christopher Sykes in Cairo, Robert explained how witnessing such a scene 'gave one an epic feeling'. The Blitz provided a closer brush with danger. As he was drinking his usual whisky one evening at the Langham Hotel, a bomb dropped on the building, failing to explode. 'Fortunately we were well under the stairs as the glass and marble descended in showers,' he told his mother. 'None of the old ladies turned a hair till panic was created by the air raid wardens who rushed in shouting to them to keep calm at all costs. Even then one of the old gentlemen went on writing letters. It was a real western front scene.' He had to climb over a mountain of rubble to get back to the BBC, where he slept like a top 'while the brutes decimated Marylebone'.

The first casualty amongst his friends was Unity Mitford. On 3 September, she had attempted suicide in the English Gardens in Munich. The bullet had failed to kill her, but she suffered irreparable brain damage. Hitler arranged for her to be moved to a hospital in Switzerland, whence, in January 1940, she was eventually brought home. Nancy kept Robert closely abreast of the news, writing within days of her return: 'She is dreadfully pathetic I keep having to go out of the room & cry – she is so ill, her teeth chatter the whole time & she can't hold anything . . . Oh dear I feel very much affected.' Three days later, Robert, with French bulldog in tow, visited the beleaguered family at their cottage in Swinbrook. 'Bobo is thrilled oh I long for Sarah,' Nancy wrote in anticipation. Despite a partial recovery and careful nursing by her mother, Unity eventually died in 1948 of meningitis.

Robert's enthusiasm for his job at the BBC scarcely lasted the summer. Soon, he was engaged in fierce battles with his superiors over the lack of a strategy for propaganda. 'The result', he complained, 'is that policy is handed out raw to the technicians, who are left to improvise the means of persuasion as they go along . . . To put it shortly there is not a single person in the whole organization whose official part is to think.' Furthermore, he had actually caught a translator censoring one of his scripts. 'For some time', he stated, 'the Hungarian Govt no doubt under German pressure have been seeking through their legation here to interfere with the freedom of the BBC . . . Last night's incident amounted in fact to a successful attempt on Germany's part to prevent the BBC from expressing views inimical to German interests.'

Hopes of a job elsewhere were raised by Italy's invasion of Greece. The attack was launched on 28 October from bases in Albania. Having knowledge of the area of conflict, Robert broadcast in person that day to the Greek people. Apologizing for his poor Greek, he spoke of the ride made on his last visit, nine years earlier, from Janina to Kalabaka:

> when I recollect the Pindus country, and the men I travelled with (Vlachs mostly) I do not find it so difficult to understand how the Greeks, though faced by enemy superiority in numbers, weapons and aircraft, have managed to inflict on these self-styled modern Romans the most signal defeat in their short, cowardly, and soon to be ended history.

After a considerable struggle with officialdom, Robert was also allowed to deliver a broadcast, entitled 'The Meaning of Greece', to the British audience. The immediacy of the opening lines commanded attention. 'It came like a breath of fresh air', he declared, 'the news that the Greeks were going to fight.

> . . . I remember like yesterday the hot August morning when I first landed in Greece – at Patras, that place the Italians have been bombing – and smelt the true Greek smell of hot sweaty dust and saw the deep blue sea and the dried-up putty-coloured earth and the white box-like houses . . . It wasn't long before I was in that sea, floating about in water as clear as a magnifying glass and sniffing the breeze from the mountains, which brought another smell, of herbs baking in the sun.

Turning to the Greeks' earlier war of independence, he described how the death of Lord Byron had revived 'the consciousness of the value of freedom in the English mind'. Herein lay the potency of the current struggle. 'Today', he concluded, 'we can draw on this inspiration again – till the time comes when Greece can share with us the task of restoring to the world the freedom that Greece first invented.'

The performance was long remembered by his friends, but it failed to secure him a posting to Greece. Hearing of vacancies in that region, he wrote to the Admiralty and the Foreign Office, but both turned him down. His search for a job continued. Sharpened by his understanding of the strategic importance of oil, he began to concentrate on the Middle East. The dangers had been spelt out in his paper on Civil Infiltration when he referred to the possibility of Nazi attacks on Asia Minor and Syria with a view to 'gaining the oil of the Middle East and opening the road to India (Persia could be conquered in a week)'. At last, someone in authority listened to his arguments. In December 1940, Robert was commissioned to travel to Meshed as an observer to keep an eye on Russian activity in the region. His cover was to proceed first to Cairo as war correspondent for the *Sunday Times*, an arrangement which was made with the blessing of the proprietor, Lord Kemsley.

His appointment to the *Sunday Times* had an authentic ring, since he had long written for the paper and was a friend of the literary editor, Cyril Lakin. Indeed, there had been discussions about a possible job earlier in the year. In December, Robert drew up a detailed proposal for his role as a war correspondent, arguing for a roving brief covering the entire area of the Middle East, even extending into Russia and as far south as the Sudan. Regardless of his role in Meshed, it was understood by the paper that he would file back reports on the region. Accordingly, he lunched with W. W. Hadley, the deputy editor, and Lakin a few weeks before his departure.

Although resigning from the BBC just before Christmas, Robert continued to work there until the end of January

1941. One of his last scripts, broadcast to the Balkans and Bulgaria, rang out across the airwaves like a personal war cry. The trigger had been a speech by Hitler made the previous day. Robert riposted thus:

> By his reference to democracy, more strident, more furiously envious than before, Hitler has made plainer than ever that there is no room in the world for him and civilization. The British people accept that position. It is war to the death. We welcome the challenge – to rid the world, on behalf of ourselves and others, of the vilest man and the vilest institutions that the history of the human race has yet recorded.

For his last few weeks in London, Robert moved into the Great Western Hotel at Paddington station. News had got out about his job as war correspondent and various friends managed to say goodbye. Nancy Mitford's last glimpse was being waved off by him on a number 6 bus, opposite C & A, in Oxford Street. For Jim Lees-Milne, the parting was more dramatic.

The war had done nothing to lessen the intensity of their friendship. In a passionately argued letter, written at the outbreak of war, Robert had been greatly influential in Jim's decision to fight rather than to become a pacifist:

> If you say you refuse to kill yr fellow men; if you maintain that the evil caused by war outweighs any good the war can preserve; if you are prepared to envisage the condition of life that wd. result from our not fighting & to accept such a prospect as preferable to war; & if you believe that by yr. personal pacifism you are contributing all you can to the avoidance of war in the future – then I will receive yr. opinions with respect & ask for you to explain them further.

Fortunately for both of them, there was no need to do so. By midsummer 1940, Jim had joined the Irish Guards.

Robert still could not suppress his feelings for him, even though these were not reciprocated. After another fraught meeting, Robert wrote to apologize. 'As for forgiveness', Jim replied, 'I feel it is rather arrogant even to assume that I have the right to grant it. Besides I daresay I too have long been to blame for insisting on seeing you so often and persistently. For this I should ask your forgiveness.' Once again, their equilibrium was restored.

A few months later, Jim found himself at Dover Castle preparing to hold back the German invasion. His ineptitude as an officer caused him agonies. 'I must say', he admitted to Robert, 'that every day I realize more acutely how utterly ill-equipped I am for a soldier. The feeling of responsibility and the constant dread of doing the wrong thing, making a fool of myself or involving our whole battalion in some ghastly muddle is a perpetual worry to me.'

That October, Jim was struck down by a bomb blast in London. The effect left him prone to mysterious fits, and weeks of hospital tests followed. As a result a planned meeting with Robert in November had to be abandoned.

Finally, Jim, passing through London, dropped into the Great Western Hotel to say goodbye. Although late in the morning, he found Robert still upstairs in his dressing gown, writing. Jim, by contrast, was in uniform. Robert took the opportunity to make one last advance. As usual, he was rejected. Later, descending in the lift together, all of Robert's frustration boiled over. He gave Jim a smart clout on the cheek which knocked off his cap. 'An American lady', Jim recalled, 'who had entered the lift with us was greatly shocked to see the plethoric civilian assaulting an officer in the Brigade.' Jim was furious. As he got out of the lift, he shouted: 'I shall never see you again, Robert. This is the end.' And it was.

A final farewell party was given for him by Michael and Anne Rosse. Also present were Ran Antrim, John Sutro and Anne's brother, Linley Messel, and his wife, Anne. The evening began in the Rosses' flat in Eaton Place. After drinks, they went on to the Café de Paris in Coventry Street. The occasion was marked by a typically Byronic row between Robert and John Sutro about Jews not standing up for themselves in Germany. Robert's bad mood did not last. He invited Anne Messel to dance. Snake Hips Johnson, the bandleader, complimented him on his partner. 'As a matter of fact', Robert quipped, 'she's my niece.'

During his last weeks in England, Robert made frequent visits to his parents in Wiltshire. On Tuesday 18 February, they came to London to see him off on the midnight train from Euston to Liverpool. He also spoke on the telephone that night to Michael Rosse, who recalled that 'He was so thrilled to be going, & was so full of energy for the job he was going to take up.' His passage had been booked on a small merchant ship called the *Jonathan Holt*. He found her to be quite new, comfortable, and captained by 'a splendid old tough'.

In a final letter home, Robert did his best to reassure his mother. 'Don't worry,' he urged her. 'We are all in this war together . . . I regard this as a glorious war and am glad to be taking a more active part in it.' His farewell carried the familiar refrain: 'Well, goodbye darling – & very best love – & think of the times we shall have when it's all over.'

On 21 February 1941, the *Jonathan Holt* sailed out of Liverpool as part of convoy OB289. Taking the northern route, they sailed through the Minches to Cape Wrath before heading into the Atlantic. Ultimately, Robert's ship was bound for the West African port of Takoradi before continuing round the Cape and on to Alexandria. Before one a.m. on 24 February, the sound of depth charges was heard from the outer edge of the convoy. A cascade of 'snowflakes' or flares illumined the sky. A German U-boat, the U-97, had surfaced, fired two torpedoes and dived. Two ships were hit almost simultaneously. Distress rockets hurtled skywards. One of the targets had been the *Jonathan Holt*. Blazing furiously she fell back from the convoy, her engine room and bridge destroyed. Still underway, she disappeared in a vast cloud of smoke and steam. Out of the thirty-eight crew, two gunners and eleven passengers, only three survived. Robert was not among them. He had been killed two days before his thirty-sixth birthday.

Naturally, the Byrons had no idea of Robert's fate. One month later, Eric was writing to Robert in Egypt bringing him up to date on various business matters, ending: 'I wish we could hear of your arrival somewhere but we are told not to worry.' Towards the end of April, the Byrons learnt about the sinking of the *Jonathan Holt* and the existence of survivors. News from the ship's owners, Holt & Co., was ambiguous. In answer to an inquiry from Margaret Byron, they wired back that 'other boats may have been picked up.'

Rumours continued to circulate for months to come. So strong was Robert's personality that people could not believe in his death. That summer, Harold Nicolson claimed to have seen him walking up St James's Street in his customary suit and bowler. His stricken mother was only finally convinced when Robert appeared to her in a dream and told her that he had been drowned. His death was officially announced, in September, in *The Times*.

Notes

Books, pamphlets and surveys by Robert Byron:

Europe in the Looking Glass, George Routledge & Sons, 1926
The Station Athos: Treasures and Men, Duckworth, 1928 (also published by Knopf in the USA)
The Byzantine Achievement, George Routledge & Sons, 1929 (also published by Knopf in the USA)
The Birth of Western Painting, George Routledge & Sons, 1930
'New Delhi', *Architectural Review*, 1931
An Essay on India, George Routledge & Sons, 1931
'Russian Survey', *Architectural Review*, May 1932
The Appreciation of Architecture, Wishart & Co., 1932
Little Innocents (containing his contribution: 'All these I learnt'), Cobden-Sanderson, 1932
First Russia Then Tibet, Macmillan & Co. Ltd, 1933
Shell Guide to Wiltshire, The Architectural Press, 1935
Innocence and Design by Richard Waughburton, Macmillan & Co. Ltd, 1935 (co-written with Christopher Sykes)
'Imperial Pilgrimage', Westminster London Transport, 1937
'How We Celebrate the Coronation', The Architectural Press, 1937
The Road to Oxiana, Macmillan & Co. Ltd, 1937

In researching and writing this book, the principal source has been the Robert Byron archive. Unless otherwise stated, all quotations derive from this source. Letters home from Robert Byron to his mother are indicated as LH. Other important archives have included the Harrod archive [RH], British Library; the Macmillan archive [MAC], British Library; the Brian Howard archive [BH] at Eton College; the archive of Nancy Mitford [NM] and Diana Mosley at Chatsworth; the John Mavrogordato [JM] archive at the Bodleian; the H. V. Yorke archive [HVY], property of the executors of H. V. Yorke; the Sacheverell Sitwell archive [SS]; the James Lees-Milne archive [JLM] at the Beinecke Library, Yale University; the

Anthony Hobson archive [AH]; the David Talbot Rice archive [DTR]; the Patrick Kinross archive [PK] at the Huntingdon Library; the Bryan Moyne archive [BM]; the Harold Acton archive [HA]; the Rosse family archive, Birr Castle [BC]; the Christopher Sykes archive [CS] at Georgetown University; the archive of the Society for the Protection of Ancient Buildings [SPAB] and the Georgian Group [GG].

Principal books referred to in the source notes are: Anthony Powell, *Infants of the Spring* (Heinemann, 1976) and *Messengers of Day* (Heinemann, 1978); Harold Acton, *Memoirs of an Aesthete* (Methuen, second impression 1970); *Brian Howard: Portrait of a Failure*, ed. Marie-Jacqueline Lancaster (Anthony Blond, 1968); Henry Green, *Pack My Bag* (Oxford University Press, 1989 edition); Evelyn Waugh, *A Little Learning* (Chapman & Hall, 1964); James Lees-Milne, *Fourteen Friends* (John Murray, 1996); Christopher Sykes, *Four Studies in Loyalty* (Collins, 1946)

1 No Relation

1 'Oh, my dear, dear Lord Byron' Cecil Clonmore to Robert Byron, September 1921.
'Lord Byron liked it' LH, March/April 1925.
'by gazing at her' Lucy Butler to the author.
2 'one of the ugliest' Robert Byron unpublished memoir, Wembley–Cardiff, 1930.
4 'Ah give him to me' Robert Byron unpublished memoir, Wembley–Cardiff, 1930.
5 'I did not learn' Margaret Robinson to Eric Byron, 1900.
'I am not what' Margaret Robinson to Eric Byron, 27 July 1902.
6 'they may be useful' Edmund Byron to Eric Byron, 26 February 1905.
'model of Queen' Memories of Little Bobbie [MLB] by Edith Robinson, May–June 1956.
7 'smart, good looking' ibid.
'I remember remembering' Robert Byron unpublished memoir, Wembley–Cardiff, 1930.
8 'Isn't that beautifully' MLB.

2 Little Innocent

9 'Flowers made deep' Robert Byron unpublished memoir, Wembley–Cardiff, 1930.
'Heard an invisible' Margaret Byron's diary, 21 July 1915.
10 'so ends the saddest' Margaret Byron's diary, 31 December 1915.
'Very sorry indeed' Margaret Byron's diary, general memoranda.
11 'easily the youngest' Lindisfarne Magazine, December 1917, Abberley School Archive.
'a horrible' 'Diary the fourth year of the Great War', 10 March 1918.
'it began to snow' ibid., 28 February 1918.
'is much intrigued' ibid., 31 January 1918.
'I'm sure mother' ibid., 9 March 1918.
12 'Thou art Peter' notebook May/June 1918.
'I live in hunger now' diary, 11 February 1918.
13 'grim shadow' Robert Byron unpublished memoir, Wembley–Cardiff, 1930.
15 'poor old Bob' Margaret Byron to Eric Byron, 12 June 1918.
'we shan't get him' Margaret Byron to Eric Byron, 12 June 1918.
'I felt as if' Robert Byron's scholarship diary, 28 June 1918.
16 'for its idiocy' ibid., 28 June 1918.
'Well done old chap!' ibid., 28 June 1918.
'classical specialist' Arthur Kilby to Eric Byron, 12 June 1918.
'Dr Alington didn't know' scholarship diary, 28 June 1918.
'It will make no difference' E. L. Vaughan to Theodore Hall Hall, 21 June 1918, enclosed in a letter to Eric Byron, 24 June 1918.
17 'for science and business' Theodore Hall Hall to Eric Byron, 19 January 1919.
'Good thing' Margaret Byron to Eric Byron, 19 January 1919.

3 Lords and Rebels

19 'Dicis-ne Latine' Robert Byron unpublished memoir, Eton I, 1930.

'so lonely' LH, January 1919.

20 'astonishing silhouettes' Robert Byron unpublished memoir, Eton I, 1930.

'historic excitement . . . In sum' ibid.

21 'The only disadvantage' Eton sketchbook, 28 June 1919.

'The experience enrolled' Robert Byron unpublished memoir, Remember the Morning, March 1938.

'a gaunt pile' Robert Byron unpublished memoir, Eton I, 1930.

22 'Parents either did not' Roger Mortimer to the author.

'a very mixed bag' ibid.

23 'a perfectly decent' Cornish Torbock to the author.

'He appears uninterested' H. E. E. Howson's report, 22 July 1920.

'I had accepted' Robert Byron unpublished memoir, Remember the Morning, March 1938.

'others would agree' H. E. E. Howson's report, 1 April 1920.

'& apparent impermeability' F. E. Robeson's report, 14 December 1920.

24 'the house, of fabricated stone' *The Station*, p. 15.

25 'fearful skill . . . sardonic disdain' Robert Byron unpublished memoir, Remember the Morning, March 1938.

'very Irish' Cornish Torbock to the author.

'the pleasure of questioning . . . we railed against' Robert Byron unpublished memoir, Remember the Morning, March 1938.

'in that emphatic' LH, summer 1921.

26 'of pretension and refinement' Robert Byron unpublished memoir, Eton II, 1930.

'was feeling so' LH, January/February 1921.

27 'a bully of a fellow' Roger Mortimer to the author.

'an old, tough house' Anthony Powell to the author.

'large pointed ears' Anthony Powell, *A Question of Upbringing* (Flamingo edn, 1986), p. 32.

28 'I liked his enthusiasms' Cornish Torbock to the author.

'He was standing' Anthony Powell to the author.

'hypnotized by the emotion' Charles Castle, *Oliver Messel: A Biography* (Thames & Hudson, 1986), p. 32.

'Lovely things' LH, January/February 1921.

'a local tart' Cornish Torbock to the author.

29 'to some people' Charles Castle, *Oliver Messel: A Biography*, p. 35.
'it was absolutely . . . was never heard' Roger Mortimer to the author.
'How is the dear' Cecil Clonmore to Robert Byron, September/October 1921.
'They were both' Cornish Torbock to the author.
'No, I don't think' Cecil Clonmore to Robert Byron, 29 September 1921.
'openly, like men of the world' Robert Byron unpublished memoir, Eton II, 1930.
30 'and every other' LH, summer 1921.
'The rest of the house' ibid.
'certainly not one' Mrs Adams to Cecil Clonmore, 28 September 1921.
31 'My dear!' Cecil Clonmore to Robert Byron, September 1921.
'a real snorter' Cecil Clonmore to Robert Byron, September 1921.
'a very stupid' Cecil Clonmore to Robert Byron, September 1921.
'I must say' Cecil Clonmore to Robert Byron, 29 September 1921.
'His young example' Robert Byron unpublished memoir, Remember the Morning, March 1938.

4 Angry Young Man

32 'fatalism and indifference' H. E. E. Howson's report, 24 July 1921.
'outrage' F. E. Robeson's report, 24 July 1921.
'every other moment' LH, September 1920.
'filled with presentiment' LH, February 1921.
33 'madness' Edmund Byron to Eric Byron, 24 May 1919.
'His brain last night' Lucy Hall Hall to Eric Byron, 19 January 1920.
34 'uprooting the traditions' Robert Byron unpublished memoir, Wembley–Cardiff, 1930.
'I feel it would' Robert Byron to Lucy Hall Hall, 18 October 1921.

'In the real answer' LH, October 1921.
'I live in one' Robert Byron to Lucy Hall Hall, draft letter, October 1921.
'These things are' Lucy Hall Hall to Robert Byron, 26 October 1921.
'brief but vulgar' Robert Byron to Margaret Byron, October 1921.
35 'Till now I have' Robert Byron to Eric Byron, October 1921.
'only you can' Robert Byron to Margaret Byron, October/November 1921.
'Why can't the Duke' ibid.
36 'How lucky father' ibid.
'to the core' Robert Byron unpublished memoir, Wembley–Cardiff, 1922.
'from the land . . . I feel' ibid.
'small thing . . . a little bit' LH, May 1921.
37 'a small square house' Knowle, unpublished description 1930.
'Do put the silver' LH, autumn 1932.
38 'that damned' LH, October 1922.
'we are now' Eric Byron's diary, 6 July 1924.

5 Aesthetes and Dandies

39 'only second' LH, January/February 1922.
40 'all other' Anthony Powell, *Infants of the Spring*, p. 28.
'extremely quick' C. M. Bowra, *Memories* (Weidenfeld & Nicolson, 1966), p. 165.
'he can talk' LH, February 1922.
'a fierce, desperate' Henry Green, *Pack My Bag*, p. 135.
'the conversation' LH, October 1921.
41 'very large' LH, February 1922.
'Wonderful dresses' LH, February 1922.
'I really don't' ibid.
'It was too' ibid.
42 'These rooms' Anthony Powell, *Infants of the Spring*, p. 43.
'intelligent and well constructed' Drawing report, Lent 1920.

'dreadfully disappointed' LH, January/February 1922.
'All of us' Harold Acton, *Memoirs of an Aesthete*, p. 92.
43 'Coming from' Harold Acton to the author.
44 'quite the most' *Brian Howard: Portrait of a Failure*, p. 120.
'singular beauty' *Brian Howard: Portrait of a Failure*, p. 9.
'brazen with' Harold Acton, *Memoirs of an Aesthete*, p. 79.
'seemed by nature' Anthony Powell, *Infants of the Spring*, p. 67.
'It was raining' *Brian Howard: Portrait of a Failure*, p. 19.
'Blue, isn't it?' Edward James, *Swans Reflecting Elephants* (Weidenfeld & Nicolson, 1982), p. 43.
'distorted form' Post-Impressionist debate, *Eton College Chronicle*, 2 November 1922.
'Do you think . . . being very like' Harold Acton to the author.
'whatever was retrograde' Harold Acton, *Memoirs of an Aesthete*, p. 92.
45 'My "Journey"' LH, February 1922.
'his inclusion' Anthony Powell, *Infants of the Spring*, p. 75.
'I very much' LH, March 1922.
'after this' Henry Green, *Pack My Bag*, p. 163.
46 'the unrivalled' Henry Green, *Blindness* (Hogarth Press, 1977 edn), pp. 14–15.
'genius' Brian Howard, *The New Poetry*.
'Robert has' Harold Acton, *Memoirs of an Aesthete*, p. 97.
'one of us' ibid.
'poor prose' LH, March 1922.
'such a frenzy' LH, March 1922.
'superlatively' Anthony Powell, *Infants of the Spring*, p. 79.
47 'painted furniture' LH, March 1922.
'the old set piece . . . extraordinarily' LH, November 1922.
'Florence was . . .' Harold Acton to the author.
'members must' *Brian Howard: Portrait of a Failure*, p. 51.
48 'The function' *Eton College Chronicle*, 3 November 1922.
'the very ticking' LH, March 1922.
'a little toy' LH, Michaelmas 1922.

'the most gargantuan' LH, November 1922.
'Lords silk' New & Lingwood bill, summer 1919.
'most delicious' LH, Michaelmas 1921.

49 'a huge black' LH, Michaelmas 1921.
'to be paid for' LH, Michaelmas 1922.
'My suit' LH, Michaelmas 1922
'I suppose' LH, June 1922.
'to dress offensively' LH, November 1922.
'aggressively' Robert Byron to Margaret Byron, undated.
'aggressive aestheticism' *Brian Howard: Portrait of a Failure*, p. 57.

50 'broad island' Percy Lubbock, *Shades of Eton* (Jonathan Cape, 1927), p. 164.
'Perfectly' LH, October 1921.
'Yyoung eenough' Robert Byron unpublished memoir, Eton I, 1930.
'the most cultivated' LH, Michaelmas 1921.
'Lubbock' LH, Michaelmas 1921.

51 'I may be' classics report, July 1920.
'Taste began' Percy Lubbock, *Shades of Eton*, p. 34.
'They are very' LH, Michaelmas 1922.
'Tudor dungeon . . . dignified' Robert Byron unpublished memoir, Remember the Morning, March 1938.
'long romantic' ibid.

52 'the critical . . . Their example' ibid.
'I do nothing' LH, Michaelmas 1922.
'refined cruelty' LH, autumn 1922.
'This worried' LH, Michaelmas 1922.
'a frantic' LH, Michaelmas 1922.
'such drink' LH, Michaelmas 1922.

53 'for nothing' ibid.
'it was there' Remember the Morning, March 1938.

6 Vivat Regina!

54 'shoved straight' LH, February 1923.
'orgies . . . a sort of' LH, January 1923.
'Still at Merton' Robert Byron to Henry Yorke, February 1923 [HVY].

55 'very nice' LH, February 1923.
'They all think' Robert Byron to Henry Yorke, February 1923 [HVY].
'unrivalled opportunity' LH, February 1923.
'one feels it' LH, 19 February 1923.
'Lord Beauchamp is one' LH, April 1923.
'Lord Beauchamp has a mania' LH, Perugia, April 1923.
56 'they were using . . .' Italian travel diary, 1923, passim.
57 'some interesting' LH, February 1923.
'filled with priceless' LH, 1 April 1923.
'dear Harold' Italian travel diary, 1923.
'something of' Lord Beauchamp to Robert Byron, 29 April 1923.
of the greatest' Evelyn Waugh, *A Little Learning*, p. 181.
'I am looking' LH, Naples, April 1923.
58 'It is so much' Lord Beauchamp to Robert Byron, 29 April 1923.
'I shall always' Robert Byron to Desmond Parsons, 1931 [BC].
60 'I did so enjoy' LH, November 1922.
'Isn't the forest' LH, summer 1923.
'an infernal fellow' LH, February/March 1923.
'all old panelling' ibid.
'egg-blue-green' LH, October/November 1923.
'the most exquisite' LH, January 1923.
61 'disgusting shop' LH, 5 June 1923.
'My room really did look' LH, October/November 1923.
'modelled with care' Robert Byron, 'The Victorian Revival at Oxford', *Cherwell*, 5 March 1924.
'a shrine of' Harold Acton, *Memoirs of an Aesthete*, p. 129.
62 'most interesting' Harold Acton to Thomas Balston, 30 November 1923 [AH].
'What a charming' Philip Guedalla to Robert Byron, 7 November 1923.
63 'it is the way' LH, May 1921.
'behave as' Robert Byron unpublished memoir, Eton I, 1930.
'at present rather' passim Robert Byron to Lytton Strachey, 28 January 1924 [British Library].
'the attractions' Lytton Strachey to Robert Byron, 29 January 1924.

64 'articles' Robert Byron to Lytton Strachey, 28 January 1924.
'fantastic innkeeper' H. G. Wells in G. P. Wells (ed.), *H. G. Wells in Love* (Faber, 1984), p. 170.
'Victorian truck' John Fothergill, *An Innkeeper's Diary* (Penguin, repr. 1939), p. 157.
'so tedious' *Cherwell*, 2 February 1924.
'the drooping lily' *Vogue*, 23 January 1929.
'Victoria shall', passim *Tatler*, 5 March 1924.

65 'instantaneous', passim Robert Byron to *Daily Mail*, 14 February 1924.

66 'They call themselves' Robert Byron, 'Some Aspects of Oxford: Epicurean', unpublished article, November 1924.
'At all hours' Harold Acton, *Memoirs of an Aesthete*, p. 123.
'uninhibited' Evelyn Waugh, *A Little Learning*, p. 180.
'subtly pornographic' Anthony Powell, *Infants of the Spring*, p. 71.
'was a kind of' Anthony Powell to the author.

67 'make the rafters' Mark Ogilvie-Grant, unpublished memoir [private collection].
'contorting' Anthony Powell, *Infants of the Spring*, p. 119.
'a disguise' Harold Acton, *Memoirs of an Aesthete*, p. 124.

68 'done for' Harold Acton to Tom Balston, 23 May 1924 [AH].
'historical notes' Harold Acton, *Memoirs of an Aesthete*, p. 127.
'red & bubbled' Robert Byron to Henry Yorke, March/April 1924 [HVY].
'darkened warehouse' Robert Byron, 'Domes', *Cherwell*, 7 February 1925.
'quite beautiful' LH, November 1924.
'You will come' LH, November 1924.
'Victorian chamber' Harold Acton to David Talbot Rice, undated [DTR].
'express the humour', passim LH, October 1924.
'the apostle' A. L. Rowse, *A Cornishman at Oxford*, p. 122.
'in our young' Mark Ogilvie-Grant to Evelyn Waugh, 28 November 1954 [University of Austin, Texas].

69 'You may divide' Robert Byron to Henry Yorke, March 1924 [HVY].

'What a blank' Robert Byron to Henry Yorke, early summer 1924 [HVY].
'Trash', passim Evelyn Waugh, *A Little Learning*, p. 199.

70 'I suppose' Mark Ogilvie-Grant, unpublished memoir [private collection].
'an enormous' Robert Byron to Henry Yorke, March 1924 [HVY].
'the best satire' LH, October/November 1924.

71 'appreciation of' Evelyn Waugh to James Laver, 3 December 1954 [Georgetown University Library].
'he was so amusing' LH, autumn 1924.

72 'If we can't' LH, June 1924.
'You would prefer' LH, 7/8 May 1924.
'The food here' Robert Byron to Anne Byron, August 1924.

73 'How horrible' Robert Byron to Henry Yorke, August/September 1924 [HVY].
'Down with abroad' Evelyn Waugh, *A Little Learning*, p. 198.
'it makes me sick' Robert Byron to Henry Yorke, spring 1925 [HVY].
'very nice to be', passim LH, October 1924.

74 'This term has been' LH, November 1924.
'an immensely wide' Robert Byron to *Daily Express*, 26 March 1925.

75 'Oxford has developed' Cecil Clonmore to David Talbot Rice, 3 March 1925 [DTR].
'bygone loves' Harold Acton, *Memoirs of an Aesthete*, p. 120.
'Robert's' Harold Acton to Evelyn Waugh, 25 September 1964 [University of Austin, Texas].
'a group of' Robert Byron to Patrick Balfour, November 1925 [PK].
'He thought' Anthony Powell to author, 27 October 1992.

76 'What a lovely time' Christine Longford, *Making Conversation* (Gollancz, 1931), p. 113.
'Eights week is begun' LH, 5 June 1923.
'If it were not' Robert Byron to Henry Yorke, spring 1925 [HVY].

77 'journeys and the food', passim Robert Byron to Henry Yorke, January 1925 [HVY].

'Please do not think' LH, January/February 1925.

78 'a press-puffed', passim 'Oxford's Young Pretenders', *Cherwell*, 21 February 1925.

'distinctly inerudite' Terence Greenidge, 'Oxford's Young Amateurs', *Cherwell*, 28 February 1925.

'petty sneers' anonymous published letter, *Cherwell*, 28 February 1925.

7 Grand Tour

All unattributed quotations up to Robert's arrival in Athens are taken from Robert Byron's diary of the journey entitled 'A Motor Tour to Athens'; thereafter they are taken from his published account of the journey, *Europe in the Looking Glass* [ELG]. Quotations from the draft of Part II, *Europe in the Looking Glass*, are acknowledged.

81 'Alf is more' LH, February 1923.

'a brilliant historian' ELG, p. 5.

'being so very well' LH, Bologna, August 1925.

82 'he cannot be left' LH, Rome, August 1925.

83 'if we get far' LH, Rome, August 1925.

'I spent yesterday' LH, Siena, August 1925.

84 'to recall not only' ELG, p. 130.

'I am all impatience' LH, Siena, August 1925.

85 'dreading this moment' draft of Part Two [ELG], p. 8.

'like an eastern bazaar' ibid., p. 43.

'Kurios Boover' ibid., p. 9.

86 'To avoid repeated' ELG, p. 118.

'Ancient Greece so far' LH, 31 August 1925.

88 'he took me', LH, Athens, September 1925.

'political interviewing' ibid.

'The Turks entered' draft of Part Two [ELG], p. 37.

'we talk of "after the war"' ibid., p. 34.

89 'an extraordinary', passim ibid., opposite p. 38.

'by ladder', passim ibid., p. 31.

'with a high pointed' ibid., p. 60 passim.

'The voices seemed' ELG, p. 222.

90 'I could honestly' draft of Part Two [ELG], p. 73.

8 Grub Street

91 'The *Cherwell* steals' 'London Letter', *Cherwell*, 7 November 1925.
'the cause may not', passim LH, November 1925.
'I am going' LH, 6 November 1925.
92 'girl men' ibid.
'a dear little' LH, January 1926.
'like a shy maiden' London diary, 18 January 1926.
'in the midst' LH, January 1926.
93 'one of Edwardian' LH, January 1926.
'a very broad lapel' 'London Letter', *Cherwell*, 20 February 1926.
'the Charleston' ibid., 13 March 1926.
'tried to send us' London diary, 28 February 1926.
94 'I am delighted' LH, early February 1926.
'Rewrote map story' London diary, 4 February 1926.
'Insulted by man' ibid., 9 February 1926.
'say nothing' ibid., 22 February 1926.
'Charming evening' ibid., 27 February 1926.
95 'an absurdly' ibid., 19 February 1926.
'graceful Gothic' ELG, p. 46.
96 'Huge sweeping contours' diary 'A Motor Tour to Athens', p. 38.
'The country was' ELG, p. 113.
97 'analogy perhaps' ELG, p. 117.
'It is most' Robert Byron to Henry Yorke, spring 1924 [HVY].
'ugly row' ELG, p. 99.
'the new sense' ELG, p. 7.
98 'with interest' ELG, p. 228.
'I shall go round' LH, March 1926.
'Where?' LH, March 1926.
99 'cattle barge' LH, April 1926.

9 The Joyous Life

100 'the whole place' LH, 2 May 1926.
'sacrificed' Alastair Graham to Claud Cockburn, May 1926 [private collection].

'all the Palaces' ibid.

101 'I have got no' Alastair Graham to David Talbot Rice, undated [DTR].

'They hate Athens' Alastair Graham to Claud Cockburn, May 1926 [private collection].

'most of them' ibid.

'One of them' Alastair Graham to David Talbot Rice, undated [DTR].

'but not really intimate' Thanos Veloudias to the author.

102 'fashioned with' ibid.

'queer hesitation' Notebook 'At Constantinople', p. 132.

'They wore' Thanos Veloudias to Patrick and Joan Leigh Fermor, 14 May 1990 [private collection].

103 'goats bells' Notebook 'At Constantinople', opposite p. 130.

'who walked away' Alastair Graham, fragment of letter [private collection].

'entrancing', passim LH, 19 May 1926.

'wonderful late' Notebook 'At Constantinople', p. 130.

104 'great boulders' LH, 19 May 1926.

'forced open' LH, 26 May 1926.

'dressing cases' ibid.

'the whole book' LH, 29 May 1926.

105 'in places' ibid.

'Light in S. Sophia' Notebook 'At Constantinople', p. 134.

'all the main' LH, 29 May 1926.

'cannon balls' Notebook 'At Constantinople', opposite p. 134.

'renegade Maltese' ibid., p. 133.

'thrown to mob' ibid., opposite p. 134.

106 'Modern Greek' LH, May 1926.

'a deliciously' LH, June 1926.

'Vous êtes' LH, 2 May 1926.

'I revel in it' Robert Byron to Roy Harrod, 1926 [RH].

'a monument of shells' LH, August 1926.

107 'hell of fleas . . . As we approached' LH, June 1926.

'more than anywhere' LH, 22 July 1926.

108 'gnashing' LH, 29 July 1926.

'was not good' LH, 3 August 1926.

'laden with' LH, 24 July 1926.

'British and South' LH, 18 July 1926.

109 'was quite quite lovely' LH, February 1925.

'to design' Robert Byron to Bryan Guinness, June 1926 [BM].
'wooded hog's' unpublished *Times* article.
'Framed in the' unpublished *Times* article, 'The Joyous Life'.
110 'You will not own', Graham Speake, *Mount Athos: Renewal in Paradise* (Yale University Press, 2002), p. 25.
'there exists', passim unpublished *Times* article, 'A Theocratic Republic'.
111 'liqueurs like', passim LH, 6 August 1926.
'The head' unpublished *Times* article.
'up the cobbled', passim ibid.
112 'Sharks?' Mount Athos notebook 1926, p. 42.
'Within fortified' unpublished *Times* article.
'like Victorian nurseries' Mount Athos notebook 1926, opposite p. 42.
'a service began' Bryan Guinness, *Dairy Not Kept* (Compton Chamberlayne, 1975), p. 175.
'Furious all asleep' Mount Athos notebook 1926, p. 32.
'Robert's name' Bryan Guinness diary, p. 174.
113 'lavishly furnished' *The Station*, p. 70.
'Today you quit' Travel diary, Mount Athos 1927, p. 64.
'whose hair' unpublished *Times* article.
'The cold . . . Slowly' *The Station*, p. 101.
'The clouds' unpublished *Times* article.
'in an indiscoverable' *The Station*, p. 103.
114 'Here is a piece' unpublished *Times* article.
'Macedonian' Mount Athos notebook 1926, pp. 60 and 62.
'lovely Cretan', passim Mount Athos notebook 1926, pp. 40 and 41.
115 'Ferment of ideas' Notebook 'At Constantinople', opposite p. 130.
'Stupid policy' Mount Athos notebook 1926, p. 29.
'one superb' LH, 19 August 1926.
'It doesn't matter' Mount Athos notebook 1926, p. 25.
116 'keep boys' Mount Athos notebook 1926, p. 24.
'in gratitude' Bryan Guinness, *Dairy Not Kept*, p. 190.
'Bonjour' LH, August 1926.
117 'devoted 16 years' LH, 29 May 1926.
'at heresy' Bryan Guinness, *Dairy Not Kept*, p. 191.

10 An English Year

118 'to a garden', passim Robert Byron, *The Station*, p. 12.
'We just' Harold Acton to the author.
'Horror' travel diary, Mount Athos, 1927.
'It is so' Robert Byron to Henry Yorke, 8 October 1926 [HVY].
119 'silly foreigners' *Spectator*, 25 December 1926.
'the review' LH, 6/7 January 1927.
'How delightful' Robert Byron to Patrick Balfour, December 1926 [PK].
'advertised' Robert Byron to Eric Byron, 11 November 1926.
'it is too' LH, December 1926.
'putting him' LH, 18 January 1927.
'terrifying' travel diary Mount Athos, 1927.
'one long' LH, 22 January 1927.
120 'the whole building' Robert Byron to Henry Yorke, 13 January 1927 [HVY].
'with a coronet' ibid.
'he was not', passim Robert Byron to Henry Yorke, 24 January 1927 [HVY].
'who are not American' travel diary Mount Athos, 1927.
121 'for the sake' Harold Acton, *Memoirs of an Aesthete*, p. 190.
'Don't do that' ibid., p. 192.
'It is such' LH, 'winter' 1926/7.
'straight out' Robert Byron to Harold Acton, 15 February 1926 [HA].
'rough-hewn' ELG, p. 75.
'more slovenly', passim Robert Byron to Harold Acton, February 1926 [HA].
'I believe' Robert Byron to Harold Acton, c. 1925 [HA].
'I must get on' LH, May 1926.
121 'experiments with words' Harold Acton, *Memoirs of an Aesthete*, p. 160.
122 'with carnivorous' ibid., p. 192, passim.
123 'out of all this' LH, 22 December 1926.
'wonder working' LH, 18 January 1927.

'blood-curdling', passim Anthony Powell, *Messengers of Day*, p. 64.

'very boring', passim Robert Byron to Henry Yorke, 15 June 1927 [HVY].

124 'golf-and-bridge world' Anthony Powell, *Messengers of Day*, p. 27.

'a grave little' Robert Byron, unpublished 'Memories of D.P.', *c.* 1937.

'I do so want' Robert Byron to Michael Rosse, 3 July 1925 [BC].

'I have got some' Michael Rosse to Robert Byron, 21 April 1925.

125 'The nineteenth century' *The Station*, p. 15.

'The garden was' ibid.

'pseudo-moat', passim Robert Byron, unpublished 'Memories of D.P.'

126 'really I am' Robert Byron to Henry Yorke, 27 May 1927 [HVY].

'freakish' *The Station*, p. 20.

'Gavin is' LH, 2 November 1926

127 'Did you ever' Robert Byron to Henry Yorke, 24 July 1927 [HVY].

11 Seat of Angels

All unattributed quotations are taken from the five volumes of travel diaries covering the trip to Mount Athos in 1927.

129 'in accordance with' Demetrios Sicilianos, tr. Robert Liddell, *Old and New Athens* (Putnam, 1960).

'a little capital' Thanos Veloudias to the author.

'squared modern' *The Station*, p. 32.

'the Greek Revival' ELG, p. 167.

'in the most exaggerated' LH, Athens, 7 July 1926.

'Before the sun is' *The Station*, p. 32.

131 'Totally argumentative' Anthony Powell to the author.

132 'to see a moth' Mark Ogilvie-Grant, unpublished memoir [private collection].

133 'So that is how' *The Station*, p. 109.

134 'My book is up to date' LH, 16 August 1927.

'to start fresh' LH, August 1927.

136 'Sometimes they are triangles' Mark Ogilvie-Grant, unpublished memoir [private collection].

138 'You, you slavering little' ibid.

139 'How I hate it' Robert Byron to Henry Yorke, 25 September 1927 [HVY].

140 'the most beautiful', passim Mount Athos notebook 1926, p. 4.

'There is no doubt . . . resemblance' *The Station*, p. 147.

141 'letters and stones', passim *The Station*, p. 34.

'Far above' ibid., p. 152.

142 'in tones of' ibid., p. 171.

Hereafter all unattributed quotations are taken from *The Station*.

145 'a dull mist' Robert Byron's 'Colour notes on Athos and Mistra', 1927.

147 'flying visit' LH, 1 October 1927.

'over and over again' LH, 16 August 1927.

'exactly like' Robert Byron to John Mavrogordato, 8 November 1928 [JM].

'After the infinite' LH, 16 August 1927.

148 'every detail' LH, 11 September 1927.

'it is as though' Mount Athos diary, 1927.

149 'was very disappointed' Robert Byron to David Talbot Rice, 8 November 1928 [DTR].

'as they don't' LH, 25 April 1928.

'do write' ibid.

150 'the splendid images' Anthony Powell, *Infants of the Spring*, p. 73.

'rash judgements' James Lees-Milne, *Fourteen Friends*, p. 143.

'the atmosphere' Steven Runciman to Christopher Sykes, 30 April 1948 [CS].

12 Dons and Counts

Unattributed quotes on the Spanish journey are taken from Robert Byron's travel diary; the same is the case for the trip to the Salzkammergut, Czechoslovakia and his sojourn in Vienna.

151 'really I think' Robert Byron to Henry Yorke, 1923 [HVY].

'the romantic spirit' Mount Athos travel diary, 1927.
'It is perhaps' Robert Byron to Henry Yorke, 24 July 1927 [HVY].
'dominion' *Brian Howard: Portrait of a Failure*, p. 242.
'To do with the mind' ibid., p. 244.
152 'Christianity' Robert Byron to Brian Howard, 18 November 1927 [BH].
'I have a God' Robert Byron to Brian Howard, 25 January 1928 [BH].
'the instinct' Robert Byron to Brian Howard, 1 December 1927 [BH].
'the pursuit' Formal Prospectus sent to Harold Acton [BH].
'Its primary intent' ibid.
'he wished' Robert Byron to Brian Howard, 20 January 1928 [BH].
153 'young Englishmen' *Brian Howard: Portrait of a Failure*, p. 241.
154 'inconceivable genius . . . small creature' J. Meier-Graefe, *The Spanish Journey* (London, 1926), p. 111 passim.
'as for El Greco' Robert Byron to Henry Yorke, April 1928 [HVY].
155 'The Alhambra' LH, 14 April 1928.
156 'but I shouldn't' LH, May/June 1928.
157 'do use it if you can' Robert Byron to Patrick Balfour, 29 October 1927 [PK].
'Mr Robert' *Daily Sketch*, 23 January 1929.
'to entertain all possible reviewers' LH, June 1928.
'Athos is an' D. H. Lawrence, *Vogue*, 1 August 1928.
158 'as their own' LH, 7 June 1928.
'It really is' LH, 25 June 1928.
160 'Everyone says' LH, August 1928.
163 'As a matter of fact' Robert Byron to Michael Rosse, 2 October 1928 [BC].
'moderately fat, short' Christopher Sykes, *Four Studies in Loyalty*, p. 81.
'in his conversation' Etienne Amyot to the author.
'a very special' *Brian Howard: Portrait of a Failure*, p. 211.
164 'There is a' Robert Byron to Henry Yorke, 30 September 1928 [HVY].

13 Byzantine Enthusiasms

166 'the high priest', passim *The Byzantine Achievement*, Part I.
167 'A thinker is' Oswald Spengler, *The Decline of the West*, vol. 2 (George Allen & Unwin, 1926), Preface to the revised edition, p. xiii.
'the great soul' mss draft, p. 7.
168 'In all history' Oswald Spengler, *Decline of the West*, Introduction, p. 30.
169 'My object' Robert Byron to John Mavrogordato, 8 November 1928 [JM].
'Seventeen miles long' *The Byzantine Achievement*, p. 69.
170 'Catholicism' ibid., p. 178.
171 'For the last time' ibid., p. 297.
'from every degree' ibid., p. 133.
'I see in place' Oswald Spengler, *Decline of the West*, p. 211.
172 'very favourable' LH, 28 January 1929.
'it is quite' Georgia Sitwell's diary, 26 January 1929 [SS].
'heavenly' LH, October 1928.
'very deep' LH, 13 February 1929.
'exhilarating' *Saturday Review*, 24 April 1929.
173 'I am supposed' LH, 24 January 1929.
174 'I had another' Margaret Byron to Robert Byron, February 1929.
'At the moment' Alfred Duggan to Robert Byron, 5 November 1928.
'I don't believe', passim Alfred Duggan to Robert Byron, 9 February 1929.
175 'talking & playing' Nancy Mitford to Tom Mitford, June 1928 [NM].
'quite brilliant' Nancy Mitford to Tom Mitford, August 1928 [NM].
'Dear Mr Byron' Nancy Mitford as told to Tom Mitford, 30 October 1928 [NM].
'Isn't Robert simply' Nancy Mitford to Tom Mitford, 2 November 1928 [NM].
176 'prejudiced' Robert Byron to Michael Rosse, 13 November 1928 [BC].
'your parents', passim Nancy Mitford to Tom Mitford, 2

November 1928 [NM].
'I would have' Nancy Mitford to Jessica Treuhaft, 18 October 1971 [NM].
'His way with' Henry Yorke to Evelyn Waugh, 22 June 1929 [University of Austin, Texas].
'I found' Nancy Mitford to Christopher Sykes, 30 January 1947 [CS].
'I think of' Harold Acton, *Nancy Mitford* (Gibson Square Books, 2002), p. 162.
'you must promise me' Henry Yorke to Robert Byron, 20 February 1928 [HVY].
'just because' Robert Byron to Henry Yorke, 27 February 1928 [HVY].
177 'loaded on fact' Henry Yorke to Robert Byron, April 1929.
'aesthetic sincerity', passim Robert Byron to Henry Yorke, 11 February 1929 [HVY].
'I do congratulate' Robert Byron to Henry Yorke, 24 April 1929 [HVY].
178 'enormous sprays' LH, October 1928.
'I find the' Robert Byron to Henry Yorke, 28 October 1928 [HVY].
'when it does thaw' LH, 15 February 1929.
179 'I could get' LH, 22 October 1928.
'classic profile' 'Spring Modes for Policital Workers', *Vogue*, 20 March 1929.
'curry of', passim *Architectural Review*, March 1929.
180 'they all leant' LH, February 1928.
'it is all so much' LH, 1 January 1929.
'I can't think' Robert Byron to David Talbot Rice, 23 February 1929.
181 'in the moment', passim Clive Bell, *Art*.
183 'Here arose' *The Birth of Western Painting*, p. 70 passim.
184 'revolutionized everything' Robert Byron to David Talbot Rice, 11 February 1930 [DTR].
'I am setting' LH, 10 February 1930.
185 'justified' Achille Kyron to Robert Byron, 16 February 1931.
186 'Baxter' description of flight entitled 'The British Evening in the Morning-lands', December 1929

14 Air Mail to India

Unattributed quotations are taken from Robert Byron's diary covering his journey to southern India.

187 'some gigantic' *Daily Express*, 11 September 1929.
'The engines' 'The British Evening in the Morning-lands'.
188 'Here' ibid.
189 'Halfway Round' *Daily Express*, 11 September 1929.
189 'here was I' 'The British Evening in the Morning-lands'.
'Tonight, of course' ibid.
191 'it is almost' Sacheverell Sitwell, *Southern Baroque Art*.
192 'the romantic tale' *The Byzantine Achievement*, p. 169.
'I am surrounded' LH, 19 August 1929.
194 'I loathe ruins' LH, 23 August 1929.

15 Into Tibet

Unattributed quotations are taken from Robert Byron's diary to Tibet and the temple of Buddh Gaya.

201 'May I' Robert Byron's handwritten words and phrases.
206 'We fell into' *First Russia Then Tibet*, p. 230.
208 'plain six miles' notes preserved in travel diary.
213 'One was in contact' LH, 24 October 1929.

16 Analysis of Empire

215 'my darling boy' Margaret Byron to Robert Byron, 30 October 1930.
216 'The fort', passim diary 'Rampur'.
217 'Delicious way' ibid.
'I can't describe' LH, 30 December 1929.
'the genius' Robert Byron to Henry Yorke, 28 December 1929 [HVY].
218 'a heavenly' LH, 30 December 1929.
'It seems scarcely' notes on conversation with Blomfield and Crittall.
'a £25' Robert Byron to Eric Byron, 11 December 1929.
'It is almost' LH, 30 December 1929.

219 'frightful' architectural notes, Delhi.
'There are moments' LH, 30 December 1929.
220 'The Taj is' LH, 11 April 1930.
'The beauty of the' *Architectural Review*, November 1930.
'The pyramids' LH, 15 April 1930.
221 'I can't think' Evelyn Waugh diary, 30 May 1930.
'Robert . . . made' ibid., 23 August 1930.
We spent the' Robert Byron to Desmond Parsons, August 1930 [BC].
'Fortunately' Robert Byron to Desmond Parsons, undated [BC].
222 'dome, tower', passim *Architectural Review*, January 1931.
223 'The architecture', passim Geoffrey Scott, *The Architecture of Humanism* (Architectural Press, 1980), p. 32.
'remarkable' Robert Byron to Michael Rosse, 1 October 1930 [BC].
224 'Your article' Sir Edwin Lutyens to Robert Byron, 7 January 1931.
'We transcribe' *Architecture of Humanism*, p. 162.
'and created' *Architectural Review*, January 1931.
225 'I shall' LH, 19 November 1929.
'The air and' LH, 6 February 1930.
'a political' Robert Byron to John Mavrogordato, 16 June 1930 [JM].
'portentous barbarism', passim *Essay on India*, p. xxx.
227 'I'm afraid' Frederick Warburg to Robert Byron, October 1931.

17 The Higher Philosophy

228 'tall, fair' Harold Acton to the author.
'the beauty of the Parsonses' Robert Byron, 'Memories of D.P.', 1937.
229 'By the time' Robert Byron to Desmond Parsons, 1 July 1928 [BC].
'I saw' Robert Byron to Michael Rosse, 7 July 1928 [BC].
'too extraordinary' Robert Byron to Michael Rosse, 30 April 1928 [BC].

'he was non-conforming' James Lees-Milne, *Fourteen Friends*, p. 149.
'filled with' Desmond Parsons to Roy Harrod, summer 1932 [RH].
230 'Life was' Desmond Parsons to Robert Byron, late summer 1932.
'I feel very deeply' Desmond Parsons to Roy Harrod, spring 1932 [RH].
'I am not' Desmond Parsons to Roy Harrod, 18 July 1935 [RH].
'super-critical' Michael Rosse to Robert Byron, 18 September 1935.
'I've had' Diana Mosley, *Loved Ones* (Sidgwick & Jackson, 1985), p. 99.
'inborn laziness' Desmond Parsons to Roy Harrod, summer 1932 [RH].
'I have been' Desmond Parsons to Robert Byron, late autumn 1931.
'invariably lying' James Lees-Milne to the author.
231 'oblivion' Desmond Parsons to Roy Harrod, summer 1932 [RH].
'The idea' Robert Byron to Desmond Parsons, 2 November 1930 [BC].
'sulky' James Lees-Milne to the author.
'buttoned up' Robert Byron to Desmond Parsons, 27 October 1930 [BC].
232 'I had' Robert Byron to Desmond Parsons, 3 November 1930 [BC].
'the prospect' Robert Byron to Desmond Parsons, 21 December 1930 [BC].
'which was' Robert Byron to Michael Rosse, 18 January 1931 [BC].
'My flat' LH, 26 February 1931.
233 'I think' Lord Hardinge to Herbert Baker, 6 July 1931 [RIBA Library].
234 'With regard' Robert Byron to Eric Byron, 13 June 1931.
235 'Harold is' Robert Byron to Evelyn Waugh, 25 February 1930 [University of Austin, Texas].
'if it happens' LH, 17 June 1931.
'After an' Robert Byron to Eric Byron, 13 June 1931.

236 'How long had' Robert Byron to Desmond Parsons, 13 May 1931 [BC].
'Tweed' Bryan Guinness, *Twenty-Three Poems* (Duckworth, 1931).
'It is all' Robert Byron to Bryan Guinness, 23 July 1931 [BM].
237 'He spent' Kenneth Matthews, *Greek Salad* (Peter Davies, 1935).
238 'one of the most' 'The Monasteries of the Meteora', *Country Life*, 21 May 1932.
239 'a radiant light' ibid.
'The time has come' LH, 22 October 1931.
'poring over . . . statement' Robert Byron to Michael Rosse, 24 October 1931 [BC].
'Various forces' official proposal submitted to Russian Embassy, 26 October 1931 [BC].
240 'and see', Robert Byron to Michael Rosse, 24 October 1931 [BC].

18 Marx and Monuments

All unattributed quotations are taken from Robert Byron's travel diary to Russia.
245 'Nothing' LH, 14 January 1932.
246 'I like him' *Inside Stalin's Russia: The Diaries of Reader Bullard*, entry for 16 January 1932.

19 Cupid's Dart

252 'Today Russia', passim *Architectural Review*, May 1932.
254 'how vividly' Mrs Weir to Robert Byron, 5 October 1932; the five articles in *Country Life* were published 30 July, 13 August, 27 August, 10 September, 8 October 1932.
256 'Wrote my' Russian travel diary.
'to compose' Robert Byron, introduction to catalogue.
257 'Osbert Sitwell' Penelope Chetwode to Robert Byron, June/July 1932.
258 Penelope Chetwode to Robert Byron, 23 November 1932.

'it really seemed' Desmond Parsons to Roy Harrod, April 1932 [RH].
'I could not help' Robert Byron to Desmond Parsons, 5 May 1932 [BC].
'a coma' Robert Byron to Desmond Parsons, 28 May 1932 [BC].
'Small coldnesses' Robert Byron to Desmond Parsons, 21 May 1932 [BC].
259 'In every other', passim Robert Byron to Desmond Parsons, 28 May 1932 [BC].
'out of my tragic', passim Robert Byron to Desmond Parsons, 1 June 1932 [BC].
260 'take over' Desmond Parsons to Robert Byron, summer 1932.
'I am terrified' Robert Byron to Desmond Parsons, 22 September 1932 [BC].
'how wonderful' Robert Byron to Desmond Parsons, 3 November 1932 [BC].
'You ask' Evelyn Waugh to Diana Mosley, 9 March 1966 [Chatsworth].
261 'Bryan invited' Robert Byron to Michael Rosse, August/September 1932 [BC].
'she collapsed' LH, 18 May 1933.
'leads a' Robert Byron to Desmond Parsons, 1934 [BC].
262 'I have done' Nancy Mitford to Robert Byron, 15 November 1932.
'Please' Nancy Mitford to Robert Byron, 17 November 1932.
'It was a', passim Robert Byron to Nancy Mitford, 25 November 1932.
'I know how' Christopher Hussey to Robert Byron, 6 October 1932.
263 'less enlightened' *Country Life*, 12 November 1932.
264 'There are some' de Cronin Hastings to Robert Byron, 15 November 1932.
'I cannot help' Christopher Hussey to Robert Byron, 14 December 1932.
266 'In all cases' 'London's Architectural Conscience', *Weekend Review* 19 September 1931.
267 'My correspondent' Russian Survey, *Architectural Review*, May 1932, p. 193.

'very much' de Croning Hastings to Robert Byron, 10 November 1932.

'Look then at' John Betjeman to Robert Byron, 19 January 1933.

'I do not feel' John Betjeman to Robert Byron, 23 January 1933.

'His character' Robert Byron to Bryan Guinness, 26 December 1930 [BM].

268 'I saw Lucy' John Betjeman to Lionel Perry, 29 March 1932 [University of Victoria].

'By good architecture', passim *The Appreciation of Architecture.*

269 'I have I think' *New Statesman*, 3 December 1932.

'my little bastard' Robert Byron to Desmond Parsons, 13 April 1934 [BC].

'rather shortly that' Christophen Sykes, *Four Studies in Loyalty*, p. 123.

20 The Charcoal Burners

270 'don't worry' Mark Dineley to Robert Byron, May 1932.

'as one gentleman' Mark Dineley, 'The Turcomans of Persia', *Geographical Magazine*, June 1935.

'some very jolly' Mark Dineley to Robert Byron, May/June 1933.

271 'I asked some' Bosworth Goldman, *Red Road Through Asia* (Methuen & Co., 1934), p. 132.

'enlivening' Boz Goldman to Robert Byron, 10 September 1932.

'a compendium' Boz Goldman to Robert Byron, undated.

'immensely learned' Robert Byron to John Mavrogordato, 7 September 1930 [JM].

'you do not know' G. M. Young to Robert Byron 21 February 1933.

'he seemed' Penelope Chetwode to Robert Byron, 3 April 1933.

272 'I think if' Mark Dineley to Robert Byron, April 1933.

'I absolutely' Mark Dineley to Robert Byron, May 1933.

273 'I do beg' Mark Dineley to Robert Byron, June 1933.

'With regard to' Mark Dineley to Robert Byron, May/June 1933.
'I could feel' Mark Dineley to Robert Byron, June 1933.
'It was Diez's' *The Road to Oxiana*, p. 227.
'it is a joy' Arthur Upham Pope to Robert Byron, 6 April 1933.

275 'I shall' LH, 3 June 1933.
'the fact is' Robert Byron to John Mavrogordato, November 1932 [JM].

276 'I was afraid' A. D. Peters to Robert Byron, 23 May 1933.
'altogether' LH, 24 February 1929.
'Parker Producer' Letter to Persian Minister in London, 26 June 1933.

277 'a most expensive' Mark Dineley to Robert Byron, 23 October 1934.
'Boz drove me' LH, 15 July 1933.

278 'I like Xtopher' Robert Byron to Patrick Balfour, 18 March 1927 [PK].

279 'engaged in serious' 8 August 1933.
'that gave me', passim Robert Byron to Desmond Parsons, 3 June 1933 [BC].

280 'I'm afraid I'm not' Robert Byron to Desmond Parsons, July 1932 [BC].
'the great' Robert Byron to Desmond Parsons, 10 June 1933 [BC].
'Theirs was' James Lees-Milne, *Fourteen Friends*, p. 150.
'You must understand' Robert Byron to Desmond Parsons, 12 July 1933 [BC].
'the roots' Desmond Parsons to Roy Harrod, undated [RH].
'I should never' Robert Byron to Desmond Parsons, 12 January 1933 [BC].

281 'I wish' Robert Byron to Desmond Parsons, 31 July 1933 [BC].
'nothing to do' Persian travel diary.

21 Persia and Beyond

All unattributed quotations are taken from Robert Byron's travel diaries of his journey to Persia and Afghanistan.

282 'Our host' LH, 20 August 1933.
'that last' Robert Byron to Desmond Parsons, 1934 [BC].
'You have sent' Robert Byron to Desmond Parsons, 23 August 1933 [BC].
283 'Twilight' Christopher Sykes, *Four Studies in Loyalty*, p. 147.
287 'I am afraid' LH, 13 September 1933.
288 'I am still' LH, 24 September 1933.
293 'a gigantic' *The Road to Oxiana*, p. 95.
294 'Robert has' Boz Goldman to Stella Buchanan, 20 November 1933.
295 'Now and then' *The Road to Oxiana*, p. 88.
300 'it may be' LH, 15 November 1933.
'I suppose' LH, 2 January 1934.
301 'I was always' Margaret Byron to Michael Rosse, 20 October 1941 [BC].
'I miss you' Robert Byron to Desmond Parsons, 3 January 1934 [BC].
'remember sometimes' Robert Byron to Desmond Parsons, 13 April 1934 [BC].

22 Towards the Oxus

All unattributed quotations are taken from Robert Byron's travel diaries to Persia and Afghanistan.
302 'I now know' LH, 2 January 1934.
'My object now', passim Robert Byron to Daniel Macmillan, 13 January 1934 [MAC].
303 'on the honourable' Harold Macmillan to A. D. Peters, 1 February 1934 [MAC].
'it wld. have been' Robert Byron to Bryan Guinness, 10 February 1934 [BM].
309 'Excuse my late' *The Road to Oxiana*, p. 178.
312 'Persian brick' LH, 24 October 1933.
313 'The thing about' LH, 25 December 1933.
314 'He did not' Christopher Sykes, *Four Studies in Loyalty*, p. 133.
'every building' Robert Byron to Daniel Macmillan, 13 January 1934 [MAC].

315 'I have just' Robert Byron to Macmillan's, 4 April 1934 [MAC].
'and addressed' LH, 19 April 1934.
317 'A tapering' *The Road to Oxiana*, p. 230.
319 'There is the' LH, 2 May 1934.

23 A Pen in Each Hand

327 'The sales of' Harold Macmillan to Robert Byron, 24 April 1934 [MAC].
'It is refreshing' *The Times*, 21 November 1933.
'The book on' *Sphere*, 11 November 1933.
'His prose is' *Sketch*, 13 December 1933.
'I think you' Harold Macmillan to Robert Byron, 18 July 1934 [MAC].
328 '[Christopher]' Persian travel diary, 20 February 1934.
'The Persian Minister' LH, 4 October 1934.
329 'Our only', passim Report on Journeys in Afghanistan 1933–4.
330 'fabulous' Persian travel diary, 12 April 1934.
'My art is' LH, 25 December 1933.
'I am all' Arthur Upham Pope to Robert Byron, 9 July 1934.
331 'If you could' Arthur Upham Pope to Robert Byron, 3 August 1934.
'Mr Robert' *Bulletin of the American Institute for Persian Art and Architecture*, no. 7, December 1934.
'an exhaustive' Arthur Upham Pope to Robert Byron, 8 August 1934.
'Mr Byron has always' *Bulletin*, no. 7, December 1934.
332 'that great menace' Mount Athos diary, 1927, vol. 1, p. 25.
'I had the American' LH, 27 February 1929.
'one of those' Persian travel diary, 6 November 1933.
'Their standard', passim LH, 17 January 1935.
333 'The lecture' LH, 19 February 1935.
'a new' LH, 19 February 1935.
334 'Chief amongst' *Innocence and Design*, pp. 119 and 120.
'the detestable' Persian travel diary, 29 September 1933.
'Teheran is' Persian travel diary, vol. 3, end notes.

'The second' Persian travel diary, 4 April 1934.
335 'I sat next' Nancy Mitford to Robert Byron, 8 April 1936.
'I think a' Harold Macmillan to Robert Byron, 12 August 1935.
'the wind out' John Betjeman to Robert Byron, 24 November 1934.
'The Wiltshire' LH, 24 October 1934.
336 'I think' John Betjeman to Robert Byron, 22 November 1934.
'I really don't' John Betjeman to Robert Byron, 24 November 1934.
'marks the', passim *Shell Guide to Wiltshire.*
337 'I am getting' Persian travel diary, 3 December 1933.
'It breaks' LH, 6 February 1935.
'and seemed' Margaret Byron to Robert Byron, 1 January 1935.
'The house is' Margaret Byron to Robert Byron, 14 February 1935.
'they must be' Anne Byron to Robert Byron, summer 1935.
'young men' Margaret Byron to Robert Byron, 26 January 1935.
338 'golden age', passim *Islamic Monuments in Afghanistan*, Part III.
'I had never' Arthur Upham Pope to Robert Byron, 29 July 1935.
339 'rapidly' *Bulletin of the American Institute of Persian Art and Archaeology*, no. 6, June 1934.
'Naturally I don't' Robert Byron to Arthur Upham Pope, 27 July 1935 [New York Public Library].
'I was dismayed' Arthur Upham Pope to Robert Byron, 29 July 1935.
'Stay' Arthur Upham Pope to Robert Byron, 3 August 1935.

24 The Grim Orient

All unattributed quotations are taken from Robert Byron's Siberian travel diary.

341 'You don't seem' LH, 24 September 1935.
'had his eye' LH, 13 September 1935.

'They gave us' Tamara Talbot Rice to the author.
'We are thinking' LH, 23 September 1935.
342 'The flights were' LH, 9 October 1935.
'smiling', passim Russian Survey, *Architectural Review*, May 1932, p. 184.
343 'that the authorities' Russian Survey, *Architectural Review*, May 1932, p. 195.
'At last after' Robert Byron to Desmond Parsons, 5 October 1935 [BC].
346 'New Russia' The articles appeared on 16, 17 and 18 March 1936.
'Russia is now' LH, 6 September 1935.
'For the moment' *The Times*, 17 March 1936.
'unselfishness' *The Times*, 16 March 1936.
347 'A low grey' *The Times*, 16 March 1936.
'You might have' Robert Byron to Desmond Parsons, 20 September 1934 [BC].
'the old Berlin' Robert Byron to Desmond Parsons, 20 January 1935 [BC].
'the pleasures' Robert Byron to Desmond Parsons, 29 July 1934 [BC].
348 'To remain in' Desmond Parsons to Roy Harrod, 11 October 1933 [RH].
'Harold was' Robert Byron to Diana Guinness, 23 July 1931 [Chatsworth].
'Unconsciously' Harold Acton, *Memoirs of an Aesthete*, p. 199.
349 'but as usual' Desmond Parsons to Roy Harrod, late autumn 1934 [RH].
'As you foresee' Robert Byron to Michael Rosse, 1 May 1935 [BC].
'life here' Desmond Parsons to Roy Harrod, September 1935 [RH].
350 'I have suffered' Robert Byron to Michael Rosse, 20 February 1933 [BC].
'Anne really' LH, 30 November 1935.
'A great blow' LH, 11 December 1935.
'an abyss' LH, 12 December 1935.
'he is, of course' Harold Acton to Roy Harrod, 14 December 1935 [RH].

'The prospect' Robert Byron to Lucy Butler, 12 December 1935.

351 'There is a wild' Robert Byron to Desmond Parsons, 21 December 1935 [BC].

'I don't know' LH, 25 December 1935.

'emerging' LH, 24 January 1936.

352 'This winter' LH, 15 March 1936.

'Harold will' LH, 20 February 1936.

'of architecture' LH, 30 November 1935.

'Don't hesitate' LH, 29 February 1936.

353 'The book is' Robert Byron to Harold Macmillan, 31 May 1936 [MAC].

'All my interest' LH, 7 June 1936.

'a friendly' LH, 15 June 1936.

'the barbarity' LH, 6 July 1936.

354 'whereas one gets' LH, 13 July 1936.

'the criticism' Robert Byron to Harold Macmillan, 6 September 1935 [MAC].

'It would be' Robert Byron to Harold Macmillan, 12 October 1935 [MAC].

'lying in a' LH, 23 July 1936.

355 'It will be' LH, 30 July 1936.

25 Travellers' Tales

356 'I have developed' Robert Byron to Harold Macmillan, 19 February 1936 [MAC].

357 'another expedition' *The Road to Oxiana*, p. 270.

'miserable' *The Road to Oxiana*, p. 98.

'where Afghanistan' Robert Byron to Harold Acton, 19 February 1936 [MAC].

'It would give' ibid.

358 'It is cold' *The Road to Oxiana*, pp. 257–8.

'As for the' Robert Byron to John Mavrogordato, 19 October 1937 [JM].

359 'throughout the book' *Architects' Journal*, 15 March 1934.

'I liked your' Norman Douglas to Robert Byron, 12 November 1934.

'the imprint' Robert Byron to Norman Douglas, 8 December 1934 [Beinecke Library, Yale University].

360 'arresting' *Spectator*, 11 August 1933.

'hope that it will' A. D. Peters to Robert Byron, 2 February 1934.

'I have just' LH, 15 June 1934.

361 '[I am] wholly' Peter Fleming, *One's Company* (Jonathan Cape, 1934), p. 33.

'I have got back' LH, 6 February 1936.

'Boz is replanning' Persian travel diary, 20 April 1934.

'an honest account' Peter Fleming, *News from Tartary* (Cardinal paperback edn), p. 169.

'True, this last' 'Unobserved Architecture', *Architects' Journal*, 27 August 1936.

362 'His prose' *The Times Literary Supplement*, 17 April 1937.

'drily instructive' *London Mercury*, June 1937.

'of outstanding' *Spectator*, 2 July 1937.

'As may be' *Observer*, 25 April 1937.

'Mr Byron' *Manchester Guardian*, 20 April 1937.

'The power of' *Sunday Times*, 25 April 1937.

'me feel' Robert Byron to Desmond Parsons, 30 April 1937 [BC].

26 Beset with Woes

364 'the best audience' Baltic travel diary, 9 March 1937.

'what a lovely' ibid., 11 March 1937.

365 'loathsome', passim ibid.

'I hardly know' LH, 10 March 1937.

'a proper' Margaret Byron to Robert Byron, 29 March 1937.

366 'I am haunted' Robert Byron to Eric Byron, 29 March 1937.

'I am getting' Margaret Byron to Robert Byron, 9 August 1936.

'there is always' LH, 6 June 1937.

'doomed either' Baltic diary, 21 December 1936.

367 'I have just' Robert Byron to Harold Macmillan, 4 April 1934 [MAC].

'that coarse' Robert Byron to Harold Macmillan, 28 May 1935 [MAC].
'as bright' Robert Byron to Harold Macmillan, 4 February 1937 [MAC].
'general travel' Harold Macmillan to Robert Byron, 18 July 1934.
'travel books with' Harold Macmillan to Robert Byron, 10 March 1936.

368 'crypto-public' typed sheet, 3 September 1938.
'we are certainly' E. F. Richardson to Robert Byron, 29 May 1937.
'it seems to me' Harold Macmillan to Robert Byron, 26 November 1937.
'I find now' Robert Byron to Harold Macmillan, 25 January 1937 [MAC].

369 'to drown' Desmond Parsons to Roy Harrod, 5 November 1936 [RH].

370 'Ghastly', passim Desmond Parsons to Robert Byron, 6 April 1937.
'I couldn't say' Robert Byron to Desmond Parsons, summer 1937 [BC].
'it has become' Michael Rosse to Robert Byron, 2 July 1937.
'What people' *The Times*, 7 July 1937.
'I think you' Michael Rosse to Robert Byron, 12 July 1937.

371 'the Roman baths' James Lees-Milne to Robert Byron, 12 January 1937.
'Don't harrow' Robert Byron to James Lees-Milne, 12 April 1933 [JLM].
'utterly' Lady Harrod to the author.

372 'repeatedly' James Lees-Milne, *Another Self*, p. 79.
'I am very sad' James Lees-Milne to Robert Byron, 28 July 1937.
'I wd so much' James Lees-Milne to Robert Byron, 10 August 1937.
'He is really' Robert Byron to Bryan Guinness, 19 February 1930 [BM].
'I'm so glad' Robert Byron to Nancy Mitford, 16 August 1933 [NM].

'he would set' James Lees-Milne, *Fourteen Friends*, pp. 133–4.
373 'an influx' *Survey of Persian Art*, vol. II (Oxford University Press, 1939), pp. 1120 and 1121.
'I think' Arthur Upham Pope to Robert Byron, 25 February 1937.
'I warn you' Robert Byron to Arthur Upham Pope, 21 June 1937 [New York Public Library].
374 'structure came', passim Arthur Upham Pope to Robert Byron, 18 June 1937.
'A more generally' *Survey of Persian Art*, vol. II, p. 1120, n. 3.
'schoolboy' Robert Byron to Arthur Upham Pope, 16 January 1938 [New York Public Library].
'In a way' LH, 28 April 1938.

27 Georgian Crusader

376 'Slowly' 'How We Celebrate the Coronation', passim.
378 'the tide of' Hansard, 2 December 1936.
'At the present' *Daily Telegraph*, 28 May 1936.
'As a result' Douglas Goldring, *Facing the Odds* (Cassell & Co., 1940), p. 23.
379 'a distinct loss' Lord Esher to Lord Derwent, 5 February 1937 [SPAB].
'wholeheartedly' Douglas Goldring to William Palmer, 18 March 1937 [SPAB].
'for the purpose' Douglas Goldring to Robert Byron, 19 May 1937 [GG].
380 'What is not' Robert Byron to Lord Derwent, 23 July 1937 [GG].
'so virile' Lord Esher to William Palmer, 31 August 1937 [SPAB].
'She would make' Robert Byron to Michael Rosse, 2 September 1937 [BC].
382 'There is really' Duke of Norfolk to Lord Derwent, 8 December 1937 [GG].
'I see the Norfolk' Lord Derwent to Robert Byron, 16 February 1938.
'a man behind' notes, December 1937.

'I was much' Robert Byron to Rudolph Palumbo, 23 December 1937.
'The answer to' Rudolph Palumbo to Robert Byron, 24 December 1937.

383 'would it be' Gwendoline, Duchess of Norfolk to the Georgian Group, April 1938 [GG].
'The Duke of Norfolk' 'The Secrets of Abingdon Street', *New Statesman*, 4 June 1938.
'corresponds, almost' broadcast 4 June 1938, copy of text supplied to author by the late Sir John Summerson.

384 'The style of the' 'The Destruction of Georgian London', *New Statesman*, 11 December 1937.
'personal attacks' Georgian Group minutes, 8 December 1937 [GG].

385 'the most enchanting' 'Notebook', *Spectator*, 7 July 1938.
'rising above' *The Times*, 16 March 1936.

386 'unexcelled' *The Times*, 15 June 1938.

387 'will have to pass' 'The Secrets of Abingdon Street', *New Statesman*, 4 June 1938.
'It is with amazement' Ewart Culpin to Kingsley Martin, editor of *New Statesman*, 8 June 1938, copy letter.

388 'nothing could be' *The Times*, 15 June 1938.
'You wouldn't' Robert Byron to John Mavrogordato, June 1938 [JM].
'the enormous' Georgian Group minutes, 17 May 1938 [GG].

389 'These architects', passim *New Statesman*, 22 January 1938.

28 Warmongering

390 'Italy is the' ELG, p. 61.
'Hitler' Persian travel diary, 25 January 1934.
'a universal' 'The European Consciousness', *Cherwell*, 7 November 1925.

391 'landmark' 'A Clerk's Apology', *New Statesman*, 26 March 1938.
'levy a blackmail' unpublished letter to *New Statesman*, 2 November 1936, relating to published letter in *The Times*, 29 October 1936.
'driven further' *The Times*, 29 October 1936.

392 'I can't help' Robert Byron to James Lees-Milne, 9 January 1937 [JLM].
'Are you for' from 'Authors take sides on the Spanish war', *Left Review* pamphlet, November 1937.
'You condemn' ibid.
393 'but my' ibid.
'Nobody's' ibid.
'[it] might help' Robert Byron to Kingsley Martin, carbon copy, 15 March 1938.
'Every writer', passim 'A Clerk's Apology', *New Statesman*, 26 March 1938.
395 'It is good' Ewan Butler to Robert Byron, 17 May 1938.
'They said' Jonathan Guinness with Catherine Guinness, *The House of Mitford* (Hutchinson, 1984), p. 410.
396 'I want to see' Christiphen Sykes, *Four Studies in Loyalty*, p. 166.
'prelude to' Robert Byron, Nuremberg diary, 3 September 1938.
'in the heart' ibid., entry dated 31 August 1938, written 3 September 1938.
397 'to which five' Charles Ritchie, *The Siren Years: a Canadian Diplomat Abroad, 1937–1945* (Macmillan, Canada, 1974), p. 38.
'among the' Nuremberg diary, 6 September 1938.
'my fingers', passim ibid., 8 September 1938.
'a feeling of' ibid., 6 September 1938.
398 'it came to me' ibid.
'published leader' ibid., 8 September 1938.
'the buoying' Virginia Cowles, *Looking for Trouble* (Hamish Hamilton, 1941), p. 149.
'I saw a red' ibid., p. 156.
399 'A pleasant scene' Nuremberg diary, 13 September 1938.
'If these' Virginia Cowles, *Looking for Trouble*, p. 161.
'As his fury' Nuremberg diary, 13 September 1938.
400 'delicious' Anthony Hobson to the author.
'It is amusing' Nuremberg diary, 7 September 1938.
'Bobo's confidence' ibid., 13 September 1938.
'should be exposed' 'Propaganda in Germany', section II.
'frenzied', passim 'Propaganda in Germany', section III.
401 'military' *The Times*, 26 September 1938.

'How horrible' *The Times*, 28 September 1938.
402 'When the war' Propaganda file.
403 'the desire' *The Times*, 1 October 1938.
'their hearts' ibid.
'Robert Byron' Percy Muir, *Minding my own Business* (Chatto & Windus, 1956), p. 215.
404 'I told him' LH, 8 January 1939.

29 Crisis Pending

405 'I dislike' American travel diary, 1 November 1938.
406 'The coastal' LH, 10 November 1938.
'a country' American travel diary, 17 November 1938.
'reasonableness' American travel diary, undated entry, p. 38.
'I am bored' American travel diary, 29 November 1938.
407 'a huge plush' LH, 22 December 1938.
'She has suddenly' LH, 28 December 1938.
'that "Herr"' Lucy Butler to David Pryce-Jones, undated.
'We will never' article by Virginia Cowles, *Sunday Times*, 1 January 1939.
408 'enemies of' *The Times*, 12 November 1938.
'It confirmed' MS diary note, 28 December 1938.
'I shall have' Christopher Sykes, *Four Studies in Loyalty*, p. 163.
409 'the goodwill' 'The Unspoken Alliance', p. 2.
'as a gesture' ibid., p. 31.
'Many people' ibid.
'a miserable' Baltic diary, 11/12 December 1936.
'or other' 'The Unspoken Alliance', final section.
'whenever the' G. M. Young to Robert Byron, 14 February 1939.
'It is everywhere' *The Times*, 10 June 1939.
410 'I have got to' Robert Byron to Colonel Medlicott, 5 April 1939, copy letter.
'I am quite' E. F. Richardson to Robert Byron, undated.
'the destiny' *The Times*, 16 March 1939.
'I cannot believe' ibid.
'any attempt' *The Times*, 18 March 1939.
'I could not help' LH, 18 March 1939.

411 'Are you in' Christopher Sykes, *Four Studies in Loyalty*, p. 173; Richard Boston, *Osbert Lancaster*, p. 118.
'the rather special' Robert Byron to D. B. Woodburn, 1 May 1939, copy letter.
'we have you' D. B. Woodburn to Robert Byron, 25 May 1939.
412 'It is not' *Sunday Times*, 14 May 1939.
'some of them' *Daily Express*, 19 May 1939.
'the methods' *Sunday Times*, 21 May 1939.
'What you mean' Christopher Sykes, *Four Studies in Loyalty*, p. 174.
413 'English governing class' 'A Clerk's Apology', *New Statesman*, 26 March 1938.
'I see you' *Evening Standard*, 4 May 1938.
'Pity you're so' 9 July 1939.
'persistently', passim Christopher Sykes, *Four Studies in Loyalty*, pp. 174–5.
414 'in the central' James Lees-Milne, *Fourteen Friends*, p. 154.
'Inside the house' LH, January 1939.
415 '[I] am sorry' Eric Byron to Robert Byron, 27 June 1939.
'I feel worried' Margaret Byron to Robert Byron, 27 July 1939.
416 'that refined' James Lees-Milne, *Fourteen Friends*, p. 152.
417 'sheaves' *Architect*, 21 July 1939.
'wear eighteenth' poster for the ball.
418 'to give our' *The Times*, 11 July 1939.
'please don't write' Robert Byron to Eric Byron, 16 August 1939.
419 'Really Agnes' Nancy Mitford to Robert Byron, 9 July 1939.
'full of' LH, 18 August 1939.
'allow her vital' *The Times*, 24 August 1939.
420 'The crisis has' LH, 25 August 1939.
'Appeasement' LH, 1 September 1939.
'Well, there's' Christopher Sykes, *Four Studies in Loyalty*, p. 175.

30 Called to Arms

421 'a slight' LH, 10 September 1939.

'the squalor' LH, 22 October 1939.
'to inform', passim memorandum, 22 September 1939.
422 'I have nearly' Robert Byron to Harold Macmillan, 7 July 1939 [MAC].
'law above', passim unfinished MS.
423 '[it] is very' Robert Byron to Harold Macmillan, 7 July 1939 [MAC].
'the highly' H. V. Hodson to Robert Byron, 24 October 1939.
'common government', passim Clarence Streit, *Union Now.*
424 'The more people' Charles Kimber to Robert Byron, July/August 1939.
'adviser' *Radio Times*, 1 September 1939.
'sufficient', passim MS of script, 12 September 1939.
425 'seems to have' unpublished diary, 10 September 1939.
426 'There are some' *The Times*, 8 November 1939.
'but for the' unpublished diary, 7 November 1939.
'a wild' LH, 4 November 1939.
'it is absolutely' text of speech, 9 January 1940.
427 'So you see' *Listener*, 17 October 1940.
'the beastly', passim LH, 4 February 1940, 26 November 1939.
'I do feel' Robert Byron to Ewan Butler, 19 April 1940.
'haphazard' memorandum sent 24 April 1940.
428 'a rude awakening' text of broadcast.
'The present' unpublished article, 'The Word and the Sword'.
'there is no new' Desmond Morton to Clementine Churchill, 27 June 1940.
429 'with the all clear' Robert Byron to James Lees-Milne [JLM].
'I really do' LH, 9 October 1940.
'To my surprise' Christopher Sykes, *Four Studies in Loyalty*, p. 176.
430 'gave one an' ibid., p. 177.
'Fortunately' LH, 1940.
'She is dreadfully' Nancy Mitford to Robert Byron, 5 January 1940.
'Bobo is' Nancy Mitford to Robert Byron, 6 January 1940.
'The result' memorandum from Robert Byron.

431 'when I recollect', passim typed broadcast text, 28 October 1940.

'It came like', passim text of broadcast, 7 November 1940.

433 'By his reference' text of broadcast, January 1941.

'If you say' Robert Byron to James Lees-Milne, 27 September 1939 [JLM].

434 'As for forgiveness' James Lees-Milne to Robert Byron, 2 June 1940.

'I must say' James Lees-Milne to Robert Byron, 6 June 1940.

'An American lady' James Lees-Milne, *Another Self*, p. 148.

435 'As a matter' Anne Renshaw to the author.

'a splendid' LH, 19 February 1941.

'Don't worry' LH, ibid.

'I wish we could' Eric Byron to Robert Byron, 27 March 1941.

436 'other boats' Margaret Byron to Cyril Lakin, 22 April 1941.

Index

Works by Robert Byron (RB) appear directly under title; works by others under author's name

Abbas (of Persian 'roads' police), 291
Abberley Hall, Worcestershire, 10, 13, 16, 19
Abdy, Diana, Lady, 234, 277, 282
Abdy, Sir Robert, 234, 256, 277, 334
Abelson, Tamara *see* Rice, Tamara Talbot
Abercorn, Mary Anna, Dowager Duchess of (*née* Curzon), 24–5, 40, 61
Abyssinia: Italy invades (1935), 390–1
Ackerman, Phyllis (Mrs Upham Pope), 274
Acton, Arthur, 42–3
Acton, Hortense (*née* Mitchell), 42
Acton, (Sir) Harold: and Clonmore, 25; on Rudolph Messel, 29; background and upbringing, 42–3; studies drawing under Evans, 42, 44; and Brian Howard, 43–4, 46; at Oxford, 54, 57, 61–2, 69, 73; RB visits at La Pietra, 57; collecting, 61–2, 68; friendship with RB, 62, 121–2; poetry published, 62; and planned Oxford Victorian exhibition, 64–5; in Hypocrites Club, 66–7; dress, 68; published in *Cherwell*, 78; visits Nina Seafield in Scotland, 118; life in London, 120–1; writing career, 120–1, 348–9; contributes to RB/Brian Howard essay collection, 152; as best man at Waugh's first wedding, 158; and Geoffrey Scott, 223; on Desmond Parsons, 228; financial resources, 235; Diana Mitford's feelings for, 261; in Peking, 348–52; *The Last Medici*, 348
Acton, William, 45, 221, 278, 369
Adams, Mrs (William Walrond's mother), 30–1
Adrianos, Father, 111
Afghanistan: RB's expedition to, 275, 292, 294–9, 319–26, 328; RB reports on roads for Military Intelligence, 328–9; RB writes on, 353–4, 357–8, 373
Ah-Chung (cook), 201, 203
Ah-Den (overseer), 201, 206
Ailesbury, George William Brudenell-Bruce, 6th Marquess of, 59
Albania: Italy invades, 411
Alexander, Tony, 154
Ali Pasha (Albanian tyrant), 237
Alington, Cyril Argentine, 15–16, 30–1
All Hallows church, Lombard Street, London, 376
Amalia, Queen of Otho of Greece, 129
American Institute: *Bulletin*, 331
Amyot, Etienne, 163
Ancient Monuments Act (1900), 377
Anglo-Hellenic League, 180, 221
Anglo-Iranian Oil Company: RB's post with, 368
Anglo-Persian Oil Company, 290
Antrim, Angela, Countess of (*née* Sykes), 419, 425–6
Antrim, Randal John Somerled McDonnell, 8th Earl of, 419, 426, 434
appeasement policy, 411, 420
Appreciation of Architecture, The (RB), 268, 273, 275
Architectural Review: RB contributes to, 179, 217–18, 220, 222–4, 233, 240, 242, 252, 254, 276, 342; Betjeman at, 257; and London architecture, 264–6; criticizes Peter Fleming's *Travels from Tartary*, 361; attacks demolition of London buildings, 376
Ardeshir I, Sassanian king, 306
Aristarchus, Father, 145
Armenian massacres, 71–2
Armstrong-Jones, Ronald, 349
Army & Navy Stores, London, 200, 202
Asia (magazine), 333
Assad, Sardar, 334
Assheton-Smith, Sir Michael ('Michael Duff'), 425
Astrakhan, Miss (Soviet guide), 242
Atatürk, Kemal, 255

Atchley, Shirley Clifford, 106, 237
Athens: RB first visits (1925), 84–7, 89; homosexuality in, 101–2; RB revisits (1926), 100–2, 106–8; (1927), 128–30; planning and building, 129; RB visits on return from India, 221
Athos Charter (1926), 110, 116, 132
Auden, Wystan Hugh, 392
Auersperg, Countess, 162
Austria, 158; Germans occupy (*Anschluss*, 1938), 393–4, 396, 413
Avisimov, Professor, 244

Baalbek, 286
Baddeley, Hermione, 384
Baghdad, 287–8
Baikal, Lake, 344–5
Baker, Sir Herbert, 217–18, 223–4, 233, 262–3, 266, 384
Baldwin, Betty, 94
Baldwin, Oliver, 71–3, 179; *Six Prisons and Two Revolutions*, 98
Baldwin, Stanley (*later* 1st Earl), 93, 391
Balfour, (Sir) John (Jock), 409
Balfour, Patrick *see* Kinross, 3rd Baron
Balkans: RB travels to (1925), 80–9; *see also* Greece
Balkh, 323
Balston, Thomas, 62, 77, 123, 147, 149–50, 180
Bamian, Afghanistan: Buddhist site and figures, 325, 338
Bankhead, Tallulah, 229
Barkhin, G., 242
Barman, Christian, 267
Barry, (Sir) Gerald, 263–4
Baynes, Norman, 182; *The Byzantine Empire*, 168–9, 172
BBC (British Broadcasting Corporation): RB talks on, 180, 216, 233; television service, 364; RB joins European News Department, 421, 423, 427–31
Beale, Stanley, 27
Beaton, (Sir) Cecil, 417
Beatty, Chester, 115
Beauchamp, Lettice, Countess of (*née* Grosvenor), 61, 216
Beauchamp, William Lygon, 7th Earl of, 55, 57–8, 91, 153–4
Beaverbrook, William Maxwell Aitken, 1st Baron, 173, 186, 189, 392
Beddington, Jack, 233, 335, 367
Bedford Square, London, 377
Bell, Sir Charles, 199–201, 203; *Tibet Past and Present*, 212
Bell, Clive, 181
Benaki, A. E., 239, 255
Bender (Intourist guide), 248–51
Bennett, Arnold, 157
Berlin: RB visits Ewan Butler in, 395, 407–8
Berlin, Mr & Mrs Irving, 405
Berners, Gerald Tyrwhitt-Wilson, 14th Baron, 230, 234
Betjeman, (Sir) John: relations with Penelope Chetwode, 257; works for *Architectural Review*, 267; and *Shell Guides*, 335–6; in Georgian Group, 380; and Wilhelmine Cresswell, 380; marriage to Penelope, 685
Birch Grove (house), Sussex, 367
Birr Castle, King's County, Ireland, 124–5, 178, 228, 260
Birth of Western Painting, The (RB, with David Talbot Rice), 134, 180–2, 184–6, 271
Blackbirds, The (US cabaret troupe), 120, 127
Blackheath: RB's childhood in, 8–9
Blomfield, Sir Reginald, 264–5
Blood, Captain (of Saugong), 208–9
Bombay, 190
Boniface, Father, 115–16
Böös (country house), 159, 161
Boothby, Robert (*later* Baron), 126
Borough, Revd (English chaplain in Constantinople), 117
Borra, Giovanni Battista, 381
Bossom, Alfred, 387
Bower, Leonard: in Greece, 85–8, 90, 100–2, 104, 106–8; tonsillectomy, 93; relations with RB, 102, 163; in London, 232
Bowra, Sir Maurice, 40
'Boz' *see* Goldman, Bosworth
Brettingham, Matthew, 381
Briggs, Lady, 178
British Council: RB's lecture tour for (1937), 364
British Museum: RB attacks over treatment of Elgin Marbles, 411–12
Brunswick Square, London, 383–4
Buchanan, Sir George, 241
Buchanan, Stella, 294
Bullard, (Sir) Reader, 244–6
Burlington Magazine, 234
Burmah Shell (company), 216, 219–20; *see also* Shell oil company
Burton, Decimus, 264
Butler, Rohan, 338, 353, 394–5, 400, 403, 407, 420, 427
Butler, Georgia (Rohan/Lucy's daughter), 407, 420
Butler, Lucy (*née* Byron; RB's sister): birth, 8; at Coulsden, 13; move to Vienna, 153;

RB visits Holland with, 221; translations, 235; Betjeman admires, 268; marriage, 338; and RB in Peking, 350; RB visits in Washington, 353–4; at Nancy Mitford's wedding, 372; RB visits in Berlin, 407–8; leaves Berlin (1939), 420
Butt, Dame Clara, 70
Butterwick, J. C., 51
Byron, Alice (Eric's sister): death, 4
Byron, Anne (RB's sister): birth, 8; move to Vienna, 153; RB visits in Vienna, 228, 232; attitude to work, 235; assists with *Shell Guide to Wiltshire*, 336; mother's anxiety over not marrying, 337; at Nancy Mitford's wedding, 372; marriage amd move to Yorkshire, 375
Byron, Arthur (Cecil's son), 33
Byron, Cecil (RB's uncle), 4, 33
Byron, Edmund (RB's grandfather), 3–4, 6, 13–15, 17, 32, 51
Byron, Edmund (RB's three ancestors), 1
Byron, Elizabeth (*née* Green), 1
Byron, Emily (*née* Jeffreys; RB's grandmother), 3–4
Byron, Eric (RB's father): birth, 3; engineering career, 4–8; weak health, 4; marriage, 5; work in Great War, 10; and RB's admission to Eton, 16; and father's death and estate, 33–5; settles at Knowle, 37; moves to Savernake Lodge, 59; moves to Vienna, 153, 158; anxiety over RB's career, 179; financial difficulties, 234, 415; considers future of Savernake Lodge, 236, 337; sells lease of Savernake Lodge and buys Overton vicarage, 356, 365; decision on Overton, 414; inherits from brother Thomas, 415; unaware of RB's death, 435
Byron, George Gordon, 6th Baron: RB associated with, 1; in Albania, 237
Byron, Julia (*née* Jeffreys), 2
Byron, Louisa (*née* Brassey), 22
Byron, Lucy Anne (*née* Whettam), 2
Byron, Lucy (RB's aunt) *see* Hall Hall, Lucy
Byron, Lucy (RB's sister) *see* Butler, Lucy
Byron, Margaret (RB's mother; 'Daisy'): background, 4–5; marriage, 5; on RB's childhood intelligence, 9; loses father and brothers, 10; and RB's admission to Eton, 15, 17–18; visits RB at Eton, 20; RB confides in, 35; and RB's extravagant dress, 49; moves to Savernake Lodge, 59; obstructs RB's trip to Russia, 72; moves to Vienna, 153, 158; and RB's presence at mock wedding, 174; anxiety over RB's career, 179; sees RB off to India, 187; letters from RB in Ceylon, 194; begs RB not to return from India by air, 215; and RB's book on India and Tibet, 225; on financial difficulties, 234; and RB's travel diary, 287; and RB's absence in Afghanistan, 300–1; influence on RB, 301; letters from RB in Persia, 302, 312–13, 319; and disposal of Savernake Lodge, 337; letter from RB in Peking, 361; moves to Overton vicarage, 365–6; troubled relations with RB, 415; in wartime Wiltshire, 429; and RB's death at sea, 435–6
Byron, Robert (Henry): background and genealogy, 1–2; life and behaviour at Eton, 1, 20–30, 32, 36–7, 39, 48–51; birth and childhood, 6–8; early education, 9–11; interest in natural history as child and youth, 9, 11–12, 37; diary and sketchbook, 11–12, 41; eating habits, 12, 322; admitted to Eton, 15–19; rowing, 20; sporting prowess, 22; appearance, 23–4, 35, 40, 163; eye trouble, 24; practical joking, 26, 30–1; homosexuality, 29, 101–2, 163, 176, 228, 353; protests at loss of Coulsden on grandfather's death, 33–6, 38; devotion to mother, 35–6; collecting, 36–7, 61, 68, 108; at Knowle, 37; hunting, 37, 118, 179, 337; friendship with Henry Yorke, 40–1; artistic interests and activities, 41–2, 44–5, 47–8; verbal aggressiveness, 45–6, 69–70, 122, 237; poetry, 46; dress, 48–9, 190; devotion to architecture, 51–2, 56, 223, 263–9, 376, 388–9; leaves Eton for Oxford, 52–3; life at Oxford (Merton College), 54–5, 60–2, 65–6, 69, 73–4; tours Italy with Beauchamp, 55–8; fondness for Savernake Lodge, 59–60, 337; interior decorating and furnishing, 60–1; plans for exhibition of Victorian age at Oxford banned, 62–4, 68; promotes Victorian revival, 62–5, 68, 70–1; mimics Queen Victoria, 67, 161; musical accomplishments, 67; travels in central Europe (1924), 72–3; sexual adventures, 75; literary ambitions, 77, 83, 98, 275–6; writes for and edits *Cherwell*, 78–9, 91, 93, 97; takes third class degree, 79; travels to Greece (1925), 80–90; travel diaries, 82, 95–7, 147, 276, 287, 352, 356; journalism and periodical articles, 83, 88, 92–4, 156, 179, 186, 189, 216, 222–4, 233, 240, 254, 288, 329–30, 351, 364, 392, 429; asked to leave Oxford, 92; fined for insulting behaviour, 94; social life in

Byron, Robert (Henry) (*cont.*)
London, 94, 118–22, 126, 236, 368–9; literary style, 95–7, 141, 356–9, 362; revisits Greece (1926), 99–103, 106–17; (1927), 128–30; visits Constantinople, 104–5; visits Mount Athos, 110–15; religious beliefs, 117, 152, 398; financial difficulties, 123, 156, 179, 216, 234–5, 275, 302–3, 327, 337, 366; literary earnings, 123, 134, 156, 216, 240, 275, 352; returns to Mount Athos (1927), 128, 131–48; luggage, 133–4; speaks Greek, 133; photography, 144, 218, 244, 256, 306, 331; writing method, 147–8; writes about Mount Athos, 148–50; collaborates with Brian Howard on essay colllection, 151–2; travels to Spain (1928), 153–6; visits Austria and Czechoslovakia, 158–64; conversation, 163; loathing of officialdom, 164–5; historical principles, 166–9; historical sources, 168–71; broadcast talks, 180, 216, 430–3; public speaking, 180; views on art, 181–5; colour critique, 185; flies to and travels in India and Ceylon, 186–98, 215, 216–20; expedition to Tibet and Sikkim, 199–214; writes bulletins for Burmah Shell, 216, 219–20; loses religious faith, 217; puts on weight, 220; returns from India, 220–1; condemns English racial superiority, 226–7; attachment to Desmond Parsons, 228–9, 231–2, 258–60, 279–82, 301; tours central Europe with Desmond Parsons, 228, 232; suffers nervous strain and depressions, 235, 258, 351, 374, 410; visits monasteries of Meteora, Thessaly, 237–8; visit to Soviet Russia, 240, 241–51; promotes Byzantine art, 255–6; exhibition of drawings and photographs (London, 1932), 256; relations with Penelope Chetwode, 256–7; tonsillectomy, 260; attempts and abandons novel, 262; Nancy Mitford dedicates *Christmas Pudding* to, 262; campaigns over London architecture, 263–6; plans expedition to Turkestan, 270–3; expedition to Persia, 275–9, 288–94, 302–19; plans history of Great War, 275, 366–7; in Middle East, 285–7; in Afghanistan, 294–9, 319–26; dispute with Herzfeld at Persepolis, 308–11; in Turkestan, 321; co-writes satirical novel with Sykes, 328, 333; reports on Afghan roads for Military Intelligence, 328–9; exhibits drawings (1934), 330; contributes to Upham Pope's *Survey*, 331, 338–9; lecture tour in USA (1935), 332–3; writes *Shell Guide to Wiltshire*, 335–6; sells horse, 337; temper, 337, 351, 366; attends Leningrad Congress (1934), 340–2; travels in Russia, 342–6; in China, 347–52, 356; stays with Desmond Parsons in Peking, 347; illness in Peking, 351; in Japan, 353; wins National Book Fair gold medal (1937), 363; lecture tour for British Council (1937), 364; appointed to post with Anglo-Iranian Oil Company, 368; elected to Garrick Club, 369; and Desmond Parsons' death, 370; relations with James Lees-Milne, 371–2; swimming, 372–3; dispute with Upham Pope over 'Persian Classical Architecture', 373–4; attacks demolition of London buildings and features, 376–8; as Deputy Chairman of Georgian Group, 379–80, 382–8; and European political situation (1930s), 390–4, 401–2, 410, 412–13; propaganda work, 394–5, 402–4, 427–8, 430; visits Germany to observe Nazism, 395–400; mission to USA (1938), 404–6, 408–9, 422; holidays in Ireland, 410, 418–19; troubled relations with mother, 415; rents house in Swan Walk, Chelsea, 416; attends Georgian Ball at Osterley Park, 417–18; on outbreak of 1939 war, 420–1; proposes wartime book on new world order, 422–3; supports Federal Union, 423–7; elected to Pratt's Club, 429; appointed war correspondent in Middle East, 432; killed at sea, 435–6

Byron, Thomas, MP, 2

Byron, Thomas (MP's son), 2–3

Byron, Colonel Thomas (RB's ancestor), 2, 33

Byron, Thomas (RB's uncle), 4, 6, 14, 32–3; death, 415

Byzantine Achievement, The (RB): completed, 166–71; publication and reception, 171–3; on scientific revolution, 189; on Nestorian missionaries, 192; US publication, 332

Byzantine art: RB studies, 114–15, 139; RB on, 134–5, 141, 182–5; Clive Bell on, 181–2; exhibition (Paris, 1931), 234, 255; rediscovery of, 255

Byzantine Renaissance, The see Birth of Western Painting, The

Byzantine Society, Athens, 255

Byzantium: civilization and history, 104–5, 119, 134; RB admires, 168–71; architecture, 207; *see also* Constantinople

Cadogan, Sir Alexander, 402
Cairo, 220
Calcutta, 198–9, 214, 215, 219
Carlton Gardens, London, 263–5
Carlton House Terrace, London, 263–6
Carol II, King of Romania, 428
Cartaliss, Sotiri, 88
Caryes, Mount Athos, 145–6
Casson, (Sir) Hugh, 255
Casson, Stanley, 131
Castle Grant, Strathspey, 125
Castolovi̇ce, Czechoslovakia, 161
Catholicism: RB's hostility to, 170, 172
Ceylon, 192–5
Chamberlain, Neville, 396, 399, 401–3, 410–11, 418, 420
Channon, Sir Henry ('Chips') and Lady Honor (*née* Guinness), 282, 413
Chapman & Hall (publishers), 152
Cherwell (magazine), 64, 70, 78–9, 91, 93, 97, 390
Cheryan, Mr (of Travancore), 196
Chetwode, Penelope (*later* Betjeman), 256–8, 268, 271
China: Desmond Parsons in, 301, 343, 347–8; RB's visit to, 343, 347–8, 350–1
Cholerton, A. T., 247–8
Church of England: RB criticizes for demolition of buildings, 376–8
Churchill, Clementine, 428
Churchill, George Spencer, 130
Churchill, (Sir) Winston, 227, 427
Cisoxiana, 338
Clark, Kenneth (*later* Baron), 341, 427
Clarke, Mrs (Chelsea landlady), 416
Clay, Reginald, 23
Cleanthes, Stamatis, 129
Clements, Mrs (cook at Savernake), 156, 178
Clewer (convent, Windsor), 48
Clonmore, William Cecil Forward Howard, Lord (*later* 8th Earl of Wicklow): at Eton with RB, 1, 22, 24–6, 28–30; background, 24–5; homosexuality, 29; practical joking, 30–1; leaves Eton, 39; friendship with Harold Acton, 43; at Oxford, 52, 54, 73–5; trip to Russia with RB, 71; infatuation with Peter Rodd, 75; RB stays with, 124; religious commitment, 221–2; friendship with Betjeman, 268
Clutton-Brock, Alan, 45
Coates, Wells, 266
Cockburn, Claud, 101
Cockerell, C. R., 264
Commissioners of Crown Lands, 263–5
Connolly, Cyril: on RB at Eton, 49; contributes to RB/Brian Howard essay collection, 152; at Glenarm Castle, 419
Constantinople (Istanbul): history, 104–5; RB visits, 104–5, 116–17, 252; Santa Sophia, 105, 254; in RB's history, 169–71
Cooch Behar, Maharanee of, 215
Cooper, Alfred Duff, 391
Coulsden Court, Surrey, 2–3, 13, 32–6, 38, 40, 63
Country Life (magazine), 224, 233, 254, 262–3, 272–3, 276, 283, 329–30, 332, 364, 429
Courtauld Institute: exhibits Byzantine icons, 255
Covel, John, 149
Cowles, Virginia, 398–9, 403, 407
Cresswell, Wilhelmine *see* Harrod, Wilhelmine, Lady
Crete, 147–8, 184
Cullen House, Banffshire, 118
Culpin, Ewart, 386–8
Cunard, Maud Alice (Emerald), Lady, 236, 254, 348, 371
Cunard, Nancy, 392
Curzon (of Kedleston), George Nathaniel, Marquess: *Persia and the Persian Question*, 290
Curzon, Robert, 149, 238
Cyprus, 282–3
Czechoslovakia, 159–62, 396, 398–9, 401, 410

D'Abernon, Edgar Vincent, Viscount, 255
Daily Express, 186, 189, 281, 412
Daily Mail: RB works for, 92–4; praises RB's published books, 157, 172; imperialist views, 227
Daily News: RB writes on Spain for, 153, 155–6
Daily Sketch, 157
Dalai Lama, 13th, 199, 202–3
Dalton, O. M.: *Byzantine Art and Archaeology*, 115
Damascus, 287
Danzig, 364–5, 418
Deakin, Ralph, 368
Delhi *see* New Delhi
D'Erlanger, Baroness, 380
Derwent, George Harcourt Vanden-Bempde-Johnstone, 3rd Baron, 378–80, 382
Dick, Sir William Reid, 385
Diehl, Charles: *Manuel d'art byzantin*, 114
Diez, Ernst, 273, 296; *Churasanische Baudenkmaler* (*Architectural Monuments of Chorassan*), 290, 293, 317
Dimbleby (*Daily Mail* news editor; 'Fatman'), 92, 94

Dineley, Mark, 270, 272–4, 277
Dnieper dam, 249
Dodecanese, 87–8, 91, 93, 98, 106
Douglas, Norman, 358–9, 393
Driberg, Tom (*later* Baron Bradwell), 369, 406
Duccio, 182
Duckworth (publishers), 77, 123, 134, 147, 149, 180, 216
Duff, Michael *see* Assheton-Smith, Sir Michael
Duggan, Alfred: at Oxford, 54, 66, 73; travels to Balkans with RB, 80–2, 89–90; background and character, 81, 120; social life in London, 119–20; meets RB at Mount Athos, 146; broken engagement to Sylvia Nairn, 174; drink problem, 174
Duveen, Joseph, Baron, 411

Eden, Anthony (*later* 1st Earl of Avon), 391
Effingham, Gordon Frederick Howard, 5th Earl of, 64
Egypt, 220
Einstein, Albert, 408
Elgin Marbles, 411–12
Eliot, T. S., 393
Elizabeth, Queen of George VI, 409
Elkins, Miss (secretary of American Institute), 332
Elmley, William Lygon, Viscount, 55, 57, 66, 69, 394
Ephesus, 107
Erskine, Hamish *see* St Clair-Erskine, Hamish
Esher, Oliver Baliol Brett, 3rd Viscount, 378–80
Essay on India (RB), 224–7
Esterházy, Count Charles, 159
Eton Candle, The (ed. Brian Howard), 46
Eton College: RB attends, 1, 18–30, 32, 37, 39, 48–51; RB admitted to, 14–18; First War casualties, 21; homosexual practices at, 29; art teaching at, 41–2, 44–5; Acton and Howard at, 43–6; dress, 48–9; classics at, 51; RB leaves, 52–3
Eton Society of Arts, 45–7
Europe: rising tensions in 1930s, 390–9
Europe in the Looking Glass (RB), 119, 121, 147, 390
Evans, Sidney, 41–2, 44–5
Everett, Henry, 379
Eyres-Monsell, Joan, 341

Fagin, Mrs (Eton dame), 30
Fallmerayer, Jakob, 168
Faringdon, Alexander Henderson, 1st Baron, 80, 155
Faringdon, Gavin Henderson, 2nd Baron *see* Henderson, Gavin
Fascism: RB's distrust of, 390, 392–3
Fay (manservant), 416
Federal Union, 423–7
First Russia Then Tibet (RB), 327, 359–60, 367
Firuzabad, 304–5, 330
Flaxman, John, 198, 226
Fleming, Peter, 359–61, 428; *Brazilian Adventure*, 360; *News from Tartary*, 359, 361
Fonseca, José Nicolau da, 191
Forbes, Lady Angela, 98
Forthampton Court, Worcestershire, 40, 54, 177
Fothergill, John, 64
Francis, Mar, 196
Fyfe, David, 164, 189, 199, 216, 258

Gabriel, Father, 284
Gandhi, Mohandas Karamchand (Mahatma), 227
Gangtok, Sikkim, 213
Gardner, Evelyn (*later* Waugh), 158
Garrick Club: RB elected to, 369
George I, King of Greece, 129
George V, King: memorial, 385–8
George VI, King: coronation (1937), 376; visit to USA, 409–10
Georgian Group: formed, 378–81; conservation activities, 382–8; at Lord Jersey's Georgian Ball, 416–18
Gerhardi, William, 215
Germany: aggression (1930s), 395–403, 410; persecution of Jews in, 407–8; pact with USSR (1939), 419; invades Poland, 420
Gibbon, Edward, 168
Gill, Arthur, 233
Giotto, 182
Glenarm Castle, Co. Antrim, 419
Goa, 190–1
Godard, André, 331
Goebbels, Josef, 395, 397, 407
Goering, Hermann, 400
Gohar Shad, Empress, 338, 357–8; mosque, 318–19
Goldman, Bosworth ('Boz'): joins RB for Turkestan expedition, 270–3, 281; invests in charcoal-burning plant, 275, 277, 293, 369; delays and problems with vehicles, 283, 285–6, 292–5, 302; forwards money to RB, 288; RB meets in Herat, 299; and RB's determination, 301; RB dismisses charcoal-burner vehicles, 357; resumes relations with RB, 369

INDEX

Goldring, Douglas, 378–80
Gothic architecture, 223–4
Graham, Alastair, 100–2, 104, 146–7, 240, 321
Gray, Basil, 354
Great War (1914–18): RB plans history of, 275, 366–7
Greco, El (Domenico Theotocopoulos), 153–4, 180, 182–5, 256
Greece: RB first visits (1925), 84–90; conflict with Turkey, 88–90; RB plans history of post-classical, 98, 106, 119, 121, 156, 162, 166, 275; RB revisits (1926), 99–103, 106–7; (1927), 128–30, 147; (1931), 236–9; Spengler on classical, 168; Italy invades, 431; RB's wartime broadcasts on, 431–2
Green, Henry *see* Yorke, Henry
Greene, Graham, 362
Grinberg (Soviet architect), 242, 253, 342–3
Guedalla, Philip, 62, 65
Guinness, Benjamin, 254
Guinness, Bryan (*later* 2nd Baron Moyne): friendship with RB, 108, 260–1; visits Mount Athos and Constantinople with RB, 108–9, 113, 116–17; religious scepticism, 117; engagement to Diana Mitford, 162–3; in Vienna, 162–4; marriage to Diana, 174–5; Henry Yorke complains of behaviour, 176; attends RB's lecture on Travancore, 221; Waugh accuses of paying for publication of poems, 236; and RB's relations with Betjeman, 267
Guinness, Diana *see* Mitford, Diana
Guinness, Lady Evelyn (*née* Erskine), 108–9
Guinness, Colonel Walter (1st Baron Moyne), 108, 116
Gumbad-i-Kabus tomb tower, Persia, 273, 278, 316, 317, 330
Gunnis, Rupert, 282–3
Gyantse, Tibet, 208–13, 218

Haardt, M., 272
Hackin, Joseph, 338
Hadley, W. W., 432
Halatoff, Mrs (Soviet guide), 249
Halifax, 1st Earl of *see* Irwin, Baron
Hall Hall, Lucy (*née* Byron; RB's aunt), 6, 14–15, 33–4, 40
Hall Hall, Owen, 15
Hall Hall, Theodore, 6, 15, 17, 33, 38
Hamber, Major, 328
Harbord, Felix, 417
Hardinge, Sir Alexander, 409
Hardinge, Charles, Baron, 233
Harrison, Miss (schoolteacher), 11
Harrison's (London printers), 402
Harrod, (Sir) Roy, 91, 95, 106, 163, 230, 348–50, 388, 419
Harrod, Wilhelmine (Lady; *née* Cresswell; 'Billa'), 371, 380, 386, 388, 419
Hartley, Leslie Poles, 327
Hasluck, F. W., 149
Hastings, Hubert de Cronin, 264, 266–7, 376
Hay, John Stuart, 86, 94, 108, 111, 115, 123, 128–9, 146
Heine, Heinrich, 408
Henderson, Gavin (*later* 2nd Baron Faringdon): at Oxford, 54; travels to Balkans with RB, 80–5, 89–90; in London, 93; RB visits Scotland with, 118; engagement and marriage, 126–7; accompanies RB to Spain, 154; in Vienna, 164; in India and Ceylon, 165, 190, 192, 194, 198, 199; suggests expedition to Sikkim, 186, 199; quarrel with RB, 196; on expedition to Tibet with RB, 199–200, 202, 206–7, 212; RB owes money to, 216; offers to drive RB and Desmond to Munich, 237; helps RB financially, 429
Henderson, Honor (*née* Phillips): marriage to Gavin, 126–7
Henderson, John, 277, 285–6
Henlein, Konrad, 396, 398, 401
Herat, Afghanistan, 199, 294–7, 320, 338, 357–8
Herzfeld, Ernst, 308–11, 315
Heygate, John, 54
Hilliard, Arden, 67
Hilton, Charles, 33
Hilton, Eva (*née* Byron; RB's aunt), 33
Himmler, Heinrich, 397
Hislop, Paul, 413
Hitler, Adolf: rise to power and aggression, 390–1, 393, 396, 401–2, 410; and Unity Mitford, 395; at Nazi rally, 397, 399, 401; Chamberlain meets, 401–3; war threats, 419; invades Poland, 420; RB attacks in broadcast, 433
Hoare, Sir Reginald and Katherine, Lady, 314
Hodson, H. V., 423
Holburn, Jimmy, 398
Holland, 221
homosexuality: at Eton, 29; RB's, 29, 101–2, 163, 176, 228, 353; at Oxford, 75
Hore-Belisha, Leslie (*later* Baron), 421
Hourmouzios, Christodoulou, 133
Howard, Brian: at Eton, 43–7, 52–3; friendship with RB, 47–8, 151; sexual

Howard, Brian (*cont.*)
adventures, 75; collaborates with RB on essay collection, 151–2; Henry Yorke complains of behaviour, 176; religious scepticism, 217; swimming bath party, 229; RB entertains, 369; on Spanish Civil War, 392
Howson, H. E. E., 22–3, 32
Hoyland, Mr & Mrs (diplomat and wife), 303
Hudson, Edward, 233, 263, 273
Hughes, Richard, 66
Hungary, 428, 431
Hussey, Christopher, 262–4, 380
Huxley, Aldous, 46
Huyn, Count, 426
Hypocrites Club, Oxford, 6, 65–7, 73, 130

India: RB flies to and travels in, 186–92, 195–8, 215–20; RB writes on, 224–7; and self-government, 227
Information, Ministry of: formed, 402; RB seeks post with, 421–2
Innocence and Design (by 'Richard Waughburton'; i.e. RB and Christopher Sykes), 333–5, 367
International Congress and Exhibition of Persian Art and Archaeology, Third , Leningrad (1934), 340, 341, 354
Ionides, Basil, 380
Ireland: RB holidays in, 410, 418–19
Irkutsk, 344–5
Irwin, Dorothy, Lady (*née* Onslow), 217–18
Irwin, Edward Frederick Lindley Wood, Baron (*later* 1st Earl of Halifax), 217, 227, 236, 426
Isfahan, 303–4, 311–14
Isham, Gyles, 78
Istanbul *see* Constantinople
Italy: RB tours with Lygons, 55–8; invades Abyssinia, 390–1; League of Nations sanctions on, 390, 422; invades Albania, 411; invades Greece, 431

Jacks, T. L., 290
Jackson, Sir Bernard, 201
James, Montague Rhodes, 50
Janina, Greece, 237–8
Japan, 353
Jarratt (schoolmaster), 11, 16
Jersey, George Francis Child-Villiers, 9th Earl of, 416–17
Jersey, Virginia, Countess of (*née* Cherrill), 417–18
Jerusalem, 284–5
Jews: and European anti-Semitism, 160; persecuted in Germany, 407–8
Joad, C.E.M., 119
Johnson, 'Snake Hips' (band leader), 434
Johnson, William, 50–1, 57
Jonathan Holt (ship), 436
Jones, John Joseph, 10
Jungman, Teresa, 173
Jungman, Zita, 173
Justinian, Roman Emperor, 105

Kabul, 325
Kahn, Mrs Otto, 332, 341
Kala-i-Dukhtar palace, Firuzabad, 306, 331
Kanarak, Bengal, 220
Kandahar, 297, 299
Kandy, Ceylon, 192–3
Karachi, 189
Kauffer, E. McKnight, 233
Keane, D. W., 244
Kemsley, Gomer Berry, 1st Viscount, 432
Kenyon, Sir Frederick, 412
Khabarovsk, 346–7
Kharkov, 249–50
Kiev, 250
Kilby, Arthur, 9–10, 16–17
Kimber, Charles, 424
Kinross, Patrick Balfour, 3rd Baron: at Oxford, 75, 78; reviews RB's *Europe in the Looking Glass*, 119; refers to RB in gossip column, 157; on Bryan Guinness/Diana marriage, 175; Henry Yorke complains of behaviour, 176; RB lodges at London house, 179; friendship with Betjeman, 268; and RB's liking for Sykes, 278; in Persia, 293–4; RB entertains, 369; RB lodges with during war, 429
Knatchbull-Hugessen, Sir Hughe, 401
Knopf (US publisher), 332
Knowle (house), Wiltshire, 37, 58
Koela Producer Gas Plant Company, 277, 369
Krefter, Fritz, 308–10
Kristallnacht (9 November 1938), 408
Kyron, Achille, 185

Laden La, 201–2, 206, 210
Lakin, Cyril, 432
Lamb, Henry, 93, 234
Lamb, Lady Pansy, 234
Lancaster, (Sir) Osbert, 386–7
Lausanne, Treaty of (1921), 87, 89, 106
Laver, James, 71
Law, Richard, 426
Lawrence, D. H.: praises RB's *The Station*, 157
League of Nations, 390–1, 422
Lecky, William, 168
Lees-Milne, James: and RB's *The Station*,

150; on Desmond Parsons, 229–31; on RB's devotion to Desmond, 280; dines with RB, 370; rejects RB's advances, 371–2, 434; in Georgian Group, 380, 386; pro-Franco views, 392; inspects Menagerie with RB, 414; as RB's temporary lodger in Chelsea, 416; and RB's wartime departure for Middle East, 433–4; war service, 433–4
Left Review, 3
Lenin, Vladimir Ilich: tomb, 242–4, 253
Leningrad, 244–5, 341
Lewis, Rosa, 93
Lhassa, Tibet: Potala, 140–1, 192, 211; Bell's mission to, 199–200; *see also* Tibet
Liberty (Indian newspaper), 219
Lifar, Serge, 282
Listener (weekly), 233
Lloyd, George Ambrose Lloyd, 1st Baron, 236, 371
Lloyd, John ('Widow'), 65–6
Locker Lampson, Oliver, 156
London: architectural disfigurement, 263–6; demolitions in, 376–8, 381–3; in Blitz, 430
London Library, 106
London Mercury, 179, 265
London Transport: RB writes guide for, 364
Lorraine, Sir Percy, 220
Lubbock, Percy, 50–1
Lubbock, S. G., 50–1
Lubetkin, Berthold, 254, 266
Luknitsky (Leningrad guide), 245
Lutyens, Sir Edwin, 217–18, 220, 223–4, 233, 266
Luxmoore, H.E., 50, 53
Lygon, Lady Dorothy, 58
Lygon, Hugh, 30, 45, 55, 57–8, 73, 75, 91
Lygon, Lady Lettice, 58
Lygon, Reginald, 27
Lygon, Lady Sibell, 58
Lygon, William *see* Elmley, William Lygon, Viscount

MacCarthy, (Sir) Desmond, 156
Macdonald (of Younghusband expedition), 203, 206, 210
Macdonell, A. C.: *England, Their England*, 335
McGrath, Raymond, 266
Mackenzie, (Sir) Compton, 275
Maclagan, Sir Eric, 255
Macmillan, Daniel, 279, 302
Macmillan, Harold (*later* 1st Earl of Stockton): signs up RB for travel book on Persia, 279, 303; secures second book from RB, 303, 327; publishes RB/Sykes's satirical novel (*Innocence and Design*), 328, 333, 335, 367; and RB's *Road to Oxiana*, 353, 356, 367; and RB's *First Russia Then Tibet*, 360, 367; and RB's proposed book on oil industry, 368; friendship with RB, 369; and postponement of 'Persian Classical Architecture', 374; and RB's proposed wartime book, 422
Macmillan, Hugh Pattison Macmillan, Baron, 386–8
Macmillan (publishers), 276, 279, 287, 302, 354
Maconochie, Sir Richard, 369
Madras, 191–2, 198
Madura, 195–6
Magdalen College, Oxford, 69
Maillart, Ella, 361
Mallet, Victor, 405
MARS Group (Modern Architectural Research), 388–9
Marsden-Smedley, Basil, 386
Marshall (Englishman in Moscow), 246–7
Marshwood House, Dinton, Wiltshire, 414–15
Martin, Kingsley, 393
Mary, Queen of George V, 384, 417
Matthews, Kenneth, 237
Mavrogordato, John, 169, 172, 180, 271, 275, 358–9, 388
Mazar-i-Sherif, Afghanistan, 320, 322–3
Medlicott, Colonel Henry Edward, 368, 410, 424
Mehmet II, Ottoman Sultan, 105
Meier-Graefe, Julius: *The Spanish Journey*, 154, 302
Melvill, Harry, 122
Menagerie (house), Northamptonshire, 414
Mercury (US magazine), 392
Meredith, George, 43–4
Merton College, Oxford: RB attends, 52, 54–5, 60, 73–4, 77–80, 91–2
Meshed, 299–300, 317–18, 330, 432
Messel, Anne *see* Rosse, Anne, Countess of
Messel, Anne (Linley's wife), 434
Messel, Leonard, 28
Messel, Linley, 28, 434
Messel, Maud (*née* Sambourne), 28
Messel, Oliver: at Eton, 28, 30–1; at Slade, 67; at mock wedding, 173; decorations for Georgian Group functions, 384, 417
Messel, Rudolph, 28–30, 50, 54, 60, 73
Meteora monasteries, Thessaly, 237–8, 255
Middle East: wartime threat to, 432
Millet, Gabriel, 114; *Monuments de l'Athos*, 135
Mistra, 102–3, 115, 123, 147–8, 185

Mitford, Diana (*later* Guinness; *then* Lady Mosley): engagement and marriage to Bryan Guinness, 162–3, 174; hears RB's lecture on Travancore, 221; on Desmond Parsons, 230; friendship with RB, 260–1; and Waugh's jealousies, 260–1; marriage breakdown and marriage to Mosley, 261, 395
Mitford, Jessica, 176
Mitford, Nancy: friendship with RB, 175–6, 261; on authorship of *Innocence and Design*, 335; marriage to Peter Rodd, 372; in campaign for Old Palace Yard, 388; bans RB from bridge parties, 413; at Georgian Ball (1939), 417; finds bulldog puppy for RB, 418–19; RB lodges with, 429; and death of sister Unity, 430; and RB's departure for Middle East as war correspondent, 433; *Christmas Pudding*, 261–2
Mitford, Thomas David, 163–4, 175–6
Mitford, Unity, 365, 369, 395, 397, 399–400, 430
Monnet, Jean, 427
Monophysite Christians, 196–7
Moon (RB's nanny), 7
Moore, George, 43
Moore, Mrs William H., 315
Morris, Cedric, 233
Morris, William, 379
Mortimer, Roger, 22, 29
Morton, Desmond, 428
Moscow: RB visits, 240, 241–4, 246–9
Mosley, Lady Cynthia, 261
Mosley, Sir Oswald, 261, 395
Mostafavi, Dr, 309–11
Mount Athos: RB visits, 98, 108–16, 118, 123, 126, 130, 132–48; buildings compared with Lhasa Potala, 140–1, 211; RB writes on, 147–50; RB broadcasts talk on, 180; art on, 183
Muggeridge, Malcolm, 253
Mughals: architecture, 219
Munich agreement (1938), 401–2, 410
Murdocke, Jack 'Che', 91, 229
Murghab, 320–1
Murray, Gilbert, 91
Murray's Handbook for India, 191–3
Mussolini, Benito, 390, 411

Nadir Shah, King of Afghanistan: assassinated, 293
Nadjibullah (Indian servant), 190, 198
Nairn, Sylvia, 174
Nash, John, 263–4
Nash, Paul, 256
Naspati, Mr (contractor of Darjeeling), 201
Nation (US magazine), 106
National Service Campaign, 411
Nazi Party: RB meets officials, 365; RB observes in Germany, 395, 397–400
Nestorians, 140, 196–7, 221
New Delhi, 217–19, 222, 223–4, 233, 257–8, 267
New Statesman (journal), 88, 93, 255, 387–8, 391, 393, 413
New York, 332–3, 404–5
New York Times, 333
Newton, Algernon, 233
Nicolson, (Sir) Harold, 269, 436
Niedermayer, Oskar von, 296
Noel, Colonel Edward, 293–4
Noel, Captain J. B. L., 202
Norfolk, Bernard Howard, 16th Duke of, 381–3
Norfolk, Gwendoline, Dowager Duchess of, 383
Norfolk House, St James's Square, London, 381–3
Northern Ireland, 418–19
Novgorod, 245–6
Novosibirsk, 342–3
Null, Bill, 406
Nuremberg, 397–400

Observer (newspaper), 179, 256
Odessa, 250
Odom, William, 282
Ogilvie-Grant, Mark: at Eton, 43; at Oxford, 64, 73; on Victorian Revival, 64, 68; and RB's verbal style, 70; and cousin Nina Seafield, 118; on visit to Mount Athos, 130–1, 136–8, 144, 146; character and qualities, 131–2; visits Crete, 147; introduces RB to Nancy Mitford, 175; visits RB at Savernake, 178; illustrates RB's articles, 179; in Cairo, 220; illustrates Nancy Mitford's novel, 261
Old Palace Yard, London, 385–8
Olivier, Edith, 337
Osterley Park, Middlesex, 416–17
Otho, King of Greece, 129
Overton, Wiltshire, 356, 365–6, 374, 406, 414–15
Ovey, Sir Esmond, 239–42, 244
Oxford: homosexuality at, 75; women at, 75–6; RB attacks architecture of, 179–80; *see also* Merton College
Oxford Broom (magazine), 62
Oxford University Dramatic Society (OUDS), 76, 78
Oxus, River, 324–5

Palestine, 284–5
Pall Mall Gazette, 179
Palmer, William, 379–80, 384
Palumbo, Rudolph, 382–3
Pangalos, General Theodore, 91, 116
Paris: Byzantine art exhibition (1931), 234; RB meets parents in, 406
Parsons, Bridget, 119, 178, 231, 370
Parsons, Charles, 249
Parsons, Desmond: RB's relations with, 228, 231–2, 237, 258–60, 279–81; background and character, 229–31, 280; gives hat to RB, 240; separation from RB during Persian expedition, 279, 301; in Venice, 282; settles in China, 301, 343, 347–9; RB meets in Peking, 347; contracts Hodgkin's disease, 350, 369–70; and reception of RB's *Road to Oxiana*, 362; death, 370–1
Pater, Walter, 48
Patras, Greece, 84
Pears, Edwin: *The Destruction of the Greek Empire*, 105, 170; *The Fall of Constantinople*, 170
Peking (Beijing), 343, 347–52, 356
Pelly, Dennis, 174
Pemba (Tibetan interpreter), 209–10
Perry, Lionel, 268
Persepolis, 307–11, 315, 330
Persia (Iran): RB's expedition to and travels in, 274–7, 288–94, 302–19; RB plans survey and book on chief monuments, 302–3, 314; RB suggests Anglo-Russian convention on, 328; political repression in, 334; RB's writings on, 352–5, 356–7, 373
'Persian Classical Architecture' (RB's proposed book with Schroeder), 355
Peters, A. D. (literary agent), 275–6, 303, 360
Petroleum Information Bureau, 404, 429
Phari, Tibet, 206–7
Phrantzes, General, 106, 128
Plethon, Gemistos, 102
Plunket Greene, Babe, 173
Plunket Greene, David, 73–4, 76, 120
Plunket Greene, Richard, 73–4
Poland: British guarantee to, 411, 418; Germany invades (1939), 420
Ponsonby, Elizabeth (*later* Pelly), 98, 173–4, 229, 250
Ponsonby, Loelia, 173
Ponsonby, Matthew, 74, 98
Pope, Arthur Upham: scholarship and background, 273–4; RB photographs Persian monuments for, 279, 289, 291–2; photographs Persepolis, 310, 315; gives money to RB, 315; visits Gohar Shad mosque, 319; arranges US lecture tour for RB, 322; welcomes RB's return home, 330; RB works for, 331, 357; Schroeder works for, 354; RB's dispute with, 373–4; *Introduction to Persian Art*, 290; *Survey of Persian Art*, 279, 315, 331, 338–9, 373–4
Powell, Anthony: on Eton, 27–8; on Maud Yorke, 40; social unease, 40; on Sidney Evans's Studio, 42; on Brian Howard, 44; in Eton Society of Arts, 45, 123; on RB's feelings for Hugh Lygon, 57; on frescoes at Hypocrites Club, 66; and RB's homosexual adventures in Oxford, 75; published in *Cherwell*, 78; at Duckworth's publishers, 123, 150; RB's friendship with, 123–4; on Michael Rosse, 124; on Reitlinger, 131; praises RB's *The Station*, 150; and RB's affair in Japan, 353
Prague, 162
Pratt's Club: RB elected to, 429
Pressburg (Bratislava; Pozony), 159–60
Prinzhorn, Dr Hans, 151–2
Pugin, Augustus Welby Northmore, 224

Quennell, Sir Peter, 152

Raghunathaswami temple, Trichinopoly, 197
Ramesvarem, Ceylon, 194–5
Rampur, Nawab of, 216
Ramsay, A. B., 19
Ramsay, Sir William, 180
Ranchi, SS, 220
Rasputin, Grigori, 143
Rathenau, Walter, 408
Ravenna, 56
Rayner, John, 173
Redesdale, David Freeman-Mitford, 2nd Baron, and Sydney, Lady, 175–6, 395, 397, 399
Reitlinger, Gerald: on trip to Mount Athos, 126, 130–2, 136–7, 139–41; and RB's expedition to Persia, 274, 277; in Peking and Japan, 352–3; *A Tower of Skulls*, 274, 352
Renaissance: architecture of, 223–4
Renishaw, Derbyshire (Sitwells' home), 221
Rennell, James Rennell Rodd, 1st Baron, and Lillias Georgina, Lady, 372
Ribbentrop, Joachim von, 395
Rice, David Talbot: at Eton, 25–6, 43, 130; at Oxford, 54, 57, 130–1; proposed trip to Russia with RB, 71; spends year abroad, 75; and Tamara Abelson, 76, 131; leads reading party on Lundy

Rice, David Talbot (*cont.*)
Island, 77; RB writes to from Athens, 101; RB stays with, 123; visits Mount Athos with RB, 126, 130, 134–7, 142–6; background and career, 130; collaborates on Byzantine book with RB, 134, 180–1; learns Russian, 142; marriage, 142; photography, 143–4, 153, 180; returns to England, 147; mounts Byzantine exhibition at Courtauld, 255; arranges loan of Persian treasures for Royal Academy exhibition, 274; grants RB free passage to Leningrad for International Congress of Persian Art and Archaeology, 340; and Eric Schroeder, 354
Rice, Tamara Talbot (*née* Abelson), 76, 131, 341
Richards, J. M., 376, 379
Richardson, (Sir) Albert, 388
Richardson, E. F., 410
Riley, Athelstan, 149
Road to Oxiana, The (RB), 317, 356–7, 361–3, 367, 373
Roberts, Cecil, 327
Robeson, F. E., 19–23, 27, 29, 32, 42, 49, 52
Robinson, Burgess (RB's uncle), 10
Robinson, Edith (RB's aunt; 'Deedie'), 7
Robinson, Gertrude (RB's aunt), 6
Robinson, Norman (RB's uncle), 10
Robinson, Wilfred (RB's uncle), 6, 10, 12
Rodd, Peter, 75, 372
Romania, 428
Rosse, Anne, Countess of (*née* Messel), 29, 349–50, 417, 434
Rosse, Michael Parsons, 6th Earl of: friendship with RB, 124, 178; RB visits at Birr Castle, 124; joins RB and family in Austria, 158; concern over Guinness's proposal to Diana Mitford, 162–3; and RB's liking for Mitfords, 176; on expedition to Tibet with RB, 199, 202–3, 206–7, 212; visits Kanarak with RB, 220; and RB's attachment to brother Desmond, 229; and proposed visits to Turkestan, 239, 272, 321; joins RB in Russia, 249–50; and RB's mother, 301; in China, 349–50; courtship and marriage, 349–50; letter from RB on Desmond in China, 349; accompanies Desmond to Zurich for treatment, 370; and Desmond's death, 370; in Georgian Group, 380; as chairman of council of Federal Union, 425; helps RB financially, 429; war service, 430; gives final party for RB, 434
Rosse, William Parsons, 3rd Earl of, 125
Rothenstein, William, 47
Round Table Conference (on India, 1931), 222, 227
Routledge (publishers), 166, 172, 181, 216, 225
Rowse, Alfred Leslie, 68
Royal Academy: Persian Art Exhibition (1931), 274
Royal Commission on Ancient and Historical Monuments for England, 377
Royal Fine Art Commission, 386–8
Rubin, Tor, 249–50
Runciman, Sir Steven, 150; *Byzantine Civilization*, 255
Runciman, Walter, 1st Viscount, 396, 398
Ruskin, John: influence on RB, 95–6; anti-Renaissance crusade, 224
Russia (Soviet Union): RB plans trip to, 71–2; RB visits, 240, 241–51, 341–6; RB writes on, 252–4; architecture, 253–4, 342–3; activities in Turkestan, 271; and Afghanistan, 328–9; pact with Nazi Germany (1939), 419
Rutter, Eldon, 277, 285–8, 292, 299; *The Holy Cities of Arabia*, 287
Rutter, Frank, 184, 256

Sackville-West, Vita, 393
St Catherine's monastery, Mount Sinai, 184
St Clair-Erskine, Hamish, 229, 372
St Panteleimon monastery ('the Russico'), Mount Athos, 142, 148
Samarcand, 324–5, 360
San Francisco, 353
Sargent, John Singer: Royal Academy exhibition, 92
Savage, Raymond, 77, 83, 95
Savernake Forest, 59–60
Savernake Lodge, Wiltshire ('The Ruins'): RB's attachment to, 59–60, 337; RB's parents move to, 59–60; RB visits and stays at, 118, 126, 147, 178–9, 221–2, 224, 231, 236, 252, 326–7; RB's parents sub-let, 153; RB entertains friends at, 234; Desmond Parsons visits, 260; RB's parents sell lease, 356
Schroeder, Eric, 354–5, 373
Schurhof, George, 157
Scotland: RB visits, 118
Scott, Colonel Bruce, 329
Scott, Geoffrey: *The Architecture of Humanism*, 223–4
Seafield, Nina, 118, 125, 175
Seville, Spain, 155
Shah Abbas I, Safavid Emperor, 311
Shah of Persia (Reza Shah Pahlavi), 288, 328, 334
Shanks, Edward, 172

Shaw, George Bernard, 240
Shell Guide to Wiltshire (by RB), 335–6
Shell oil company, 232–3; *see also* Burmah Shell
Shiraz, 304, 306–7
Sikkim: Henderson proposes expedition to, 186; RB visits, 213
Silex, Dr (Nazi newspaper editor), 398
Sime, S. H., 137
Simopetra, Mount Athos, 140–1, 192
Sinkiang, 271, 361
Sissons (backer of *Cherwell*), 91
Sitwell family, 46, 97, 123
Sitwell, (Dame) Edith: *Façade*, 61
Sitwell, Georgia (*later* Lady), 221, 282
Sitwell, Sir Osbert: Acton visits, 61–2; RB meets in Spain, 155; in Athens, 221
Sitwell, (Sir) Sacheverell: RB meets in Spain, 155; RB takes as model, 170; reads proofs of RB's *Byzantine Achievement*, 172; in Athens, 221; visits RB at Savernake, 234; in Venice, 282; rents house to Desmond Parsons, 369; *Southern Baroque Art*, 97, 190
Sladen, Algy and Freddie, 159, 161–2
Smith, Eleanor, 173
Smyrna, 88, 98, 104, 107–8
Society for the Protection of Ancient Buildings (SPAB), 378–80
South Africa House, London, 262–3, 364
Soviet Union *see* Russia
Spain, 153–6
Spanish Civil War (1936–9), 392–3
Spectator (journal), 334
Spencer, John, 27, 30, 49
Spender, (Sir) Stephen, 392
Spengler, Oswald: *The Decline of the West*, 167–8, 171, 192, 194
Spyridon, Dr (of Great Lavra monastery, Mount Athos), 134–5
Squire, Sir John C., 265, 333, 335
Stalin, Josef Vissarionovich, 342, 346
Stanhope, James Richard, 7th Earl, 402
Station, The (RB), 149–52, 156–8, 175, 180, 211, 332
Stchousev (Soviet architect), 243, 253, 342–3
Stein, Marc Aurel, 305
Sternberg, Count, 161
Stiris: monastery of St Luke, 106–7
Stockley, Ralph, 283
Stokes, Adrian, 369
Storrs, Sir Ronald, 282, 335
Stoughton, Simon, 26
Strachey, Lytton, 68, 70, 234; *Eminent Victorians*, 63
Streit, Clarence, 423–4
Stuart, Sir Campbell, 404
Stuart-Richardson, Gladys, 89, 102
Sudetenland, 396, 398, 401, 403
Summerson, (Sir) John, 380, 383
Sunday Times, 411–12, 429, 432
Sutro, John, 41, 64, 78, 158–61, 187, 425, 434
Sverdlovsk, 342, 346–7
Swinbrook (house), Oxfordshire, 175
Syddall, Joseph, 5
Sykes, Camilla (*née* Russell), 417
Sykes, Christopher: and Steven Runciman's view of RB's *The Station*, 150; on RB's appearance, 163; RB forbids to read *The Appreciation of Architecture*, 269; in Persia and Afghanistan with RB, 278–9, 283–5, 288–93, 304–9, 314–15, 317–20, 323–4; recruited as spy, 305; co-writes satirical novel with RB, 328; accompanies RB to Leningrad, 340; on RB's *Road to Oxiana*, 362; RB entertains in London, 369; anti-Zionism, 408; and RB's views on war threat, 412–13; and RB's wartime activities, 429–30; *Changed* (unpublished), 278; *Four Studies in Loyalty*, 314; *Innocence and Design* (novel; with RB), 333; *Wassmuss*, 304
Sykes, Freya (Christopher's sister), 305
Sykes, Sir Mark, 278, 285
Sykes, Sir Percy: *Ten Thousand Miles in Persia*, 290

Taj Mahal, Agra, 219–20
Talbot Rice *see* Rice
Tallents, Sir Stephen, 394, 400–4, 409
Teheran, 289–90, 292, 303–4
Tehring, Jigmed, 210, 212, 214
Tehring, Mary, 212, 214
Tehring, Rajah, 210, 212–14
Teleki, Count, 428
Theodoric, King of the Ostrogoths, 56
Theodosius, Roman Emperor, 104
Tibet: British interest in, 199–200; RB's expedition to, 199–214; architecture, 211, 218; RB writes on, 225
Times Literary Supplement, The, 362
Times, The: RB submits articles to, 83, 115, 118, 148, 179, 254, 328; attacks Carlton Gardens scheme, 264; reports RB's departure for Persia, 281; reviews RB's *First Russia Then Tibet*, 327; BR represents at Third International Congress of Persian Art, Leningrad (1934), 340–1; RB reports to on Russia, 351; payments to RB, 352; RB writes obituary for Desmond Parsons in, 370;

Times, The (*cont.*)
letter announces formation of Georgian Group, 379; RB writes to on impending war, 391; attitude to Second World War threat, 404; commissions articles on oil industry from RB, 408, 410; on George VI's visit to USA, 410; on cleaning of Elgin Marbles, 412; announces RB's death, 436
Timurid dynasty, 295–6
Todd, Miss (editor of *Vogue*), 98
Todd, Mr (Eton housemaster), 14–17, 19
Toledo, Spain, 154–5, 184
Torbock, Cornish, 22–3, 25, 27–9
Town and Country Planning Act (1932), 377
Toynbee, (Sir) Arnold, 180
Tranquebar, India, 198
Trans-Siberian Railway, 346–7, 350
Travancore, 196–7, 221
Trew, Christine, 78; *Making Conversation*, 76
Tun-Huang caves, 349
Turkestan, 239, 249, 270–2, 274–5, 297–8, 320–43
Tyler, Royall, 255

U-97 (submarine), 435
Ubrye, Annelisa, 241, 244
Ubrye, Miles, 241
United States of America: RB's 1935 lecture tour in, 332–3; RB criticizes, 353; RB's mission to (1938), 404–6, 408–9, 422

Vardy, John, 385–8
Vatopedi, Mount Athos, 144–5
Velasquez, Diego de Silva y, 154
Veloudias, Thanos, 101–2, 129
Venice, 282
Vichlitz-Amade, Count and Countess, 159–61
Victoria, Queen, 63, 161
Victoria and Albert Museum, London, 239, 255
Vienna, 72, 153, 158, 162–4
Villa La Pietra, Florence, 42–3, 57
Vivian, Daphne, 119
Vladivostok, 347
Vogue (magazine), 98, 179, 216

Walker, Alan, 242
Walker's Gallery, New Bond Street, London, 330
Walrond, William, 30
Walton, W.G., 242, 244
War Office: RB seeks post with, 421, 423, 427
Warburg, Frederic, 95, 98, 156, 166, 181, 216, 225, 227, 276
Washington, DC, 353–4
Wassmuss, Wilhelm, 304–5, 307
Waugh, Arthur, 152
Waugh, Evelyn: on Hugh Lygon, 57; in Hypocrites Club, 66; embraces Victorian Revival, 70–1; on RB's behaviour, 70, 73; on new fashions, 74; romantic passions, 75; published in *Cherwell*, 78; Alastair Graham and, 101–3; contributes to RB/Brian Howard essay collection, 152; friendship with RB, 158; marriage to Evelyn Gardner, 158; and RB's relations with Nancy Mitford, 176; rift with RB, 176; attends RB's lecture on Travancore, 221; joins Catholic Church, 221; and Harold Acton's finances, 235; spreads rumour of Guinness paying for publication of own poems, 236; jealousy of Diana Mitford's feelings for RB, 260–1; praises Peter Fleming's *Brazilian Adventure*, 360; praises RB's use of dialogue, 362; on Spanish Civil War, 393; *Black Mischief*, 221; *Decline and Fall*, 158; *Vile Bodies*, 174
Weekend Review, 263–4, 266, 276
Weir, Colonel J. L. R., 200, 214
Weir, Thyra, 214, 254
Wellesley, Lord Gerald (*later* 7th Duke of Wellington), 382
Wells, H. G., 393
Weymouth, Daphne, Viscountess (*later* Fielding), 186
Whistler, Rex, 233
White, Gilbert, 11
Whittemore, Thomas, 254
Wicklow, Ralph Francis Forward Howard, 7th Earl of, 24–5, 31
Wiener Neustadt, 164
Wilkinson (Shell representative in New York), 405
Williams-Ellis, (Sir) Clough, 233
Williamson (of Indian Intelligence), 271
Willingdon, Marie Adelaide, Marchioness of (*née* Brassey), 257
Windsor Castle, 51
Windsor, Edward, Duke of, 409
Wishaw (of Anglo-Persian Oil Company), 311
women: at Oxford, 75–6
Woodburn, D.B., 411
World Review (magazine), 425
World War I (1914–18) *see* Great War
World War II (1939–45): outbreak, 420
Worthington, Diana and Greville, 403, 419
Wortley, Mrs Stuart, 352

Xenophontos, Mount Athos, 143
Xeropotamou monastery, Mount Athos, 146

Yate, Major C.E.: *Northern Afghanistan*, 296
Yorke, Adele (*née* Biddulph; 'Dig'), 177, 369
Yorke, Henry (Henry Green): at Eton, 39–41; friendship with RB, 39–41, 54–5, 77, 178; on Brian Howard, 44; in Eton Society of Arts, 45; literary ambitions and career, 45; RB reports to on Oxford, 69; at Oxford (Magdalen), 73; RB complains of Europe to, 73; and RB's reaction to David Plunket Greene, 76; RB praises Sacheverell Sitwell to, 97; letter from RB in Scotland, 118; and Alfred Duggan's behaviour, 120; and Anthony Powell, 123; and RB's book on history of Greece, 123; RB complains of depression to, 126; works in family factory, 126; and RB's preoccupation with Byzantine art, 139; and RB's comments on Brian Howard, 151; contributes to RB/Brian Howard essay collection, 152; RB writes to from Spain, 154; and RB's view on Vienna, 164; on RB's attachment to Nancy Mitford, 176; rift with RB, 176–7; marriage, 177, 187; RB dislikes writings, 177; visits Byrons in Vienna, 177; RB praises Lutyens to, 217; RB entertains, 369; *Blindness*, 45; *Living*, 177
Yorke, Maud (*née* Wyndham), 39–41
Yorke, Vincent, 39
Young, George Malcolm, 271, 362, 409
Younghusband, Sir Francis, 140, 199

Zagorsk, Russia, 248
Zervos, Dr Skevos, 87–8, 106
Ziller, Ernst, 129
Zimmern, Sir Alfred, 424
Zitsa monastery, Thessaly, 237
Zographou, Mount Athos, 148